Curriculum Internationalization and the Future of Education

Semire Dikli
Georgia Gwinnett College, USA

Brian Etheridge
Georgia Gwinnett College, USA

Richard Rawls
Georgia Gwinnett College, USA

A volume in the Advances in Educational
Technologies and Instructional Design (AETID)
Book Series

Published in the United States of America by
IGI Global
Information Science Reference (an imprint of IGI Global)
701 E. Chocolate Avenue
Hershey PA, USA 17033
Tel: 717-533-8845
Fax: 717-533-8661
E-mail: cust@igi-global.com
Web site: http://www.igi-global.com

Library of Congress Cataloging-in-Publication Data

Names: Dikli, Semire, editor.
Title: Curriculum internationalization and the future of education / Semire
   Dikli, Brian Etheridge, and Richard Rawls, editors.
Description: Hershey PA : Information Science Reference, [2018]
Identifiers: LCCN 2017010717| ISBN 9781522527916 (hardcover) | ISBN
   9781522527923 (ebook)
Subjects: LCSH: International education--Curricula--Handbooks, manuals, etc.
   | Curriculum change--Handbooks, manuals, etc. | Education and
   globalization--Handbooks, manuals, etc.
Classification: LCC LC1090 .C87 2018 | DDC 370.116--dc23 LC record available at https://lccn.loc.gov/2017010717

This book is published in the IGI Global book series Advances in Educational Technologies and Instructional Design (AE-TID) (ISSN: 2326-8905; eISSN: 2326-8913)

British Cataloguing in Publication Data
A Cataloguing in Publication record for this book is available from the British Library.

For electronic access to this publication, please contact: eresources@igi-global.com.

Advances in Educational Technologies and Instructional Design (AETID) Book Series

Lawrence A. Tomei
Robert Morris University, USA

ISSN:2326-8905
EISSN:2326-8913

MISSION

Education has undergone, and continues to undergo, immense changes in the way it is enacted and distributed to both child and adult learners. From distance education, Massive-Open-Online-Courses (MOOCs), and electronic tablets in the classroom, technology is now an integral part of the educational experience and is also affecting the way educators communicate information to students.

The **Advances in Educational Technologies & Instructional Design (AETID) Book Series** is a resource where researchers, students, administrators, and educators alike can find the most updated research and theories regarding technology's integration within education and its effect on teaching as a practice.

COVERAGE

- Instructional Design
- E-Learning
- Social Media Effects on Education
- Online Media in Classrooms
- Bring-Your-Own-Device
- Virtual School Environments
- Digital Divide in Education
- Classroom Response Systems
- Adaptive Learning
- Game-Based Learning

IGI Global is currently accepting manuscripts for publication within this series. To submit a proposal for a volume in this series, please contact our Acquisition Editors at Acquisitions@igi-global.com or visit: http://www.igi-global.com/publish/.

Titles in this Series

For a list of additional titles in this series, please visit: www.igi-global.com/book-series

Supporting Multiculturalism in Open and Distance Learning Spaces
Elif Toprak (Anadolu University, Turkey) and Evrim Genc Kumtepe (Anadolu University, Turkey)
Information Science Reference • ©2018 • 381pp • H/C (ISBN: 9781522530763) • US $195.00 (our price)

Innovative Technology Training Frameworks in CALL Emerging Research and Opportunities
Sandra Morales (Newcastle University, UK)
Information Science Reference • ©2018 • 100pp • H/C (ISBN: 9781522537649) • US $125.00 (our price)

Handbook of Research on Pedagogical Models for Next-Generation Teaching and Learning
Jared Keengwe (University of North Dakota, USA)
Information Science Reference • ©2018 • 454pp • H/C (ISBN: 9781522538738) • US $295.00 (our price)

Handbook of Research on Mobile Technology, Constructivism, and Meaningful Learning
Jared Keengwe (University of North Dakota, USA)
Information Science Reference • ©2018 • 454pp • H/C (ISBN: 9781522539490) • US $265.00 (our price)

Deviant Communication in Teacher-Student Interactions Emerging Research and Opportunities
Eletra Gilchrist-Petty (The University of Alabama in Huntsville, USA)
Information Science Reference • ©2018 • 133pp • H/C (ISBN: 9781522527794) • US $125.00 (our price)

Culturally Engaging Service-Learning With Diverse Communities
Omobolade O. Delano-Oriaran (St. Norbert College, USA) Marguerite W. Penick-Parks (University of Wisconsin – Oshkosh, USA) and Suzanne Fondrie (University of Wisconsin – Oshkosh, USA)
Information Science Reference • ©2018 • 359pp • H/C (ISBN: 9781522529002) • US $225.00 (our price)

Enhancing Education and Training Initiatives Through Serious Games
John Denholm (The University of Manchester, UK & University of Warwick, UK) and Linda Lee-Davies (The University of Manchester, UK & Wroxton College of Fairleigh Dickinson University, USA)
Information Science Reference • ©2018 • 311pp • H/C (ISBN: 9781522536895) • US $185.00 (our price)

A Simplex Approach to Learning, Cognition, and Spatial Navigation Emerging Research and Opportunities
Pio Alfredo Di Tore (University of Salerno, Italy)
Information Science Reference • ©2018 • 116pp • H/C (ISBN: 9781522524557) • US $125.00 (our price)

701 East Chocolate Avenue, Hershey, PA 17033, USA
Tel: 717-533-8845 x100 • Fax: 717-533-8661
E-Mail: cust@igi-global.com • www.igi-global.com

Editorial Advisory Board

Table of Contents

Detailed Table of Contents

Section 1

Chapter 1

> *Michael A. Lewkowicz, Georgia Gwinnett College, USA*
> *Laura D. Young, Georgia Gwinnett College, USA*
> *Dovilė Budrytė, Georgia Gwinnett College, USA*
> *Scott A. Boykin, Georgia Gwinnett College, USA*

This chapter documents a group of political scientists' attempts to internationalize an introductory course surveying the essentials of American government. This course is a required course for every student at Georgia Gwinnett College (and other state colleges and universities in Georgia). The content in this course, unfortunately, tends to privilege domestic political institutions and political development and does not take the diversity of students into account. The chapter, therefore, starts out with the definitions and a discussion of "internationalization" and "individualization" approaches and how to incorporate them into the course through active learning activities. Next, the authors describe five activities that attempt to shift the focus from "covering the material" to student experiences. They believe that these activities can help students acquire communication and intercultural competence skills and help avoid the unintended consequences of the use of the comparative method which can result in divisions between "us" and "them."

Chapter 2

> *Clemente Quinones, Georgia Gwinnett College, USA*

The purpose of this chapter is to analyze the possible factors that determined a relatively relaxed process of transforming the author's two courses into i-courses. The argument is that some GGC's institutional mechanisms smoothed the process. To support the argument, the chapter first introduces a conceptual framework, followed by the presentation of other scholars' findings on factors of internationalization of the curriculum. The introduction of GGC's process approach to internationalization and the author's intrinsic motivation were the major institutional arrangements and natural factors, respectively, that explain the relatively relaxed process of transforming the author's two courses into i-courses. The chapter concludes with a description of venues for future research and some student evaluations of the two i-courses.

This chapter explores questions of methodology and pedagogy in dealing with diverse student populations in a freshman-level human geography class by highlighting a multi-tiered exercise that encourages students to investigate and to articulate their own feelings and beliefs about migration in a series of low-risk classroom exercises complemented with an out-of-class assignment. The self-reflective portion of this exercise provides the instructor insight into student feelings, attitudes, and knowledge of students' migration histories and knowledge. Lessons and examples from the author's classroom experiences are detailed in this chapter to call upon instructors to implement multi-tiered approaches to controversial and international topics, particularly in a multi-cultural, multi-ethnic, twenty-first century college classroom.

The purpose of this chapter is to provide an example of internationalizing an Introduction to Human Geography course. This mostly consists of translating the material normally found in such a class into the explicit language of internationalization. This is accomplished by modifying the course to include less theoretical descriptions and more concrete examples of globalism at work. Topics normally found in an introductory Human Geography course are well suited for this. Religion, global development, foreign direct investment, immigration, language, and political conflict are avenues of investigation that overlap between geography and international or global studies.

Chapter 5

This chapter investigates the process of internationalizing a course on ancient history. It suggests ways that a course can be created, examines important issues, and provides examples of assignments to help meet course, discipline, and institutional outcomes. Informed by the work of Fink, it commences by arguing for the significance of course outcome goals, disciplinary outcome goals, and additional institutional goals related to internationalizing the curriculum. Without these various outcome goals as building blocks for the course, it will be both difficult to assess the educational effectiveness of the class and challenging to organize the content. The chapter next discusses pedagogical issues before moving into internationalizing the course. It then investigates the work of two ancient authors, Herodotus and Tacitus, who commented upon foreign cultures. Their histories support exercises designed to help learn outcome goals. Contrary to what some may think, internationalizing a course on ancient history is easier than one might initially anticipate.

The process of internationalizing a music appreciation class is discussed. The role of music appreciation in an internationalized curriculum is examined and a philosophy of music education is developed. Curriculum design, assessment practices, and teaching and learning activities are viewed through the framework of Fink's Taxonomy of Learning, including descriptions of specific practices and assignments and their relationship to the taxonomy of learning the philosophy of music education. Special consideration is given to the power of music, the arts, and aesthetic experiences to cultivate knowledge of the self and of the other.

This chapter presents the author's experiences working with international content in the higher education classroom to explore successful examples of intercultural material that can benefit students pursuing a degree in any field. The author explores how social science courses in general, and anthropology courses in particular, that work from a foundation of cultural relativism and standpoint theory can equip students with important knowledge and skills that promote tolerance and respect of cultural difference. Finally, the author demonstrates that students finish courses like these with a better understanding of and appreciation for the cultural differences that exist all around them.

To internationalize the campus, a Language Exchange Pal Project was developed to enhance students' cross-cultural experiences in a beginner's Chinese foreign language course. The Language Exchange Pal Project, using Skype or QQ (similar to Skype), is a great tool to increase students' global perspective by working in communities of practice with individuals in China who are learning English as a foreign language. Through the technology, students enjoy the opportunity to use the target language in an authentic communicative context and collaborate with their international partners. These two groups collaborate about their language and culture through messages and/or live connections via Skype, chat, or other software systems such as QQ. This chapter shares the process of transforming Chinese 1001 into an i-course, present the Language Exchange Pal Project, describe its challenges, and discuss the preliminary results of the research findings of the Language Exchange Pal Project based on students' survey and interview.

    Priya Shilpa Boindala, Georgia Gwinnett College, USA
    Ramakrishnan Menon, Georgia Gwinnett College, USA
    Angela Lively, Georgia Gwinnett College, USA

This chapter focuses on the redesign of a traditional History of Mathematics course as an internationalized course and its early implementation. This redesign of the course incorporates significant learning experiences and includes the learning goals of both the college and the discipline. The design of these learning experiences using the backwards design model, the framework based on a blended taxonomy of Bloom and Fink, are elaborated on. How these learning experiences are supported by active learning strategies and forward assessments is also presented. The pilot implementation by an author not involved in the design process provides for an objective perspective of this redesign. The chapter elaborates on the learning experiences within the initial implementation and concludes with ideas for future iterations of the course.

    Boyko Georgiev Gyurov, Georgia Gwinnett College, USA
    Mark Andrew Schlueter, Georgia Gwinnett College, USA

In 2014, the authors of this chapter joined forces to create a unique STEM study abroad experience for Georgia Gwinnett College students, and that experience grew into a model worthy to be examined and replicated. The model addresses the main objectives of U.S. Senator Paul Simon Study Abroad Program Act to bring the demographics of study abroad participation to reflect the demographics of the United States undergraduate population and to implement the study abroad programs in nontraditional study abroad destinations, and in particular in developing countries. Further, the model contains six important components (bundle setup, faculty led, interdisciplinary academic content delivery, undergraduate research, low cost, and cultural component added). The characteristics of all of which are explained in details in the paper. Finally, the successes and challenges of the program are discussed through the prism of it successful implementation in the summers of 2015 and 2016.

    Semire Dikli, Georgia Gwinnett College, USA
    Richard S. Rawls, Georgia Gwinnett College, USA
    Brian C. Etheridge, Georgia Gwinnett College, USA

This chapter aims to describe the mandatory training program (Internationalized Learning Essentials) offered to the new faculty as part of the internationalization of the curriculum process at four-year colleges in the U.S. The chapter presents survey results regarding faculty perceptions on the training program. The results of this study suggest important implications for research in internationalization by providing further insights regarding faculty training about internationalized education.

Chapter 12

Curriculum internationalization (CI) has shifted from U.S. student and faculty mobility, foreign language offerings, and interdisciplinary programming to the delivery of content and the role of international students in the method of delivery. Although CI is still about developing students' international and intercultural perspectives, it is not only about teaching or students. Broadly speaking, it is about learning and involves every member of the campus community through purposeful curriculum planning and campus programming. Curriculum internationalization is also about exposing American students, scholars, faculty, staff, and administrators to their overseas counterparts as well as to international settings and perspectives through co-curricular programs. This chapter discusses Georgia Gwinnett College's path towards campus internationalization through a quality enhancement program, education abroad programming, international students and partnerships, and campus programming—a purposeful blend of an internationalized curriculum and a co-curriculum.

Section 2

This chapter explores the internationalization of higher education at four-year institutions in the Rocky Mountain West (Idaho, Montana, Wyoming, Colorado, Utah, Nevada, Arizona, and New Mexico) through the lens of James Peacock's grounded globalism. As global forces increase and impose upon higher education, administrators and faculty must remain mindful of best practices in internationalizing curriculum. This chapter draws on surveys of senior international officers at four-year colleges in the Rocky Mountain West states. It examines existing literature to apply Peacock's concept of grounded globalism. The authors provide shared characteristics of states in the Rocky Mountain West to add context to the challenges and strengths of internationalization in this region. The authors provide recommendations for future research and best practices in internationalizing curriculum.

Most curriculum internationalization studies have been focusing on international students and study abroad programs, which has excluded the majority of non-mobile students on American campuses. In addition, the existing studies have been conducted from administrator and faculty perspectives. This chapter generates a substantive theory of intercultural curriculum and teaching methods from the experiences of students who have taken intercultural classes in American classrooms. Active interview theory and grounded theory were utilized for data collection and data analysis. Based on the pure voices from both domestic and international students, this chapter has identified three core categories and eight sub-categories representing student-preferred internationalized curriculum. These categories or themes offer new angles to look at curriculum internationalization.

Twenty-first century teachers can become more culturally competent through thoughtfully planned opportunities designed to develop global perspectives. Cultural competence can be cultivated through service-learning experiences such as study abroad, thus maximizing pre-service teachers' global preparation and future success within diverse classrooms. In this chapter, the authors discuss preparing undergraduate and graduate students for fieldwork in Liberia, South Africa, and Belize. The purpose of trips to developing countries is to teach and serve but also requires planning that acknowledges issues experienced by pre-service teachers such as anxiety and low efficacy. Upon completion of the Mercer on Mission trips, several pre-service teachers expressed their views about the usefulness of the preparation activities, which are explored within student narratives. Ultimately, the goal of the service-learning program is to support the completion of fieldwork requirements in exceptional contexts while adequately preparing students to be effective across a variety of diverse settings and activities.

Software development is the process to produce an information technology solution to a real-world problem. Teaching and integrating non-technical software engineering skills into the curriculum is considered one of the most challenging tasks in an academic environment. This becomes even more challenging when the curriculum is supposed to be internationalized and applied in different countries because of the cultural difference, policy difference, and business model difference. In this chapter, the authors present their experience of teaching a software engineering course both locally and globally, where two universities of USA and China are chosen for this study. Specifically, they describe how they adjust homework assignments and student performance evaluations to reflect different government policies, different business environment, and different real-world customer requirement. The chapter shows that it is possible to create an internationalized computer science curriculum that contains both common core learning standards and adjustable custom learning standards.

Foreword

In this special collection, faculty from a range of disciplines engage questions of how to best design and deliver an educational program that will prepare students for their futures in an increasingly diverse and globalizing world. Internationalization is changing our institutions. Faculty in the United States and Canada over the past number of years have wrestled with how our internationally interconnected reality is changing the landscape for teaching in higher education. Faculty are looking for a coherent set of skills that will prepare them and their learners for the challenges of the present and future.

The work of internationalization, and the approach of integrating intercultural perspectives and skills in teaching and learning, is both global and local, as my background attests. Prior to my work in higher education, I spent a decade based in Tokyo designing and facilitating a range of intercultural training programs for major Japanese and international corporations. My work with teams and leaders focused on building their capacity for growing relationships and achieving their goals. The experience showed me how working across worldviews can make the exchange of information, critical thinking, and communication across cultures much more complex. It taught me how difference matters and that engaging across multiple disciplines and jurisdictions demanded a new set of intercultural skills and attitudes to achieve success.

After returning to North America, I was struck by the clear need for change in teaching practices brought about by the increasing diversity of the college classroom and the integration of our domestic economy with the rest of the world. The internationalization of our campuses is a response to our global era's challenges through its incorporation of a blend of activities including student and faculty mobility, international student recruitment, research, transnational programs, and joint projects to list a few. These initiatives take the institution out into the world and welcomes a wider experience into the institution and its programs. Faculty who become involved with the international activities of their discipline and institution recognize how important it is to prepare their students to more effectively engage, understand and appreciate the world. Similar to what I discovered overseas, faculty at home can see how graduating learners with skills that enable them to think critically and problem solve across different national, regional, cultural worldviews will lead to better responses to the challenges of a more interconnected and interdependent global era. Faculty I meet and work with on this path often speak of their early attempts to add international content and case studies to their programs as the way to achieve these aspirations. Over time, however, they recognized that the intercultural component is a vital missing piece in this approach.

Faculty want to prepare graduates that can form relationships with people, ideas, and practices from widening geographic and cultural distances. They admit they do not feel as well prepared for this task as they would like and that this is more complex than simply adding international content to a reading list. They share that both the diversities inside their classrooms as well as the global complexities outside of the classroom need to be addressed and that a more intercultural mindset and skillset holds the potential to transform internationalization into interculturalization. They are looking for a union of the best of the internationalized curriculum with intercultural skills and perspectives. Internationalization has a bias in how it emphasizes the international. Interculturalization is the integration of international and intercultural content and approaches and holds the potential to improve how students communicate, problem solve, critically engage and understand their own position in relation to what they are learning. Faculty share how they observe that their graduates are better prepared for the challenges their future careers will present them with. We need to prepare all of our graduates, whether they come from abroad or from the local community, to succeed wherever they live and work.

Our campuses, communities, and workplaces are becoming more diverse and students are increasingly influenced by ideas, media and trends from around the world. What we do in our classrooms with our students related to internationalization is not only about preparing our learners to travel, live and work abroad. Our domestic populations increasingly mirror the diversity and complexity of the global. Graduates must be effective working with difference at home and abroad.

For faculty developing the skills to teach across differences, it can be intellectually and emotionally challenging. They regularly share how the curriculum and teaching process associated with their disciplinary tradition has not always prepared them to design and deliver their teaching content so that it is relevant to the challenges their learners will encounter. They want to teach and model the personal and professional competencies that will empower and enrich all of their students. To improve student outcomes, we recognize that much of the challenge moving forward, therefore, involves faculty development. Working with our faculty at multiple levels, over a sustained period of time, to increase their own ability to navigate cultural difference is a critical first step toward interculturalizing their teaching and curriculum.

We know the majority of our graduates will remain at home while a few will grow lives internationally. Regardless, all will work and live with the resulting complexity of our world and engaged faculty want to prepare their students with the knowledge, skills and attitudes to be successful. The approaches explored and shared in this collection represent a range of disciplines and ways of achieving this necessary goal.

Todd Odgers
British Columbia Institute of Technology, Canada

Preface

Internationalization is a critical issue in higher education today. Many colleges and universities are transforming their curriculum by integrating international perspectives and providing professional development to faculty and staff so that they can effectively participate in today's increasingly global environment. A major reason for internationalization in higher education is that college graduates are expected to become global citizens to be able to successfully communicate in diverse workplace. Students who take courses with international content are believed to be better equipped to effectively communicate in global contexts. Therefore, employers are looking for candidates who not only have appropriate degrees for the job but also foreign language skills and intercultural competence. Furthermore, many colleges and universities are admitting more and more international students, and this makes it necessary to train fellow students as well as faculty and staff about intercultural awareness and multiculturalism.

This book stems from internationalization of curriculum efforts at a higher education institution (Georgia Gwinnett College-GGC). The goal of this book is to provide a platform for faculty not only at GGC but also in other colleges and universities to share their experiences with curriculum internationalization and research. Our target audience are faculty and administrators who are invested in globalizing education in higher education institutions and looking for ways to incorporate international content into their curricula. We believe that this book fills in a gap internationalized education as most books focus solely on the theory or policy with little or no emphasis on actual faculty experiences and challenges they face. This book, however, is one of the handful publications that focuses on the perspectives of faculty and includes examples of successful classroom practices.

There are two sections to this book. Section 1 is a collection of chapters that are written by faculty and staff at GGC, whereas Section 2 consists of chapters written by authors from other higher education institutions in the U.S. and/or abroad. The first 10 chapters in Section 2 describe internationalization process of various undergraduate-level college courses. Chapters 11 and 12, however, discuss programs that help faculty and staff internationalize the curriculum. Also, all chapters in Section 1, with the exception of Chapters 9 and 10, focus on internationalizing social science courses. Below includes a more specific description of each chapter in the book.

- Chapter 1 explains the steps that are taken to internationalize an introductory level American Government course, which surveys the essentials of American government at GGC. The authors discuss the concepts of "internationalization" and "individualization" and explain how they incorporate these concepts into their course using various active learning techniques to help students acquire intercultural competence.

- Similarly, Chapter 2 describes the process of transformation of two Political Science courses into internationalized courses. The author shares successful classroom practices.
- Chapter 3 investigates classroom experiences with international focus in an introductory level human geography class. While teaching the "migration" subject, the author utilizes a multi-tiered activity and promotes intercultural sensitivity awareness among students.
- Like Chapter 3, Chapter 4 explains the author's experiences working with international content in an Introduction to Human Geography course while focusing less on theoretical descriptions but more on concrete examples of globalism.
- Chapter 5 discusses the inclusion of international content in an undergraduate-level ancient history. The author underlines the important role of course, program, and institution goals as they relate to internationalization of this history course.
- Chapter 6 explains the process of curriculum internationalization of an introductory level Music Appreciation course. The author describes the development of philosophy of music education with international focus and explains curriculum design, assessment practices, and teaching learning activities utilized in class to promote intercultural sensitivity.
- Chapter 7 presents various examples of intercultural material that promote cross-cultural awareness in college classrooms. The author provides sample classroom activities from her anthropology class and points out the importance of exposing students to international and intercultural content to help them develop a better understanding of and appreciation for the cultural differences.
- Chapter 8 describes steps that the author has taken to internationalize a foreign language course through a Language Exchange Pal Project. The author provides detailed description of the project and examines some of the challenges while discussing the preliminary results of a research project.
- Chapter 9 analyzes the process of restructuring a traditional History of Mathematics course as an internationalized course using a Backwards Design model. The authors present active learning strategies and forward assessment techniques to accomplish this goal.
- Chapter 10, on the other hand, presents a successful implementation of a STEM study abroad experience in a nontraditional study abroad destination. The authors address the challenges as well as the strengths of the program and suggest valuable insights about this experience.
- Chapter 11 focuses on one of the training programs (Internationalized Learning Essentials) offered to the GGC faculty as part of the internationalization of the curriculum process. The authors describe the mandatory training program offered to the new faculty and present the survey results regarding faculty perceptions on the training program.
- Chapter 12 describes the efforts of GGC towards internationalization of its curriculum through faculty training programs, study abroad programs, international student and scholar visits and partnerships, and various college-wide international activities and events.
- Chapter 13 investigates the internationalization of higher education curriculum at four-year institutions in eight states including Idaho, Montana, Wyoming, Colorado, Utah, Nevada, Arizona, and New Mexico. The authors identify existing challenges and strengths of internationalization in these institutions and conduct a study applying Peacock's concept of Grounded Globalism. Their findings suggest innovative practices in internationalized curriculum.
- Chapter 14 explores the process of curriculum internationalization from student point of view in two higher education institutions in the U.S. The authors use a Grounded Theory and an Active

Interview approach to collect data on student perceptions of integrating intercultural competence into curriculum. Participating students shared opinion on the type of elements (i.e., intercultural awareness, intercultural knowledge, intercultural skills, study abroad opportunities, etc.) they would like to see as a part of an intercultural program.

- Chapter 15 explains the process of preparing teacher education students in one university in the U.S. to do fieldwork in other countries including Liberia, South Africa, and Belize and draw upon narratives written by the students after the trip. The chapter underlines the value of training culturally competent pre-service teachers and helping them develop a global perspective in education.

- Finally, Chapter 16 describes the experience of including intercultural content in an undergraduate-level software engineering course both in the U.S. and China. The author presents a problem-based learning methodology to internationalize this course.

Section 1

Chapter 1
Bringing the Study of American Government to Life in a Diverse Classroom:
Internationalization and Individualization

Michael A. Lewkowicz
Georgia Gwinnett College, USA

Laura D. Young
Georgia Gwinnett College, USA

Dovilė Budrytė
Georgia Gwinnett College, USA

Scott A. Boykin
Georgia Gwinnett College, USA

ABSTRACT

This chapter documents a group of political scientists' attempts to internationalize an introductory course surveying the essentials of American government. This course is a required course for every student at Georgia Gwinnett College (and other state colleges and universities in Georgia). The content in this course, unfortunately, tends to privilege domestic political institutions and political development and does not take the diversity of students into account. The chapter, therefore, starts out with the definitions and a discussion of "internationalization" and "individualization" approaches and how to incorporate them into the course through active learning activities. Next, the authors describe five activities that attempt to shift the focus from "covering the material" to student experiences. They believe that these activities can help students acquire communication and intercultural competence skills and help avoid the unintended consequences of the use of the comparative method which can result in divisions between "us" and "them."

DOI: 10.4018/978-1-5225-2791-6.ch001

INTRODUCTION

An often daunting challenge for college instructors is attracting and retaining student interest, particularly in survey courses, which may serve as a student's only exposure to a subject. This challenge may enhance when the course is a general education course that students are taking only because it is required. Such is the case for American government courses in several states like Georgia. Thus, instructors must develop ways to generate and maintain student interest in the material, particularly given that a key objective of American government courses is the promotion of civic engagement.

Making the challenge of attracting student interest even greater is the fact that American government instructors may face students who lack confidence in American political institutions, a problem prevalent in American society. According to Gallup data, the percentage of people who believe that "you can trust the government in Washington to do what is right most of the time" has been decreasing since 2002, dropping to 19% in 2009 (2016a). In 2016, trust in the three branches of government was lower than a decade ago (2016b, 2016c). This lack of confidence in American political institutions may translate into apathy in courses that address those institutions.

To successfully address these challenges, the instructor should incorporate two approaches into survey courses in American government: internationalization and individualization.

INTERNATIONALIZATION OF AMERICAN GOVERNMENT CURRICULUM

Betty Leask defined internationalized curriculum as the incorporation of material with an international component (2009, p. 209; 2014). Including an international component requires integrating global and comparative perspectives in the classroom, placing emphasis on diverse cultures, social groups, and types of governments. Understanding how these components affect politics is also important for internationalized curriculum because that understanding can help students better analyze their own cultures, social groups, and governments. However, internationalized curriculum is not just about incorporating international elements into course material. Rather, internationalized curriculum should also encourage students to develop critical thinking skills that challenge their own views and help them recognize the merit of alternative perspectives (Crichton et al, 2004; Zimitat, 2008). By engaging alternative perspectives, students can better understand the course material in a twenty-first century context (Hudzik & McCarthy, 2012).

What does it mean to internationalize a survey course in American government? After all, many instructors teach this course from a purely "American" perspective, as they rarely include comparisons with other governments and often leave topics such as United States foreign policy for the end of the semester. In contrast to that traditional approach, we argue that American government courses could benefit from utilizing an internationalized curriculum.

In other words, an internationalized approach to an American government course should help students become familiar with and appreciate the importance of other cultures, countries, and regions while increasing the student's awareness of their own cultural identity. According to Eric LeBlanc, curriculum should therefore "embody contrasting perspectives and be understood in different ways depending on the context" (as cited in Takagi, 2015, p. 350). Cross-cultural experiences and interactions among students are also critical components of the learning process since they help build international competencies, especially regarding contrasting perspectives (Wamboye, Adekola, & Sergi, 2015). For example, the

"Special Places" icebreaker in Activity 1 below helps increase student interactions on the first day of class by requiring students to consider the meaning of a "special place." Such a discussion helps highlight classroom diversity since even students from similar backgrounds will have distinct places of meaning and distinct reasons as to why those places are special. In addition, through sharing, students are forced to reflect on how their values, as well as the values of others, may shape the selection of those "special places." Creating a platform for student interactions that enhance cross-cultural experiences such as this is important for increasing internationalization in the classroom.

Another way to incorporate international dimensions into an American government course is to develop activities that facilitate comparisons between America and other nations. Such comparisons would achieve several significant learning outcomes, including a better understanding of the institutions and challenges of American government (Reitano & Elfenbein, 1997; Engstrom 2008; Gelbman, 2011) and a greater understanding of the factors involved in decision-making of various political actors, both inside and outside of government (Reitano & Elfenbein, 1997). Furthermore, an internationalized approach to civic engagement would not be complete without incorporating comparisons of the roles played by the public in various democratic societies (Reitano & Elfenbein, 1997; Gelbman, 2011). Activities 5 and 7 below allow for such comparisons, with the former activity exploring differences between diverse democratic (or perhaps non-democratic) political systems, and the latter activity comparing voter participation levels amongst various countries. Giving students the ability to make such comparisons allows them to critique the American political system more closely. This approach also provides students an opportunity to achieve a greater appreciation of the benefits of the American political system itself (Gelbman, 2011), as well as those of other countries. This appreciation, in turn, can facilitate greater civic engagement, a key learning outcome for the political science discipline.

On the other hand, this comparative approach invites risks of turning the classroom discussion into a debate as to which governmental institutions are deemed superior, especially if the instructor appears to take sides in the discussion. In turn, such a debate could sow alienation from recent immigrants and those who may be critical of the United States of America, particularly if the classroom discussion implies that the political institutions of their "homeland" (or another country) are inferior to those of the United States. Such alienation could lead students to become disengaged from the class, and, by extension, from the material. Thus, it is incumbent upon the instructor to develop and implement activities in a way that provide sources of comparison, but do so in a way that highlights the tradeoffs between different institutions and approaches to government. This approach prevents labeling one country's system as inherently superior to another.

For example, any comparisons of presidential versus parliamentary systems should frame the discussion in a manner so that students can understand the benefits of both systems, such as the facilitation of input from diverse viewpoints in the separated-powers presidential system, versus the streamlining of policy decisions in the fused-power parliamentary system (Carey, 2008). In a similar fashion, a discussion of majoritarian and consociational democracies, as found below in Activity 6, should focus on the tradeoffs between process efficiency and policy consensus. This type of discussion reduces the possibility of biasing some students against the material, while providing opportunities for critical analyses of distinct types of political and government systems.

In short, internationalized courses should focus on activities that help students become familiar with their own culture and identity while instilling a sense of understanding and importance of other cultures and political institutions as well. Cross-national comparisons--such as the ones presented in the subsequent activities--help students view the American government, political systems, domestic society, and culture with a critical perspective. In turn, that perspective produces a more nuanced approach that leads to a deeper understanding of various aspects of American government.

INDIVIDUALIZATION OF AMERICAN GOVERNMENT CURRICULUM

In addition to developing a nuanced approach to cross-national comparisons, the instructor should seek to incorporate an individualization approach to the material. Individualization approaches are necessary for internationalized courses because they help students relate the course material to their own lives. This ability to relate is particularly helpful for enhancing student interest in the material. Furthermore, individualization promotes self-awareness and enhances cultural awareness. This approach also produces a bottom-up understanding of social interactions, institutions, and society in general. In other words, repeated interactions among individuals shape norms and institutions in society. This process occurs because "individuals act based on the meanings objects have for them" and because events "must be defined or categorized based on individual meaning" (Carter & Fuller, 2015, p. 2). Similarly, constructivism also argues "meanings are embodied in the language and actions of social actors" (Schwandt, 1998, p. 222). In short, individuals socially construct the world in which they live. Since it is this social construction that leads to the rules and norms that guide individual behavior, it is important for students of American government to more closely explore this relationship. Individualization approaches provide the opportunity for this kind of examination.

Individualization approaches to American government should encourage students to examine their own views, including how those views are shaped. In addition to the icebreaker in Activity 1, the group-based exploration of definitions of "human rights" in Activity 3 achieves the goal of highlighting how students' backgrounds and experiences shape their understanding of which rights are most important.

It is also important for students to place themselves in the role of others to gain a clear understanding of viewpoints other than their own. This approach can help students understand various elements that mold one's views, which in turn can facilitate discussions regarding why differences exist, and the impact those differences can have when it comes to shaping their societies. The role-playing scenario in Activity 4 achieves this outcome by having students consider the impact of their assigned factions' values upon those factions' approaches to government censorship of various forms of speech.

In individualization approaches to American government, the instructor should also develop activities that connect students to the material through the exploration of real lives, real people, and real stories. By incorporating such stories into a variety of activities, the instructor moves away from the notion of lecturing on purely abstract concepts and toward facilitating a greater understanding of how those concepts have played a role throughout U.S. history and today. This approach makes the material much more vivid and relatable to the students.

For example, "Reacting to the Past" scenarios involve the reconstruction of historical events by creating character roles for students to fill. These roles are related to a variety of different topics, but all serve to immerse students into a specific time and place in history in order to understand not only the historical context of an event, but also the individual perspectives of people during the event. More specifically, "The Reacting method entails elaborately designed role-playing games set in pivotal moments of clashing ideas and interests. Students are assigned distinctive roles and 'victory objectives' that they pursue, in alliance with some students and in competition with others" (Higbee, 2009, p. 43).

These types of games enable students to think through events from a given perspective, particularly one that may be unfamiliar or even uncomfortable for them. In *Greenwich Village, 1913: Suffrage, Labor and the New Woman* (Treacy, 2015), for example, men are often placed in female roles, whereas minority characters are usually filled by students who are not in a minority group. Placing them in roles that challenge their own views empowers students to consider the viewpoints of others in contrast with their own. In a similar fashion, Activity 2 below introduces students to the story of Sylvia Mendez, an overlooked figure in the civil rights struggle. Focusing on individual struggles helps the instructor make the civil rights narrative more vivid and compelling. This compelling narrative can also get students to consider the impact of these historical struggles on their daily lives.

Approaches that focus on individualization, like those described in the *Greenwich Village* book and in Activity 2, are beneficial because they deepen one's understanding not only of his or her own values (including how those values are formed), but also the values of others. This awareness can open a dialogue regarding the divisions in the viewpoints that exist among individuals, and how people can overcome those obstacles to cooperation. Doing so can also lead to discussions regarding alternative policy options that yield greater benefits to all since a greater awareness about others' needs is achieved.

Although it is possible to include elements of individualization in a course without the added components of internationalization, as seen with the *Greenwich Village* example or in Activity 2, it is not possible to successfully internationalize a course without including at least some elements of individualization. Without individualization, it is much more difficult for students to think critically about their own views vis-à-vis others. As discussed earlier in this chapter, critical thinking and the ability to shift perspectives are essential elements of the internationalization of curriculum. Thus, internationalization must combine with individualization to achieve the best results.

ACTIVE LEARNING ACTIVITIES

The dual pedagogical approaches of internationalization and individualization lend themselves to utilizing various active learning techniques. It is not enough for the instructor to give a traditional lecture where students would do little more than listen and take notes (Felder, 2009). Instead, active learning requires that students be "actively engaged in building understanding of facts, ideas, and skills through the completion of instructor directed tasks and activities" (Bell & Kahrhoff, 2006, p, 1). Such activities are designed to promote classroom engagement, so that as students become more involved with the course, they more clearly comprehend the underlying concepts and themes. Studies have shown that active learning techniques contributed to improved student performance in STEM courses--science, technology, engineering and mathematics (Freeman et. al, 2014), as well as other disciplines such as English and the Social Sciences (Mello & Less, 2013).

Utilizing a variety of activities to engage the students is particularly important when the instructor incorporates an internationalization approach to American government. For example, a student may expect an American government course to focus only on subjects relevant to the study of domestic politics. Thus, lectures that incorporate descriptions of other governments and societies may result in students tuning out the material, falsely concluding that such descriptions have little to do with an American government course. On the other hand, an activity that has students complete a task that addresses other governments can facilitate student engagement in a way that would not only help them to understand those governments, but also the American government as well.

The active learning approach is also significant when it comes to incorporating individualization into the curriculum. It is not enough for the instructor to relate the stories of other people; the instructor should utilize activities to better connect those people to the students, and to have students incorporate their own experiences into the material.

The remainder of this chapter is devoted to describing several examples of activities that incorporate the internationalization and individualization approaches to the curricula. These activities range from a brief icebreaker to an extended role-playing activity on civil liberties, to an online activity exploring the nature of democratic systems to a combination game/discussion activity exploring variances in voter participation.

Activity 1: "Special Place" Icebreaker

The first day of any academic course provides an opportunity for instructors to attract students' interest in the course material. The need for instant engagement is particularly significant for survey courses (including American government) in which students may not be otherwise familiar with, or even interested in, the course material. Furthermore, many survey courses can also be students' first experience with higher education. For such students, there may be an additional level of anxiety, as they may not know what to expect from the higher education experience, let alone any specific course. Thus, at a minimum, the first day provides the opportunity, and indeed the impetus, for the instructor to not only set the tone for the course, but also to make students feel comfortable with the material, with the instructor, and with each other.

In any given college classroom, there are bound to be a diverse range of student backgrounds and experiences. This variety can challenge the instructor on day one, as it easy for subtle biases (on behalf of the instructor and fellow students) to trigger feelings of anxiety and shame, which in turn can limit students' levels of concentration and learning abilities (Tedrow, 2017). One way to minimize those biases is to develop an icebreaking activity in which students learn more about each other and about themselves.

One such activity would take place during the classroom introductions, which typically cover relatively basic information such as the students' names, where they are from, their majors, and other details that are often forgotten by the end of the session, if not the end of the introductions themselves. Instead, the instructor could ask a question that gets students to more thoroughly consider their response and the responses of others.

For example, the instructor could ask students to briefly describe a place that has a special meaning in their heart, including reasons why this place is so significant for them. Through a description and explanation of their "special place," the student goes beyond mere recitation of a location as a simple fact, but instead goes into a deeper analysis intended to connect the fact (location) with an experience. This activity has several benefits. First, it helps students to become more fully engaged on the first day of class. Second the activity provides an interesting range of experiences for students to consider as they listen to other students' "special places." Finally, the activity incorporates individualization as it requires students to reflect upon how their values (as well as the values of others) may shape the selection of those "special places."

Activity 2: Immigration and Civil Rights in America

In addressing the impact of identity on politics, few topics are as vital to a course on American government as civil rights, a term which has numerous definitions and interpretations. However, at its most fundamental level, "civil rights" refers to "the rights of individuals to receive equal treatment (and to be free from unfair treatment or discrimination) in many settings -- including education, employment, housing, and more -- and based on certain legally-protected characteristics" (Findlaw, n.d.).

Beyond providing the underlying definition and the descriptions of various forms of civil rights, lessons in this topic often focus on historical and current struggles of members of various identity groups to achieve equality. Describing and discussing those struggles provides an opportunity for the instructor to highlight notable individuals who have used society's oppression of their identities as motivation for those individuals to fight for fundamental changes in the law and/or societal attitudes towards their identity group.

The history of civil rights is filled with such stories, ranging from Susan B. Anthony's efforts to promote equality for women to Rosa Park's arrest for refusing to give up her bus seat to a white man to Martin Luther King's promotion of civil disobedience to Malcolm X's more confrontational approach to promoting African-American rights. By providing a focus upon these individual struggles, the instructor can make the civil rights struggle more vivid and compelling, and thus attract a diverse group of students to the topic.

Beyond the iconic civil rights struggles, the history of civil rights in America has also involved many individuals who have not received as much attention. One unsung hero was Sylvia Mendez, whose immigrant family (her father from Mexico, and mother from Puerto Rico) fought for her right to education in a white school in California at a time when schools there were still segregated (U.S. Courts, n.d.).

Sylvia's story is compelling; her family moved into a ranch previously inhabited by Japanese Americans who were treated as potential traitors during World War II and placed in detention camps. Although the family had become successful in agriculture, the parents' long-term dream was to ensure a quality education for their daughter. Their dream was hampered by legal requirements that Sylvia attend a school exclusively for Mexican-Americans. Seeking to ensure that their daughter could get the best educational opportunities possible by attending a whites-only school, the family filed a lawsuit against the Orange County school district. Their lawsuit was consolidated with four other cases in *Mendez et. al v. Westminster School District of Orange County* (1947) where the California Court of Appeals ruled in favor of desegregation. Although the direct impact of the decision was limited in that it only applied to California schools and it only addressed the status of Mexican-Americans, it was the first court decision in the United States to support desegregation of public schools. Furthermore, the *Mendez* case paved the way for the nationwide desegregation of all public schools in *Brown v. Board of Education of Topeka, Kansas* (1954).

Analyzing the story of Sylvia Mendez is a way for both students and instructors to consider efforts to achieve political empowerment, for a variety of identity groups, such as Latinos, African-Americans, Native Americans, individuals with disabilities, and the LGBT community. Most importantly, this story helps to show similarities in fights that various groups had to undertake to achieve equal treatment in society. Focusing on engaging storytelling of individuals struggling to achieve equality helps to invite stories from the class members and to make a case that individuals can make a difference to society.

An ideal classroom activity that works towards that end would involve a brief (1-2-minute) response paper in which students would respond to a question that asks them to consider how Sylvia Mendez's struggles affect their lives today. That paper would serve as a springboard for a classroom discussion that allows students to tell stories regarding their connections to civil rights struggles. Such stories would demonstrate that although the *Mendez* case (and others like it) took place generations before, it continues to facilitate education opportunities for those who might not otherwise have had it. In turn, such a discussion would get students to think about how diversity in the education system not only affects their lives, but also society (Lewkowicz, 2017).

Activity 3: Defining Human Rights

With origins dating back to Franz Boas' early 20th Century anthropological studies (Brown, 2008), the concept of cultural relativism focuses on the notion that people's values, beliefs and activities are best understood by examining those people's cultures. In other words, we can best understand people not through the lens of our own values and culture, but through the values and cultures of the people we seek to understand.

This approach incorporates both an internationalized and individualized perspective. However, instructors often face the problems of helping students understand and, more importantly, appreciate the value of this approach. The topic of human rights provides an opportunity to introduce this concept and to engage students in a way that helps them better understand and appreciate the merits of cultural relativism. By starting a discussion of cultural relativism, the instructor can transition into a discussion of the impact of cultures and values upon the creation and maintenance of different political systems, including institutions those systems have in place to protect individual rights.

Before students are exposed to any material or any discussion on the topic of human rights, it is useful to start with an introductory activity. One suggested activity would entail that students be divided into groups based on their similarities, such as students who were born in or lived in another country other than the United States. Dividing students into these groups is beneficial because the shared background and experiences of these individuals provides them insight regarding what rights are most important. Significantly, the different outcomes produced by each group can highlight how experiences can shape perceptions as to the necessity for certain rights over others. It is important, however, for the instructor to be careful about assigning students to these groups as it could introduce an element of bias which leaves some students feeling alienated from the perspective of the group to which they are assigned.

Once students are divided into their groups, the instructor assigns the groups the task of preparing a list of the ten most important human rights that all individuals should have. In developing these lists, students would not be allowed to use outside material. Following the group discussion, each group would share their list of rights with the class. Once each group has shared its list, the instructor would then compare the group lists with the actual list of rights spelled out in the Universal Declaration of Human Rights (UDHR). From there the instructor could highlight discrepancies between the group lists and the rights listed in the UDHR by facilitating a discussion that explores not only the variances between the lists, but also the reasons behind such variances.

In previous applications of this activity, students from Africa, Eastern Europe, or Latin America have identified freedom from torture, political persecution, and the right to life as high on their list of important human rights. In a similar fashion, students from less affluent backgrounds (including countries of origin that are often described as "developing") tended to include rights to material goods such as food and clean water. On the other hand, students who have lived in the United States for almost all of their lives often take such rights for granted, and thus rarely mentioned them in this activity. Instead, American students focused on the right to education and health care, along with more abstract rights such as those listed in the Bill of Rights such as freedom of speech and religion.

An exploration of the different perspectives regarding human rights can provide an engaging introduction to the concept of cultural relativism. By explaining how people's backgrounds can shape their understandings of right versus wrong, needs versus wants, and to what, if anything, humans are entitled, students are awakened to how cultures and values can shape the granting of rights in various societies. Furthermore, the activity can also provide an opportunity for the class to address the historical contexts that shape the development of different political institutions, along with the corresponding set of human rights and protections accorded by those institutions.

Activity 4: Exploring Civil Liberties Via Role-Playing

Cultural relativism can also play a significant role in a classroom discussion of civil liberties. As with civil rights, there are many varied definitions of civil liberties. In their essence, civil liberties relate to the notion of freedom from interference by government, at least not without some form of due process. Civil liberties are significant insofar as government suppression of the people often begins with substantial restrictions upon various forms of expression such as speech and the press. By seeking to restrict access to information, governments can assert their control over the populace, particularly minority groups that may already struggle to assert themselves and to spread their message throughout a society.

Beyond providing a mechanism of control for those in power, limits to free expression can also be reflective of the underlying values shared by members of that society. However, a society with diverse values and points of view may face numerous conflicts and tensions about the types of expression considered "acceptable" by that society, and the types of expression that should be restricted through punishment or outright censorship. Over time, each country has developed its own unique set of traditions in how its citizens and government approach free expression. Thus, what may be a perfectly acceptable form of expression in one society is deemed offensive in another, sometimes to the point of being subject to criminal or civil penalties.

One challenge in addressing the topic of free expression in an introductory American government course is that students often may not fully appreciate how generous free speech protections are in America, let alone understand the underlying historical motivations behind this relatively generous approach. Thus, a classroom discussion of free speech could involve exploring not only the types of speech and expression that are given protection in America, but also the underlying foundations and traditions behind the American approach to free speech, especially compared to other democracies.

The instructor could start the classroom discussion of civil liberties in America by highlighting the latitude given to various forms of expression. The First Amendment to the United States Constitution protects various forms of speech that are deemed offensive by many in a society. The language of the First Amendment's Speech Clause states "Congress shall make no law…abridging the freedom of speech…" This approach to free speech appears to be absolute, as suggested by the phrase "no law means no law," offered up by Supreme Court Justice Hugo Black in *New York Times Co, v. United States* (1971), in which the Court rejected a federal government request for an injunction blocking publication of classified materials.

Despite the absolutist language of the First Amendment, various United States federal courts (including the Supreme Court) have imposed some limits on speech in various case rulings. For example, the courts have allowed for criminal penalties for "fighting words" (*Chaplinsky v. New Hampshire*, 1942) and for obscenity (*Miller v. California*, 1973). Still, these are very minimal restrictions on speech, as the U.S. still permits certain forms of expression deemed offensive by some, such as the burning of the American flag in protest, the publication of pornographic material, and the dissemination of hate speech. Considering how many forms of potentially offensive speech are allowed by the courts, some students may feel that this interpretation of the free speech clause of the First Amendment may be too permissive.

Other countries may have constitutions in which the wording appears to be as absolutist of the United States, but may not be as generous in how they interpret that wording. For example, Article 5 of the Basic Law of Germany provides that "[e]very person shall have the right freely to express and disseminate his opinions in speech, writing, and pictures." However, in practice, the German Criminal Code allows for restrictions on numerous forms of speech. For example, paragraph 130, section 1 of the German Criminal Code provides a fairly broad definition of racial incitement:

1. incites hatred against a national, racial, religious group or a group defined by their ethnic origins, against segments of the population or individuals because of their belonging to one of the aforementioned groups or segments of the population or calls for violent or arbitrary measures against them; or

2. assaults the human dignity of others by insulting, maliciously maligning an aforementioned group, segments of the population or individuals because of their belonging to one of the aforementioned groups or segments of the population, or defaming segments of the population (Bohlander, 1998).

Violating this law could result in a prison sentence of up to five years (Bohlander, 1998). Clearly, Germany's approach towards hate speech is quite different than that of the United States, where hate speech is usually given a great deal of latitude unless accompanied by action.

What are the reasons for the differences in the scope of protections for free speech (including speech that offends) in the United States and other democracies? Important historical, cultural, and ideological differences between the United States and other democracies help to account for these differences. For example, Germany's stricter approach to hate speech is rooted in that country's history with various forms of racism, particularly anti-Semitism, which culminated in the Holocaust. In fact, denial of the Holocaust is also subject to criminal penalties in Germany (Bohlander, 1998), as well as many other European nations that have all directly or indirectly faced the consequences of Nazi anti-Semitism during World War II, such as France and Italy.

One approach to stimulating discussion on the impact of societal values upon free expression is a role-playing scenario involving a mythical country considering several proposals regarding the protections (or lack thereof) of different forms of expression. During this scenario, the expressive activities of various minorities are under siege as hostile majorities might wish to ban forms of speech they deem offensive, such as religious proselytism or political expression.

In a basic version of this game, the class would be divided into three factions. The first faction is culturally refined, sophisticated and agnostic to the point of being hostile to religious proselytism and enjoys expressing pride in their sophistication and sometimes ridiculing the less sophisticated factions. The second faction is devoted to religious proselytizing, with its members also advocating for the secession of their region from the country. The third faction is historically minded, and thus favors celebrations of the unification of the country via military victories over the other factions.

Each faction would have the opportunity to select from one of three operational rules concerning how the country would address offensive speech. The first option, otherwise known as the "freedom rule" would allow for all types of speech. The second, known as the "majority rule" would allow restricted speech if a majority of the country agrees to restrict that form of speech. The third rule, known as the "safety rule" would restrict all forms of potentially offensive speech.

Once the class is informed about the framework of the simulation, members of each faction would then have to develop a consensus as to which rule their faction supports. At the completion of the deliberations, a representative of each faction would present their faction's consensus selection, including the explanation behind that choice. These explanations can be particularly significant because they can reveal the extent to which each group is willing to consider limitations to this presumably core value of free speech. Even factions that reach a consensus on adopting a "freedom rule" may do so less because of a general predisposition to free speech by members of that faction, but because limiting certain forms of speech would go against that faction's interests. Thus, by giving students the opportunity to make collective decisions based on a set of values and beliefs assigned to their factions, students can explore the impact of cultural relativism in action.

Activity 5: A Comparative Approach to Discussing Democracy

A crucial topic for introductory American government is "democracy," which is described by the *Oxford Dictionary* as the exercise of power by the public, typically through elected officials (n.d.). However, each country differs in how (or even if) they allow the public to exercise influence over their government. For example, although many countries hold elections on a regular basis, some do not allow a genuine choice to be offered to the people. In those countries, competition can be limited through manipulation of election laws, intimidation of the voters and even the arrest or murder of opponents of the country's leadership. Thus, although leaders of those countries may claim adherence to democratic principles, elections would only be a means by which those leaders retain their power while giving their government the appearance of public support. Not surprisingly, such systems also tend to be restrictive towards various rights and liberties, particularly when such restrictions also serve the interests of those in power.

Even countries that fully adhere to democratic principles by allowing the public to have a genuine impact upon outcomes will vary in their institutional frameworks, which in turn will produce different methods of accountability to the public. For example, in parliamentary systems, the voters select the parliament, which in turn selects the prime minister and other members of the executive branch. This fused-power approach allows voters to hold political parties accountable for policy successes and failures, since a single party (or a coalition of parties) will control both the executive and legislative branches. On the other hand, in presidential systems, voters choose among a group of candidates for executive offices, particularly the chief executive. Thus, presidential systems may result in reduced voter accountability as separated powers can lead to one party controlling the legislature and another controlling the executive branch. When there is the potential for divided government, voters may struggle to hold their leaders accountable for policy outcomes, whether good or bad (Carey, 2008).

Beyond the procedural aspects of democracy that ensure the voice of the people is heard, countries also can vary in the extent to which policy outcomes are reflective of the demands and the interests of the people, otherwise known as substantive democracy. Those two types of democracy may not always go hand in hand. Mary Kaldor argues that even as procedural democracy has expanded in Europe, substantive democracy has actually contracted (2014).

The varying facets of procedural and substantive democracy lend themselves to an activity whereby students could evaluate the United States as a democracy as compared to other countries. Since non-international introductory American government students are likely to have less experience with, let alone knowledge of, other democracies, the best approach is to give students the opportunity to conduct outside research on the subject. An online discussion assignment is ideal, as it gives students the opportunity and the time to conduct research about other countries which can be chosen by either the students or the instructor. In their responses, students would describe aspects of a society they would consider to be important for that society and/or its government to be truly democratic. From there, the students would provide an analysis of how the United States and at least one other country live up to their subjective democratic ideals. Through the assignment instructions, the instructor would encourage students to think about the things the countries have in common, as well as those aspects in which the countries differ.

Once students have completed the online assignment, the instructor would then lead the class in a discussion about various facets of democracy. In addition to addressing comparisons between procedural and structural democracies, the instructor can also promote a discussion of how much influence the public has upon policy decisions, including whether the public can vote upon policies directly via ballot referenda. Furthermore, the instructor could examine comparisons of specific types of representative democracies, such as presidential versus parliamentary systems, and majoritarian versus consociational democracies.

Activity 6: Majoritarian and Consociational Democracies

The previous activity provides one avenue in which American government instructors can facilitate a discussion of various aspects of democracy. Another activity would focus upon a specific set of comparisons, that of majoritarian versus consociational democracies.

Majoritarian democracies usually enable slim legislative majorities to govern without sharing power. Features in majoritarian democracies are useful in ensuring that governments of homogenous societies are accountable to majoritarian preferences. The United Kingdom is a good example of a majoritarian democracy. By contrast, consociational democracies include features such as multi-party systems and proportional representation that encourage power sharing and consensus development among minority interests. These features are useful in diverse societies with numerous minority interests such as Germany and Switzerland (Lijphart, 2008).

After providing an explanation of these two approaches to democracy, along with accompanying examples, the instructor would then divide the class into groups. Each group is asked to list features of the United States political system that would lend themselves to majoritarian democracy (such as single-member-district elections) and features that would lend themselves to consociational democracy (such as the Electoral College or the Senate filibuster). Next, the groups would share their responses as a class and the class could come to a consensus as to where the United States system fits on the majoritarian-consociational spectrum.

The post-activity discussion can provide an opportunity to highlight those features the United States shares with other democracies. Students would consider how the United States political system shares commonalities with both majoritarian and consociational systems around the world. From there, the instructor can facilitate a discussion of the tradeoffs of each system, such as the greater accountability in a majoritarian democracy versus the need for consensus and compromise in a consociational democracy.

Activity 7: Comparing Voter Participation Rates

One implication of the different governmental frameworks involves the extent to which elected officials are held accountable by the public. For example, the divided government in a presidential system may reduce accountability to the voters (Carey, 2008), who in turn may become alienated and less willing to participate in a range of elections. The lack of a direct link between elections, partisan power, and policy outcomes might be one reason why average voter participation rates in the United States are relatively low compared with those of other countries. For congressional (legislative/parliamentary) elections[1] from 1945 to 2015, the United States has an average voter turnout rate of 46.89% of the voting age population (VAP), ranking it at 164th of 195 nations.[2]

Rather than giving students the aforementioned voter participation statistic as part of a lecture on political participation, the instructor can liven up the discussion of voter participation by turning it into a game, whereby students would be asked to guess where the United States ranks among 195 nations. At the beginning of the activity, the instructor would hand out a set of index cards and briefly explain the IDEA data set used to calculate the average turnout rates. He/she would then ask students to write down their guesses as to where the United States ranks in average turnout rates among the 195 nations in the data set. After a few minutes, students would share their guesses with the class.

Next, the instructor would divide the class into discussion groups. Each group would then have 5-10 minutes to come up with a list of explanations as to why United States voter participation might be so low (or conversely, why participation in other democracies is so high). Ideally, this activity would provoke a discussion of the various causes of low participation rates in the United States. Furthermore, this activity can serve as a springboard for a discussion of comparative institutional differences such as presidential versus parliamentary systems and compulsory voting laws that impose penalties upon those who abstain from voting (Solijonov 2016).

Beyond highlighting institutional differences between political systems, the instructor can also ask students to relate their attitudes towards process of voting, including the navigation of any registration hurdles. Such a discussion can be particularly useful during those semesters that include a major election, particularly a presidential election, which receives a great deal of attention from the media and the public. During the presidential election season, students' memories and attitudes regarding the election would be particularly fresh, which would hopefully facilitate an energetic discussion regarding topics such as attitudes towards voting and whether students voted (or intended to vote) in a given election.

CONCLUSION

Internationalization and individualization of American government courses are a way to keep today's diverse students engaged in material that may otherwise seem dry and boring. Connecting course material to their lives in ways that help them draw comparisons between their experiences and others is also needed to help facilitate a deeper understanding of the issues facing individuals within their own country and in societies around the world. The activities presented in this chapter are just a few examples of how one can incorporate both internationalization and individualization into an American government course. Adopting these kinds of activities creates an active-learning approach to a class that may not appeal to every student, but which is likely to be more engaging than more traditional lecture-based methods.

Promoting internationalization strictly through adoption of comparative elements without including elements of individualization may produce unintended consequences, such as division into "us" versus "them" camps among students, or feelings of national superiority and exceptionalism (for example, a belief that "our" democracy is "better" and more developed than everyone else's in the world). Incorporating life stories may help to challenge such dichotomies and myths, bringing the level of analysis down to an individual and reminding us about the complexity of social realities. In addition, developing activities with a focus on the rights of individuals (civil rights and civil liberties in the context of the United States and human rights in the international context) can also help to reduce divisions amongst "us" versus "them" that can be an unintended consequence of the use of the comparative method to internationalize the study of U.S. government.

To conclude, our chapter argues that effective internationalization of American government courses (and probably other political science courses) must be accompanied by thoughtful individualization of carefully planned activities. We suggest including activities that address various levels of analysis (individual, domestic, international, and global), thoughtfully use comparisons, and demonstrate cultural embeddedness of individual rights and respect for individual no matter where they are located.

REFERENCES

Bell, D., & Kahrhoff, J. (2006). *Active learning handbook*. Retrieved February 26, 2017, from http://www.cgs.pitt.edu/sites/default/files/Doc6-GetStarted_ActiveLearningHandbook.pdf

Bohlander, M. (1998), *Bundesministerium der Justiz und für Verbraucherschutz: GERMAN CRIMINAL CODE* [Federal ministry of justice and consumer protection: GERMAN CRIMINAL CODE]. Federal Ministry of Justice, Germany, para. 130 sec. 1. Retrieved June 11, 2017, from http://www.gesetze-im-internet.de/englisch_stgb/englisch_stgb.html#p1241

Brown, M. F. (2008). Cultural relativism 2.0. *Current Anthropology, 49*(3), 363–383. doi:10.1086/529261

Brown v. Board of Education of Topeka, Kansas, 347 U.S. 483 (1954).

Carey, J. (2008). Presidential versus parliamentary government. In C. Menard & M. Shirley (Eds.), *Handbook of new institutional economics* (pp. 91–122). Berlin: Springer-Verlag. doi:10.1007/978-3-540-69305-5_6

Carter, M. J., & Fuller, C. (2015). Symbolic interactionism. *Sociopedia.isa*. Retrieved March 13, 2017, from www.sagepub.net/isa/resources/pdf/Symbolic%20interactionism.pdf

Chaplinsky v. New Hampshire, 315 U.S. 568 (1942).

Crichton, J. A., Paige, M., Papademetre, L., & Scarino, A. (2004). *Integrated resources for intercultural teaching and learning in the context of internationalisation in higher education (University of South Australia, Research Centre for Languages and Cultures Education) The role of language and culture in open learning in international collaborative programs: A case study*. Retrieved June 23, 2017, from: https://www.researchgate.net/publication/224807122_The_role_of_language_and_culture_in_open_learning_in_international_collaborative_programs_A_case_study

Democracy. (n.d.). In *Oxford dictionary*. Retrieved June 11, 2017, from https://en.oxforddictionaries.com/definition/democracy

Engstrom, R. N. (2008). Introductory American government in comparison: An experiment. *Journal of Political Science Education*, *4*(4), 394–403. doi:10.1080/15512160802413675

Felder, R. M., & Brent, R. (2009). Active learning: An introduction. *ASQ Higher Education Brief, 2*(4).

Findlaw. (n.d.). *What are civil rights?* Retrieved June 10, 2017, from http://civilrights.findlaw.com/civil-rights-overview/what-are-civil-rights.html

Freeman, S., Eddy, S. L., McDonough, M., Smith, M. K., Okorafor, N., Jordt, H., & Wenderoth, M. P. (2014). Active learning increases student performance in science, engineering and mathematics. *Proceedings of the National Academy of Sciences of the United States of America*, *111*(23), 8410–8415. doi:10.1073/pnas.1319030111 PMID:24821756

Gallup. (2016a). *Confidence in institutions*. Retrieved February 12, 2017, from http://www.gallup.com/poll/1597/confidence-institutions.aspx

Gallup. (2016b). *Trust in government*. Retrieved February 12, 2017, from http://www.gallup.com/poll/5392/trust-government.aspx

Gallup. (2016c). *Americans trust in political leaders at new lows*. Retrieved February 12, 2017, from http://www.gallup.com/poll/195716/americans-trust-political-leaders-public-new-lows.aspx

Gelbman, S. M. (2011). A qualitative assessment of the learning outcomes of teaching introductory American politics in comparative perspective. *Journal of Political Science Education*, *7*(4), 359–374. doi:10.1080/15512169.2011.615187

Higbee, M. D. (2009). How reacting to the past games 'made me want to come to class and learn': An assessment of reacting pedagogy at EMU, 2007- 208. *The Scholarship of Teaching and Learning at EMU, 2*(4).

Hudzik, J. K., & McCarthy, J. S. (2012). *Leading comprehensive internationalization strategy and tactics for action*. NAFSA: Association of International Educators. Retrieved June 23, 2017, from http://www.nafsa.org/pubs

International Institute for Democracy and Electoral Assistance (IDEA). (n.d.). *Voter turnout database*. Retrieved June 16, 2017, from http://www.idea.int/data-tools/data/voter-turnout

Kaldor, M. (2014). The habits of the heart: Substantive democracy after the European elections. *Open democracy*. Retrieved June 10, 2017, from https://www.opendemocracy.net/can-europe-make-it/mary-kaldor/habits-of-heart-substantive-democracy-after-european-elections

Leask, B. (2009). Using formal and informal curricula to improve interactions between home and international students. *Journal of Studies in International Education*, *13*(2), 205–221. doi:10.1177/1028315308329786

Leask, B. (2014, December 12). Internationalising the curriculum and all learning. *University World News*. Retrieved February 19, 2017, from http://www.universityworldnews.com/article.php?story=20141211101031828

Lewkowicz, M. (2017). The law as the language of civil rights: using Supreme Court cases to facilitate an inclusive classroom dialog on difference and equality. In D. Budrytė & S. Boykin (Eds.), *Engaging difference: Teaching humanities and social science in multicultural environments* (pp. 19–30). Lanham, MD: Rowman & Littlefield.

Lijphart, A. (2008). *Thinking about democracy*. London: Routledge Press.

Mello, D., & Less, C. A. (2013). *Effectiveness of active learning in the arts and sciences*. Retrieved February 24, 2017, from http://scholarsarchive.jwu.edu/cgi/viewcontent.cgi?article=1044&context=h umanities_fac

Mendez, et al *v. Westminster [sic] School District of Orange County, et al,* 64 F.Supp. 544 (S.D. Cal.1964), aff'd, 161 F.2d 774 (9th Cir. 1947) (en banc).

Miller v. California, 413 U.S. 15 (1973)

New York Times Co. v. United States, 403 U.S. 713 (1971).

Reitano, R., & Elfenbein, C. (1997). American government: A comparative approach. *PS, Political Science & Politics, 30*(3), 540–552. doi:10.1017/S1049096500046801

Schwandt, T. A. (1998). Constructivist, interpretivist approaches to human inquiry. In N. K. Denzin & Y. S. Lincoln (Eds.), *The landscape of qualitative research: theories and issues* (pp. 221–255). Thousand Oaks, CA: Sage Publications.

Solijonov, A. (2017). *Voter turnout trends around the world. Institute for Democracy and Electoral Assistance.* Retrieved March 26, 2017, from http://www.oldsite.idea.int/vt/compulsory_voting.cfm

Takagi, H. (2015). The internationalisation of curricula: The complexity and diversity of meaning in and beyond Japanese universities. *Innovations in Education and Teaching International, 52*(4), 349–359. doi:10.1080/14703297.2013.820138

Tedrow, B. (2017). Favorite place mapmaking and the decolonization of teaching. In D. Budrytė & S. Boykin (Eds.), *Engaging difference: Teaching humanities and social science in multicultural environments* (pp. 75–82). Lanham, MD: Rowman & Littlefield.

Treacy, M. J. (2015). *Greenwich Village, 1913: Suffrage, labor, and the new woman (reacting to the past).* New York City: W. W. Norton & Company.

United States Courts. (n.d.). *Background. Mendez v. Westminster reenactment.* Retrieved March 5, 2017, from http://www.uscourts.gov/educational-resources/educational-activities/background-mendez-v-westminster-re-enactment

Wamboye, E., Adekola, A., & Sergi, B. S. (2015). Internationalisation of the campus and curriculum: Evidence from the US institutions of higher learning. *Journal of Higher Education Policy and Management, 37*(4), 385–399. doi:10.1080/1360080X.2015.1056603

Zimitat, C. (2008). Student perceptions of the internationalisation of the curriculum. In L. Dunn & M. Wallace (Eds.), *Teaching in transnational higher education* (pp. 135–147). London: Routledge.

KEY TERMS AND DEFINITIONS

Active Learning: A process that engages students in activities that promote problem solving, critical analysis, and deeper comprehension of course content.

Civil Liberties: Those rights of citizens protected by law from unjust government (or other) interference.

Civil Rights: The rights of citizens to political and social freedom and equality.

Comparative Method: A technique for studying two or more political systems, including domestic politics and political institutions.

Cultural Relativism: The notion that people's values, beliefs, and activities are best understood by examining those people's cultures.

Human Rights: Rights that promote dignity and belong to every person simply because they are human.

Individualization: The promotion of greater self-awareness of one's own values and opinions as well as those of others.

Internationalization of the Curriculum: The incorporation of an international and intercultural dimension to course content to promote greater student awareness and appreciation of other cultures, countries, and regions while increasing the student's awareness of their own cultural identity.

ENDNOTES

[1]   Average turnout rates were even lower for congressional elections in years in which the United States presidency was not on the ballot. For those midterm elections, the average voter turnout rate was 37.68%.

[2]   Data used to calculate average voting rates in parliamentary elections was obtained through the International Institute of Democracy and Electoral Assistance (International IDEA) website.

Chapter 2
Process of Transforming Regular Courses Into I-Courses:
The Case of Two Political Science Courses at GGC

Clemente Quinones
Georgia Gwinnett College, USA

ABSTRACT

The purpose of this chapter is to analyze the possible factors that determined a relatively relaxed process of transforming the author's two courses into i-courses. The argument is that some GGC's institutional mechanisms smoothed the process. To support the argument, the chapter first introduces a conceptual framework, followed by the presentation of other scholars' findings on factors of internationalization of the curriculum. The introduction of GGC's process approach to internationalization and the author's intrinsic motivation were the major institutional arrangements and natural factors, respectively, that explain the relatively relaxed process of transforming the author's two courses into i-courses. The chapter concludes with a description of venues for future research and some student evaluations of the two i-courses.

INTRODUCTION

Due to globalization of communication technology, social media, and multiple free trade agreements, national borderlines all over the world are disappearing. This demands that our universities must transcend their local or national focus to address the changing educational landscape that globalization has created. At the same time, the ability to work with people from other countries and cultures has become a key factor for such interactions to succeed. Related to this globalization, in the area of education, we have two different terms that are very often exchangeable: *international dimension of education* and *global dimension of education*. However, there is a fundamental difference between these two concepts. The former refers to "the process of integrating an international/intercultural dimension into the teaching, research and service functions of the institution" (Knight, 1993, p. 21). This means that *international*

DOI: 10.4018/978-1-5225-2791-6.ch002

dimension of education implies infusion of other cultural values and traditions into specific teachings, e.g. political science, at home. *Global dimension of education,* meanwhile, denotes a dimension that goes beyond the particular concerns targeted by the international dimension of education to reach general concerns, like the philosophy of a school and global interdependence.

By 2009, Georgia Gwinnett College (GGC) initiated a generalized effort to internationalize the curriculum by focusing on the *international dimension of education* as defined above. A few years later, those efforts culminated with the origination of the current Global Studies Certification" program. Three years of college-wide research and planning led to the design of the certification program and the development of a two-part program by the Center for Teaching Excellence (CTE). The first one exposes GGC faculty members to the implementation of concepts of internationalized learning on their own teaching and their students' learning. The second part consists of a semester-long "deep" training faculty development program designed to help faculty gain the knowledge, skills, and attitudes needed to successfully convert their courses into *i*-courses (GGC.b, 2016).

The author of this chapter participated in the college's efforts to internationalize the curricula. Then, he actually got two of his regular courses approved as internationalized courses (or *i*-courses). The purpose of this chapter is to analyze the possible factors that determined a relatively relaxed process of transforming the author's two courses into *i*-course. The argument is that some institutional mechanisms created by the college administration smoothed the process. To support the argument, the chapter, first, provides definitions of some concepts related to internationalization of the curriculum, followed by the presentation of other scholars' findings on factors of internationalization of the curriculum. The introduction of GGC's *process approach to internationalization* will be next, followed by an analysis of the process of transforming the author's two regular courses into *i*-courses. The chapter concludes with some challenges, several student evaluations of the two *i*-courses, and directions for future research.

BACKGROUND. LITERATURE REVIEW

Meaning of IoC

Internationalization of the curriculum may refer to a variety of internationalization activities including study abroad programs, foreign language courses, interdisciplinary or area programs, or the provision of programs or courses with an international, intercultural, or comparative focus (Bremer & van der Wende, 1995). This is the *"what"* we teach. Following influential scholars in the literature of internationalization of education (Adams, 1992; Bond, 2006; DeVita & Case, 2003; Leask B., 2001; Marchesani & Adams, 1992; Maidstone, 1995; Mckellin, 1998; McLoughlin, 2001), our concept of internationalization of the curriculum also includes the pedagogy approach, that is, the *how* we teach. This way, our conception of IoC is comprehensive by including both the *what* we teach and *how* we teach it (Bond, 2006).

Professor Betty Leask conceives *internationalization of the curriculum* as a *process* that incorporates "an international and intercultural dimension into the content of the curriculum as well as the teaching and learning arrangements and support services of a program of study" (Leask, 2009, p. 209). As we see, Leask's concept of *internationalization of the curriculum* as a *process* includes both the *"what"* and the *"how"* we teach (Bond, 2006). However, Professor Leask goes beyond this by providing us with the concept of *internationalized curriculum* as a *product,* which "engages students with internationally informed research and cultural and linguistic diversity and purposefully develop their international and intercultural perspectives as global professionals and citizens" (Leask, 2009, p. 209). Thus, this conception departs from and includes IoC, but it goes beyond that to emphasize the active involvement of students in both the learning process and the development of international and intercultural learning outcomes (Leask, 2014).

On his part, Bond (2003a; 2003b) associates internationalization of the curriculum with three approaches: add-on, infusion, and transformation. The add-on approach consists of adding "Content, concepts, themes, and perspectives…to the curriculum without changing its structure" (Banks, 2004, p. 246). Thus, Bond's 'add-on' concept is similar to Leask's (2009) notion of *internationalization of the curriculum*, except that Bond does not include the pedagogical element in her approach (the *how* we teach). Bond's infusion approach tries to include "an international, multicultural, and if possible intercultural dimension [in the curriculum]" (Maidstone, 1995, pp. 63-64). However, this approach focuses on disseminating knowledge based on West paradigms of domination. The absence of critical learning, in this approach, obstructs the development of intercultural skills and attitudes (Williams, 2008). Finally, Bond's transformative approach focuses on "enabling students to move between two or more worldviews" (Bond, 2003a, p. 5). In words of Bond herself, this approach promotes counter-hegemonic view of curriculum reforms and promotes social justice through the education process.

In sum, IoC involves "crossing boundaries into cultures and subjectivities beyond our own experience" (Bates, 2005, p. 107). This, in turn, assumes two basic characteristics: internationalization at home (IaH) and internationalization abroad (Knight, 2008). The former consists of awareness activities. These activities may take place both on campus and in classrooms, including internationalizing the curriculum (*i*-courses at GGC), new inclusive pedagogy (teaching-learning process or *how* we teach), local collaboration with others of different ethnic and racial backgrounds, '*different from us*-ethnic/racial groups (Latinos, Asians, etc.) and scholarly activities, such as research, conferences, lectures, faculty professional development training, and the like.

Internationalization abroad, meanwhile, embraces crossing boundaries beyond our society and cultures, as Bates (2005) argues, "only by the redress of exclusion and disadvantage on a global scale can we truly imagine a global curriculum…" (p. 108). Activities in this category may include study abroad programs for students and faculty exchange programs, among others (Agoston & Dima, 2012). However, we should very careful, because Internationalization abroad could both portray west values of domination and promote the development of submitted minds (non-critical thinking development).

Based on this literature, internationalization of the curriculum has two dimensions: "Orientation" and "Content and Pedagogy." The orientation of internationalization of the curriculum may be carried out through different tasks at home (at the institution) and/or via activities abroad (see Table 1). At home and/or abroad, the essential elements of IoC are the subject (*what* we teach) and *how* we teach it (pedagogy), (refer to Table 1). In a few words, it is important that courses with international content are included in our curricula, while at the same time, academic exchanges such as study abroad programs and faculty visits are essential to a successful story of internationalization of the curriculum and of the institution itself.

Determinants of Internationalization of the Curriculum

According to Herzberg, Mausner and Snyderman (1959), there are two factors of motivation: one is intrinsic, or *motivator* and the other one is extrinsic, or *hygiene*. The former includes 'job satisfiers' that fulfil the psychological development of a worker. This is to say the intrinsic-motivator factor is the

Table 1. Internationalization of the Curriculum (Author's elaboration based on Bates, 2005)

		Content and Pedagogy of IoC	
		The *What* We Teach **(the *subject matter*)**	The *How* We Teach **(Pedagogy)**
Orientation of IoC	*(1)* **Internationalization at Home (IaH)** consists of awareness activities that may take place both on campus and in classrooms.	*(2)* -*internationalization of the curriculum as a product* (includes: activities on campus like foreign language courses, and other courses and/or programs with a comparative, intercultural, and international component like the *i*-course at GGC; international recruitment; international research collaboration and preparing students to excel in a multicultural and global environment	*(3)* -*internationalization of the curriculum as a process* Activities include: -new inclusive pedagogy of teaching and learning (the *how* we teach) that encourage the inclusion of international students, collaboration with local '*different from us-ethnic/racial groups* (Latinos, Asians, etc.) and scholarly activities, such as research, conferences, lectures, faculty professional development training, and the like, **on campus.**
	(4) **Internationalization Abroad:** embraces crossing boundaries beyond our society and cultures.	*(5)* -*internationalization of the curriculum as a product.* Activities include -study abroad programs that include foreign language courses and other courses and/or programs with a comparative, intercultural, and international component taught abroad (semester or semesters abroad), faculty exchange programs, and any other activities and/or programs to develop a global citizenship in both our students and faculty.	*(6)* *internationalization of the curriculum as a process* Activities include: -new inclusive pedagogy of teaching and learning (the *how* we teach) that encourages the immersion of local students in other cultures, collaboration with different institutions around the world, and scholarly activities, such as research, conferences, lectures, faculty professional development training and the like, **abroad.**

natural inclination to exercise a specific profession, task, or activity. In Political Science, an example is a comparativist accepting a teaching position because it is a comparative politics position. Regarding IoC, it may happen that the same comparativist also has international/comparative insight. Deci and Ryan (1985) calls this factor simply *intrinsic motivation* that encourages an individual to participate in an activity merely for a sense of duty or self-fulfillment. The *hygiene* factor embraces 'job satisfiers' that are related to the work environment. This latter includes incentives, whether they are economic or symbolic (like academic rewards, honorific mentions, etc.), that is, anything that may help prevent worker's dissatisfaction (Castillo & Cano, 2004). Several scholars have found that intrinsic factors, in fact, have been determinant for faculty involvement in higher education (Rockwell, Schauer, Fritz, & Marx, 1999; Parker, 2003; Serow, Brawner, & Demery, 1999; Tang & Chamberlain, 2003). The assumption here is that by extension, the intrinsic factors may also affect faculty involvement in internationalization of the curriculum.

Backman (1981), however, argues that both intrinsic and extrinsic motivations are a barrier for faculty involvement in internationalization of the curriculum. Nevertheless, Backman does not provide solid arguments or evidence to support his argument. Differing from Herzberg, Mausner and Snyderman (1959) and Deci and Ryan (1985), De-Zan, Paipa-G, and Parra-M (2011) argue that it is not the intrinsic motivation nor the extrinsic one that affects IoC. It rather is the concept of skills. This concept, according to them, facilitates the psychological communication, the integration in the institutional networks, and it actually promotes the legitimate cultural and social differences. The problem with this conception is that it focuses on economic rather than on academic-intellectual matters, as some scholars argue: "earning money is a key motive for all internationalization projects in the profit sector and for some traditional nonprofit universities with financial difficulties" (Altbach & Knight, 2007, p. 292).

The assumption in this chapter is that all the GGC faculty members who have converted their regular courses into *i*-courses were naturally inclined to do so (motivator factor or intrinsic motivation) because their courses had already some international or comparative content and/or they—the faculty—have some international background of training. Then these faculty members received the skills, not the skills to which De-Zan, Paipa-G, and Parra-M (2011) refer. The faculty attended the Internationalized Learning Program (ILP), which is a two or one semester long workshop on course design, which includes strategies, dynamics, and even some pedagogy to internationalize the curriculum. It is relevant to point out here that the author of this chapter had and has the intrinsic motivation: he is from abroad (naturalized USA) and his academic training is in comparative politics. In addition, he attended the ILP program at GGC.

The literature behind institutional rationales to internationalize the curriculum is limited, but very important. For example, Hor and Matawie (2006) found "the size of the university, the number of PhD staff in the faculty, the number of international students attending the university, the size of the university, and student faculty ration" (p. 1) to be the variables that determined internationalization of the business and accounting curricula.

For Childress (2010), however, the institutional factors affecting internationalization are financial incentives, support staff and personnel to facilitate international initiatives, internationalization policy, and the like. GGC's internationalization structural organization (extrinsic motivation) is an institutional arrangement similar to Childress' *support staff and personnel to facilitate international initiatives*. The argument here is that GGC internationalization structural organization represents a real extrinsic motivation for faculty participation in IoC. The internationalization structural organization certainly was an extraordinary extrinsic motivating factor for the author of the chapter to participate in IoC.

GGC'S PROCESS APPROACH TO INTERNATIONALIZATION: ORGANIZATION AND PROGRAM OR THE EXTRINSIC MOTIVATION

Since early in the 1990s, the foreign-born population in Georgia has been growing significantly: it rose from 2.7% in 1990, to 7.1% in 2000, to 9.7% in 2013 (American, 2015). Georgia was home to 970,979 immigrants in 2013, representing 9.7 percent of the state's overall population of 9.9 million (Redmon, 2014). This state foreign-born population growth has affected Gwinnett County significantly: today, a majority of the county residents belongs to minority groups, including foreign-born minorities (Vasilogambros, 2015) with Latinos representing 20.4 percent of the county population (IndexMundi, 2013). In total, the foreign-born population in Gwinnett represents 25 percent of the county total population (Atlanta-Regional, 2013). This makes Gwinnett the most diverse county in the Southeast (Vasilogambros, 2015).

Given this population diversity in Georgia, especially in Gwinnett County (home of Georgia Gwinnett College), it was imperative for GGC to internationalize its curriculum and transcend any local focus to cup up with this population trend. In doing this, intentionally or unintentionally, GGC followed a *"process approach to internationalization"* of its curricula, as we will see in this section. First, according to Leask (2001), Knight and De-Wit (1995) define *process approach* "as consisting of two main types of strategy: organization and program. Policies and administrative systems comprise the focus of organization strategies. Academic activities and services embrace the focus of program strategies" (Leask, 2001, p. 101).

Consistent with the college's principle of encouraging *diversity and building a multicultural environment to prepare students to succeed in a global society*" (Webmaster, 2006), GGC created the Office of Internationalization. Precisely, this office represents both part of the 'organization strategies' of Knight and De-Wit's '*process approach*' and Herzberg, Mausner and Snyderman's (1959) extrinsic motivation. The main goal of this office is "to develop globally competent citizens by initiating, coordinating, and maintaining campus and overseas programs. These programs are designed to provide students, faculty and staff opportunities for intercultural awareness and mutual understanding and respect, and prepare students to serve in the global community…" (Internationalization, 2007). In sum, the creation of this office indicates both the serious institutional internationalization commitment of the college administration and its clearest internationalization strategy to remain loyal to that commitment.

Regarding the "academic activities and services that comprise the focus of program strategies" of Knight and De-Wit's '*process approach,*' the college established a strategic plan first: the 2013-2018 Quality Enhancement Plan (QEP). Concerning the students, the plan intended to equip them with abilities to describe and evaluate their *own* and *other* cultures in relation to history, values, politics, communication styles, economy, beliefs, and practices. A second intention was that students obtained the ability to communicate effectively with individuals from different cultures, demonstrate ability to interact effectively and productively in situations involving people from diverse cultural and national backgrounds. A third goal of QEP consisted of giving the students the ability to apply intercultural knowledge to intercultural or global problems (GGC, 2016a).

To reach these objectives, GGC first developed a curriculum that contained sufficient internationalized courses (GGC, 2016c). Secondly, GGC created a professional development program. The purpose of this program was to equip the GGC faculty and staff with the appropriate knowledge and skills needed to design, deliver (or support the delivery) of an internationalized curriculum (GGC, 2016c). Third, GGC created the current Global Studies Certification in international competence whose main objectives are to equip the students with "greater depth and breadth of content and experience than the standard curriculum provides" (GGC, 2016d). Precisely, this certification is the clearest instrument and strategy through which GGC is successfully trying to reach the QEP objectives, especially those related to providing the students with the ability to communicate effectively with people from different cultures. Finally, the GGC's plan intended to equip the students with proper abilities for them to be able to interact effectively and productively in situations involving people from diverse cultural and national backgrounds, while at the same time GGC authorities wanted the students to demonstrate the ability to apply intercultural knowledge to intercultural or global problems (GGC, 2016e). In a few words, the goal of the program is to help students become able to, feel comfortable with, and even enjoy-love understanding and interacting with people from other cultures both at local—on campus and off campus—and global level.

QEP offered the GGC faculty members the opportunity to obtain the knowledge and skills necessary to design and deliver an internationalized curriculum (GGC, 2016b). To reach this objective, GGC initiated a two-part professional development program: The Internationalized Learning Program (ILP). The first part of ILP consists of a forum, the Internationalized Learning Essentials Forum, which is a four-hour orientation session required of all faculty members. GGC offers this part of the ILP at new faculty orientations in August of each year. Faculty members have the opportunity to review some strategies to implement concepts of internationalized learning in their teaching and their students' learning (GGC, 2016b). The second part of ILP originally consisted of an academic yearlong program. Starting in the 2015-16 academic year, the length of the program changed to a semester. Delivered by the Center for Teaching Excellence (CTE), ILP offers a very deep training on internationalization of the curriculum, covering both the subject (the *what* we teach, including instructional design) and the corresponding pedagogy (the *how* we teach). During the semester, and as part of the training, the Faculty members participating in the program apply the acquired knowledge (skills and tools) to one of their courses. At the end of the semester, the participants submit the course as an internationalized course (*i*-course) to the QEP Assessment Committee via the "QEP Portfolio Course Repository" web page. At that time, the committee reviews "the [submitted] course against the operational definition of an *i*-course" (GGC, 2016b) to approve it or otherwise to recommend the next course of action. Following this procedural path, the author of the present chapter submitted two of his regular courses, Comparative Politics and Comparative Political Institutions, as *i*-course candidates. The QEP Assessment Committee has approved the two courses as *i*-courses.

Thus, using (intentionally or intentionally) Knight and De-Wit's (1995) *"process approach to internationalization,"* GGC administration has been seriously working on internationalizing the college curricula and eventually the whole institution. Specifically, the process of internationalization is taking place by attacking two avenues: internationalization at home (the certification) and internationalization abroad (the Office of Internationalization). Special attention is paid to the subject matter (*what* we teach) and *how* we teach it (pedagogy) both at home and abroad (see Table 1).

The important fact of the GGC's internationalization effort is that the way GGC has been applying the "process approach to internationalization" is an amazing, encouraging, facilitating factor for many of the Faculty to convert some of their regular courses into *i*-courses. Certainly, it was a determinant factor for the author of this chapter to convert his two regular courses into *i-courses, as we will see next.*

PROCESS OF TRANSFORMING REGULAR COURSES INTO I-COURSES

Description of "Comparative Politics" and "Comparative Political Institutions" as Regular Courses

Comparative Political Institutions and Introduction to Comparative Politics are two GGC political science courses with a significant international focus. For example, the primary course materials and the teaching-learning activities used in more than 50% of the two courses come from international sources and/or have an international focus. In theory, this particular feature should simplify the work to convert these courses into *i*-courses. For example, political systems around the world were the primary sources to analyze the political institutions covered in the 'Comparative Political Institutions' course. Meanwhile, the content of the introductory course in Comparative Politics is also international in nature as its specific topics demonstrate. Such topics include 'States, Nations, Nation-States, and Nationalism;' 'Democracy VS Authoritarian Rule;' 'World Political Participation: Mass VS Elite, Gender Participation;' 'Political Socialization in the World: Influences on Beliefs and Actions;' 'World Political Institutional Arrangements' including political structures, political parties, and political institutions;' and 'Comparative Public Opinion and Public Policy.'

Although these courses are comparative-international in nature, we needed to do some specific arrangements, especially regarding their pedagogy, if we really wanted them to be *i*-courses. However, their comparative-international dimension per se converted them into natural candidates to become *i*-courses. With the application of the appropriate pedagogy, the instructor was able to carry out two important aspects of internationalization of the curriculum. First, he could place the teaching learning process in a clearer and more appropriate international context, and second, the teacher facilitated an environment where students developed a better understanding among or between different cultures. The following section presents a full explanation.

Impact of Institutional Arrangements on The Process of Transforming "Comparative Politics" and "Comparative Political Institutions" Into *i*-Courses.

First, to assess the comparative-international nature of the courses, GGC faculty must use a scale that the QEP team created. The scale goes from zero to four in four categories: course teaching material, lectures, course evaluation material (e.g., tests, exams, research papers, presentations, and the like), and assignments (see Table 2). The two courses that the author of this chapter submitted reached score of three in each of the four categories (refer to Table 2). For example, the primary materials used in 30-60% of course in the first category 'course teaching material' come from international sources. In the second category, 'lectures,' the primary focus of class presentations in 30-60-% of course is international-multinational in nature. Related to the third category, 'course evaluation material,' the primary focus of tests or exams for 30-60% of course is on international affairs, including political culture, socialization, political systems, and the like. Finally, between 30% and 60% of assignments in the fourth category, 'assignments,' have an international perspective (see Table 2, columns 1 and 5).

In sum, the 'QEP scale' was one of the institutional elements that decisively facilitated assessing the comparative-international nature of the courses. This is to say the instructor of these two courses already knew that his courses had international dimension. The QEP scale institutional factor greatly facilitated measuring the nature of internationalization of the courses, while at the same time, the instructor was sure that this first step (assessing the comparative-international nature of his courses via the QEP scale) complied with the college's guidelines to internationalize his courses.

Once the courses met the level of international-comparative content, we still needed to assess their depth of internationalization so that we could convert them into *i*-courses. This meant that still it was necessary to identify the QEP student learning outcomes under three categories, 'intercultural aware-ness,' 'communication and collaboration,' and 'problem solving' (refer to Tables 3 and 4) that were appropriate to the two courses and the level of performance that the students were expected to execute in these outcomes. These two courses reached the levels of 'developing' (level 2) in the outcome of the 'intercultural awareness' category (see Table 3) and 'mid stage,' level 2, in the outcomes of 'communication/collaboration' and 'problem solving' (see Table 4). The next paragraphs describe the specific pedagogy and strategy that the teacher used to reach this internationalization depth.

First, to reach the internationalization level, we used the critical pedagogy approach, whose relevant argument is that culture and mass media play a preponderant role in the creation, promotion, and main-tenance of conditions of ideological hegemony for the legitimacy and smooth working of a system of manipulation and alienation (Burbules & Berk, 1999). Advertising, for example, promotes both con-sumption and industries as agents driven only by a desire to serve the needs of their customers. Satisfied consumers, this way, would be 'happy' citizens. As consumers, as workers, and as winners or losers in the marketplace of employment, citizens soon will learn that their role is to work within the 'happy' limits imposed by this consumption society (Burbules & Berk, 1999). The case is that according to several scholars (Bowles & Gintis, 1976; Apple, 1979; Popkewitz, 1991), some educational institutions promote and reinforce this order of domination, "through the rhetoric of meritocracy, through testing, through tracking, through vocational training or college preparatory curricula, and so forth" (cited in Burbules & Berk, 1999, 4/17). In this context, we understand Critical Pedagogy (CP) as a reaction to

Table 2. Content rubric to convert regular course into I-Courses (GGC's QEP committee)

Categories:	Score	Level 0	Level 1	Level 2	Level 3	Level 4
Course materials drawn from international sources or locations		None	Isolated items inserted into course in individual class session	Supplemental materials used in 10-30% of course	Primary materials used in 30-60% of course	Primary materials used in >60% of course
Lectures (including guest lectures) or other classroom presentations focused on international or multinational perspectives or comparisons		None	Isolated comments or individual class sections inserted into course, but not related to broader content	Primary focus of class presentations in 10-30% of course	Primary focus of class presentations in 30-60-% of course	Primary focus of class presentations in >60% of course
Tests, Exams, Research Papers, Presentations, or other work requiring consideration of international or multinational perspectives		None	Isolated items on one or more test or exam	Primary focus on tests or exams for 10-30% of course	Primary focus of tests or exams for 30-60% of course	Primary focus of tests or exams for >60% of course
Homework/Class assignments or other student work (e.g. papers, discussions, cultural experiences, research assignments) requiring consideration of international or multinational perspectives		None	None	10-30% of assignments are internationally related	30-60% of assignments are internationally related	Primary and substantive student work product for course requires taking international focus across full scope of course
Overall						

Table 3. Student learning outcomes in international courses. intercultural awareness (GGC's QEP committee)

Course Name: Comparative Political Institutions. Course Prefix and Number: POLS 4050. Reviewer's Name: Clemente Quinones					
Category	Outcome	Novice (Level 1)	Developing (Level 2)	Capstone (Level 3)	Row Total
Intercultural Awareness	Students will be able to describe and evaluate their own cultures in relation to history, values, politics, communication styles, economy, or beliefs and practices.	Identifies own cultural rules and biases (e.g. with a strong preference for those rules shared with own cultural group and seeks the same in others.)	Recognizes new perspectives about own cultural rules and biases (e.g., not looking for sameness; comfortable with the complexities that new Perspectives offer.)	Analyzes own cultural rules and biases and how own experiences have shaped these rules and biases.	2
	Students will be able to describe and evaluate other cultures in relation to history, values, politics, communication styles, economy, or beliefs and practices.	Identifies elements important to members of another culture in relation to its history, values, politics, communication styles, economy, **or** beliefs and practices.	Articulates basic understanding of the complexity of elements important to members of another culture in relation to its history, values, politics, communication styles, economy, **or** beliefs and practices.	Analyzes the complexity of elements important to members of another culture in relation to its history, values, politics, communication styles, economy, **or** beliefs and practices.	2

this institutionalized order of domination (Burbules & Berk, 1999) by developing critical consciousness (Freire, 1970). This consciousness includes raising awareness "about inequalities of power, about the false myths of opportunity and merit for many students, and about the way belief systems become internalized to the point where individuals and groups abandon the very aspiration to question or change their lot in life" (Burbules & Berk, 1999, p. 5/17). For this reason, the CP places strong emphasis on change and collective action to achieve it (Freire, 1970).

Table 4. Student learning outcomes in international courses: communication, collaboration, and problem solving (GGC's committee)

Category	Outcome	Early Stage (Level 1)	Mid Stage (Level 2)	Capstone (Level 3)	Row Total
Communication and Collaboration	**Students will communicate effectively with persons from different cultures.**	Articulates the verbal and nonverbal communications used in own culture; identifies some cultural differences in verbal and nonverbal communication.	Recognizes and participates in cultural differences in verbal and nonverbal communication and begins to negotiate a shared understanding based on those differences.	Articulates a complex understanding of cultural differences in verbal and nonverbal communication (e.g., demonstrates understanding of the degree to which people use physical contact while communicating in different cultures) and is able to skillfully negotiate a shared understanding based on those differences.	2
	Students will demonstrate ability to interact effectively and productively in situations involving people from diverse cultural and national backgrounds	Identifies components of other cultural perspectives but responds in all situations with own worldview.	Recognizes intellectual and emotional dimensions of more than one worldview and sometimes uses more than one worldview in interactions	Interprets intercultural experience from the perspectives of own and more than one worldview and demonstrates ability to act in a supportive manner that recognizes the feelings of another cultural group.	2
Application/ Problem Solving	**Students will demonstrate the ability to apply intercultural knowledge to intercultural or global problems**	Defines challenge or problem in basic ways, describing a limited number of systems, beliefs, and solutions.	Formulates practical yet elementary solutions to challenge or problem from a disciplinary perspective, using at least two cultural lenses	Applies knowledge and skills to generate sophisticated, appropriate, and workable solutions to address complex problems from a disciplinary perspective, using multiple cultural lenses	2
	Column Totals: # marked or Row Total Sum				10

So given that the teacher was going to use the just described Critical Pedagogy to reach the internationalization depth of these two courses, he needed to find the specific strategies or ways of delivering his course content to meet enough and deep 'intercultural awareness,' 'communication and collaboration,' and 'problem solving.' The specific strategies include teamwork, student panels and dialogues, simulations, glocal projects, and open assembly. The instructor also found it useful to open the class sessions with a very brief lecture, simply to lay the groundwork for the rest of the time. This brief introduction is basic and takes up only about 10%-15% of the total teaching time if discussion in small groups is used; and 15%-20%, if open assembly is used. From there, the class progresses into some sort of other activity (i.e. student panels, dialogues, and open assembly). The activity changes from day to day or week to week, simply to "mix it up" and keep the course fresh and non-repetitive: empowering the students with internationalization consciousness *a la Freire* must be a motivating, pleasant, lovely, and always fresh adventure for both the student and the instructor. As a final project, the students may submit a teaching-learning portfolio, a poster, or an essay about an international problem affecting local communities and families (glocal project). The common characteristic of these projects is that students must summarize critically what they consider were the most important components of the course, present an analysis of how important it is to know other cultures and interact with people of those cultures.

Intercultural Awareness Through Teamwork

In 5-to-6 member teams, students share their opinions on the specific components of the assigned readings. Right before the class starts, the instructor posts one or two questions tapping the main idea/purpose of the assigned readings. After 10 minutes, a member from each team shares his/her **team** conclusions with the rest of the class. Then, in open assembly, the class analyzes each team conclusion so that the teacher provides a general conclusion at the end of the class. In the Comparative Politics course, for example, to analyze comparative public policy, the teacher asks each team to identify the same public policy in two different countries of their choice. Then, in their teams, they must focus on policy differences and why such differences. This latter is the most important part, given that the goal of this exercise is to appreciate other sociopolitical cultures (e.g., political values) and institutions, as well as the role that both of them play in the policy making process.

Communication and Collaboration Via Student Panels and Dialogue

This is a quasi-team presentation by one of the teams previously formed, with the difference that the members of this quasi-team have a *dialogue* on a specific topic selected from the readings of the day. This is not a discussion. It rather is a talk, during which each member builds upon what his/her colleague or colleagues who preceded him/her said. In a debate / discussion format, students tend to disqualify the other. In a dialogue format, the key to success is sharing ideas and opinions, comparing them against others' opinions and ideas, listening to others, and encouraging one another. This is a process or a model of caring communication and constructive collaboration for the students to better understand and communicate with people from other cultures. At the end of the class period, the instructor posts a general conclusion for the students to consider it. To analyze the world electoral systems in the Comparative Political Institutions course, for example, a team (student panel) leads us in a dialogue on the most beautiful components of the three general electoral systems: plurality, proportional representation, and mixed-member. Then, the students describe the problems they think the current electoral system may have. Next, they propose one of the three systems that they think would work better than the one that is in place. This exercise helps the students appreciate other political cultures in general and other electoral systems in particular. On the way, the students see the contribution of the electoral systems to national peaceful coexistence of people in socially and racially diverse countries.

Problem Solving

Depending on the topic of the day or week, simulations or student panels or both help students find solutions to practical problems. As described above, in the panels, students hold dialogues (no discussions or debates) on specific topics previously assigned by the instructor. For this purpose, we use the classic problem-solving process whose main components are definition and identification of the problem, generation of alternatives, evaluation of alternatives, selection of an alternative, and implementation of alternatives (or solution of the problem). For example, when the student panel discus the electoral system currently in place in their respective counties, they first tried to see if the USA plurality system still serves properly our sociocultural diversity. In 'the identification of the problem' phase, generally the students have found that indeed the system is not working in that direction. The students, then, carefully analyze the group of electoral systems they previously covered in the readings. Then, the students mostly select a mixed member proportional system that, according to them, would better serve our current sociocultural diversity in USA. Usually, the students see a major approval and implementation problem: none of the two major parties in the national Congress would be willing to do something to change the current plurality system because it has been serving the interests of the two parties. Usually, then, the students conclude that we should start trying the change at state level where it may be less difficult for the citizens to influence their state authorities, especially their state representatives.

In sum, applying or using the Critical Pedagogy approach to comply with the QEP student learning outcomes under the three mentioned categories helped the instructor reach the required internationalization depth for the two courses. At the end, this institutional element (organization strategy) led the process to the final destination: internationalization of the curriculum of the two courses, as we will see next.

Transforming these two courses into *i*-courses was a relatively smooth process for three reasons: the comparative-international dimension of the two courses, the author's participation in both the QEP program and ILP. First, the chapter already presented the process-criteria that the courses had to go through for the instructor to prove that the courses were international in nature and had enough depth of internationalization so that the QEP Assessment Committee approved them as *i*-courses.

Second, since 2012 the instructor of these courses had been part of the Quality Enhancement Program (QEP) committee, whose members represented different GGC disciplines. The committee was involved in college-wide research and planning whose result was the creation of the Global Studies Certification. Our specific role was to ask our colleagues in our own discipline to indicate if their courses had some international content, or if they wanted to convert their courses into *i*-courses. We provided them with the respective rubric (see Table 2). As a result, in Political Science we identified at least nine courses as possible *i*-courses: Current Global Issues, Comparative Politics, International Relations, International Organizations, Comparative Foreign Policy, Comparative Political Institutions, Topics in Comparative Politics, International Law, and Political Negotiation and Conflict Resolution.

Third, being involved in this committee and being teaching international-in-nature courses converted the instructor into a natural candidate to take the Center for Teaching Excellence's Internationalized Learning Program (ILP). He took the program during the 2014-15 academic year. The central piece and requirement of this program was that each participant had to submit a course to the QEP Assessment Committee. The committee then would convert the course into an *i*-course. The author of the chapter submitted the Comparative Politics course. About six months later, he submitted the other one: Comparative Political Institutions. In sum, the process of converting these two courses into *i*-courses was relatively soothing due to the institutional mechanism and arrangement established by the college administration to internationalize the curriculum. Part of these mechanisms, as we just saw, included both the QEP and ILP programs.

In sum, the factors that facilitated a relative relaxed process of transforming the author's two regular courses into *i*-courses are the intrinsic motivation of the author and the amazing GGC internationalization structural organization or extrinsic motivation. The components of the former include the insight of the author (he is from abroad), his doctoral training (comparative politics), and his passion for internationalization. The elements of the extrinsic motivation include the administration commitment to internationalization expressed through the creation of the well-structured internationalization plan, which embraces the Office of Internationalization, the Quality Enhancement Program, and the Internationalized Learning Program.

The possible challenges that the author found along the way were not directly associated with his efforts to internationalize his courses. For example, replacing two professors that were teaching political science *i*-course was problematic. The Political Science faculty members who substituted for the departing faculty members were not willing to teach the courses as *i*-courses, even when it was obvious that Political Science was going to lose some *i*-courses. Some of the arguments included the following: "I will not teach this course using other faculty member's syllabus. Ask other colleagues if they are interested…" "I am not interested in teaching this course as *i*-course." It was necessary that a member of the QEP Steering Committee came to one of the Political Science meetings for several of the instructors to become interested in converting some of their courses into *i*-courses. In sum, the problem was to convince members of the Political Science discipline to convert their courses (those courses including already some international content) into *i*-courses. However, as indicated above, this situation was not directly associated with the process of converting the author' two regular courses into *i*-courses.

Some Results

Good student evaluations indicate, first, that the students appreciate this innovative teaching – learning process and, second, that they are willing and prepared to interact with people from other cultures, as comments from the students demonstrate. A presentation of comments from all the students is far beyond the scope of this chapter. For this reason, the chapter introduces some selected commentaries:

Undoubtedly, we—in the USA—love other people and want them to do well, but if we really want to help them in this endeavor, we first need to understand their cultures, to appreciate and love these cultures, and to interact with these people. …The panels every Friday are a great model too. I liked that you made us look at all aspects of our solutions so like why people would support the issue (for example, cultural explanations), and why other people would not (cultural explanations?). This class did me wonder on how I viewed the people of the world and how I saw all the conflicts…

If we wanted to get a conclusion from these comments, it would probably be that the students in these courses are convinced that culture matters. It was even clearer in the following one-paragraph short essay that one of the students wrote:

I learned about different cultures and how that can impact a policy or a regime. … . Since Georgia Gwinnett College has the most diverse student body in the southern region, I had classes with people from different countries. This was something that helped me understand and interact with students who know and have experienced different regimes. For this class, our professor put us in different groups for presentations. This put me in contact with people of different countries and different cultures, different from my own culture. I became more aware of the cultural differences that are around me. …. I realized how many of us carry misinformation and stereotypes about people in different cultures. Especially, when we are young, we acquire this information in bits and pieces from TV, music or from listening to people talk, but this class helped me understand, appreciate other cultures and enthusiastically communicate with people from other cultures.

Precisely, one of the goals of the course this student is referring to (POLS 3100-Comparative Politics) is helping the students be aware of other cultures, understand people from other cultures and be able to communicate with those people. The fact that the instructor of these courses is originally from abroad has helped the students enjoy the walk through other cultures, especially political cultures.

WHERE TO GO FROM HERE: DIRECTIONS FOR FUTURE RESEARCH

This chapter has presented a qualitative analysis about the impact of institutional arrangements on internationalization of the curriculum at Georgia Gwinnett College. Transforming two regular political science courses into *i*-course was relatively easy due to these institutional arrangements. The next step must be to conduct a public opinion survey whose sample should come from the group of students who have already taken the two courses since the time the instructor started teaching the courses. Specifically, we will be looking for the expected level of internationalization through the three categories described above: 'intercultural awareness,' 'communication and collaboration,' and 'problem solving.'

This wider research endeavor is about the two courses presented here, but they are part of a college wide effort: an institutional internationalization process. For this, a larger or wider future research should be about internationalization of GGC's curricula, that is, a research evaluating results of our current Global Studies Certification (GSC) through the three mentioned categories. A second component of this wider project should include an assessment of the Office of Internationalization work. This latter component is to measure the level of institutional internationalization, that is, up to what degree GGC as institution is committed to internationalization. Thus, for this proposed public opinion survey, the target population should include students, instructors, and administrators. The first one will include students who already finished the certification, students who are currently registered in the program, and those who are taking *i*-course or have been in a 'study abroad' program but are not registered in the certification program. The administrator population will include all administrators: President, Vice-Presidents, Deans, Assistant Deans, and the like. Finally, the instructor target population will embrace the entire faculty who are teaching *i*-courses. If our samples are too small, we may include as many subjects from each population as we can. The risk is that our results would not be scientific, but still we will have an idea about how the internationalization process is working, while at the same time, the administrators will have some empirical analysis for them to change the current organization strategies, if necessary. In any case, we could treat the study as a pilot study. The questionnaire will include questions tapping the different issues of Knight and De-Wit's (refer to Leask, 2001, 101) *process approach to internationalization* as the presented in this chapter.

CONCLUSION

The purpose of this chapter was to analyze the possible factors that determined a relatively relaxed process of transforming the author's two courses into *i*-course. For this purpose, the chapter defined IoC, first, as incorporation of "an international and intercultural dimension into the content of the curriculum as well as the teaching and learning arrangements and support services of a program of study" (Leask, 2009, p. 209). This concept includes both the *what* and the *how* we teach (Bond, 2006). Then, the existent literature indicates that institutional arrangements affect IoC. In fact, the chapter showed that GGC's 'Process Approach to Internationalization' (Organization and Program) or the 'extrinsic motivation' in the form of internationalization structural organization (institutional arrangement) was determinant for the author of this chapter to convert his two regular political science courses into *i*-courses. Internationalization structural organization includes the QEP student learning outcomes under the three mentioned categories: intercultural awareness, communication and collaboration, and problem solving. The author's intrinsic motivation was another variable that affected this conversion. Good student evaluations indicate that these two *i*-courses are in the right direction: helping the students be aware of other cultures, understand people from other cultures and be able to communicate with those people. Finally, the author suggest two future lines of research: first, conducting a public opinion survey whose sample should come from the group of students who have already taken the two courses since the time the instructor started teaching the courses. The second line is an evaluation of the Global Studies Certification and the work by the Office of Internationalization.

REFERENCES

Adams, M. (1992). Cultural inclusion in the American college classroom. In L. L. Border, & E. N. Van Note Chism. *Teaching for diversity New Directions for Teaching and Learning, 49*(49), 5–17. doi:10.1002/tl.37219924903

Agoston, S., & Dima, A. M. (2012). Trends and Strategies within the Process of Academic Internationalization. *Management & Marketing Challenges for the Knowledge Society, 7*(1), 43-56. Retrieved August 30, 2016, from http://www.managementmarketing.ro/pdf/articole/254.pdf

Altbach, P., & Knight, J. (2007). The Internationalization of Higher Education: Motivations and Realities. *Journal of Studies in International Education, 11*(3-4), 290–305. doi:10.1177/1028315307303542

American, I.-C. (2015, January 1). *New Americans in Georgia: The Political and Economic Power of Immigrants, Latinos, and Asians the Peach State.* Retrieved September 2, 2016, from American Immigration Council: https://www.americanimmigrationcouncil.org/research/new-americans-georgia

Apple, M. (1979). *Ideology and Curriculum.* New York: Routledge and Kegan. doi:10.4324/9780203241219

Atlanta-Regional, C. (2013, March). *Regional Snapshot.* Retrieved September 2, 2016, from ARC: Atlanta Regional Commission: http://documents.atlantaregional.com/arcBoard/march2013/dr_regional_snapshot_3_2013_foreignborn.pdf

Backman, E. (1981). The development of an international commitment: A case study. *Occasional Paper Series in International Education, 1*(1), 3-17.

Banks, J. (2004). Approaches to multicultural curriculum reform. In J. A. Banks & C. M. Banks (Eds.), *Multicultural education: Issues and perspectives* (5th ed.; pp. 242–264). Hoboken, NJ, USA: John Wiley & Sons, Inc.

Bates, R. (2005). Can we live together? Towards a global curriculum. *Arts and Humanities in Higher Education, 4*(1), 95–109. doi:10.1177/1474022205048760

Bond, S. (2003a). *Engaging educators: Bringing the world into the classroom: Guidelines for practice.* Ottawa, Canada: Canadian Bureau for International Education.

Bond, S. (2003b). *Untapped resources: Internationalization of the curriculum and classroom experience: A selected literature review (CBIE Research Millennium Series No. 7).* Ottawa, Canada: Canadian Bureau for International Education.

Bond, S. (2006). *Transforming the culture of learning: Evoking the international dimension in Canadian university curriculum.* Retrieved June 30, 2016, from http://international.yorku.ca/global/conference/canada/papers/Sheryl-Bond.pdf

Bowles, S., & Gintis, H. (1976). *Schooling in Capitalist America.* New York: Besic Books.

Bremer, L., & van der Wende, M. (1995). Internationalizing the curriculum in higher education: Experiences in the Netherlands. Amsterdam: Academic Press.

Burbules, N., & Berk, R. (1999). *Critical Thinking and Critical Pedagogy: Relations, Differences, and Limits. In Critical Theories in Education.* New York: Routledge.

Castillo, J., & Cano, J. (2004). Factors explaining job satisfaction among faculty. *Journal of Agricultural Education, 45*(3), 65–74. doi:10.5032/jae.2004.03065

Childress, L. (2010). *The Twenty-First Century University: Developing Faculty Engagement. In Intrinsic motivation and self-determination in human behavior.* New York: Plenum.

De-Zan, A.-T., Paipa-G, L.-A., & Parra-M, C. (2011). Las Competencias: Base para la Internationalicion de la Educacion Superior [The Skills as a Basefor Internationalization of Higher Education]. *Revista Educacion en Ingenieria,* (11), 44-54. Retrieved August 1, 2017, from www.acofi.edu.co

DeVita, G., & Case, P. (2003). Rethinking the internationalization agenda in UK higher education. *Journal of Further and Higher Education, 27*(4), 383–398. doi:10.1080/0309877032000128082

Freire, P. (1970). *Pedagogy of the Oppressed.* New York: Seabury Press.

GGC. (2016a). *Academics: Program Goals.* Retrieved Sept 2, 2016, from Georgia Gwinnett College: http://www.ggc.edu/academics/qep/program-goals/

GGC. (2016b). *Academics: Faculty Professional Development.* Retrieved Sept 4, 2016, from Georgia Gwinnett College: http://www.ggc.edu/academics/qep/faculty-professional-development/

GGC. (2016c). *Academics: Internationalized Courses.* Retrieved September 4, 2016, from Georgia Gwinnett College: http://www.ggc.edu/academics/qep/internationalized-courses/

GGC. (2016d). *Academics: Global Studies Certification.* Retrieved September 4, 2016, from Georgia Gwinnett College: http://www.ggc.edu/academics/qep/global-studies-certification/

GGC. (2016e). *Academics: Student Learning Outcomes.* Retrieved September 5, 2016, from Georgia

Herzberg, F., Mausner, B., & Snyderman, B. (1959). *The motivation to work.* New York: Johjn Wiley & Sons.

Hor, J., & Matawie, K. (2006). An Examination of Institutional Factors for Internationalizing the Business and Accounting Curricula. *International Journal of Learning, 13*(5), 1–7.

IndexMundi. (2013). *Georgia Hispanic or Latino Origin Population Percentage, 2013 by County.* Retrieved September 2, 2016, from Index Mundi: http://www.indexmundi.com

Internationalization, O. o. (2007). *Office of Internationalization Mission and Vision.* Retrieved July 21, 2017, from Georgia Gwinnett College: http://www.ggc.edu/academics/academic-opportunities-and-support/office-of-internationalization/mission-vision/

Knight, J. (1993). Internationalization: Management strategies and issues. *International Education Magazine*, 21-22.

Knight, J. (2008). Internationalisation: key concepts and elements. In M. Gaebel (Ed.), *Internationalisation of European Higher Education: an EUA/ACA Handbook* (pp. 1–24). Berlin, Germany: Raabe Academic Publishers.

Knight, J., & De-Wit, H. (1995). Strategies for Internationalization of Higher Education: Historical and conceptual perspectives. In *Strategies for Internationalization of Higher Education: A comparative study of Australia, Canada, Europe and the United States of America* (pp. 5–33). Amsterdam: European Association for International Education.

Leask, B. (2001). Bridging the gap: Internationalizing university curricula. *Journal of Studies in International Education, 5*(2), 100–115. doi:10.1177/102831530152002

Leask, B. (2009). Using formal and informal curricula to improve interactions between home and international students. *Journal of Studies in International Education, 13*(2), 205–221. doi:10.1177/1028315308329786

Leask, B. (2014, July 25). Internationalising the curriculum and all learning. *University World News.* Retrieved July 25, 2016, from University World News: http://www.universityworldnews.com/article.php?story=20141211101031828

Maidstone, P. (1995). International literacy: A paradigm for change. A manual for internationalizing the post-secondary curriculum. Victoria, Canada: Ministry of Skills, Training, and Labour.

Marchesani, L., & Adams, M. (1992). Dynamics of diversity in the teaching-learning process: A faculty development model for analysis and action. In New directions for teaching and learning (Vol. 52, pp. 9-20). San Francisco: Jossey-Bass. doi:10.1002/tl.37219925203

Mckellin, K. (1998). *Maintaining the momentum: The internationalization of British Columbia's post secondary institutions.* Victoria, Canada: The British Columbia Centre for International Education.

McLoughlin, C. (2001). Inclusivity and alignment: Principles of pedagogy, task and assessment design for effective cross-cultural online learning. Distance Education. *Distance Education, 22*(1), 7–29. doi:10.1080/0158791010220102

Parker, A. (2003). Motivation and incentives for distance faculty. *Distance Learning Administration, 6*(3). Retrieved August 1, 2017, from http://www.westga.edu/~distance/ojdla/fall63/parker63.htm

Popkewitz, T. (1991). *A Political Sociology of Educational Reform*. New York: Teachers College Press.

Redmon, J. (2014). *Georgia's foreign-born population up by 5 percent since 2009*. Retrieved September 2, 2016, from AJC.com: http://www.ajc.com/news/news/state-regional-govt-politics/georgias-foreign-born-population-up-by-5-percent-s/nhQGZ/

Rockwell, S., Schauer, J., Fritz, S., & Marx, D. (1999). Incentives and Obstacles Influencing Higher Education Faculty and Administrators to Teach Via Distance. *Online Journal of Distance Learning Administration*, 2(3). Retrieved from http://www.westga.edu/~distance/rockwell24.html

Serow, R., Brawner, C., & Demery, J. (1999). Instructional reform and research universities: Studying faculty motivation. *Review of Higher Education*, 22(4), 411–423. doi:10.1353/rhe.1999.0018

Tang, T., & Chamberlain, M. (2003). Effects of rank, tenure, length of service, and institution on faculty attitude toward research and teaching: The case of regional state universities. *Journal of Education for Business*, 79(2), 103–110. doi:10.1080/08832320309599097

Vasilogambros, M. (2015, April 2). *The Most Diverse County in the Southeast Is Run Almost Entirely by White Politicians*. Retrieved September 2, 2016, from The Atlantic: http://www.theatlantic.com

Chapter 3
Active Learning and the "Teaching" of Migration in Geography:
A Critical Reflection on the Twenty-First Century Multicultural College Classroom

Todd Lindley
Georgia Gwinnett College, USA

ABSTRACT

This chapter explores questions of methodology and pedagogy in dealing with diverse student populations in a freshman-level human geography class by highlighting a multi-tiered exercise that encourages students to investigate and to articulate their own feelings and beliefs about migration in a series of low-risk classroom exercises complemented with an out-of-class assignment. The self-reflective portion of this exercise provides the instructor insight into student feelings, attitudes, and knowledge of students' migration histories and knowledge. Lessons and examples from the author's classroom experiences are detailed in this chapter to call upon instructors to implement multi-tiered approaches to controversial and international topics, particularly in a multi-cultural, multi-ethnic, twenty-first century college classroom.

INTRODUCTION

Though not the exclusive domain of the discipline, migration as a topic features prominently in most human geography texts and is considered compulsory material for introductory courses in nearly every college/university in North America. Regardless of political affiliation or personal background, the topic often invokes heated debate among undergraduate students and sometimes results in "discussion as spontaneous combustion" (Brookfield 1995, 12). Academic freedom encourages faculty to 'teach' the topic in a myriad of ways, and this chapter presents a critical reflection on the author's classroom experiences at a suburban college in the South, where students represent a diverse set of linguistic, cultural, class, ethnic, and racial backgrounds. The chapter explores questions of methodology, pedagogy, and

DOI: 10.4018/978-1-5225-2791-6.ch003

active learning (Fink 2013) as they apply to diverse student populations by highlighting a multi-tiered exercise (Figure 3) that invites students to investigate and to articulate their own feelings and beliefs about migration in a series of low-risk classroom exercises complemented with a more intimate out-of-class assignment. The self-reflective portion of this exercise provides the instructor insight into student feelings, attitudes, and knowledge of their students' migration histories.

The exercise assesses intercultural competence but does not penalize or reward students with more or less international experience. African American students whose families have never left the South, for example, tend to have less specific knowledge about their families' migration (his)stories, while recent immigrants or children of immigrants tend to have the most direct knowledge (but not always). Moreover, student narratives suggest that less knowledge of one's own family's migration path tends result in more simplistic narratives and understanding of migration in general. Students with more knowledge of their family's migration tend to describe the complexities of migration in more nuanced terms that might be difficult for other students to fully grasp. Moreover, this case study suggests that affording students multiple platforms of expression results in more profound learning experiences – particularly for those with painful, recent, and/or complicated migration histories.

Oversimplification and generalization remain inherent problems with introductory courses in all disciplines, but they are particularly problematic in geography, where most students will never take an upper level course that would allow for greater scrutiny and more critical thinking. Those students may never have another scholastic opportunity to parse, analyze, and meaningfully synthesize the content on migration presented by their textbooks. As such, it is imperative that students develop a deeper understanding of migration in their introductory course. While many instructors welcome and facilitate debate and/or classroom discussion, such an activity does not always result in thoughtful reflection and/or discourse. Certain students tend to dominate the conversation. Meanwhile, others tune out and/or may not share at all. They may be timid, pensive, or protective or their own thoughts and ideas, leaving the discussion to be dominated by others. The exercise presented in this chapter borrows from both partner sharing techniques and from reflective writing and facilitates learning to occur regardless of pre-existing student knowledge or experience. The author argues that it is incumbent upon instructors to apply pedagogically informed approaches that are mindful of the diversity of student experiences in order to engage the class and facilitate deep learning in introductory general education courses.

TEACHING MIGRATION IN HUMAN GEOGRAPHY

Students are routinely exposed to the core principles and theories of migration in introductory geography classes across North America. The Association of American Geographers annual meeting from 2014 boasted independent papers presented on the topic, compared to just 187 results for 'region', 215 for 'place', and 217 for 'map'! The most popular textbooks include large amounts of empirical data including colorful world maps of annual migration flows, historical immigration trends for the U.S., historical overviews of U.S. legislation, brief treatments of migration around the world, and explanations of neoclassical gravity and econometric models. While textbooks vary, most introduce Ravenstein's 'Laws of Migration' (1876) and link generalized economic and demographic patterns between countries and regions in which people move from LDC's to MDC's, often in stepwise processes or as a part of chain migration. Some textbooks offer vignettes, case studies, and/or first-person accounts of migration from alternative perspectives (e.g. refugees, forced immigrants, or undocumented immigrants).

Traditional content delivery includes class readings reinforced with lecture, video, case studies, and/or other in-class activities designed to achieve content mastery. Such traditional approaches are demonstrable effective for content mastery, but often fall short in terms of critical thinking, transformative learning, and deep engagement. Unfortunately, *confirmation bias* (Nickerson 1998, Gilovich 1991) often tempts students to unwittingly misinterpret or selectively interpret data presented in the text/lecture to actually strengthen pre-conceived views regarding the patterns, processes and policy implications of international migration in the 21st century rather than leading learners to deeper multi-faceted understandings. Liberal arts instructors that understand the complicating and powerful effect of confirmation bias are compelled to push students beyond the stage of content mastery in the case of controversial and complex topics.

For example, student views on immigration are often diffused through the powerful lens of American exceptionalism (Lipset 1991; Koh 2003). Common student comments include, "everybody wants to come here", "why don't they just stay and fix their own country", or "if every country just followed the example set by the US, then people wouldn't have to leave". Even edited and vetted textbook graphics sometimes serve to perpetuate a certain power-laden discourse surrounding the topic of immigration. For example, Figure 1, depicts a typical textbook graphic of global interregional migration used in introductory classes.

Students' initial responses to the map often tend to reinforce the mental maps of those who believe that all of the world is seeking to enter the United States as an immigrant, compromising its border security, and bringing potential danger to American citizens. Well trained geographers and students of geography, of course, treat maps with suspicion, owing to the vast body of literature on the historical deceptive use of maps by those in power (Harley and Cosgrove 1988; Monmonier 1991). Many college freshmen and sophomores, of course, have not yet honed the skills of map interpretation and/or intel-lectual skepticism, so the confirmation bias effect is predictable. The inconsistencies (note the arrow of US migration to Australia and larger arrows from Asia to North America than from Latin America) provide a unique discussion platform as the map in Figure 1 seems to imply that everybody is leaving Asia and that most international migration is from poor countries to the wealthy countries in spite of the fact that most migration flows are actually *between* poor and middle tier countries (United Nations

Figure 1.

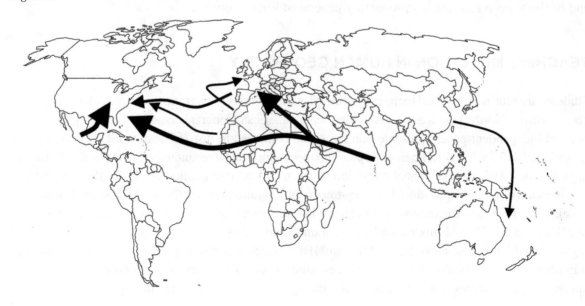

2013). Facile interpretations of such maps are a favorite activity of geography professors but they meet with varying degrees of 'success' in the classroom.

The temptation among faculty members to constantly 'correct' myths and misunderstandings of controversial and complex topics is no doubt commonplace, but does such an approach actually lead students to heightened critical thinking? Such a question is difficult to answer. Over ten years, the author has incorporated in-depth documentary films, assigned research papers, and presented countless datasets from the academic literature dispelling common factual misconceptions and should alleviate unsubstantiated nativist fears on the topic of migration. Examples include empirical studies on immigrant criminality, lower than expected consumption of social services by immigrant groups, demographic imbalances in labor supply offset by immigrants, and a variety of other visual data-driven interventions. As a researcher and educator, the author (and most academics) place a premium on research findings and the compelling power of raw data. However, when it comes to certain controversial topics like (im)migration, data and critical examinations of facts are insufficient to transform overly simplistic, ideologically driven, and fiercely unwavering opinions. Classroom discussions on the topic tend to affirm the recent exhaustive scholarship by (Hainmueller and Hopkins 2014), which finds that negative attitudes towards immigration are shaped much more strongly by 'sociotropic concerns' and by perceived threats to group identity than by economic concerns. Moreover, lessons from failed public health interventions prove illustrative here. In attempting to combat misperceptions regarding vaccination in the US in recent years, the CDC set about to re-educate those who stand in staunch opposition (namely highly educated middle and upper middle class young parents and prospective parents). Simply stated, the CDC's strategy of data-centric education intervention failed, leading researchers to conclude that, "corrections of misperceptions about controversial issues… may be counterproductive in some populations. The best response to false beliefs is not necessarily providing correct information" (Hendrix et. al 2014; Nyhan et. al 2014).

Students tend to quickly take sides when it comes to migration, and discussion of the topic may devolve into polarized hyperbole in the absence of proper gatekeeping by the instructor. On occasion, the author conducts the following short in-class exercise. At the front of the class the word, 'MIGRATION' is written on the board. Students then break students into groups (4 minimum) and are instructed to compose two lists based upon the words: *Pro* and *Con*. No further instructions are provided, so that questions, definitions, and debates may percolate among and between students. Next, each group's responses are placed on the board. Invariably, the same broad themes emerge from students across multiple classes and years. The most common themes appear in Figure 2.

Usually, students begin to disagree about various components on the list. Varying by students' experiences, they share anecdotes, family histories, and personal encounters. Others rely on news stories, media reports, and/or political ideology to inform their opinions. Nevertheless, classroom discussion

Figure 2.

Pros: cheap labor, better restaurants/food, enhanced culture/diversity of the population, workers willing to perform undesirable jobs, new energy/ideas/entrepreneurialism among migrants, migrants spur economic activity even if they don't pay taxes, language skills.

Cons: increased crime, drain on social services, bring in disease, less educated, links to terrorism, don't pay taxes, take jobs away from Americans, don't speak English, sometimes don't assimilate/may not adapt culturally, drive down wages, overpopulation/higher birth rates.

moves quite quickly from one subtopic to the next (i.e. undocumented/legal/illegal migration, crime, lack of English, governmental policy to name a few). Such a free-flow of information/opinion/hearsay does not come without risk. On occasion, the dialog devolves into exaggerated and ill-informed claims (e.g. Migrants will do ANY kind of work, because even the worst job here is better than anything they have back in their own country; Migrants don't pay taxes, but they have more kids than non-migrants, which is not fair)[1]. Another problem is that a handful of outgoing students dominate the discussion at the exclusion of others in what has been termed "Discussion as Spontaneous Combustion" (Brookfield 1995, 12). Those who don't contribute may do so for a variety of reasons. Some feel unsure of their own opinions, while others are shy, and still others need more time to digest, comprehend, and/or synthesize the ideas presented by their classmates before electing to speak. Invariably, the emergent themes from Figure 2 frame the issue entirely from the viewpoint of the receiving country, thus ignoring sending country perspectives (e.g. brain drain, negative demographic repercussions) and the effects on migrants themselves (e.g. family separation, depression, danger of detention).

In a highly diverse classroom, however, even more complicated factors mitigate the discussion. Some of the most well-informed students often don't participate in the open conversation at all. Students may be children of migrants or they may, in fact, be migrants, in which case the stark differences in cultural frameworks rise to the surface. These may include notions of power knowledge (Foucault 1980), student/teacher relationships, collective/individualist cultural backgrounds, gender/age deference, and/or language boundaries (Hall 1989; Oyserman et. al 2002). Nonetheless, the open exchange allows some students to articulate the source of their opinion, whether it is steeped in personal experience, hearsay, reading, stereotype, or careful consideration, and it affords others the opportunity to consider the issues silently. Once the source of students' knowledge/opinion is clarified, the instructor and class at least have acquired a better understanding of the overall student 'positionality' on the topic of migration (however each group chose to define it). For example, one student who worked in a restaurant kitchen with 'immigrants' informed others of the importance of remittances by citing how much of those workers' wages are sent home to care for family members or to pay for basic needs. Another student viewed this as further evidence that migrants serve as a strain on the economy (by sending money away), while others acknowledge the significance of labor migration as an articulation of commitment to family, which is a noble virtue. Overall, however, the open forum exercise fails to illicit meaningful input from those students with perhaps the most insight – migrants and children of migrants. The next section of this chapter describes the unique student body at the author's institution and then offers an alternative, active learning approach for these particular students in order address some of the inherent limitations with the afore-mentioned teaching methodologies (maps, graphs, text, lecture, and debate) to explicitly include those voices often muffled, silenced, and/or misunderstood during the traditional class discussion and/or open forum/debate[2].

CUSTOMIZED CONTENT DESIGN AND PREACHING TO THE CHOIR

Should teaching methods be modified to meet students where they are? Should students be required to 'do' things rather than just 'learn' things? These questions have occupied a great deal of debate and contemplation among those advocating for active learning techniques (Barkley 2010; Fink 2013) defined by Bonwell and Eison (1991) as "anything that involves students in doing things and thinking about the things they are doing" (2) and further refined by Fink (2013) to include a purposeful combination of 1)

Figure 3.

receiving information 2) experiencing/doing/observing and 3) reflecting/making meaning (116-117). Such ideas form the pedagogical underpinnings of the following discussion into the migration exercise presented next, but the design of this particular instrument/class activity is undoubtedly mediated by the unique composition of students in suburban Atlanta, and therefore a short accounting of the student body is helpful.

The student body at the author's institution reflects what Audrey Singer describes generally as an 'Emerging 21st Century Gateway', where immigrant populations have grown very rapidly during the past twenty-five years alone (Lichter and Johnson 2009; Singer 2013). Gwinnett County specifically, is one of the most diverse in the South with a foreign-born population of 25%, where 33% speak a language other than English at home. Sixty percent of those between the ages of 25 and 44 are foreign-born, so the number of 2nd generation (children of) immigrants is very high, though hard data is difficult to ascertain. Those under the age of 18 who identify as white alone (not Hispanic or Latino) comprise just 35% of the population. Figure 3 displays the author's students' origins (or their parents) from just a single semester, further demonstrating breadth of immigrant populations present here. It's particularly noteworthy that no single source country dominates numerically or symbolically as is often the case elsewhere.

As such, a huge reserve of knowledge and experience lays dormant in the student body just waiting to be mined and refined into a very valuable commodity! This institution [modified to maintain anonymity] opened in 2005 with the mission to offer a four-year degree experience in this decidedly sprawling suburban county (population: 880,000) that has undergone rapid and unfettered growth for more than two decades. Predictably, the undergraduate student population grew from 50 in 2005 to nearly 11,000 in 2015. Campus diversity is framed as both an opportunity and a challenge, and the cornerstone of the institution's quality enhancement plan (QEP) is "Internationalization of the Curriculum: Engaging the World to Develop Global Citizens." Meanwhile, most of the enrolled students have grown up in a school system characterized by ethnic, racial, and linguistic diversity on the one hand and massive amounts of standardized testing and common core driven pedagogy on the other.

Within the context of such recognized diversity, then, the topic of migration could be taught in a way that borrows from student centered learning approaches advocated by 'active learning' scholars in which active knowledge construction is just as important as knowledge accumulation. Added to the mix of the diverse cultural capital inherent in immigrant/child of immigrant students can be found a heterogeneous brew of Southern style conservatism, large numbers of socioeconomically diverse African American students (~25%), and a mostly commuter student body lacking in cohesion, common purpose, and shared experiences. This is not the stereotypical 20th century classroom. Rather, it represents the future of American society and very likely foreshadows the kind of college experience that will continue to dominate the 21st century as traditional college costs soar, middle class wages stagnate, and the age of migration (Castles 2000) further proliferates. The exercise described in the next section of this paper, then, is conceptualized and designed with such specific circumstances in mind.

TEACHING MIGRATION AS REFLECTION

Oversimplification and generalization remain inherent problems with introductory courses in all disciplines, but they are particularly problematic in geography, where most do not take upper level geography courses and may never have another scholastic opportunity to parse, analyze, discuss, and/or meaningfully synthesize the global-scale data, maps, and policies presented by their textbooks and/or instructors. As such, I argue here that it is imperative for students develop a more meaningful understanding of migration in the introductory course, particularly in a community with such diverse members. To address this limitation, a multi-tiered class exercise is offered in order to provide an opportunity for deeper and more nuanced understandings of this topic through controlled discussion, investigation, and reflection. The method centers upon a process of critical reflection that challenges and replaces the decontextualized reflection of more cognitive approaches. Moreover, reflecting critically means not only "learning to learn in the tradition of androgogy, but . . . understanding how relevant knowledge has been constructed and managed, and how what is deemed to be 'relevant' or 'common sense' has been arrived at" (Reynolds, 1997:129). Students are assessed a grade for the assignment based on demonstrating understandings of core concepts such as migration push and pull factors, demographic patterns, and knowledge of pertinent data points. The more significant learning occurs, however, through more personal questions that challenge students to contemplate and to investigate their own family's migration experience(s), be they real or 'imagined'. They are also required to compare/contrast with classmates, and then finally to contemplate the impact of migration upon their personal educational experience.

Though this model may not be applicable to all post-secondary classrooms, the North American student body is rapidly transforming and higher education needs to acknowledge the changes that are ocurring. Across the US, one in four children under 18 have at least one foreign-born parent (US Census Bureau Report 2014). Increasing numbers of college classrooms, then, are imbued with a rich tapestry of (sometimes hidden) culture, language, and migration stories that should be meaningfully integrated into transformative learning activities. Recent literature on active learning approaches suggest that retention of material, depth of understanding, and ability to communicate effectively are all improved when interactive modules are introduced (Freeman et. al 2014), so reflective and active learning approaches are essential. Notably, geographers have skillfully incorporated and facilitated debate and classroom discussion through problem based learning (PBL) models that prove very innovative and produce notably positive outcomes (Fournier 2002; Pawson et. al 2006; Spronken-Smith 2005). Depending upon the implementation approach, such models still may unintentionally mute certain students, especially those with very personal connections to the issues associated with migration (e.g. documented status, Dream Act, and remittances). In fact, framing migration as a 'problem to be solved' may run counter to the learning objectives related to deeper and more nuanced understandings of the topic. When framed as a problem, certain students tend to dominate the conversation, while those potentially with the most relevant personal experience do not share at all. They may be timid, pensive, or guarded about their own experiences, thoughts and ideas, leaving the discussion to be dominated by those with no such reservations or cultural constraints or direct insight (Brookfield 1995, Fink 2013). Instructors, then, need be tactful, respectful, and acutely cognizant of individual sensitivities and group dynamics in leading discussions or guiding student interactions.

The exercise presented in this paper (Figure 4, 5, 6) combines partner sharing techniques with reflective writing to meet course objectives, achieve learning outcomes, and facilitate rich learning experiences that transcend policy and patriotism. The order of questions are purposely ordered to commence with lower risk activities progressing towards more contemplative, personal, and higher order questions in the end.

Basic concepts and terms regarding migration theory are included in the exercise but are limited to content mastery. The more meaningful elements assign three basic tasks to each student: 1) track one's own history of mobility and migration; 2) interview a classmate and compare experiences; 3) reflect on deeper meanings of migration pertaining to identity, educational experiences, and world view. Though unoriginal, task 1 allows for inclusivity and low-risk individual contemplation. Most have moved at some point, regardless of gender, citizenship, ethnicity, or socioeconomic status, so students quickly find commonality in a shared experience. The simple action of filling out the boxes tends to invoke questions such as, "What if I can't remember the move?" or "Do short-distance or short-term moves count?" (answer: any and all moves count), or "What if I've never moved?" The author highly recommends other instructors to acknowledge the non-movers and rare-movers to validate that experience and to be sure they don't feel alienated by the discussion. Often, those who have never moved find it difficult to interrogate the topic of migration from multiple lenses. The topic of 'not moving' opens the door to a short discussion

Figure 4.

Part II. Migration Effects

As defined by your textbook, **migration** is "a form of relocation diffusion involving a permanent move to a new location." Formerly, migration was studied only in terms of permanent moves, but in recent years, scholars and policy makers have begun to acknowledge that many moves involve shorter time frames and distances. In the table below complete your own migration (all moves) history from birth to the present moment (add more rows as needed). If you have never moved, then you may interview a parent or other close relative **(1 pt)**

Age	From	To	Main Reason	Effect on you/your life

Figure 5.

Next, interview a classmate and compare/contrast your migration histories. Enter the name of your partner below and briefly describe how your histories are different and/or similar? **(1/2 pts)**

_____

_____

Figure 6.

Answer one of the following, depending upon your situation:

A) If you or your parents are/were foreign-born, describe in greater depth the impact of your migration experience upon your current life. How does/did this experience affect the way you see the world? How/why? Have you returned to your (or your parents') birth country? Why or why not? How does you/your family's migration experience affect your educational experience? Finally, what is something that you wish you knew about your family's migration history or experience but don't?

B) If you or your parents did not migrate (internationally), then investigate your family's migration experience. You may need to interview relatives to answer this question. What country/region of the world did they come from originally? When? Why? What do you know about the circumstances of that migration? How does this knowledge affect your identity today? Describe how *you think* your family's migration experience might have been different from those who migrate today. Finally, what is something that you wish you knew about your family's migration history or experience but don't? **(1.5 pt)**

on 'cultures of migration' (Sowell 1997) around the world. After all, the central question for migration scholars is not, "Why do people migrate?", but rather "Why is that that most do not?" Acknowledging the non-movers, then invites them into the discussion and also encourages their participation of the next section of the activity. Students are given a limited time to complete the timeline portion (Figure 4) before moving on to the interview section (Figure 5).

For task 2, students are separated into pairs or groups to share, contrast, and compare their own history of mobility and/or movement or lack thereof. Invariably, some find common ground and others do not. Prior to the interview, it is essential that instructor set good ground rules for the engagement. For example, nobody is required to answer questions that make them uncomfortable and nobody should ask deeply personal questions. Rather, interviewees should make the choice about how much they wish to share or withhold. Nonetheless, active learning requires that students do something with the knowledge they have gained, so participants are primed to utilize textbook and lecture terms throughout the interview activity (e.g. step migration, chain migration, and cultural/economic pull/push among others). Students are given only 5-8 minutes for the sharing portion in order to keep them on point and focused[3]. Proper priming for this task allows students to ask questions in skillful and culturally sensitive ways. Students are given specific questions that should not be asked. A partial list includes, "Were you adopted? Are you or your family illegal/undocumented? Don't you feel lucky that you were able to come to the US?" Through targeted conversation, this task often leads to meaningful storytelling, student bonding, and greater awareness of the complexities associated with migration.

The next portion (task 3) of the exercise (Figure 6) is completed outside of class and asks students to describe what they know about their families' or their own experiences and to further contemplate/explain the impact of that experience and/or knowledge upon their own lives, education, identity, and world views (a lofty set of questions to be sure).

Those who are more removed from migration experiences often resist this question initially and suggest that there is no connection. On some occasions, students tell me their family has never moved (e.g. "My family's always been in Georgia and will always be in Georgia!"), but when pushed, most find that they are able to construct a mental map of their family's past and are quite capable of articulating a logical construct that connects individual identity to an imagined or actual migration path at some point in the past. African American students, particularly those from the South find this portion of the exercise daunting for obvious reasons, and so they are encouraged to focus instead upon domestic moves rather than cross-border ones. Foreign-born and children of foreign-born, on the other hand, often craft long, detailed responses to this question, citing specific examples of how their identities, educational experiences, and worldviews are mediated by connections to migration. With rare exceptions, those with direct experience provide more contemplative answers. More importantly, they offer insights that expand on, contradict, and complicate the narratives offered by many textbooks. Many instructors find such student outpourings to be moving, but how might they be transformed into classroom learning opportunities? The following section provides a road map for how these rich, first-person accounts of migration may be utilized in the classroom to facilitate learning for all.

REFLECTING ON REFLECTION: MINDFUL USE OF STUDENT RESPONSES

Reading lengthy, in-depth, deeply personal responses from students on the topic of migration for the first time can make an instructor uneasy or overwhelmed. Do I reach out individually to particular students to show support and express sympathy for difficult situations? Do I ignore intimate personal and family details in order not to compromise student-teacher protocol? During four years of implementing this activity in class, this author has encountered horrific stories of family members left behind, death, family fragmentation, impossible decisions, torture, financial hardship, guilt, and daily struggles associated with living as undocumented. Others share stories of triumph, success, sacrifice, perseverance, and assimilation. Compelling as the narratives may be, a central challenge for this activity is to meaningfully integrate student knowledge(s) into learning for the whole class. The following section suggests three distinct ways in which this activity (and other similarly designed ones) can facilitate deep and active learning.

Building Student-Instructor Linkages

First, this chapter argues strongly that the instructor can and should use the narratives to connect directly to those who share details of their families' (or their own) struggles quite simply because it improves the quality of teaching. Students sometimes report that they don't speak openly about their migration experiences because nobody ever asks or they are embarrassed or they worry about their classmates' reactions. One non-traditional student thanked the instructor personally for requiring her to write out her responses, because it provided her an outlet to express burdens she has carried in silence for a long time. Forging direct connections to students simply makes for more effective instructor, educator, and professor. For example, reading student migration details has forced the author to re-conceptualize and re-evaluate the very notion of student participation to the point that he no longer attaches a grade to verbal class participation because of the tangible barriers that some students have to 'participate'. Students remain silent during class discussion not because they have nothing to say, but sometimes because they have too much to say!

Addressing the overwhelming task of internationalizing the curriculum, Odgers and Giroux (2006) offer the Three Pillars Model in which educators must seriously assess their own 1) values/assumptions/ philosophy 2) classroom dynamics/management 3) curriculum (course content) before they attempt to 'internationalize' their own courses. Part of that self-reflection may lead different instructors to engage with their students in different ways. The instructor must reflect upon his or her own family, academic fieldwork, and non-traditional travel experiences, for example, that may give the instructor direct knowledge of the pain that accompanies long-distance and cross-border migration. In some cases this author shares this intimate connection with individual students as a way to encourage their active participation in class, particularly in those cases where the student may be struggling academically due in part to their complicated past and transnational existence. One student from Pakistan shared her experience with arranged marriage and explained in her essay that her spouse migrated to the US specifically for that purpose. However, she stipulated before marrying him that she be permitted to pursue her undergraduate degree even after she becomes pregnant. Over time, however, her husband continually pressured her to quit. Her absences in my class became more frequent, but owing to my insight of her situation, we negotiated a way for her to complete the course in spite of her problematic situation. Other examples are too numerous to mention here, but the main point is that the student-instructor link can absolutely be strengthened through the acknowledgment of migration stories shared by students with instructors.

Students as Active Constructors, Discoverers, and Transformers of Knowledge

Second, the content provided by students' written answers can and should be used to question the overgeneralizations inherent in introductory texts and also to re-inforce general theories of migration (e.g. most moves are driven by economic opportunity, most migrants are of working age, etc.). Student responses are, of course, protected by long established confidentiality policies and procedures, but usually students are willing to share their insights with classmates when encouraged to do so or alternatively to allow the instructor to utilize student responses during lecture without calling out the individual student. Upon reading student responses, the instructor should take notes of insightful and instructive experiences that may facilitate learning and then invite those students to share their insights with the class or to allow the professor to summarize responses for class discussion (completely optional for the student of course). Some students prefer not to share at all, but most appreciate being included and allow their responses to be shared with classmates and others, so they can be used across classes and even semesters. Students are also given the option to remain anonymous, if they wish. This simple approach to sharing experiences has had a transformative effect in how the class discusses migration after the activity is completed and assessed by the facilitator. Because the instructor has a fairly broad understanding of each student's migration past, he/she can selectively bring those students into particular discussions as the semester progresses (note: this should be done with extreme care as students should not be made to continually speak on behalf of an entire nation, race, or ethnic group, of course). A few examples of student-driven themes are included to illustrate how it might be used for further student classroom learning.

As mentioned previously, world maps and figures may actually serve to reinforce overly simplistic understandings of immigration rather than to challenge conventional views, particularly in relationship to the US. This student's response, however, wonderfully articulates a more complex narrative of tied migration and downward social mobility that upends conventional discourse and re-frames discussions of the American Dream.

Togo-Benin-USA. Sometimes I question my decision of coming here because of the hard and harsh realities that still, are disappointing me. I used to be a working mom. I had a great job that I loved. I had people taking care of my daughter when I was at work. Here I became a housewife.... Moreover my diplomas are not accredited here, thus, I am here again as a student. [the university] only transferred one of my courses that will count as elective. I had to start everything over. The discrimination of the treatment that I receive sometimes because of that is choking. The silence[sic] treatment, the expression on a face, the response to a question and more… are destined to make me recall I am a foreigner.

The theme of downward mobility associated with migration (Papademetriou et. al, 2009) is something not generally contemplated by non-migrants and yet takes a huge toll on the lives of those directly affected like the student above. Another student explained in class that his father works as a nurse in the US in though he was an experienced physician in his native Philippines. Another student added that, although his parents were granted work visas to the US, they returned to the UAE because their certifications were unrecognized in this country and they were too old to start all over with their education. As a result, the student was living alone and feeling increasingly isolated without any family support or social capital though he comes from family of doctors, businessmen, and other professionals. Class discussion emanating from such first-person accounts elicits more nuanced understandings of migration as deeply embedded in global labor demands mediated by nationally defined understandings of 'education', 'certification', and 'skilled/unskilled labor'. The emergent theme changes with each class, based upon student experiences and written responses, but paramount to the specific content, is the active engagement of the class with lived experience that challenge oversimplified binaries such as skilled/ unskilled, documented/undocumented, legal/illegal, good/bad. Over a period of several semesters the instructor can readily accumulate a variety of first-person accounts from students that can be shared, not just with one class but across multiple sections, semesters, and years. The practice, of course, requires explicit permission of contributing students, but they too usually feel empowered by adding their own content and knowledge to others, most of whom they will never meet directly.

Classroom Discussion as Skill-Building (Intercultural Competence)

Third, sharing and discussing student-generated content with the class can increase intercultural competence (IC) among students by allowing them to encounter direct experiences that may contradict existing ideological positions. Higher education institutions across the globe increasingly embrace internationalization as a key objective for providing excellence in education (Biles and Lindley 2009; Egron-Polak 2014; Horta 2009; Kim 2011; Yang 2014). Such pursuits have also been criticized as "policy agendas that facilitate… the corporatization [through commodification] of higher education" (Biles and Lindley 2009, 150; Pandit 2009). Nonetheless, internationalization efforts typically involve study abroad programs, international invited lectures, language instruction, and international student recruitment. An often overlooked and incredibly important component piece of strategies also seeks to achieve intercultural competence among students. The examples cited in the previous paragraphs deal substantively with content mastery by using student experiences as course material. However, direct discussion and engagement with multiple perspectives related to that content can also help students develop the skill of intercultural competence (Deardorff 2009; Deardorff et. al 2012; Fink 2013; Leask 2015). Measures of such a complex skillset are outside the scope of this paper, but in general they require students to move from a place of 'not knowing what they don't know' to a condition in which 'they know that they don't know what they don't know' (Bennett 1986; Bromberger 1992). Rather than structuring a debate on migration, it is suggested that the instructor frame the discussion as an open forum, the goal of which is to consider the topic from multiple perspectives, geographic scales, and places. One way to do this is by verbally thanking the class for sharing their family stories with and then describing what the author learned from reading them[4]. It usually goes something like this:

I was blown away by the huge diversity in migration experiences reported by this class. In my multiple sections, students or their families come from 21 different countries and while some students have never moved at all, one student has moved 14 times! Wow! I have learned that I really cannot assume anything about any of you! For example, we have a student who used to be considered as 'white' until arriving in the US, where everybody told him that he was Latino and another whose family never considered race at all until her family filled out the census form for the first time. Would others like to share anything you discovered about your family's migration history from doing this activity?

Open-ended questions can result in ambiguous and ill-formed responses, but in this case, students have already been given the opportunity to interrogate, synthesize, crystalize, and articulate their own ideas in written form before speaking up in class. Many who had been unprepared to discuss the topic during previous phases of the exercise have now had time to organize their thoughts and are more likely to add to the discussion at this point, and many do. In asking an open-ended question, it is essential that the discussion leader/instructor be skilled and proactive in mediating the discussion, encouraging marginalized voices and perspectives, and gatekeeping when just a small number of students dominate the discussion. One strategy that works well is to communicate directly with a handful of students through email, direct conversation, or via text message and to encourage (but not require) them to share their insights with the class. In so doing, the instructor can prepare for those themes and the ensuing questions/controversies that are most likely to emerge. Meanwhile, otherwise silent students experience empowerment through their participation. A number of students, for example, have recounted narratives of multiple moves across multiple countries (e.g. China-Cambodia-Thailand-U.S.). Knowing this ahead of time, the instructor prepares to present lecture materials on the topics of step-migration, tied migration, globalization from below, and transnationalism to the class (a series of lecture slides are also pre-loaded and ready to display). Such a simple practice allows students with migration histories to connect their own experiences to a wider body of knowledge and theory, and it also enhances learning for non-migrant students, who are made to directly encounter classmates who put a human face on an otherwise disembodied set of concepts in a textbook.

The open-ended nature of the class discussion has the potential to break down barriers in communication, reduce stereotypes, and to find common connections. Sharing knowledge does not necessarily compel students to alter their own entrenched viewpoints, but it creates opportunities for students to grapple with difficult topics from multiple perspectives. Students begin to learn that, "where you stand is instrumental in determining what you see" (Somdahl-Sands 2015, 31), an essential skill to increasing intercultural competence at even the most basic level. Moreover, students with more direct experiences and perhaps more advanced levels of IC also have the opportunity to practice and hone the skill of intercultural communication by learning to share their experiences and framing them in meaningful, compelling, and relatable ways to their classmates. Migration alone does not increase intercultural understanding, but the practice of active oral communication and in some cases storytelling to those outside of one's own cultural framework does in fact hone the skills of intercultural communication, which is a high order skillset according the Developmental Model of Intercultural Sensitivity (Bennett, 1986; Mahoney and Schamber, 2004).

BENEFITS, RISKS, LIMITATIONS

The benefits associated with the teaching model presented in this chapter are most associated with deeper learning that stays with the student long after the semester ends. As such, assessment of students longitudinally proves difficult. The conclusions reached in this chapter are grounded primarily in student accounts of their own classroom experiences rather than via a codified assessment measure.

The purpose of this chapter, then, is to articulate one process by which instructors may take advantage of existing student knowledge by applying it to classroom learning. Such an effort is not limited to migration, but given the author's current student body, that topic serves as a natural conduit for active student learning and knowledge construction. Similar approaches may also be applied for nearly all topics in human geography courses (i.e. presenting agriculture to students in the Midwest, urban geography to students who live in suburbs, population geography to students from large and/or small families, etc.) Of utmost importance for the instructor are mindful preparation, flexibility, and ongoing communication with students. As professors/teachers/lecturers/adjuncts, we are no longer the lone vessels of knowledge and certainly not the sacred guardians of truth. Student experiences and access to information have far exceeded those from the pre-Internet generations. In any given day, an average student has access to more information than a student from 1970 had in an entire year. Our job as educators has changed and our methods need take account of and also take an active role in this ongoing paradigm shift. However, such personalized approaches to 21st century education also carry certain risks, presented in this final section of the paper.

First, not all students in freshman level courses are developmentally or academically prepared for deeper learning. Many first generation college students are already overwhelmed with concepts such as 'credit hour', 'add-drop date', and 'cumulative gpa'. To thrust such students into a deep/active learning environment entails risk. Some students tune out or are intimidated by meaningful engagement because of their limited school or life exposure. For example, at the end of what this author believed to be a really meaningful hour-long class discussion on migration recently, a student approached privately and asked, "How many Muslims would be in the United States, if there were no immigration?" Such a question indicated that the student really didn't grasp the idea that everybody in North America is an immigrant – just from a different time frame, so some students are not yet prepared to think critically in an introductory course and instructors need to plan/modify accordingly. There is a risk to overplaying your hand in an introductory course.

Second, protecting student confidentiality supersedes every other aspect of this approach, no matter how interesting, compelling, or insightful the student experience may be. Most instructors feel tempted to share student details with others when they are particularly compelling, and in many cases the practice is justified (student is endangered, other staff members need to be informed about particular situations, etc.). However, it is essential not to fetishize such stories or share them in class or with colleagues at all unless the student has explicitly approved. The author has certainly made this mistake before with very negative results. In discussing the service economy in class, for example, the lecturer described to the class the system of after-school institutes (termed *hagwons)* that dominate Korean students' lives. Having had discussed this system at length with a specific Korean student in my class (privately), the instructor asked her if she wished to elaborate on the after school system in Korea for her classmates. I believed the opportunity would serve to empower and position her as an 'expert' on the topic, but instead she felt ashamed and embarrassed that she was called out in front of her peers. In the end, she was very open in speaking to instructor privately, but she was very uncomfortable to discuss such things with her classmates. The risk of 'outing' a student is very real, and instructors should take extreme care to never violate student confidentiality in our out of the classroom.

Third, African American students (particularly those in the American South) represent a special case pertaining to the topic of migration in this country. What seems like an obvious reality becomes particularly salient in a classroom discussion or lecture utilizing terms like 'forced', 'tied', 'chain', and/or 'labor' migration. Those African American students with parents from Togo, Ghana, Haiti, Ivory Coast, and Senegal openly share their family experiences. But others feel completely disconnected from the migrant experience or associate their ancestors' brutal forced migrations as a source of shame, pain, and loss. Is it ethical for instructors (particularly non-Black ones) to induce such students to discuss, write about, and engage with this experience in an introductory geography course? Students may tune out and/or disengage with the topic that evokes such negative feelings for them. They also may feel left out of the discussion without their own meaningful stories to tell. Slavery is embedded in forced and brutal forms of labor migration. Yet, more importantly, its legacy has embezzled family history from an entire set of people. Meanwhile, Euro-ancestry students consistently construct/imagine/discover narratives of glory, honor, and empowerment among their ancestors' immigration pathways. They started businesses, conquered the land, escaped religious persecution and were welcomed at Ellis Island. African American students are robbed of such fanciful tales, instead imbued with a collective story, equally devoid of verifiable documentation, but one that evokes pain and loss and reaffirms fractures in a past that can never be undone. Such students represent a unique and serious risk in the methodological approach presented here. Proper preparation, mindfulness, and sensitivity to such risks are essential for successful weaving of student knowledge into the tapestry of any classroom. Students should certainly not be penalized or marginalized for having been robbed of their family migration story or for not knowing anything about the details of a long ago forced displacement.

CONCLUSION

While foreign-born and children of foreign-born tend to be demarcated as 'underperformers' or as challenges to educational delivery and mastery (Schleicher et. al, 2004), this chapter argues that their knowledge, experiences, and insights should be viewed as assets and valuable resources in the case of human geography, particularly in an institution that places tangible value on 'internationalization of the curriculum'. The innate sensitivities and complications associated with the use of intimate and personal student narratives in the classroom ought not be taken lightly, but the benefits outweigh the cost in the author's assessment and experience.

Taking seriously Fink's (2013) call for significant learning experiences that embrace experiential learning and reflection, this chapter offers a praxis by which "learning is regarded not as the acquisition of information, but as a search for meaning and coherence in one's life" (Candy, 1991, 415). Moreover, the chapter, via the subtopic of migration, seeks to foster a classroom dynamic in which students actively construct, discover, and transform knowledge rather than subsisting as passive vessels to be filled by truth of an omniscient 'expert' (Campbell and Smith 1997). By creating a series of short activities that require self-assessment (recording family moves), pair share discussion (compare/contrast family histories of migration), deep reflection (critical thinking and self-reflection in written form on the meaning of migration), and finally informed and prepared class discussion mediated by the instructor, students are led through a self-guided learning progression/trajectory (Huynh et al. 2015) that is flexible enough to facilitate learning among students with varying degrees of content expertise by meeting them where they are. As the discipline of geography continues to engage in such initiatives as "Where Faculty Live: Internationalizing the Disciplines" and emphasis is placed upon international collaboration and curriculum (Klein and Solem 2008; Ray and Solem 2009; Bednarz et al. 2013; Whalley et. al 2011), the case presented here suggests yet another important but missing dimension of this larger ongoing project. Demographically, more of our students each year are the direct products of the *Global Shift* (Dicken, 2011), the *Age of Migration* (Castles and de Haas 2013), the *Network Society* (Castells 2004), and the *Runaway World* (Giddens, 2004). It's imperative that academically minded instructors skillfully include their stories, experiences, and knowledge as an important micro-brew of internationalization from within.

REFERENCES

Barkley, E. F. (2010). *Student Engagement Techniques: A Handbook for College Faculty*. San Francisco: Jossey-Bass.

Bednarz, S., Heffron, S., & Huynh, N. (2013). *A Road Map for 21 Century Geography Education: Geography Education Research*. Washington, DC: Association of American Geographers.

Bennett, M. J. (1986). A Developmental Approach to Training for Intercultural Sensitivity. *International Journal of Intercultural Relations, 10*(2), 179–196. doi:10.1016/0147-1767(86)90005-2

Bonwell, C. C., & Eison, J. A. (1991). *Active Learning: Creating Excitement in the Classroom*. Washington, DC: School of Education and Human Development, George Washington University.

Bromberger, S. (1992). *On What We Know We Don't Know: Explanation, Theory, Linguistics, and How Questions Shape Them*. Chicago: University of Chicago Press.

Brookfield, S. (1995). *Becoming a Critically Reflective Teacher*. San Francisco: Jossey-Bass.

Campbell, W. E., & Smith, K. A. (1997). *New Paradigms for College Teaching*. Edina, MN: Interaction Book Co.

Candy, P. C. (1991). *Self-Direction for Lifelong Learning: a Comprehensive Guide to Theory and Practice*. San Francisco: Jossey-Bass.

Castells, M. (2004). *The Network Society: a Cross-Cultural Perspective*. Cheltenham, UK: Edward Elgar Pub. doi:10.4337/9781845421663

Castles, Miller, & de Haas. (2013). The Age of Migration: International Population Movements in the Modern World. New York: Guilford Press.

Deardorff, D. K. (2009). *The Sage Handbook of Intercultural Competence*. Thousand Oaks, CA: Sage Publications.

Deardorff, D. K., de Wit, H., & Heyl, J. (2012). *The SAGE Handbook of International Higher Education*. Thousand Oaks, CA: SAGE Publications.

Dicken, P. (2011). *Global Shift: Mapping the Changing Contours of the World Economy*. New York: Guilford Press.

Egron-Polak, E., & Hudson, R. (2014). *Internationalization Of Higher Education: Growing Expectations, Fundamental Values. In Internationalization Of Higher Education: Growing Expectations, Fundamental Values*. Paris: International Association of Universities. Retrieved from http://www.iau-aiu.net/sites/all/files/iau-4th-global-survey-executive-summary.pdf

Fink, L. D. (2013). *Creating Significant Learning Experiences: an Integrated Approach to Designing College Courses*. San Francisco, CA: Jossey-Bass.

Foucault, M., & Gordon, C. (1980). *Power/Knowledge: Selected Interviews and Other Writings, 1972-1977*. New York: Pantheon Books.

Fournier, E. J. (2002). World Regional Geography And Problem-Based Learning: Using Collaborative Learning Groups in an Introductory-Level World Geography Course. *The Journal of General Education*, *51*(4), 293–305. doi:10.1353/jge.2003.0011

Freeman, S., Eddy, S. L., Mcdonough, M., Smith, M. K., Okoroafor, N., Jordt, H., & Wenderoth, M. P. (2014). Active Learning Increases Student Performance in Science, Engineering, and Mathematics. [abstract]. *Proceedings of the National Academy of Sciences of the United States of America*, *111*(23), 8410–8415. doi:10.1073/pnas.1319030111 PMID:24821756

Giddens, A. (2003). *Runaway World: How Globalization Is Reshaping Our Lives*. London: Routledge.

Gilovich, T. (1991). *How We Know What Isn't so: the Fallibility of Human Reason in Everyday Life*. New York, NY: Free Press.

Hainmueller, J., & Hopkins, D. J. (2014). *Public Attitudes Toward Immigration*. SSRN Journal SSRN Electronic Journal.

Hall, E. T. (1989). *Beyond Culture*. New York: Doubleday.

Harley & Laxton. (2001). *The New Nature of Maps: Essays in the History of Cartography*. Baltimore, MD: Johns Hopkins University Press.

Harley, J. B., & Cosgrove, D. E. (1988). Maps, Knowledge and Power. Cambridge, UK: Cambridge University Press.

Hendrix, K. S., Finnell, S. M. E., Zimet, G. D., Sturm, L. A., Lane, K. A., & Downs, S. M. (2014). Vaccine Message Framing And Parents' Intent to Immunize Their Infants for MMR. *Pediatrics*, *134*(3), e675–e683. doi:10.1542/peds.2013-4077 PMID:25136038

Horta, H. (2009). Global And National Prominent Universities: Internationalization, Competitiveness and the Role of the State. *High Educ Higher Education*, *58*(3), 387–405. doi:10.1007/s10734-009-9201-5

Kim, T. (2011). *Globalization And Higher Education in South Korea: Towards Ethnocentric Internationalization or Global Commercialization of Higher Education?* Handbook On Globalization and Higher Education.

Koh, H. H. (2003). On American Exceptionalism. *Stanford Law Review*, *55*(5), 1479–1527. Retrieved from http://www.jstor.org/stable/10.2307/1229556?ref=no-x-route:c6cf276eeb26e8f80e47cb2d574528e5

Leask, B. (2015). *Internationalizing The Curriculum*. Taylor and Francis.

Lichter, D. T., & Johnson, K. M. (2009). Immigrant Gateways And Hispanic Migration to New Destinations. *The International Migration Review*, *43*(3), 496–518. doi:10.1111/j.1747-7379.2009.00775.x

Lipset, S. M. (1996). *American Exceptionalism: a Double-Edged Sword*. New York: W.W. Norton.

Mahoney, S. L., & Schamber, J. F. (2004). Exploring The Application of a Developmental Model of Intercultural Sensitivity to a General Education Curriculum on Diversity. *The Journal of General Education*, *53*(3), 311–334. doi:10.1353/jge.2005.0007

Monmonier, M. S. (1991). *How To Lie with Maps*. Chicago: University of Chicago Press.

Nickerson, R. S. (1998). Confirmation Bias: A Ubiquitous Phenomenon in Many Guises. *Review of General Psychology*, *2*(2), 175–220. doi:10.1037/1089-2680.2.2.175

Nyhan, B., Reifler, J., Richey, S., & Freed, G. L. (2014). Effective Messages In Vaccine Promotion: A Randomized Trial. *Pediatrics*, *133*(4), e835–e842. doi:10.1542/peds.2013-2365 PMID:24590751

Odgers, T., & Giroux, I. (2006). York University Annual International Conference On Internationalizing Canada's Universities. In *Internationalizing Faculty: A Phased Approach To Transforming Curriculum Design and Instruction*. Retrieved from https://www2.viu.ca/internationalization/docs/odgersgirouxic-paper.pdf

Oyserman, D., Coon, H. M., & Kemmelmeier, M. (2002). Rethinking Individualism and Collectivism: Evaluation of Theoretical Assumptions and Meta-Analyses. *Psychological Bulletin*, *128*(1), 3–72. doi:10.1037/0033-2909.128.1.3 PMID:11843547

Pandit, K. (2009). Geographers and the Work of Internationalization. *The Journal of Geography*, *108*(3), 148–154. doi:10.1080/00221340903099557

Papademetriou, D., Somerville, W., & Sumption, M. (2009). *The Social Mobility Of Immigrants and Their Children*. Migration Policy Institute. Retrieved from http://www.migrationpolicy.org/research/social-mobility-immigrants-and-their-children

Pawson, E., Fournier, E., Haigh, M., Muniz, O., Trafford, J., & Vajoczki, S. (2006). Problem-Based Learning in Geography: Towards a Critical Assessment of Its Purposes, Benefits and Risks. *Journal of Geography in Higher Education*, *30*(1), 103–116. doi:10.1080/03098260500499709

Ravenstein, E. G. (1876). The Birthplaces of the People and the Laws of Migration. London: Academic Press.

Reynolds, M. (1997). Learning Styles: A Critique. *Management Learning*, *28*(2), 115–133. doi:10.1177/1350507697282002

Rubenstein, J. M. (2010). *Contemporary Human Geography*. New York: Prentice Hall.

Rui, Y. (2014). China's Internationalization Strategy. *Global Opportunities And Challenges for Higher Education Leaders*, 95–98.

Schleicher, A., & Shewbridge, C. (2004). *What Makes School Systems Perform?: Seeing School Systems through the Prism of PISA*. Paris: Organisation for Economic Co-operation and Development.

Singer, A. (2013). Contemporary Immigrant Gateways In Historical Perspective. *Daedalus, 142*(3), 76–91. doi:10.1162/DAED_a_00220

Somdahl-Sands, K. (2014). Combating The Orientalist Mental Map of Students, One Geographic Imagination at a Time. *The Journal of Geography, 114*(1), 26–36. doi:10.1080/00221341.2014.882966

Sowell, T. (1997). *Migrations And Cultures: a World View*. New York: Basic Books.

Spronken-Smith, R. (2005). Implementing a Problem-Based Learning Approach For Teaching Research Methods in Geography. *Journal of Geography in Higher Education, 29*(2), 203–221. doi:10.1080/03098260500130403

United Nations. (2013). *Migrants by Origin and Destination: The Role of South-South Migration*. Department of Economic and Social Affairs: Population Division.

United States Census Bureau. (2014). *The Foreign-Born Population in the United States: US Census Bureau*. Retrieved from https://www.census.gov/newsroom/pdf/cspan_fb_slides.pdf

Whalley, W. B., Saunders, A., Lewis, R. A., Buenemann, M., & Sutton, P. C. (2011). Curriculum Development: Producing Geographers For the 21st Century. *Journal of Geography in Higher Education, 35*(3), 379–393. doi:10.1080/03098265.2011.589827

ENDNOTES

[1] These examples are not direct quotes attributed to specific individuals, but rather they are representative of the types of claims/arguments witnessed firsthand by the author from students over a 5 year period.

[2] The open forum portion of this exercise is followed by a lecture in which migration terms are defined and several common pieces of misinformation generally are corrected, such as migrant criminality, fertility rates, social service usage. Rather than challenging specific students' contentions directly, I have found that a prepared lecture allows for certain misinformation from the open forum to be 'corrected' without direct confrontation with any particular student.

[3] In my experience, students feel more comfortable sharing in groups of 3 than in pairs or in a large group, so I construct the groups of three, giving students the option to choose either member of the group on which to report. These exchanges may, on occasion, become uncomfortable, so it is essential that the instructor remain active and ready to interject where necessary.

[4] There are too many other parts to the class exercise to describe in detail here, but students have multiple opportunities to share various components of their own family migration stories in various formats.

Chapter 4
Using International Content in an Introductory Human Geography Course

David Dorrell
Georgia Gwinnett College, USA

ABSTRACT

The purpose of this chapter is to provide an example of internationalizing an Introduction to Human Geography course. This mostly consists of translating the material normally found in such a class into the explicit language of internationalization. This is accomplished by modifying the course to include less theoretical descriptions and more concrete examples of globalism at work. Topics normally found in an introductory Human Geography course are well suited for this. Religion, global development, foreign direct investment, immigration, language, and political conflict are avenues of investigation that overlap between geography and international or global studies.

INTRODUCTION

It is fair to start a discussion of internationalization with a few questions. What is internationalization? At its most basic it is the process of instilling an international perspective in a course or curriculum. Why should curricula and courses get internationalized? To produce more globally literate citizens and perhaps, more effective workers. Institutions are attempting to internationalize curricula to create a cohesive international narrative. It is no longer enough to randomly provide courses that may or may not provide the material needed by students to understand the world beyond their own borders. Students benefit from an organized effort to provide an internationalized education. Why should this particular course human geography be internationalized? At this institution, this course is part of the general education curriculum and it might be the only internationalized course that students ever take.

This chapter describes the path taken to integrate an Introduction to Human Geography course into a campus-wide internationalization initiative. It begins with a description of what prompted the drive for internationalization, discusses the types of courses that were initially put through the internationalization

DOI: 10.4018/978-1-5225-2791-6.ch004

process, and then moves to the procedures for certifying this course as international. This work contains a general guideline to internationalize an introductory geography course as well as some examples of the materials used. It is not the only possible method, but it is a method that survived the certification process, was implemented and has been successful in teaching international content. The chapter introduces important geographic concepts and relates them to internationalization. The penultimate section provides an overview of some of the specific assignments that were used to certify this course as international. Finally, the chapter discusses what was learned during the process of internationalizing a human geography course.

Internationalization in the contemporary context is an institution-wide undertaking. In the context of this institution, internationalization was undertaken as a quality enhancement plan (QEP) associated with reaccreditation (Southern Association of Colleges and Schools, 2011). As part of the QEP, students have the option of taking a certain number of designated international courses.

Courses were suggested for internationalization by their hosting disciplines or by individual instructors. In the case of this course, both the discipline and the administration believed that the course should be certified as international. The certification process was straight forward. Five student learning outcomes were presented and a rubric was created to determine whether a course was sufficiently international. If the course scored well enough on the rubric, it was international. Other courses that were part of this process were introductory political science courses, anthropology courses, international business courses and world history courses. The common thread among all these courses were their emphases on humanity, which puts human geography within the current intellectual foment surrounding internationalization.

INTERNATIONAL STUDENT LEARNING OUTCOMES

The process of internationalizing this course began by evaluating the ways in which the course met the institutional student learning outcomes for the institution. Internationalization of the curriculum at Georgia Gwinnett College for the Quality Enhancement Program (QEP) was defined by the following Student Learning Outcomes, taken from the Georgia Gwinnett College Internationalization website (GGC 2017).

1. Describe and evaluate their own cultures in relation to history, values, politics, communication styles, economy, or beliefs and practices;
2. Describe and evaluate other cultures in relation to history, values, politics, communication styles, economy, or beliefs and practices;
3. Communicate effectively with persons from different cultures;
4. Demonstrate ability to interact effectively and productively in situations involving people from diverse cultural and national backgrounds;
5. Demonstrate the ability to apply intercultural knowledge to intercultural or global problems.

Although no geographers were involved in the formulation of these Student Learning Outcomes, these outcomes fall within the range of classic and contemporary geographical pedagogy. The evaluation rubric included three levels of performance of the Student Learning Outcomes- Early Stage (Level 1), Mid Stage (Level 2) and Capstone (Level 3). Although an introductory human geography implements all the associated student learning outcomes, the level of performance is only Level 1, the lowest. This is not unexpected for a course that is generally taken in the first semester of undergraduate study and is designated by the institution as fulfilling a global culture requirement.

The following section broadly relates the student learning outcomes with their associated geographical topics.

Describe and Evaluate Their Own Cultures in Relation to History, Values, Politics, Communication Styles, Economy, or Beliefs and Practices

Geographers use the word culture to designate that which is human-induced. Anything that is a learned human behavior would fall under the category of cultural phenomena, as opposed to natural phenomena. Geographers have been exploring and teaching about the relationship between people, places, and cultures for quite some time. The term we use to encapsulate this complex relationship is cultural ecology. Cultural ecology includes the total of all human processes in a place working interactively with the natural attributes of a place. Since each place has a different set of characteristics and interactions, then each place is different. Geographers study the differences between places as well as the causes of those differences. All the attributes listed in the previous student learning outcomes are cultural in nature, and all the referenced phenomena vary across space. Geography is the study of variation across space. Cultural geography is the study of human variation across space.

Cultural landscape is another important geographical term. It includes the purposefully-built environment- houses, office buildings, farms- but it also adds the element of inadvertent constructions- fragmented forests, agricultural monoculture or mine tailings. Different economic activities or levels of political power can produce wildly different landscapes, even when the underlying natural characteristics are the same.

This student learning outcome is logically first. Before students can make any comparisons with other places, they must first understand something about their own. College freshmen have not generally been expected to visually dissect their own cultural landscape. The introductory human geography class is the opportunity to begin the process of comparing the familiar to the unfamiliar. One problem with starting with the local cultural landscape is that students have few opportunities to problematize their own culture.

The materials addressing SLO 1 and SLO 2 are taught together. This course often uses local and international cultural processes. In much the same way that learning another language can help someone understand their first language, switching between examples of spatial phenomena can help illuminate a concept.

Describe and Evaluate Other Cultures in Relation to History, Values, Politics, Communication Styles, Economy, or Beliefs and Practices.

By the time students have reached college, they are aware of the concept of diversity. Unfortunately, the understanding of diversity tends to be superficial and simplistic. Culture itself is often reduced to religion, language, and governance. In many instances the archaic notion of environmental determinism, the idea that an environment creates a particular culture, has been replaced by a form of cultural determinism. Culture is used as an explanation for human variability with little understanding of the relationships between the components of culture or the influence of other factors, such as levels of development. Students can connect cultural processes like politics, religion, and economics in their own lives- the challenge is getting them to make the same connections when thinking of other places.

Comparing a suburbanized place in the United States with a place that is poor and rural is fraught with problems. Places that are profoundly different across many categories lack an obvious starting point. Comparisons can start with places that are similar to the United States, such as Canada, Australia or Western Europe. Controlling for variables such as levels of development or settler history allows for meaningful comparison.

Communicate Effectively With Persons From Different Cultures

The most direct way of accomplishing this is to send students to other places. That is not available in this course, but that does not mean that this goal cannot be reached. This college is in a suburban area with a tremendous diversity of immigrants. The college, like many, has also managed to attract sizeable numbers of international students. Assignments that help the students talk to one another about migration, religion, or other international subjects can be the fastest way to getting students to think outside of their immediate surroundings.

The nonverbal aspect of this SLO relates directly to a geographical concept known as "landscape as text." This is the idea that the built environment is a form of communication. It tells a person where wealth is concentrated, who has political power and what places are considered valueless. This idea can also be approached with the use of videos from other places. Students can already read visual cues that denote realities such as "dangerous neighborhood" or "wealth."

Demonstrate Ability to Interact Effectively and Productively in Situations Involving People From Diverse Cultural and National Backgrounds

This section is related to the SLO 3, and it is accomplished in a similar manner, by leveraging the high percentage of foreign-born students. Added to this, are many more interactions that are virtual in the form of watching videos and engaging with music or news broadcasts from other places.

Many face-to-face courses will struggle with this SLO, and it has been implemented in this college in an expansive manner. Even in institutions with large and established study abroad programs there is some utility to preparing students for the perspectives (cultural or otherwise) that may be found in other places.

Demonstrate the Ability to Apply Intercultural Knowledge to Intercultural or Global Problems

This is the general task of this course. We create a situation in which students learn enough about the world that they can begin to form meaningful questions, then look for answers to those questions. In-depth investigations of world problems are left to courses that specialize in a subject. An introductory human geography course makes students understand some of the dynamics of international migration or flows of investment, but if cannot cover every topic in depth. That's not the purpose of a survey course. These are the general ways in which the course was determined to be sufficiently international. The following section looks specifically at some of the course materials that were used to internationalize the course.

Geographers have been teaching students to think outside their immediate situations for decades. Geography is also well suited to help in this process because geographers have been working with other disciplines for a very long time. As one of the smaller disciplines on many campuses, interdisciplinarity has been a matter of survival. Geographers have always had an international mindset, but what qualifies as international has moved well beyond geography. Geography courses reflect geographic ideals, but they can also be completely idiosyncratic, reflecting the expectations of a professor. They may or may not be useful as part of the metanarrative of internationalization in an institutional context.

In terms of internationalization, the gold standard is immersion in another place (Mazon, 2009). For multiple reasons study abroad is simply not an option for most students. The second-best option is to immerse a student in content from another place. This is far easier and cheaper, and it is the intellectual premise of internationalizing courses. It has the advantage over study abroad in that a much greater range of places can be represented than a student could realistically visit. This content can also be presented at much greater depth than can be accomplished by rushed tours that often lack context.

The process of transforming a college human geography course into an internationalized one is not as involved as transforming other curricula. International or global thinking is geographical thinking. The modern curriculum for geography courses has been international in focus for over a century. Geography is also inherently interdisciplinary, making it ideal for relating other disciplines to international content, themes and methods (Baerwald, 2010). The current difficulty within the geography academe is the fact that many people do not know what geography is. Interest in internationalization has often grown at the same time that interest in teaching geography globally has waned (Butt & Lambert, 2014).

WHAT IS HUMAN GEOGRAPHY?

Before going further, it is necessary to describe this course. Introductory human geography courses are survey courses that attempt to cover the major sub-disciplines of human geography. A typical text for the course will include chapters on the historical geography, human population dynamics, language, religion, migration, the interactions between folk and popular culture, ethnicity, political geography, development, food and agriculture, industry, human settlement patterns and human interactions with the environment. This course is about people around the world and the ways in which they live. It is well-suited for integration into an internationalized curriculum.

Every human geography course has its own goals. These are likely to be somewhat divergent, so it is useful for this exercise to revert to a general definition of an introduction to human geography course. The following is taken from the definition document for AP Human Geography (College Board, 2015). The value of this list of course content is that it represents a standard implementation of human geography. It also has the value of demonstrating the degree of congruence between geographical content and international/global content. Generally, the theoretical framework is geographical and the case studies are international or global.

An introductory human geography course investigates:

1. Problems of economic development and cultural change
2. Consequences of population growth, changing fertility rates, and international migration
3. Impacts of technological innovation on transportation, communication, industrialization, and other aspects of human life
4. Struggles over political power and control of territory
5. Conflicts over the demands of ethnic minorities, the role of women in society, and the inequalities between developed and developing economies

6. Explanations of why location matters to agricultural land use, industrial development, and urban problems
7. The role of climate change and environmental abuses in shaping the human landscapes on Earth

All of these themes are international in perspective. In fact, it would be very difficult to construct an internationalized course without using many of the preceding themes. The goals of geographical education overlap significantly with the goals of international education. This particular implementation of a human geography course has the following course goals as its basis (taken from the syllabus):

1. Students will be able to describe the relationship between humans and the Earth.
2. Students will be able to identify geographic attributes and components.
3. Students will be able to interpret the relationship between people and places.
4. Students will be able to comprehend the dominant characteristics of the cultural landscape.
5. Students will be able to develop an integrated concept of the Earth as a place.

Geography is a chorological (spatial) epistemology providing a spatial perspective, as opposed to a chronological or thematic epistemology. Human geography concerns itself with the things people do: language, politics, religion, economics, etc. The other side of geography is physical geography which concerns itself with landforms, climate, and human-environmental interaction.

The spatial perspective is the most useful means of understanding differences and similarities across the globe (Massey, 1995). It is the lens that best explains the distributions of wealth, conflict, communication, and every other phenomenon that varies from place to place. Geography is to space what history is to time. It is about products like Disney World and processes like technological diffusion. It asks the kinds of questions that are best answered at the global scale. Why is this thing here and not there? What is the relationship between these places?

The spatial element of geography provides fertile ground for cross disciplinary studies (Hinde, 2014). The geographical perspective applied to a content area produces a geographic subdiscipline. A common graphic in geography text books present the idea that geography + anthropology = cultural geography or geography + geology = physical geography. This symbiotic relationship forms the core of contemporary geography. This relationship is also the greatest problem for the discipline- geography cannot be easily broken into natural and social science categories, since the discipline is defined by its epistemology, not its subject matter (Kriewaldt, 2010).

The core concepts of geography are Place, Space, Scale, and Connections. These four words have a common usage, but they also have specific meanings in geography, and those meanings relate directly to internationalization. Space is the medium that we as people navigate every day. It can be empty or full or any state in between. A person's ability to navigate and use space is contingent upon many factors- wealth, gender, ethnicity, and relationship to power are just some of them. Every person has limited mobility to some degree, but the limit is highly variable. The ability to use space for a poor child is far less than that of a wealthy adult (Thompson & Clay, 2008).

Place is a point on the Earth (a site) plus the interactions within this site, plus this site's relationship to other places (situation). All places are made of different people, interactions, and physical characteristics. This means that they look differently, act differently, and think differently. These expected differences are the intellectual basis for all five of the international student learning outcomes stated at Georgia Gwinnett College. In an age of instantaneous communications and an encroaching homogeneity of landscape, there has even been some discussion of the end of place (Sorkin, 1992) and that eventually the world will be an unbroken strip mall of fast food and coffee shops. There is no evidence that this is true, and an underlying reason to internationalize a curriculum is the assumption of spatial variation.

Scale is the relationship between distance on a map and the corresponding distance on the ground. It also describes the space required for a process to function. For example, infectious disease operates at many scales. It can operate at the cellular level where infection occurs, at the individual scale of a body as organs sicken, at the local level as cultural practices may induce or inhibit dissemination, and at the global level as political decisions can help or hinder the transmission process. Different scales require different methods of investigation.

Connections are the relationships between places. There can be physical connections between places, such as bridges or roads. Historical connections tie some places together, for example, the British Commonwealth is a connection based on a shared colonial history. Economic relationships tie places together, both between countries, but within them as well. Contemporary technological connections allow distant communication at minimal expense. The modern collection of connections has produced the ability to move goods rapidly and cheaply, and ideas instantaneously and freely. In geography this is called space-time compression. This compression is the process most responsible for globalization. It has allowed the development, production, and consumption of products to occur at completely different places and to operate at different scales.

Introductory human geography courses are the first glimpse that many students get of the wider world (DaSilva & Kvasnak, 2012). It is also a time to discuss the evolving relationship between the local and the global, and how can students understand the relationship between where they live and the rest of the world. The curriculum for an introductory geographical can be jargon-ridden and model-heavy, but that is all the more reason to include content that bridges the gap between the abstract and the experiential. Engaging the senses as much as possible transforms dry text into lived experiences, with the added benefit of context.

An important part of any discussion of globalization is the local context of internationalization (Meyer, Mudambi, & Narula, 2011). Internationalization is not just a process affecting other places. It is a global force that manifests itself locally. There are many available tools to teach lessons regarding similarity and difference across space, which help students understand their positions (figuratively and literally) within the global network.

FUNCTIONAL CONSIDERATIONS OF THE COURSE

In some institutions, individuals will be responsible for internationalizing their own courses. In others, decisions will be made by teams or committees. Faculty have varying degrees of freedom in their choice of materials. In the case of this course, the institutional goals were not solidified in time to allow an extended faculty discussion regarding the international goals for all sections the human geography course. An informal process was used to reconcile differences between courses taught by different faculty.

This course relied mostly on content that had already been used by the instructor, modified in order to meet the previously mentioned institutional needs. Some assignments focused on local ethnic populations, whereas others drew upon sources in other countries. This mix of assets was important as it provided the basis of understanding the spectrum of processes that range from the local to the global. Due to the expansion of communication technology, the quantity of accessible international material has become almost unlimited. Online material was useful in two ways. First, it was relatively easily accessible. The difficulty was not a scarcity of information, but instead a surfeit. Sorting through the material and looking for useful items was time consuming, but there was no substitute for it. Second, since there was so much material available, it is possible to be very narrow in searching for international content. The greatest problem with the quantity of information was the fact that much of it was of low quality, or erroneous. There was also the problem of link rot, the process by which web resources are subject to being abandoned or updated so rarely that they fall quickly out of date.

Technology proved useful in another way. Students themselves have grown up expecting access to information. In many ways the job of an educator, and particularly a geographic educator, has become the art of replacing incorrect information with correct information, and students see professors in this role. Educators can use this expectation to feed students the information they need and want. Content that is engaging and interesting will be used by students, and content that is not will simply be ignored. The selection of highly engaging and relevant content, then, was paramount.

Once the content had been selected it needed to be assembled in a way that made it cohesive and logical. All courses have a metanarrative, and the content of a course must fit that metanarrative. If some of the material did not fit with the rest of the material, it was usually possible to find something that worked better. The importance of telling a coherent story through the content of a course is not unique to international courses. This is just a reminder that these courses are not made by cutting and pasting random pieces of information together in the desperate hope that students might gain some utility from them.

Each assignment served to illuminate a particular type of connection between places- be it cultural, economic, or historical. In this institutional setting, the narratives of the students in the class who were immigrants or descendants of immigrants were integral to the explicit relationship between local lives and global processes. The purpose of this was not to exoticize students in a classroom setting, but instead to start a discourse that explicitly linked the lives of students in the United States with other places and illuminate the relationships between places.

Internationalization is an iterative process and it never ever fully ended for the course, there will always be tweaks that can be made to the material and updates have periodically been necessary. Once the content had been selected, it was presented to students for feedback regarding its utility and appropriateness. Some content resonated and some did not. Each time the course has been taught has been an opportunity to implement new content, change old content, or discard content entirely. In terms of this course, the content that was most useful was that which explicitly tied geographical concepts such as diffusion of a cultural characteristic (for example, a musical style) with a recognizable product (dancehall in Denmark) (Eaggerstunn, 2012). Both visual and musical content has proven useful, as have newscasts from other countries. The students have preferred content that allows them to feel as though they are in a different place.

In terms of accessing far-away places and content generated by non-American sources, it was easy to find suitable material for intellectual and academic exploration. There were limitations, however. It should be understood that many sources of material may be catering for the North American market. This is particularly true of some news websites (e.g. RussiaToday.com, PressTV.com), which can be heavily invested in influencing North American thinking on a range of topics.

Another consideration of the range of available materials was cost. The ability to provide students with access to high quality information and materials for free shifted power away from publishing companies toward instructors. One of the most readily available resources for internationalization was video. Content generators, such as the British Broadcasting Company, Non-Governmental Organizations, film studios, and other groups have made innumerable videos available on almost any possible subject. Websites such as Vimeo and YouTube have become repositories of this material. This was particularly true for international subjects and topics pertaining to globalization. As is the case with so many available resources, instructors are forced to sift through a tremendous number of inappropriate, often low quality videos.

One significant complication with sourcing videos was not the most obvious- whether or not it is offensive. The primary problem was whether or not the video has been posted without the owner's approval, in which case it could not lawfully be used in a course, and it would likely be removed from the site hosting it. Fair use for education is permissive, but it does have limits.

Videos can also be a problem in that a college course should be more than just a video feed. The need for context in the selection of material was important, as well as the imperative of assessing whether and what the students have learned. Video has been an element of education in the United States for decades, but it has not replaced the need for other sources of information, even at a time of such abundant video sources. The videos are used to begin discussions and to prepare for other activities.

SELECTED ASSIGNMENTS

This last section describes some of the assignments used in the course. Not all are included, for the sake of brevity. These assignments represent key components of the international aspect of human geography – global connections, geospatial technology, international popular culture, world news, global economics, world religion, and environmental pollution. These subjects not only represent important concepts; they are also subjects that are resonant with students. These assignments align with the stated course goals for this geography class.

Our Connected World Computer Assignment

Internationalization Student Learning Outcomes Numbers 1 and 2

Assignment Student Learning Outcomes:

1. Students will be able to identify examples of geographic data and assess the usage of such data.
2. Students will be able to articulate the significance of scale for the analysis of spatial phenomena.
3. Students will be able to analyze the relationship between population and migration.

Spatial data are now generated by any number of governments, companies and even private individuals. Having the students view and interpret data from space programs of other countries exposes them not only to the range of data that are available, but also to the range of uses for that data (Rindfuss & Stern, 1998). Because countries have their own expectations regarding data collection, spatial data generated by individual countries is perhaps the most contextualized international data available.

Online data can also be used to explore demographic changes such as population growth, depopulation, and migration (Kim, Kim, & Lee, 2013). Using freely available spatial data from other countries, for example the space agencies of the following countries- India, Japan, Canada, China, France, the United States, and from private companies such as Google, Microsoft and Yahoo, the student will make a series of maps that exemplify the changing population dynamics of the world and explore other maps and data that have been produced. Students are often surprised to discover the extent to which some places in the United States are depopulating or that one country, Russia, is in the top five countries for both immigration and emigration.

Google Earth Assignment

Internationalization Student Learning Outcomes Numbers 1 and 2

Assignment Student Learning Outcomes:

1. Students will be able to collect data and produce a simple map.
2. Students will be able to access, manage, process, and analyze spatial data.
3. Students will become familiar with platforms and formats of spatial data.

Probably no other technology has been more useful in providing context to discussions of global topics than Google Earth (Patterson, 2007). It represents tremendous investments in geographical information science (GIS), remote sensing, data visualization, content production and computer graphics (Lamb & Johnson, 2010). It's also available completely for free. It uses data formats that are easily shared with all GIS packages. Simply seeing the spatial implications of migrants streaming to Spanish territories in Africa, or using the historical imagery function to assess deforestation in Malaysia makes this product useful, but the fact that students can also generate their own content and save it for later use makes this tool invaluable for internationalizing a course. When looking at data being presented on an actual rendered globe, it is easier for students to contextualize both the data and the human stories that they are given during a course (Rundquist, 2013) .

Being able to zoom across levels allows students to investigate for themselves notions of scale and density. Since this technology platform is free it is possible for students to continue using it outside the confines of this course. As such it allows students to apply their newfound skills to other classes as well. Since the maps created by the students are representative of the students' own weekly routines, the students can relate directly to the product (Boschmann & Cubbon, 2014).

Top Ten Music Lists and Music Videos Assignment

Internationalization Student Learning Outcomes Numbers 1, 2 and 3

Assignment Student Learning Outcomes:

1. Students will be able to differentiate between global popular music and its local equivalents.
2. Students will be able to articulate the function of scale as it relates to a globally marketed commodity.
3. Students will be able to recognize the dominant languages of popular music.

Students find the music industry more interesting than other industries (Waldron, 2012). It is more familiar, since they have been subject to music marketing for most of their lives. Other industries such as vehicle manufacturing, agriculture, etc. do not generate the same level of interest (Smiley & Post, 2014).

Students are given the assignment to simply list the current top ten songs for twenty countries. The global nature of music distribution will become immediately apparent to the students as country after country has charts dominated by American and British pop stars. However, it is also apparent that not every name on the charts will be familiar. Most countries will have some local artists in the top ten. The charts are diagrammatically *glocal*- a mashup of the global and the local. The importance of students placing themselves within the global music marketplace is important as it allows students the opportunity to relate their knowledge, that of popular music in the United States, to other places. Music charts are momentary, changing at weekly intervals. A characteristic of modern popular culture is that it tends to homogenous across space while being heterogeneous across time. This characteristic describes music charts perfectly ("Charts All Over the World," 2016).

Music videos can be used to show diffusion of a cultural artifact. Showing reggae videos from Jamaica, Germany, The United States, and Brazil allows students to assess diffusion in the form of direct and indirect cultural relationships between music producers and music consumers. Having students interpret the built environment evident in music videos is an entertaining way to get students to look at the landscape. This allows students to then use the same spatial analytical skills to analyze the landscapes they themselves inhabit in order to tease apart power structures built into the environment. It begins a conversation about representation that later will help to explain to them why they see statues commemorating long dead soldiers in some neighborhoods (Winberry, 2015), and airports and garbage dumps in other neighborhoods.

This assignment that seems best suited for helping students understand the interrelated world they live. Lecturing about diffusion, talking about the global lingua franca, showing charts of foreign direct investment, none of these things are as effective as just having students explore music charts around the world. The feedback posted below demonstrates that the goals of the assignment were met. Beyond that quoted feedback were other comments such as:

The differences in these charts are most likely due to language and cultural demographics/preferences. For instance, the Spain top ten includes a lot of Latin music that you most likely wouldn't ever see on the chart in Ireland. The similarities lie in the more mainstream (usually pop) music category, where you see the same songs or artists on every chart. Even if the songs aren't identical, there are artists who are popular enough and appeal to a broad enough audience to be included on charts of different countries... It was great to see yet another example of the differences and similarities among countries and cultures.

Or

Germany and Australia have all but a couple of the same exact songs as the US chart. Australians speak English so it makes sense for them to enjoy American music. Not many German music stars have popped up recently and a majority of the population speaks English as a second language so enjoying American songs is not that strange. Overall, the internet has trafficked American culture all around the world.

When the assignment is interesting to students, they complete it. When it has relevant content, they learn. Not every assignment can approach the material in the same manner as this, music provides an easy introduction to studying similarity and difference across space. The following assignment asks the students to again study similarity and difference across space, but exploring a different medium.

World News Reading Assignment

Internationalization Student Learning Outcomes Numbers 1, 2 and 3

Assignment Student Learning Outcomes:

1. Students will be able to demonstrate knowledge of current national and global issues for the worlds' regions.
2. Students will develop an appreciation and respect for the diversity of perspectives world-views, and cultures.
3. Students will be able to apply knowledge of global issues to answer a pressing world problem.

The most obvious sources of international content are free, easily accessed and updated every day. Entire courses could be devoted to reading international headlines on a daily basis. These assignments start by introducing students to basic geographical concepts- differences across space or the importance of place, then move to specific examples of divergence of news across space. World news is another powerful tool for helping students absorb international messages (Aspaas, 1998). English is the world's lingua franca. English speakers can read news sources from such diverse sources as Qatar, the United Kingdom, France, Singapore, Russia, India, Iran, and China. Obviously, each of these places have different ideas regarding which topics are of global importance, but they all present the news in a manner that furthers their own interests, in the same fashion the US news sources do. Once again, the goal of this assignment is to foster a more global understanding of the interconnected nature of the news cycle as well as helping students understand that what counts as "world" news is spatially and culturally variable. This assignment induces comparisons and contrasts between news agencies that may be state-owned, politically biased, or culturally propagandistic. All of these positions and more are part of the spectrum of news, and as such should be used in any attempt to teach students to recognize a more global perspective.

Looking at the world news generated by other countries allows students to experience the internal conversations within other places on a range of topics. News topics are public discourses within a particular country. People in other countries not only discuss the topics that are considered newsworthy, they rank them in terms of placement on a website. Students note not only what the news sources in particular countries choose to talk about, but also those events that are not covered. Ideas about free speech, religious freedom, propaganda, and dissidence may or may not be familiar to American college students. Events may be filtered with a different set of parameters than would be used in the United States. The differences in perspectives available from different news sources can serve as the prompt for a discussion on the nature of truth and how public opinions can be manipulated by media outlets of any origin.

Economics Activity

Internationalization Student Learning Outcomes Numbers 1, 2 and 5

Assignment Student Learning Outcomes:

1. Students will be able to discuss the relationship between geography and development.
2. Students will have a basic understanding of global economic activities and networks.

3. Students will have a general understanding of how the physical environment, human
4. societies, and local and global economic systems are integrated.

Economic integration is a global phenomenon that necessarily manifests locally (Meyer et al., 2011). This relationship can be difficult to see in the daily lives of students. Although products may be labelled with their country of origin, it doesn't necessarily mean that global economic networks will be understood by students. True globalization, in which the forces of design, production, and consumption are completely spatially disconnected from one another, is by its very nature seamless and invisible (Dicken, 2014). If it were not, the system probably would not work, as it requires tight tolerances for communication. The best way to teach this to students is through their own investigation, and the best place for them to start is in their home states.

Every state in the United States has examples of foreign direct investment (FDI). These local investments are a translation between the local workforce and the global production and consumption chain. One of the recurrent problems in teaching an international perspective is the idea that something international is necessarily somewhere else. Transnational corporations are familiar to students and most can name some of them (McDonald's, Microsoft), but these are companies that grew from the United States outward. Getting students to find companies that started elsewhere and eventually came to the United States can be more useful in that it represents the internationalization of "right here."

The conversation surrounding offshoring in the United States can often simply be a narrative of fear and unemployment. Showing that the two largest contributors of FDI are the same as the two largest recipients (the United States and the European Union) helps students internalize the reality of the footloose nature of investment and production, as well as help them recognize that there is a balance struck between the return of an investment and the assumed risk of the investment (World Bank, 2015). The students find foreign based transnational corporations in their own state, which helps them understand that their communities have gained from someone else's offshoring.

The student must also research and report on what resources are produced and exported from his or her home state. This section serves to reinforce the fact that the global system requires inputs from innumerable, often redundant places. The global market for anything survives by incorporating local goods and services. Globalization is a process involving resources, labor, capital and consumption, none of which exists outside of the context of local places.

Pollution Scavenger Hunt

Internationalization Student Learning Outcomes Numbers 1, 2 and 4

Assignment Student Learning Outcomes:

1. Students will be able to describe human-environment interactions as well as global environmental issues.
2. Students will be able to evaluate the changing impacts of pollution on natural environments.
3. Students will be able to assess the past, present, and future impacts of pollution.

This assignment closely connects to the assignment on economics. Although they are usually presented as separate topics, the case could be made for combining them, since the global economic system is the root cause of the global pollution problem.

Of all the topics that are covered in an introductory geography course, pollution often is one that is considered most locally applicable. Advertising campaigns and volunteer opportunities stress the need to contribute locally to picking up litter or cleaning a stream. Pollution or deforestation are local problems, but they are driven by global forces. Demand for paper, palm oil, or simply cheap consumer goods drives pollution across the globe. Therefore, it is important to frame the problem as a global one. The assignment looks at pollution within the United States, then shifts overseas. It looks at types of pollution that drift beyond the confines of a state. It asks about environmental justice and the relationships between environmental despoliation and natural disasters. Often activities that are presented as being environmentally beneficial in one place are disastrously damaging in other places, for example recycling electronics waste in places with little environmental regulation (Michel, 2013).

In a globalized world it can be difficult to understand the environmental impact of a product when its production occurs on another continent. Mines, oil wells, and clear-cut forests that are out of sight can be out of mind. Further inhibiting a full assessment of environmental impact is that after a product has been used its disposal may carry it even farther from the consumer than its production and marketing.

Just as pollution has become an international problem, it also requires international, or at the least super-national solutions. The last part of this assignment has students investigating possible solutions for reducing or mitigating pollution's harmful effects. It is worth noting that few of the solutions presented are actually global-level activity, but instead are local activities within a global organizational umbrella.

Religion Assignment

Internationalization Student Learning Outcomes Numbers 1, 2 and 5

Assignment Student Learning Outcomes:

1. Students will demonstrate a basic understanding of the spatial distributions, conflicts, and landscapes related to a variety of religious traditions.
2. Students will investigate the relationship between religion, ethnicity, socioeconomic class, and access to political and social power.
3. Students will be able to contextualize particular religious conflicts at a global level.

Probably the subject that is most likely to generate resistance and distrust is the subject of religion (Haynes, 1990). It can be difficult to convince students to separate their own values and beliefs from any discussion of other religions and belief systems.

This assignment encourages students who have already been made aware of the general distribution of religions around the world to investigate religious conflict. Much of the subtext of such an assignment is that often religious tags serve as a shorthand for non-religious struggles. For example, ethnicity and religion are closely tied, and what can appear as a religious conflict may be in fact a political disagreement, or a struggle over resources that has become defined as a religious war. The underlying cause of the tendency to define ethnic or economic struggles as religious can be understood through the notion that leadership often relies on religion as a motivator.

Carefully analyzing religiously-defined strife in many places across the world, using a wide mix of religions, can allow students an opportunity to develop an understanding of the factors that lead to this conflict. Other than examples of inter-sectarian strife (conflict over heresy or doctrine), most of this conflict can be better explained through the lenses of nationalism, economic competition, or access to political power.

In order to provide balance, students will also make a list of local religious establishments. Local religious context in the United States is generally one of diversity and tolerance. The local narrative of cooperation can serve as the starting point of a discussion of tolerance around the world, which of course is generally the norm.

Supermarket Assignment

Internationalization Student Learning Outcomes Numbers 1, 2, 3 and 4

Assignment Student Learning Outcomes:

1. Students will acquire an understanding of the role that food can play in ethnic identity.
2. Students will briefly immerse themselves in the culture of another place.
3. Students will assess the global connections that allow food to be profitably transported long distances.

One of the most obvious hallmarks of the arrival of an ethnicity into the United States, or any other country, is the diffusion of a food from the group of origin (Pillsbury, 2008). Pizza in the United States, curry in the United Kingdom, and doner kebab in Germany all exemplify the degree to which a food brought by immigrants can reach the status of adopted national cuisine. Long after the language of an immigrant group has been lost the cultural value of food remains. Food is also the cultural element that is most accessible to outsiders. Food must be part of any effort to internationalize a curriculum. Foodways are used to construct a spatial sense of one location as a reflection of the entire world.

Foodways refer to the types of food that people eat, the ways they are prepared, and the cultural factors that surround and contextualize the food. Food is the most resilient cultural artifact. In countries undergoing language unification foods can define ethnic groups. In monolingual countries, foods may indicate geographical origins or social class. Food is easily bought, tried, and accepted or rejected. It is multisensory. As such it is the most accessible cultural element (Jarosz, 1996). This is not the same as a discussion of agriculture, although the two are related. In many ways the consumption of a food and its production have been divorced by the modern restaurant industry and international food conglomerates. Americans have eaten foods they consider Chinese or Mexican for generations, while few know the histories of said foods. Questions of whether or not a food is authentic are difficult to answer when the cooks in a restaurant are of a completely different ethnicity from the stated cuisine.

Books such as Hungry Planet (Aluisio & Menzel, 2005) provide students with resources to compare foodways between places and groups. Quantities of food, the ratio of prepared foods, and consumption of tobacco and alcohol all help students get inside the lives of people in different places, at different states of technological development, and different socioeconomic classes.

Waves of migration to U.S. cities and suburbs have created landscapes of tremendous ethnic difference embedded in architectural homogeneity (Frazier & Margai, 2010). The supermarket assignment sends students into this mix. It is another way of approximating travel abroad in a closer setting (Olsson,

2007). Students must visit ethnic grocery stores to see products of another ethnic group. This assignment builds on the previous ones, but instead of being through the internet, this assignment moves a student into a new space, with different signs, smells, and products. It is a personal field trip (Krakowka, 2012). For many students this may be the first time they have been in a place not designed to appeal to their own sensibilities. Unfamiliar products, or familiar products in unfamiliar brands allow students to see a store with fresh eyes. This perspective will be even more useful when the students look at their familiar stores in the same way that they looked at the ethnic grocery store.

Students are forced to interact with products from another place, made for another market, but in a non-threatening manner in a location that they may pass every day (Jang & Yao, 2014). With low stakes and the familiar settings of their own local neighborhoods, barriers for investigating unfamiliar foods, medicines, and consumer goods are lowered. One advantage that this assignment has over travel abroad is that it can be performed without overwhelming a student in the way that many people may feel while visiting places outside their home country. There are fewer disorienting details to digest.

CONCLUSION

The aim of internationalization at the course level and the institutional level are practically synonymous with education itself- to expose students to a wider world than they have likely seen before. Internationalization provides a venue for examining the sorts of problems and opportunities that students will experience throughout their lives, while also providing the tools to best navigate the world around them.

Education reflects the society in which it is embedded. On the one hand, we widely recognize the importance of learning other perspectives, but on the other hand we have limited time and resources. If it is important to teach students about the culture, politics, religion, and economies of the world, then we must do that in the time allotted in general education. Introductory human geography courses have been doing this for decades.

The process of recasting a human geography course into an international course required a reimagining of the course. The emphasis shifted from being a course designed to recruit students into a geography program to a course that supported majors in English, business, computer science and others. This philosophical shift necessitated a change in teaching materials. These materials were selected to apply as widely as possible to other disciplines.

Internationalization is probably best taught as an applied perspective across the curriculum. This was the goal in the stated internationalization plan for this institution, but truly campus wide internationalization is likely impossible. It's imperative that there be some courses that cover a range of international topics, since these may be the only international courses that students ever take. Human geography is just such a course.

It is entirely possible that the idea of internationalization will shift over time and different interpretations of the meaning of the word will arise. It is unlikely that the concept will lack a spatial element. The assignments used for this class will need periodic updating, but the underlying concepts are unlikely to change much. The international student learning outcomes became implementations of the overall course goals. Sometimes the interaction between a course goal and the SLOs of an assignment were indirect. For example, the supermarket assignment sought to reinforce the understanding that food is a direct product of the environment (Goal 1), but it is also a cultural construct (Goal 4), and an economic product (Goal 3). In the same ways that course goals can overlap, so too can different assignments serve different purposes. Looking at different phenomena through different spatial lenses (such as human-environment interaction or political geography) provided a fuller picture of the world as a functioning system with different inputs.

The assignments were used to allow the students to draw conclusions about the world around them by interacting with data, videos, images, music, and stories. The content was compelling when it allowed the students to make the connections between places and phenomena on their own, using their own intellectual frameworks. As students were transitioned from the more familiar toward the less familiar they were able to integrate what they had learned into a cohesive set of ideas.

The previously detailed course assignments and decisions regarding internationalization were only a starting point for internationalizing a course. As was mentioned earlier, the context of internationalization was also important. Part of this process consisted of talking with colleagues in other disciplines that were internationalizing, as well as sharing material and ideas with others. The process of internationalization also allowed the human geographers at this college to teach the other faculty what we do. A positive side effect of the internationalizing process was that it was used to further the general institutional goals of interdisciplinary teaching and research.

REFERENCES

Aluisio, F., & Menzel, P. (2005). *Hungry Planet*. New York: Material World Books.

Aspaas, H. R. (1998). Integrating World-views and the News Media into a Regional Geography Course. *Journal of Geography in Higher Education*, 22(2), 211–227. doi:10.1080/03098269885912

Baerwald, T. J. (2010). Prospects for Geography as an Interdisciplinary Discipline. *Annals of the Association of American Geographers*, 100(3), 493–501. doi:10.1080/00045608.2010.485443

Boschmann, E. E., & Cubbon, E. (2014). Sketch Maps and Qualitative GIS: Using Cartographies of Individual Spatial Narratives in Geographic Research. *The Professional Geographer*, 66(2), 236–248. doi:10.1080/00330124.2013.781490

Butt, G., & Lambert, D. (2014). International perspectives on the future of geography education: An analysis of national curricula and standards. *International Research in Geographical and Environmental Education*, 23(1), 1–12. doi:10.1080/10382046.2013.858402

Charts All Over the World. (n.d.). Retrieved March 9, 2017, from http://www.lanet.lv/misc/charts/

College Board. (2015). *AP Human Geography Course Description Effective 2015*. College Board. Retrieved from http://media.collegeboard.com/digitalServices/pdf/ap/ap-human-geography-course-description.pdf

DaSilva, E. B., & Kvasnak, R. N. (2012). Multimedia Technology and Students' Achievement in Geography. *Geography Teacher*, 9(1), 18–25. doi:10.1080/19338341.2012.635080

Dicken, P. (2014). Global Shift: Mapping the Changing Contours of the World Economy. *Sage (Atlanta, Ga.)*.

Frazier, J. W., & Margai, F. M. (2010). *Multicultural Geographies: The Changing Racial/Ethnic Patterns of the United States*. Global Academic Publishing.

Georgia Gwinnett College International Student Learning Outcomes. (n.d.). Retrieved from http://www. ggc.edu/academics/qep/internationalized-courses/index.html

Handbook for Institutions seeking reaffirmation.pdf. (n.d.). Retrieved from http://www.sacscoc.org/ pdf/081705/Handbook%20for%20Institutions%20seeking%20reaffirmation.pdf

Haynes, C. C. (1990). Religion in the Classroom: Meeting the Challenges and Avoiding the Pitfalls. *Social Education*, *54*(5), 305–306.

Hinde, E. R. (2014). Geography and the Common Core: Teaching Mathematics and Language Arts from a Spatial Perspective. *Social Studies Review*, *53*, 47–51.

Jang, W., & Yao, X. (2014). Tracking Ethnically Divided Commuting Patterns Over Time: A Case Study of Atlanta. *The Professional Geographer*, *66*(2), 274–283. doi:10.1080/00330124.2013.784952

Jarosz, L. (1996). Working in the global food system: A focus for international comparative analysis. *Progress in Human Geography*, *20*(1), 41–55. doi:10.1177/030913259602000103

Kim, M., Kim, K., & Lee, S.-I. (2013). Pedagogical Potential of a Web-Based GIS Application for Migration Data: A Preliminary Investigation in the Context of South Korea. *The Journal of Geography*, *112*(3), 97–107. doi:10.1080/00221341.2012.709261

Krakowka, A. R. (2012). Field Trips as Valuable Learning Experiences in Geography Courses. *The Journal of Geography*, *111*(6), 236–244. doi:10.1080/00221341.2012.707674

Kriewaldt, J. (2010). The Geography Standards Project: Professional Standards for Teaching School Geography. *Geographical Education*, *23*, 8.

Lamb, A., & Johnson, L. (2010). Virtual Expeditions: Google Earth, GIS, and Geovisualization Technologies in Teaching and Learning - ProQuest. *Teacher Librarian*, *37*(3), 81–85.

Massey, D. B. (1995). *Spatial Divisions of Labor: Social Structures and the Geography of Production*. Psychology Press. doi:10.1007/978-1-349-24059-3

Mazon, B. (2009). Creating the Cosmopolitan US Undergraduate: Study abroad and an emergent global student profile. *Research in Comparative and International Education*, *4*(2), 141–150. doi:10.2304/ rcie.2009.4.2.141

Meyer, K. E., Mudambi, R., & Narula, R. (2011). Multinational Enterprises and Local Contexts: The Opportunities and Challenges of Multiple Embeddedness. *Journal of Management Studies*, *48*(2), 235–252. doi:10.1111/j.1467-6486.2010.00968.x

Michel, B. (2013). Does offshoring contribute to reducing domestic air emissions? Evidence from Belgian manufacturing. *Ecological Economics*, *95*, 73–82. doi:10.1016/j.ecolecon.2013.08.005

Olsson, T. C. (2007). Your Dekalb Farmers Market: Food and Ethnicity in Atlanta. *Southern Cultures*, *13*(4), 45–58.

Patterson, T. C. (2007). Google Earth as a (Not Just) Geography Education Tool. *The Journal of Geography*, *106*(4), 145–152. doi:10.1080/00221340701678032

Pillsbury, R. (2008). No Foreign Food: The American Diet. In *Time And Place*. Westview Press.

Rindfuss, R., & Stern, P. (1998). Linking Remote Sensing and Social Science: The Need and The Challenges. In People and Pixels: Linking Remote Sensing and Social Science (pp. 1–28). National Academies Press.

Rundquist, B. C., & Vandeberg, G. S. (2013). Fully Engaging Students in the Remote Sensing Process through Field Experience. *The Journal of Geography*, *112*(6), 262–270. doi:10.1080/00221341.2013. 765902

Smiley, S. L., & Post, C. W. (2014). Using Popular Music to Teach the Geography of the United States and Canada. *The Journal of Geography*, *113*(6), 238–246. doi:10.1080/00221341.2013.877061

Sorkin, M. (Ed.). (1992). *Variations on a Theme Park | Michael Sorkin* (1st ed.). Macmillan. Retrieved from http://us.macmillan.com/variationsonathemepark/michaelsorkin

Thompson, L., & Clay, T. (2008). Critical literacy and the geography classroom: Including gender and feminist perspectives. *New Zealand Geographer*, *64*(3), 228–233. doi:10.1111/j.1745-7939.2008.00148.x

Waldron, J. (2012). Conceptual frameworks, theoretical models and the role of YouTube: Investigating informal music learning and teaching in online music community. *Journal of Music. Technology and Education*, *4*(2–3), 189–200. doi:10.1386/jmte.4.2-3.189_1

Winberry, J. J. (2015). "Lest We Forget": The Confederate Monument and the Southern Townscape. *Southeastern Geographer*, *55*(1), 19–31. doi:10.1353/sgo.2015.0003

World Bank. (2015). *Foreign direct investment, net inflows*. Retrieved November 1, 2016, from http:// data.worldbank.org/indicator/BX.KLT.DINV.CD.WD?year_high_desc=true

APPENDIX OF ACTIVITIES AND FEEDBACK

Assignment #1

Our Connected World

Complete this assignment and submit it digitally by the due date.
  For all of these sites, I would also like you to visit the main pages of each site, if you do not start there.

https://www.planet.com/gallery/
http://www.realtor.com
http://www.theverge.com/2016/8/4/12369494/descartes-artificial-intelligence-crop-predictions-usda
http://nationalmap.gov/

  What kinds of data are available here?

http://water.usgs.gov/edu/photo-gallery/large/sinkhole-guatemala.jpg

  What is a sinkhole?

http://www.asc-csa.gc.ca/eng/satellites/disasters.asp

  What environmental disaster is in the first image?

http://www.intelligence-airbusds.com/en/5751-image-detail?img=34292&search=&market=0&world
    =1176&sensor=0&continent=0&keyword=#.V7zuU_krKt8

  Where is this?
  What is that on the center right?

http://www.terraserver.com/

  Type in your address. What are the Lat/Longs for your house in decimal degrees?
  Also+++ Click resolution and watch scale change+++

http://www.fastcompany.com/3062560/the-recommender/a-look-at-the-olympics-from-outer-space

  What do the photos in the article show?
  Also check out the main site.... http://www.digitalglobe.com

https://zoom.earth/#40.748434,-73.985809,18z,sat

  Play with the buttons for different data sets.

Which data set do you prefer and why?

http://modis.gsfc.nasa.gov/gallery/showall.php

What is the most recent image of the day?
What are three of the others on the page?

http://www.eorc.jaxa.jp/ALOS/img_up/jdis_opt_tohokueq_110324-3.htm

What country runs this site?

Assignment #2

Google Earth Activity

Complete this assignment and submit it digitally by the due date

1. Time to think about your daily routine. Give me at least fifteen (15) places (restaurants, parks, etc) where you regularly go.
2. Fill out the data sheet. I need at least 15 places. If you need to, use google to find the address of the places you have been.
3. Make sure your data are properly placed in your Data Document spreadsheet.
4. Go to the following URL:
   http://batchgeo.com/
5. Following the directions on the webpage paste your data into their form.
6. Click map now
7. Save and continue.
8. If necessary, use a screenshot program like the Windows Snipping tool to save the image. Each of you save it as your own name.
9. Upload the image and this sheet to Assignments in D2L.

   Please remember that Feedback is not graded, nor will your opinion be held against you!
   Feedback:

1. On a scale of 1 to 5, 1 being the least useful, I would rate this assignment a _____
2. What is the most useful aspect of this assignment?
3. What is the least useful aspect of this assignment?
4. How would you improve this assignment?
5. Please comment on this assignment.

Activity #3

The Top of the Charts: Popular Music

Complete this assignment and submit digitally by the due date

US Top Ten

1._____

2._____

3._____

4._____

5._____

6._____

7._____

8._____

9._____

10._____

_____ Top Ten

1._____

2._____

3._____

4._____

5._____

6._____

7._____

8._____

9._____

10._____

_____ Top Ten

1._____

2._____

3._____

4._____

5._____

6._____

7._____

8._____

9._____

10._____

_____ Top Ten

1._____

2._____

3._____

4._____

5._____

6._____

7._____

8._____

9._____

10._____

Discussion:

How are do these charts differ? Why do you think that is?
>   How are they similar? Why do you think that is?
>   Why are so many of the songs in English?

Assignment #4

News Activity

Complete this assignment and submit it digitally by the due date
>   Visit the following websites:

http://www.cnn.com/WORLD/
http://www.presstv.ir/
http://www.france24.com/en/
http://www.bbc.co.uk/news/
http://rt.com/
http://www3.nhk.or.jp/nhkworld/
http://www.aljazeera.com/
http://www.ndtv.com/
http://www.dw.de/
http://www.straitstimes.com/Breaking+News/World/World.html

>   Answer the following questions.
>   All of these pages are showing World News, but World News is different from place to place.

1.   What do **all** these sites think is truly global in importance?
2.   In your opinion, what is a topic on each site that is not global in any way?

>   Add your answers to the questions (in this document) and return it to me via Assignments on D2L by the due date.
>   Please remember that Feedback is not graded, nor will your opinion be held against you!
>   Feedback:

1.   On a scale of 1 to 5, 1 being the least useful, I would rate this assignment a _____

2.   What is the most useful aspect of this assignment?
3.   What is the least useful aspect of this assignment?
4.   How would you improve this assignment?
5.   Please comment on the News Assignment.

Assignment # 5

Economics and Development

Complete this assignment and submit it digitally by the due date.

Give me a list of ten (10) foreign plants (factories) in Georgia. Explain what they do, where they are located, and their country of origin. Tell me when this company opened a location in Georgia.

If you can determine this, tell me if their only presence in the United States is in Georgia.

ON YOUR OWN, find the World Bank data regarding FDI inflows and outflows. Who are the 5 largest investors?

Who are the 5 largest recipients?

Watch the container ships move around the world

http://www.marinetraffic.com/en/ais/home/centerx:-82/centery:31/zoom:8

Assignment #6

Pollution Scavenger Hunt

Complete this assignment and submit it digitally by the due date

Find me 1 link per question on the stated topic.

1.   What are the 10 most polluted places on Earth?
2.   What is the most polluted place in the US? Justify your answer.
3.   What form of pollution causes the most deaths in China?
4.   What is the current state of the ozone layer?
5.   Describe the total pollution impact of the earthquake/tsunami/reactor leak in Japan.
6.   Why are our perceptions of pollution risk so distorted?
7.   What are pollution sources in this area?
8.   Is organically produced food inherently better? Why or why not?
9.   What is the concept of environmental justice?
10. What is the link pollution and economic development?
11. 11.   Asian brown cloud

http://www.nature.com/news/take-responsibility-for-electronic-waste-disposal-1.20345

Assignment # 7

Religious/Ethnic Strife Activity

Complete this assignment and submit it digitally by the due date

1. Nigeria
    http://www.futod.net/2011_04_01_archive.html
    http://api.ning.com/files/g4uwOmFeoZdaN5hHRmSaPhLIvh5S6A7Wb1D-0oGL3ZI7L8M
        OW8b0rTx*8UOsp8SYPWgxIgMhLoPaPzQSMVRh7xw12YEfeLIr/NIGERIA_MAP.
        jpg?width=500
2. India
    http://en.wikipedia.org/wiki/Religion_in_India#mediaviewer/File:India_religion_map_1909_en.jpg
3. Islamic State
    http://www.bbc.com/news/world-middle-east-27838034
4. Syria
    http://www.washingtonpost.com/blogs/worldviews/wp/2013/08/27/the-one-map-that-shows-why-
        syria-is-so-complicated/
5. Philippines
    http://en.wikipedia.org/wiki/Philippines#mediaviewer/File:Philippine_ethnic_groups_per_province.
        PNG
    http://en.wikipedia.org/wiki/Religion_in_the_Philippines#mediaviewer/File:ReligionPhilippines.
        png
6. Indonesia
    http://www.bbc.com/news/world-asia-22165159
7. Myanmar
    http://www.amnesty.org.au/refugees/comments/35290/
8. Sri Lanka
    https://news.vice.com/article/hardline-buddhist-violence-flares-against-muslims-in-sri-lanka

Activity # 8

Supermarket Assignment

Supermarket Name and Address _____

 Your job is simple- Go to an ethnic supermarket, preferably one unfamiliar to you and select five products that are unknown to you. For each product provide the following details:

1. What is it called?
2. What do you do with it?
3. Where did it originate?
4. Does it look appealing to you?
5. Would you consider eating it?

Chapter 5

Internationalizing a Course on the Cultural and Intellectual History of the Ancient World

Richard S. Rawls
Georgia Gwinnett College, USA

ABSTRACT

This chapter investigates the process of internationalizing a course on ancient history. It suggests ways that a course can be created, examines important issues, and provides examples of assignments to help meet course, discipline, and institutional outcomes. Informed by the work of Fink, it commences by arguing for the significance of course outcome goals, disciplinary outcome goals, and additional institutional goals related to internationalizing the curriculum. Without these various outcome goals as building blocks for the course, it will be both difficult to assess the educational effectiveness of the class and challenging to organize the content. The chapter next discusses pedagogical issues before moving into internationalizing the course. It then investigates the work of two ancient authors, Herodotus and Tacitus, who commented upon foreign cultures. Their histories support exercises designed to help learn outcome goals. Contrary to what some may think, internationalizing a course on ancient history is easier than one might initially anticipate.

INTRODUCTION

This chapter will examine the process of internationalizing a course on ancient history. Some might think that a class on ancient history would not lend itself well to the process of "internationalizing the curriculum." After all, one cannot have a face-to-face conversation with someone from a different culture if that person is long dead. One cannot resurrect the ancient Medes no matter how much one tries. It is thus an intimidating enterprise to interrogate the texts and artifacts of people from "then and there." Contrary to the hesitations one might have, this chapter argues that it is in fact possible to internationalize a course on ancient history. If, as White (1965) asserted, "History is a means of access to ourselves" (p. 201), then our study of the ancients will be an act of self-revelation and discovery.

This chapter will further suggest ways that a course can be created or changed, examine issues to be considered, and provide examples of assignments to help meet course, discipline, and institutional

DOI: 10.4018/978-1-5225-2791-6.ch005

outcomes. Informed by the work of Fink (2013), it will start by suggesting the importance of course outcome goals, disciplinary outcome goals, and additional institutional goals related to internationalizing the curriculum. Without these various outcomes in mind, it will be both difficult to assess the educational effectiveness of the class and challenging to organize the content. The chapter will discuss a series of pedagogical issues before moving into internationalizing the course. It will show some ways that two ancient authors commented upon foreign cultures, and it will discuss exercises designed to help learn outcome goals.

A study conducted in 1993 surveyed student reactions to university-level instruction, especially to the overall quality of their in-class experiences. In the summary of their study, Courts and McInerney (1993, pp. 33-38) reported that students did not understand themselves as self-directed learners. Students generally lacked confidence in their overall abilities to approach, conceptualize, and discover a way to figure things out on their own. In commenting on the Courts and McInerney study, Fink (2013) observed that students feel fragmented and isolated, and that this isolation stems partly from "not having much interaction with other students, either in class or out of class, about course-related matters" (p. 6). Fink (2013) proposes "significant learning experiences" as a partial remedy for the problems of isolation, segmentation, and for student inability to figure out how to approach problems.

Fink's (2013) definition of significant learning remains ambitious in how he defines it: "significant learning is learning that makes a difference in how people live – and the kind of life they are capable of living" (p. 7). Although this definition may sound flowery or highly aspirational, the intentions of significant learning remain easily grasped yet tough to implement. For Fink (2013), significant learning remains so vital that it merits its own taxonomy precisely because the phrases, words, and concepts captured by Bloom's taxonomy no longer prove as helpful as they once did. Fink (2013) argues, "Individuals and organizations involved in higher education are expressing a need for important kinds of learning that do not emerge easily from the Bloom taxonomy" (p. 34). Fink (2013) maintains that significant learning involves inter alia a classroom setting characterized by: high levels of student engagement and in-class participation; different and multiple types of learning experienced by students (p. 33); interaction (p. 37); the acquisition of "foundational knowledge" (pp. 34-39); learning how to learn; and (new) ways of applying knowledge. Although it is beyond the scope and intentions of this chapter to summarize everything Fink suggests, it is nonetheless evident that professors must engage in careful planning if they wish for their students to acquire these experiences and content. The connection between significant learning and internationalization will be made more explicit below, but oral assignments remain especially vital for achieving several of Fink's recommendations.

Oral assignments feature prominently in this course, and for several reasons. They help with significant learning and internationalization. Oral assignments permit students to both share knowledge and interact so that a variety of skills can be assessed (Joughin, 1998; R. Rawls & J. Rawls, 2017). No single assessment mechanism can possibly measure all that students have learned or whether they are fulfilling the various learning objectives (Angelo & Cross 1993; Fink 2003; J. Rawls, Wilsker, & R. Rawls, 2015). Oral assignments satisfy Fink's encouragements for interaction, different types of engagement, participation, and dialogue. Oral assignments thereby close a feedback loop. Students can easily get lost with the ideas and not even realize that they are not keeping up. The interactive nature of oral assignments and debates helps the professor to monitor student progress and to provide additional information if necessary. These assignments not only help students to interact more but they also develop their oral presentation skills and foster an engaged "learning community."

The formulation of course goals and/or outcomes (what the professor intends for students to take away from the course) remains central to internationalizing a course. In fact, outcomes and goals constitute a vital component in the success of any course, but especially so with respect to internationalized courses. The demands of changing a course to reflect internationalized perspectives can prove difficult for faculty precisely because professors are socialized into modes of disciplinary thinking, training, and assuming (Becher, 2001). Professors must therefore focus upon *what* they want students to learn and *how* they hope to help their students achieve these desired goals. Failure to do so will result in a reversion to habits, disciplinary thinking, and the inertia of what has been done in the past. This author therefore took to heart not only the idea that proverbial thinking outside of the box was necessary but also that the design of the curriculum, the selection of course outcome goals, and assessment of student learning required a series of intentional choices in designing the course (Leask, 2012).

While development of course outcome goals remained vital to internationalizing a course on ancient history, it was equally important to insure that course goals integrated well with departmental goals and institutional goals. In the absence of such harmony, conflicts might develop between competing goals and interests. Similarly, one might teach only to one set of goals to the detriment of others. Cognizance of such goals is frequently viewed as a nuisance in teaching undergraduate courses, but properly viewed, they can assist the professor in making certain that the course strives to achieve its stated goals and that the goals are explicit and in harmony with each other. A course reflecting such harmony ought also to display a relationship between course content, skills, intercultural development, and other intangibles.

The syllabus can reinforce goals, skills, and other objectives related to intercultural competence (Lee, Poch, Shaw, & Williams, 2012). Syllabi communicate the values of a professor and the institution. They inform students, administrators, accreditation specialists, and others about the class. For example, syllabi: 1) provide cues to students about the value of the knowledge and skills they will acquire; 2) communicate the intentions of faculty; 3) hint at the significance of assignments intended to help students learn, apply, and communicate knowledge; and 4) syllabi communicate values by what they exclude (Anderson, 2008). Professors must remain attentive on this last point. If syllabi stress the significance of group projects but exclude anything else about them in a schedule that highlights only lecture and content, then students will interpret this as suggesting that only the content is important (Lee et al., 2012). Desired student outcomes ought to be reinforced and modelled by the professor. Moreover, the content (learning) and the delivery (teaching) should align with assessments, because most students will presume that assessed items are the most important (Sinnema & Aitken, 2012).

Another consideration for faculty internationalizing their course relates to the extent of learning. The depths at which one can reach or even assess outcomes and goals depends upon both the course and the professor. Some courses may lend themselves more readily to deeper levels of significant learning. Other courses may not naturally enable professors to explore certain topics in depth. Consider, for example, the student learning outcomes for IOC at Georgia Gwinnett College. The outcomes include five separate areas. According to the college website (Georgia Gwinnett College, 2017):

Students will be able to: 1 - Describe and evaluate their own cultures in relation to history, values, politics, communication styles, economy, or beliefs and practices; 2 - Describe and evaluate other cultures in relation to history, values, politics, communication styles, economy, or beliefs and practices; 3 - Communicate effectively with persons from different cultures; 4 - Demonstrate ability to interact effectively and productively in situations involving people from diverse cultural and national backgrounds; and 5 - Demonstrate the ability to apply intercultural knowledge to intercultural or global problems.

These five outcomes enable a variety of possibilities for both *what* gets taught and *how* the content might be conveyed and learned. No course is expected to achieve the deepest levels of learning in all five areas. Few courses can be expected to even touch on all five student learning outcomes. For example, the course proposed here aimed at meeting outcomes 1, 2, and 5; none are at the deepest level. A robust internationalization of the curriculum plan within any college or university will insure that students receive exposure to all outcomes in a combination of courses.

ADDITIONAL CONSIDERATIONS FOR INTERNATIONALIZING A COURSE

The ancient history course designed for internationalization was a senior-level course titled "Cultural and Intellectual History of the Ancient Mediterranean World." The course not only fulfilled departmental/disciplinary (history), school (liberal arts), and institutional outcomes for internationalized courses, but it also met the applicable recommendations of the *American Council of Education* (ACE). The ACE website (http://www.acenet.edu/news-room/Pages/Intlz-in-Action-2013-December.aspx) listed examples of internationalized courses that in some way met four separate criteria of: 1) content, 2) materials, 3) activities and assignments, and 4) student outcomes (Helms, n.d.). The case study or sample class on their website furnishes examples for a course on United States history, but it still helps concretize how the content, materials, activities and outcomes integrate into the course. It should be readily apparent in what follows that Cultural and Intellectual History of the Ancient Mediterranean met these four recommendations.

Bonds (2003) suggested three methods or approaches to internationalizing courses. The first, "Add-on," seeks to include guest speakers or supplementary readings on international topics, but otherwise leaves the remainder of the curriculum untouched. The second, "Infusion," aims to infuse intercultural skills and knowledge throughout the entire course. This approach likely demands that professors refashion parts of their syllabi and course goals to reflect the incorporation of intercultural approaches. The third, "Transformation," suggests a complete reorientation of the course so that the course is transformed by the incorporation of significant levels of intercultural material. In a course taking a transformative approach, students should be able to demonstrate the capacity to understand and even move between two or more worldviews as a consequence. It is important for faculty to keep these distinctions explicitly in mind as they develop their courses, just as cognizance of course outcome goals, disciplinary goals, and the institutional IOC goals can be helpful for constructing one's course.

Before moving into the course content, one further recommendation about course construction merits scrutiny. Course outcome goals can help instructors to avoid becoming bogged down among the competing interests of various institutional stakeholders and well-intentioned administrative and academic offices. This may sound counterintuitive at first, so some explanation is required. Various college and university offices are entrusted with overseeing different functions both within the institution and in representing it to outsiders. Sometimes these functions overlap. Usually they harmonize, but not always. Sometimes they maintain competing views and agenda. It is important to stress that conflicting views might need to be held in tension rather than resolved. Sometimes the tensions caused by institutional stakeholders can hinder individual course development. At other times such tensions reflect not only the lack of institutional consensus but also the existence of a greater national or even international disagreement.

The literature regarding the purpose of internationalizing courses can further reflect myriad and sometimes contradictory inquiries. For example: 1) Should internationalized curricula promote global citizenship or even "good" national citizens (Fordham, 2012; Peterson, 2011)? 2) Ought all curricula to aim at modern public policy awareness (Barber, 2007)? 3) Should curricula promote international cooperation and exchange in order to forestall widespread global conflict (Altbach & de Wit, 2015)? 4) Ought we to strive for creating a culture of peace as part of the formation of social identity (Korostelina, 2013)? Should we focus on educating in order to promote human rights and global citizenship (Abdi & Shultz, 2008)? All of these are legitimate questions, but not all courses can answer or seek to address them. It is in this sense, then, that disciplinary/departmental, school, institutional, and university IOC goals can help a course to stay focused. Certainly, the aforementioned themes can constitute a big part of a course, but they do not of necessity need to do so in order to be an "internationalized" course. Teaching to the specific course goals will help one to stay focused. No class can do it all, and none should be expected to cover everything.

INTERNATIONALIZING THE ANCIENT HISTORY COURSE

The front cover of a *Time Magazine* special edition featured the following words on its cover: "The New Face of America: How Immigrants are shaping the World's First Multi-Cultural Society" (*Time* 1993). *Time* can be forgiven for engaging in a bit of journalistic overreach because its mission is to sell magazines. Indeed, the magazine cover featured an attractive woman created by a computer simulation combining the beautiful features of women from numerous ethnic groups. In the midst of its self-congratulatory tone, the editors seemingly forgot that the Persian and Roman Empires spanned three continents. The editors further overlooked the intentional creation of a short-lived but equally significant Macedonian Empire, not to mention the creation of the twentieth-century communist land-mass behemoths of the Soviet Union and the People's Republic of China, both of which were cognizant of the "multiculturalism" and multi-ethnic natures of their nations long before *Time's* editors bestowed their recognition upon the United States. The point is that the world has been diverse, multi-ethnic, and cognizant of differences between people for as long as human records go back and speak to us from the past. One of the biggest hurdles in "internationalizing" a modern history course based on the ancients is simply to pay attention to what the ancients were saying and to temporarily suspend judgments about either the present or the past in light of the present.

The ancient history course description creates the possibility of intercultural exploration: "An historical investigation into the cultures and ideas of the Mediterranean world and of the historical role of these in the synthesis of cultures, politics, ideas, and the human view of the world (as manifested in religion and philosophy) from 800 BCE to 600 CE." The course commences from the course description and then proceeds both chronologically as well as thematically.

Herodotus and the Course

Several assignments help the course reach its internationalization goals. Two assignments particularly help meet the IOC goals. The first assignment requires students to write a paper based on Herodotus' monumental story of the struggle between Persia and Greece, the *Histories*. The paper encourages reflection on intercultural relations, not military tactics, battles, or even questions about Herodotus as a historian. Instead, it requires students to do the following:

Compare and contrast Herodotus' portrayal of the Persians with that of the Greeks. How do the Persians understand Greek culture? In what ways does Herodotus' portrayal of the Persians reflect Greek understandings of Persian culture? What are the ways that Herodotus misunderstands these cultures? Is this misunderstanding intentional or done out of cultural unfamiliarity? In a final paragraph, discuss the types of cultural misunderstandings that a modern historian might exhibit when writing about other cultures?

This assignment works toward three of the five institutional IOC goals in that the class assignments require students to: 1 - Describe and evaluate their own cultures in relation to history, values, politics, communication styles, economy, or beliefs and practices; 2 - Describe and evaluate other cultures in relation to history, values, politics, communication styles, economy, or beliefs and practices; 5 - Demonstrate the ability to apply intercultural knowledge to intercultural or global problems. The assignment must be examined in order to demonstrate how it is possible to fulfill these outcomes.

Examining the second outcome first, students are required to do three things in quick succession. They must evaluate Herodotus' understanding of Greek and Persian culture, they must understand something about Persian and Greek culture, and they must analyze what Herodotus related to his audience in terms of these cultures. Class discussion, oral presentations, debates, and carefully selected readings (in addition to Herodotus) help prepare for the assignment. Oral presentations by students especially prepare the class to acquire additional skills in cultural analyses.

The past thirty years of studies of Herodotus also proven helpful in cultural analysis. Even those who do not specialize in ancient history recognize that Herodotus occupies both a special place among historians and a controversial legacy. Some view Herodotus as inventing portions of his history or as being completely unreliable where the Persians are concerned (Sancisi-Weerdenburg, 2002). Others have lamented that he remains a source upon which Persian specialists have had to rely and that he remains behind the "hostile press" the western tradition gives to Persia (Brosius, 2006, p. 2). Notwithstanding valid concerns, a number of scholars have argued persuasively that Herodotus remains far more informed and helpful about Persians than one might think (Momigliano, 1966). Munson (2009) suggests that Herodotus usually had Persian sources and that, "Even some of his inaccuracies are illuminating as they are rooted in Persian traditions or discourse" (p. 458).

Despite their diverging opinions, nearly all scholars concur that Herodotus made a unique contribution in that his work exhibited an unprecedented interest in culture. In her review of Burkert's (1990) *Hérodote et les peoples non grecs*, West (1992) commented, "Despite living at a period when the Hellene/Barbarian antithesis crystallized, [Herodotus] retained a lively sense of the intrinsic value and interest of non-Greek ways" (p. 279). Even Sancisi-Weerdenburg (2002) observed, "Herodotus at least made a very serious attempt to give the Persians a fair deal" (p. 583). When Momigliano (1966) commented that "Herodotus has really become the father of history only in modern times" (p. 141), Schorske (1990) later added that "The reason for this is that Herodotus allowed culture (in the wide, anthropological sense) to play a critical role in his *Histories*" (p. 409). Even if we concede the argument of Hartog (1988) that Herodotus used some cultures as a mirror by which he could examine the Hellenes themselves, we can nonetheless agree and reply that Hartog's work mostly investigated Herodotus' treatment of the Scythians, about whom Herodotus knew vastly less. The Persians were another story. Herodotus knew well certain aspects of Persian life and culture. He was, in the words of Munson (2009), "fascinated by the Persians and confident in his access to informants who can clarify for him who the Persians are as a culture and where they came from ideologically" (p. 457). It was precisely Herodotus' attention to ethnicity that makes him valuable for internationalizing a course.

In a journal article, McWilliams (2013) elaborated upon the concept of hybridity. In contrast to *stasis*, the condition of the world has been one of the movement of its peoples. It is hybrid, in motion. McWilliams (2013) asseverates that Herodotus remains one of the key contributors to our knowledge of this dynamic in antiquity: "Through his elaborate descriptions of a globe that is overwhelmed by motion – the motion of all peoples and cultures through time – Herodotus draws a picture of the world that draws the hybrid to the fore" (p. 745). The movements of people then and now suggests cross-cultural contact and differing political systems. Even if we factor myriad conceptions of political borders, political systems, and other forms of social identification, we still arrive at cross-cultural interaction. Herodotus' biography is a bit of an open question, but it seems clear that he was from Halicarnassus, a Greek city in Asia Minor that fell under Persian domination. That he traveled the Aegean, if not the Mediterranean, is relatively clear too. He was thus uniquely poised to talk with, understand, and interact with a wide range of cultures, and especially Persians and Greeks.

Having established that Herodotus is viewed by many scholars as being one of the first historians to notice and comment upon cultural differences, it is time to look at what he actually did. In other words, how and in what ways can Herodotus help to achieve the internationalization objectives? Since it must be remembered that students were asked to comment upon both Persian and Greek understandings of each other and misunderstandings, it becomes necessary to help them notice how the ancients observed cultural differences. This requires an understanding of the concept of "surface" and "deep" culture, which the class has covered through student-led oral presentations.

Scholars attributed the metaphor of "culture as an iceberg" to E. Hall's (1976) *Beyond Culture*, but that attribution was incorrect. Hall (1959) actually discussed the iceberg metaphor in *The Silent Language,* where he lamented the inadequacy of the metaphor or model of culture (pp. 85-87). The metaphor suggests that approximately ten percent of the iceberg rises above the water's surface. The remaining ninety percent remains below water (Katan, 1999). By analogy then, what we can see is often called "surface or visible or explicit" culture, and what stays hidden is "deep or internal or implicit" culture. Surface or visible culture obviously includes such things as language, style of dress, some behaviors, music, games, economic activities, etc. Deep or hidden culture might include the reasons for these activities, which are not always explicitly stated. It might also include assumptions about topics as diverse as gender roles, religion, myth, the "why" of "how" things are done, ideas about interpersonal relationships and sexuality, ways of ordering and conceptualizing time, collective and individual approaches, ideas about personal space, competitiveness, among other things (Brake, D. Walker, & T. Walker, 1995). It is frequently the case that people who live within a culture understand how their culture proceeds with doing a particular action, but they may not be capable of elucidating why their own culture engages in this behavior. Although Hall does not explicitly apply the label "culture as an iceberg" in *Beyond Culture*, and in fact his work in *Silent Language* questions its usefulness, his work on hidden culture certainly supported the metaphor.

With this in mind, we arrive at one of the first episodes in Herodotus. In an early scene of interaction between Persians and Greeks, the Spartans sent an envoy to the Persian king, Cyrus, to warn him about harming other Greek cities, for "the Spartans would not allow it [ὡς αὐτῶν οὐ περιοψομένων]" (Herodotus 1. 52. 3, trans. R. Rawls). In what constituted a tacit admission of his own ignorance, Cyrus inquired about the Spartans: who were they and how large was their city that they might make such demands of him. Upon learning more, Cyrus responded accordingly (Hdt. 1. 153. 1, trans. 2007): "I have never yet feared any men who have a place in the center of their city set aside for meeting together, swearing false oaths, and cheating one another..."(Hdt. 1. 153. 1, trans. 2007). Lest his readers/auditors not understand, Herodotus (hereafter trans. 2007) further interpreted Cyrus' statement: "Cyrus thus insulted the Hellenes because of their custom of setting up agoras in their cities for the purpose of buying and selling, which is unknown among the Persians, who do not use markets and… have no such place as an agora in any of their cities" (153. 2).

Cyrus' retort reflected a surface level awareness not of Spartan culture in particular but of Greek culture in general. Taking Herodotus' text at face value, Cyrus remained aware of Hellenic customs of holding market days in their agora. The irony, of course, is that the Spartans of all the Greeks were least likely to hold such markets. Cyrus' statement thus shows a surface level cognizance of Greek culture, but an ignorance of surface level Spartan culture. Of all the people to insult, Cyrus had insulted those Greeks whose regime was perhaps most like that of his own Persians (Green, 1996, p. 12)!

Cyrus' misunderstanding is instructive for another reason. It suggests that he did not understand the purpose and function of market cultures. To him, they were designed for people to cheat one another. Even worse, they provided the opportunity for people to get together and exchange not just goods and services but also ideas. Ideas could be subversive. Cyrus gave little thought to the polis, its need for citizens to rub shoulders, market-based economies, the interactive nature of democracy, etc. Why ought he to have considered these things when he was king of an emerging and mighty empire, not one of several *archons* of a tiny Greek polis tucked out of the way in some remote corner of Greece? According to Shenefelt (2003), "Most intellectual and literary history is actually focused on small and divided places, especially marketplaces, where equals crowd upon equals and where new creeds are hard to suppress" (p. B11). It was precisely this freedom as represented by the *agora* that Persian kings disliked, because the *agora* not only meant "market" in ancient Greek but also a locus of assembly of citizens. In contrast, the Persian king constituted the state, as revealed not just in Greek sources but also in Persian ones (Green, 1996; Rahe, 2015).

In addition to helping students consider differences between economies in ancient Hellenic cities and the Persian Empire, this moment in history helps students to analyze the present. The assignment therefore facilitates IOC objective 1 as well, because conversation inevitably turns toward bartering in American and Canadian contexts. Students may instinctively know that one can barter for automobiles and houses but not for items at the grocery store chain, for example. When pressed why this is the case, they have no answer. "It is just the way we do things," they respond. They become tenuous when asked to turn the microscope on themselves, which is not surprising because it is uncomfortable.

Another reason why students find it difficult to begin to assess their own cultures is because they do poorly at it. As E. Hall observed (1959), "Culture hides much more than it reveals, and what it hides, it hides most effectively from its own participants" (p. 53). In other words, it might be easier for students to intuit and understand ancient marketplaces than it would to understand modern markets. Class discussion and graded presentations on markets, haggling, and other cultural practices help students to put ancient and modern practices in perspective. The key in persuading North American students to notice the cultural aspects at work in Herodotus thus relates as much to their own cultural judgments as to anything else. When they can set them aside for a moment, then they can begin to relate to ancient texts. The ancients are different enough that students understand them better when they do not assume that "they are just like us." Even so, noticing the hidden or surface dynamics in Herodotus is difficult enough, to say nothing of uncovering the hidden or deep cultural levels. As E. Hall commented elsewhere (1976), "The surface problem in analyzing any culture is that people maintain rather stereotyped pictures of themselves that may not fit the multiple facts, levels, and dimensions of which all cultures or composed" (p. 193). In other words, the problem may be as much with the subject as the object!

The Persian invasion of Greece in 480 BCE provides another moment for discussion of cultural understanding and misunderstanding. Herodotus portrayed King Xerxes with an advisory council consisting not only of some of his relatives and leading Persians but also some important Greek exiles such as the former Spartan king, Demartus. Nobody doubts that the Persian king consulted with such a council even if the actual vicissitudes may have transpired differently than portrayed in Herodotus; we shall never know actual details for certain. Still, the council's interaction, as portrayed by Herodotus, inevitably leads to other inquiries.

One of the questions the class entertains comes only after a week or so of exposure to Herodotus: how did he conceptualize culture? The answer to this question soon turns murky because Greek language actually contained no such word for culture. This raises another inquiry: did the Hellenes have a conception of culture? Of course, but the concept and the thing itself are not necessarily the same thing. According to Lasky (2002), "One could have culture in ancient Athens but not the word; one can have, nowadays, the word – it is ubiquitously around us – and not be referring to the real thing" (p. 77). Lasky's assertion raises a profound point: how did the Greeks understand themselves? It took Jaeger (1939) three volumes to explain the ideals of Greek culture, and one suspects that despite his monumental achievement, he still could not encapsulate it all. Jaeger's (1939, vol. 1) early definition of culture as, "simply the aristocratic ideal of a nation, increasingly intellectualized" (p. 4), left him commenting on *paideia* and *arête*, but still no closer to a modern, anthropological sense. Students thus begin to appreciate the complexity of the inquiry about Herodotus' definition of culture: perhaps he never quite defined "culture" even as he described it in operation all around him.

Some have argued that Herodotus' greatest contribution was actually defining Greek culture by observing what it was not. Burkert (1990) averred that Herodotus sympathized with Persian views, a position backed by the ancient writer Plutarch (*Moralia* 857a), who went so far as to call him a *"philobarbaros."* Herodotus portrayed the various Hellenic *poleis* as the independent political and cultural entities that they were, complete with different personalities, customs, religious practices, and ways of understanding the world. They remained far from homogenous; heterogeneous in fact. According to J. Hall (1997), "The only way in which cultural heterogeneity could appear more uniform was by contrasting with practices that were even more heterogeneous, and this is precisely what Herodotos [sic] achieved through the barbarian[s]" (p. 45). Thus, the value of Xerxes' retinue of advisors who accompanied him relates to the dialogical and comparative nature of what constitutes and differentiates a Persian from a Greek. The irony is that Herodotus here uses Greeks to explain Greeks to a Persian king, all the while actually explaining Greeks to the other Greeks who constituted his audiences!

Xerxes' advisors maintained mixed opinions on an invasion of Greece, and the "debate" Herodotus presented gave him the opportunity to suggest both sides of the same coin regarding Hellenic styles of waging war. Namely, fighting in the hoplite-phalanx fashion likely seemed ridiculous to some who were unfamiliar with it. In the view of the Persian general, Mardonius, Hellenic fighting reflected Greek pugnaciousness and a simultaneous lack of rationality: since the Greeks can understand each other, accents notwithstanding, they ought to make peace (Hdt. 7. 9. β 2). Instead, of utilizing the advantage of geographical or topographical features, they seek out level ground, line up opposite each other, and then rush at each other in a scrum and inflict heavy injuries on one another. To a Persian general with a massive army comprised of multi-national forces and myriad fighting styles, the ancient Greek style of fighting would indeed seem irrational.

Hanson (1989) and others (Green, 1996; Strauss, 2004; Cartlege, 2006; Rahe, 2015) have suggested not only that Greek warfare was rational but that it actually suited Greek topography, social conditions, and agricultural needs. Although hoplite-phalanx fighting involved scenes of incredible carnage, it actually kept casualties lower than they might otherwise be if battle was protracted for hours (Hanson, 1989). The fighting usually finished within an hour. Citizen-soldier-farmers preferred decisive infantry battle over long, drawn-out campaigns, in which the Persians would find themselves embroiled. At this point in the narrative, however, the Persians did not know this. Herodotus' later auditors and readers would have recognized the lengthy nature of Persia's invasion, however, and the irony would not be lost on them. Whether by literary artifice, custom, or pure invention we cannot know, but Herodotus records that Artabanus, Xerxes' uncle, rose to argue against Mardonius. Artabanus suggested that one cannot choose from a menu of options without cognizance of the possibilities, and he felt duty-bound to present the case against invading Greece. He referred not only to the vagaries of warfare, nature, and chance, but he also suggested that the Greek reputation for warfare surpassed that of the Scythians, whom the Persians already fought and found most difficult of opponents (Hdt. 7. 10). Warfare is an uncertain enterprise and its unpredictable results can neither be anticipated nor controlled. Xerxes obviously ruled against his uncle's advice.

With the invasion well under way, we find Xerxes continuing to solicit advice from various commanders. Additional insights into cross cultural understandings arise. A few additional examples will suffice. While scholars have been quick to understand Herodotus' passages as attributing the Hellenic victory to love of freedom (7. 133-136), superior cunning (7. 144; 8. 75. 2-3), better armaments and superior military strategy (9. 62, 7. 211), there is yet another reason that emerges upon careful textual analysis. Namely, the Persians failed to take advantage of the persistent and ongoing Hellenic disunity. Episode after episode of Greek disunity appear. When we take into consideration the advice that Hellenes and others give Xerxes, combined with the prominence of the theme in Herodotus, we are left to marvel at Persia's inability to take greater advantage. Herodotus frequently reported disunity in the Hellenic world, and there is no reason to doubt it.

Several episodes of disunity featured prominently. The former Spartan king, Demartus, advised Xerxes to occupy Cythera, which would instigate a Spartan retreat to the Peloponnesus out of fear of outright insurrection (Hdt. 7. 235). Demartus advised bypassing the isthmus and sailing directly to the Peloponnese (Hdt. 7. 234-237), with the result that the Spartans and Peloponnesians would be rendered useless to the rest of Greece. Artemisia counselled Xerxes to avoid a pitched naval battle at Salamis in favor of a coordinated army and naval investiture of the Peloponnesus (Hdt. 8. 68). She argued that the resistance of the Peloponnesians would fade away as they retreated in order to defend their individual *poleis*; given the right pressure, they would refuse to fight on behalf of the Athenians (Hdt. 8. 68).

The most significant instance when we can visibly see Persia militarily taking advantage of Greek disunity was the episode Themistocles manufactured at Salamis. For those who may not know, Themistocles sent a slave to Xerxes encouraging him to attack while the Greeks were quarrelling and disunited. Themistocles' actions raise the prospect that he knew the Persians were cognizant of Greek disunity and thereby turned this weakness into a strength by establishing the time and place of the naval battle. By this point readers are aware of the Theban betrayal of the Greek cause (Hdt. 7. 233), the actions of Themistocles in etching graffiti in the Greek language onto rocks in order to sow suspicion about the loyalties of those Greeks subjected to the Persian cause (Hdt. 8. 22), and the discussion among the Greeks about abandoning Salamis (and thereby abandoning Athens too) and retreating to the Peloponnesus (Hdt. 8. 60-62). As Athenian commander, Themistocles threatened to take the formidable Athenian fleet and depart to Italy, thus leaving the Greeks to their own fate (Hdt. 8. 62). Finally, the Thebans submitted a strategy to the Persian commander, Mardonius, about another possibility of conquering Greece without a fight: namely, bribe the leading men of each of the cities (Hdt. 9. 2). Herodotus reported once again that sound advice from Greeks to Persians was ignored.

Students almost always conclude the same thing after investigating course material, completing assignments, and engaging in debates and oral presentations: the Persians probably should have won the war, but they continued making strategic mistakes (Lazenby, 1992). Moreover, these mistakes could have been avoided if Persian kings and senior commanders had listened and accepted the advice of those foreigners in Persian service as opposed to listening to the advice of Persian commanders who had less knowledge of the cultural, geographical, political, and topographical landscape.

In order to further investigate intercultural competence and IOC goal 5, we move to an examination of how the armed forces of the United States train their service branches to understand "foreign culture." This includes but is not limited to topics as diverse as language training, cultural sensitivity, and intelligence gathering. In exploring how various military branches train their personnel to understand culture, we arrive at a more nuanced idea of the dynamics at work in Herodotus. We also fulfill our IOC objective number 5: "Demonstrate the ability to apply intercultural knowledge to intercultural or global problems."

The class specifically explores the efforts of the various branches of the U.S. military to understand, disseminate, and train service members and others about "culture." The U.S. Army's efforts since 2005 to increase Cultural Awareness since 2005 are integrated into the overall TRADOC (Training and Doctrine Command) structure (Hajjar, 2006). The Army located the TRADOC Culture Center (TCC) at the U.S. Army Intelligence Center (USAIC), at Fort Huachuca, Arizona. The TCC, in addition to working on the dissemination of cultural awareness education, cooperates both with the American government's militaries and with other countries, including British, Canadian, and Australian (ABCA) Programs and experts (Hajjar, 2006). The U.S. Marine Corps maintains its Center for Advanced Operational Culture and Learning (CAOCL) for similar reasons. According to its website and as of 2014, the CAOCL was providing cultural training to 33,000 people annually (Center for Advanced Operational Culture and Learning, 2014). The U.S. Air Force houses its cultural education efforts within the Air Force Culture and Language Center (AFCLC). The AFCLC's efforts have culminated, among other ways, in the "Expeditionary Culture Field Guides (ECFG)" which remain available for download via "Google Play" or the "iPhone App Store." According to the webpage (AFCLC, 2017), the ECFGs aim at what are called the "3Cs," cross-cultural competency: "This model encompasses 12 cultural domains that account for every aspect of a society's cultural identity." The ECFG guides further divide into two separate sections regarding culture: Culture General (CG) and Culture Specific (CS). The CG portion addresses foundational aspects of culture across a broad-spectrum of considerations and on a world wide scale. The Culture Specific portion remains directed at identifiable cultures and societies, taking into account their nuances and particularities. Finally, the United States Navy maintains its cultural education efforts partially through the Center for Language, Regional Expertise, and Culture (CLREC). According to its website, the CLREC "provided language and culture support to over 80,000 Navy personnel and managed the Navy Foreign Language Testing Program at more than a 100 testing facilities worldwide with more than 11,000 Defense Language Aptitude Battery tests, Defense Language Proficiency Tests, and Oral Proficiency Interviews in FY16" (United States Navy, n.d.).

While we understand that these centers represent only a small portion of what the military and American government attempt in terms of training for cultural awareness, these examples nonetheless illuminate the extent to which the American government tries to train its military personnel for cultural awareness (Watson, 2010). This training might not have prevented the types of misunderstanding shown in Herodotus. Indeed, this training neither prevents nor precludes modern cultural misunderstandings.

However, this training intimates a parallel between the American government's efforts and GGC's concern to address its goal outcome number 5: "Demonstrate the ability to apply intercultural knowledge to intercultural or global problems."

We conclude this section with a two-page essay and in-class discussion on individual experiences. Each student identifies an instance of cultural misunderstanding. In addition to suggesting what they think went wrong, students are then required to suggest some ways that additional training or intercultural knowledge might have helped the situation. It is also permissible for students to recognize that they might still not understand what happened or what additional knowledge might ameliorate the situation. This is because sometimes the route to knowledge begins with our recognition that we neither know something nor understand how to fix it. This is especially true with respect to cultural misunderstandings.

The Tacitus Assignment

Completion of the Herodotus assignment prepares students for the later project on Tacitus. Cornelius Publius Tacitus lived approximately from 56-120 C.E., or nearly five hundred years after Herodotus. Like Herodotus, "foreign" peoples frequently appeared in Tacitus' works. Like Herodotus, little is known about Tacitus, whose name in Latin appropriately means "silent" (*tacitus*). Like Herodotus, he maintained deep, complex, and sometimes impenetrable (to us) reasons for writing. There the comparisons end. Whereas Thucydides and even Herodotus provided a detached and at least an attempt at an objective-style historical account, Tacitus furnished opinion-laden pieces. In this he was in good company amongst Roman historians, who, as R. Mellor (1993) argued, scarcely concealed their views: "Romans regarded as impractical the detachment so prized by Greek thinkers; theirs is a subjective, confessional literature" (p. 2).

Tacitus' "Germania" *De origine et situ germanorum (On the origin and situation of the german [peoples])* received its final composition circa 98 C.E. The work reflected the literary tradition known today as "ethnography," which meant that ancient authors sometimes included geographical information, reflections on the customs of indigenous peoples, tales of religious myths/beliefs, accounts of political structures and organization, and stories that "other" people told about their reality (Thomas, 2009). We have no record of Tacitus ever spending time in the region Romans called *Germania*, nor does it seem likely that Tacitus maintained any German friends. Instead, he depended upon accounts previously written by Caesar, Poseidonius, Pliny the Elder, and others. Although some scholars propose that he may have acquired additional information from soldiers (Mellor, 1993), most concur that nearly all of the *Germania* portrayed the peoples living prior to 69 C.E. While the *Germania* might be of questionable use as a reliable source on the specifics of the history of the people living in *Germania*, this does not mean it lacks historical value. Rather, it means that one must use, in the words of Rives (1999), "careful evaluation and a willingness to acknowledge uncertainty" (p. 66).

It is precisely this uncertainty that makes Tacitus so valuable in an assignment on observing culture and the judgments that others make (IOC goal 1). The assignment calls upon students to address the following questions:

Tacitus frequently refers to foreign peoples and somehow compares them to Rome. In what ways does he compare and contrast Romans and "barbarians?" Do you think he understands barbarian peoples? Does he portray them fairly and accurately? In what areas is he seeing them through the lens of "surface" culture, and in what areas has he grasped "deep" culture? How does he use foreign people to make a point to a Roman audience? In a final paragraph or two, tell how you think the English-speaking media, politicians, and even film-makers use foreigners as a foil by which to critique their own society. In what ways might this create "real-world" problems?

The assignment therefore requires students to address GGC's IOC goal outcomes 1, 2, and 5. In inquiring about Tacitus' understanding of German culture, we seek goal 2. In asking about the English speaking media and use of foreigners as a foil, we delve into IOC goal 1. Finally, in inquiring about the real world problems whereby people use foreigners as foils to critique society, we begin to identify possible solutions to real world problems. Without identifying what the problems are, one can scarcely "solve" them.

The assignment requires that students address three basic questions: 1) To what extent did Tacitus understand the "Germans?" 2) To what extent did he portray them accurately? and 3) Why? It has already been suggested that Tacitus' "Germans" were likely a reflection of earlier writers. Scholars think that he never journeyed north of the Alps in his entire life. Even the least perceptive of students quickly conclude that Tacitus is engaging in broad-brush stereotyping. Krebs (2011) asserted, "The *Germanen* who roam Tacitus's pages are in many ways typical representatives of the northern barbarian, sketched within the Greek and Roman ethnographical tradition by a writer with at least one eye toward Rome and the empire" (p. 49). Through oral presentations and various assignments, the students also discover the truth of Krebs' observation that the real intention of the *Germania* had less to do with the barbarians north of Rome's frontiers than it did with Tacitus' Roman audience. Krebs' conclusions notwithstanding, it is important to note that "ethnography" is a modern term with no correspondence to words in Greek or Latin. Rives (1999) instead calls the tendency by authors to comment about other peoples "a somewhat standardized set of topics and interpretative strategies for writing about other peoples, which justify the idea of an actual ethnographic tradition" (p. 12).

Tacitus praised the "Germans" as a type of noble primitive. They were simultaneously savage and virtuous. In his account they did not live in cities (Germania 16). They constructed buildings not out of stone or brick but timber (Germ. 16). They remained prone to violence. Still, Tacitus thought they provided positive examples to compare with morally questionable Roman behaviors. "German" women nursed their babies at their own breast, in contrast to Roman aristocrats, who hired wet nurses (Germ. 20. 1). "Germans" scarcely ever had affairs; both women and men respected their marital bonds (Germ. 18-19). "Germans" spoke their minds repeatedly so that their secrets and innermost thoughts became exposed over time to all (Germ. 22). The "Germans" were many things, some of which might have been true or possibly true but greatly exaggerated.

One problem remained with Tacitus' Germans: they did not exist. If you were to ask a "German" by what signifying label he identified himself in the first century or the fifth century, for that matter, he might have responded that he was a member of a particular "tribe" such as the Ubians or Batavians or Suebi (Rives, 1991). He might respond that he was the son of a particular father and mother. He might reply that he was a member of a particular war band. If a member of the Roman military by his own volition, he might later describe himself as a Roman soldier. He might answer in any number of different ways, but he would not have responded that he was a "German." *Germania* referred to a region north of Rome's imperial borders, east of the Rhine River, and hemmed in by the Baltic Sea and in most authors, the Vistula River. It was not yet an ethnic identity. Moreover, there were "Germanic" speaking peoples who lived outside of these boundaries. No pan-Germanic consciousness existed among the various speakers of the ancestor of the modern German language. The notion of an "ethnic" German "people" is purely a late medieval and early modern construct that has stuck into the post-modern world, and sometimes for chilling reasons (Rives, 1999; Goffart, 2006; Etherington, 2011; Krebs, 2011). A group referred to as *Germani* first occurred in the writings of Julius Caesar (Gallic War 2. 4.), circa 57 B.C.E., but Caesar made careful efforts to divide them into tribes that did not appear unified.

The "Germans" also functioned as the yardstick by which the Roman Empire's internal political workings could be criticized (Jones, 1971). The fact that there was no such thing as pan-Germanic consciousness made no difference to Tacitus. Rome's northern neighbors offered a safe contrast to the oppression the Roman aristocracy felt at home. Even if the earliest emperors in the Julio-Claudian (32 B.C.E. – 68 C.E) dynasty had been competent leaders, Caligula (37-41 C.E.) and Nero (54-68 C.E.) demonstrated the dangers of absolute power. Then, what we call the "year of four emperors" (68-69 C.E.) further manifested the dangers. The Flavians (69-96 C.E.) only heightened anxieties in Rome, especially Domitian (81-96 C.E.). Tacitus gave full voice to his fears and judgment in his work about his father-in-law, titled the *Agricola* (1991 trans.). Since it was not safe or advisable to overtly criticize the emperor, including a "good" one like Nerva (96-98 C.E.), Tacitus resorted to the "Germans" as his "foil." Whereas Rome's aristocracy suffered from the capricious imperial system that gave little autonomy and even less voice to selecting emperors, the "Germans" enjoyed their freedom. By way of summarizing Tacitus, we might suggest that his depiction (Germ. 11-13) portrayed "Germans" as electing their leaders over a stout beer. Unlike Romans, all German warriors were entitled to an equal voice in their assemblies.

Whatever the veracity of Tacitus, his "Germans" reflected what he wished his Roman aristocracy would be when it came to certain forms of morality and political liberty. The scholarly consensus on this view of Tacitus has held sway for a long time. Beare (1964) commented, "When Tacitus speaks of the virtues of the Germans, he is thinking not only of the imperfect Rome which he knew, but of the ideal Rome of past ages which he imagined" (p. 73). Tacitus' praise of the "Germans" did not mean that he admired them. They also received their share of criticism from him (Rives, 1999). For example, they indulged in frequent drunkenness (Germ. 23). Their living conditions reflected a primitive material culture to which no affluent Roman would ever want to return. In a jeremiad about the corrupting influences of civilization, the "Germans" made a nice point of comparison, but nobody would have wanted to inherit their dirt floors. In Tacitus' words (Germ. 20. 1), they "grow up naked and filthy."

Students can discover much of this on their own simply by researching Tacitus and *Germania*. Part of the exercise therefore is not only to learn something about Rome and its northern neighbors, but also to begin to think about how we (and obviously, the Romans) pass judgment on their own culture and country via exaggerated, unrealistic, and unknowledgeable comparisons with "other" peoples. Several in-class exercises help students achieve this. The first exercise aims to take students completely out of the context of the ancient world. The intention is to help students begin to understand that our disciplinary modes of thinking, our modern "tribes," shape the way we view and understand things. Students receive a brief ten-minute lecture on shipbreaking in India. Shipbreaking is the practice whereby old ships are beached upon land, disassembled, and then sold off in various pieces for scrap metals, wires, and other items (Buerk, 2006; Gwin, 2014). We examine shipbreaking in its historical context. Then, having already handed out note cards with the name of different academic majors and fields of study written on the card, I ask the students to gather with all of those who have the same area of study as printed on their card. I ask them next to consider how an economist, biologist, public health specialist, chemist, political scientist, historian and accountant would explain and investigate this phenomenon. We then take turns sharing how the various disciplines within a university might approach ship breaking. Students immediately begin to see that even people from the same culture can understand things very differently. In other words, a university's own academic "tribes" will have radically different ways of examining, conceptualizing, and explaining the same phenomenon.

A final exercise brings students together in pairs to discuss the assignment, especially with discerning the ways in which "foreigners" are used today as a measuring guide by which Americans can critique their own society. Students provide fascinating instances and insights. Some of the examples include higher education, tax rates, medical systems, crime rates, cost of living, commitment to social welfare, public transportation, and several other issues. One topic that inevitably arises relates to unfavorable comparisons between American university and college students and their foreign counterparts. Given the wider American levels of access in comparison with the more restricted access of other countries, comparisons can be made but are not necessarily fair or accurate. Students note that the comparisons tend to correspond with lamentations about the decrepit state of American education *and* political agendas to fix higher education or even secondary education (Ryan, 2013). Some students object by pointing out that the literature frequently compares different types of institutions, and that therefore the research is inaccurate. They may have a point. Marginson and Smolentseva (2014) observed, "Some countries, such as the USA and Canada, include two-year community college and shorter post-school learning programmes under the heading of 'higher education'" (p. 26). Regional and even continental locations further influence the effectiveness of the "what" and "how" that universities accomplish their missions. For example, European universities boast the longest existences, and therefore have enjoyed larger stretches in which to develop synergies with the locations in which they find themselves. Benneworth and Osborne (2014) commented, "European universities have been inextricably tied up with their host societies since their foundation, and universities' institutions and ideas have evolved along with their host societies" (p. 219). Colleges and universities in other regions have not enjoyed such longevity and history, and are therefore likely to witness the result in some forms of statistical measurement.

Some students locate research that questions the entire tradition of comparative higher education. For example, Teichler (2014) argues that higher education remains such a, "relatively small area of research—possibly too small to encourage the development of clearly distinct branches such as comparative research as compared, for example, to educational research where a sub-discipline of comparative education has emerged" (p. 394). This does not mean that comparing higher educational systems in various international contexts lacks merit. However, many policy makers, politicians and people lacking expertise cannot resist the temptation to pull a "Tacitus-style comparison" (phrase mine) as part of a lamentation about the decrepit state of their home country. Teichler (2014) avers, "Further, a comparative discourse is often loaded with values —notably beliefs that higher education in the home country has many strengths or, in reverse, complaints that higher education in the home country is extremely weak and in need of reform" (p. 397). In this sense, students reveal and learn the limitations of applying "real world" solutions to problems based off research comparing countries or cultures. Higher education is definitely internationalizing in scope, but it still remains the prerogative of nation-states. This fact makes comparisons subject to second guessing and the cautious application of research methodologies.

CONCLUSION

This chapter has suggested that "internationalizing" a course on ancient history remains difficult but not impossible. By focusing upon outcomes, involving students in their own education through varied pedagogical exercises, paying attention especially to the institutional goals for internationalization, and by not trying to cover all outcomes at the deepest levels, a professor can get students to begin noticing such things as difference, assumptions, values, customs, and cultural practice. Moreover, students can engage the content of the class in such a way that they learn about both the "then and there" of the ancient world as well as the "here and now" of the world they inhabit.

REFERENCES

Abdi, A., & Shultz, L. (Eds.). (2008). *Educating for Human Rights and Global Citizenship*. Albany, NY: State University of New York Press.

AFCLC. (2017, October 20). *Expeditionary Culture Field Guides*. Retrieved October 26, 2017, from http://culture.af.mil/ecfg/index.html

Altbach, P., & de Wit, H. (2015). Internationalization and Global Tension: Lessons from History. *Journal of Studies in International Education, 19*(1), 4–10. doi:10.1177/1028315314564734

American Council of Education. (2013). *Internationalization in Action*. Retrieved from http://www.acenet.edu/news-room/Pages/Intlz-in-Action-2013-December.aspx

Anderson, J. (2008). *Driving change through diversity and globalization: Transformative leadership in the academy*. Sterling, VA: Stylus.

Barber, B. (2007, January). Internationalizing the Undergraduate Curriculum: Opening Commentary. PS. *Online (Bergheim)*, 105.

Beare, W. (1964). Tacitus on the Germans. *Greece & Rome, 11*(1), 64-76.

Becher, T. (2001). *Academic tribes and territories: intellectual enquiry and the cultures of the disciplines*. Buckingham, UK: Society for Research into Higher Education and Open University Press.

Benneworth, P., & Osborne, M. (2014). Knowledge, Engagement, and Higher Education in Europe. In *Global University Network for Innovation, Higher Education in the World 5* (pp. 219–232). New York: Palgrave Macmillan.

Bonds, S. (2003). *Engaging Educators: Bringing the World into the Classroom: Guidelines for Practice*. Ottawa, Canada: Canadian Bureau for International Education.

Brake, T., Walker, D., & Walker, T. (1995). *Doing Business Internationally: The Guide to Cross-cultural Success*. Burr Ridge, IL: Irwin Professional Publishing.

Brosius, M. (2006). *The Persians: An Introduction*. London: Routledge.

Buerk, R. (2006). *Breaking Ships*. New York: Chamberlain Bros.

Burkert, W. (1990). Herodot als Historiker fremder Religionen. In W. Burkert et al. (Eds.), *Hérodote et les peoples non grecs* (pp. 1–32). Geneva: Foundation Hardt.

Caesar, J. *Comentarii de bello gallico*.

Cartlege, P. (2006). *Thermopylae: The Battle that changed the World. Woodstock*. Overlook Press.

Center for Advanced Operational Culture and Learning. (2014). Retrieved from https://www.marinecorp-sconceptsandprograms.com/programs/investing-education-and-training-our-marines/center-advanced-operational-culture-and

Courts, P. L., & McInerney, K. H. (1993). *Assessment in Higher Education: Politics, Pedagogy, and Portfolios*. Westport, CT: Praeger.

Etherington, N. (2011). Barbarians Ancient and Modern. *American Historical Review, 116*(1), 31-57.

Fink, L. D. (2013). *Creating Significant Learning Experiences: An Integrated Approach to Designing College Courses, Revised and Updated*. San Francisco: Jossey-Bass.

Fordham, M. (2012). Disciplinary History and the Situation of History Teachers. *Education in Science, 2*(4), 242–253. doi:10.3390/educsci2040242

Georgia Gwinnett College. (2017). *Quality Enhancement Plan Student Learning Outcomes*. Retrieved from http://www.ggc.edu/academics/qep/student-learning-outcomes/index.html

Goffart, W. (2006). *Barbarian Tides: The Migration Age and the Later Roman Empire*. Philadelphia: University of Pennsylvania Press. doi:10.9783/9780812200287

Green, P. (1996). *The Greco-Persian Wars*. Berkeley, CA: University of California Press.

Gwin, P. (2014). The Ship-Breakers. *National Geographic*. Retrieved from http://ngm.nationalgeographic.com/2014/05/shipbreakers/gwin-text

Hajjar, R. (2006). The TRADOC Culture Center. *The Free Library*. Retrieved from https://www.the-freelibrary.com/TheTRADOC Culture Center.-a0190700220

Hall, E. (1959). *The Silent Language*. Garden City, NY: Doubleday & Company.

Hall, E. (1976). *Beyond Culture*. Garden City, NY: Anchor Books.

Hall, J. (1997). *Ethnic identity in Greek antiquity*. Cambridge, UK: Cambridge University Press. doi:10.1017/CBO9780511605642

Hanson, V. D. (1989). *Western Way of War: Infantry Battle in Classical Greece*. New York: Knopf.

Hartog, F. (1988). *The Mirror of Herodotus: The Representation of the other in the writing of History* (J. Lloyd, Trans.). Berkeley, CA: University of California Press.

Helms, R. M. (n.d.). *Internationalization in Action: Internationalizing the Curriculum, Part 1 - Individual Courses*. Retrieved from http://www.acenet.edu/news-room/Pages/Intlz-in-Action-2013-December.aspx

Herodotus, . (2007). *The Landmark Herodotus: the Histories*. New York: Pantheon Books.

Jaeger, W. (1939). *Paideia: The Ideals of Greek Culture* (G. Highet, Trans.). Oxford, UK: Oxford University Press.

Jones, W. R. (1971). The Image of the Barbarian in Medieval Europe. *Comparative Studies in Society and History, 13*(4), 376–407. doi:10.1017/S0010417500006381

Joughin, G. (1998). Dimensions of Oral Assessment. *Assessment & Evaluation in Higher Education, 23*(4), 367–378. doi:10.1080/0260293980230404

Katan, D. (1999). *Translating Cultures.* Manchester, UK: St. Jerome Publishing.

Korostelina, K. (2013). *History Education in the Formation of Social Identity: Toward a Culture of Peace.* New York: Palgrave Macmillan. doi:10.1057/9781137374769

Krebs, C. (2011). *A Most Dangerous Book: Tacitus's Germania from the Roman Empire to the Third Reich.* New York: W. W. Norton & Company.

Lasky, M. J. (2002). The Banalization of the Concept of Culture. *Society, 39*(September/October), 73–81. doi:10.1007/s12115-002-1008-2

Lazenby, J. F. (1993). *The Defence of Greece 490-479 B. C.* Warminster: Aris & Phillips.

Leask, B. (2012). *Internalisation of the curriculum (IoC) in action: A guide.* University of South Australia.

Lee, A., Poch, R., Shaw, M., & Williams, R. D. (2012). *Engaging Diversity in Undergraduate Classrooms: A pedagogy for Developing Intercultural Competence.* San Francisco: Jossey-Bass.

Marginson, S., & Smolentseva, A. (2014). Higher Education in the World: Main Trends and Facts. In *Global University Network for Innovation, Higher Education in the World 5* (pp. 26–31). New York: Palgrave Macmillan.

Mellor, R. (1993). *Tacitus.* London: Routledge.

Momigliano, A. (1966). *Studies in Historiography.* London: Weidenfeld and Nicolson.

Munson, R. V. (2009). Who are Herodotus' Persians? *Classical World, 102*(4), 457–470. doi:10.1353/clw.0.0116

Peterson, A. (n.d.). *Civic Republicanism and Civic Education: The Education of Citizens.* London: Palgrave Macmillan.

Rahe, P. (2015). *The Grand Strategy of Classical Sparta: The Persian Challenge.* New Haven, CT: Yale University Press.

Rawls, J., Wilsker, A., & Rawls, R. (2015, Spring). Are You Talking to Me? On the Use of Oral Examinations in Undergraduate Business Courses. *Journal of the Academy of Business Education, 16,* 22–33.

Rawls, R., & Rawls, J. (2017). Intersectionality and the Spoken Word. In D. Budryte & S. Boykin (Eds.), Engaging Difference: Teaching Humanities and Social Science in Multicultural Environments (pp. 11-17, 134-135). Lanham, MD: Rowman & Littlefield.

Rives, J. B. (1999). *Tacitus, Germania.* Oxford, UK: Oxford University Press.

Ryan, J. (2013). American Schools vs. the World: Expensive, Unequal, Bad at Math. *The Atlantic Monthly.* https://www.theatlantic.com/education/archive/2013/12/american-schools-vs-the-world-expensive-unequal-bad-at-math/281983/

Sancisi-Weerdenburg, H. (2002). The Personality of Xerxes, King of Kings. In E. J. Bakker & H. de Wees (Eds.), *Brill's Companion to Herodotus* (pp. 579–590). Leiden: Brill.

Schorske, K. (1990). History and the Study of Culture. *New Literary History, 21*(2), 407-420.

Shenefelt, M. (2003). Why Study the Greeks? *The Chronicle of Higher Education, 49*(26), B 11.

Sineema, C., & Aitken, G. (2012). Effective pedagogy in social sciences. Brussels: International Academy of Education, and Geneva: International Bureau of Education.

Strauss, B. (2004). *The Battle of Salamis: the Naval Encounter that saved Greece – and western Civilization.* New York: Simon & Schuster.

Tacitus, . (1991). *Agricola* (H. Benario, Trans. & Ed.). Norman, OK: University of Oklahoma Press.

Tacitus, . (1999). *Germania* (J. B. Rives, Trans. & Ed.). Oxford, UK: Clarendon Press.

Teichler, U. (2014). Opportunities and problems of comparative higher education research: The daily life of research. *Higher Education, 67*(4), 393–408. doi:10.1007/s10734-013-9682-0

Thomas, R. (2009). The Germania as a Literary Text. In A. J. Woodman (Ed.), *Cambridge Companion to Tacitus* (pp. 59–72). Cambridge, UK: Cambridge University Press.

Time Magazine. (1993, November 18). Special Issue: The New Face of America: How Immigrants are shaping the World's First Multi-Cultural Society. *Time, 142*(21).

United State Navy. (n.d.). *Center for Language, Regional Expertise, and Culture.* Retrieved from http://www.netc.navy.mil/centers/ciwt/clrec/

United States Air Force. (n.d.). *Expeditionary Field Guides.* Retrieved from http://culture.af.mil/ecfg/index.html

Watson, J. R. (2010, March). Language and Culture Training: Separate Paths? *Military Review*, 93–97.

West, S. (1992). Herodotus and Foreign Cultures [Review of the book *Hérodote et les peoples non grecs: Neuf exposés suivis de discussions* by G Nenci & O. Reverdin]. *The Classical Review New Series, 42(2),* 277–279.

White, L. Jr. (1965). The Legacy of the Middle Ages in the American Wild West. *Speculum, 40*(2), 191–202. doi:10.2307/2855557

Chapter 6
Internationalizing Music Appreciation

Marc Gilley
Georgia Gwinnett College, USA

ABSTRACT

The process of internationalizing a music appreciation class is discussed. The role of music appreciation in an internationalized curriculum is examined and a philosophy of music education is developed. Curriculum design, assessment practices, and teaching and learning activities are viewed through the framework of Fink's Taxonomy of Learning, including descriptions of specific practices and assignments and their relationship to the taxonomy of learning the philosophy of music education. Special consideration is given to the power of music, the arts, and aesthetic experiences to cultivate knowledge of the self and of the other.

INTRODUCTION

Georgia Gwinnett College was founded in 2006. The first Music Appreciation section, taught by the author, was offered in January of 2008. A committee of Film and Anthropology professors initially developed this class, and over the course of the next several semesters the author more fully developed the course. The committee proposed the course, wrote the course description, chose a textbook, and created the syllabus. It is important to note that from its inception, Music Appreciation as taught at Georgia Gwinnett College was never conceived as a history of Classical Music as it is often taught. Instead it reflected an intentional multi-cultural mindset present at Georgia Gwinnett College from its inception. For several years this was the only music class offered Georgia Gwinnett college. It was purposefully designed to allow students in Student Success programs take the class while bringing their Math and English skills up to a college level. In this way the course diverged from prevalent norms. This deviation allowed for, and even inspired, experimentation and development from the beginning. The environment in which this class was created and in which it is taught naturally led the author to several realizations.

DOI: 10.4018/978-1-5225-2791-6.ch006

That General Education classes such as Music Appreciation in fact have the single largest impact on the student body, regardless of the size or quality of a music program. That in many cases this class might be the last formal instruction in the arts that a college student might encounter. And finally, that these classes have the power to be transformational for students and that they should be transformational classes.

When Georgia Gwinnett College began its Quality Enhancement Program based on internationalized education the course had already incorporated elements of world music at its core through use of Bonnie C. Wade's *Thinking Musically* (2013). This text takes an elements based approach and uses the musical elements as a lens to view the musical practices of cultures from around the world. Additionally the author is a practicing musician who performs regularly in a variety of musical styles and approaches the class with the understanding that cultural practice and understanding are best developed through experiential and active learning techniques. The course already had many hallmarks of an internationalized course- 85-90% of the music discussed was of international origin, the instructor made us of sitars, mbiras, kudu horns, antiphonal flutes, and ewe drums regularly in class and had students interacting with and performing on those instruments. It was very easy to conceive of this class as already "internationalized." As the author developed the fully internationalized course it became apparent that while the content of the course was of an international nature, course design and pedagogy could be refined to a much higher standard.

Georgia Gwinnett College has one of the most diverse student populations in the south (Georgia Gwinnett College, 2015), which is reflected in the student population taking Music Appreciation. Furthermore, as GGC is an open enrollment institution, Music Appreciation is open for registration by students who have not met college level English and Math requirements, leading to a wide variety of experiences and scholastic abilities in each iteration of the class. From the very beginning the author endeavored to reach a wide variety of students in a meaningful way, to maintain academic standards yet allow students of differing abilities to engage with the material in a way accessible to all, and most importantly to impact their education with the most positive experience possible. The author felt that as taught the class could provide the resources to create a transformative experience, but that as often as not fell short of that goal.

The Center for Teaching Excellence at Georgia Gwinnett College provided a useful framework to develop this course more fully. The Author took part in a two-semester program designed to help guide the Internationalization process. Resources used in this program included works by Leask (2012) who identified two attributes of Internationalized learning that are directly applicable to Music Appreciation: 1) Internationalized education is multi-dimensional and incorporates curriculum design, content, pedagogy, learning activities, and assessment, and 2) it is evolutionary and cyclical in nature. Another important element of this two-semester workshop was the text *Creating Significant Learning Experience,* by L. Dee Fink (2013). Fink's text focuses on creating a learning-centered curriculum. The Taxonomy of Learning proposed in the text provides a meaningful framework to guide the Internationalization effort. Fink (2013) developed a Taxonomy of Learning that both reinforces transformational education and provides a framework for assessment including: Foundational Knowledge, Application, Integration, Human Dimension, Caring, and Learning How to Learn (p. 31). Fink's Taxonomy provides a framework for integrated, learning-centered, course design balancing three factors (Learning Goals, Feedback and Assessment, Teaching and Learning Activities) that are informed by overall situational factors found in the teaching the environment and learning situation (p.69-70).

BACKGROUND

The broader situational factors include the recent decline in arts education in primary and secondary schools (Prasad & Spiegelman, 2012), which is particularly problematic for underserved African American and Hispanic populations for whom waning arts access is most dramatic; for this demographic only 26-28% of students have access to arts education (Rabkin & Hedberg, 2011). The diverse student population of Georgia Gwinnett College is affected at a higher rate than more traditional school populations. Additionally, Music Appreciation is a General Education core-class. The Southern Association of Colleges and Schools stipulates that a bachelor's degree comprised of 30 semester hours of coursework include at least one class in the arts and humanities, however "the courses do not narrowly focus on those skills, techniques, and procedures specific to a particular occupation or profession" (SACS 2012, pg. 20).

Taking these broad parameters into account the purpose or intent of Music Appreciation should be well defined including the role of Internationalization and a philosophy of general music education should be developed to guide the transformation of the course.

Jorgensen, in her work *The Aims of Music Education* (2002), provides a concise and thorough exploration of the contemporary issues and aims of music education from a societal perspective. This work provides several valuable "philosophical keys" (pg. 32) that serve as conceptual touchstones when considering the philosophy and aim of music education. Jorgensen asks should Music Education aim to: 1) create musical communities (music creators and music listeners), 2) transform musical traditions (transmit tradition to the young with the purpose of surpassing the past), 3) enrich culture (celebrating the resonances, ambiguities, and clashes of cultures expressed in music as a window into the other's conception of the world), 4) enrich society (are aesthetic, artistic, and ethical ends inter-related), 5) ennoble people (supporting character formation, enriching personal experience, developing spirituality and aesthetic sensibility, educating for moral and ethical responsibility). In conjunction with the Situational Factors present surrounding this course these philosophical prompts help guide the process of course development. The class cannot teach practical skills, but it can develop student's skill as a listener. The class presents a wide range of musical traditions for consideration using an elements based approach as the framework. This framework can provide a scaffolding on which encounters with other cultures can take place including historical practices, differing aesthetic and cultural values, and a variety of human experiences. This class can introduce the role of ethics as expressed through music, aesthetic values, and artistic expression. The class can introduce varieties of spirituality as expressed through music as well as moral concerns, and through the wide variety of music introduced, this class can introduce rich, personal experiences.

The challenge of each of these philosophical concerns is one of refraining from judgment based on the existing expectations of the students (or professor) in the class. In freely discussing conflicting aesthetics, ethical considerations, spiritual practices, reserving judgment is paramount. For example, as Jorgensen asks, what characteristics should be identified as ennobling? The answer to that question can vary greatly. In a more specific example, in a reading assignment Doubleday (2008) provides a wide-ranging survey of the many roles that gender can play across a myriad of musical traditions, specifically as gender impacts the understanding of musical instruments. For a 1xxx level class this concept can be quite unfamiliar. The discussion that follows this reading is often a wide-ranging discussion focusing on unfamiliar practices and later illuminating some aspects of the paradigm of gender in Western musical culture. Great care had to be taken to ensure that this unfamiliar concept was not mistaken as advocacy for one tradition over another and especially to prevent students from extrapolating incorrect or unsound uniform concepts such as low pitched or loud instruments universally and directly referring to maleness. Each cultural tradition had to be examined through the lens of Cultural Relativism (Devale, n.d.), from the perspective of an outsider. It is had to be made clear that to avoid misunderstanding one must avoid rash judgment.

When combined with Fink's Taxonomy of learning (2013) this philosophical framework becomes a powerful organizational tool. Foundational knowledge can be viewed through the lens of transmitting and transforming traditional practices (Western and otherwise). Application can be viewed through the lens of creating a musical culture, listeners who are aware of and participate in multiple international musical traditions. Integration can connect musical traditions to other areas of study such as ethics, history, social issues, and the physical sciences, enriching the academic experience of participating students. Engaging in meaningful examination of the practice other cultures can support and develop the human dimension of learning, connecting students to their fellow beings in meaningful ways and can help students to further develop their capacity to care for the subject, for their fellow man, for the past and the future. Finally, the many analytical concepts and learning skills developed and used in the class can have a specific impact on the student's ability to learn. This class can teach how to learn, and the foundational knowledge and experience can provide the bedrock on which a student can build a meaningful engagement with the world as their lives develop.

From the perspective of the individual, a piece of music is a significant human document. It transmits knowledge, history, narrative, and elements of the human experience such as emotion, movement, and the passage of time. It is metaphorical, it is literal, and it is abstract. It is a personal expression and it is a communal expression. It is a product of culture and of people and so it is localized and it is ubiquitous. Beyond its own intrinsic value as a topic of study, music then becomes a meaningful arena in which to consider the human condition and a locus around which internationalized, multi-cultural learning can take place. There are many avenues to connect the study of music across disciplines, deepening the impact of discussions around music: historical issues, social issues, lyrical writing as text, the development of the neuroscience of music, the biography of musicians, the physics of musical sound, the biology and psychology of hearing, etc… The aesthetic discussion of music provides a unique window through which to view these connections. As Arts Education Scholar Eisner states (1985),

What we are able to see or hear is a product of our cultivated abilities. The rewards and insights provided by aesthetically shaped forms are available only to those who can perceive them. Not only is competence a necessary condition for experiencing the form in works we have access to, but the particular quality of life generated by the forms encountered will, to some degree, differ from individual to individual. All experience is the product of both the features of the world and the biography of the individual. Our experience is influenced by our past as it interacts with our present. Thus, not only must a certain kind of competence be acquired in order to perceive the qualities of form in the objects available to us, but the nature of our experience with these forms is influenced not only by the form itself but by our past. (pp. 25-26)

In addition to the multi-disciplinary connections to be made through music the unique aesthetic forms of music include the combination and organization of time and pitch and timbre, which act as the medium through which those many meanings are transmitted. As the field of neuroscience delves into the perception and understanding of music and the mind, this connection between the meaning and expression of music and the aesthetics, or order, of the fundamental elements of music becomes even more important. Philosopher of Art Dutton (2009) writes,

Nothing can substitute for a sense of emotional expression derived from the experience of a complex aesthetic structure created by another human being. To speak in metaphors, the work of art is another human mind incarnate: not in flesh and blood but in sounds, words, or colors. (p. 235)

From the perspective of the listener new research supporting the embodied cognition of music suggests that a musical work is not only "another human mind incarnate" but also is a metaphor for the human experience of the physical world itself, allowing the logic, or aesthetic structure, of the experience of music "to make sense of another kind of experience" (Cox, 2016, p.80). The conceptual metaphor theory suggests that the experience of music pertains to auditory, physical, and visual imagery, and in fact that musical actions have an affective dimension, so that the conception of music in a listener includes the feeling of the physicality of the music. The listener makes physical in their own body what was first created by a musician (Cox, 2016). Dutton's statement above might be updated to read that "the work of art is another human mind incarnate" *and is embodied within the listener.*

The meaningful study of music should elevate the perceptions of the listener. It should refine the ability to listen and inform the mind so that the listener can more fully meet another human mind, so that the listener can bring their own past to converse with this expressive human document and its creators, so that the listener can more fully embody the expression and experience of another.

MAIN FOCUS OF THE CHAPTER

Fink's Taxonomy of Learning supports a learning centered approach reinforces the philosophy stated above. It also reinforces the individual expression of the student's interests, resulting in a holistic approach both to the student and to the subject a number of specific learning goals.

The foundational knowledge of the course is based on an elements of music approach, defined for this purpose of this course as: Instruments, Rhythm, Pitch, Form, and Meaning. Through this framework a variety of cultures and traditions as well as important figures, historical and contemporary can be viewed. The student should be able to remember the fundamental elements of music. They should be able to identify unique features of a piece of music and understand how those features are and are related to the expression of a person and culture.

Learning how to learn becomes a fundamental part of this class, especially considering that many of the students in this class are in learning support programs and are not working at the typical college level. The challenge in all of this is to approach topics so that all may actively participate. The first week of class is spent introducing the learning techniques described in Make it Stick (Brown, 2014), including spaced retrieval, low stakes quizzing, self-evaluation, etc... Teaching and assessment elements are fundamentally designed around the practice of learning. The student has areas of influence so that they can set a learning agenda for themselves. They are asked to construct knowledge beyond the specific music formally presented to them. This includes evaluating sources of information and framing useful questions.

Application includes aural analysis and critical listening skills. The student should be able to make a meaningful statement about the music including its musical and stylistic features, its precise meaning presented in lyrical content and its larger meaning connected to the life of the individual who made it and the culture from which that person originated.

The elements of music, cultural traditions, aesthetic values, and distinct expressions are presented in a holistic fashion throughout the course. Though the discussion of instruments as a unit occurs at the beginning of the semester, as new topics and music are introduced, the discussion of the instruments used is always a part of the conversation. The same can be said of the other elements. Every effort is made to place the subject of study in the larger world inside and outside the academy.

The Human Dimension is developed through the treatment of music as a product of a person, or of a people, and those people are always present in the discussion of a work. Furthermore, the choice of music to be studied is informed by compelling human elements. For example the parent offspring relationships of Ravi Shankar and Anoushka Shankar, or Ustad Alla Rakha and Zakir Hussein, or the Mozart family dynamics, provide many ways to discuss the human dimension of music making at the personal level. Some readings are chosen specifically because of their human perspective, Oliver Sacks's numerous works on disorders of the mind involving music have proven very valuable, as have the letters written by Mozart to his father and sister. The writings on rhythm by Grateful Dead drummer Mickey Hart are both personal and inter-cultural by nature, and approachable by first year college students. The students should come to see themselves and the variety of people and cultures presented in class as part of a continuum of the total human experience. The student should understand others in terms of their individual and cultural expressions in the universal human practice of music making.

Caring is developed in a number of ways. Readings are chosen so that no matter their chosen major students will find something that speaks to them, whether it be the neurology of the perception of music, an academic treatise on the gender imposed on instruments, or personal letters written by a historical or contemporary personality. Much of the music chosen for the final project is left to the student, allowing them the freedom, and impetus to develop their work along personally meaningful lines. There is the opportunity to learn to value the unique modes of expression available through the practice of music and value the message itself as a communication from one valuable being to another. The student should be introduced to the concept of music as a significant document that transmits knowledge and experience. The student should be excited about the possibilities inherent in communicating through means other than purely written or spoken language, communicating the essence of the human experience at a more fundamental level.

These learning goals are to be achieved by creating a predictable and educative pattern of assessment and feedback. Using low stakes quizzing and testing designed around analytical practice rather than the pure recall of accumulated knowledge. These practices should be space out through time, be predictable in nature, and holistic in their treatment of specific topics. And all of these practices and topics should support divergent learning rather than convergent learning, always asking the students to take and active role in choosing the music that they will deal with beyond what is presented in the class.

Once situational factors are identified and learning goals are defined Integrated course design demands that attention be paid to the semester as a whole including teaching and learning activities and assessment activities, and that these are thoughtfully and coherently organized.

The structure of the course should reflect the subject being taught. This class takes place over the course of a sixteen-week semester, though it has been successfully adapted for an 8 week summer semester. The large-scale structure of the course is organized around four fundamental areas: introducing the course, developing knowledge of the fundamental elements of music individually, understanding them as a whole, and moving forward. Each of these areas addresses the whole Taxonomy of Learning, uses a consistent pattern of teaching and learning activities, and encourages focused feedback.

The introduction provides and overview of the course including concepts to be discussed, course activities, grading scheme, and a schedule for the semester. Foundational knowledge to be introduced in the class is given a cursory discussion. Care is taken to allows the students time to define what music means to them, to discuss its purpose, its value, and its definition. This allows students to encounter the experiences of their classmates and to express their own experiences. Intentional connections are made between the study of music and other subjects, and the wider experience of life. Importantly, time is spent discussing study habits, and introducing best practices described by Brown (2014) including study techniques such as retrieval by memory, self-quizzing, spaced retrieval. Student input is taken during the Initial online discussion assignments lay the groundwork for the conclusion of the class. Later assignments will capitalize on this groundwork. This component of the class takes the first two weeks, allowing for drop-add students time to catch up, and for students to acclimate to the learning environment of the class.

The largest amount of time over the course of the semester is spent on the fundamental concepts in music as defined for this class: instruments, rhythm, pitch, followed by form, which incorporates each of these elements into a whole. Each unit lasts approximately 3 weeks. Once each unit is completed the concepts is retained throughout the class, reinforcing the holistic approach of the course. Once the class moves from instruments as its focus to rhythm, the instruments used in each example remain topics for instruction, analysis, and discussion. Each unit follows consistent teaching and learning activities, assessment activities, and feedback practices consisting of related readings with related short answer and online critical listening exercises, alternating with in-class Listening ID quizzes spaced every other week. Throughout these units time is taken for prompted discussion, reflection, and open discussion sessions. As each unit draws to a close a component of the final project is implemented, asking students to discover new works on their own, to analyze those works in a focused way related to each unit, and to document them as one would in the works cited portion of an academic paper. Subjects studied in the class are introduced in an integrated fashion, connecting them to historical or social concerns and developments in the wider world they coincide with their work. Intention is given to ensuring that ever continent is represented for each unit, and connections are drawn between units and cultural practices as appropriate.

A discussion of musical form follows the focused instruction on each unit integrating these disparate concepts together into a coherent. Form is discussed as an analytical tool to understand the other elements of music, all of which, taken with the biography of the musicians, the cultures from which they originate, and the time in which they were created, contribute to the meaning of a work. Meaning is understood to be divergent in nature, related to how the musical elements are used expressively, how an individual musical work relates other output from the individual musician, from that musician's culture, and how it relates to the human experience including the experiences of the students themselves. This focused period lasts two weeks. Students refer back to their early discussion topics and relate to them with new knowledge and experiences.

Moving forward is characterized by the final expression of the learning goals, especially focusing on caring and self-directed learning. Students choose works that particularly resonate with them for further study, research and analysis. Best practices and resources are presented in-class. The final project becomes the focus for the remaining weeks of the course in which the student analyzes works, researches their origins including biography, expressions of culture, and relationship to the larger world.

It is important to note that the long-term structure of the class mimics the long-term structure of a piece of music. The first two weeks present the main themes of the class, including student experiences and expectations. The middle section develops the themes through a focus on individual elements as expressed in a variety of cultures, mimicking the development found in the symphonic Sonata Form. Once each unit has been addressed they are reassembled into a coherent whole, mimicking the return of the main themes in a Sonata Form, including the original student experiences and expectations, now hopefully more deeply informed. The last several weeks activity act as a Coda bringing the entire exercise to a graceful end, with an eye on what comes after as expressed through the student's self-directed analysis and research. . Form in music, the organization of the fundamental elements into a coherent whole, suggests to us that repetition of a theme, the development of that theme, and a return to that theme are powerful ways of infusing "content" with meaning. Over several iterations of this course this idea of development and return have become central to the structure of the class, which lends itself to the idea of a learning based structure rather than a purely content based structure. The structure has several overlapping and complementary elements.

In practical terms every topic begins with a prompt or question. A very basic question. What is pitch? How do we hear? Can you describe a saxophone? The aim is to create a dialogue rather than find an answer, to develop the skill of framing useful questions and formulating modes of learning and knowledge.

The assessment activities are grouped into 5 fundamental assignments. A long-term project. A concert attendance requirement. A series of in-class Listening ID Quizzes. In-class work and Homework consisting fundamentally of readings and online quizzes. The readings and online quizzes alternate with the Listening ID Quizzes.

Readings beyond the text are carefully chosen to resonate with the element currently being discussed class, instruments, rhythm, pitch, etc... and are also chosen for the widest variety of authors and writing styles, academic and popular, personal and general, though the quality of writing is of great concern. In one semester students read an academic overview of gender associations applied to instruments across many world cultures (Doubleday, 2008), a letter from Mozart to his father while he was composing *Die Entfuhrung* (Strunk, 1998, pp. 965-969), a chapter on mystical associations of rhythm from Mickey Hart (1990, pp. 117-128), and watched video by Daniel Levitin discussing the neuroscience of music along with musician Alex de Grassi (2011), and others.

The online quizzes are educative in nature, and designed around practice of skills rather than memorization of content. Once a topic has been completed in the classroom the student will complete an online quiz over that topic, and any previous topics. After discussing pitch (melody and harmony), using the D2L quizzes function, students will hear a short 30 second to 1 minute selection of audio and be asked to describe it- usually using multiple choice options such as: In this excerpt the melody 1) ascends by leap, ascends by step, descends by leap, descends by step. At this point the class will have dealt with rhythm and meter, and also instruments, and so there will be further questions concerning those elements as well. Multiple attempts are offered for the quizzes, stressing that these are for practice, that the students should engage a thoughtful response to the quiz, keep track of their progress, look up terms that may have been misunderstood, and take it again if their initial grade was unsatisfactory. The goal is to practice analytical skills as one might practice a musical instruments. Three attempts are offered initially and during the last weeks of the class, a fourth attempt is allowed, reinforcing the idea of practice, the idea of a learning focused environment, and the idea that effort leads to improvement.

The long-term project components are triggered by completion of each topic. When the instrument focus comes to completion students are asked to find and document music that has specific rhythmic features: Duple meter, Triple meter, prominent syncopation, polyrhythm, etc... additionally each of the 5 populated continents must be represented at least once in the final list. Students are asked to discover music from a variety of places, featuring a variety of specific features, use their analytical skills to determine the appropriateness of inclusion, and research the piece to create a citation for it. This is done for instruments, rhythm and pitch, generating a list of 30 songs discovered by the student. This list becomes the raw materials for the last stage of the project, a written analysis an research paper focusing on a piece of music, covering the five elements specifically, the biography of its creator, the culture and time from which it originated. The student is asked to create a portrait of the piece of music, to tease out meaning and resonance and to try and understand it as a coherent whole, created by and person or people, that communicates with that student's individual experience and history.

For each unit there is a standard teach and learning scheme and assessment. Each unit is designed to address all categories for the Taxonomy of Significant Learning. The teaching, learning, and assessment plan for each three-week period is as follows. The introduction to the unit typically lasts one full week and is followed by elaboration on that unit over the next two weeks. The introductory period address foundational knowledge for the unit including concepts, vocabulary, and historical development. In each unit the focus moves from familiar western musical traditions to less familiar traditions found around the world. During the following two weeks, elaboration includes detailed discussion of variations, discrepancies, and alternative expressions found through focused work based on carefully chosen musical examples. Once the initial foundational week has been completed assessment activities begin. The second week is taken up with educative online quizzes focused on developing critical listening skills. Assignments for the third week include related readings and an in-class listening ID designed to familiarize students with music related to the unit at hand. As the course moves into the next unit a capstone assignment is introduced. It is considered to be a part of the long-term large-scale project for the class. This pattern repeats for each of the three units, Instruments, Rhythm, and Pitch.

The categories of the Taxonomy of Significant Learning are individually addressed in each unit. During the Instruments unit Foundational Knowledge is based on the Hornbostel-Sachs Instrumental classification system including Chordophones, Aerophones, Idiophones, Membranophones, and Electrophones (Montagu, n.d.). Each is defined and discussed in detail down the first level of categorization. Students are given low-stakes in-class quizzes on the details of the system following the procedures outlines in Make it Stick (Brown, 2014).

Application is addressed through two means. Initially students are assigned several online quizzes that require the aural identification of instruments from recorded excerpts and categorize them according to the Hornbostel-Sachs system, including familiar western musical instruments and less familiar world instruments. These quizzes are designed to be educative in nature. Students are given 3 attempts. The highest grade of the three attempts is recorded. Using the process of music making as a metaphor for the class, these quizzes are described as "practice," and students are instructed in best practices for this type of task (Duke, 2009, p.318). The method of focused and disciplined practice has been shown to increase both the speed and quality of improvement among professional musicians and athletes. This type instruction is especially important for students who have had no previous musical training. Best practices include: identifying an initial problem related to a mistake, addressing that problem in a focused and coordinated fashion, and implementing newly developed technique and ideas consistently. The capstone assignment for each unit serves as a point to address application and self-directed learning as well. Students are required to discover and document music that prominently features specific types of instruments in each of the Hornbostel-Sachs categories, and each continent must be represented. This serves as a simple way to require diversity of thought and experience for the student. Examples include: Reed Aerophones, Trumpet/Horn Aerophones, Flute Aerophones, Lute bodied Chordophones,

Harp Bodied Chordophones, Zither Bodied Chordophones, etc… Individual works are documented in APA citation style.

Once the Foundational Knowledge of the Instrument unit is presented, Integration is addressed through focused study of several differing instruments. Care is taken to discuss individual musical instruments in a focused manner. The author is a professional saxophonist and time is taken in-class to discuss the history and development of the Saxophone including the biography of its inventor, its capabilities as a musical instrument including range, expressive capabilities, and uses in a variety of musical genres, and important performers of the instrument. The goal is to make this artifact both real and meaningful for the student and to show in detail the human interaction involved in playing an instrument at a high level. Students are also introduced to the Theremin, the world's oldest successful electronic instrument (Orton, n.d.). The biography of Leon Theremin is discussed, as well as the history of the instrument including its role in the development of the contemporary Moog synthesizers. More importantly this instrument provides the perfect opportunity to introduce students to the act of playing an instrument. The Theremin is manipulated by disrupting a radio frequency oscillator with the natural capacitance of the human hand, which is moved around two antennae. These antennae control volume (controlled with the left hand), and pitch (controlled with the right hand). The experience of playing this instrument is entirely intuitive, immediately expressive and perfectly inviting. Time is taken to explain the workings of the instrument as well as the analogue radio technology from which it was developed.

Finally students are introduced to the mbira of Zimbabwe, the *mbira dza vadzimu (Kubik)*. Care is taken to instruct students on the proper way to hold the instrument and the proper way to play the instrument including a distinctive, traditional and unfamiliar way of crossing the index finger over the thumb to reach the upper range of keys. This instrument has a history dating back 3000-5000 years, and is an example of an instrument that has survived on the continent of Africa in recognizable form through all of modern history including colonialization, conflict, and independence (Berliner, 1978). Mbira music of Zimbabwe is discussed and listened to in class, including relevant musical features such as the use of ostinato patterns and African yodeling techniques. Among the Shona of Zimbabwe the instrument takes on significant cultural meaning. It is a spiritual instrument. The mbira calls the spirits of ones ancestors to come and bestow wisdom on their descendants during a ceremony called Bira. This depth of meaning is explored in class. It is noted that the mbira is both an artifact of a culture, a musical instrument, and it is a conduit through which the culture performs one of its most fundamental acts, connecting present to the past.

The progression of the presentation of instruments is very important, moving from familiar to unfamiliar. Moving from the experience of the other through the saxophone to the personal experience of playing the Theremin to the profound depth of experience represented by the mbira. Moving from two modern instruments that were invented by individuals, each of whom has a uniquely compelling biography, to a traditional instrument where the origin can only be guessed at and that has come to be associated so closely with a deeply meaningful ceremony.

The Human Dimension and the Integration of the subject are further developed through related readings. Recently students have read Sounds of Power (Doubleday, 2008), an academic article that introduces the role gender plays in understanding instruments in a wide variety of world cultures. This fundamental concept is has more often than not proven very unfamiliar to students. A short worksheet of 3-4 short answer questions is required to complete the assignment, and time is taken to discuss the reading in class.

Caring reinforced through the long-term project. Students discover music on their own, their analysis is self-directed. They document these pieces of music precisely. Caring is more directly achieved through the act of learning a precise group of instruments intimately, putting the instrument in the students' hands. Discussing the origin and development of the instrument, and making a connection to its role and meaning in a given society.

Several concepts organize this and each unit of the course. The unit moves from broad definitions to focused examination of precise instrumental examples. Care is taken that the compelling examples are chosen. The unit begins by discussing the familiar western traditions, creating a context, and then the subject deliberately moves beyond this boundary, coming to terms with several distinctive cultures from around the world. This unit moves from the experience and practice of the instructor to a unique experience for the student. The assessments follow a similar course, moving from memorization of terms and concepts, to practice analysis of recorded material, to self-directed discovery and documentation of a variety of different world music that meet defined criteria. Rhythm and Pitch share the same organization.

Foundational Knowledge in Rhythm consists of the fundamental concepts and definitions of western musical meters consisting of Duple, Triple, and Additive meters, presented in the first week. Each meter is defined precisely and heard in carefully chosen representative musical pieces. Conducting patterns are introduced as well as important concepts such as rubato and syncopation.

The second and third week are characterized by the introduction of several world meters including Indian Tala, the Rhythmic Modes of the Middle East, the Colotomic meter of Indonesian Gamelan, and West African Polyrhythm. Each meter is defined precisely and heard in carefully chosen representative musical pieces. Care is taken to provide cultural context for each meter such as the connection of Indian Tala to the instruments performing it including the spoken syllabic language associated with Tabla and other percussion instruments, the use of Polyrhythmic drumming in rights of passage in West Africa, and the emotional context of Rhythmic Modes in the Middle East. Students practice analyzing each meter through low-stakes in-class quizzes covering vocabulary and concepts. Drums such as the Darbuka, a family of Ewe drums from Ghana, and Indian Tabla are presented in class as well as important musicians on each instrument. Students use these instruments and are taught appropriate playing techniques.

Application is addressed through online analytical quizzes that present students with prompts such as: The meter in this excerpt is best described as A) Duple, B) Triple, C) Additive, D) Polyrhythmic. The quizzes follow the same procedure as in the previous unit allowing three chances to take the quiz understanding that only the highest grade will be factored into the final grade. In addition to questions about meter, questions about the instruments heard on these excerpts are also included, building on the progress of the previous unit. The concept of each quiz as practice is reinforced through meta-cognitive exercises including one-minute papers asking, "What strengths and weaknesses were exposed during the last set of quizzes? What better technique for taking each quiz can implemented immediately? What successful strategy should I continue to use?" The capstone project asks students to discover and document music featuring distinct rhythmic features. Each of the five continents should be represented as before, and selections are documented in APA citation style.

The progression from western meters to world meters is important, moving from familiar to unfamiliar, but also connecting related rhythmic styles such as the influence of West African polyrhythm on the music of the Caribbean and North and South America including the development of Rumba, Salsa, and Jazz. The concept of Middle Eastern Rhythmic Modes that carry emotional information draws attention to the contrasting way in which Western music connotes emotional meaning through harmonic content. Indian Tala as a spoken language draws attention to the oral traditions that preserve and continue that music contrasting with the written musical notation of the west.

The Human Element and Integration are developed through related readings including the writings Mickey Hart, the drummer for the Grateful Dead and ethnomusicologist. (Hart, 1990). These writings are chosen precisely because of their accessibility, introducing students to another way of thinking about rhythm and instruments and the lives and concerns of musicians. A written response is required consisting of 3-4 short answer questions. Time is set-aside in class to discuss the reading. Discussion prompts include: "when you think back over the reading what stands out as the most surprising, or most important, ideas presented? what question can I answer about the reading for you?" Provocative and accessible readings such as this reliably promote excellent in-class discussions. Further Integration takes place by drawing attention to cultural and historical connections related to the meters and music presented. The Atlantic slave trade is the mechanism that introduces Polyrhythm to the New World (Ramsey, n.d.). The Sitar originates in Persia and is introduced to India through trade (Sitar, n.d.). Ravi Shankar influences multiple Western musical genres decades apart through his personal relationships and influence on the music of John Coltrane, Philip Glass, and the Beatles (Slawek, n.d.). Personal relationships are highlighted such as Ravi Shankar's daughter and final student Anoushka Shankar coming into her on the world stage and the relationship between Ravi Shankar's Tabla player Alla Rakha and his son Zakir Hussain, widely regarded as one of the great living Tabla players. The music serves as a lens through which one can view the full expression of the human experience.

Caring and self-directed learning are further developed through the long-term capstone project for the rhythm unit. Students are required to discover music on their own, their analysis is self-directed. They document these pieces of music precisely. Caring is more directly achieved through the act of experiencing the aesthetics and cultural values as expressed through rhythm including Polyrhythm as a way of building community and Indian Tala as a way of connecting the present to the ancient through oral tradition.

As before this unit moves from the familiar, which is defined in academic terms, to the unfamiliar. Care is taken to connect these disparate traditions, to illustrate similarities and differences, and to expose the complexities of the human experience that emerge from that discussion. Assessments follow a similar course moving from simple memorization of terms and concepts to analysis of recorded music to self-directed discovery and documentation of music from around the globe. Instruments themselves are brought into class and used to demonstrate performance techniques, to discuss their construction, to show how they are related to the meters themselves. Additionally students take an even more physical role during this unit, clapping out polyrhythm, and singing colotomic meter patterns.

Foundational Knowledge in pitch is divided into two equal parts addressing a scientific, or physical understanding of pitch (Dostrovsky) and an experiential, human understanding of pitch (Deutsch). Pitch is introduced through these two lenses simultaneously. Each discussion enhances the understanding of the other.

The first week of the unit introduces pitch and is guided by the Aristotelian concept of First Principles (Irwin, 1990). Pitch has two parallel definitions: 1) a specific frequency with measurable characteristics of amplitude, duration, and timbre, 2) a precise point of a scale of audible sound, characterized by volume, duration, and timbre. This broad approach allows for a divergent application of these concepts. Further foundational concepts are taught including the workings of the human auditory system, the octave as an organizing principle in pitch, the organization of pitches into scales and the creation of melody (and western harmony) from those scales, the related concepts of consonance and dissonance, and texture including world textures such as biphony (melody over a drone as in Indian Classical music). Each concept is defined and discussed so as to nourish divergent thinking. The next two weeks are spent analyzing the melodic content of different eras and cultures. Care is taken to present examples in carefully chosen contexts such as the 5 and 7 notes scales of Indonesian Gamelan (Kartomi, n.d.), the micro-pitch scales used in Bulgarian Folk music (Singing with two voices, 2011), and the unique timbre and texture of Tuvan Throat singing (Pegg, n.d.). More than in previous units Pitch is taught and assessed through analytical and written descriptive means. Students are asked to first define melodic areas, analyze melodic pitch content through melodic contour, and describe them in both written and spoken exercises in class.

Application is addressed through online analytical quizzes that present students with prompts such as: The melody present in this excerpt is best described as A) Ascending by step, B) Descending by Step, C) Descending by Leap, D) Ascending by Leap. The quizzes follow the same procedure as in the previous unit allowing three chances to take the quiz understanding that only the highest grade will be factored into the final grade. In addition to questions about pitch, questions about the instruments heard on these excerpts are also included as well as questions on the rhythmic structure of the excerpt, building on the progress of the previous units. Finally, the capstone project asks students to discover and document music featuring distinct melodic features. Each of the five continents should be represented as before, and selections are documented in APA citation style.

The variety of melodic styles presented is important, both for the purpose of exposing the student to a variety of musical cultures and also to expose the student to the variety of human expression. Melodic content presents an opportunity to illuminate the connection between lyrical meaning and the other sometimes abstract elements of music. An analysis of the melodic contour of "I want to hold you hand" by the Beatles reveals one simple, common technique for drawing attention to an important word or concept. The highest note in each verse corresponds to the word "hand." Not only is this the highest word, but it is reached by an upward leap, drawing the attention of the listener and reinforcing the weight or meaning of that word. This simple example can lead the way to more sophisticated and nuanced discussion of the relationship that pitch has with "meaning" and from there how rhythmic content and instrumentation can further enhance and support the lyrical meaning of a piece of vocal music. While this simple example can open a door, it serves the student well to move quickly to more substantial works, and to works of a variety of cultures. As in everything else, modes of expression vary from culture to culture.

The Human Element is developed outside of class through readings and short answer worksheets. The letters of W. A. Mozart to his father provide a good example (Strunk, 1998, pp. 965- 969). In two letters Mozart details the concerns facing him as he completes his first Opera in Vienna and he details how he specifically created a melody that features the voice of and impressive Bass vocalist. Other concerns of expression are related as well, from dramatic pacing to narrative to the role of lyrical content versus purely musical content.

Integration is developed through another suggestive reading by concerning the Chaconne progression (Ross, 2010). This essay follows the Chacona from its origin in the sixteenth century through historical styles, development, and expressions to the modern era, suggesting that pitch content, though ephemeral in some senses, is also lasting in another sense. Pitch content can exist as a cultural artifact and can be examined as such, resonating with the concept of Boas's principle of cultural relativism (Devale). At a more fundamental level, the dualities of pitch, which are presented as a physical phenomena capable of being studied by the physical sciences and as a experience of the human body and mind allow for a wide range of discussion topics, especially with the advent of contemporary neuroscience and its study of music and the brain (Levitin, 2011). Extra time is given to the many divergent connections between the concept of pitch and its resonance with many other strains of thought.

Caring and self-directed learning are further developed through the long-term capstone project for the pitch unit. Students are required to discover music on their own, their analysis is self-directed. They document these pieces of music precisely. Caring is more directly achieved through the act of experiencing the aesthetics and cultural values as expressed through pitch as well as the science of the human experience through the field of neuroscience and the use of descriptive and analytical assessments, and finally through the planting of sound and pitch in the physical world, suggesting that music is real on multiple levels and in multiple ways. It must be reinforced that these disparate modes of thought about pitch are centered around the simple concept that sound/pitch/music is fundamentally a mode of human communication, as complex and humanity itself, capable of expressing thought, experience, emotion, and spirit.

Unlike previous units the unit on pitch does not move in a clear direction from familiar to unfamiliar. It presents at once a holistic view of this element of music, leading to a deeper understanding of the other elements and of music itself, and it develops the analytical skills of the students in a way the previous units do not. This unit asks students for more creativity, more descriptive expression, and more divergent thinking than in previous units. It serves as an introduction to the final section of the class and its conclusion.

The unit on pitch's focus on analysis is further developed in the discussion of form and musical structure. Like pitch form is not presented as concrete list of examples to be learned as it might in a class covering the history of classical music. Form is presented as an opportunity to analyze music and to help discover meaning, both specific and broad. Some precise forms are presented during the first week of this section including: Rondo, Sonata Form, twelve-bar blues, and AABA form. The focus of form in this context is as a concept that organizes and connects all of the fundamental elements in such a way as to create meaning, to create music.

Form is understood as the organization of distinct melodic areas, defined by pitch content, rhythmic style, and instrumental arrangement. Mood and expression play a role, as does lyrical content when present. The student is instructed to listen for change, to identify what has changed, how it has changed, and to theorize why it changed, or what the effect of the change is from one area to the next. Each area is labeled using the familiar letter system to identify distinct section of a work. In essence the student is creating a detailed outline of a piece of music, or metaphorically painting a portrait of a piece of music as it moves through time. Students are asked to describe the piece in detail, focusing on audible events in a work, and to construct a holistic description of a piece. This approach requires effort from the students. Music from multiple cultures are presented for analysis, stressing that each piece must be considered on its own terms, that each analysis is an act of analytical listening, creativity, focus, and resonance with the student's personal experience, the composer or performer's experience, the culture from which that person originates, the time period, and other areas of meaning. Supporting research is introduced including elements of biography, history, and cultural practices that inform a given work. *Esta Plena*, a work by Miguel Zenon (2009) presents a good example analysis and integration of elements leading to meaning. The song incorporates elements of modern jazz and the plena music of Puerto Rico, Zenon's home. Instruments include a jazz quartet (piano, bass, drums, and saxophone), Puerto Rican hand drums, and lyrics written by Zenon that deliberately describe this musical integration:

This Plena warms up my/ Heart This Plena gives me Satisfaction/ With the Requinto, the Seguidor/ And this melody I make the combination/ From Borinquen I bring this to you/ And I sing it even in New York /With the Requinto, the Seguidor / And this melody I make the combination.

The form begins with voices in call and response accompanied by drums and quickly moves into an improvised second section featuring jazz improvisation, with no voices or traditional drums. As the piece moves forward, elements of Puerto Rican plena are introduced one at a time eventually leading to a lively cora section where all of the elements, modern jazz and traditional Puerto Rican, are fully integrated. The form, in a clear and audible way, uses elements of instrumentation, rhythm, and melody to combine these two disparate forms of music into a meaningful and coherent whole. Further more in the album liner notes and interviews Zenon indicates that this work serves in many ways as an autobiography, that the music mirrors his own development into a respected jazz musician and MacArthur Fellowship recipient.

Teaching form as a method to discover meaning, to make connections, to develop understanding, informs the final element of the capstone project in which students choose individual works previously documented for a holistic analysis. They are asked to look for music that has a special resonance for them, to research that music, and to create a portrait of that piece of music in writing- to develop a nuanced understanding of this music as a significant human document, an expressive product of a person, of a culture, of a time and of a place, that is in dialogue with their own experiences, culture, time, and place. This project by its nature self-directed. Students are required to overtly address elements of cultural diversity in their choices. It is advantageous for the student to choose well-constructed music of depth that rewards closer examination. Students are assessed on the quality of their analysis and presentation of their ideas, the presentation of new concepts discovered through their own research rather than relying purely on what has been introduced in class, and in the integration of this music with other elements of the human experience.

While the discussion of each unit has referenced specific examples it should be noted that this framework allows for variety and personal development by the professor as well, the one requirement being high quality, well-constructed music. In the internationalization of this class several themes developed that informed the music selected for focused presentation in class. It became important that each piece support each category of Fink's taxonomy while exposing the student to a wide variety of cultural expressions and musical styles, and that each piece guide the student towards a divergent understanding of the world of music. In addition to universal concern covering thorough presentation of knowledge, this course considers Integration with the wider world, the Human Element, and Caring are as important factors. Music with a connection to a compelling individual, or that expresses the human experience in a particular way, music that offers a non-western viewpoint, that widens the perception of the interconnectedness of the human experience becomes valuable. Some suggestions include the importance of the family connection as exemplified by the career of Anoushka Shankar, Ravi Shankar's daughter who continues to practice Indian Classical music at the highest level, but also strives to create an original mode of expression connected to many traditions found around the world. The father son dynamic found between Ustad Alla Rakha Khan and Zakir Hussain illuminates a similar multi-generational story. The developing legacy of Yo-Yo Ma in classical music can be balanced against his long time collaborators the Silk Road Ensemble, as well as more disparate collaborations with Chris Thile on the Goat Rodeo Sessions album. The history of passion, love, and personal disaster found in the marriage of Robert and Clara Schumann and the profound influence of Clara on Johannes Brahms illustrates in very personal terms the human connection in music. The story of Leon Theremin and Adolfe Sax connect the development of musical instruments to the technical and scientific world, while Albert Einstein's well-known love of music, and Max Planck's lengthy study of vibration on a string connect music and modern science from the other direction. The syncretic musical culture of the United States reflects its origins as a nation of immigrants and that story can be told through the development of Gospel, Blues, Jazz, and Rock and

Roll, connecting these contemporary music to those music introduced from west Africa and from the British Isles. This divergent approach allows the class to respond well to surprising real-time developments. For example as this chapter was written Bob Dylan became the first musician to be awarded the Nobel Prize for Literature. Examples such as these lend themselves to the human experience expressed through music, to the integration of this subject with the rest of the student's lives, and hopefully they help to develop new, wider, and deeper understanding of the human condition.

FUTURE RESEARCH DIRECTIONS

Further development can come from deepening the connections of each musical example to one another and to the wider human experience through subject Integration and the Human Dimension, as well as creating more opportunities for students to develop their own interests and self-directed learning skills. Meta-cognitive elements are in place but the power of these techniques to develop a meaningful educational experience has just barely been tapped, much more work can be done to integrate them into the course structure. The world of neurological science is opening up new ways to understand how and why music plays such an important role in the human experience and how aesthetic expression, musical expression, can open up in the listener other modes of experience, other points of view, and guide the way to a new understanding. *Music and Embodied Cognition* (Cox, 2016) provides a focused introduction to this concept with suggested applications. Contemporary neurological studies into the affect of the arts can lead the way to a deeper understanding of how these significant human documents can change, inform, and grow the listener, and can in turn inform teaching and learning practices.

CONCLUSION

The approach taken in this chapter is not intended as a precise roadmap to Internationalization. It presents one experience. The fundamental ideas and practices of this paper, presented in specific examples, express one point of view. First an instructor must articulate a philosophy of education. This philosophy can and should change as the instructor's understanding of the subject deepens. The ultimate goals of the course should be clearly defined. In this particular example the goals are informed by the Taxonomy of Learning presented by Fink. Focused curriculum design is a powerful tool that can and should be used in support of these ultimate goals. Teaching and learning activities, assessment, and situational factors should be taken into account when designing the curriculum. The course design itself should reflect the subject being taught at a fundamental level. Each instructor is an individual and within the confines of a specific subject of study that individuality should be expressed. Student engagement emerges from the meaningful dialogue between the personal experiences of the student and the larger subject at hand. The student should develop a personal relationship with the material. Content is important but the focus should be on learning.

REFERENCES

Berliner, P. (1978). *The soul of mbira: Music and traditions of the Shona people of Zimbabwe*. Berkeley, CA: University of California Press.

Brown, P. C., Roediger, H. L., & McDaniel, M. A. (2014). *Make it stick: The science of successful learning*. Cambridge, MA: The Belknap Press of Harvard University Press. doi:10.4159/9780674419377

Cox, A. (2016). *Music and Embodied Cognition: Listening, Moving, Feeling, and Thinking*. Bloomington, IN: Indiana University Press.

Deutsch, D., Gabrielson, A., Sloboda, J., Cross, I., Drake, C., Parncutt, R., . . . Zatorre, R. (n.d.). Psychology of music. In *Oxford Music Online*. Retrieved from http://www.oxfordmusiconline.com.libproxy.ggc.edu/subscriber/article/grove/music/42574

DeVale, S. C. (n.d.). Boas, Franz. In *Oxford Music Online*. Retrieved from http://www.oxfordmusiconline.com.libproxy.ggc.edu/subscriber/article/grove/music/03328

Dostrovsky, S., Cambell, M., Bell, J., & Truesdell, C. (n.d.). Physics of music. In *Oxford Music Online*. Retrieved from http://www.oxfordmusiconline.com.libproxy.ggc.edu/subscriber/article/grove/music/43400

Doubleday, V. (2008). Sounds of Power: An Overview of Musical Instruments and Gender. *Ethnomusicology Forum, 17*(1), 3-39. Retrieved from http://www.jstor.org.libproxy.ggc.edu/stable/20184604

Duke, R., Simmons, A., & Cash, C. (2009). It's Not How Much; It's How: Characteristics of Practice Behavior and Retention of Performance Skills. *Journal of Research in Music Education, 56*(4), 310–321. doi:10.1177/0022429408328851

Dutton, D. (2009). *The art instinct: Beauty, pleasure and human evolution*. New York: Bloomsbury Press.

Eisner, E. W. (1985). *Learning and teaching the ways of knowing*. Chicago: National Society for the Study of Education.

Fink, L. D. (2013). *Creating significant learning experiences, revised and updated: An integrated approach to designing college courses*. San Francisco, CA: Jossey-Bass.

Georgia Gwinnett College. (2015). *Student demographics. About GGC*. Retrieved from http://www.ggc.edu/about-ggc/at-a-glance/ggc-facts/

Hart, M., Stevens, J., & Lieberman, F. (1990). *Drumming at the edge of magic: A journey into the spirit of percussion*. San Francisco: Harper San Francisco.

Irwin, T. (1990). *Aristotle's first principles*. Oxford, UK: Clarendon Press. doi:10.1093/0198242905.001.0001

Jorgensen, E. (2002). The Aims of Music Education: A Preliminary Excursion. *Journal of Aesthetic Education, 36*(1), 31-49. Retrieved from http://www.jstor.org/stable/3333624

Kartomi, M., & Mendonça, M. (n.d.). Gamelan. In *Oxford Music Online*. Retrieved from http://www.oxfordmusiconline.com.libproxy.ggc.edu/subscriber/article/grove/music/45141

Kubik, G., & Cooke, P. (n.d.). Lamellophone. In *Oxford Music Online*. Retrieved from http://www. oxfordmusiconline.com.libproxy.ggc.edu/subscriber/article/grove/music/40069

Leask, B. (2012). *Internationalization of the curriculum: A guide*. Sydney, Australia: University of South Australia.

Levitin, D., & de Grassi, A. (Nov. 3, 2011). Your brain on music: a story of song meets science. In *Inforum: connect your intellect*. San Francisco: The Commonwealth Club. Retrieved from https://www. commonwealthclub.org/events/2011-11-03/your-brain-music

Montagu, J. (n.d.). Instruments, classification of. In *Oxford Music Online*. Retrieved from http://www. oxfordmusiconline.com.libproxy.ggc.edu/subscriber/article/opr/t114/e3431

Orton, R., & Davies, H. (n.d.). Theremin. In *Oxford Music Online*. Retrieved from http://www.oxford-musiconline.com.libproxy.ggc.edu/subscriber/article/grove/music/27813

Parsad, B., & Spiegelman, M. (2012). *Arts education: In public elementary and secondary schools 1999*. Academic Press.

Pegg, C. (n.d.). Overtone-singing. In *Oxford Music Online*. Retrieved from http://www.oxfordmusiconline.com.libproxy.ggc.edu/subscriber/article/grove/music/49849

Rabkin, N., & Hedberg, E. C. (2011). *Arts education in America: What the declines mean for arts participation 2000 and 2009-2010*. Washington, DC: National Endowment for the Arts.

Ramsey, G. (n.d.). African American music. In *Oxford Music Online*. Retrieved from http://www.oxfordmusiconline.com.libproxy.ggc.edu/subscriber/article/grove/music/A2226838

Ross, A. (2010). Chacona, lamento, walking blues: bass lines of music history. In *Listen to this*. New York: Farrar, Straus and Giroux.

Shelemay, K. (2015). *Soundscapes: Exploring music in a changing world*. New York: Norton.

Shields, C. (2016). Aristotle. In *The Stanford Encyclopedia of Philosophy*. Retrieved from http://plato. stanford.edu/archives/win2016/entries/aristotle/

Singing with two voices. (2011). In *Get mouthy*. London, UK: Wellcome Collection. Retrieved at https:// www.youtube.com/watch?v=-o31Yg936Ac

Sitar. (n.d.). In *Oxford Music Online*. Retrieved from http://www.oxfordmusiconline.com.libproxy.ggc. edu/subscriber/article/grove/music/25900

Southern Association of Colleges and Schools Commission on Colleges. (2012). *Resource manual for the principles of accreditation: foundations for quality enhancement*. Decatur, GA: Southern Association of Colleges and Schools Commission on Colleges. Retrieved from http://www.sacscoc.org/pdf/ Resource%20Manual.pdf

Strunk, W. O., Treitler, L., Mathiesen, T. J., McKinnon, J. W., Tomlinson, G., Murata, M., & Allanbrook, W. J. (1998). Source readings in music history. New York: Norton.

Wade, B. C. (2013). *Thinking musically: Experiencing music, expressing culture*. New York: Oxford University press.

Zenón, M., Perdomo, L., Glawischnig, H., Cole, H., Matos, T., Allende, O., & Gutiérrez, J. (2009). *Esta Plena*. Cambridge, MA: Marsalis Music.

Chapter 7
Cultivating Global Citizens:
Classroom Tools to Reduce Cultural Judgment and Foster Intercultural Understanding in Higher Ed

Jenna Andrews-Swann
Georgia Gwinnett College, USA

ABSTRACT

This chapter presents the author's experiences working with international content in the higher education classroom to explore successful examples of intercultural material that can benefit students pursuing a degree in any field. The author explores how social science courses in general, and anthropology courses in particular, that work from a foundation of cultural relativism and standpoint theory can equip students with important knowledge and skills that promote tolerance and respect of cultural difference. Finally, the author demonstrates that students finish courses like these with a better understanding of and appreciation for the cultural differences that exist all around them.

INTRODUCTION

Students undertaking a four-year undergraduate degree program stand to benefit immensely from international and intercultural content that is integrated into higher education curricula – perhaps now more than ever. A number of scholars have documented this increased need, emphasizing that success in an ever-globalizing world relies in part on students' development in the areas of intercultural competence (Deardorff, 2006) and cross-cultural empathy (Haigh, 2007). While campus communities increasingly see the value of international and intercultural opportunities, the process of changing curricula or introducing new programming is not always an intuitive one. In fact, a surprising number of undergraduate students still outwardly bristle at ideas and practices unlike their own. On college campuses, where ideals of open-mindedness and diverse opinions and experiences are meant to encourage interdisciplinary thought, efforts to promote intercultural perspectives are too often unsuccessful, and fall short of providing a holistic perspective that encourages the development of competent, global citizens.

DOI: 10.4018/978-1-5225-2791-6.ch007

What all of this seems to signal is that in spite of various tropes touting the importance of blurry, vague ideas like "diversity" and "multiculturalism" in creating a more tolerant and inclusive society, there still exists a good deal of ethnocentrism and closed-mindedness in a typical college classroom. One might argue (as many scholars do, see Homan et al., 2015) that this indicates that token attempts at increasing international and cross-cultural understanding via "diversity training" and the like are not working well. And if this is indeed the case, what happens when these students take jobs and become leaders in the global marketplace? More often than not, they are inadequately prepared to move forward as empathetic, productive global citizens.

Exposure to international or intercultural information is an important step in the process of internationalizing college curricula – and in, by extension, college students' training – but it is only one of many. In fact, many scholars have noted the dangers inherent in such an approach: treating cultural diversity as an addendum to "real" course material is not doing justice to the process (e.g. Leask, 2001). Instead, what needs to occur is careful integration and investigation that encourages students to appreciate and to question why particular cultural practices or ideologies exist – what Milton Bennett called "ethnorelativism" in his influential Developmental Model of Intercultural Sensitivity (DMIS) work (Bennett, 1993).

This chapter explores the role that cultural relativism and standpoint theory have played in the author's curriculum design and teaching thus far, focusing primarily on the author's work at Georgia Gwinnett College, a new four-year liberal arts institution with an access mission near Atlanta, Georgia. The author argues that using pedagogical tools that counter ethnocentrism with cultural relativism and standpoint theory can result in a more advanced level of intercultural understanding for many students. The chapter demonstrates that, even though a few undergrads come into their first anthropology class expecting to talk about digging up dinosaur bones, they end the semester with a better understanding of and appreciation for the cultural differences that exist all around them.

BACKGROUND

Institutions of higher education, if they are to successfully fulfill their responsibility to students' holistic development, must carefully consider how to train students and faculty alike on the effects of globalization; first and foremost is the increasing need to negotiate intercultural relationships. Globalization functions today as both ideology and fact; that is, it simultaneously frames transnational policy and international agendas (e.g. NAFTA, the World Bank), and impacts how individual people engage with the world around them (e.g. Facebook, WhatsApp). Both facets of globalization influence higher education, in that students are seeking training and skills they will need to work in a swiftly changing globalized economy *and* they are seeking this skill set while surrounded by cultural information from a myriad of places. Faculty and administrators are thus faced with negotiating the wildly diverse economic and cultural impacts of globalization on both fronts, as well. A growing number of scholars from various campuses and institutes around the world have made the case for adopting a framework of internationalization in higher education to deal with this complicated task (Leask, 2001; Knight, 2004; Altbach & Knight 2007). As the author posits here, anthropology is a productive place to do this work – especially if the ultimate goal of such a framework is to foster a sense of intercultural empathy and understanding (and not merely to prepare workers for the global economy) that students can then adapt to a wide variety of disciplines, careers, and life situations they may encounter.

Students at community colleges and four-year undergraduate institutions with an access mission often have little exposure to anthropology before entering the classroom. But a foundational course in anthropology can serve these students exceedingly well, as it welcomes culturally diverse perspectives of both self and "other" and as a discipline, anthropology is well-equipped to call upon diversity within the classroom itself as a learning experience (Muir, 2016). Teaching in this context, especially at the introductory level, led the author to cultivate a hybrid approach of sorts to help students comprehend and learn to embrace cultural similarities and differences. This informal approach combines some of the most accessible, applicable theories from the author's own professional training, research, and scholarship: cultural relativism and standpoint theory. These perspectives from Anthropology and Women's Studies, plus a healthy dose of empathy and humor, offer a classroom-based reprieve from the lip service that so often takes the form of traditional diversity or cultural sensitivity training.

Cultural relativism is a notion that was popularized in American anthropology by Franz Boas in the late nineteenth century. Its primary purpose was to situate knowledge and experiences firmly within a particular cultural context, and to emphasize that an outsider looking into a new culture may not be equipped to fully understand that culture when they carry with them a set of culturally-specific biases and experiences themselves. Cultural relativism has evolved a bit from its earliest usage in the discipline, and now carries with it particular ideas about how researchers approach such tasks as garnering informed consent, and it increasingly evokes postmodern or feminist ideologies with its emphasis on context-specific epistemology.

It is important to note that cultural relativism has faced criticism from some scholars for its perceived disregard for human rights (especially in regard to its problematic "moral relativism" conflation) (e.g. Gellner, 1995; Rachels, 2003). Scholars using overly simplified, incomplete versions of cultural relativism do indeed run the risk of rationalizing harmful or violent behavior as a valid component of culture. A fuller, more nuanced understanding of how cultural relativism can lead to ethically responsible research (or cross-cultural interactions, more generally) reminds us that cultural relativism does not preclude moral criticism (Dundes Renteln, 1988; Ulin, 2007). Rather, it calls out cultural hegemony and problematizes theories like unilineal evolution or so-called "human nature", which often espouse extreme bias and leave little room for reflexivity or cultural critique. Demonstrating that some empirically different cultural trait exists and "makes sense" for its practitioners does not, in the end, negate widely shared moral standards such as human rights and equity.

Some academics and theoreticians have posited that renaming or throwing out cultural relativism altogether might assist in distancing the theory and the discipline of anthropology from some of these negative implications (e.g. Norris, 1996). But others have argued – and rather more successfully – that cultural relativism was not a tool created for repressive or violent aims, and any such usage must be condemned in an effort to create and promote philosophical and practical frameworks that leave room for both human rights and cultural rights (Donnelly, 1984; Fleuhr-Lobban, 1995, 1998, 2005). To this end, the American Anthropological Association approved a Statement on Human Rights, first in 1947, and later updated in 1999. This large, influential professional organization also maintains a Committee on Human Rights, whose primary role is to respond to reports of human rights abuses (see http://humanrights.americananthro.org/category/human-rights/).

Indeed, it is the author's perspective that cultural relativism stands in strong opposition to colonial and imperialist attempts to paint Western cultural models as some pinnacle of cultural development, and reminds scholars and students alike that there is value in understanding all cultural perspectives. As such, most cultural anthropologists maintain that cultural relativism remains a productive way to consider cultural diversity. Many academic anthropologists and other social scientists treat this as an invaluable – if, perhaps, imperfect – introductory pedagogical concept to help students begin to grasp the value of other perspectives and to begin to guide students away from ethnocentrism.

Careful attention to cultural context is key to understanding why people do not behave the in the same way from one place or time to another, though this idea is often not quite clear to students until they also begin to consider that their own behaviors and thoughts are culturally-situated. To this end, cultural relativism is complimented nicely by feminist standpoint theory. Standpoint theory is a perspective popularized by feminist scholars seeking to emphasize the intersection of gender, class, and ethnicity (among other powerful components of identity) in shaping how one interacts with people or institutions (Collins, 1990; Harding, 1993, 2004; Haraway, 2004). Thus, both relativism and standpoint highlight the utility of thoughtful consideration of how one's perspective on the world is fashioned. In fact, feminist scholars have long used the notion of standpoint in cross-cultural studies to demonstrate, for instance, that experiences of gender differ from place to place and over time, and are thus culturally constructed and cannot be adequately studied or understood without taking into account the local cultural context (e.g. Oakley, 1985). Further, feminists of color and feminists in the Global South use the theory to highlight the disparate impact postcolonial, Western epistemology (and Western feminism) has had on their experiences – namely, that owing to gendered and racialized marginalization, the experiences of people of color or people in the Global South often differ markedly from those of people occupying more privileged social locations (Collins, 1997; Jaggar, 2016). Thus standpoint theory, when integrated into a supportive classroom environment, encourages students to consider how their own perspective, social location, and experience might influence the way they view the world around them.

Carefully curated examples and experiences of cultural relativism and standpoint theory in the classroom can help students begin to work their way from ethnocentrism toward a better model of intercultural understanding. Developmental models such as Bennett's DMIS strive to aid learners along a trajectory of personal growth with the goal of increasing learners' ability to comprehend different worldviews (Bennett, 1993). It is the author's experience that the combined approach described above accomplishes this goal, thereby providing students with an invaluable (and transferable!) set of skills to empower their own critical intercultural understanding. Many students, upon completing an introductory anthropology course, demonstrate great success in moving into subsequent stages, e.g. Bennett's "Acceptance" stage, wherein cultural identity and difference are acknowledged and considered valuable (though some, to be sure, fail to move this far along the spectrum over the course of one class). The following section offers a discussion of the author's classroom tools in practice, using examples of specific activities to illustrate the utility of relativism and standpoint.

IN THE CLASSROOM: CULTIVATING GLOBAL CITIZENS

The real challenge is to develop courses and curricula that embed and validate the thought of cultures other than the Western and present them to local learners without making them seem exhibits in a museum (Haigh, 2009).

Thus far, discussion of intercultural awareness in this chapter has been largely theoretical. The following sections offer descriptions of the author's experience integrating internationalized content and encouraging cultural relativism in the classroom. Narratives of classroom experiences such as these are important resources; too often, higher education scholarship glosses over firsthand accounts from students and instructors in favor of generalized analyses that, while theoretically useful, may fall short of providing practical, detailed examples of work that can be integrated into a course (Scutt & Hobson, 2013). Narrative approaches, such as what follows, are often used in ethnographic research and allow for a richer and arguably more accurate description of events, what anthropologist Clifford Geertz, himself a proponent of cultural relativism, called "thick description", that can shed contextualized light on specific attributes of an activity that went well (or not so well) in the classroom (Geertz, 1973). This level of interpretation is key if scholars are to ferret out successful avenues for internationalization and put them into practice.

Classroom Context

Georgia Gwinnett College took on the task of internationalizing the curriculum for its most recent (and first – the school opened its doors in 2006) Quality Enhancement Plan in 2013. The objective, in part, is to teach students to "describe and evaluate their own [and other] cultures in relation to history, values, politics, communication styles, economy, or beliefs and practices" (GGC QEP Student Learning Outcomes). While the school primarily uses the term *internationalize*, some goals of the program are very much in line with what other scholars have termed *intercultural competence* or *sensitivity* (e.g. Bennett & Bennett, 2004). Administrators of the campus-wide program identified existing courses with "significant" international content, and assisted faculty members, via workshops and individualized training, in their efforts to internationalize additional courses. Those courses that make it through a careful internal verification process earn the designation of "*i*-course", and appear as such on students' transcripts; additionally, if they wish, students may count designated *i*-courses toward a Global Studies Certificate.

The author received *i*-course designation for two courses, a four-field Introduction to Anthropology course and an upper-level course in Cultural Anthropology. The introductory course is a popular way for students to fulfill one of their general education requirements, and as such, it needs to reach students from an especially wide variety of majors and experience levels. To do this well, the author utilizes several teaching methods with the ultimate goal of increasing all students' understanding of – and appreciation for – the human diversity that is all around them. Students are encouraged to see how class material will complement their chosen major or career, whatever the field, because students will all encounter people different from themselves. The upper-level course serves a variety of majors (GGC does not offer an Anthropology major) and considers cultures and cultural diversity with the primary goal of broadening students' personal experiences and encouraging thoughtful, critical analysis of human diversity.

The *i*-course verification process is in place largely to ensure that international content is fully integrated into a course, not merely added on haphazardly to a lecture or reading assignment here and there. When faculty are encouraged to think about international content in such terms, they may have better results both teaching students from diverse backgrounds *and* encouraging students to consider what it means to learn and think in a particular cultural context (Trahar, 2013). It is important to avoid offering international content as some exotic "other" way of life and present the material instead as an equally valuable perspective on the world. As such, international content can more broadly impact students' development as critical thinkers and empathizers by encouraging (requiring?) them to ponder the way their own culture and experience shapes how they interact with the world. This is, in a nutshell, the goal of standpoint theory.

In a similar vein, when students learn about another culture or epistemological perspective thanks to campus-wide internationalized curriculum plans, they simultaneously and often unconsciously compare that perspective with their own. This comparison risks ethnocentrism and without the tools to more empathetically process their response, students may never move beyond an initial gut reaction that paints the "other" as strange or backwards. But when the framework of cultural relativism is an integrated part of the curriculum along with that wonderful international, intercultural content, students become increasingly conscious of biases and are more apt to think critically about why they do things the way they do them.

Anthropology courses offer students in a wide variety of major programs of study the opportunity to examine humans and culture. Material in these courses ranges from human evolution to sociolinguistics to global gender diversity. And students are provided with a framework that allows them to *process* this material that is easily transferred to intercultural experiences outside of the classroom. The following subsection details successful examples of activities and topics – "tools" – that engage students in international content via standpoint theory and cultural relativism.

Classroom Tools

The realizations that students and instructors experience together over some new level of understanding – moments in which students (or, indeed, their instructor) seem to light up with excitement at connecting novel concepts or recognizing that a new vocabulary term applies to something they have experienced in their own lives – are undoubtedly rewarding, but sometimes difficult to come by. Specific examples of internationalized material from the author's courses that evoke or require cultural relativism and/or standpoint theory in these sorts of "lightbulb moments" include ideas presented in the following formats: traditional lecture; student-centered small group discussion; in-class student presentations; local ethnographic research; and written reflection.

Lecture topics in introductory anthropology courses cover an exceedingly broad range of material. Anthropology is, after all, the study of humankind. But it is often precisely this diversity that makes an impact on students. For example, the discussion of *language* begins with an overview of the adaptive utility of communication and the genetic traits that accumulated over 150,000 years ago that would eventually allow anatomically modern humans to develop linguistic complexity unparalleled in other primate species. This discussion transitions into considering the linguistic practices of the instructor and students present, focusing particularly on accent and dialect. There are a number of online tools, results of the Harvard Dialect Survey and the Dictionary of American Regional English among them, that support this discussion. Via these tools, students in class listen to others' speech, look at demographics that can impact someone's linguistic patterns, and consider how their own regional linguistic tendencies developed. To further expand this topic, the author introduces segments of a documentary demonstrating language loss and efforts to salvage dying languages. This helps students expand their recent experience in class of comparing (and often laughing and playfully arguing about) regional American English to consider global language diversity and why indigenous languages, with their local dialects and specialized vocabulary, continue to disappear at an alarming rate. After proceeding through these steps – from objective comprehension of the biological beginnings of language to self-reflection on local language diversity to the implications of global language loss – students report a deeper understanding of the importance of language overall and a greater appreciation for linguistic diversity. A significant outcome of this process is reduced judgement and increased comprehension of that difference.

To reach students who may benefit from peer learning experiences more than lectures and large group discussion, small group discussions of various intercultural themes are integrated into the course as well. An important advantage of requiring students to discuss anthropological themes and concepts amongst themselves is that, very often, they enter into conversation with another student whose cultural background and experiences differ markedly from their own. It is important, of course, that the instructor not call out individual students to exemplify difference. Instead, leaving room for students to self-identify and share their own story creates an empathetic classroom environment in which students (and the instructor) feel more comfortable acknowledging difference and learning from one another. This practice sets an example of respect in the classroom that students can model elsewhere in their lives.

One example of a successful small group discussion format is a guided ethnographic interview exercise that introductory students complete. They are instructed to first decide which student in their small group will play the role of the anthropologist. The "anthropologist" then asks the other group members (the "interviewees") questions they have carefully constructed to elicit responses about the interviewees' upbringing and hometown culture/s in order to determine if and why differences may exist across their experiences. The interviewees are aware that they do not have to answer any question that is uncomfortable or poorly posed. After a set time, students change roles to experience both sides of the interview. The whole exchange typically takes approximately thirty minutes, and it can easily be added into an otherwise traditionally formatted class, no matter the size. The goal of this exercise is threefold: first, students gain a deeper understanding of an important anthropological method and its ethical implications; second, students learn about one another and how one's upbringing or hometown culture may impact their cultural perspective; and third, students reflect upon how their own upbringing and hometown culture shaped their cultural perspective. Across all three outcomes, the exercise acts as a reminder of cultural relativism and one's standpoint, and very often it introduces internationalized content via the classroom community itself.

Another teaching method that has met with a significant level of success in introductory courses is student presentations. The author, after sitting through a few too many traditional presentations, in which a student reads from a painfully wordy slide presentation, made a conscious effort to change the way presentations were conducted in her courses. For a final project, students select a contemporary cultural group (with consultation with the instructor), then conduct research using a variety of sources to answer a variety of basic questions about that cultural group (where are they? how many people? what language/s do they speak? what kind of religious practices exist? how are families arranged? are there any surprising cultural traits or issues this group faces?). Library and online sources comprise the majority of sources students consult, but they are advised to consider alternative sources such as firsthand accounts as well. Students compile this research into an essay, including an explanation for why they chose the group they did and what can be learned from studying a group in this manner. Finally, students select information from their research paper to share with the class. This presentation follows a creative, engaging format, similar to that of a science fair, during which students set up a display of their material, speak informally about what they learned, and interact with others' displays. These displays range from trifold posters and demonstrations of some notable cultural trait or local language to raucous games that get everyone (the instructor included!) involved. Many students dress in attire or play music that reflects the culture they researched, and even more prepare and share traditional foods. Students routinely comment that they have fun with this presentation format and that they learn more from each other this way than they might from a more traditional PowerPoint-style presentation.

Novel formats like this for what might otherwise be a very traditional college-level project encourage reflexivity. That is, students must consider their own role in the project, both in terms of how they conduct research and what they choose to present AND how their own membership in a particular cultural group might influence their work. Additionally, the presentation format welcomes some degree of experiential learning, of the sort that rarely shows up in many lower level or introductory college courses. This embodiment of culture – via dress, food, language, play, and music, in particular – is a simple but powerful way to experience cultural difference. And when it occurs in a classroom, a space that students have occupied for weeks or months, they may feel safer encountering and engaging with that difference.

Students in the upper level course engage in classroom discussions and lectures as well, but additionally, they are tasked with designing and carrying out their own ethnographic research project, in stages, over the semester. They are also responsible for presenting their results to the class or at a regional conference in an engaging way. The bulk of students' data comes from ethnographic observation and interviews they arrange, record, and analyze. To prepare for this work, students receive instruction on how to take field notes, how to craft good interview questions, how to select the best methods and theory for one's research question/s, and how to gain the proper permissions when working with people. Along with this instruction, students have time in class to practice the methodology they hope to use in "the field". An important compliment to teaching and supervising student ethnographic work like this is ethics training; it is imperative that students participate in a range of discussions about ethics both in terms of their role as researchers and around responsible analysis and presentation of the data they might gather. Part of ethical research and presentation is recognizing standpoint and the role it plays in science; that is, students must learn to recognize and address their own biases and how those biases might influence what others tell them (in the case of interviews) and how they analyze and present information. Cultural relativism is closely linked to this process as well: one cannot hope to be a good scientist or researcher if they are consistently and uncritically judging others' behaviors or practices.

As a compliment to their own research, upper level students also select an ethnographic text (a case study of some particular cultural community). After reading their chosen text, they complete a reflexive writing assignment and an informal presentation on the text and their response to it. Ideally, this exercise sheds light on the students' research, if only by providing a model for how to successfully and respectfully share ethnographic data with the public. Other reading, lecture, discussion, and films that comprise the course cover a wide range of global and international examples and experiences (along with eliciting the students' own) across a number of theoretical and practical realms.

Classroom Successes

One theme that permeates all of the successful tools discussed in the preceding section is empathy – directed toward students and encouraged in students – and one especially important component of empathy is humor. Humor plays a significant role in an internationalized, intercultural classroom as students begin to learn how to process and appreciate differences. It helps prevent "excessive resistance, and deal with it more effectively when it occurs" (Bennett & Bennett, 2004). One initial way humor might appear, for instance, is intentionally directed at the instructor. The author habitually shares stories from field research with students that illustrate ways she "messed up" when attempting to negotiate an unfamiliar culture. Modeling this behavior creates a classroom space in which students feel more comfortable making mistakes. After all, learning or experiencing something new is bound to result in a misstep or two along the way. And this is something essential; the ability to laugh at oneself establishes the ability to perhaps consider another's point of view, which is at the core of cultural relativism.

Next, one must push students to decode the reasons for some behavior or practice that may occur differently across cultures. For example, one way this unfolds in the author's classroom is through an analysis of one of the universal behaviors across all human groups, past and present (well, all living beings, actually): eliminating waste. First, students are asked to list all the materials required to go to the bathroom "correctly" in the United States. They list such things as fluffy toilet paper, clean running water, a sink and soap, privacy, and a toilet one can sit on and flush. Then, the instructor shares a story of one of the most embarrassing intercultural bathroom experiences she ever had, in which a broken-down bus and privacy-free outdoor pit toilet with a top too high to reach on her own take center stage. Students quickly begin to share their own "bathroom stories" from travels or home countries or stories friends have relayed. The classroom environment frequently becomes a bit boisterous at this, but soon students begin to realize that all of these practices accomplish the same simple goal.

The most important step of this exercise is then to consider *why* this very basic act occurs in so many different ways across cultures. For instance, the students are instructed to think about the context in which our bathroom practices are possible; one needs a reliable supply of potable water, a complex infrastructure of water and sewer or septic facilities, imported and dyed wood pulp in the form of rolls of special soft paper, and a rather large area within homes or other buildings that must be devoted to this activity. Very quickly, students come to the realization that the way they have always done some task is just one of many. And, in fact, that the practice many students are accustomed to might be quite wasteful. In such cases, cultural relativism and standpoint theory lead to critical thinking about one's own customs, which can further encourage empathy and cross-cultural understanding.

Anthropologists quite often compare stories from the field amongst themselves, trying to one-up one another with tales of the unexpected, the supremely difficult, or the simply fantastic. This tendency sometimes comes across in textbooks, as well, in the form of seemingly "exotic" examples of various human activities or behaviors that anthropologists have named or categorized. For instance, a commonly cited example of a collective rite of passage is that traditionally practiced by the Sambia people of Papua New Guinea. In this rite, boys in the same age set were put through a number of challenges, and successful completion validated their passage into manhood. Many of these challenges are relatively easy for Western students to understand, based on their familiarity with pop culture depictions of indigenous peoples; portions of the ritual include trials like learning the ways of the forest and demonstrating bravery in the face of fear or pain. But the part of this rite that grabs students' attention every time is the oral transfer of masculine life force, called *Jerungdu*, from older boys to the younger initiates in the form of semen (Herdt, 2006). Once murmurs of disapproval quiet, the responsible instructor's job is to steer the classroom discussion toward a culturally relative perspective on this ostensibly unusual cultural trait. In this case, the particular value of Jerungdu has a lot to do with the same kinds of patriarchal norms and ideas about female pollution (especially linked to menstruation and reproduction) that have been commonly documented in Western societies. Situating such a fantastic example of cultural difference in terms of cultural relativism and empathy models for students how very simple a task this can be – that with a little practice, they too can quickly move beyond common initial, negative reactions to difference and look instead toward a deeper level of understanding that underscores our common humanity.

Similarly, cross cousin marriage, a relatively common practice in which people who share a set of grandparents will marry to shore up alliances and access to resources, elicits grumbles or shock from many students at first blush. But upon further inspection, students come to see that the institution of cross cousin marriage makes sense to those who use it owing to unilineal kinship reckoning – simply put, those so-called "cousins" do not consider themselves related to one another (Levi-Strauss, 1969). Yet another example, and one that students often feel a connection to, is body modification. This is a practice that has been around since humans have had the capacity for complex, symbolic thought, albeit in a variety of ways and with diverse rules for members of various cultures. Students are often more than happy to talk about the meanings behind their own tattoos or piercings or dyed hair – this, again, is their standpoint. When one then compares tattoos, for instance, across cultures, similar reasons for painful body modification become apparent: tattoos commonly signify belonging, individualism, and/or bravery across a wide range of social and cultural contexts. Other types of body modification highlight additional similarities between mainstream Western cultural practices and practices that are part of cultures that may at first seem quite different: lip plates compare to lip injections; scarification to breast augmentation; and brass neck rings to stilettos.

Students provide some of the most meaningful feedback on the author's anthropology courses via an in-class written exercise that has far reaching impact for them, as well. Toward the end of each semester, students are asked to consider their career goals and reflect upon how they might integrate anthropology concepts, perspectives, and/or methods in their chosen profession. Overwhelmingly, students recognize – often with a degree of surprise – that anthropology has positively impacted how they now interact with people from diverse backgrounds, especially in terms of increased feelings of empathy and acceptance. And in a rapidly globalizing world, when students are progressively more aware that their future (or present) colleagues will in fact *not* come from the same cultural background, this recognition is incredibly heartening.

The result here is that students, from their standpoint, may initially feel disapproval or even disgust at practices that are different from their own, but anthropology also gives them a set of methods – cultural relativism perhaps first among them – to step back and consider how a given behavior makes sense to those who practice it. Indeed, it is the differences between cultures that make life so very rich and interesting; cultural relativism is not about erasing difference, but about understanding it. Students develop this holistic ability through thoughtful, empathetic examination and analysis of diverse cultural practices, and it is this ability that is transferrable to other academic or professional intercultural contexts those students may one day find themselves in.

SOLUTIONS AND RECOMMENDATIONS

Anthropology courses approach teaching and learning about human diversity from a range of perspectives that consider the biological, (pre)historical, linguistic, and cultural bases for the fascinating differences and similarities that exist between and within human groups. So it follows that the author's first recommendation is to integrate anthropology and anthropological perspectives – especially cultural relativism – into courses undergoing a shift toward more internationalized curricula with the aim of increasing students' intercultural sensitivity. This serves as a solution to the common problem of simply tacking on international material to a course, without giving students the tools they need to more fully understand why that material is important. Cultural relativism serves as that much-needed tool, and it provides an exceedingly easy-to-use model that would not be out of place in higher education classrooms teaching within disciplines ranging from algebra to zoology.

A second and related suggestion, which can work as a stopgap measure while instructors in other disciplines are coached to revise their courses to contain more international perspectives, would be to simply encourage all students across a given institution to enroll in an anthropology or other social science course that has this sort of perspective by default. Self-serving though this suggestion may seem, if one of the goals of internationalization is to truly increase intercultural understanding and reduce judgement, one cannot ignore how anthropology is already situated to meet that demand. By studying and teaching students to carefully analyze the reasons for human differences, anthropologists highlight the cross-disciplinary utility of cultural relativism. In fact, cultural relativism is not only taught to students via traditional pedagogies like lectures or textbook reading, it is *modeled* by any anthropologist worth their salt.

Of course, if students are to benefit from new international materials, they really need to have a foundation for how to critically engage with their own perspectives, as well. That understanding can come from a degree of familiarity with standpoint theory, which reminds students and instructors alike that, epistemologically speaking, there are many vantage points from which to experience and understand the same thing. When this perspective is coupled with cultural relativism, students begin to see that their standpoint is relative to others'; it is not objectively better or more accurate than another point of view. One caveat, which *must* be integrated into any classroom environment that evokes these perspectives, is that cultural relativism and standpoint serve to increase awareness of the multitude of ideas and practices in the world today, but certainly not to the point where one can ignore violence or abuse that occur because of some cultural ideology.

FUTURE RESEARCH DIRECTIONS

Institutions of higher education in the U.S. now host approximately one million international students, most of whom pay full, out-of-state tuition. And according to a handful of experts at international education marketing and research firms, U.S. schools must continue to change with the times if they are to continue reaping the economic benefits of this particular consequence of globalization (Scott, 2016). One very promising way to do that, of course, is to integrate internationalized courses into all students' programs of study, such that the campus culture is welcoming and empathetic. Anthropology courses, especially those taught in an introductory capacity that reach a broad range of students, are well situated to accomplish such a task.

Subsequent research on the internationalization of college curricula will necessarily vary based on context. That is, scholars and administrators must first consider the particular impacts of globalization that they and their institutions (and their students) face. Is the primary impact an increase in international students? Or is it the growth of some new international industry that may employ graduates? Only then can the process of internationalization hope to prove beneficial to those involved: the outcomes must be mapped to the process itself.

In addition to adequately addressing the particular, contextual outcomes for internationalization that a given institution might desire, future scholarship on internationalizing higher education curricula must inevitably deal in terms of practicable examples. Narrative accounts of successful classroom activities or discussion topics or assignments represent one way to perhaps ease this important transition. Indeed, there is no need for each instructor or institution to reinvent the wheel; scholars working on this topic would do well to provide substantive suggestions for their audience, apart from jargon or theory. To this point, details about a school, a student body, a discipline, or an instructor can approximate the standpoint from which a given piece was written, which can subsequently assist readers in determining which portions of some published account might be best suited to their own learning and teaching context.

Interdisciplinary perspectives can also play a key role in scholarship on internationalization. The author's own perspective from her training and research in anthropology and women's studies have influenced how she views the process and outcomes of internationalization at the classroom level.

Perspectives from scholars and professionals that evoke additional discipline-specific techniques are a necessary contribution if scholarship is to reach the widest audience possible and have the most positive impact on students.

CONCLUSION

Students from a range of backgrounds and life experiences who are enrolled in a degree-granting higher education program clearly stand to benefit from international content that is integrated into the college curriculum. This need is documented in a variety of case studies and other publications, which tend to emphasize that success in an ever-globalizing world relies on students' development in the areas of intercultural competence and cross-cultural empathy (Deardorff, 2006; Haigh, 2007). But the process of changing curricula or introducing new programming is not always an easy or intuitive one, and it depends on the precise goals of a given institution. Often, initial efforts to promote international perspectives are unsuccessful, and fail to provide a holistic perspective that encourages the development of competent, global citizens.

This chapter has put forth a series of perspectives and methods to successfully integrate international and intercultural content into the classroom so that students are well-versed in cultural diversity when they graduate. The author has also suggested that institutions seeking to internationalize students' experience more generally look to anthropology as a model for how to accomplish that goal. In an era when natural science-, technology-, engineering-, and math-oriented courses and careers so often have a stranglehold on resources and imaginations, it is important to remember that students pursuing any kind of career need to be equipped to work with *people* from a variety of backgrounds and life experiences. Indeed, the tide may be turning; employers are now recognizing that students with experience in interdisciplinary liberal arts programs are often more adept at working in a flexible environment, which means those graduates make valuable, adaptable employees in a range of professional fields (Chopp, Frost, & Weiss, 2014; Jacobs, 2015). One highly successful avenue for this kind of exposure is via the social sciences in general, and perhaps anthropology in particular. Students who complete courses in these fields with international content and critical intercultural training are likely to be more empathetic to their future colleagues and better equipped to act as conscientious global citizens.

REFERENCES

Altbach, P. G., & Knight, J. (2007). The internationalization of higher education: Motivations and realities. *Journal of Studies in International Education, 11*(3/4), 290–305. doi:10.1177/1028315307303542

Bennett, J. M., & Bennett, M. J. (2004). Developing intercultural sensitivity: An integrative approach to global and domestic diversity. In D. Landis, J. M. Bennett, & M. J. Bennett (Eds.), Handbook of intercultural training (pp. 147-165). Thousand Oaks, CA: Sage.

Bennett, M. J. (1993). Towards ethnorelativism: A developmental model of intercultural sensitivity. In R. M. Paige (Ed.), Education for the intercultural experience (pp. 21-71). Yarmouth, ME: Intercultural Press.

Boas, F. (1887). Museums of ethnology and their classification. *Science, 9*, 589. PMID:17779725

Chopp, R., Frost, S., & Weiss, D. H. (2014). *Remaking college: Innovation and the liberal arts*. Baltimore, MD: The Johns Hopkins University Press.

Collins, P. H. (1990). *Black feminist thought: Knowledge, consciousness and the politics of empowerment*. New York: Routledge.

Collins, P. H. (1997). Comment on Hekman's "Truth and method: Feminist standpoint theory revisited": Where's the power? *Signs (Chicago, Ill.)*, *22*(2), 375–381. doi:10.1086/495162

Deardorff, D. K. (2006). Identification and assessment of intercultural competence as a student outcome of internationalization. *Journal of Studies in International Education*, *10*(3), 241–266. doi:10.1177/1028315306287002

Donnelly, J. (1984). Cultural relativism and universal human rights. *Human Rights Quarterly*, *6*(4), 400–419. doi:10.2307/762182

Dundes Renteln, A. (1988). Relativism and the search for human rights. *American Anthropologist*, *90*(1), 56–72. doi:10.1525/aa.1988.90.1.02a00040

Fleuhr-Lobban, C. (1995, June 9). Anthropologists, cultural relativism, and universal rights. *The Chronicle of Higher Education*, pp. B1–2.

Fleuhr-Lobban, C. (1998). Cultural relativism and universal human rights. *Anthro Notes*, *20*(2). Retrieved from http://anthropology.si.edu/outreach/anthnote/Winter98/anthnote.html

Fluehr-Lobban, C. (2005). Cultural relativism and universal rights in Islamic law. *Anthropology News*, *46*(9), 23. doi:10.1525/an.2005.46.9.23

Geertz, C. (1973). Thick description: Toward an interpretive theory of culture. In C. Geertz (Ed.), The interpretation of cultures: Selected essays (pp. 3-30). New York: Basic Books.

Gellner, E. (1995). *Anthropology and politics: Revolutions in the sacred grove*. Oxford, UK: Blackwell Publishers.

Georgia Gwinnett College Quality Enhancement Plan. (n.d.). *Student Learning Outcomes*. Retrieved from http://www.ggc.edu/academics/qep/student-learning-outcomes/index.html

Haigh, M. (2009). Fostering cross-cultural empathy with non-western curricular structures. *Journal of Studies in International Education*, *13*(2), 271–284. doi:10.1177/1028315308329791

Haraway, D. (2004). Situated knowledges: The science question in feminism and the privilege of partial perspective. In S. Harding (Ed.), The feminist standpoint theory reader (pp. 81-102). New York, NY: Routledge.

Harding, S. (1993). Rethinking standpoint epistemology: What is strong objectivity? In L. Alcoff & E. Potter (Eds.), Feminist epistemologies (pp. 49-82). New York, NY: Routledge.

Harding, S. (Ed.). (2004). *The feminist standpoint theory reader*. New York, NY: Routledge.

Herdt, G. H. (2006). *The Sambia: Ritual, sexuality, and change in Papua New Guinea*. Belmont, CA: Thomson/Wadsworth.

Homan, A. C., Buengeler, C., Eckhoff, R. A., van Ginkel, W. P., & Voelpel, S. C. (2015). The interplay of diversity training and diversity beliefs on team creativity in nationality diverse teams. *The Journal of Applied Psychology*, *100*(5), 1456–1467. doi:10.1037/apl0000013 PMID:25688641

Jacob, W. J. (2015). Interdisciplinary trends in higher education. *Palgrave Communications*, *1*, 1–5.

Jaggar, A. M. (2016). *Just methods*. New York, NY: Routledge.

Knight, J. (2004). Internationalization remodeled: Definition, approaches, and rationales. *Journal of Studies in International Education*, *8*(1), 5–31. doi:10.1177/1028315303260832

Leask, B. (2001). Bridging the gap: Internationalizing university curricula. *Journal of Studies in International Education*, *5*(2), 100–115. doi:10.1177/102831530152002

Levi-Strauss, C. (1969). *The elementary structures of kinship*. Boston, MA: Beacon Press.

Muir, K. (2016). So what is anthropology anyway? *Anthropology News Teaching and Learning Blog*. Retrieved from http://www.anthropology-news.org/index.php/2016/09/29/so-what-is-anthropology-anyway/

Norris, C. (1996). *Reclaiming truth: Contribution to a critique of cultural relativism*. Durham, NC: Duke University Press.

Oakley, A. (1985). *Sex, gender and society*. London: Gower.

Rachels, J. (2003). *The elements of moral philosophy*. Boston, MA: McGraw Hill.

Scott, A. (2017, October 17). *Foreign students eye U.S. election with caution. Marketplace*. National Public Radio.

Scutt, C., & Hobson, J. (2013). The stories we need: Anthropology, philosophy, narrative and higher education research. *Higher Education Research & Development*, *32*(1), 17–29. doi:10.1080/07294360.2012.751088

Trahar, S. (2013). Autoethnographic journeys in learning and teaching in higher education. *European Education Journal*, *12*(3), 367–375.

Ulin, R. C. (2007). Revisiting cultural relativism: Old prospects for a new cultural critique. *Anthropological Quarterly*, *80*(3), 803–820. doi:10.1353/anq.2007.0051

KEY TERMS AND DEFINITIONS

Anthropology: An academic discipline that approaches the holistic study of humans as a species from combined biological, historical, linguistic, and cultural perspectives; also has a robust practical component.

Cultural Relativism: A perspective that emphasizes the need to consider some practice, experience, or ideology relative to the culture in which it occurs; opposite of ethnocentrism.

Empathy: The ability to understand and identify with the experiences of another; a particularly important component of cultural relativism and intercultural sensitivity.

Globalization: A condition in which human groups are increasingly in contact with processes and people that originate elsewhere; also has a strong economic component that leads to an integrated—though unequal—global economy.

Intercultural: Of or relating to a practice, experience, or ideology that occurs across cultural groups.

Internationalization of the Curriculum: The process of integrating international material, themes, and content into college-level courses, whether by adding new content, international learning experiences, or addressing international diversity that is already present.

Standpoint Theory: Recognizes that each person has their own perspective, related to their socio-cultural location, and that all perspectives should be valued equally.

Chapter 8
Transforming a Beginner's Foreign Language Course Into an Internationalized Course:
Language Exchange Pal Project

Rong Liu
Georgia Gwinnett College, USA

ABSTRACT

To internationalize the campus, a Language Exchange Pal Project was developed to enhance students' cross-cultural experiences in a beginner's Chinese foreign language course. The Language Exchange Pal Project, using Skype or QQ (similar to Skype), is a great tool to increase students' global perspective by working in communities of practice with individuals in China who are learning English as a foreign language. Through the technology, students enjoy the opportunity to use the target language in an authentic communicative context and collaborate with their international partners. These two groups collaborate about their language and culture through messages and/or live connections via Skype, chat, or other software systems such as QQ. This chapter shares the process of transforming Chinese 1001 into an i-course, present the Language Exchange Pal Project, describe its challenges, and discuss the preliminary results of the research findings of the Language Exchange Pal Project based on students' survey and interview.

INTRODUCTION

In response to the call to internationalize the campus and to rethink the curricula to meet the changing needs of students in the new century, a Language Exchange Pal Project was developed to enhance students' cross-cultural experiences in a beginner's Chinese foreign language course. Three key objectives of this i-course are for students to be able to describe and evaluate their own cultures, describe and evaluate the target cultures, and communicate with persons of different cultures. The Language Exchange Pal Project, using Skype or QQ, a social networking tool similar to Skype, is a great program to increase students'

DOI: 10.4018/978-1-5225-2791-6.ch008

global perspective by working in communities of practice with individuals in China who are learning English as a Foreign Language. Through the technology, students enjoy an opportunity to use the target language in an authentic communicative context and collaborate with their international partners who teach each other their language and culture through messages or live connections via Skype, chat, or other software systems such as QQ.

This chapter will share the process of transforming Chinese 1001 into an internationalized course, i.e., an i-course, present the Language Exchange Pal Project, describe its challenges, and discuss the initial results of the research findings of the Language Exchange Pal Project based on students' survey and one student's interview. The data collection is very limited and ongoing. However, based on past research (Darhower, 2007; O'Dowd, 2006; Ware & Kramsch, 2005), the project has great potential on helping students achieve communicative and cultural competence in the target language.

Background

Educators and policy makers increasingly acknowledge the value of global competence and intercultural understanding. The National Education Association (NEA) declared in 2010 that "Global competence is a 21st century imperative" (NEA, 2010). Other educators and organizations caution that global competence "is not a luxury, but a necessity" (National Geographic-Roper, 2002; The Asia Society, 2008). The National Intelligence Council (2008) in its report Global *Trends, 2025: A transformed World* asserts that global challenges will constitute most if not all of the incoming challenges humankind will face. Indeed, the U.S Census Bureau reported that 20% percent of the jobs is tied to international trade (U.S. Census Bureau, 2005).

Despite the importance of global competence, the American Council on Education (ACE), in its most recent assessment report of internationalization on US campuses, states that "This optimism about the progress of internationalization is not always grounded in reality (ACE, 2012). The 2012 data show solid gains in some areas, but stagnation or even declines in others, and that progress varies widely by institutional sector." One of the dramatic declines is the percentage of colleges with an undergraduate foreign language requirement for graduation: it has dropped from 53% in 2001 to only 37% in 2012. This contrasts rather sharply with the research findings in the second and foreign language field that the study of a second language enhances global competence and also cultivates cognitive development, critical thinking, and creativity (Cooper, 1987; Olsen and Brown, 1992; Saville-Troike, 1984). In 2007, the Modern Language Association of America (MLA) issued its report "Foreign Languages and Higher Education: New Structures for a Changed World", which made recommendations to transform foreign language curriculum, including course redesign around cultural rather than exclusively literary-historical (MLA Ad hoc Committee on Foreign Languages, 2007). Since the publication of the report, many projects have conducted to transform the curriculum with different approaches ranging from integrating a foreign language and content (i.e., the Languages Across the Curriculum movement) to study abroad programs (Gehlhar, 2009; Klee, 2009). However, no formal report is found regarding internationalizing a beginner's foreign language course. When discussing foreign languages' role in internationlizaiton, it is clear that foreign language departments do not play a major role in internationalization efforts and are often not invited at the internationalization meetings (Swaffar & Urlaub, 2014). The current chapter is going to fill a gap in the research by documenting one example of transforming a beginner's Chinese foreign language course into an internationalized course.

Internationalizing an entry level foreign language course is a direct response to one of the initiatives for Georgia Gwinnett College's (GGC) 2013-2018 Quality Enhancement Plan (QEP): Internationalization of the Curriculum: Engaging the World to Develop Global Citizens. The focus of the QEP is assisting students in developing intercultural competence. I-courses are offered by GGC to promote student learning and development in intercultural competence and skills. Currently 65 courses are verified as i-courses at GGC. GGC, the most diverse college (public or private) in the entire Southern region as rated by U.S. News & World Report magazine, is an ideal place to carry out the internationalization of the curriculum to reflect the increasingly globalization and diversity needs in the community.

Despite the agreement on the importance of global competence, researchers have less consensus on the definition of global competence. Different definitions of global competence have been proposed. NEA defines it as " the acquisition of in-depth knowledge and understanding of international issues, an appreciation of and ability to learn and work with people from diverse linguistic and cultural backgrounds, proficiency in a foreign language, and skills to function productively in an interdependent world community" (NEA, 2010). It also points out that global competence includes four areas: international awareness, appreciation of cultural diversity, proficiency in foreign languages, and competitive skills. The American Council on Education describes global competence as the knowledge, skills, and attitudes needed to live and work in a multicultural and interconnected world. The American Council on Teaching (ACTFL) explains global competence as the ability to:

Communicate in the language of the people with whom one is interacting;

Interact with awareness, sensitivity, empathy, and knowledge of the perspectives of others;

Withhold judgment, examining one's own perspectives as similar to or different from the perspectives of people with whom one is interacting;

Be alert to cultural differences in situations outside of one's culture including noticing cues indicating miscommunication or causing an inappropriate action or response in a situation;

Act respectfully according to what is appropriate in the culture and the situation where everyone is not of the same culture or language background, including gestures, expressions, and behaviors;

Increase knowledge about the products, practices, and perspectives of other cultures. (The American Council on the Teaching of Foreign Languages, 2014)

This paper uses intercultural competence and global competence interchangeably to refer to the global mindset and skills to be competitive in a global society.

Many educators assume that a foreign language course is international in nature because leaning another language broadens one's views and fosters intercultural competence and skills in the target language. This is true in general, however, this does not automatically make it an i-course. An i-course at GGC has to meet the following standards.

Operational Definition of an i-Course

A course is considered an i-course if:

1. Has a score of three or four on the Content Rubric (See Appendix I), indicating that over 30% of the course material is international or global in focus;
2. Addresses a minimum of two of the QEP SLOs, drawn from two separate SLO categories as determined by the Outcomes Rubric (See Appendix II);
    a. Category 1 is Cultural Awareness and includes SLOs 1 and 2,
    b. Category 2 is Communication and Collaboration and includes SLOs 3 and 4, and
    c. Category 3 is Application/Problem Solving and includes SLO 5.
3. Expects students to demonstrate competence at a developmentally appropriate level, i.e.:
    a. For lower level courses, a minimum of two SLOs (in 2 of 3 categories) must be met at least at the novice level.
    b. For upper level courses, a minimum of two SLOs (in 2 of 3 categories) must be met at least at the developing level.

(Georgia Gwinnett College, 2015)

MAIN STEPS TO DEVELOPING AN I-COURSE IN CHINESE 1001

To develop an i-course in Chinese 1001, the author attended a semester long Internalized Learning Program (ILP) training program organized by Center for Teaching Excellence (CTE). At the beginning of the ILP program, a three-day Intercultural Workshop, led by Todd Odgers, an intercultural relations specialist and the Principal of NorQuest College's Centre for Intercultural Education in Edmonton, prepared faculty to revise or design courses to help students achieve the QEP learning outcomes around intercultural communication, collaboration, and problem solving. On the final day of the Intercultural Workshop, the author and other participants prepared presentations about how to integrate learning from the workshop into their teaching and course design. The ILP also conducted several group meetings followed by individual consultative sessions with ILP facilitators. In the semester following the Intercultural Workshop, the ILP faculty revised or designed a course as an internationalized course. The following describes the theoretical orientation and the steps of internationalizing Chinese 1001.

Intercultural Workshop

The workshop started with an assessment of intercultural competence by Intercultural Development Inventory (IDI) developed by Dr. Michell Hammer. The assessment tool describes intercultural competence as the ability to understand and adapt behavior to cultural difference and commonality. The intercultural development continuum, originally developed Dr. Milton Bennett in the Developmental Model of Intercultural Sensitivity, identifies specific orientations ranging from more monocultural to more global mindsets (Bennett & Bennett, 2004; Bennett, Bennett, & Allen, 2003). On this intercultural development continuum, there are five stages: Denial (People at this stage only recognize surface cultural differences),

Polarization (two different orientations: Defense refers to people view one's own culture uncritically and other cultures overcritically; Reversal refers to people view one's own culture critically and other cultures uncritically), Minimization (People emphasize commonality and may overlook deeper cultural differences), Acceptance (People accept one's own and other cultures), and Adaptation (People are able to adapt and behave culturally appropriate). IDI reports a sixth dimension, cultural disengagement, which evaluates the degree of detachment from a primary cultural group. Surprisingly, results showed a large gap between the perceived orientation and the developmental (actual) orientation for the author. In other words, there was an overestimate of the level of intercultural competence on the continuum. Having been in the country for more than ten years and having been teaching languages for more than five years in the States, the author was reluctant to accept the findings at first. However, after consultation and self-refection, the result can be quite common and understandable, especially for educators.

Many instructors tend to emphasize commonalities for bridging across cultural diversity when using teaching strategies to make sure everyone can participate in classroom discussions. Doing so makes instructors have a blind spot because they may not be attending to how cultural differences need to be recognized and adapted to help students learn effectively. Furthermore, the author has taught English as a Second Language for many years, and this might have impacted the orientation as well since one of the tasks in the class is to teach students to adapt to the dominant American culture, i.e., what most Americans typically do, for example, writing conventions in composition classes. During this process, it is common for instructors to minimize the differences and utilize strategies that seems to work for most students, most of whom come from a different background. What this IDI assessment revealed is that even a language teacher with many years of experience could benefit from the assessment and need further training in intercultural competence. The workshop helped the author further understand the concepts of intercultural competence, and develop skills to cope with diversity and stereotypes, and reflect on how to use the concepts in teaching. The workshop also motivated the author to develop the current project, an i-course in Chinese.

12 Steps Integrated Course Design Process (GGC ILP Program)

The major theoretical orientation adopted when transforming the course is the Model of Integrated Course Design proposed by Dr. Fink (2003). This model takes a systematic, learning centered approach to course designs. The approach is widely adopted because it addresses a key question about how educators enhance students' significant learning. Interested readers can download and follow a self-directed guide to designing a course for significant learning (See references, Fink, 2005). Within this model, several important concepts are backward course design---outcomes first (Wiggins and McTighe, 2005), significant learning---long term, lasting learning (Fink, 2003), educative assessment---learning enhancing assessment (Juwah et al, 2004), and active learning---doing and thinking (Bonwell and Eison, 1991). Those concepts will be further illustrated in the following as the author discusses the twelve steps of the course design. The 12-step approach needs time and efforts but it is inspiring and rewarding as shown by the author's experience.

There are four major components in the model: Situational Factors, i.e., circumstances and context of the course that will be used to make important decisions about the course; Learning Goals, i.e., what should students learn?; Feedback and Assessment, i.e., how will we know if those goals are achieved?; Teaching and Learning Activities, i.e., what should students and the instructor do to accomplish the goals. Lastly, the model emphasizes that the four components should support and reinforce each other.

Step 1

Identify Situational Factors. Situational Factors will be used to make important decisions about the course such as course outcomes and expectations. For example, question #2: General Context of the learning situation: What learning expectations are placed on this course or curriculum by: the university, college and/or department? Society? Answering this question on the worksheet #1 helped the author identify learning expectations: the author's college emphasizes global competence and multi-perspectives (QEP) and the foreign language profession employs the national standards for language education, i.e., world-readiness standards for learning languages (The National Standards Collaborative Board, 2015). The world readiness standards contain five global areas (5Cs): Communication, cultures, Connections, Comparisons, and Communities. Communication refers to the ability to communicate effectively in more than one language in order to function in a variety of situations and for multiple purposes; Cultures mean to interact with cultural competence and understanding; Connections are the ability to connect with other disciplines and acquire information and diverse perspectives in order to use the language to function in academic and career-related situations; Comparisons are to develop insight into the nature of language and culture in order to interact with cultural competence; Communities stand for the skills to communicate and interact with cultural competence in order to participate in multilingual communities at home and around the world. Clearly, the foreign language education's national standards are in line with the need to develop global competence at the current institution.

Step 2

Formulate Significant Learning Goals. This step is helpful for the author because in the past, the focus was primarily on what topics or lessons to cover in the class. The new model recommends instructors move beyond "understand and remember " types of learning and add more significant learning goals such as critical thinking, learning how to apply knowledge from the course, learning to solve real world problems, changing the way students think about themselves and others, realizing the importance of life-long learning. Fink (2003) listed a taxonomy of six major types of significant learning: Foundational Knowledge (understanding and remembering information and ideas), Application (skills and thinking and projects), Integration (connecting ideas, people and realms of life), Human Dimension (learning about oneself and others), Caring (developing new feelings, interests and values), Learning How to learn (becoming better students and self-learning skills). When answering the question "What would the impact of this course be on students, 2 or 3 years later?" The author would like the students to be able to move along the intercultural competence continuum. Considering this course is the beginning level, specific goals were proposed. For example, the author would like the students to build up an understanding of and sensitivity to the cultural foundations of some Chinese language usages and develop some basic knowledge of Chinese culture, traditions, and society (e.g., politeness in Chinese culture, i.e., how to show respect, express modesty).

Step 3

Feedback and Assessment Procedures. In contrast to the traditional two mid-terms and a final exam assessment, the integrated course design features educative assessment, which incorporates assignments to enhance learning (Anderson et al, 2001). What characterizes educative assessment is learning-centered and it composes of four components: Forward-looking Assessment, which uses assessment that replicates real-life contexts; Criteria and Standards, which distinguish excellent accomplishment from poor performance; Self-assessment, which asks students to assess their own work; FIDeLity Feedback, which give students feedback that is Frequent, Immediate, Discriminating, and Lovingly delivered. One example assignment came out of this step was that: After learning major cities in China, students are asked to sell a US product in China and decide which city to use to enter the Chinese market and why? This task is authentic because many companies face this question when entering the Chinese market.

Step 4

Teaching and Learning Activities. In this step, active learning is preferred over traditional lectures and discussions, which are mostly passive learning. Active learning is described as doing things and thinking things (Bonwell and Eison, 1991), and it entails providing a variety of activities of getting information and ideas, providing experience and reflection. Examples of active learning are debates, problem solving activities, case studies, and simulations. One task the author designed using this step is that after students present a cultural characteristic about China, and compare and contrast this cultural characteristic with a cultural aspect of the United States, they teach three key words in Chinese. Students reflect on what three items they have learned, two items they do not know or understand, and one item they would like to know more (a 3-2-1 reflection task). This reflective dialogue gives students in-depth reflective experience about understanding the target culture and their own culture.

Step 5

Integration. The goal of this step is to integrate steps 1 to 4, making sure all components are aligned. To ensure that the situational factors, learning goals, feedback and assessment, and the teaching and learning activities all support each other, the author followed the worksheet by listing each major learning goal for the course, designing ways of assessing the learning, actual teaching and learning activities, and helpful resources. For example, one significant learning goal of this course is cultural understanding and sensitivity: Students will build up an understanding of and sensitivity to the cultural foundations of some Chinese language usages and develop some basic knowledge of Chinese culture, traditions, and society. One teaching and learning activity is a weekly student presentation about Chinese culture and comparing and contrasting that particular phenomenon with American culture. The formal assessment and feedback is a rubric and a 3-2-1 refection, and the informal assessment is answering other students' questions and discussions at the end of the presentation.

Steps 6 to 8

Course Structure, Instructional Strategy and Creating the Overall Scheme of Learning Activities. This is the intermediate phase to organize and assemble the components into a whole course. Important questions are when to introduce each topic, what instructional strategy to use, and how to integrate the course structure and the instructional strategy for the class. The result is a week-by-week schedule for the course with topics or concepts and learning activities. What is important during this phase is to ensure that the type of learning activities vary and the complexity of learning progresses through the semester. One of such example activity is the Language Exchange Pal Project, in which students gradually complete more challenging tasks with their pals. More details about this project will be discussed in the following sections.

Steps 9 to 12

Grading and Grade Book Design, What could Go Wrong? Course Syllabus Planning, Course Evaluation, and Self-assessment. During this final phase, the goals are to coordinate the grading system, de-bug problems, write a syllabus and design a thorough evaluation of the course and teaching. One important lesson the author learned from this phase is that there is no need to grade everything formally because grading is supposed to enhance leaning and not assigning a grade to some activities can actually provide low stake tasks for students to grow. Another lesson is that problems may arise and it is always wise to have an alternative plan such as using different software or giving students more time to complete key assignments. This was the case for this course as shown in the challenges of the project section.

Specific Considerations of the Course to Meet QEP Student Learning Outcomes (SLOs)

As shown in the operational definition of an i-course section, to be an i-course, a course needs to have at least 30% in global content and should address at least two SLOs from three different categories including cultural awareness (SLOs 1 and 2), communication and collaboration (SLOs 3 and 4), and application and problem solving (SLO 5). Since Chinese 1001 is an elementary foreign language course, the content is international in nature. The course is also a lower level class, it aims to meet the novice level of the SLOs chosen (SLOs 1, 2 and 3). To align the course with the discipline of national standards, the course focuses on communicating with native speakers; developing communicative competence over studying grammar for grammar's sake, providing students with valuable cultural knowledge and skills about the target language and their own culture; experiencing the culture, and discussing global events and international news. One of the important significant goals is that the course debunks common stereotypes about China using the techniques learned from the intercultural workshop, i.e., D.I.E, which stands for describe the phenomenon, interpret it and evaluate. Another technique useful for students' intercultural competence development is when something is up, students can suspend their judgment first and then try to make sense and inform further action. For example, students see a video about young Chinese men in the street holding hands together or holding shoulders and they may be surprised and conclude that there are so many gay men in China. However, this is a myth. Students should suspend their judgment first by trying to make sense of the phenomenon. Considering the circumstances and the cultural norms helps inform the evaluation or action. This technique can be summarized as: I notice something is up; I suspend my judgment; I decode what is actually happening; I act culturally appropriately. Using this I- suspend-my-judgment technique and critical incidents like this will help students cultivate their intercultural competence.

Sample Activities and Materials

The following table presents sample materials designed for the i-course using the above 12 steps integrated course design.

Table 1. Sample course goals, teaching and learning activities, and assessment for Chinese 1001

Course Goals	QEP SLOs	Teaching/Learning Activities	Assessment
Cultural understanding & sensitivity. Students will build up an understanding of and sensitivity to the cultural foundations of some Chinese language usages and develop some basic knowledge of Chinese culture, traditions, and society (e.g., politeness in Chinese culture (e.g., how to show respect, express modesty);	SLO 1: Students will be able to describe and evaluate their own cultures in relation to history, values, politics, communication styles, economy, or beliefs and practices. SLO Level: Novice Identifies own cultural rules and biases (e.g. with a strong preference for those rules shared with own cultural group and seeks the same in others.)	• Students discuss questions in English about greetings in their own culture/community—1. How do people greet each other when meeting for the first time? 2. Do people say their given name or family name first? 3. How do acquaintances or close friends address each other? • Students learn to say formal and informal greetings in Chinese. • Students compare and contrast greetings in Chinese and in English: focus on what is considered polite in each culture. • Students discuss questions in English about shaking hands in the Chinese manner, exchanging hand shaking, personal space in Chinese, and when one must use a formal or informal greeting to show respect and politeness. The readings and discussions explicitly highlight differences in personal distance and physical contact in terms of what is expected in China and what is expected in the U.S. and notes how an interaction between individuals from the two different cultures could be awkward, if they weren't aware of one another's social norms. One discussion question really focuses on this point. • Students are asked to perform greetings with each other and with the professor, paying attention to the dictates of familiarity and gender. Students also pay attention to body languages. • Students watch a video in which native speakers of Chinese greet each other and begin conversations. For each encounter in the video, students identify the likely relationship between the speakers, based on their nonverbal communication. • Students discuss the meaning of their names and then discuss the meaning of Chinese names. • Students choose their own Chinese names; • Students make a name/business card in Chinese and in English; • Students learn most common Chinese family names and the appropriate way to ask someone's names—it is polite to ask for family names rather than the full name when meeting someone for the first time. • Students learn the concept of intimacy when using first names in China. The use of given names in China often suggests a much higher degree of intimacy than is the case in the west.	• Students post their Chinese names/English names to d2l (course management system); Students write a short paragraph about their English name: the origin and meaning and what is in a name; they write about why they choose the Chinese name; The names must be meaningful and be a good name according to the Chinese customs; • Students turn in the business card both in English and Chinese and will receive a grade for the appropriateness and accuracy; • Students fill in forms before watching a video showing Chinese people interacting, during watching the video and after watching the video (see sample form below) This activity is conducted for each unit for this course **Sample form:** LESSON 1: Greetings Previewing Activity How do people greet each other in your culture? (Answer in English.) Situation What do people do? What do people say? First time meeting your teacher Running into an old friend Interviewing a candidate for a job PostViewing Activity Compare the way people introduce themselves in your own culture to the Chinese way.
Cultural understanding & sensitivity: visiting friends in China	SLO 2: Students will be able to describe and evaluate other cultures in relation to history, values, politics, communication styles, economy, or beliefs and practices. SLO Level: Novice Identifies elements important to members of another culture in relation to its history, values, politics, communication styles, economy, or beliefs and practices.	• Students learn to use Chinese to: welcome a visitor; introduce one person to another; compliment someone on his/her house; ask for beverages as a guest; offer beverages to a visitor politely; chitchat; tea culture; learn about privacy in China. • Students discuss questions in English about visiting friends in their own culture/community—1. Is it common to pay a visit to a friends' house without advance notice? 2. Do people bring anything when visiting a friend's home? What is considered a poor/taboo gift? 3. What are some of the common beverages and foods offered to visitors? • Students compare and contrast visiting friends in Chinese and in English: focus on what is considered polite in each culture. For example, never bring a clock as a gift in China because the word clock in Chinese sounds like Chinese character Zhong, which means death or end. This gift could be perceived as death threatening. • Students discuss questions in English about privacy in the Chinese manner, and when one must constantly answer "private questions" such as your age, marital status, salary, the price of your house. The readings and discussions explicitly highlight differences in privacy in terms of what is expected in China and what is expected in the U.S. and notes how an interaction between individuals from the two different cultures could be awkward, if they weren't aware of one another's social norms. Appointments are not necessary for visiting friends in China. Requiring an appointment can alienate your friends in China. Sharing personal information in China is an important gesture of trust. • Students discuss the proper way to compliment in both cultures. The responses to compliments are different. Chinese people tend to be modest and will typically deny your compliments. Students will experience this awkwardness of responding by using the Chinese way when speaking English or vice versa. • Students are asked to perform introduction, being a host with each other and with the professor, paying attention to the dictates of privacy and politeness. • Students watch a video in which native speakers of Chinese or English visiting each other and begin conversations. For each encounter in the video, students identify the politeness between the speakers, based on their topics nonverbal communication.	• Students fill in forms before watching the video, during watching the video and after watching the video. Sample activities: **Viewing Activities** A. Watch the video. Check True (对) or False (错). 1. This is the first time that Gao meets Liyou. **PostViewing Activity** Write a short paragraph in Chinese about Li You and Wang Peng's visit from Gao Wenzhong's perspective. **Culture Minute Viewing Activity** Watch the video. Answer the questions in Chinese. 1. Does Sufei greet appropriate to the family? **PostViewing Activity** Compare the way people behave when they visit friends' houses in your own culture to the Chinese way. • Students take tests/quizzes about privacy, complementing, and politeness in both spoken test and written test: For example, students are asked to be a host/hostess or a visitor when taking a speaking test in Chinese. They will make a compliment to each other and respond in Chinese; They will chat about some sensitive topics such as age, salary and etc. • Students take written tests. Sample items are: Which of the following is NOT an appropriate gift when visiting a friend in China? A.a clock B. a watch C. spirits D. some fruits (the actual test will be in Chinese). • Other sample cultural related items are: Chinese Culture Quiz Who was the Chinese girl warrior that fought against the Huns?

continued on following page

Table 1. Continued

Course Goals	QEP SLOs	Teaching/Learning Activities	Assessment
Language functions. Students will acquire basic knowledge of socioculturalinfluences on Chinese language use, and will be able to apply the knowledge to conduct spoken and written communication appropriately in some daily situations (e.g., greetings, talking about one's family, talking about dates and time, dinner table conversation, talking about hobbies, and visiting friends). Cultural understanding & sensitivity. Students will build up an understanding of and sensitivity to the cultural foundations of some Chinese language usages and develop some basic knowledge of Chinese culture, traditions, and society	SLO 3: Students will communicate effectively with persons from different cultures. SLO Level: Novice Articulates the verbal and nonverbal communications used in own culture; identifies some cultural differences in verbal and nonverbal communication.	• Group and partnered conversation in a language other than English with language pals from China or online chatting forums: **Language Exchange Pal Program guidelines (see below for more details)** Students have a Chinese native speaking college student in China who is studying English as your language exchange pal. Students use QQ, software similar to Skype, or other online tools such as Wechat. First assignment: email your language pal in China and introduce yourself using Chinese: including your Chinese name, your occupation, your nationality. Tell him/her that you are learning Chinese. • In class context based written exercises in a language other than English • In class context based oral exercises in a language other than English • In class vocabulary and grammar drills in a language other than English	• Individual oral presentation about a cultural topic in the target language: Students choose a topic of their interest about Chinese culture and do a PPT presentation; Students are required to teach the class 5-10 words in Chinese. Students must use Chinese when possible (introduce themselves, introduce key concepts). Students write a short one minute paper after each presentation: 321: 3 things I have learned; 2 things I want to know more; 1 thing I do not understand. • Submit sample chatting with native speakers of Chinese to d2l • Individual Exam/Test/Quiz (M/C & Short Answer & Short Essay) • Individual writing assignment in a language other than English • Individual oral exam in a language other than English

THE LANGUAGE EXCHANGE PAL PROJECT (LEP)

Going through the training and the 12 steps of course design, the author found that the Language Exchange Pal project is perfectly aligned with the significant learning outcomes and the QEP SLOs—combining intercultural competence and language skills with active learning. In this LEP project, students interact with Chinese college students in China using internet-based technology such as email, Skype and QQ (an instant messenger system similar to Windows Messenger and Skype). The project has the potential to bring the world to the classroom. To get the most out of the project, the author assigned tasks related to the course goals, including introducing family members, comparing visiting friends in both countries, and other activities. . Moreover, students complete a reflection journal each week and submit sample recordings of the conversation, which provides students a chance to reflect on their learning.

Potential Benefits of the LEP Project

- Help students achieve communicative and cultural competence in Chinese;
- Cultivate students' language skills in real communication;
- Provide students' opportunities of application of what have learned in class and give them chances to learn new language skills: new vocabulary, grammar and colloquial Chinese, listening comprehension;
- Bring the world of Chinese culture and language to American students using internet based technology; enhanced learning takes place in and beyond the confines of the traditional classroom
- Break the constraining boundary of geographical conditions;
- Students also take control of their own learning because they need to be proactive in the program: find topics, ask questions, and seek their partner's guidance and collaborate to make it happen.

Guidelines of the LEP for Students

You will have a Chinese native speaking college student in China who is studying English as your language exchange pal. Sign up today. You will use QQ, software similar to Skype.

- Each week: use Chinese for 30-45 minutes first and then use English for 30-45 minutes;
- Sometimes, I will assign activities/tasks; When there are no assigned tasks, it is free chat time.
- CC me when emailing each other; Record at least one session of your conversation.
  Four Steps:
  Step 1: Conversation About One or Many Topics (Approximately 20-25 Minutes):
  + Partners talk about whatever they wish and whatever there is of their interest. Participant 1 (proficient speaker) should pay attention to WHAT and HOW participant 2 (student) says things in the target language. Participant 1 should be a good listener and respond to what participant 2 says in order to keep the conversation going. At the same time (and this will take practice!) the proficient speaker should keep taking SOME (not all) notes of the vocabulary that his / her student needs, his /her grammar mistakes and pronunciation problems (ONLY those that affect comprehension). These notes will function as guidelines for the next step.
  Step 2: Language Feedback (Approximately 10-15 Minutes)
  + It is necessarily done in the last 10-15 minutes. Do not overwhelm your partner. This is the period of the lesson in which the participant 1 (the proficient speaker) will use the notes he/ she has taken while his /her partner was talking with him/her. The partner, who is playing the role of the teacher (the language expert), should not give long grammar explanations, but be objective and focus his /her comments on the grammar, vocabulary, or pronunciation problem, preferably.
  Step 3: Shared Reflection on Session (Approximately 5-10 Minutes):
  + First, the proficient speaker can ask his /her partner how he/ she felt while speaking the target language. The proficient speaker should listen attentively to his /her partner's feelings, fears and problems. Only after he/ she has expressed his /her point of view about his /he performance, the proficient speaker should start making brief comments about it. The proficient speaker should be encouraging, look for positive points, and praise his /her partner's risk taking and accomplishment s. He/she should be attentive to possible competition and comparison between his /her partner's performance and his /her own, and remember that the *program* is a cooperative, reciprocal and mutual endeavor, not a destructive competition for one partner to show off that he/ she is better than the other. Shared reflection on the session is important for reviewing common agreements and building team identity, in the sense that partners can talk about how they wish their learning story of the program to unfold. Between one session and another, both partner s should take a few minutes to leave the room, to stretch, to relax and /or to have something to drink.
  Step 4: Post Session Activity: Fill in the Reflection Journal (15 to 25 minutes) (See Appendix III)

This step will help you reflect what you have achieved in each session.
(Guidelines adapted from Telles and Vassallo, 2006)

Initial Students' Perceptions

Although the author only has very limited preliminary data regarding the LEP program, past research suggest that it is likely to make a positive impact on students' learning (Darhower, 2007; O'Dowd, 2006; Ware & Kramsch, 2005). Based on the end of course evaluation survey, students expressed their positive opinion about the project. When answering the course survey question at the end of the semester in 2015: What I found most valuable about this course was: Some sample comments are:

- *I was able to apply what Ilearned (sic) to the outside world.*
- *Learning new chinese (sic) words*
- *Learning the culture and values of China and how to apply Chinese language on an international scale.*
- *What I found most valuable about the course is the history of chinese(sic) culture.*
- *Loved this course. Professor Liu was very engaging and informative.*
- *Our trip to China Town.*
- *learning a different language.*
- *the new ideas and insight into Chinese culture through the learning of their language.*

Other positive outcomes are: at least two students still keep contact with their pal in China and they became friends; Students are motivated to learn more; students are satisfied with the course. The overall global index of the course in 2015 is 3.9 out of 4. Students rated 3.9 for instructional design, 3.8 for instructional delivery, 3.9 for student-teacher engagement and 3.9 for overall evaluation.

When responding to a survey for this project, students made the following comments regarding their experience:

- *Learning about Chinese from a native speaker in mainland China was very interesting.*
- *I was concerned about the video exchange. I was worried that he wouldn't understand me when I spoke Chinese to him, but he said I talked well and also corrected me.*

The writer also interviewed one student and recorded the interview. The student provided his perspective about the LEP project, showing the activity is aligned with the significant learning goals in this i-course. His overall experience is very positive because he said that he was immersed in the Chinese language and culture, his pal taught him Chinese, and he learned much more out of class. He also got to know more people, global friendship and an opportunity to share and talked about pop culture including Walking Dead. What is most valuable for him is that he gained a better understanding of the target culture and people. He observed the difference between collectivism versus individualism because his pal is more family oriented and every time they talked his pal used "we Chinese people". His pal quoted Confucius for many cases while he would just use his own words. What is considered cliché here in the States may be so in China. The interviewee also liked the activity because they shared cultures including movies, food and pictures. Both of them love food and they exchanged pictures of food. He tried to explain the differences between Mexicans and Latinos but his pal did not recognize the differences even after his explanation. They also shared history of the U.S., love stories and music. The student highly recommends this activity to future students because to him language is the expressions of the culture and to learn a language one has to learn its culture. He urges students to come out of their comfort zone and go out there interacting with people using the target language. The activity clearly provides rich learning experiences for the student based on the topics and cultural values he discovered during the cross-cultural interaction.

Challenges of the Project:

When asked about the difficulties, students provide the following comments:

- *Finding the time we're we are both awake*
- *Time difference between China and America is 12 hours thus making it very difficult to communicate live. Most communication/replies were done one or two days after each message was sent.*
- *I was concerned about the time difference. I was worried if I was disturbing my language pal because I kept forgetting his schedule.*

This echoes the writer's concern that due to the time zone difference, finding common time for the activity can be challenging, especially for the synchronous video conferencing. The best time for both parties is either in the early morning or in the evening since there is a 12 or 13 hours difference in time (13 during summer time in Georgia). One possible solution is that students sent asynchronous messages or voices using Wechat (the mobile version of QQ) or QQ. Another way is to use an event organizer for both pals and send reminders in advance. A third solution is to find students in the US who are studying English and can speak Chinese.

Another challenge is that American students have limited language proficiency in Chinese while their Chinese counterparts are more advanced in English because they have been learning English since middle school. It is easy for students to rely on English for the conversation. To tackle this problem, more scaffolding or materials are needed to support a meaning conversation. Small and manageable tasks can also help in this situation. The student the author interviewed also mentioned that miscommunication can be a problem because of limited language proficiency and sometimes they used an online translator. One particular example he cited is that in Chinese one puts two verbs together (去上班 go work literally, meaning go to work) while in English it does not make sense. It is also due to the fact that Chinese relies on the context to make sense. He gave one example: When he asked his pal about what he usually would like to do on his usual time. The pal said just the usual but for Americans what that meant. His pal had to explain further. So he explained to his pal that in America people do not just say the usual but tell what they actually do. His pal was shocked about the cultural difference. In fact, this communication breakdown is a learning experience for both parties. They realized a specific cultural difference: high context versus low context.

A third challenge is getting pals actively involved from the other institution. The instructor from the other school did not assign specific tasks for their students to complete and this sometimes makes it hard for pals to be engaged in the activity. American students sometimes got no response. One improvement can be that all participants are required to complete certain tasks and their performance or completion of the tasks will be part of their course grade.

FUTURE RESEARCH DIRECTIONS

Although foreign language education is considered a pivotal part of the global competence, the number of learners and programs are declining in the U.S. As the need to internationalize college curriculum is increasingly recognized in the higher education sector, foreign language educators need to seize the chance to participate in the internationalization process. Transforming a current course into an i-course takes time and efforts, and it should not be taken for granted as shown by the current study. Even an experienced language teacher could still benefit from intercultural competence training. Further investigation is needed to inform the revision process. What role should foreign language programs play in the current internationalization movement? How do we know if a transformed course is truly international? What is the best model for a fully internationalized foreign language course? Language Across Disciplines seems to regain interest but more studies are needed to examine its impact. Those are important questions for future studies because as curriculum internationalization is not just about content and it requires pedagogical change as well (Zimitat, 2008).

Future studies should gather more data about the LEP project to make it possible to generate generalizations. The current study is limited in sample size and only provides some preliminary data; broad generalizations and definitive conclusion are not possible. Future studies should also exam what really happens when students engage in the LEP activities. How do instructors move students along the intercultural competence continuum? What is the best approach for dealing with stereotypes? One danger of interacting with native speakers is that it only reinforces students' stereotypes. How do we debunk stereotypes?

CONCLUSION

The chapter documents the author's efforts to transform a beginner's foreign language course into an i-course. As shown by the author's experience, even a foreign language course needs revision to meet the criteria of an i-course. Using a 12-step integrated course design model, the author first identified situational factors, selected significant learning goals, chose assessment measures and designed teaching and learning activities; then, the author created the course structure, instructional strategy, and integrated them into the overall sequence of learning. Last, the author debugged the course design, picked grading system, planned course syllabus and course evaluation. The process has been guided by several important theoretical notions including backward design, significant leaning goals, educative assessment, and active learning. During the process of searching for an engaging learning and teaching activity, the LEP project stands out because it matches the definition of a rich learning experience. The whole process is time consuming, but inspiring and rewarding as well. Students' initial feedback about the course is positive, and that is the best reward an educator can hope for.

REFERENCES

Adams, T. M. (1996). Languages across the curriculum: Taking stock. *ADFL Bulletin, 28*, 9–19. doi:10.1632/adfl.28.1.9

Anderson, L. W., Krathwohl, D. R., Airasian, P. W., Mayer, R. W., Pintrich, P. R., Raths, J., & Wittrock, M. C. (Eds.). (2001). *A taxonomy for learning teaching and assessing*. New York: Longman.

Bennett, J. M., & Bennett, M. J. (2004). Developing intercultural sensitivity: An integrative approach to global and domestic diversity. In D. Landis, J. Bennett, & M. Bennett (Eds.), *Handbook of intercultural training* (3rd ed.; pp. 147–165). Thousand Oaks, CA: Sage. doi:10.4135/9781452231129.n6

Bennett, J. M., Bennett, M. J., & Allen, W. (2003). Developing intercultural competence in the language classroom. In D. L. Lange & R. M. Paige (Eds.), *Culture as the core: Perspectives on culture in second language learning*. Greenwich, CT: Information Age Publishing.

Bennett, M. J. (2004). Becoming Interculturally Competent. In J. Wurzel (Ed.), *Toward multiculturalism: A reader in multicultural education* (2nd ed.; pp. 62–77). Newton, MA: Intercultural Resource Corporation.

Bonwell, C. C., & Eison, J. A. (1991). ASHE-ERIC Higher Education Report: Vol. 1. *Active Learning: Creating Excitement in the Classroom*. Washington, DC: George Washington University.

Cooper, T. C. (1987). Foreign Language Study and SAT Verbal Scores. *Modern Language Journal*, *71*(4), 381–387. doi:10.1111/j.1540-4781.1987.tb00376.x

Darhower, M. (2007). A tale of two communities: Group dynamics and community building in a Spanish-English telecollaboration. *CALICO Journal*, *24*, 561–589.

Elia, A. (2006). Language Learning in Tandem via Skype. *The Reading Matrix*, *6*(3), 269–280.

Fink, L. D. (2003). *Creating Significant Learning Experiences: An Integrated Approach to Designing College Courses*. San Francisco, CA: Jossey-Bass.

Fink, L. D. (2005). *A Self-Directed Guide to Designing Courses for Significant Learning*. Academic Press.

Gehlhar, J. (2009). Of course they want us at the curriculum internationalization table. *Modern Language Journal*, *93*(4), 616–618.

Georgia Gwinnett College. (2015). *Internationalized Courses*. Retrieved October 21, 2016, from http://www.ggc.edu/academics/qep/internationalized-courses/

Green, M. F., Luu, D., & Burris, B. (2012). *Mapping internationalization on U.S. Campuses* (2012 edition). Washington, DC: American Council on Education.

Hudzic, K. (2011). *Comprehensive internationalization: From concept to action – executive summary*. Washington, DC: NAFSA.

Juwah, C., Macfarlane-Dick, D., Matthew, B., Nicol, D., Ross, D., & Smith, B. (2004). *Enhancing Student Learning Through Effective Formative Feedback*. York, UK: Higher Education Academy.

American Council on Education. (2012). *Mapping Internationalization on U.S. Campuses: 2012 Edition*. Retrieved October 21, 2016 from https://www.acenet.edu/newsroom/Documents/Mapping-Internationalizationon-US-Campuses-2012-full.pdf

American Council on the Teaching of Foreign Languages. (2014). *Global Competence Position Statement.* Retrieved October 21, 2016, from https://www.actfl.org/news/position-statements/global-competence-position-statement

Asia Society. (2008). *Going Global: Preparing Our Students for an Interconnected World.* Retrieved October 21, 2016, from http://asiasociety.org/files/Going%20Global%20Educator%20Guide.pdf

Klee, C. (2009). Internationalization and Foreign Languages: The resurgence of interest in languages across the curriculum. *Modern Language Journal, 93*(4), 618–621. doi:10.1111/j.1540-4781.2009.00936.x

Levy, M. (2007). Culture, culture learning and new technologies: Towards a pedagogical framework. *Language Learning & Technology, 11*(2), 104–127.

Liaw, M.-L. (2006). E-learning and the development of intercultural competence. *Language Learning & Technology, 10*(3), 49–64.

MLA Ad hoc Committee on Foreign Languages. (2007). *Foreign languages and higher education: New structures for a changed world. Profession.* Academic Press.

National Education Association (NEA). (2010). *Global Competence Is a 21st Century Imperative.* Retrieved October 21, 2016, from http://www.nea.org/assets/docs/HE/PB28A_Global_Competence11.pdf

National Geographic-Roper. (2002). *Global Geographic Literacy Survey.* Retrieved October 21, 2016, from www.nationalgeographic.com/roper2006/pdf/FINALReport2006GeogLitsurvey.pdf

National Intelligence Council. (2008). *Global trends 2025: A transformed world.* Washington, DC: U.S. Government Printing Office.

National Standards Collaborative Board. (2015). *World-Readiness Standards for Learning Languages* (4th ed.). Alexandria, VA: Author.

O'Dowd, R. (2006). The use of videoconferencing and e-mail as mediators of intercultural student ethnography. In J. Belz & S. L. Thorne (Eds.), *Internet-mediated intercultural foreign language education* (pp. 86–119). Boston, MA: Thomson Heinle.

Olsen, S. A., & Brown, L. K. (1992). The Relation Between Foreign Languages and ACT English and Mathematics Performance. *ADFL Bulletin, 23*(3), 89–93.

Savile-Troike, M. (1984). What Really Matters in Second Language Learning for Academic Achievement? *TESOL Quarterly,* (18): 2, 199–219.

Schenker, T. (2012). Intercultural competence and cultural learning through telecollaboration. *CALICO, 29*(3), 449–470. doi:10.11139/cj.29.3.449-470

Swaffar, J., & Urlaub, P. (Eds.). (2014). *Transforming Postsecondary Foreign Language Teaching in the United States.* Springer. doi:10.1007/978-94-017-9159-5

Telles, J. A., & Vassallo, M. L. (2006). Foreign language learning in-tandem:Teletandem as an alternative proposal in CALLT. *The ESPecialist, 27*(2), 189–212.

Truscott, S., & Morley, J. (2001). Cross-cultural learning through computer-mediated communication. *Language Learning Journal, 24*(1), 17–23. doi:10.1080/09571730185200171

U.S. Census Bureau. (2005). *Exports from manufacturing establishments.* Retrieved October 21, 2016, from www.census.gov/mcd/exports/arp05.pdf

Ware, P., & Kramsch, C. (2005). Toward an intercultural stance: Teaching German and English through telecollaboration. *Modern Language Journal, 89*(2), 90–105. doi:10.1111/j.1540-4781.2005.00274.x

Wiggins, G., & McTighe, J. (2005). *Understanding by design.* Alexandria, VA: Association for Supervision and Curriculum Development.

Woodin, J. (2001). Tandem learning as an intercultural activity. In M. Byram, A. Nichols, & D. Stevens (Eds.), *Developing Intercultural Competence in Practice* (pp. 189–203). Toronto: Univ. of Toronto Press.

Yanguas, I. (2010). Oral computer-mediated interaction between L2 learners: It's about time. *Language Learning & Technology, 14,* 72–79.

Zimitat, C. (2008). Internationalisation of the undergraduate curriculum. In L. Dunn & M. Wallace (Eds.), *Teaching in Transnational Higher Education.* London: Routledge.

KEY TERMS AND DEFINITIONS

Active Learning: A type of learning process whereby students engage in activities that require doing and thinking. It is often contrasted with passive learning such as listening to lectures.

Backward Design: A course design method in which starts from the desired outcomes of the course first and then works back towards the assessment and activities.

Educative Assessment: A type of assessment that emphasizes helping students learn rather than assigning students a grade. The purpose of the assessment is mainly to enhance learning.

Language Exchange Pal Project: A learning project whereby students teach each other's native language through online technologies.

Significant Learning: A type of learning that is lasting and long term. It is more than just learning basic facts and information. Examples of significant learning are: Critical thinking, connecting ideas and people, and application of concepts.

APPENDIX 1

Rubric for Internationalization Review of GGC Courses (Content Rubric)

Course Number _____ Course Name_____ Completed by_____ Date____

Directions: Faculty members should enter an X on the line provided to indicate your choice for each of the rows 1-4. Then answer the three questions below.

1. What is your overall assessment of the international intensity of the course (0-4)? _____
2. Do you think the international content in this course could be increased to a higher level? _____
3. If so, to what level (1-4)? ____

Table 2.

	Level 0	Level 1	Level 2	Level 3	Level 4
Course materials drawn from international sources or locations	None _____	Isolated items inserted into course in individual class sessions _____	Supplemental materials used in 10-30% of course _____	Primary materials used in 30-60% of course _____	Primary materials used in >60% of course _____
Lectures (including guest lectures) or other classroom presentations focused on international or multinational perspectives or comparisons	None _____	Isolated comments or individual class sections inserted into course, but not related to broader content _____	Primary focus of class presentations in 10-30% of course _____	Primary focus of class presentations in 30-60-% of course _____	Primary focus of class presentations in >60% of course _____
Tests, Exams, Research Papers, Presentations, or other work requiring consideration of international or multinational perspectives	None _____	Isolated items on one or more test or exam _____	Primary focus on tests or exams for 10-30% of course _____	Primary focus of tests or exams for 30-60% of course _____	Primary focus of tests or exams for >60% of course _____
Homework/Class assignments or other student work (e.g. papers, discussions, cultural experiences, research assignments) requiring consideration of international or multinational perspectives	None _____	None _____	10-30% of assignments are internationally related _____	30-60% of assignments are internationally related _____	Primary and substantive student work product for course requires taking international focus across full scope of course_____

APPENDIX 2

Rubric for Identifying Student Learning Outcomes in International Courses (Depth Rubric)

Course Name: _____ Course Prefix and Number: _____ Reviewer's Name: _____

Faculty members should use this rubric to identify all of the five QEP Student Learning Outcomes listed in the Outcome column that are appropriate to the course being reviewed and, for those outcomes, each level of student performance/capability the course requires. In the far right column, place the number

Table 3.

Category	Outcome	Novice (Level 1)	Developing (Level 2)	Capstone (Level 3)	Row Total
Intercultural Awareness	Students will be able to describe and evaluate their own cultures in relation to history, values, politics, communication styles, economy, or beliefs and practices.	Identifies own cultural rules and biases (e.g. with a strong preference for those rules shared with own cultural group and seeks the same in others.)	Recognizes new perspectives about own cultural rules and biases (e.g., not looking for sameness; comfortable with the complexities that new perspectives offer.)	Analyzes own cultural rules and biases and how own experiences have shaped these rules and biases.	
	Students will be able to describe and evaluate other cultures in relation to history, values, politics, communication styles, economy, or beliefs and practices.	Identifies elements important to members of another culture in relation to its history, values, politics, communication styles, economy, **or** beliefs and practices.	Articulates basic understanding of the complexity of elements important to members of another culture in relation to its history, values, politics, communication styles, economy, **or** beliefs and practices.	Analyzes the complexity of elements important to members of another culture in relation to its history, values, politics, communication styles, economy, **or** beliefs and practices.	
Category	Outcome	Early Stage (Level 1)	Mid Stage (Level 2)	Capstone (Level 3)	Row Total
Communication and Collaboration	Students will communicate effectively with persons from different cultures.	Articulates the verbal and nonverbal communications used in own culture; identifies some cultural differences in verbal and nonverbal communication.	Recognizes and participates in cultural differences in verbal and nonverbal communication and begins to negotiate a shared understanding based on those differences.	Articulates a complex understanding of cultural differences in verbal and nonverbal communication (e.g., demonstrates understanding of the degree to which people use physical contact while communicating in different cultures) and is able to skillfully negotiate a shared understanding based on those differences.	
	Students will demonstrate ability to interact effectively and productively in situations involving people from diverse cultural and national backgrounds	Identifies components of other cultural perspectives but responds in all situations with own worldview.	Recognizes intellectual and emotional dimensions of more than one worldview and sometimes uses more than one worldview in interactions	Interprets intercultural experience from the perspectives of own and more than one worldview and demonstrates ability to act in a supportive manner that recognizes the feelings of another cultural group.	
Application/ Problem Solving	Students will demonstrate the ability to apply intercultural knowledge to intercultural or global problems	Defines challenge or problem in basic ways, describing a limited number of systems, beliefs, and solutions.	Formulates practical yet elementary solutions to challenge or problem from a disciplinary perspective, using at least two cultural lenses	Applies knowledge and skills to generate sophisticated, appropriate, and workable solutions to address complex problems from a disciplinary perspective, using multiple cultural lenses	
	Column Totals: # marked or Row Total Sum				

Table 4.

value for the highest student performance level for that outcome (e.g., 1, 2, or 3). Total the row values at the bottom to yield an overall score for each course. This will be combined with the score previously assigned for amount of international content to generate a QEP Curriculum Map to support further QEP planning.

APPENDIX 3

QQ/Skype Language Pal Exchange Portfolio

QQ1. Macro Goals & Priorities

Here write down your priorities to be reached in your QQ/Skype tandem language exchange program. Tick the relevant objectives and specify their degree of importance (Box 1).

1. not important **2.** some importance **3.** quite important **4.** important **5.** very important
- □ **Broaden vocabulary** 1 □ 2 □ 3 □ 4 □ 5 □
- □ **Improve grammatical accuracy** 1 □ 2 □ 3 □ 4 □ 5 □
- □ **Improve pronunciation** 1 □ 2 □ 3 □ 4 □ 5 □
- □ **Get better listening skills** 1 □ 2 □ 3 □ 4 □ 5 □
- □ **Improve reading skills** 1 □ 2 □ 3 □ 4 □ 5 □
- □ **Develop speaking skills** 1 □ 2 □ 3 □ 4 □ 5 □
- □ **Develop cultural understanding** 1 □ 2 □ 3 □ 4 □ 5 □

QQ2. General Objectives

Keeping a record of what you have learned during your Skype tandem learning exchanges will help you to reflect on your progress and increase your awareness about how you learn a foreign language. At the end of every QQ/Skype session try to summarize what you wanted to learn and what you have actually learnt.

When you start a new session it is essential to define your goals clearly. Try to set objectives that you can pragmatically achieve in your "virtual meetings".

It is essential that you share them with your QQ/Skype tandem partner.

What would I like to be able to do?
In how long?
How often?
Day and time schedule

QQ3. Learning Log

DATE: _____ SKYPE EXCHANGE Number._____
Length of the sessions:_____(at least 30 minutes for Chinese; 30 minutes for
    English)

1.   Today's objective(s): *Fill in this box by trying to answer the following questions:*
   - Did I succeed in reaching the objectives I had set out for today?
   - What did I learn?
   - Was (or not) the QQ/Skype session good, useful, fun or motivating?
   - What worked well, what didn't? Why?
   - Am I satisfied with my personal performance and with my partner's performance?
   - Did I ask for help?
   - Did I get enough help?
   - Did I use other tools such as QQ/Skype chat or on line dictionaries for help?
2.   Main meeting discussion topic(s):
3.   New words and expressions learned:
4.   New cultural information:
5.   Reflections on grammar and accuracy:

    Fill in this box by trying to answer the following questions:

- Did I correctly adopt and imitate grammatical structures used by my QQ/Skype tandem partner?
- Did I imitate my tandem partner's pronunciation?
- Did I use newly learnt words and structures?
- Did my tandem partner use language learning strategies that I would like to adopt?
6.   Self-observation:
7.   **Observation of tandem partner:** What do you think your partner has learnt from you today? Any other general comments/observation of your partner.
    Adapted from Elia (2006).

Chapter 9
How Is Mathematics Humanistic, Culturally Rich, Relevant, and Interesting?
Seeking Answers Through the Redesign of an Undergraduate Mathematics Course

Priya Shilpa Boindala
Georgia Gwinnett College, USA

Ramakrishnan Menon
Georgia Gwinnett College, USA

Angela Lively
Georgia Gwinnett College, USA

ABSTRACT

This chapter focuses on the redesign of a traditional History of Mathematics course as an international-ized course and its early implementation. This redesign of the course incorporates significant learning experiences and includes the learning goals of both the college and the discipline. The design of these learning experiences using the backwards design model, the framework based on a blended taxonomy of Bloom and Fink, are elaborated on. How these learning experiences are supported by active learning strategies and forward assessments is also presented. The pilot implementation by an author not involved in the design process provides for an objective perspective of this redesign. The chapter elaborates on the learning experiences within the initial implementation and concludes with ideas for future iterations of the course.

INTRODUCTION

In this chapter, the authors describe the redesign of a STEM course, namely the History of Mathematics course, as part of their institution's internationalization initiative. They begin with a discussion of relevant literature related to internationalization of curriculum: the assessment of intercultural and global learning outcomes, the emerging paradigm of student-centered learning outcomes as a means to student

DOI: 10.4018/978-1-5225-2791-6.ch009

engagement and achievement and the challenges in teaching and learning mathematics. They describe the theoretical framework used to redesign the course, namely, the Backwards Design model with a blend of Bloom's Taxonomy and Fink's model of creating significant learning experiences and elaborate on the various phases of the framework in the context of the History of Mathematics course. The authors further illustrate how the course goals and institutional learning outcomes were used to develop the learning activities for the internationalized course with the goal of making mathematics less static and more humanistic. The human element is emphasized by examining how the study of math was used to solve real world problems, exploring how scholars grappled with academic challenges that were demanding to solve, and finally by exploring the very human qualities of the lives that notable mathematicians lived. The chapter further summarizes the pilot implementation of the internationalized course for the first semester including synopses of student work. It concludes with a reflection upon how the course may evolve, including additional assessment strategies for future implementation.

BACKGROUND

Internationalization of Curriculum and Assessment of Intercultural and Global Learning Outcomes

Given the increased and varied challenges in the world including a growing number of mobile employees as well as the trend of global employability, it is no surprise that institutions of higher learning are placing more emphasis on internationalization of the curriculum and initiating appropriate assessment measures of intercultural competence. On examining a plethora of studies on the concept of intercultural competence, it was found that there have been as many as 20 different definitions and frameworks (Spitzberg & Changnon, 2009), such as Cross's cross-cultural continuum, Bennett's Developmental Model of Intercultural Sensitivity, and King and Baxter Magolda's intercultural maturity model (Cross, 1988; Bennett, 1993; King, 2005). While a few of these models were not strictly research-based, Deardorff was one of the first to have a research-based definition of intercultural competence (Deardorff, 2006), and that was followed by a synthesis of related work published in the *Sage Handbook of Intercultural Competence* (2009). Subsequently, there were many publications all over the world on this topic, not only in the United States but also in many other countries around the world.

These intercultural competence models identify characteristics of intercultural competence for use by institutions of higher learning to translate into measurable student learning objectives. There are two means by which postsecondary education internationalizes the campus in order to bring an intercultural and global dimension to students' educational experiences: through the curriculum, and through co-curricular activities (Deardorff, 2011). According to Bok (2006), fewer than 10 percent of undergraduates take a course in international relations, and fewer than 20 percent of four-year colleges require more than two years of foreign language study. He further suggests that postsecondary institutions can maximize the intercultural competence by integrating intercultural experience throughout the undergraduate course work (Bok, 2006). Deardorff continues this theme by suggesting that an infusion of intercultural competence and global learning into courses is more than just an inclusion of some international readings, or taking a single course in international studies. To ensure the development of intercultural competence, this process must span many undergraduate courses, including the STEM (science, technology, engineering, and mathematics) fields, with faculty invested in the efforts of internationalization. Such infusion of intercultural competence and global learning into courses provides opportunities for students to see issues from diverse perspectives, providing exposure to diverse cultures through either local immersion experiences or study abroad opportunities that relate to the major (Deardorff, 2011).

Given that intercultural competence depends in part on the field of study, it becomes important for academic departments to reflect and collaborate around a number of questions related to internationalization and intercultural competence related to the discipline. Colleges can better equip students for a more global, interdependent world, through courses that provide a framework for understanding a variety of perspectives on global issues, including foreign and comparative material into courses, and requiring foreign language (Bok, 2006).

While many terms such as global citizenship, intercultural intelligence, are used interchangeably with the term intercultural competence, this terminology includes, with different levels of emphasis, the knowledge, skills and attitudes needed to interact successfully with those from diverse backgrounds. If it is accepted that intercultural competence is the ability to interact successfully with those from diverse backgrounds, then, the assessment of intercultural competence must be multi-modal, and assess both the process and end result (Deardorff, 2012; Deardorff & Edwards, 2012; Gordon & Deardorff, 2013). This competence has been assessed in various ways, such as questionnaires, reflection papers, interviews, project presentations and scenarios. Therefore, while intercultural competence can be assessed, most of the available extensive assessment tools do not result in a complete picture, as the instruments are mainly self-report instruments, and do not measure communication and behavior that need to be measured by perspectives other than self-reports (Deardorff, 2011; Fantini, 2009 ; Stuart, 2009). Furthermore, most assessments instruments of intercultural competence rely on indirect evidence, such as a survey instrument, resulting in an incomplete picture of intercultural competence. Even though the American Association of Colleges and Universities provides a sample rubric for measuring direct evidence of intercultural learning, they are not aligned with specific learning objectives within intercultural competence development (Deardorff, 2009). Therefore, no one method of assessment can be considered the best.

Concerning the authors' home institution, the Intercultural Development Inventory (IDI) was used to measure the intercultural competence among incoming freshmen, and outgoing seniors, to assess any difference between their competencies. The instrument was used to determine whether the institution itself is contributing to any positive change in students' intercultural competence. However, to determine such intercultural competence in a specific course such as the History of Mathematics, the course was redesigned with specific learning objectives related to intercultural competence in the course as discussed in the following section. Assessments were created to measure these learning objectives, the details of which are discussed later in the chapter.

THE REDESIGN PROCESS

Theoretical Framework

The framework of this course redesign uses the backwards design (B-D) model (Wiggins and McTighe 2005) and a blend of taxonomies of Bloom (Bloom, 1956; Anderson et al., 2001) and Fink (Fink 2003) of significant learning experiences. This approach was adopted previously in redesigning a flipped Pre-Calculus course (Brewley et al., 2014) with a similarly diverse student population.

The B-D model (Wiggins and McTighe 2005) essentially requires one to visualize the course with the end goals in mind. It has three stages –

Stage 1: Identify the Desired Results or Goals for the Course

In this stage, one establishes the content standards for the course at the discipline/college/state level. Also of priority at this stage are the long-term performance goals the instructor would like their students to have after completion of the course.

Stage 2: Identify the Evidence Students Need to Demonstrate for the Achievement of These Goals

In the second stage, the instructor/designer takes on the role of an assessor and considers the types of assessment that would be necessary for the course. Considered here are the facets of understanding that will be assessed in the course and the types of assessments such as quizzes, tests, presentations and rubrics that will align with the first stage.

Stage 3: Identify the Learning Plan That Will Facilitate This Achievement

In the final stage, instructors design the activities for the course that will target items enumerated in the first and second stages. The activities are designed to give the learner many opportunities to not just learn the content but also be able to actively construct meaning and draw inferences. This model helps to design activities that are more focused with clear priority and purpose. It supports a student-centered learning environment.

Bloom's taxonomy (Bloom, 1956; Anderson et al., 2001) has also been a significant resource to inform course redesign. The elements of its cognitive domain have been used to develop and evaluate course objectives and student learning for over a half century in various educational settings. Bloom's cognitive domain included the six levels of learning namely: knowledge, comprehension, application, analysis, synthesis and evaluation.

On the other hand, Fink's taxonomy for significant learning experiences helps capture other important kinds of learning such as, communication skills, tolerance and interpersonal skills. It helps incorporate elements such as caring, learning how to learn and human dimension of the affective domain as part of the design process. By adding components to a course that will enable students to discover something about themselves or others informs the human dimension of the subject they are learning. Including components that improve student interest in the course help build a sense of community within the classroom, which can aid in developing a higher energy and contributing to greater motivation to learn.

Dee Fink's methodology for constructing an integrated course consists of three phases. The first phase of the integrated course design includes several preliminary planning factors. The elements of situational factors, student-learning goals, and assessment and learning activities are considered individually as well as how they interrelate within the educational process. This first phase of Fink's integrated course design intersects the three stages of the B-D model. Taking it further, Fink's integrated course design considers a second phase where the structure for the course is developed and the instructional strategy is chosen. This is integrated with the learning activities developed in the first phase. The final phase includes developing the grading scheme, preparing the course syllabus, constructing the course and teaching evaluation (Fink, 2013).

Following this blended framework, the authors began by contextualizing what internationalization meant at the college and discipline level. At the course level, it was more focused on the situational factors. How these three elements feed into the design of assessments and learning activities can be visually presented as in Figure 1, with further exploration in the following sections.

In the context of the History of Mathematics course, it was necessary to incorporate Fink's learning goals of human dimension and caring. In order to achieve this, elements such as, an inquiry-based approach to learning and faculty-student and peer-peer discussions needed to be included.

What Does Internationalization Mean in the Context of the Institution?

The authors began by considering what internationalization meant in the context of an educational institution and, in particular, their home institution. The National Council for Social Studies states that the pertinent goal of a global education is to develop in youth the knowledge, skills, and attitudes needed to live effectively in a world possessing limited natural resources and characterized by ethnic diversity, cultural pluralism, and increasing interdependence (Merryfield, 2012)

Internationalization at the institutional level can be considered as a spectrum. On one end of the scale, it could be as limited as having the presence of international students on campus, whereas on the other end, it could be a harmonious and collaborative process among the faculty, students, administrators and the community with the capability of influencing positive transformations. (Bartell, 2003)

Universities serve two primary goals, teaching and research, as well as servicing the surrounding community. This requires the university to understand where its student population comes from, the careers they will prepare for, and the skills they will need to function as effective citizens with global competence in the society and community they live in. The university will therefore have to communicate its identity within the community to all stakeholders and make a choice on the objectives of their internationalization that will consider all the various facets described above. To enhance the effectiveness of this process, the leadership has the task of identifying any contradictions and designing appropriate solutions (Bartell, 2003). It is important to see this broader perspective when redesigning a course in order to see how different pieces fit together to affect a transformative change.

Figure 1. Contextualizing "Internationalization" and its role in the design of student and classroom learning goals

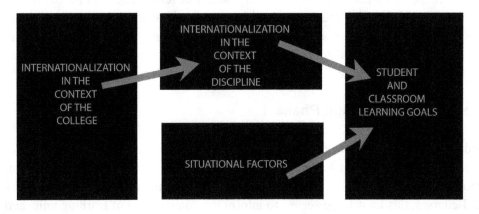

The authors' home institution serves a very diverse community of students. The choice of Internationalization as the institution's Quality Enhancement Program (QEP) topic and its plan was developed in partnership with faculty, staff and students over a period of three years.

As a result, students have the opportunity to participate in a credit-bearing study abroad program in an international location. On campus, students are given the opportunity to complete internationalized courses (I-courses) that provide them with a broad global awareness and perspective related to the discipline of study. The courses are designed to address student- learning outcomes (SLOs) under three broad areas of competencies as below.

- **Cultural Awareness:**
  - Describe and evaluate their own cultures in relation to history, values, politics, communication styles, economy, or beliefs and practices;
  - Describe and evaluate other cultures in relation to history, values, politics, communication styles, economy, or beliefs and practices;
- **Communication and Collaboration:**
  - Communicate effectively with persons from different cultures;
  - Demonstrate ability to interact effectively and productively in situations involving people from diverse cultural and national backgrounds; and
- **Application and Problem Solving:**
  - Demonstrate the ability to apply intercultural knowledge to intercultural or global problems.
  - A course at the author's home institution is considered an I-course if more than 30% of the course material content has a global focus and addresses a minimum of two of the SLOs from separate areas of competencies, at the novice level for lower level courses and at least at the developing level for upper level courses.

A systematic process was designed by the QEP office to enable I-course development across the campus, which involved faculty enrolling in a yearlong faculty development institute that culminated in a proposal for the I-course in their respective disciplines. The resulting proposal was peer reviewed by the QEP committee on campus before the I-course was made available for students the following semester. This project was the result of one such endeavor. The proposal was developed by the first two authors of this chapter who underwent the yearlong faculty development institute and implemented by the third author who was not involved in the initial redesign of the course. This allowed for a very objective perspective, and a lens that was uncluttered by previous versions of the course. While the third author had experience in other History of Mathematics courses, she had not previously taught this at their home institution, allowing for a fresh perspective.

Integrated Course Redesign Phase 1

Understanding what internationalization meant at the college level gave the redesign team a glimpse of alignment needs that would facilitate the support of institutional goals. The year-long institute provided exposure to the college's prescribed student learning outcomes and competencies for all courses designated as I-courses; this knowledge served to inform the construction of learning units and activities specific to the History of Mathematics course.

Situational Factors

An important component of the first phase of an integrated course design, as outlined by Dee-Fink, are the situational factors that play into the dynamics of a course. Details considered by the authors in this context included the course meeting time, frequency of meetings, number of credit hours and student demographic information.

The History of Mathematics course at the authors' home institution is targeted to mainly students earning a Bachelor's degree in Mathematics with a concentration in Teacher Certification (pre-service high school teachers). Knowing the student population of a classroom helped tailor the redesign by considering any subject-related challenges students face (discussed in the following sections) as well as consequences with possible broader impact beyond the course level. The results from a recent study suggest that pre-service teachers who took courses with global content had a better-developed global perspective than those who took fewer globally enriched content courses (Cyndi, 2015). It has been shown further that such pre-service teachers are more likely to integrate global content into their future classrooms (Merryfield, 1994; Rapoport, 2010).

The History of Mathematics was a two-credit hour course offered once yearly and classes met for a period of seventy-five minutes once per week. There were at most ten students per class. Either an instructor from the School of Education or an instructor from the mathematics discipline housed within the School of Science and Technology taught the class. The credit hours, face-to-face meeting times and their duration played an important role in determining the type of activities appropriate for the course and the time students are required to invest outside of class. In addition to these situational factors, the redesign also considered enough flexibility for instructors (other than the authors who redesigned the course) so that academic freedom is preserved.

Identifying the Course Goals

Under the broad umbrella of the first phase of Fink's integrated course design are the three stages of the B-D model. In the first stage, the outcomes of the course are identified; in the context of the History of Mathematics course, the goals were pre-determined. They consisted of the course outcome goals (COGs) at the discipline level as well as the college-wide QEP Student learning outcomes (SLOs). These informed the design of the learning activities, feedback and assessment for the course.

It was therefore important to determine how the COGs feed into the SLOs. The COGs outlined what students would be able to do after completion of the course. Specifically, students would be able to:

1. Explore the utility of mathematics from a historical and cultural perspective.
2. Solve problems of historical significance.
3. Develop their sensitivity to the diversity of cultures contributing to the development of mathematics and to the unique perspectives of students for groups underrepresented in the mathematical sciences
4. Develop and share curricular materials and teaching strategies to promote knowledge and appreciation for historical and cultural foundations of mathematics
5. Explicitly address the designated National Council of Teachers of Mathematics (NCTM) content standards

Considering internationalization in the context of both the institution as well as the discipline, the SLOs that were best captured through this course fell under the themes of cultural awareness and application/problem solving, namely SLO 1, 2 and 5.

SLO 1: Describe and evaluate their own cultures in relation to history, values, politics, communication styles, economy, or beliefs and practices.
SLO 2: Describe and evaluate other cultures in relation to history, values, politics, communication styles, economy, or beliefs and practices.
SLO 5: Demonstrate the ability to apply intercultural knowledge to intercultural or global problems.

The mapping of the SLOs to the COGs is visually depicted in Figure 2. This diagram provides clarity into the rationale behind the re-design of activities and their corresponding assessments.

Identifying Relevant Challenges

In addition to the course objectives, the authors also considered specific difficulties faced by the pre-service teachers taking this course. While there were many challenges inherent to the teaching and learning of mathematics, the authors focused on those that were most relevant to the student population under consideration: students' attitude towards mathematics, mathematics anxiety, lack of a positive self-concept, identity, and development of their pedagogical and content- related skills.

Figure 2. Mapping of the QEP student learning outcomes to the course outcome goals

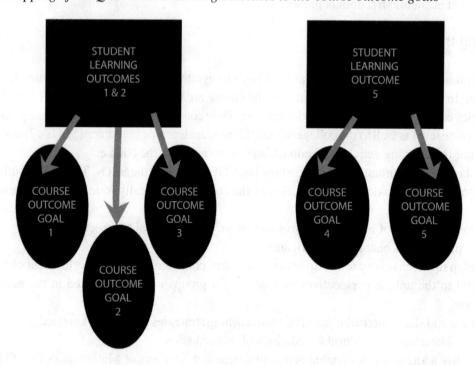

Attitude Towards Mathematics

The following excerpt from a study, gives a telling example of students' attitude towards mathematics. Written by a student who feared mathematics, the apprehensive feelings expressed continue to be prevalent today.

Math does make me think of a stainless steel wall -- hard, cold, smooth, offering no handhold; all it does is glint back at me. Edge up to it, put your nose against it; it does not give anything back; you cannot put a dent in it; it does not take your shape; it does not have any smell; all it does is make your nose cold. I like the shine of it -- it does look smart, intelligent in an icy way. But I resent its cold impenetrability, its supercilious glare. (Buerk, 1982, p. 19)

Research shows that there is a close relationship between attitudes towards mathematics and the learning of mathematics (Mubeen, 2013; Kazemi, 2013). It is important that as future mathematics educators, the student population under consideration developed a positive attitude towards math; this mindset could be fostered within this course. A larger study considering the causal relationship between attitude and achievement was conducted with data from the Longitudinal Study of American Youth (LSAY) that included 60 randomly selected seventh graders who were followed through high school. This study revealed that prior attitudes and achievement had a significant effect on later attitude, suggesting the importance of the academic experience in improving student achievement and consequently their attitude towards mathematics (Ma & Xu, 2004).

A potential route to developing this positive attitude was by providing these students meaningful classroom experiences that engage them in activities that allowed them to see mathematics in a broader context. By providing them opportunities to observe how mathematics aligned with their field of education as well as eliminating their perception that mathematical ability is innate, both of which have been shown to be factors affecting students' mathematical learning. Teachers can reinforce the idea that mathematics is an interesting subject, used in other disciplines, and is an admission ticket for colleges and careers (Anderson, 2007).

Furthermore, if this course were presented in a way that created awareness of the contributions of diverse cultures towards the field of mathematics (Greer, 2009), students might be more inclined to develop an appreciation for both the cultures as well as their corresponding contribution to the field. These students, who will be employed in future mathematics classrooms, may find it beneficial to explore how mathematical techniques originated out of cultural need and by the exchange of ideas between the east and west. This may lead to more positive student attitudes and less tendencies to consider mathematics as depersonalized and an asocial science.

Mathematics Anxiety, Self-Concept, and Identity

Closely related to students' attitude towards mathematics is their own self-concept, mathematical identity as well as any associated anxiety.

It has been demonstrated in studies that a differential variable such as mathematics anxiety in students affects their memory spans. They suggest that the working capacity used for skilled tasks is now occupied by the worries generated by their anxiety towards the subject. This consequently increases their errors on assessments (Arp, 1999 and Ashcraft & Kirk 2001). Beilock & Carr (2005) who showed that interferences such as anxiety-related pressure and mental distractions compete for working memory space, which would otherwise be devoted for skill tasks, further support this work. They also claimed that individuals that were likely to fail under pressure were those that had a higher likelihood for success in the absence of such interferences.

In a study that focuses on pre-service teachers, it has been shown that differences in self-concept among the genders influences how both primary and secondary teachers view the nature of mathematics as well as their attitudes towards teaching and learning mathematics (Relich, 1996). Improving the self-concept among these novice teachers would help them identify themselves as problem solvers and mathematicians in their classroom, which in turn may have a positive effect on the cognitive and affective development of their students. This suggested that it was essential in the development of curricula to consider not just the cognitive but also the affective needs of teachers in training.

Mathematics identity is the perception of the student as a capable or incapable mathematics learner resulting from interactions and experiences with others (peers, teachers, etc.). Most often this occurs in an academic environment, and develops through the learner's perception of mathematics itself in a broader context (such as whether it makes sense, is relevant, or useful).

Since identities are dynamic and depend upon interactions between the learner and the classroom environment, paying attention to a student's mathematical identity can be as important as paying attention to the student's cognitive knowledge and performance. Therefore, to better facilitate proficiency in mathematical concepts and skills, it benefits the student to develop a more positive identity as a mathematician.

The identity as a math learner is dependent upon instructional methods. For example, if quick answers are the expected norm in a math classroom, and some students cannot answer quickly, then their identity as a math learner is compromised, even if they might be able to give the correct answer when given more time. Since there is a great potential to influence students' identities in the mathematics classroom, teachers need to engage students by giving mathematical tasks where students are actively involved in the creation of mathematics and students need to feel that their contributions are valued by both their classmates and teacher (Anderson, 2007; Solomon, 2007).

A realization of the importance of identity can enable future teachers to present their math lessons in a way that empowers the development of a positive identity by their own students. Such a development can be facilitated by studying the sociopolitical aspects of math, and the attendant factors of equality, equity, identity, power, and emancipation that are highlighted by a critical discussion of developments within the history of math.

Teaching as a Cultural Activity

Teaching is a highly contextualized cultural activity where teachers use teaching routines that have evolved over time to create learning opportunities for students that socialize student beliefs, values, and behaviors that in turn define students as learners (Gallimore, 1996; Hiebert, 2013; Stigler, 1999). Moreover, teachers learn these practices implicitly, drawing on their own experiences as students themselves, and such practices are resistant to change, even if these teachers go through teacher education programs or in-service workshops that offer alternative methods of teaching. In other words, students from different cultures view mathematics differently, mainly due to the different practices of teaching they were exposed to (Lortie, 1975).

Part of the cultural activity of math teaching seemed to be the type of math problems students were given to work on. The three types of problems could be classified as the following: *stating properties, using procedures, and making connections*. An example of the *stating properties* type of problem is, "What is the formula for the area of a parallelogram?" An example of the *using procedures* type of problem would be practicing finding the area of a parallelogram, after first being shown how to use the formula, then giving various dimensions of parallelograms, and then computing the corresponding areas. An example of the *making connections* type of problem would be giving students examples of parallelograms presented as compound figures, composed of familiar shapes such as rectangles, squares, and triangles. Students then construct a method to make connections among these figures to determine the area of the parallelogram instead of relying on a provided formula, thus strengthening their conceptual knowledge.

There was no clear evidence that one type of problem was instrumental in students' higher achievement in math; what was clear was that *how the teacher implemented the problem*—namely, *the cultural practices of teaching* did affect the outcome. The results indicate that if the teacher did not quickly jump in to help students figure out the problem (as was a prevalent practice by teachers in the United States), students would continue to struggle and think deeply, thereby building connections that would not be formed by merely using provided formulas.

Stigler continues by describing how different teaching routines resulted in different student views about what mathematics is. Students in Japan were given problems that they had not seen before or ones that the teacher had not previously explained, and given time to try to solve the problem, while the teacher circulated around the class, giving hints and encouragement. Students with erroneous solutions were called up to the front of the class, and, together with the help of their classmates, came to a suitable solution. The experiences in the Japanese classrooms, as portrayed in this study, illustrated that when students were given problems for which no previous solution path was explained by the teacher, they took time to try to solve the problems themselves, or in cooperation with other students. In addition, when students were encouraged to discuss their wrong solutions, they were able to arrive at a correct solution with the help of their classmates. The implicit message seemed to be that in a positive classroom culture, students are capable of solving previously unseen problems by themselves, and they can learn from mistakes, without feeling shame at having an erroneous solution.

The students from Japan viewed mathematics as requiring effort on the part of the student and success was not based on innate mathematical ability. However, students in the United States seemed to believe that math is merely a set of rules to follow or problems that can be solved once the teacher guides them, and that mathematical ability was genetic and not dependent upon students' efforts.

Furthermore, this study pointed out that a teacher in Japan did not feel that confusion and struggle on the part of the student needed immediate resolution by the teacher—instead they considered these struggles as contributing to mathematical thinking. Many teachers from the United States believed that it was counterproductive to let students struggle while solving a problem.

These international studies demonstrated that teaching is a cultural activity arising from localized rituals that result in students having different attitudes toward the learning of mathematics. The redesign team believed that, such studies were useful for the History of Mathematics students, as they can begin to appreciate how culture—in this case, the culture of teaching—affected the learning of math, and even how approaches to solving problems varied according to the teaching culture students had been exposed to. Such an awareness that teaching culture affects student learning would then be a precursor to an awareness of how the different cultures in history have contributed to the field of math, and is aligned with the courses objectives.

Learning the History of Mathematics helps teachers answer the oft-repeated question by students, "Why study math?" The awareness that historically, math was utilitarian in nature and not accessible to all also helps students challenge preconceived notions of mathematics. The commonly accepted perception of math as a universal, rational and objective discipline can now be reconsidered as affected by contemporary socio-political issues and subjectivities (Harouni, 2015).

In terms of the utilitarian nature of math, early humans kept track of regular, natural occurrences such as the phases of the moon and the seasons. Those adept at these practices often were elevated to positions of authority, as they seemed capable of predicting events such as seasons, eclipses and tides.

Later in history, mathematics developed largely as a response to bureaucratic needs when civilizations settled and developed agriculture, such as to measure plots of land, to compute the taxation of individuals, and conduct censuses. Such uses of math first occurred in the early civilizations of Mesopotamia, such as those of Sumeria, Babylonia and Egypt. Here again, math was limited to a select class of people. Becoming aware, that math initially was used to fulfill utilitarian needs and subsequently evolved to sociopolitical purposes might allow students to view math as more than a mere abstraction, and serve to engage them more fully in math.

These socio-political issues affecting math also included inequities, specifically regarding who was permitted access to learning mathematics. History is full of these examples: with examples ranging from exclusivity of royal courts to the cultish Pythagoreans to academia's denial of entry into the field of higher mathematics for women (as recently as the 20th century)! These inequities perpetuated by those in power, still exist today in the field of mathematics education. The fact that mathematics is a human practice means it is inherently political, rife with issues of domination and power, just like any other human practice (Gutierrez, 2013; pg. 40). Potential educators becoming more aware of inequity as a historical issue can become more sensitive and proactive in their teaching practices to promote more socially just practices. Affirming students' diversities will enable teachers to engage students by drawing on students' knowledge that is related to their culture, and making students aware of issues of power and identity (Guttierez, 2013).

By discussing how mathematics was used in various cultures, historically and more recently, the hope is that students will become more aware that mathematics has a sociopolitical context, with respect to equality, equity, identity, power, and emancipation (Frankenstein, 1990, 1995; D'Ambrosio, 1990; Gutstein, 2006; Gutierrez, 2009; Walshaw, 2013.)

Ironically, in an increasingly global environment, globalization of curriculum development has resulted in an exclusion of contributions from non-western cultures (Applebaum, 2008). This leads to a great opportunity: internationalizing the History of Mathematics course aids in highlighting these non-western contributions, thereby laying a foundation that increases student interest and performance in the subject by considering individual students and the diversities inherent in their cultural backgrounds.

The authors claim that the redesign of the History of Mathematics course at their home institution could be instrumental in giving mathematical achievements a diverse cultural context in addition to supporting the goal of their institution's QEP. Such a redesign would give students the opportunity to take courses (not restricted to general education) which offer discipline-relevant content that will improve their global awareness and make them increasingly aware of varied cultural perspectives.

In addition to awareness of diverse cultural perspectives, this redesign would create an experience that makes mathematics less static and more humanistic. The authors expect to achieve this goal by examining how mathematics was historically used to solve real-world problems, by investigating how scholars grappled with academic challenges, and by exploring the very human qualities of the lives of notable mathematicians.

Developing the Themes for the Teaching and Learning Activities: I-Course Recommended Curriculum

Considering the course-outcome goals and the QEP student learning outcomes the following broad range of topics/themes were suggested for the course. They are listed below by the CoG and SLO they target.

- **CoG1 and SLO 1, 2:**
  - Mathematics from a historical and cultural perspective. Development of Number Systems and Symbols (for example. Egyptian, Sumerian, Babylonians, Chinese, Greek, Roman, Incas, Mayan, Hindu).
  - Some applications and uses of mathematics (example, cartography, predicting weather, internet transaction security/encryption, stopping distance of vehicles, tomography, cell phones, radio and TV, computers, actuarial tables, radar, X-ray, scanners, automobile design and fabrication, GPS, archeology, finding the authors of the Federalist papers, using the geometric and harmonic means, Apportionment of the House of Representatives, polls, taking the Census, best way to pack oranges, medical tests, DNA).
- **CoG 3 and SLO 1, 2:**
  - Ethno mathematics (diversity of cultures, including non-Western cultures, contributing to the development of mathematics—for example, Arabic, French, Chinese, Hindu, African, Mexican, Native American).
  - Mathematics of the Renaissance and Women Mathematicians (for example., Cardano, Tartaglia, Hypatia, Germaine, Kovalevskaya, Noether)
  - Using history of math and math education to inform the teaching of specific math topics (for example, areas and perimeters, theorems, algebra, trigonometrical functions, statistics and probability, proofs).
  - Problems/theorems of historical significance (for example quadrature of the lune and circle, Pythagoras theorem, proof that is irrational, infinitude of the primes, Herons' formula, approximations of π, solution of equations, Binomial theorem, Divergence of the harmonic series, Euler's sum of the reciprocals of the squares of whole numbers).
- **CoG 2, 4, 5 and SLO 1, 2, 5:**
  - Greek Mathematics (for example., Thales, Archimedes, Pythagoras), Mathematics of the East (for example., Chinese, Hindu, Islamic), Mathematics of medieval Europe (for example, Fibonacci, Oresme)
  - History of Mathematics Education (for example, Polya, Cuisenaire, Brownell, Freudenthal, van Hiele, Gagne, Dienes).
  - Precalculus, calculus and beginning of modern math (for example, Biggs, Napier, Descartes, Pascal, Viete, Fermat, Leibniz, Newton)
  - Math of the 18th century (for example, Euler, Lagrange, Laplace)
  - Probability Theory (for example, Pascal, Bernoulli, and Laplace)
  - Number Theory (for example, Fermat, Euler, & Gauss)
  - Math of the 19th century (for example, Cantor, Lobachevsky, Hilbert)
  - Math of the 20th & 21st centuries. (for example, Gödel, von Neumann, Bourbaki, Thom, Mandelbrot, Turing, Ramanujan, Erdös, Noether, Cantor, Kronecker, Hardy, Hausdorff and Shelling)

The review of the background research and consideration of what internationalization meant in the context of the institution and the course, suggests that the themes developed above, implicitly explore how challenges such as mathematics anxiety, self-concept, attitude towards the subject and approach to problem solving are affected by factors such as gender, ethnicity, race and past experiences. Since this is a course where the majority of students are pre-service teachers, it is important to consider these themes from both a student and instructor perspective.

Integrated Course Redesign Phase 2:

Instructional Strategy Focused on Student Centered Learning Outcomes

Research (Barr & Tagg, 1995) shows there was a paradigm shift in American undergraduate education, shifting from an "instruction paradigm" – characterized by an emphasis on delivering lectures and providing students with the means to learn – towards a "learning paradigm" in which the emphasis is no longer on the means but on the end, i.e. supporting the learning process of students. Essentially, colleges now attempt to produce learning, not just through instruction, but emphasize a mission to produce student learning using whatever means work best (Barr & Tagg, 1995). This shift towards a learning paradigm has also shifted to a learner-centered pedagogy (Cornelius-White, 2007; Weimer, 2002), many faculty have started embracing the principles of this philosophy in the United States and are willing to change their practices to adopt new classroom strategies (Webber,2012 ; Scott, 2009). Chung (2011) gives an example of such a shift in the context of engineering education, where, under the impact of globalization, the approach and orientation in engineering courses shifted from objective-based/input-based education to outcome-based education. Moreover, according to the American Psychological Association (1997), and McCombs and Miller (2007), this changing emphasis on student-centered learning leads to better understanding of the interrelationship between teaching and learning, and helps identify effective teaching strategies and tests new ideas to enhance students' learning outcomes (American Psychological Association, 1997; McCombs and Miller, 2007). In addition, Brock's review of systematic research findings on the effectiveness of various interventions designed to help at-risk students remain in college shows that some student-centered programs and interventions do improve student outcomes (Brock, 2010). It is therefore recommended that the learning environment for this course employ activities that involve discussions (in class/online) as a team or as a classroom, involve student presentations as well as individual student reflections in addition to the traditional lecture.

Structure of the Course and Assessment

The themes for the activities emerged from the consideration of the situational factors and relevant challenges faced by the student population taking the History of Mathematics course. To facilitate a student-centered learning environment, the following three phases were recommended as the course structure. The first phase focuses on the individual student becoming informed on a given topic using resources provided by the instructor prior to class meetings. The second phase includes a learning experience using knowledge acquired in phase one in deepening the understanding through discussion or other activities. The third phase involves individual and/or group reflections that integrates the prior two phases. An example of this structure has been presented in Table 1.

Table 1. Activities corresponding to targeted QEP SLOs

	SLO 1	SLO 2		SLO 5		
	Activity 1	Activity 2	Activity 3	Activity 4	Activity 5	Activity 6
Phase one	Readings based on Hindu Arabic Numeric System	Additional Reading – choose number system of another culture or time	Read and evaluate a non-European culture's contributions to Math	Prepare a presentation on one female mathematician.	Prepare presentation on one real life application of math by tracing the history.	Prepare a presentation on the History of Math and math educators and their contributions.
Experiential phase	Full class discussion and creation of concept maps	Give a 10 min presentation with relevant handouts.	Present posters of their findings. Students will walk around and take notes	Give a 7-minute presentation on the female mathematician they have chosen.	Give a 10-minute presentation to the class on their findings.	Give a 7-minute presentation and provide relevant handouts.
Reflection phase		Summary comparing & contrasting cultures based on class.	200 word reflection on findings based on the poster sessions.	Complete an exit ticket before end of class.	Complete an exit ticket before end of class.	Complete an exit ticket before end of class.

Integrated Course Re-Design Phase 3

An important aspect of a learning-centered course is a good feedback and assessment procedure that goes beyond the traditional assessment procedures used to assign student grades. Forward-looking assessments that incorporate assignments with a context of a topic under discussion and clearly outline criteria and standards expected on completion are recommended. A good way to outline criteria and standards for assignments or activities is via rubrics.

A rubric for the experiential phase can be constructed like the one below. This specific rubric was designed for activity two targeting SLO1 (See Table 1).

- **Outstanding (90% to 100%):**
  - Presentation is clear, interesting, involves active participation from audience, accurately describes the number system, and states explicitly how the number system met the needs of the culture, and the handouts are appropriate.
- **Credit (80% to 89.9%):**
  - Presentation does not involve active participation from audience but is clear, interesting, accurately describes the number system, and states explicitly how the number system met the needs of the culture, and the handouts are appropriate.
- **Pass (70% to 79.9%):**
  - Presentation is clear, accurately describes the number system, and states explicitly how the number system met the needs of the culture, and the handouts are appropriate.
- **Fail (below 70%):**
  - Presentation is unclear, does not describe the number system accurately, and does not state explicitly how the number system met the needs of the culture, and the handouts are inappropriate.

The following rubric can be modified for an activity in the reflection phase. This was customized for activity three targeting SLO 2 (See Table 1).

- **Outstanding (90% to 100%):** The summary is free from major language errors, is about 200 words, is submitted on time, states clearly what was learned during the presentations, states the utility of math from a historical and cultural perspective, describes how the present day cultural needs are met by the binary and decimal numeration systems, and briefly describes how a historical knowledge of the numeration system might impact their future teaching.
- **Credit (80% to 89.9%):** The summary is mostly free from major language errors, is about 200 words, is submitted on time, states clearly what was learned during the presentations, states the utility of math from a historical and cultural perspective, describes how the present day cultural needs are met by the binary and decimal numeration systems, but does NOT briefly describe how a historical knowledge of the numeration system might impact their future teaching.
- **Pass (70% to 79.9%):** The summary has a few language errors, is about 200 words, is submitted on time, states clearly what was learned during the presentations, states the utility of math from a historical and cultural perspective, or describes how the present day cultural needs are met by the binary and decimal numeration systems, but does NOT briefly describe how a historical knowledge of the numeration system might impact their future teaching.
- **Fail (below 70%):** The summary has many language errors, is about 200 words, is submitted on time, but neither states clearly what was learned during the presentations, nor states the utility of math from a historical and cultural perspective, and does NOT describe how the present day cultural needs are met by the binary and decimal numeration systems, nor briefly describes how a historical knowledge of the numeration system might impact their future teaching.

THE IMPLEMENTATION: DETAILS

The internationalization of this course, planned by the first two authors in the spring of 2015, was implemented for the first time in its internationalized format in the fall of 2015. At their home institution, the History of Mathematics course is a requirement for all math educator candidates, but can also be used as an elective for any pure or applied students. The college averages about 3-4 candidates entering the program per semester, and the course is scheduled to be offered in the fall semester each year (this has since been adjusted to be fall semesters every other year based upon recent changes to their education program). During this semester, the course met once per week, on Fridays from 2:00-3:15pm. This time frame proved challenging in three respects:

- Being a weekly course, students procrastinated work for this class, often resulting in work that was not of the desired caliber,
- Being a weekly course, the instructor had limited opportunities to build relationships with students, and
- Being offered at the end of the week on Friday afternoons proved challenging, especially for the Teacher Certification students who already had rigorous weekly time commitments with their field experiences, pedagogical instruction, and other content instruction.

During the fall of 2015, there were five students enrolled in this course; four of whom were Teacher Certification candidates at various stages of progress toward their degree, but each of these students was either a junior or a senior. The fifth student was a math major with a pure mathematics concentration, taking the course as an elective. The demographics represented within the course setting were four males, 1 female of whom three were Caucasian, one African-American, and one student from India. The gender makeup was disproportionate to the Teacher Certification program, which is predominantly female. However, the student diversity in the course was representative of the educator preparation program. Such diversity enriched course discussions and interest, as illustrated in discussions that follow.

The goals of the course previously stated are repeated here as an easy reference for the reader. This course presents a historical development of various areas in mathematics and important figures in mathematics from ancient to modern times. Upon completion of this course, a student will:

1. Explore the utility of mathematics from a historical and cultural perspective.
2. Solve problems of historical significance.
3. Develop their sensitivity to the diversity of cultures contributing to the development of mathematics and to the unique perspectives of students for groups underrepresented in the mathematical sciences.
4. Develop and share curricular materials and teaching strategies to promote knowledge and appreciation for historical and cultural foundations of mathematics.
5. Explicitly address the designated NCTM Content Standards.

The resources for this course relied heavily on *The History of Mathematics: An Introduction*, by David Burton, *Algebra in Context: Introductory algebra from origins to applications* by Shell-Gellasch & Thoo, and several online resources including,

- **History of Math (TAMU)**
  - http://www.math.tamu.edu/~dallen/masters/hist_frame.htm
- **History of Math (Steven Krantz, 2006)**
  - http://www.math.wustl.edu/~sk/books/newhist.pdf
- **History of Math Topics**
  http://www-history.mcs.st-and.ac.uk/Indexes/HistoryTopics.html

Learning Experiences Within the Pilot Implementation

This course was structured, both in planning phases, and in implementation, to provide varied learning opportunities that allowed students exposure to multiple cultures, contributions and the impact these cultures made upon the field of mathematics.

The following themes from the recommended curriculum were covered during this pilot implementation.

- **CoG1 and SLO 1, 2:**
  - Mathematics from a historical and cultural perspective. Development of Number Systems and Symbols (ex. Egyptian, Sumerian, Babylonians, Chinese, Greek, Roman, Incas, Mayan, Hindu).
  - Explored the application and use of mathematics to security/encryption.
- **CoG 3 and SLO 1, 2:**
  - Ethno mathematics (diversity of cultures, including non-Western cultures, contributing to the development of mathematics namely Egyptian and Chinese).

- ◦ Female Mathematicians
- ◦ Using history of math and math education to inform the teaching of specific math topics such as volumes and completing squares.
- ◦ Problems/theorems of historical significance explored were the Pythagoras theorem and proof that what is irrational
- CoG 2, 4, 5 and SLO 1, 2, 5
  - ◦ Greek Mathematics (Pythagoras), Mathematics of the East (Chinese), Mathematics of medieval Europe (Fibonacci)
  - ◦ History of Mathematics Education Polya, Cuisenaire, Brownell, Freudenthal, van Hiele, Gagne, Dienes.
  - ◦ Precalculus, calculus and beginning of modern math (Descartes, Pascal, Fermat, Leibniz, Newton)
  - ◦ Math of the 18th century (Euler)
  - ◦ Probability Theory (Pascal)
  - ◦ Number Theory (Fermat, Euler)

While there was some direct instruction (lecture) within the course, this made up only about 40% of the format of instruction, with other formats including group mini-research/presentations, textbook and website investigations, and problem-solving opportunities, formal independent research projects, and analysis of pop culture's treatment of famous mathematical advancements. This is aligned with the active learning approach prescribed during the course redesign. Included below are synopses of some of these activities, as well as selected student reactions and responses.

Mini-Research/Presentations

As this course is targeted to the aspiring teacher candidate, direct instruction was present, but minimized in favor of a more student-centered learning experience. Students were encouraged to be active participants in their acquisition of knowledge; one such way to facilitate this was to offer opportunities for mini-research/mini teaching presentations. In this setting, students were expected to arrive at class with some minimal knowledge on a given topic (addressed phase 1). Upon arrival to class, students were split into small groups (2-3 students) and were directed to use the first part of class time to investigate more rigorously a subset of the previously previewed topic. After a given amount of time, they were to present an informal demonstration and dialogue revolving around their given subject (addressing the experiential phase). There was a follow-up assignment given by the instructor that reinforced the presented material (addressing the reflection phase).

An example of this was used during Week 2 of the course:

- Students were expected to skim Chapter 2 of the Burton text focusing on Sections 2.3, 2.4 and 2.5 prior to coming to class:
- Upon arrival to class, students could self-select into one of three groups:
  - ◦ Group 1 focused on Using Early Egyptian methods of Multiplication and Division
  - ◦ Group 2 focused on the Egyptian Method of False Position
  - ◦ Group 3 focused on the use of Geometry in Early Egypt

- Each group was given a set of instructions to complete during the first 40 minutes of class, followed by a 10-minute presentation of their topic to the rest of the class. The instructor had previously created a set of guided notes for class members to utilize in synthesizing and summarizing these presentations.
- For example, the directions given to Group 1 were as follows:
  - Demonstrate understanding of how to multiply using the Egyptian method. Utilize the example of 18*25 in both orders to illustrate in your instruction. Have students perform 85*21 in both orders and be prepared to answer questions.
  - Demonstrate understanding of how to divide using the Egyptian method. Include a discussion of the use of unit fractions (p. 39) in answers, making sure to touch on the usability of repeated unit fractions and the rules stated on page 41. Utilize the examples of 184/8 and 19/8 to illustrate. Have students perform 46/9 and be prepared to answer questions.
  - Verify the three splitting algorithms (pages 40, 41, 43) and show how they can be used to find unit fractions that sum to non-unit fractions.

During the time that students were preparing these presentations, the instructor circulated among the groups and was available for clarifications or answering questions.

Students were actively engaged in these activities, not only in the preparation of the mini-presentations, but in support of their classmates' presentations as well. Their depth of knowledge was greater; especially for the topics, they were responsible for presenting. They were amazed by the abilities of these early cultures to use mathematics for practical purposes.

Formal Independent Research Projects

Another mode of active learning was given in the form of an independent research project. These were utilized in various forms three times within the semester. In one case, students would choose a topic (a specific culture or individual) and prepare a presentation for their classmates. The research for this would take place outside of class. An example of this was an exploration of ancient civilizations' use of number, utilized during Week 4 of the course:

The directions to students were as follows:

For this multicultural presentation, each student will choose a different ancient culture to research its number system. Use three reputable sources (one can be your textbook). Create a 10-12-minute presentation on the number system, especially how it was used by and how it met the needs of that culture. Use a PowerPoint or Prezi to guide your presentation (do not read it), and provide a handout that supports the presentation and assists in class understanding (handouts should not be the PowerPoint notes sheet). We will conclude the presentations by having a discussion contrasting the various number systems to those used in the present day. Suggestions for Cultures to Investigate: Prehistoric, Egyptian, Babylonian, Chinese, Greek, Roman and Mayan.

Your follow up assignment will be a 200-word summary of your overarching knowledge acquisition through your (and your classmates') presentations, highlighting a culture other than the one you personally researched. Also, discuss how a historical knowledge of these numeration systems might influence your future teaching.

Students did a fantastic job in presenting these cultures and it was evident that they were enlightened by and developed a respect for these cultures' use of number and mathematics. By providing guided notes in prior weeks, the instructor modeled what a good handout might look like that may engage the class and encourage synthesis of the presented material. These were all essential components of a forward-looking assessment as outlined during the course redesign.

One student, presenting on China, presented not only numbering, but also on stick multiplication, which is interesting and a very different to the way multiplication is taught in the United States. This, in particular, was commented on by the presenter's classmates.

I learned a lot about the earliest forms of writing during our presentations. One culture that I was really fascinated by is the ancient Chinese number system. They had writing system for numbers that was logical and easy to understand. The Chinese had recorded their mathematics into a collection, in a way similar to what other cultures did.... Historical knowledge of mathematics, especially this methods helps me appreciate another way to multiply numbers. When teach multiplication, this might be one of the ways I might be able to reach out to students who are more visual learners; they might try a lot of these stick problems before being made to memorize their tables.

Since the population of China was growing, they needed to have systems in place that allowed them to make calculations, especially in order to collect taxes. The Chinese also had some cool methods for multiplying numbers like the stick method....

Historical knowledge of mathematics, especially this method helps me appreciate another way to multiply numbers. When I teach multiplication, this might be one of the ways I might be able to reach out to students who are more visual learners; they might try a lot of these stick problems before being made to memorize their tables.

Rubrics like the ones suggested during the design phase were used to evaluate these presentations and follow-up reflections.

Analysis of Pop Culture's Treatment of Famous Mathematical

Achievements

Recently, a movie was produced that documented and celebrated the cryptographic achievement of breaking the code of the Enigma machine (previously thought to be unbreakable) during World War II. In Imitation Game (2014), the achievements and life of Alan Turing were treated through the lens of Hollywood. Students were guided through the process of differentiating between the factual and fictional aspects of this movie.

Prior to viewing this film, they were given a list of questions to facilitate their research before class. They were to arrive to class with these questions answered, and the sources they used to find the answers to these questions were to be documented. They watched this film as a class (class time was extended for this day), and while watching the film, students were on the lookout for instances that were fictionalized for the film or reinforced documented fact. This experience allowed them to use a critical eye to analyze popular treatment of mathematical achievement. While this achievement did occur in a Western country, it is a country with cultural differences from those of the United States, and the context of this achievement is interesting.

AFTERTHOUGHTS AND CHANGES TO THE COURSE

Several adaptations have occurred since the time this course was originally planned to be internationalized. These adaptations were prompted by two factors: curricular adjustments due to program/standard changes, and feedback from the pilot implementation in fall of 2015. These changes are currently in use (fall of 2016) and seem to be positive adjustments to the course.

Curricular Changes

As the state and nation focuses their attention increasingly on the preparation of its educators, the requirements and standards for these students continue to evolve. The National Council of the Teachers of Mathematics recently added historical standards to the document NCTM CAEP Mathematics Content for Secondary Addendum to the NCTM CAEP Standards 2012. These additions, revised in March of 2015, added the following standards to those recommended for aspiring teachers:

- A.1.5 Historical development and perspectives of number, number systems, and quantity including contributions of significant figures and diverse cultures
- A.2.7 Historical development and perspectives of algebra including contributions of significant figures and diverse cultures
- A.3.10 Historical development and perspectives of geometry and trigonometry including contributions of significant figures and diverse cultures
- A.4.6 Historical development and perspectives of statistics and probability including contributions of significant figures and diverse cultures
- A.5.6 Historical development and perspectives of calculus including contributions of significant figures and diverse cultures
- A.6.5 Historical development and perspectives of discrete mathematics including contributions of significant figures and diverse cultures

These explicitly stated standards provided a rationale to include more material and cultural discussion in the course, and suggested a move from a two-credit learning experience to a three-credit learning experience.

As the state in which the authors' home institution is located also adjusted several requirements, the Teacher Certification programs had to be re-aligned to the most current State and National standards. One result of this was the change in course offerings leading to the History of Mathematics course being offered bi-annually, during the fall semesters of even-numbered calendar years. A consequence of this change was the doubling in size of the class compared to the prior enrollments. The student enrollment at the beginning of Fall 2016 was 10 students, and while this number is still small enough to provide quite an intimate tone within the class, it also allows for more interesting discussions from varied perspectives; better group work, and more occasions for collaborative learning opportunities.

Instructor-Related Changes

As previously stated, there were certain challenges inherent in a class that is offered once weekly. Students were more likely to procrastinate work related to this course, thereby producing less-quality work products and lacking a good understanding of some of the materials that were presented. In addition, the student-instructor relationships were not optimal because of the decreased frequency of meetings. Because of these factors, the instructor requested a different learning format for this course: instead of meeting once weekly for an extended period, the course is currently offered three times per week. This change facilitates increased frequency in exposure and interaction, thereby encouraging greater understanding and facilitating rewarding relationships within the learning environment.

Ideas for Future Iterations of the Course

As this course is targeted to future educators, and exposure to international cultures is a specific objective, an experience that could be of benefit to these students would be to end the course with a culminating project that allows them to be exposed to the way that contemporary math is addressed, taught, and embraced by other cultures. As suggested during the planning phase, this would allow the historical spectrum to run the range from ancient civilizations to current times.

Another suggestion would be for this research project to take on different forms. For example, students may be tasked with investigating the culture, curriculum and teaching methods of another country. Additionally, with current technological capabilities, instructors could encourage students use synchronous or asynchronous communication with international communities that allows them to witness cross-cultural curricular and pedagogical treatment of mathematics. Such activities would expand perspectives limited by their own experiences regarding the teaching and learning of math.

CONCLUSION

The goal of the project was to develop an internationalized undergraduate History of Mathematics course that supported the Quality Enhancement Plan of the home institution. This chapter elaborated on the theoretical framework used in the redesign process (B-D model, Bloom and Fink's taxonomies). It described how the framework was used to develop appropriate learning activities for the current I-course that can be used by others to design similar courses. The authors continued by giving a snapshot of the initial iteration of the course so that the reader can compare the intent of the redesign team with the actual student experiences. Student work, informal feedback and reflections were included to enhance the vicarious experiences.

In the process of the redesign, the authors reflected on a more fundamental question of "why teach History of Mathematics?" Specifically, it was noted how this course has the potential to positively build students' mathematical attitudes and identities while concurrently minimizing their mathematical anxiety. These positive byproducts of the course would complement the mathematical curricular knowledge gained by studying the history of mathematics.

Additionally, background research conducted during this course redesign indicated how enabling future educators to be informed beyond their own cultures would equip them to be more versatile and open in their future classrooms. Such knowledge would also facilitate more culturally accepting attitudes and appreciation for mathematics in future generations because of these experiences.

In summary, this chapter has provided a glimpse into the process and initial implementation of internationalizing an undergraduate history of mathematics course. This could serve as a road map for others considering similar course redesigns. The methodology and framework presented here can be extrapolated to course redesigns in other disciplines as well.

REFERENCES

American Psychological Association. (1997). *Learner-Centered Psychological Principles: Guidelines for School Redesign and Reform*. Author.

Anderson. (2007). *Being a Mathematics Learner: Four Faces of Identity*. University of Georgia.

Anderson, L. W. (2009). *A taxonomy for learning, teaching, and assessing: A revision of Bloom's taxonomy of educational objectives*. New York.

Ascher, M. (2010). *Ethno mathematics: A multicultural view of mathematical ideas*. Boca Raton, FL: CRC Press.

Ashcraft, M. H., & Kirk, E. P. (2001). The relationships among working memory, math anxiety, and performance. *Journal of Experimental Psychology. General*, *130*(2), 224–237. doi:10.1037/0096-3445.130.2.224 PMID:11409101

Barr, R. B., & Tagg, J. (1995). From Teaching to Learning —A New Paradigm for Undergraduate Education. *Change: The Magazine of Higher Learning*, *27*(6), 12–26. doi:10.1080/00091383.1995.10544672

Beilock, S. L., & Carr, T. H. (n.d.). When High-Powered People Fail: Working Memory and Choking Under Pressure in Math. *PsycEXTRA Dataset*. doi:10.1037/e537052012-380

Bok, D. C. (2006). *Our underachieving colleges: A candid look at how much students learn and why they should be learning more*. Princeton, NJ: Princeton University Press.

Bolhuis, S., & Voeten, M. (2004). Teachers' conceptions of student learning and own learning. *Teachers and Teaching*, *10*(1), 77–98. doi:10.1080/13540600320000170936

Breninger, B., & Kaltenbacher, T. (2012). Intercultural Competence in the 21st Century: Perspectives, Issues, Application. In Creating cultural synergies: Multidisciplinary perspectives on interculturality and interreligiosity (pp. 7-23). Newcastle upon Tyne, UK: Cambridge Scholars Pub.

Brewley, N., Boindala, P., & Sinclair, J. (2014). *Ideation to Execution: Flipping an Undergraduate Pre-Calculus Course to Create Significant Learning Experiences* (pp. 26–41). IGI Global Publications.

Brock, T. (2010). *Young adults and higher education: Barriers and breakthroughs to success*. Ann Arbor, MI: National Poverty Center.

Clayton, P. H., Bringle, R. G., & Hatcher, J. A. (2012). Research on Intercultural Learning of Students in Service Learning. In Research on Service Learning V2A: Conceptual Frameworks and Assessments (pp. 157-186). Sterling, VA: Stylus Pub.

Cornelius-White, J. (2007). Learner-Centered Teacher-Student Relationships Are Effective: A Meta-Analysis. *Review of Educational Research, 77*(1), 113–143. doi:10.3102/003465430298563

Deardorff, D. K. (2006). Identification and Assessment of Intercultural Competence as a Student Outcome of Internationalization. *Journal of Studies in International Education, 10*(3), 241–266. doi:10.1177/1028315306287002

Deardorff, D. K. (2009). *The Sage handbook of intercultural competence*. Thousand Oaks, CA: Sage Publications.

Deardorff, D. K. (2009). Assessing intercultural competence: Issues and tools. In *The Sage handbook of intercultural competence* (pp. 456–476). Thousand Oaks, CA: Sage Publications.

Dee, F. L. (2013). *Creating Significant Learning Experiences: An Integrated Approach to Designing College Courses*. Wiley.

Fennema, E., & Sherman, J. A. (1976). Fennema-Sherman Mathematics Attitudes Scales: Instruments Designed to Measure Attitudes toward the Learning of Mathematics by Females and Males. *Journal for Research in Mathematics Education, 7*(5), 324. doi:10.2307/748467

Frankenstein, M. (1990). Incorporating Race, Gender, and Class Issues into a Critical Mathematica Literacy Curriculum. *The Journal of Negro Education, 59*(3), 336. doi:10.2307/2295568

Gutierrez, R. (2013). The Sociopolitical Turn in Mathematics Education. *Journal for Research in Mathematics Education, 44*(1), 37–68. doi:10.5951/jresematheduc.44.1.0037

Gutstein. (2006). *Reading and Writing: The World with Mathematics, Towards a Pedagogy for Social Justice*. CRC Press.

Harouni, H. (2015). Toward a Political Economy of Mathematics Education. *Harvard Educational Review, 85*(1), 50–74. doi:10.17763/haer.85.1.2q580625188983p6

Heiede, T. (1992). Why Teach History of Mathematics? *The Mathematical Gazette, 76*(475), 151. doi:10.2307/3620388

In Greer, G. B. (2010). *Culturally responsive mathematics education*. New York: Routledge.

Johnson, R. M., Smith, K. H., & Carinci, S. (2010). Preservice Female Teachers' Mathematics Self-Concept and Mathematics Anxiety: A Longitudinal Study. *Global Pedagogies*, 169-181. doi:10.1007/978-90-481-3617-9_11

Kazemi, F., Shahmohammadi, A., & Sharei, M. (2013). The survey on relationship between the attitude and academic achievement of in-service mathematics teachers in introductory Probability and Statistics. *World Applied Sciences Journal, 22*(7), 886–891.

King, P. M., & Baxter Magolda, M. B. (2005). A Developmental Model of Intercultural Maturity. *Journal of College Student Development, 46*(6), 571–592. doi:10.1353/csd.2005.0060

Leatham, K. R. (2013). *Vital Directions for Mathematics Education Research*. Dordrecht, The Netherlands: Springer. doi:10.1007/978-1-4614-6977-3

Lortie, D. C. (2007). Schoolteacher: A sociological study; with a new preface. Chicago: Univ. of Chicago Press.

Ma, X., & Xu, J. (2004). The causal ordering of mathematics anxiety and mathematics achievement: A longitudinal panel analysis. *Journal of Adolescence, 27*(2), 165–179. doi:10.1016/j.adolescence.2003.11.003 PMID:15023516

McCombs, B. L., & Miller, L. (2007). *Learner-centered classroom practices and assessments: Maximizing student motivation, learning, and achievement*. Thousand Oaks, CA: Corwin Press.

Moodian, M. A. (2009). Assessment instruments for the global workforce. In *Contemporary leadership and intercultural competence: Exploring the cross-cultural dynamics within organizations* (pp. 175–190). Los Angeles, CA: SAGE. doi:10.4135/9781452274942

Mubeen, S., Saeed, S., & Hussain Arif, M. (2013). Attitude towards mathematics and academic achievement in mathematics among secondary level boys and girls. *IOSR Journal of Humanities and Social Science, 6*(4), 38–41. doi:10.9790/0837-0643841

Paige, R. M. (1993). *Education for the intercultural experience*. Yarmouth, Me: Intercultural Press.

Powell, A. B., & Frankenstein, M. (1997). *Ethno mathematics: Challenging eurocentrism in mathematics education*. Albany, NY: State Univ. of New York Press.

Relich, J. (1996). Gender, self-concept and teachers of mathematics: Effects on attitudes to teaching and learning. *Educational Studies in Mathematics, 30*(2), 179–195. doi:10.1007/BF00302629

Russell, W. B. (2011). *Contemporary social studies: An essential reader*. Charlotte, NC: Information Age Pub.

Schubring, G., & Karp, A. P. (2014). History of Mathematics Teaching and Learning. Encyclopedia of Mathematics Education, 260-267. doi:10.1007/978-94-007-4978-8_70

Secada, W. G., Fennema, E., & Byrd, A. L. (1995). *New directions for equity in mathematics education*. Cambridge, UK: Cambridge University Press.

Solomon, Y. (2007). Not belonging? What makes a functional learner identity in undergraduate mathematics? *Studies in Higher Education, 32*(1), 79–96. doi:10.1080/03075070601099473

Speece, D. L., & Keogh, B. K. (1996). *Research on classroom ecologies: Implications for inclusion of children with learning disabilities*. Mahwah, NJ: Lawrence Erlbaum Associates.

Stigler, J., & Thompson, B. J. (2009). Thoughts on Creating, Accumulating, and Utilizing Shareable Knowledge to Improve Teaching. *The Elementary School Journal, 109*(5), 442–457. doi:10.1086/596995

Stigler, J. W., & Hiebert, J. (2009). *The teaching gap: Best ideas from the world's teachers for improving education in the classroom*. New York: Free Press.

Van Maanen, J. (2004). The Role of History of Mathematics in the Teaching and Learning of Mathematics: Presentation of the ICMI Study and the Study Book. *Proceedings of the Ninth International Congress on Mathematical Education*, 374-377. doi:10.1007/1-4020-7910-9_96

Walshaw, M. (2013). Post-Structuralism and Ethical Practical Action: Issues of Identity and Power. *Journal for Research in Mathematics Education*, *44*(1), 100–118. doi:10.5951/jresematheduc.44.1.0100

Webber, K. L. (2012). Learner-Centered Assessment in US Colleges and Universities. *Research in Higher Education*, *53*(2), 201–228. doi:10.1007/s11162-011-9245-0

Weimer, M. (2002). *Learner-Centered Teaching: Five Key Changes to Practice. the Jossey-Bass Higher and Adult Education Series*. Jossey-Bass.

Wiggins, G. P., McTighe, J., Kiernan, L. J., & Frost, F. (2000). *Understanding by design*. Alexandria, VA: Association for Supervision and Curriculum Development.

KEY TERMS AND DEFINITIONS

Affective Domain: The affective domain includes feelings, values, appreciation, enthusiasms, motivations, and attitudes.

Backwards Design: Backward design is a method of designing educational curriculum beginning with the end in mind (i.e., by setting goals before choosing instructional methods and forms of assessment).

Cognitive Domain: The cognitive domain includes content knowledge and the development of intellectual skills.

History of Mathematics: The area of study that is primarily an investigation into the origin of discoveries in mathematics, and to an investigation into the mathematical methods and notation of the past.

Internationalization: Internationalization is the process of planning and implementing products and services, specifically educational curriculum, so that they can be adapted to specific local situations, languages, and cultures.

Mathematics Attitude: A positive or negative emotional disposition towards mathematics.

Mathematics Identity: The perception of the mathematics learners about mathematics, arising from the relationships and experiences with their peers, teachers, family, and community.

Significant Learning: Significant learning is learning that facilitates the construction of ideas and conceptual understanding.

Chapter 10
Creating a Vibrant STEM Study Abroad Program With a Cultural Component

Boyko Georgiev Gyurov
Georgia Gwinnett College, USA

Mark Andrew Schlueter
Georgia Gwinnett College, USA

ABSTRACT

In 2014, the authors of this chapter joined forces to create a unique STEM study abroad experience for Georgia Gwinnett College students, and that experience grew into a model worthy to be examined and replicated. The model addresses the main objectives of U.S. Senator Paul Simon Study Abroad Program Act to bring the demographics of study abroad participation to reflect the demographics of the United States undergraduate population and to implement the study abroad programs in nontraditional study abroad destinations, and in particular in developing countries. Further, the model contains six important components (bundle setup, faculty led, interdisciplinary academic content delivery, undergraduate research, low cost, and cultural component added). The characteristics of all of which are explained in details in the paper. Finally, the successes and challenges of the program are discussed through the prism of it successful implementation in the summers of 2015 and 2016.

INTRODUCTION

Over the past two decades, colleges and universities have made a significant effort to provide study abroad opportunities for their students. Most higher education institutions feel that students should be interculturally competent and exhibit global awareness. Universities have even inserted terms such as global society, globalization, and international awareness into their students' educational goals. Focusing on internationalizing the curriculum has become a priority in higher education in the USA, with over 90% of all colleges and universities offering study abroad (Hoffa & DePaul, 2010). Studies suggest that study abroad experiences have significant beneficial outcomes for students, such as becoming more

DOI: 10.4018/978-1-5225-2791-6.ch010

interested in academics (Malmgren & Galvin, 2008) and becoming more globally aware (Dolby, 2007; Fuller, 2007; Clarke, Flaherty, Wright, & McMillen, 2009).

Many students have taken advantage of study abroad opportunities. During the 2014-2015 academic year, 313,415 students participated in study abroad programs, an increase of over 150% from just 10 years ago (Institute of International Education (IIE), 2015). The number of undergraduates who studied abroad in the same period was 274,551, and despite the 3.6% increase over the participants in 2013/2014, the overall percentage of U.S. students who study abroad remains below 2 percent of total U.S. undergraduates. These incremental successes highlight the complexity and the hardship of successfully setting up and executing study abroad opportunities. Many academic institutions spend significant time and effort creating study abroad programs, yet only a small fraction of their students take advantage of these programs. On a federal level, in 1990, The National Task Force on Undergraduate Education recommended that, by the year 2000, 10% of North American college and university undergraduates should have a significant educational experience abroad before graduating (Burn & Smuckler, 1990). The recommendation was given federal support by the passage of the National Security Education Act of 1991, which sought to facilitate study abroad, among other things. A simple extrapolation from the data shows, however, that at the current participation rate at around 2% and the average graduation rate of over 5 years, the National Task Force recommendation would miss its mark by at least two decades. One may argue that this is proof of the inefficiency of the federal government to execute and deliver on its programs, and another - that this is proof of the complexity of the undertaking. However, all would agree that in an economically and digitally shrinking world, a cross-cultural awareness and exploitation of the advantages that it gives is a must for a nation that wants to be at the leading edge.

In 2016, a revised goal on study abroad was proposed by the passage of the Senator Paul Simon's Study Abroad Program Act, in which the conjecture of one million U.S. college students engaged in studying abroad each year was proposed. However, at the current growth rate of around 3% per year (IIE, 2015), the goal of 1 million students studying abroad per year, cannot occur for at least another generation.

Student diversity, both socially and financially, of participating U.S. students is very restricted, with a low percentage of males and minorities participating in study abroad programs. The vast majority of current study abroad students are financially comfortable, white females without disabilities (Stallman, Woodruff, Kasravi, & Comp, 2010; Sweeney, 2013). Furthermore, most study abroad students major in social sciences and humanities (Stroud, 2010), and despite the reversal of trends in the last 5 years with STEM and business taking the lead and accounting for about 44% of study abroad participants, still only (slightly under) one out of four attending students is in the field of the natural sciences, engineering, or math (IIE, OpenDoors® "FastFacts", 2016).

One of the main hurdles preventing students from participating in study abroad is finances. A second big hurdle for Science, Technology, Engineering, and Math (STEM) majors is a lack of study abroad courses that fit into their major or program of study. Both of these conditions have kept many STEM students and minority students from participating in study abroad altogether. However, several schools have developed highly specific biology or natural history courses that take students on study abroad trips to visit the flora and fauna of target ecosystems, but these experiences often lack a cultural component (Malloy & Davis, 2012).

In 2014, the authors of the current chapter joined forces to create a unique STEM study abroad experience for Georgia Gwinnett College (GGC) students, and that experience grew into a model worthy to be examined and replicated. The model addresses all objectives of U.S. Senator Paul Simon's Study Abroad Program Act of 2016 (114th Congress, 2nd Session Issue: Vol. 162, No. 144, S6041), namely:

"(i) not less than 1,000,000 undergraduate students will study abroad annually;

(ii) the demographics of study abroad participation will reflect the demographics of the United States undergraduate population;

and

(iii) an increasing portion of study abroad will take place in nontraditional study abroad destinations, with a substantial portion of such increases in developing countries".

Even more so, this model adds two additional and hard to obtain objectives, namely:

(iv) the study abroad program is specifically designed for STEM majoring students to address the growing need of globally aware scientists and engineers;

(v) the program has an extensive cultural component that enhances the STEM curriculum with international and intercultural exposure, as well as, discussions and reflections with the ultimate goal of creating a STEM global citizen.

The next sections provide an in-depth explanation of the model. They give the flows of ideas, goals, challenges, and successes of the program as it successfully ran in the summers of 2015 and 2016.

THE MODEL: FACULTY LED STEM COURSE BUNDLE APPROACH WITH A CULTURAL COMPONENT

Motivation

Georgia Gwinnett College (GGC) is an open-access, public 4-year college, with over 12,000 students. Situated in the second most populous county in Georgia – Gwinnett, and one of the most diverse counties in the state, in 2016, US News and World Report ranked GGC as the most ethnically diverse Southern regional college. As a member of the University System of Georgia (USG) and the Southern Association of Colleges and Schools (SACS), a successful implementation and completion of the Quality Enhancement Plan (QEP) is required for reaffirmation of accreditation from the SACS Commission on Colleges (SACS-COC). In 2011, GGC selected the topic of the institutional QEP to be "Internationalization of the Curriculum: Engaging the World to Develop Global Citizens" and set the 2012-2013 academic year to be the pre-QEP year during which infrastructure and models for the implementation of the programs were to be established. The notion of an "I-course" (Internationalized course) was created to be the main vehicle to deliver intercultural content to students and to serve as a tool to internationalize the curriculum. Since, among other requirements, a minimum of 30% intercultural content in any given course was imposed as a requirement for a course to be an I-course, it became apparent that for (most) STEM courses, which have rigid scientific content, an approach that involves extra curriculum activities was needed.

Thus, the School of Science and Technology (SST) at GGC concentrated its efforts on creating study abroad programs with an embedded cultural component that would allow the science classes to cover all of their specific scientific curriculum, and would also include (or extend) a cultural discussion, as well as reflection and assessment. In that way, through the experiences garnered from pre-departure and post travel meetings and the opportunities U.S. students have while interacting abroad with their foreign counterparts in learning, studying, and solving problems together, the 30% intercultural content could easily be achieved. That would allow a robust, culturally enhanced science I-courses to be put in place, with the ultimate goal of creating an inter-cultural competent and internationally competitive STEM workforce.

Besides the practical reasons explained above behind the SST decision for moving into the study abroad model, there are a series of studies that show that students in study abroad programs demonstrate greater gains in intercultural competence compared to students studying on campus during the same semester (Vande Berg, Connor-Linton, & Paige, 2009), (Anderson & Lawton, 2012). Successfully running the currently discussed STEM model for two consecutive years, makes the authors of this research believe that the gains are not only in intercultural competence, but in academic competence in general. All the GGC students who participated in the program spent a substantial number of hours working on math homework and project problems, both individually and in groups, with their Vietnamese counterparts. Significant academic improvement, infused by the intercultural interactions with their peers, can be measured by the American students' performances on their class assessments (quizzes, tests, projects etc.), with grades consistently averaging above 80%. These averages were above the students' individual academic GPA averages, and thus the improvement in their performance can be considered significant. Similar findings about improved academic performance and increased interest in academic activities for participants in study abroad were reported elsewhere (Malmgren & Galvin, 2008). The dedication and hard work that students demonstrated during the study abroad can be partially explained by the natural competition that occurs when American students are set to perform alongside or against their foreign counterparts. Additional factors are due to other specific design components of the program explained later in the chapter.

Setting up a successful "in-house" study abroad program requires addressing specific challenges and needs throughout the process. There are five main steps in the development and implementation of such a program: (1) proposal submission and institutional program approval; (2) recruitment of students; (3) academic setup at the foreign host university (country); (4) travel and cultural component set up; and (5) program implementation with post program administration.

The first stage, the proposal submission, needs to be in conjunction with the university mission and vision, and also in conjunction with the needs of the student population at the school. A good proposal (after approval) should seamlessly lead to fast recruitment, since the students' *intent, availability, and ability* to participate will be addressed in the program setup. Extensive research on students' intent, found that various forms of capital (financial, human, social, and cultural) attained before attending college influence students' predispositions to study abroad and that females and whites are more likely to plan to study abroad (Salisbury, Umbach, Paulsen, & Pascarella, 2009). This same study also found differences in intent to study abroad based on institutional type, with students at research universities, regional institutions, and community colleges less likely than students at liberal arts colleges to consider study abroad.

Despite being a regional institution, GGC has the advantage of being situated in a very diverse county and thus has a very diverse student population. A large number of those students are from immigrant families from Asia and Latin America, and by the virtue of their family ties, they have built-in cultural capital and an anthropological connection with the different countries of those regions. So the intent to travel abroad and, as a subsequence, the intent to travel to study abroad is organically built into a good portion of the GGC student population.

This intent, based on cultural connections, was manifested in the two GGC Math and Biology Study Abroad Vietnam programs that the authors executed in 2015 and 2016. Students with links or family ties to the Vietnamese culture participated in the former programs, and the current recruitment for 2017 shows a similar trend of 10% to 20% of the participating students being first or second generation immigrants from Vietnam. Furthermore, over 50% of the participating students in both programs are children of first generation immigrants, and thus have built-in social and cultural capital of traveling abroad to visit other cultures, in part fueled by travels to the home country of their parents.

Thus, setting up programs at GGC that address the second and third objectives of Senator Paul Simon's Study Abroad Act - to diversify the study abroad groups and to implement them in non-traditional destinations and, in particular, developing countries is a relatively simple task, given the inherited advantages that the school has.

The main disadvantage for students at regional colleges, including GGC, is not a lack of offered study abroad programs, but rather the students' availability and ability to participate in study abroad programs.

As a majority commuter college with only around 10% of the student population residing on campus, many GGC students work full time off campus jobs, with little to no (paid or unpaid) vacation. Thus, most students are not available to travel for longer than a week or two away from their workplace, let alone for month long or semester long study abroad programs. As a result, most employed students who desire to participate in study abroad must take into consideration the possibility of losing their job in order to participate. Clearly, providing them with an academic opportunity that would significantly enrich their education and accelerate their graduation can work as a justification for losing a month long revenue or losing a job altogether. So, the idea of offering a bundle of 2 or 3 classes, all of which fit into students' degree plans naturally occurred. Additionally, a large number of GGC students are first generation college students, and as such, have much lower levels of built-in social and human capital for proactively searching for opportunities, or even being comfortable and confident in unfamiliar environments, which implies that the most natural set up for the bundles are faculty led, GGC study abroad programs, rather than outsourced study abroad opportunities. Participating in a program with well-known GGC faculty who (1) recruit students, (2) proctor the pre-departure meetings and the post travel reflection meetings, and (3) travel with the students the entire travel time, provides a natural shelter and comfort (both academically and personally) to the participating students and addresses any social and human interaction deficiencies there might be.

Next, an inherent advantage of the faculty led bundle program is the possibility of incorporating an interdisciplinary approach in the teaching of the courses, specifically incorporating class materials and techniques from one course into the other discipline's course. For instance, in our model, biology and mathematics courses are put to work in unison. In the biology course, the students perform scientific measurements, and then in the mathematics course, the biological data gathered is analyzed and interpreted using mathematical methods and techniques. This teaching technique improves individual student interest in learning the mathematical methods, since the relevance of those methods is directly apparent. Furthermore, this educational technique allows a natural gateway to understand the motivation behind the mathematical methods, and it is a useful tool for learning and retaining mathematical knowledge, a common struggle for undergraduate students.

The fact that the faculty leaders are from the same institution, and complement and support each other in the preparatory and recruitment part of the study abroad, allows for close cooperation in the preparation of the study abroad program, at both a science and at a cultural level. The close faculty cooperation and interdisciplinary approach allows the program to be naturally enhanced by the addition of an undergraduate level research component – an opportunity that we took in our model.

Rooted into the availability of math and science courses and the interdisciplinary approach taken for the content delivery, it is a low hanging fruit, at that point, to add a research component to the program. Even more so, stepping on the developed interdisciplinary materials, the undergraduate research could be easily steered in the direction of either of the science classes, or both. From the point of view of the program developer, adding the research is technically seamless, and it just requires several well-planned activities. Moreover, while additional effort and ambition from students willing to take the challenge is needed, the financial burden to them is marginal (the cost of one additional institutional credit in the case of our program).

In the view of these authors, the research opportunity should be delivered through a separate course, which is not necessarily taken by all participating students. After careful prescreening, only those who feel confident in their abilities to cope with the harsh reality of taking two science classes, while traveling extensively and still finding the time that the research requires, should be encouraged to take the class.

For dedicated students, there is an additional benefit, namely, the opportunity for the students to continue and present the research after returning to their home institution. In the GGC program, most students were very enthusiastic to take the research class, due to its obvious benefits, but some students underperformed during the implementation of the program. A good number of the actively participating students, on the other hand, polished the research in the fall semester following the study abroad and presented it at regional or national conferences. Those students stay vested into the program way after its completion as well, and are the best ambassadors on campus for subsequent recruitments.

While the intent and the availability, as well as the social ability of students to participate in STEM study abroad were addressed with some of the previously discussed techniques, the ability of a student to raise the funds needed to participate is their next big hurdle. Additionally, each student's physical and mental ability to participate in an intense, multi-course STEM program, enhanced with a cultural and research component, is also worth considering, discussing, and addressing. As an open enrollment and relatively inexpensive higher education institution, GGC attracts a big number of first generation students and students with lower incomes. Yet, it is clear that in order for the U.S., as a country, to even get close to the federal goal of 1,000,000 undergraduates participating in study abroad annually, much bigger numbers of middle class and lower middle class students need to be inspired and supported to participate in such travels. Thus, keeping the price of a program as low as possible for students is a major consideration for a school such as Georgia Gwinnett College.

There are two main techniques to keep the price of a month long program at its lowest possible range – one is to constitute it in a country with substantially lower life standards than the U.S. and/or two - to cooperate with institution(s) in the destination country, which can absorb some of the expenses, by providing direct (in the form of a financial support) or indirect support (in the form of providing housing, board, or services for free or at discounted rates). In particular, many hosting institutions in developing countries are often willing to absorb some of the cost for programs that are mutually beneficial and would allow their students and faculty to participate in academic activities that are novice for them, such as flipped classrooms, team learning projects, team research projects and so on, an advantage that was used in the currently discussed program.

A third way to keep the price of a program as low as possible is the removal of "the middle man". The idea is rather controversial, since clearly big travel companies can provide a good product at a reasonable price, due to their buying power and contacts in the regions where the product is delivered. However, most of those reasonably priced travel packets are in counties and areas that are top choices for study abroad, and by default, out of reach for a student with limited means. For example, in the academic 2014/2015, UK, Italy, Spain, France and China were the top 5 travel destinations, with 42% of all study abroad participants. If we add the next 5 – Germany, Ireland, Costa Rica, Australia and Japan, it is apparent that only one of the top ten countries qualifies as a developing country, and none qualifies as a non-traditional study abroad destination. Furthermore, the top 10 travel destinations constitute roughly 60% of all study abroad travels (IIE, OpenDoors®, "FastFacts", 2016), and the living standard in all but two of those are comparable (if not higher) than that of U.S, which clearly makes a month long program at such destinations relatively expensive for a middle class student. Finally, most of those program and destination providers have rigid rules and travel packets, and it is hard to accommodate the specific needs of a small STEM study abroad. So, while we do not argue against great study abroad travel providers such as STA Travel, or academic study abroad providers such as the Council of International Educational Exchange (CIEE) Asia, CIEE Europe, and others, the specifics of our model require us to set up the travel components ourselves in order to accommodate the specific academic needs of our students, while keeping the price of the program affordable for a larger part of the student population at our institution.

Capitalizing on the cultural angle that any study abroad program presents, the addition of a cultural component is a must for any study abroad, including those in the STEM area. Stepping on the goals of the Georgia Gwinnett College, Quality Enhancement Program, a cultural component was embedded into our program and executed through a series of pre-departure discussions and lectures, on site discussions and observations, and shortly after the return, a post arrival reflection, and assessment.

The long-term connections of one of the authors with Thai Nguyen University of Technology (TNUT) in Vietnam and the University's willingness to subsidize the study abroad program, made TNUT a natural host for the GGC program. The hosting institution agreed to provide free rooms and to also pay for some of the transportation and cultural events for the U.S. students in exchange for allowing their students to participate in classroom activities and the cultural workshops. Thus, a study abroad program bundling biology, mathematics, and interdisciplinary undergraduate research was put together to constitute the GGC Math and Biology study abroad program. The study abroad program consisted of 3 and a half weeks of academic and cultural activities in Vietnam and 4 days of cultural activities in Tokyo, Japan. All travel components were designed to maximum academic and cultural impacts, while keeping the price of the program down. The originating institution also provided $800 per student for travel support to help boost the participation in the program in 2015 and 2016 and pave the road for future programs. This innovative study abroad program provides a typical STEM major at GGC the opportunity to study abroad, while taking useful courses at affordable prices. The details of the model are discussed next followed by a discussion of its successes and setbacks.

The Model

The Georgia Gwinnett College Math-Biology Study Abroad model is designed to include two institutional faculty (one biology and one mathematics) and up to 15 (due to hosting university constrains), but no less than 10 (due to home institution requirements) students enrolled (preferably) in all 3 classes of the program.

The Academic Design

The academic part of the model implements the different ideas mentioned in the motivation – bundle, faculty led, interdisciplinary, undergraduate research. In the program, we bundle three courses: (1) a biology course, (2) a mathematics course, (3) a research course. Students can sign up for as little as one or all three courses offered. However, during the recruitment process, students taking all three courses were given priority in registration for the limited spots in the program. The program is a month long study abroad experience set in the first of the two summer semesters at GGC, typically the last week of May and the first three weeks of June. The course bundle includes a 4-credit Calculus I (MATH 2200) course, a 3-credit Tropical Biology (BIOL 3050) course, and a 1-credit research experience (STEC 2500). The STEC 2500 experience is an undergraduate research class with an interdisciplinary design, where the mathematical methods and techniques covered in the Calculus I course are used in conjunction with the biological knowledge and research methods covered in the Tropical Biology course. The research project provides students with a unique opportunity to connect and implement theoretical and quantitative knowledge in real-life scientific experiments, data gathering, and analysis. Furthermore, the course advances another innovating GGC initiative implemented at the School of Science and Technology – the course-embedded undergraduate research experience (CURE).

In order to successfully provide thorough academic coverage and practice of the mathematical skills taught during study abroad, the schedule and curriculum are designed to allow students to be in a traditional classroom 4 days a week at a foreign university and to participate in biological field trips and cultural trips the other 3 days a week. The academic experience is designed for a time that adds up to 3 weeks (non-consecutive) of the program time. The remaining program time that is the equivalent to one week (non-consecutive seven days) is devoted to cultural fieldtrips, which give students the opportunity to experience, and compare and contrast developed and developing Asian countries, in particular - Japan versus Vietnam. Even within the same country, regional comparisons can be drawn between the north and south of Vietnam, since travels are done in both parts of the country. Additionally, there is an academic requirement from the Biology course for the students to keep a field journal in which to reflect on their biology related observations, as well as cultural connotations and findings.

The Calculus I course is set to be taught in a classroom on the campus of the hosting institution in Vietnam, with a mix of both American and Vietnamese students. This academic framework provides the opportunity for students to interact both inside the classroom and outside of class. Mixed teams of American/Vietnamese students work on joint Calculus problems and projects, creating an environment of group cooperation and friendly competition between groups. Student presentations and competitions create additional opportunities for students to learn from one another, while also reflecting on their own opinions and methods of learning Calculus. Due to the relatively low number of in classroom meeting days (around 10 to 12), the course is rather intensive with two session per day on the days it meets, usually 2.5 hours in the morning and 2.5 hours in the afternoon. A full week (5 meetings) of pre-departure sessions are setup to update the students' Pre-Calculus knowledge and math-algebraic abilities.

Approximately 35% of the Tropical Biology content is provided to students prior to the study abroad course. We refer to this as "pre-teaching" of the course. The "pre-teaching" allows students to be more academically prepared and ready to be fully engaged in biological research activities, field trips, and hands-on activities. Pre-teaching consists of 5 class meetings, which are held two weeks prior to the beginning of the study abroad experience. During the "pre-teaching" period, each student is assigned 2 topics (1 tropical plant and 1 tropical animal) to prepare two, 10-minute oral presentations, to be given to their fellow students in the foreign country. Students are also assigned a brief reflective essay on the topics of biodiversity, ecotourism, and conservation biology. All of these assignments prepare the students to jump right into the hands-on activities and experiences provided in the natural areas explored in Vietnam (e.g. Cat Tien National Park). Approximately 30% of the Tropical Biology course is taught at the university in host institution. (See Table 1 for an example of topics covered and scheduled). The remaining 35% of the course is taught during hands-on field experiences while on biological field trips in Vietnam, where students implement research techniques and sample organisms.

Table 1. Tropical biology schedule for math-biology study abroad program Vietnam 2015. Pre-teaching was an important method in both covering content and preparing students for the biology portion of the study abroad experience.

Date	Class Topics	Exams & Activities	Homework
Pre-teaching (GGC -Day 1) 8 AM- 5 PM	(1) VIETNAM: Its People, History, Culture, and Geography. (2) Ecology & Introduction to Ecosystems	Work on: Animal Presentation	Chapters 1-2
Pre-teaching (GGC-Day 2) 8 AM- 5 PM	(3) Tropical Animals in Vietnam (4) Tropical Plants in Vietnam	Work on: Plant Presentation	Chapters 3-4 Essay – Biodiversity
Pre-teaching (GGC-Day 3) 8 AM- 5 PM	(5) Tropical Ecosystems (Rainforest to Savanna to Limestone Forests) (6) Field Guides	Using Field Guides to Identify Organisms	Chapters 5-6 Essay – Ecotourism
Pre-teaching (GGC-Day 4) 8 AM- 5 PM	(7) Research/Field Techniques (8) Conservation Biology: Balancing Environment vs. Economy	Nature Hike	Chapters 7-8 Both Essays Due
Pre-teaching (GGC-Day 5) 8 AM- Noon	Review of Major Concepts Final Instructions & Preparations	**EXAM**	None
6/2 (Vietnam) Afternoon	Introduction to Vietnam	Set-up Experiments	None
6/3 (Vietnam) Afternoon	Field Sampling and Biology Projects	Field Experiments	None
6/4 (Vietnam) Afternoon	Biology of Ha Long Bay (Vietnam)	Field Experiments	None
6/9 (Vietnam) Afternoon	Animal and Plants of Vietnam	Field Experiments	Animal Oral Presentation
6/10 (Vietnam) Afternoon	How to sample and identify insects (Butterfly sampling)	Field Experiments	Assigned Readings
6/11 (Vietnam) Afternoon	Biology of Ba Be (Vietnam)	Field Experiments	Plant Oral Presentation
6/16 (Vietnam) Afternoon	Biology of Cat Tien Rainforest (Vietnam)	Field Experiments	Assigned Readings
6/17(Vietnam) Afternoon	Discussion of results and data collected	Field Experiments	Data Analysis
6/18(Vietnam) Afternoon	Discussion of results and data collected	Data Analysis	Project Summary
7/1 (GGC)	Class Reunion/Party	Field Notebook Due	None

The 1-credit STEC 2500 research project provides students opportunities to connect and implement theoretical and quantitative knowledge. Students perform a 3-week long experiment on the university campus in Vietnam and are asked to use the skills, techniques, and methods taught in both the Calculus and Tropical Biology classes.

The travel design. The travel part of the program is planned in a way to serve both – the academic needs of the model, in our case, the biology field trips, and the cultural needs of the model – developing an understanding of the Far East by experiencing the vibrant culture of Vietnam. More so, a reflection on the contrasts: developed versus developing, democratic versus single party rule, homogeneous versus multi-ethnic and so on is required by design through the visits of Japan and Vietnam. The trips start with a 4 day visit to Tokyo, Japan. Furthermore, visits to both the north and south of Vietnam are included which gives students the opportunity to experience the mountainous regions of the north, the Pacific Ocean and limestone formations of the north east, and the rain forests and the Mekong delta on the south of Vietnam. In detail, the trips for the program are:

1. A 4 days, 3 nights trip to Tokyo, Japan done at the beginning of the program. The trip is mostly a cultural experience and also serves as a decompression period after the long 16-hour flight to East Asia. The first day is, upon arrival in Tokyo, an introduction of the students to the metro system of the city and a visit to the lively and youthful Shibuya district. The second day is packed with cultural explorations – starting with the Hie Shrine in the heart of Akasaka, through a daytime city observation from the Tokyo Metropolitan Government building in Shinjuku, and a visit to the Tokyo National Museum in Ueno and the Sensoji Temple in Asakusa. The day ends with a night time observation of the city from the Tokyo Skytree in Sumida. The day time exploration also includes a visit to one of the many botanical gardens in Tokyo, which serves as an initial glimpse at the flora and fauna in Asia. The third day of the program includes a visit to the Imperial Palace, after which students are allowed to explore whatever excites them the most in that cosmopolitan city. The same rule applies for the fourth day, with the awareness of the afternoon flight to Vietnam.

2. A 3 days, 2 nights trip to the Ha Long Bay area, with combined biological field trip that explores limestone forests and caves along the coast of Ha Long Bay, and a cultural filed trip that includes Quang Ninh museum, local temples, and night markets. The Quang Ninh museum is a multi-theme exposition, which includes the geomorphological formation of Ha Long Bay and the region's flora, fauna, as well as, the region's culture and religion, and Quang Ninh's path to industrialization.

3. A 5 days, 4 nights trip to the Ho Chi Minh area, that includes an extensive 2 day biological field trip to the rain forest in Cat Tien National park and a 2 day cultural trip in the area of the Mekong Delta. One night in between the two parts is spent in Ho Chi Minh City, which provides opportunities for students to explore one of the most vibrant cities of South-East Asia. The visit to the National Palace and Ben Thanh night market are highlights of the day.

4. A 2 day biological field trip to BaBe Lake - a fascinating ecosystem in the Limestone Mountains in the north, which is the largest natural lake in Vietnam and is a UNESCO recognized site.

5. A day trip to Hanoi, just before departure back to the USA, where students explore the capital of Vietnam and visit a series of sites to complete their exploration, as well as, expand their understanding of the country. The itinerary includes visits to the Temple of Literature, the one pillar pagoda, the Hanoi museum, and a water puppet show – an art form unique to Vietnam.

The Cultural Design

The cultural goals of the program are naturally embedded into the academic and travel designs, as discussed previously. For maximum impact, however, a series of culture nights are planned by the leading faculty in coordination with the hosting institution to engage students during the week nights. Such events are needed to stimulate students to interact and form friendships with their foreign counterparts early in the program, a technique that is required for students who are less culturally curious or too culturally shy to explore, learn, understand, and accept the other.

Through a variety of sponsorships and budgeted planning, the program is designed to cost approximately $3,000 (institutional tuitions and fees not included).

Despite the relatively low price for a month-long program with most activities and excursions expenses covered, the price tag is high for many GGC students. For that reason, as well as to encourage broader student participation in the study abroad programs, GGC provides through its Office of Internationalization a fixed $800 scholarship (reduced to $700 for the programs run in 2017) for all travels that are between 4 and 8 weeks long. The minimal requirement of a 2.5 GPA and 24 institutional credits completed makes the travel scholarship easily accessible for a majority of school students.

Implementation of the Model in the GGC Vietnam Math/Biology Study Abroad Program

We ran the bundle approach for two years (2015 and 2016) with a total of 23 student participants. The program enrolled 5 white (USA born), 3 black (USA born), 2 Asian (USA born), 2 non-white (USA born), 6 Latino (USA born), and 5 Latino (USA residents).

As mentioned in the motivation, GGC has a natural advantage to run its study abroad programs in a more diversified pool of students due to the broad diversity of its student population. Thus, our program had roughly half of its participants being Latino versus 8.3% nationally (IIE, 2013/2014 data), and while the participation of the Asian students is comparable to the national, we had almost three times as many Black students participating as the national averages (see Figure 1).

The bundle has proven to be a superior model for the students to choose versus the one class program. The enrolment doubled from 2014, when the Calculus course was offered as a standalone course, and the recruitment for the 2015 and 2016 offering of the Math-Biology bundle was substantially easier. Furthermore, the 2016 recruitment was practically seamless due to the successful execution of the program the previous year. The participated students were the most valuable ambassadors in spreading the details of the program's benefits to their school peers. It quickly became apparent to all STEM students that getting eight credits of courses closely aligned to their degree, while also participating in a study abroad that greatly enhances their resume, is a rewarding endeavor. Other studies also show that students are becoming increasingly more sensitive to time-to-degree, indicating that the lack of academic integration continues to be an impediment to participation in study abroad (Doyle, et al., 2010; Stroud, 2010). This program allows ambitious students to complete their travel, obtain 8 credits towards their degree, and be back in time to take classes offered in the second summer session at GGC, resulting in completing up to 12 credits in that summer, giving the proposed study abroad a high level of academic integration.

The study abroad program's foreign host university in both years was Thai Nguyen University of Technology (TNUT) located in Thai Nguyen, Vietnam. Thai Nguyen is a moderate to large size city

Figure 1. GGC Math and Biology study abroad Vietnam aggregated 2015/2016 participation by ethnic group (first pie graph) versus the national study abroad participation by ethnic group 2013/2014 (second pie graph) (IIE 2015 data)

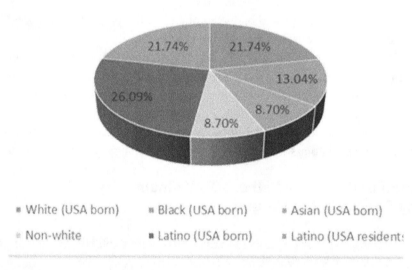

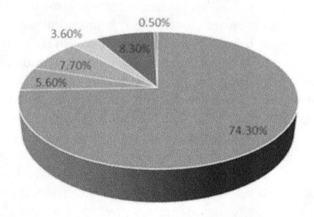

in Northern Vietnam. It is the capital city of northeast Thai Nguyen province, which is a mountainous, midland province, with a multi-ethnic society composed of eight ethnic groups.

Thai Nguyen University of Technology is a midsize (11,000 students) university in a system of universities jointly called Thai Nguyen University (TNU). The system is comprised of 7 universities and several other academic and non-academic units, and the system is considered a leading regional university system in Vietnam.

The mission of Thai Nguyen University as per their official website is stated as: *"The University is mandated to pursue the following: training high quality human resources, conducting researches on scientific technologies and management, verifying and proposing solutions and sustainable development policies, and contributing to the socio-economic development of the region towards industrialization and modernization."*

Moreover, the vision of the system states: *"To become a world class University system within Vietnam and the Southeast Asia in providing higher education in the fields of agriculture and forestry, teacher education, technology, economics and business administration, medicine and pharmacy, information and communication technology, foreign languages, among others. In addition, it envisions to enhance the advancement of research and development strategy in its various fields of expertise to complement the university's educational distinction and excellence."*

Thai Nguyen University of Technology is the engineering school within the system, which grants degrees in mechanical and electrical engineering and thus contributes directly to the socio-economic development part of the mission of TNUT. Furthermore, TNUT was selected to be one of the few universities throughout the entire country to participate in the so called "Advanced Program" – a government subsidized initiative that requires selected schools to put in place an innovative educational program taught entirely in English with the goal of modernizing the educational system in Vietnam. The program specifically targets the areas of Engineering, Agriculture, and Business with the ultimate goal of modernizing the country's economy and engineering workforce. Since 2009, TNUT has actively sought to cooperate with American schools to help develop and implement the initiative. Since its inception, the university has invited U.S. professors, including one of the current authors, to teach its science and engineering classes. Furthermore, the university invites foreign engineering graduate students to their campus to work with TNUT faculty and students in research projects. The university also searches for opportunities to bring foreign undergraduate students to bolster student engagement, both academically and culturally, for their students admitted in the Advanced Program.

During the two consecutive GGC Math-Biology Study Abroad programs that ran in 2015 and 2016, the Calculus I course was taught in a classroom on the campus of Thai Nguyen University of Technology, with a mix of both American and Vietnamese students taking the class together. Mixed teams of American/Vietnamese students worked on joint Calculus problems and 2 major Calculus projects that created an environment of group cooperation and friendly competition between groups. The calculus projects used data collected during the STEC2500 insect study, and thus an interdisciplinary activity was put into place. Using actual data collected from a hands on biological experiment to demonstrate calculus concepts such as rate of change, instantaneous rate of change, linear approximation, optimization and integration, and created a great learning opportunity for both groups of students.

Significant benefits from American and Vietnamese students taking the math course together were observed, but there were several negative aspects as well. Calculus I, being a 4-credit course, required a good amount of time to conduct class lectures and activities. Thus, it was difficult to find optimal class times for the Calculus course, Biology course, research activities, and additional activities. Furthermore, the course meeting times had to be aligned with the GGC students' travel schedule and the TNUT students' academic schedule, which led to rather intensive 2 class sessions per day (5 academic hours) in class interaction (See Table 2).

Further, all of the Vietnamese students in the Calculus class were engineering majors, and each had taken an extensive and rigorous mathematics examination as an entrance test to their university. Conversely, most GGC students enrolled in the Calculus course were science majors with different mathematical

Table 2. Calculus I schedule for Math-Biology Study abroad program Vietnam 2015.

Date	Sections covered	Quizzes and Tests	Homework
06/2 Morning session	Chapter 1. Functions and Modeling – Functions and graphs, Linear, Exponential, Logarithmic Functions; Chapter 2. Limits and Derivatives – Limits Graphically and Numerically; Chapter 2. Limits and Derivatives – Limits Analytically, One-sided and infinite limits		Homework 1 assigned due 06/9 afternoon session
06/2 Afternoon session	Chapter 2. Limits and Derivatives – Limits Analytically, One-sided and infinite limits – Derivatives and tangent line problems;		
06/3 Morning session	Chapter 2. Limits and Derivatives – Limits Analytically, One-sided and infinite limits – Derivatives and tangent line problems;		
06/3 Afternoon session	Chapter 3. Differentiation Rules – Derivatives and tangent line problems; Basic differentiation rules		Homework 2 assigned due 06/11 afternoon session
06/4 Morning session	Chapter 3. Differentiation Rules – Derivatives and tangent line problems; Basic differentiation rules	Quiz 1. Functions and Limits Morning session	
06/4 Afternoon session	Chapter 3. Differentiation Rules – Derivatives and tangent line problems; Basic differentiation rules		
06/9 Morning Session	Chapter 3. Differentiation Rules – Product and Quotient Rules; Chain rule		
06/9 Afternoon Session	Chapter 3. Differentiation Rules – Implicit Differentiation and higher order derivatives	Quiz 2. Derivatives	Homework 3 assigned due 06/17 afternoon session
06/10 Morning Session	Chapter 3. Differentiation Rules – Implicit Differentiation, Rates and related rates	Test 1. Over chapter 1 and 2, 3 – Functions, Limits and Derivatives	
06/10 Afternoon Session	Chapter 4. Applications of Differentiation – Extrema and increasing, decreasing, Concavity		
06/11 Morning session	Chapter 4. Applications of Differentiation – Extrema and increasing, decreasing, Concavity		
06/11 Afternoon session	Chapter 4. Applications of Differentiation – Mean value and Intermediate value Theorems, L'Hopital Rule		
06/16 Morning session	Chapter 4. Applications of Differentiation – Mean value and Intermediate value Theorems, L'Hopital Rule		Homework 4 assigned due 06/19
06/16 Afternoon session	Chapter 5. Integration – Areas, Riemann Sums, Fundamental Theorem of Calculus	Quiz 3. Derivatives and applications (Chapter 4)	
06/17 Morning session	Chapter 5. Integration – Fundamental Theorem of Calculus applications and integration techniques (substitution)		
06/17 Afternoon session	Chapter 5. Integration –Integration techniques. Trig Functions	Quiz 4. Derivatives and Integration	
06/18 Morning session	Chapter 5. Integration –Indefinite integrals. Trig Functions		
06/18 Afternoon session	Finishing Chapter 5 and Review	Test 2. Differentiation and Integrals (Chapter 3, 4, 5)	

Created by Boyko Gyurov at TNUT May-June 2015

exposure and ability varying from good, to moderate, to weak. So, the GGC student's mathematical performances were, on average, lower than that of their Vietnamese counterparts. To compensate this disparity, a balance in the formation of the teams was sought. Yet, the before mentioned friendly competition, as well as working in groups and having the teaching faculty at their disposal, technically the entire day, helped the GGC students to overcome any mathematical hardships and to score on their assessments at a level above their academic GPA average.

The 3-credit Tropical Biology class did not have the same impact as the Calculus class, since it is not a class on the curriculum at the Vietnamese institution. However, there were several opportunities in the course for both Vietnamese and American students to interact. Students gave their oral presentation on specific tropical Vietnamese animals and plants to both Vietnamese and American students. This allowed for additional follow-up discussions and inquiries as to if the Vietnamese students had ever seen the target plant or animal. Even though all of the Vietnamese students in the Calculus class were engineering majors, they demonstrated a high level of curiosity in the results of the biology experiments and were interested in seeing the insect collections, especially the butterflies collected by the American students during the biology field trips.

The 1-credit STEC 2500 research project provided students with the opportunity to connect and implement theoretical and quantitative knowledge. Students performed a 3-week long experiment on the university campus in Vietnam. For the experiment, 5 sets of bowls (yellow, blue, and white) were set up 10 meters apart, starting at one flower patch of yellow flowers and extending for 40 meters to a patch of purple flowers, in order to investigate flower color preference in insects. The bowls samples were collected 2 times per week, and the collected insects were sorted, classified, and the data recorded. In addition, 5 malaise traps were also set around the campus, close to insect food sources (flower patches), and their data was also collected. Next, the students were asked to use skills and methods taught in both the Calculus and Tropical Biology classes in order to analyze the data that had been collected. In particular, (1) calculus optimization methods were used to perform different computations to maximize the area on which insect traps were installed, while keeping the circumference of the region constant; (2) calculus rate of change studies were used to model the relationship between the distance of a trap from an insect food source (particular color flower patch) and the number of insects caught in the traps; (3) different biological techniques were used to collect, sort, and classify different species of insects. Figure 2 visualizes some of the specimens collected during the experiment.

The program provided numerous diverse cultural experiences in both Japan (developed Asia country) and Vietnam (developing Asian country) with all preset trips discussed in the model, successfully executed. Students were exposed to important historical sites, different religions, temples and shrines, unique art forms (Vietnamese Water Puppet Theater), museums, exotic foods, ethnic music and dances, language, and cultural attitudes.

Both times the program ran, students experienced Japanese culture for 4 days and then proceeded to Vietnam. In Japan, students visited the Imperial Palace, the Tokyo National Museum, various temples and shrines, and many other sites. Students were introduced to the Tokyo subway and were encouraged to explore Tokyo using the subway during their free day in Japan. For some of the participating students, the trip to Tokyo was the first visit to a cosmopolitan city and first introduction to a complex metro system. The only change we implemented in 2016 versus 2015 was the replacement of the Koishikawa Korakuen garden with the Hamarikyuu garden, since the latter provided the addition of a riverboat trip and thus a time for the students to relax during the intense walking day. The first execution of the program showed that while the average age of the participating students was 21.4 years, many of the

Figure 2. STEC 2500 Undergraduate research - classified collection of insects, Math-Biology Study abroad program, Vietnam 2015

students didn't have the stamina to endure full day of activities, thus some additional relaxation time was needed during of the program.

In Vietnam, students spent the majority of their time at Thai Nguyen University of Technology (TNUT). At the university, students interacted with their Vietnamese peers and were directly exposed to Vietnamese culture. Students ate at local restaurants, shopped in local markets, and visited local vendors for snacks and supplies. In the 2015 program, there was only one grand culture night during the last weekend before departure. Despite its multicultural components, with participation of students from 4 countries – USA, Vietnam, Thailand and the Philippines as well as various stage performances including a popular USA band, the culture night lacked a major ingredient – namely, the opportunity for students to bond in a non-formal setting as early as possible in the duration of the program. The U.S. students reported that the grueling academic schedule consumed a lot of their energy, and this combined with the natural reluctance of some students to break out of their comfort zone, made it harder for them to intentionally look for opportunities for social interactions. Consequently, in the 2016 execution of the program, these authors introduced two smaller in scope cultural activities. There were two culture nights – one towards the beginning of the program and the other – two thirds into it. The first culture night took place at the Thai Hai Ethnic Village. This village is the home of the Tay Ethnic minority group and showcases 30 houses built on stilts. There, the students observed the traditional music, dances, and culture of the largest minority group in a list of 54 minorities present throughout the country. The American students were encouraged to invite their favorite Vietnamese classmate to join them at the village, and thus an opportunity for non-formal bonding was created, which strengthened academic groups and resulted in improvement of their academic performance.

The second culture night was a Vietnamese food cooking competition, where mixed teams of American and Vietnamese students competed against one another to complete various culinary tasks. The event was planned, sponsored, and executed by the hosting, TNUT, university.

The three preplanned weekend trips (ranging from 2 to 5 days) were executed accordingly. The first trip was to the UNESCO World Heritage Site of Ha Long Bay for 4 days. Students explored a limestone forest, caves, and the coast of Ha Long Bay. The second trip was to Ba Be National Park for 2 days. Students performed a butterfly survey and studied the river systems in the National Park. The third trip investigated the South Vietnam sites of Ho Chi Minh City, Cat Tien National park, and the Mekong Delta for 5 days. Students explored the rainforest, took nature hikes, went on night jeep safaris, and explored the Mekong Delta by boat. In Ho Chi Minh City, the National Palace and other important historical and cultural sites were visited. At the conclusion of the study abroad experience, students explored the cultural areas of Hanoi during a 1-day field trip to the capital.

As part of the tropical biology course, students were to create a field journal of their cultural and biological experiences of the trip. The journal was to be about 40-60 pages in length. Each day, students wrote one to two pages reflecting on the biological and/or cultural event experienced that day and included one or more photos of the events. The field journal promoted student discussions and reflections of past, present, and future experiences during and after the study abroad program. They were submitted to the biology faculty after the completion of the program, as a final academic assignment of the class. Those journals are a priceless treasure trove for a multi-angle academic research on the students' thoughts, feelings, observations, and reflections during a study abroad of this type, and it is our strong recommendation for any program to require them as a part of the academic syllabus.

Challenges and Successes

The challenges to a program like the one described here come from many directions – originating and host institutions' "red tape", meeting students' needs, navigating travel conditions and specifies in the destination countries, unexpected students' health and personal issues, potential natural disasters, political or social unrest at the visiting countries, terrorism and so on. The successes are all measured by the students' satisfaction and their academic achievements, and by their cultural and intellectual growth.

As mentioned in the introduction, the five main steps in the development and the implementation of a study abroad program are: (1) proposal submission and institutional program approval; (2) recruitment of students; (3) academic setup at the foreign host university (country); (4) travel and cultural component set up; and (5) program implementation with post program follow ups and reflections.

The institutional program approval and paperwork at GGC took a significant amount of time to fill out and prepare. Since this was the first STEM faculty led program at the school, many new forms and procedures were created. While clearly such programs need to comply with the school, university system and the state requirements, often it seemed that the program faced more administrative hurdles than help. This was in part and due to the unique administrative structure at GGC. As per the vision of its charter president, Dr. Kaufman, the college has a flat administrative structure without separate departments, which allows a great flow of interdisciplinary communication and cooperation. Faculty from the different disciplines are at constant discussions and meetings with each other, and all ideas and intendent projects are quickly executed within the individual schools due to the one level approval needed from the dean of the particular school. When a project is outside of the school of one school, however, and requires the coordination and input from several (semi)-autonomous administrative units, the speed of interaction, decision making, and implementation of the project, decreases substantially. When putting together a study abroad program, the faculty proposing the program should start as early as possible, perhaps even an entire year in advance. In addition, it would be helpful for the faculty to perform a site visit (scout out the sites in advance) without students, prior to the study abroad program, so as to be able to address all inquiries, requirements, and needs for the different administrative units that have to approve the program. Setting up a bundle program with a courses from different disciplines is much easier at GGC, as per the mentioned advantages of the flat, one level administrative structure of the college.

The recruitment process was difficult, especially for the first year of the program. The second year of the program, recruiting was much easier, since past students acted as ambassadors for the Math-Biology Study abroad program. The financial ability and the time-constrained availability served as an obstacle for the recruitment, while the build in cultural intent served as a booster. Numerous students were attracted to the program. The biology field trips and cultural experiences of the study abroad program seemed to be the most attractive features. Many students were concerned about taking Calculus I in a foreign country. Many students viewed Calculus as a difficult course, and believed that taking the course in a tough environmental setting would make learning and passing Calculus, virtually impossible. Through a series of recruitment meetings, however, the students understood the advantages of taking math class, and Calculus in particular, in such a setting. The small number of participants and the availability of the teaching faculty the entire day make it easy for the students to ask questions and revisit the material. The study abroad format results in faculty and students learning, traveling, and eating most meals together, which means that students have constant access to faculty members who can provide academic help and answer students' questions. It is like having 24/7 office hours. And while such setup is intense for faculty members, it is a great resource for both struggling and good students alike. Thus, this is not a tough setting, but rather, an ideal setting for learning Calculus. Additionally, in study abroad programs of this type, students have peer support from both American and Vietnamese students, some of whom are very capable in the field of mathematics. It is much easier to ask questions of students who are constantly around and with whom you spend a good part of the day. In addition, working in groups on projects allows students to understand the material better, while earning points, and building ground towards a good final grade. Once this was understood, the recruitment was easier, especially after having returning students to testify the case.

The study abroad interactions between student and faculty for our bundle are quite in contrast to typical on-campus GGC faculty-student interactions. For the majority of the students at Georgia Gwinnett College, being a student at a commuter college with a very small number of on campus residing students, the constant academic interaction with faculty and peers is often limited. Thus, this study abroad experience provides an enriching academic tool and emphasizes students' intellectual, social, and personal development.

The academic setup at the foreign host university went relatively smoothly. This occurred because the former author had already served as a visiting professor at TNUT for five years, which allowed for GGC and TNUT to cooperate and sign a formal Memorandum of Understanding for academic cooperation, including the exchanges of students and hosting study abroad programs. TNUT agreed on and provided free dorm housing for the students and an air conditioned classroom in which the Vietnamese and American students met and studied Calculus together and where some biology presentations were made. In addition, the hosting institution organized and subsidized culture night activities, beneficial for all participating students. The only problem arose in coordinating the schedules of the American and Vietnamese students to fit the intense time requirements for the jointly taken Calculus class. Due to the busy travel program of the GGC students and the regular academic activities of the Vietnamese students who were taking other academic classes as per their regular academic calendar, the commonly available times led to an intense calculus schedule, which caused some unease among the American students. (See table 2).

The travel and cultural component involved a lot of time and effort by the study abroad faculty. The first year, once again, was much tougher than the second year. Planning involved 4 major steps: (1) faculty needed to outline the target cultural and biological sites that would provide the greatest impact to students, (2) travel logistics and costs had to be examined for each site, (3) faculty needed to determine whether outside vendors were needed for a given site, and (4) outside vendors had to be contacted and quotes for excursions provided for more extensive and/or distant sites. The huge time and effort devoted to these four steps by the study abroad faculty significantly reduced the financial cost of the study abroad program, which is one of our main goals by design. After forming partnerships with outside vendors in the first year, it was much easier to plan and implement subsequent study abroad programs.

The program implementation was fun yet challenging. Numerous surprises (e.g. lost keys, passports, sick students, etc.) will always take place on month long study abroad programs. Well-trained and prepared faculty can often solve these types of problems quickly and effectively. In addition, having clear guidelines and rules for students can often help circumvent problems. These rules should be clear, promote student safety, and encourage group cohesion. Obviously, rule number 1 is that no student should wander outside the University/hotel alone. Students should always travel in groups.

The academic challenges faced during the implementation were twofold. First, there was a relatively big gap in the mathematical ability and knowledge among the participating American students. While this is expected, based on the type of schooling and the diversity of the group in many aspects – racially, socially, educationally, the math component created challenges and unease for the less prepared students. The fast pace of the delivery of the Calculus material (in conjunction with the constant travel), the homework assignments, team work participation and so on, created a stressful environment for the students at the beginning. The advantages of the program – constant faculty access, properly selected (based on ability) mixed teams and so on, described earlier, quickly helped to reduce stress and provided a venue for all students to excel. The second academic challenge was the time compression derived from the very dense academic calendar. In a program timed almost to perfection, classes followed on field experiment setups, specimen collection, data collection, modeling, project designs and on and on, which left only small fluctuations in time to move, replace, or cancel some activities. This, combined with the academically diverse student participants, poised challenges to execute all preplanned academic goals. So, while the program as initially constructed is a perfect academically-cultural endeavor, it also requires a perfect collection of students who are all highly academically motivated and culturally curious, something that is clearly hard to materialize. Possible fixes to this challenge are specific GPA requirement for all applicants to the program, and/or more extensive pre-teaching in all aspects – academic, cultural, and research and/or loosening of some of the planned activities or classes – for example replacing a 4 credit Calculus class with a 3 credit Statistic class.

The most common nonacademic problems we faced during implementation were: (1) students lost room keys and small items (passports, cell phones, sunglasses, etc.) and (2) students showed up late for group events. The easy solution to the first problem is to issue one key for each hotel/dorm room. This way, only one person (ideally the most responsible person) is in charge of keeping the key safe and secure. In addition, students should be told that when possible, they should leave any small, unnecessary items in their room, especially during field trips. As for student tardiness, the easy solution is to develop a policy that penalizes students who are more than 10 minutes late, by dictating that the individual(s) miss the field trip (he/she will be left at the hotel or dorm). Alternatively, assigning buddies who will make sure their buddy arrives at the correct meeting time also reduces tardiness. Using social networking to send messages and reminders also proved effective. For example, in our program we created a WhatsApp group for the study abroad and constantly kept the entire group up to date.

The biggest challenge for faculty leading in-house designed study abroad programs is that the faculty do everything, which can lead to faculty burn out. When students get sick or hurt, it is up to the faculty to fix the problem and spend time with the sick student. This can be very tough, since the other students need that faculty member to lead the study abroad program. Thus, the here proposed bundle shows another clear advantage, since at least two faculty lead the program at the same time.

The faculty leaders set one post arrival reunion to reflect and assess the students' thoughts, satisfaction and suggestions about the program. During that meeting the students also submit their field journals which is the last class assignment for their biology class. (See Figure 3). The university also collects post travel assessment data from the students to be used to improve the study abroad experiences at GGC, as well as, reporting data for the Quality Enhancement Program (QEP) at the school – the Internationalization of the Curriculum. The lack of good assessment tools however, poses a challenge to the program coordinators to collect good and meaningful data and to effectively measure the benefits and successes of the program.

The most important success of the program does not need to be measured, however. It can be seen written in the students' journals. In the words of one participant "I often think of what I experienced and learned in this study abroad. I made some friends, I traveled everywhere in amazing foreign country. I learned about its culture and its people. I ate their food. I love Pho! But most importantly, I realized I

Figure 3. GGC Math and Biology study abroad Vietnam field journals required class assignment for BIOL3050 class

love biology and I want to become biologist. I understand what rate of change is and I can take derivative of everything:) I am not afraid of math!"

CONCLUSION AND FURTHER MODEL IMPLEMENTATIONS

We developed a successful, low budget study abroad program using the course bundle method, with added interdisciplinary content delivery, research, and cultural components. This approach involves a significant amount of time, work, planning, and patience on the part of the faculty members running the program. However, students greatly benefit from: (1) taking courses they can use in their major; (2) learning through innovative interdisciplinary teaching techniques; (3) observing in person on field trips biological diversity and exotic species in their natural habitats; (4) visiting cultural and historical sites, (5) experiencing new cultural ideas and behaviors in person, (6) having in-class interactions with foreign peers. All of these experiences and interactions in this cross-cultural learning and interdisciplinary study abroad program provide a greater culture and academic impact than just a travel visit to a country.

Students form new intercultural friendships and grow academically, culturally, and personally, while in the protective environment of the study abroad program.

This new method of study abroad lowered the cost (financial commitment) for the students, since the travel component of the program was organized by the GGC faculty and not third-party vendors. Significant cost savings were passed onto the students. The lower study abroad program price tag made it possible for more GGC students, including some from the lower income brackets, to participate in the study abroad experience. In addition, incorporating required science and math courses into the study abroad program, opened the door for STEM majors to study abroad.

Inspired by the success of the first two Vietnam study abroad program implementations and armed with the experience gained in overcoming the obstacles, we designed a second, similar program. Its destination is the Kingdom of Thailand, with a cultural stop in South Korea. The successful implementation of this program will get us that much closer to the United States' goal of 1,000,000 undergraduate students studying abroad annually.

Results to be reported soon.

REFERENCES

Anderson, P. H., & Lawton, L. (2012). Intercultural Development: Study Abroad vs. On-campus Study. *Frontiers: The Interdisciplinary Journal of Study Abroad, 21*, 86–108.

Burn, B., & Smuckler, R. (1990). *A National Mandate for Education Abroad: Getting on with the Task.* Washington, DC: National Association of Student Affairs.

Clarke, I. III, Flaherty, T. B., Wright, N. D., & McMillen, R. M. (2009). Student intercultural proficiency from study abroad programs. *Journal of Marketing Education, 31*(2), 173–181. doi:10.1177/0273475309335583

Dolby, N. (2007). Reflections on nation: American undergraduates and education abroad. *Journal of Studies in International Education, 11*(2), 141–156. doi:10.1177/1028315306291944

Doyle, S., Gendall, P., Meyer, L. H., Hoek, J., Tait, C., McKenzie, L., & Loorparg, A. (2010). An Investigation of Factors Associated With StudentParticipation in Study Abroad. *Journal of Studies in International Education, 14*(5), 471–490. doi:10.1177/1028315309336032

Fuller, T. L. (2007). Study abroad experiences and intercultural sensitivity among graduate theological students: A preliminary and exploratory investigation. *Christian Higher Education, 6*(4), 321–332. doi:10.1080/15363750701268319

Hoffa, W. W., & DePaul, S. C. (2010). *A history of U.S. study abroad: 1965–present.* Carlisle, PA: Forum on Education Abroad.

Institute of International Education (IIE). (2015). *Open doors 20/12 "fast facts."* Retrieved from http://www.iie.org/Research-and-Publications/Open-Doors/Data/US-Study-Abroad#.WARf8YVYWt8

Malloy, M. N., & Davis, A. J. (2012). The University of Georgia Avian Biology Study Abroad Program in Costa Rica. *North American Colleges and Teachers of Agriculture (NACTA) Journal, 56*(3), 24–29. PMID:23097857

Malmgren, J., & Galvin, J. (2008). Effects of study abroad participation on student graduation rates: A study of three incoming freshman cohorts at the University of Minnesota, Twin Cities. *NADADA Journal, 28*(1), 29–42.

Salisbury, M. H., Umbach, P. D., Paulsen, M. B., & Pascarella, E. T. (2009). Going global: Understanding the choice process of the intent to study abroad. *Research in Higher Education, 50*(2), 119–143. doi:10.1007/s11162-008-9111-x

Stallman, E., Woodruff, G. A., Kasravi, J., & Comp, D. (2010). The diversification of the student profile. In W. W. Hoffa & S. C. DePaul (Eds.), A history of U.S. study abroad: 1965–present. Lancaster, PA: Frontiers: The Interdisciplinary Journal of Study Abroad.

Stroud, A. H. (2010). Who plans (not) to study abroad? An examination of U.S. student intent. *Journal of Studies in International Education, 20*(10), 1–18.

Sweeney, K. (2013). Frontiers: The Interdisciplinary Journal of Study Abroad. Inclusive Excellence and Underrepresentation of Students of Color in Study Abroad. *Frontiers: The Interdisciplinary Journal of Study Abroad, 23*, 1–21.

Vande Berg, M., Connor-Linton, J., & Paige, R. M. (2009). The Georgetown Consortium Project: Interventions for Students Living Abroad. *Frontiers: The Interdisciplinary Journal of Study Abroad, 18*, 1–75.

Chapter 11
Reflecting on New Faculty Training:
Internationalized Learning Essentials

Semire Dikli
Georgia Gwinnett College, USA

Richard S. Rawls
Georgia Gwinnett College, USA

Brian C. Etheridge
Georgia Gwinnett College, USA

ABSTRACT

This chapter aims to describe the mandatory training program (Internationalized Learning Essentials) offered to the new faculty as part of the internationalization of the curriculum process at four-year colleges in the U.S. The chapter presents survey results regarding faculty perceptions on the training program. The results of this study suggest important implications for research in internationalization by providing further insights regarding faculty training about internationalized education.

BACKGROUND

There is no doubt that developing sensitivity toward people from other cultures and communicating effectively with them are important characteristics that every college graduate should possess in to-day's diverse workplace. As Leask (2009) suggested, "an internationalised curriculum (product) will purposefully develop the international and intercultural perspectives (skills, knowledge and attitudes) of all students." An ideal way to help college students gain intercultural sensitivity and intercultural communicative skills is to expose them to different cultures through study abroad programs. Study abroad programs have gained popularity among higher education institutions by allowing students to explore a culture in its most authentic form. However, their costly nature does not make these programs favorable for a great number of college students. Therefore, many higher education institutions have been looking

DOI: 10.4018/978-1-5225-2791-6.ch011

into offering classes that help students learn these skills without having them travel long distances, while simultaneously making efforts to internationalize the curriculum and provide internationalized experiences on campus. In this framework, faculty training becomes an essential component of internationalization because faculty have the power to decide whether or not to incorporate international perspectives into their classes (Green & Olson, 2003). In order to help their students appreciate diversity, faculty must become aware of the basic concepts of internationalization. Similarly, the higher-education institution discussed in this study, Georgia Gwinnett College (GGC), prioritizes the role of faculty development in the successful implementation of an internationalized curriculum. The focus of this chapter is to describe one of those training programs (Internationalized Learning Essentials (ILE) Forum), and draw upon survey results regarding faculty perceptions of this training process. This effort offers some thoughts about how one institution has used faculty development to support the internationalization of the curriculum.

LITERATURE REVIEW

The effort to internationalize the curriculum required familiarity with the literature. Since internationalizing the curriculum was part of GGC's Quality Enhancement Plan (QEP) – and the QEP constituted part of the basis of accreditation from the Southern Association of Colleges and Schools – finding the literature and theoretical bases remained a significant early task. It was recognized that while GGC hosts one of the most diverse student bodies and faculty in the southeastern United States, not all of the literature would be relevant to institutional stakeholders. Administrators and faculty quickly identified three distinct areas, broken down in this literature review as the following interrelated concepts: 1) internationalization of the curriculum; 2) intercultural competence; and 3) training university faculty in both internationalizing the curriculum and in intercultural competence.

The literature addressing internationalization of the curriculum (IOC) has expanded both in quality and scope in the last fifty years. Since internationalization itself can mean different things to different people, one of the tasks scholars have attempted to address relates to its meaning. For example, does internationalizing the curriculum suggest enlarging the faculty with higher numbers of professors from foreign countries? Does it include adding larger numbers of international students to courses? Does it involve sending students to other countries for a portion of their higher education, or even bringing branch campuses of foreign universities to one's national shores? Does it require adding international content to courses? Internationalization raises questions and provokes confusion about its relationship to globalization: are they the same thing? If not, how do they differ? As Knight observes, "This reflects the realities of today and presents new challenges in terms of developing a conceptual model that provides some clarity on meaning and principles to guide policy and practice" (2004, p. 6).

Although scholars agree that a universal definition of "internationalization" proves elusive, they also concur that arriving at a commonly held definition is important for helping an institution to understand what it is hoping to achieve. One can detect an evolution in definition since the late 1970s. In the 1980s and early 1990s, internationalization frequently intimated activities, programs, services, exchange, or even "studies" (Arum & van de Water, 1992, p. 202). As the 1990s progressed, a definition assuming a more institutional and integrative approach began. Internationalization could not just remain the preserve of a few offices on a university campus. Knight (1997) wrote at the time that "integrating an international and intercultural dimension into the teaching, research, and service functions of the institution" was necessary (p. 7). H. de Wit (2002) later furnished a fascinating summary of the waning decades of "Internationalization of Higher Education as a Research Area" in the late 20th century.

Georgia Gwinnett College never adopted an "official definition" of internationalization of the curriculum, let alone internationalization, but Knight's definition came close: in its efforts, GGC focuses on the "process of integrating an international, intercultural or global dimension into the purpose, functions or delivery of postsecondary education" (Knight, 2003, p. 2). Knight (2004) cautioned elsewhere, however, that the definition ought not to specify outcomes of internationalization. While that might be true of a working definition applicable to a wide range of contexts, her stipulation could not possibly work at Georgia Gwinnett College because the entire QEP was tied to accreditation, which implied both outcomes goals and assessment of those goals.

A similar concept that informed the development of GGC's internationalization of the curriculum efforts was "Comprehensive Internationalization." Comprehensive internationalization in the scholarly literature also enjoyed numerous definitions. NAFSA, the Association of International Educators, defined it on a national level, but its definition works equally well on a singular campus: "Comprehensive internationalization is a commitment, confirmed through action, to infuse international and comparative perspectives throughout the teaching, research and service missions of higher education. It shapes institutional ethos and values and touches the entire higher education enterprise" (Hudzik, 2011, p. 6). The wisdom of making internationalization a comprehensive venture across campus is manifest, since the relationship between accreditation and the QEP remained tightly linked. Arguments such as that put forth by NAFSA resonated and were shared across campus. Moreover, other academic literature recommended much the same as NAFSA (Knight, 1999, p. 14).

A second area pertaining to internationalizing the curriculum related to teaching Intercultural Competence (IC). As one might expect, the theories and assumptions behind the attempts to define this concept are legion, and they remain beyond the scope of this literature review to comprehensively suggest. A cursory outline will nonetheless prove helpful. The term "intercultural" suggests levels of interactions between peoples of various and differing cultures. Few would disagree with this statement, but the moment one begins researching these interactions one encounters myriad difficulties: cultural misunderstandings, biases of researchers, research design issues, serendipitous findings from research, disagreements about terms (such as "democracy" for example), data collection problems, and so on (Johnson & Tuttle, 1989). For our purposes, the key element of "intercultural" focuses on the idea of interaction. A university cafeteria with three different cultural groups might witness them all inhabiting the same space, sharing the same refectory, and taking the same classes. However, if they sit and dialogue only with those from their same group, we can assume low levels of intercultural interaction.

The literature in the 1980s affirmed that IC involved a person's capabilities in effectively communicating with people from differing cultural backgrounds (Spitzberg & Cupach, 1984). Research into IC continued to provoke a variety of questions: in instances of successful IC does the competency belong to individuals, is it located within a broader social arena, or is it a matter of the interpersonal skills of individuals quite apart from cultural considerations (Koester et al., 1993). These might remain merely "academic questions" were it not for the fact that many people in higher educational institutions seek to help others gain greater competencies when it comes to helping others who are different from them. In fact, as Yershova, DeJaeghere, and Mestenhauser (2000) suggest, "From its inception, the study of intercultural competence has been largely fueled by very practical concerns..." (p. 43).

The academic literature increasingly recognized that greater distinctions needed to be drawn between intercultural education and international education. Crichton et al. (2004) argued that "Intercultural education, as opposed to international education, is a more inclusive formulation, in that interculturality includes both international and domestic students. All students… need to develop the capability to contribute in the intercultural construction, exchange and use of knowledge" (p.11). This line of argumentation resonated well at institutions where the student body consisted of a large percentage of first-generation college and university students who were also simultaneously working. Foreign travel, an "international experience" away from home was not an option. However, the increasingly diverse nature of the campus and metropolitan Atlanta meant the opposite: the "world" had come to our campus. The question nevertheless remained: how to train our students and simultaneously utilize this diversity to become better contributors, exchangers, and constructors of the knowledge of interculturality?

Milton Bennett provided not only a definition but also a model of intercultural competence that has informed not only GGC's approach but also the praxis of many other universities (Odgers & Giroux, 2006). Bennett (1993) created the Developmental Model of Intercultural Sensitivity (DMIS) as a way of describing how people move along a continuum in terms of their experience of intercultural difference from ethnocentrism to ethnorelativism. As individuals become capable of accommodating cultural differences, they move along the scale through three stages of ethnocentrism (Denial of Difference; Defense Against Difference/Reversal; and Minimization of Difference) to three stages of ethnorelativism (Acceptance of Difference; Adaptation to Difference; Integration of Difference). Bennett's articulation of this insight was not unique, but it recognized a complexity that had not always been appreciated. Bennett (2004) argued that the "more ethnocentric orientations can be seen as ways of avoiding cultural difference" (p. 63). One might deny cultural differences by asserting that their own culture is the correct standard and that others "don't get it," one might create an "us versus them" system of thought, or one might even downplay differences by insisting that all people remain basically the same. As one encounters other cultures one's worldview hopefully shifts, but this is not always the case. Bennett thus began to utilize insights into how to help people move from one stage to the next (Bennett & Bennett, 2004). He maintained that working on the worldview remained key: "Developmental interventions such as training programs are appropriately aimed at the worldview, not at any particular knowledge…, any particular attitude…, or any particular skill acquisition" (2004, p. 75).

Mitchell Hammer (1999) applied psychometrics to the study of intercultural competence and coping mechanisms, and he helped develop the Intercultural Development Inventory (IDI). While the IDI remains a proprietary enterprise, Hammer's insights echoed those of Bennett (with some differences and modifications). Hammer proposed five responses to intercultural difference instead of the six of the DMIS: Denial, Polarization, Minimization, Acceptance, and Adaptation. Hammer proposed the utility of an instrument such as the IDI because it measures an individual or group approach to intercultural difference. Once contextualized, an individual or group can then begin taking steps to move along the continuum from a monocultural to an intercultural mindset (Hammer, 2009). Indeed, those taking the IDI receive encouragements for ways to move from one stage of openness and intercultural development to the next stage. In Hammer's words the IDI "…provides a blueprint for how to encourage and assist individual and group development toward greater capability to shift cultural perspective and adapt behavior to cultural context" (2009, p. 215).

While universities and researchers arrived at an understanding of IC, they also studied the implications for preparing higher education institutions for its instruction. Not surprisingly, they discovered that a diverse context was not enough to automatically render faculty (or students) interculturally competent. In a recent study backed by the Association for the Study of Higher Education, scholars found that "just as research indicates that intercultural competency skills do not 'naturally' develop as the result of structurally diverse environment, faculty do not 'naturally' develop the awareness, skills, or knowledge to effectively support students' capacity to engage diversity" (Lee et al., 2012, p. 14).

It was recognized when GGC began to consider training its faculty in IOC and IC that an inherent tension would develop surrounding a central question: ought we to teach a skill or content? This is a decidedly ambiguous question because the two are not always and neatly separable. The ambiguity surrounding this question has been reflected in the literature, but GGC acknowledged from the start that the literature might help in some areas. For instance, the college followed the recommendation that the entire institution take internationalization seriously: "Faculty, students, and employers can encounter mixed messaging within institutional curricula when important skill-based intercultural development is emphasized... in some places within an institution and not in others" (Lee et al., 2012, p. 15). The co-curricular "side of the house" was included from the beginning, which included not only Student Affairs but also those entrusted with assessment for Student Affairs. In this, GGC followed the description of Leask (2009, p. 209), when she observed, "Internationalisation of the curriculum is the incorporation of an international and intercultural dimension into the content of the curriculum as well as the teaching and learning arrangements and support services of a program of study."

In addition to utilizing the insights of Bennett and Bennett (2004) and many others (Pusch 2009, Hofstede 2009, & Krutky 2008), GGC also implemented the insights of Deardorff. Her model of intercultural competence (2006) argued for a recognition that intercultural competence was developmental, required a long-term commitment from the institution, necessitated the development of both skills (knowledge and comprehension) and content, and involved the tolerance of ambiguity. Another theorist's work influencing the implementation of GGC's faculty training was Kolb's *Experiential Learning: Experience as the Source of Learning and Development* (1984). Kolb's articulation of the learning process as occurring in four stages informed GGC's *praxis*: 1) Concrete Experiences frequently occurring the direct encounter with a new idea, person, or perspective; 2) Reflective Observation of the experience; 3) Abstract Conceptualization which involves describing and applying theories and rules to articulate it; 4) Active Experimentation in terms of testing the experience and description of it in order to modify it later. As one might imagine, the four stages in the process can repeat again as new experiences warrant. Moreover, even though there is not a direct link between assessment and Kolb's theories, one can easily imagine how these stages might be engaged in educational practices capable of assessment.

The literature assured and reinforced our assumptions about instruction in IC and in the efforts to internationalize curriculum. Deardorff observed, "Intercultural competence development is a lifelong process – one doesn't become magically interculturally competent after completing one course or going on an education broad experience in another country." The training for IOC therefore reflected and continues to reflect this reality. The prevailing commitment is to longitudinal training. Odgers and Giroux (2006, p. 14), further writing about the efforts at training faculty at Malaspina University, developed the "Three Pillars of Internationalization," which describe the training sessions of faculty: 1 ME (my values, assumptions, experience, and philosophy); 2) MY TEACHING (classroom dynamics); and 3) MY CURRICULUM (course content). Helping faculty to recognize their "ME" values, assumptions, attitudes, philosophy) will further foster cognizance of how this influences their teaching and curriculum.

IMPLEMENTATION PROCESS

Armed with these perspectives, the institution's teaching and learning center offered two types of trainings—its Internationalized Learning Essentials (ILE) forum and its Internationalized Learning Program (ILP)—to faculty in order to provide them with the knowledge and resources needed to expose them to these ideas and concepts, and thereby achieve internationalization of the curriculum through the internationalization of the faculty. The latter, the ILP, is a training program for faculty who would like to gain the deep knowledge and skills necessary to design and deliver internationalized courses (what GGC calls i-courses). Interested faculty attend a mandatory three-day professional-development seminar led by external professionals, and then attend additional workshops on course design in small groups.

The Internationalized Learning Essentials (ILE) forum, on the other hand, is a mandatory training program to ensure that all faculty on the campus are, to some degree, internationalized. Following Odgers and Giroux, the designers of the ILE sought to achieve the following objectives: 1) familiarize all faculty with the basic concepts regarding internationalization and intercultural competence; 2) prompt critical self-reflection; and 3) help them understand their place within both the framework of the Quality Enhancement Plan and the internationalization of the curriculum. For the first two years, the forum was a four-hour workshop held just before the beginning of the fall semester. Based on faculty feedback, the format has been different for the last two years; the forum now consists of three sessions (one 90 minute session and two 75 minute sessions). It is required that all full-time faculty at GGC participate in the Internationalized Learning Essentials forum.

Over the course of the four hours, the main goals are to examine why the college is engaged in internationalizing its curriculum, introduce the student learning outcomes of internationalization and its relationship with the college's institutional student learning outcomes, discuss possible ways to accomplish this initiative, and motivate faculty to show interest and engage in these efforts to internationalize the curriculum at GGC (ILE Training Guidelines, 2017). The forum seeks to achieve these goals through a highly interactive format that models many of the active learning strategies demanded by the internationalization initiative. The forum begins with a brief presentation that emphasizes the importance of internationalization within the context of a globalizing world. Following the recent trends in the literature, the presentation stresses the efficacy and efficiency of comprehensive internationalization over older notions of internationalization. This brief presentation is followed by a series of activities in which faculty become aware of their own biases and limitations in trying to understand and navigate cultural differences. They play a BINGO game in which they try to assess the intercultural experiences of one another, and they reflect on previous missteps in their own efforts to navigate difference in the classroom.

Following these exercises designed to raise awareness, they are provided some cultural frameworks for understanding the differences that they encounter. Through a series of games and simulations, they are sensitized to the challenges and feelings of frustrations students from a non-dominant culture may experience attempting to understand and fit into a dominant culture. The "Aunt Bonnie" game simulates the challenges and rewards of understanding and cracking cultural codes by presenting participants with a simple, but not obvious, pattern to discern; those that are able to replicate the pattern are invited to sit in a circle of chairs, and those who are not able to do so (or do not try) are forced to stand on the outside until the end of the game. At the end, the participants are invited to reflect on how it felt to be unable (or unwilling to try) to understand and act according to the cultural code; for those who did it successfully, they are invited to discuss the feeling of privilege this knowledge afforded them. Finally, they are familiarized with Bennett's Developmental Model of Intercultural Sensitivity (DMIS) through an on-boarding simulation at the institution, in which different groups of participants are asked to inhabit a particular mindset along the DMIS continuum and then offer advice to a new employee based on the characteristics of the assigned outlook. As they go through each of these exercises, they are repeatedly reminded of the student learning outcomes associated with the internationalization of the curriculum.

DATA COLLECTION, PROCEDURES, AND FINDINGS

Faculty who have received the Internationalized Learning Essentials (ILE) training are asked to complete anonymous surveys after each training. These surveys are provided by the college to gain insights about the Quality Enhancement Plan (QEP) at GGC. We have compiled the results of the survey as part of this study as our goal is to find out about faculty perceptions about the training they received on internationalization as part of the ILE program. The results revealed that the training program was generally successful.

Year 1 (2013)

The Results of Year 1 were considered promising. For the 9 questions, 8 responses ranged from 75.2% to 95%. While the results of item 9, "interest in participation in the ILP (av.=2.6)," is much lower than others, it was still considered very good because 46.2% (or 153 faculty) were strongly interested and very interested. Table 1 below shows the survey results of Year 1.

Year 2 (2014)

In Year 2, the survey results were slightly better than Year 1. The agree/strongly agree rate ranged from 88.1% to 95.5% with the exception of two questions (items 5 and 6). The number of faculty who participated in the ILE forum was smaller in Year 2 compared to Year 1 as all of the continuing faculty were trained in Year 1, yet only the newly hired faculty were trained in Year 2. Please see Table 2 below for more information.

Table 1. Year 1 survey results

ILE Survey 2013 (N=331)	Agree & Strongly Agree (%)	Disagree & Strongly Disagree (%)
I understand the intent of GGC's QEP.	95.3	1.8
I am aware of the QEP's 5 Student Learning Outcomes.	91.1	2.4
I am aware of the various levels of faculty involvement in internationalizing the curriculum.	85.0	3.0
I am aware there are various pathways for i-course development and/or documentation.	77.8	7.4
I am more interested in being involved in QEP efforts.	57.0	14.1
I am interested in participating in year-long faculty development program, the Internationalized Learning Certificate, in the future.	46.2	27.7
The "Faculty Resource Guide" from this Forum will be useful.	75.2	6.5
The forum was well-organized.	89.8	2.4
Overall, the facilitators were effective.	93.2	0.9

Table 2. Year 2 survey results

ILE Survey 2014 (N=67)	Agree & Strongly Agree (%)	Disagree & Strongly Disagree (%)
I understand the intent of GGC's QEP.	95.4	3.0
I am aware of the QEP's 5 Student Learning Outcomes.	95.5	3.0
I am aware of the various levels of faculty involvement in internationalizing the curriculum.	88.1	3.0
I am aware there are various pathways for i-course development and/or documentation.	86.5	3.0
I am more interested in being involved in QEP efforts.	66.7	10.6
I am interested in participating in year-long faculty development program, the Internationalized Learning Certificate, in the future.	53.7	25.4
The "Faculty Resource Guide" from this Forum will be useful.	86.6	4.5
The forum was well-organized.	92.5	3.0
Overall, the facilitators were effective.	93.8	3.0

Year 3 (2015)

In Year 3, the ILE forum was divided into three parts, one being a 90-minute-long session and the following two sessions being 75-minutes-long. The assessment results of the 90-minute-session that was administered during NFO were less favorable compared to those in the previous years. Of particular concern is the 42.2% on item 4, "awareness of various pathways for i-course development and/or documentation." One reason was that this topic was not the focus of the first session of the ILE series. However, unlike in Years 1 and 2, a higher percentage of faculty showed interest in item 6 in Year 3.

Table 3. Year 3 survey results

ILE survey (2015/2016)	Year 3/Session 1 (Fa15) (N=46)		Year 3/Sessions 2 and 3 (Sp16) (N=28)	
	Agree & Strongly Agree (%)	Disagree & Strongly Disagree (%)	Agree & Strongly Agree (%)	Disagree & Strongly Disagree (%)
I understand the intent of GGC's QEP.	93.3	4.4	72.0	12.0
I am aware of the QEP's 5 Student Learning Outcomes.	86.1	2.3	61.6	15.4
I am aware of the various levels of faculty involvement in internationalizing the curriculum.	82.3	4.4	66.6	18.5
I am aware there are various pathways for i-course development and/or documentation.	42.2	13.4	55.5	18.5
I am more interested in being involved in QEP efforts.	79.5	6.8	24.0	36.0
I am interested in participating in year-long faculty development program, the Internationalized Learning Certificate, in the future.	72.1	7.0	25.0	41.6
The "Faculty Resource Guide" from this Forum will be useful.	69.8	9.3	50.0	20.8
The Forum was well-organized.	83.8	2.3	52.0	24.0
Overall, the facilitators were effective.	90.9	0.0	64.0	20.0

The Spring 2016 assessment had markedly lower results overall than the fall assessment, especially regarding "being more interested in being involved in QEP effort" (24%), "interest in participation in the ILP (25%), and "the Forum was well organized" (52%). One reason was the length of time that elapsed between the sessions and the assessment. Participants were asked to complete one survey for two sessions several months after the training. This also adversely affected the response rate. Table 4 below shows the survey results in Year 3.

Year 4 (2016)

In Year 4, a survey was administered following each session. A couple of survey questions were changed depending on the main focus of the session. For example, unlike the first and last sessions, Session 2 highlighted the role of Developmental Model of Intercultural Sensitivity (DMIS). One drawback regarding Year 4 surveys was that the response rate of Session 3 was not as high as the first two sessions. Overall, Year 4 assessments results were more positive than those in Year 3, and they were as favorable as Year 1 and Year 2 results. The results revealed that 86.83% of the participants met the main goal of the ILE program and stated that they understand the intent of GGC's QEP on internationalization (average of item #1 in three sessions). Please see Tables 4, 5, and 6 for the survey results of all three sessions in Year 4.

LIMITATIONS AND RECOMMENDATIONS

The ILE Forum was originally designed as a 4-hour session and assessments were completed at the end of the session during the first couple of years. In the following years, the forum was divided into three parts (one 90-minute and two 75-minute sessions), and the assessments were given at different times, sometimes in combination with other assessments for other programs. The time lapse between the training day and the survey date is one variable that may have affected the assessment results. For example, unlike in Year 1 and Year 2, in Year 3, the survey was not administered at the end of the first

Table 4. Year 4 survey results (session 1)

ILE Survey 2016 (N=30)	Agree & Strongly Agree (%)	Disagree & Strongly Disagree (%)
I understand the intent of GGC's QEP.	100.0	0.0
I am aware of the QEP's 5 Student Learning Outcomes.	100.0	0.0
I am aware of the various levels of faculty involvement in internationalizing the curriculum.	93.3	3.3
I am aware there are various pathways for i-course development and/or documentation.	78.6	3.6
I am more interested in being involved in QEP efforts.	90.0	3.3
I am interested in participating in year-long faculty development program, the Internationalized Learning Certificate, in the future.	74.0	7.4
The "Faculty Resource Guide" from this Forum will be useful.	96.5	3.4
The Forum was well-organized.	100.0	0.0
Overall, the facilitators were effective.	100.0	0.0

Table 5. Year 4 survey results/session 2

ILE Survey 2016 (N=40)	Agree & Strongly Agree (%)	Disagree & Strongly Disagree (%)
I understand the intent of GGC's QEP.	77.5	15.0
I am aware of the QEP's 5 Student Learning Outcomes.	60.0	22.5
I understand the importance of raising intercultural awareness among ourselves and our students.	84.6	7.7
I have greater understanding of the Development Model of Intercultural Sensitivity (DMIS) as a means of measuring an individual's intercultural competence.	72.5	10.0
I am more interested in being involved in QEP efforts.	61.5	12.8
I am interested in participating in year-long faculty development program, the Internationalized Learning Certificate, in the future.	40.1	28.2
The "Faculty Resource Guide" from this Forum will be useful.		
The Forum was well-organized.	60.5	13.2
Overall, the facilitators were effective.	78.9	13.2

Table 6. Year 4 survey results/session 3

ILE Survey 2016 (N=12)	Agree & Strongly Agree (%)	Disagree & Strongly Disagree (%)
I have a greater understanding of the intent of GGC's Quality Enhancement Plan (QEP) on Internationalization.	83.3	0.0
I am aware of the diversity of GGC's student population.	100.0	0.0
I have a greater understanding of some of the challenges in dealing with cultural difference in the classroom.	90.9	0.0
I have a greater understanding of the role of i-courses and the Global Studies Certification in GGC's internationalization effort.	70.0	0.0
I am more interested in being involved in QEP efforts.	75.0	12.5
I am interested in participating in year-long faculty development program, the Internationalized Learning Certificate, in the future.	77.0	0.0
The Forum was well-organized.	90.9	0.0
Overall, the facilitators were effective.	90.9	0.0

90-minute session, yet it was given several weeks later as part of the New Faculty Orientation (NFO) assessment. It is unknown whether or not the participants were able to recall this particular ILE session and assessed the training accordingly among many other training sessions and workshops. Furthermore, the assessments for the remaining two 75-minute fall sessions were not administered until the spring semester, several months after the conclusion of the ILE-Forum.

Response rate is another variable that may have affected the results adversely. For instance, in Years 1 and 2, the response rate was 100%. However, in Year 3 and Year 4, the response rate to the 90 minute session was 55%, and the assessment result for spring was only 48%. The facilitators are aware of these limitations and determined to overcome them during the 5th year of implementation.

Despite these limitations, the faculty was generally satisfied with ILE forums. The main goal of the ILE forums has been to create intercultural sensitivity and awareness among the new faculty. The survey results showed that new faculty consistently met this objective (see items 1 and 2 in all surveys).

CONCLUSION

This chapter aims to provide insights regarding faculty training on internationalized education at a four-year-college while drawing upon survey results regarding this training process. The college offers various programs for internationalizing the curriculum, yet the focus of this chapter has been on one of the two training programs (ILE Forums). ILE is a particularly important program as it is the first step toward cross-cultural training of faculty. This program is specifically designed to familiarize faculty with basic concepts on internationalized education and help them become aware of the diverse   student body in their classrooms. As Odgers and Giroux (2006) highlighted, faculty may have different experiences, assumptions, and values, which have an impact on their teaching, leadership style, and service. It is imperative for faculty to understand their own culture and that of others before they can develop inter-cultural competency in students. In order for students to become global learners, they need to be able to effectively communicate across cultural boundaries. This is hard to achieve without the help of faculty who themselves have cross-cultural awareness and intercultural sensitivity. We hope that this chapter inspires other higher education institutions to offer similar professional development opportunities for faculty and make internationalization of curriculum their priority.

REFERENCES

Bennett, J. M., & Bennet, M. J. (2004). Developing intercultural sensitivity: An integrative approach to global and domestic diversity. In D. Landis, J. m. Bennett, & M. J. Bennet (Eds.), *Handbook of intercultural training* (3rd ed.; pp. 147–165). Thousand Oaks, CA: Sage. doi:10.4135/9781452231129.n6

Bennett, M. J. (1993). Towards Ethnorelativism: A Developmental Model of Intercultural Sensitivity. In R. M. Paige (Ed.), *Education for the Intercultural Experience* (pp. 21–71). Yarmouth, ME: Intercultural Press.

Bennett, M. J. (2004). Becoming Interculturally Competent. In J. Wurzel (Ed.), *Toward multiculturalism: A reader in multicultural education* (2nd ed.; pp. 62–77). Newton, MA: Intercultural Resource Corporation.

Crichton, J. P. M., Papademetre, L., & Scarino, A. (2004). *Integrated resources for intercultural training and learning in the context of internationalization of higher education.* Retrieved from http://www.unisa.edu.au/staff/gratns/archive/2003-integrated-report.doc

de Wit, H. (2002). *Internationalization of Higher Education in the United States of America and Europe.* Westport, CT: Greenwood Press.

Deardorff, D. K. (2006). Identification and assessment of intercultural competence as a student outcome of internationalization. *Journal of Studies in International Education, 10*(3), 241–266. doi:10.1177/1028315306287002

Deardorff, D. K. (2009). Exploring interculturally competent teaching in social sciences classrooms. *Enhancing Learning in the Social Sciences, 2*(1), 1–19. doi:10.11120/elss.2009.02010002

Green, M. F., & Olson, C. L. (2003). *Internationalizing the campus: A user's guide.* Washington, DC: American Council on Education.

Hammer, M. R. (1999). A Measure of intercultural sensitivity: The Intercultural Development Inventory. In S. M. Fowler & M. G. Mumford (Eds.), *Intercultural sourcebook: Cross-cultural training* (Vol. 2, pp. 61–72). Yarmouth, ME: Intercultural Press.

Hammer, M. R. (2009). The Intercultural Development Inventory. In M. A. Moodian (Ed.), *Contemporary leadership and Intercultural Competence.* Thousand Oaks, CA: Sage.

Hofstede, G. J. (2009). The Moral Circle in Intercultural Competence. In D. Deardorf (Ed.), *Handbook of Intercultural Competence* (pp. 85–99). Thousand Oaks, CA: Sage.

Hudzik, J. K. (2011). Comprehensive Internationalization: From Concept to Action. Washington, DC: NAFSA: Association of International Educators.

Johnson, J. D., & Tuttle, F. (1989). Problems in Intercultural Research. In Handbook of International and Intercultural Communication (pp. 461-483). Newbury Park, CA: Sage Publications.

Knight, J. (1999). *A Time of Turbulence and Transformation for Internationalization.* Ottawa, Canada: Canadian Bureau for International Education.

Knight, J. (2003). Updated Definition of Internationalization. *Industry and Higher Education, 33*(Fall), 2–3.

Knight, J. (2004). Internationalization Remodeled: Definition, Approaches, and Rationales. *Journal of Studies in International Education, 8*(1), 5–31. doi:10.1177/1028315303260832

Koester, J., Wiseman, R. L., & Sanders, J. A. (1993). Multiple perspectives of intercultural communication competence. In R. L. Wiseman & J. A. Koester (Eds.), *Intercultural Communication competence* (pp. 3–15). Newbury Park, CA: Sage.

Kolb, D. A. (1984). *Experiential learning: Experience as the source of learning and development.* Englewood Cliffs, NJ: Prentice-Hall.

Krutky, J. (2008). Intercultural competency: Preparing students to be global citizens. *Effective Practices for Academic Leaders, 3*(1), 1–15.

Leask, B. (2009). Using formal and informal curricula to improve interactions between home and international students. *Journal of Studies in International Education, 13*(2), 205–221. doi:10.1177/1028315308329786

Lee, A., Poch, R., Shaw, M., & Williams, R. D. (2012). *Engaging Diversity in Undergraduate Classrooms: A Pedagogy for Developing Intercultural Competence.* San Francisco: Jossey-Bass.

Odgers, T., & Giroux, I. (2006). *Internationalizing Faculty: A Phased Approach to ransforming Curriculum Design and Instruction.* Paper presented at the York University Annual International Conference on Internationalizing Canada's Universities, Toronto, Canada.

Pusch, M. D. (2009). The interculturally competent global leader. In D. Deardorff (Ed.), *Sage Handbook of Intercultural Competence* (pp. 66–84). Thousand Oaks, CA: Sage.

Spitzberg, B. H., & Cupach, W. R. (1984). *Interpersonal communication competence.* Beverly Hills, CA: Sage.

Yershova, Y., DeJaeghere, J., & Mestenhauser, J. (2000). Thinking Not as Usual: Adding the Intercultural Perspective. *Journal of Studies in International Education, 4*(1), 39–78. doi:10.1177/102831530000400105

Chapter 12
Beyond Curriculum Internationalization:
Globalization for Intercultural Competence

Funwi Ayuninjam
Georgia Gwinnett College, USA

ABSTRACT

Curriculum internationalization (CI) has shifted from U.S. student and faculty mobility, foreign language offerings, and interdisciplinary programming to the delivery of content and the role of international students in the method of delivery. Although CI is still about developing students' international and intercultural perspectives, it is not only about teaching or students. Broadly speaking, it is about learning and involves every member of the campus community through purposeful curriculum planning and campus programming. Curriculum internationalization is also about exposing American students, scholars, faculty, staff, and administrators to their overseas counterparts as well as to international settings and perspectives through co-curricular programs. This chapter discusses Georgia Gwinnett College's path towards campus internationalization through a quality enhancement program, education abroad programming, international students and partnerships, and campus programming—a purposeful blend of an internationalized curriculum and a co-curriculum.

INTRODUCTION

Curriculum internationalization (CI) in the early decades of systematic campus internationalization in the United States—particularly in the 1970s-1990s—referred primarily to U.S. student and faculty mobility (through study, service, and research abroad), foreign language offerings, and interdisciplinary programs—mainly area studies or comparative studies. Starting in the late 1990s and early 2000s, the focus broadened markedly to encompass the delivery of content and the role of international students in the method of delivery (McLoughlin, 2001; De Vita & Case, 2003; Bond, 2006; Leask, 2011; & Leask, 2015)—a broadening which Bond characterizes as "changing fundamentally what we teach and how we teach it" (2006, p. 3). Curriculum internationalization is still about developing students' international

DOI: 10.4018/978-1-5225-2791-6.ch012

and intercultural perspectives, but it is not only about teaching or students. Broadly speaking, CI is about learning, and it involves every member of the campus community through purposeful curriculum planning and campus programming. It is also about exposing American students, faculty, staff, and administrators to their overseas counterparts as well as international settings and perspectives. This chapter discusses Georgia Gwinnett College's path towards campus internationalization through a quality enhancement program, education abroad, international students and partnerships, and general campus programming.

Georgia Gwinnett College (GGC) was founded in 2005 as the thirty-fifth member of the University System of Georgia. The establishment of the college arose from a realization that Gwinnett County was the most populous county east of the Mississippi River lacking a four-year college. In March 2005, the Georgia legislature authorized the establishment of GGC as an access institution to "serve the broadest range of students, including those whose level of academic preparation limited their options for higher education" (initial mission and vision statement). Georgia Gwinnett College is a liberal-arts institution which provides select bachelor's and associate's degree programs in a student-centered, technology-enriched learning environment which meet the needs of the Northeast Atlanta metropolitan region. Gwinnett County has a population of over 907,000 residents and is home to various businesses, including those involved in health care, education, and information technology. GGC is accredited by the Southern Association of Colleges and Schools Commission on Colleges and has over 12,000 students enrolled in programs in six schools: Business, Education, Health Sciences, Liberal Arts, Science and Technology, and Transitional Studies. GGC opened its doors to students in 2006 and began creating many aspects of student life, such as the Student Government Association, student clubs, honor societies, and other organizations, including intercollegiate (NAIA) sports. In fall 2013, GGC received its first international students.

GGC's choice of a topic for a Quality Enhancement Plan ensued from three years of assessment and planning involving research and input from across the campus community. At a June 2011 planning retreat, one of the five recommendations adopted was that the QEP include international content and focus in co-curricular programming; however, because GGC had just been selected to participate in the American Council on Education Laboratory to develop internationalized co-curricular programming, the college determined that including co-curricular programs to the QEP charge would be redundant. In the final design of the QEP, the QEP Committee decided the program would "focus only on internationalization of the academic curriculum and [...] [i]nternationalized courses [would] be infused throughout the curriculum by revising or developing courses in the core curriculum, majors, and upper level electives" (Quality Enhancement Plan, n.d., p. 23). As a result, the QEP Committee maintained a primarily curricular charge focusing on creating internationalized courses, a Global Studies Certification Program, and faculty development, whereas the Internationalization Committee maintained a primarily co-curricular charge focusing on study abroad, international student recruitment, and campus programming (*Quality Enhancement Plan*, n.d. p. 23). GGC had already established the Office of Internationalization in 2010 to shepherd the co-curricular component of its internationalization mission. Internationalization of the curriculum aligns well with GGC's mission to produce globally competent graduates—those who are "inspired to contribute to the local, state, national, and international communities and are prepared to anticipate and respond effectively to an uncertain and changing world" (current mission statement).

Georgia Gwinnett College's approach to internationalization was informed by, and is modeled after, the American Council on Education's Center for Internationalization and Global Engagement (CIGE) model for comprehensive internationalization. The model defines comprehensive internationalization as "a strategic, coordinated process that seeks to align and integrate policies, programs, and initiatives to position colleges and universities as more globally oriented and internationally connected institutions" (American Council on Education, 2017). The model comprises six pillars: articulated institutional commitment; administrative leadership, structure, and staffing; curriculum, co-curriculum, and learning outcomes; faculty policies and practices; student mobility; and collaboration and partnerships. Prior to establishing the Office of Internationalization, the College participated in the American Council on Education's Internationalization Laboratory over a twenty-month period. The participation culminated in an articulated mission and vision and a plan for campus internationalization which emphasizes co-curricular programs and complements the quality enhancement plan, whose focus is internationalization of the academic curriculum.

This chapter scales down and restructures the American Council on Education pillars into these four components: the Quality Enhancement Plan, education abroad programming, international partnerships, and campus programming in terms of intercultural competence. The chapter does not address ACE's articulated institutional commitment; administrative leadership, structure, and staffing; or faculty policies and practices in part because of the inchoate nature of comprehensive internationalization at GGC and for the sake of focus. The four components addressed here are GGC's main vectors of intercultural competence. The QEP constitutes the academic underpinning of the internationalization plan by laying out the requisite knowledge, skills, and attitudes of global citizenship which permeate the curriculum and are verifiable through student learning outcomes. Education abroad is an extension of students' knowledge base in their respective disciplines, but is anchored within a relevant international setting to enable students to apply their skills, deepen their awareness, and develop appropriate attitudes and dispositions. International partnerships facilitate academic and intercultural exchanges and education programming as they promote international study and service learning, joint programs, and student and scholar exchanges. Campus programming is an opportunity for all members of the campus community to share their various academic and cultural experiences with one another. The events are usually open to all members of the campus community, and primary presenters tend to be education abroad returnees, education abroad program directors, international students/scholars, and foreign-born students, faculty, and staff. This chapter is meant to shed light on how purposefully the curriculum is interwoven with the co-curriculum to develop the intercultural competences of all members of the campus community. Given the economic profile of the student population—with 76% receiving need-based scholarships—GGC's internationalization plan is appropriate and cost effective.

GEORGIA GWINNETT COLLEGE'S QEP AND INTERNATIONALIZATION

As an integral part of Georgia Gwinnett College's reaffirmation for continued accreditation from the Southern Association of Colleges and Schools Commission on Colleges, GGC's Quality Enhancement Plan (QEP), titled "Internationalization of the Curriculum: Engaging the World to Develop Global Citizens," is a five-year plan designed to enhance student learning and the student learning environment. The QEP supports GGC's mission to produce global citizens and constitutes the curricular component of the college's internationalization plan. The college began by examining assessment data on student learning outcomes to identify appropriate QEP topics related to student performance or institutional educational effectiveness. Such an assessment was to draw on GGC's eight Integrated Educational Experience student learning outcomes (SLOs)—college-level competencies which articulate the knowledge, skills, and attitudes GGC graduates should demonstrate (*Quality Enhancement Plan*, n.d., p. 5). The learning outcomes are as follows:

1. Clearly communicate ideas in written and oral forms;
2. Demonstrate creativity and critical thinking in inter- and multidisciplinary contexts;
3. Demonstrate effective use of information technology;
4. Demonstrate an understanding of diversity and global perspectives leading to collaboration in diverse and global contexts;
5. Demonstrate an understanding of human and institutional decision making;
6. Demonstrate an understanding of moral and ethical principles;
7. Demonstrate and apply leadership principles;
8. Demonstrate competence in quantitative reasoning.

The QEP was crafted through the leadership of a 34-member campus-wide committee constituted in spring 2011 and charged with, among others, developing a QEP topic. Based on input from topic development sessions, five recommendations emerged, including establishing "multiple curricular encounters" for all students, incorporating international content and focus in co-curricular programs, fostering faculty and staff professional development in internationalization, and building processes and infrastructure (*Quality Enhancement Plan*, n.d., p. 15). Convinced of the need for more engaging course work in global learning, the QEP Committee and QEP Steering Committee recommended the establishment of a certification program which would strengthen students' global citizenship skills. A Global Studies Certification Subcommittee tasked with doing the necessary research ultimately recommended the creation of a Global Studies Certification Program, which would ensure student participation from various disciplines, integration between the program and existing academic programs, and tracking of student retention and persistence throughout the program (n.d., pp. 18-19).

While benchmarks or "targets" by themselves do not define internationalization, it is important to identify the key elements of GGC's plan: internationalized courses (also called *i*-courses) and the Global Studies Certification Program. For this chapter, one core component of the curriculum will be discussed: internationalized courses—those which "are intended to provide students with opportunities to build intercultural competence and skill. As such, *i*-courses contain both an elevated level of international content and the requirements and activities needed to promote student success in achieving the desired learning outcomes at an appropriate level for a given course" (Georgia Gwinnett College, 2016). The College already offered many courses with international content before the onset of the Quality Enhancement Plan. The QEP Steering Committee established guidelines for developing *i*-courses and put in place a process for verifying the courses. Much of this section is a restatement of the work of that committee, chaired by the Associate Vice President for Quality Enhancement Programs and Institutional Policy. Below too are the course attributes:

1. Has a score of three or four on the Content Rubric (indicating that over 30% of the course material is international or global in focus);
2. Addresses a minimum of two of the QEP student learning outcomes (SLOs), drawn from two separate SLO categories as determined by the Outcomes Rubric;
3. Expects students to demonstrate competence at a developmentally appropriate level as follows:

a. For lower-level courses, a minimum of two SLOs (in 2 of 3 categories) must be met at least at the novice level;

b. For upper-level courses, a minimum of two SLOs (in 2 of 3 categories) must be met at least at the developing level.

The QEP Student Learning Outcomes (SLOs) address three broad areas of competence: intercultural awareness (SLOs 1 and 2), communication and collaboration (SLOs 3 and 4), and application (SLO 5). Having decided to focus the QEP on internationalization of the academic curriculum and not on the co-curriculum, the QEP Steering Committee needed to "equip appropriate faculty and staff with the knowledge and skills needed to design, deliver or support the delivery of an internationalized curriculum" (*Quality Enhancement Plan*, pp. 21-22)—a goal which parallels those of providing *i*-courses and the Global Studies Certification Program.

EDUCATION ABROAD AND INTERCULTURAL COMPETENCE

Intercultural competence, as used here, follows Deardorff's 2006 definition: "the ability to communicate effectively and appropriately in intercultural situations, shift frames of reference appropriately and adapt behavior to cultural context" (qtd. in Leask 2015, p. 249). At GGC, education abroad is promoted as a potential life-changing experience. It is central to developing intercultural competence in that it provides students opportunities to come face to face with foreign cultures and different modes of expression, increase their interpersonal communication skills, examine American culture from a foreign lens, take a course in a different environment, make new friends overseas, challenge themselves physically and psychologically by living outside their comfort zones, and examine the United States from the vantage point of non-Americans. Ultimately, education abroad constitutes a good opportunity for students to engage personally with their peers overseas. At GGC, education abroad programming is decentralized, primarily faculty led, and sponsored by the respective schools or departments. All study abroad programs are credit bearing, while service-learning programs may or may not be credit bearing. There are college-wide policies and procedures for establishing and running the programs, and the process begins with the interested faculty or staff member and requires approval by various officials, from the dean or supervisor to the President.

GGC's first study abroad program was established in 2008 by a faculty member in the School of Business. It was followed by another in 2010 led by a faculty member in the School of Science and Technology. Since then, there has been growing interest in faculty-led programs, with programs now in four of the five degree-granting schools: Business, Health Sciences, Liberal Arts, and Science and Technology. For academic year 2016/2017, the following nine faculty-led study abroad programs have been approved: Belgium/France/Switzerland: International Business; China: Biology and Natural History of China; China: Global Issues; Costa Rica: Biology; Ecuador: International Conservation Biology; Ecuador: Spanish and Nursing; Thailand: Calculus and Biology; United Kingdom: Criminal Justice and Criminology/British Studies; and Vietnam: Calculus and Biology. In addition, GGC faculty members have been approved to teach in two University System of Georgia "Council" programs in summer 2017—a European Council Paris Program (France: A Cultural History through Art, Literature, and Film) and an Asia Council Program (Japan: Japanese Spiritual Traditions).

Corresponding to the growth in education abroad programming is a spike in enrollment, from 30 in academic year 2010/2011 to 111 in academic year 2016/2017. While the figures seem statistically impressive, they do no justice to an institution with over 12,000 students. That is why, when GGC joined the Council for International Educational Exchange Generation Study Abroad, it pledged not to double its study abroad number within five years but to triple it. That still was a rather easy commitment to make. To help move students from their disciplinary silos, for the past two years, faculty proposing new programs have been encouraged to work with their peers in other disciplines to establish broader-based, interdisciplinary programs. As the above list shows, there has been a shift in that direction. Interdisciplinary programming engenders more collaboration between faculty and a better appreciation among students and faculty for other disciplines. Students may also study abroad through other third-party affiliates of their choice, with prior approval by the college.

Financial aid and scholarships (based primarily on a mandatory international education fee) are available to all students. In fall 2016, the Office of Internationalization (OI) received additional scholarship funding—the Cole Blasier Award—from the University of Pittsburgh's Center for Latin American Studies. It helped fund a student's study in Costa Rica in summer 2016. Two of the study abroad programs—Vietnam and Thailand—are based on university campuses. The programs offer the best opportunities for intercultural learning as the classes are open to Vietnamese and Thai students, so both domestic and visiting GGC students interact with one another in and outside the classroom.

Complementing study abroad and to fulfill Georgia Gwinnett's service pillar is international service learning. Georgia Gwinnett's service-learning program is a five-year-old non-credit program called Global Civic Engagement. Established in 2012 by the founding director of the Office of Internationalization, the program examines the concept of service learning as it relates to issues of social justice in a global context. Global Civic Engagement seeks to goad participants to engage with difference. It enables students to examine the societal effect of service around the world through hands-on learning experiences with local and international communities, relevant course readings, and interactive reflection. Every spring break since 2012, students have participated in an intensive service project abroad with these learning outcomes: an ability to:

1. Enhance one's experiences, which foster intercultural understanding and communication;
2. Appreciate and develop respect for people from other backgrounds;
3. Identify one's self and one's cultural context in relation to others';
4. Demonstrate social responsibility in the global sphere;
5. Develop leadership skills anchored through active involvement with diverse communities and real-world challenges;
6. Gain an in-depth understanding of social justice issues in a global context;
7. Provide a critical analysis of how/why socioeconomic, political, and cultural factors affect the nature and value of civic engagement within a community;
8. Identify ways in which individuals/groups can enhance or challenge approaches to working for the common good in a global society;
9. Discuss and be aware of the motivations for, and possible consequences of, doing service in a community.

The 2012 trip was to Ecuador, the 2013 trip to South Africa, the 2014 one to Spain, and the 2016 and 2017 to the Dominican Republic. The 2015 trip was canceled. Each trip includes a hands-on project and a project with children. Over the years, community projects have included the following: distributing donated service project supplies at a school and working with high school students to plant trees in a city park (Ecuador), constructing community health clinics (South Africa), working in a soup kitchen and touring an organic dairy farm (Spain), and helping to build a "bottle school" out of discarded plastic bottles and serving at a local orphanage (Dominican Republic).

Among common observations by GGC education abroad returnees are a greater appreciation for the opportunities and resources they have at home and a better understanding of the distinction between needs and wants. Such shifts in perspective would be more difficult to inculcate in students within a conventional educational setting. Short-term faculty-led programs are an initial step towards facilitating longer-term study abroad—one of the underlying reasons for international partnerships, to which we now turn.

INTERNATIONAL PARTNERSHIPS AND INTERCULTURAL COMPETENCE

One of the primary charges of the Office of Internationalization is recruiting and integrating international students into the GGC community. The need to increase GGC's international student numbers was urgent—both to take advantage of external forces and to meet the College's own internal dynamics. Even though Georgia Gwinnett College is the most diverse college in the U.S. South (*U.S. News and World Report*, 2013, 2014, 2015, and 2016) and though 10% of the student population identify as "international" in the broad sense that they have at least one immigrant parent, the nonimmigrant international students currently number only 125. Prior to 2016, there was no systematic international student recruitment. The mission of the recently elaborated international student recruitment plan is to grow the number of international students attending Georgia Gwinnett College–as degree-seeking students, exchange students, short-term visiting students, or English as a second language students. Increasing the number of international students would further diversify the campus, expose GGC students to more global perspectives inside and outside the classroom, and engender a more vibrant campus culture. International student recruitment has four objectives: grow the international student population; enhance the campus cultural environment; enhance student persistence, completion, and graduation; and enhance domestic students' ability to embrace change and deal with otherness.

Crucial to campus internationalization is Georgia Gwinnett's endeavor to further internationalize its student body. Developing an international student recruitment plan involved the input of colleagues from various departments, including the offices of Enrollment Management, Athletics, and Internationalization, as well as the contributions of members of the International Admissions Task Force and the Internationalization Committee. Several factors shaped GGC's international recruitment: internal and external. Among the internal factors was the commitment to grow the general student enrollment to 11,700 in academic year 2015/2016 and 13,000 in 2016/2017. With this planned growth was a need to look beyond Georgia and the United States for students. Another internal factor was the opportunity to promote GGC's academic programs such as nursing, business, and the science, technology, engineering, and mathematics disciplines. The third factor was intercultural—the College's Integrated Educational Experience (IEE) outcomes (IEEs), five of which are as follows: demonstrate creativity and critical thinking in inter- and multidisciplinary contexts (IEE 2); demonstrate an understanding of diversity and global perspectives leading to collaboration in diverse and global contexts (IEE 4); understand the role of history in human development and national and world affairs (IEE 7); understand human and institutional behavior from a political, social, and global perspective (IEE 8); and appreciate human endeavors in literature or the arts (IEE 9).

Among the external factors were these: the popularity and reputation of American higher education; a dearth of opportunities for post-secondary education in several world regions, especially Asia and Southeast Asia; dominance of American English as a world lingua franca; and a need to look beyond the county and state to frame how to tell the GGC story. Because GGC is only eleven years old, has no international alumni base, and has limited resources, the Office of Internationalization has been strategic in establishing overseas partnerships. Based on the 2016 census, the Asian population comprises 11.9% of Gwinnett County's 907,135 residents, corresponding to a headcount of 107,949 residents. It is the fastest-growing demographic group in the county, and Vietnamese is the fourth most commonly spoken language at home after English, Spanish, and Korean (statisticalatlas.com). Asia and Southeast Asia are the primary regions for GGC's initial recruitment phase (2016/2017). GGC established its first partnership with a Vietnamese institution—Thai Nguyen University of Technology (TNUT). The partnership is a combination of five programming types: a student tuition and fee exchange, a short-term scholar program, and an English as a second language program. TNUT is also host to GGC's month-long math and biology faculty-led study abroad program.

Georgia Gwinnett has hosted three scholar cohorts from Thai Nguyen University of Technology, of which the first comprised three faculty members who shadowed their counterparts in the School of Science and Technology in fall 2015. The second cohort—in spring 2016—included two faculty members who participated in a similar shadowing program. Simultaneously, seven other faculty members took intensive English language in GGC's English Language Institute. Of the two faculty members who shadowed in the School of Science and Technology in spring 2016, one of them—a biochemist—observed five GGC faculty members teaching Principles of Chemistry I, Principles of Chemistry II, and Survey of Chemistry I. Even after returning to Vietnam, this TNUT faculty member has maintained contact with her GGC counterparts. Besides working with GGC faculty, she collaborated with a faculty member at Georgia Institute of Technology (Georgia Tech) in the area of atmospheric chemistry. The second TNUT faculty member shadowed his counterparts in these upper-level math classes: Math 4900 (Capstone), Math 4250 (Topology), and Math 4100 (Differential Equations). He also visited two lower-division math classes: Calculus II and Calculus III. This faculty member was a regular participant in the faculty mathematics seminar, which met every Friday afternoon. At the end of the visit, all nine visiting faculty members made a joint campus-wide presentation on various aspects of life in Vietnam, including family life, education, religion, dress, and marketing.

A third cohort from Thai Nguyen University of Technology visited GGC in fall 2016 as short-term scholars—two in the School of Science and Technology and one in the School of Transitional Studies. Two of the scholars were biochemists and one a Humanities lecturer. They had more robust research agendas than did the preceding cohorts, though the overarching purpose of the program was essentially the same—to enable TNUT faculty to familiarize themselves with GGC's academic culture and pedagogical practices, participate in joint research and teaching activities at GGC, and observe classes and consult with GGC faculty. This type of engagement reflects Leask's approach to curriculum internationalization in terms of "incorporation of international, intercultural, and global dimensions into the content of the curriculum as well as the teaching methods, learning outcomes, and support services of a program of study" (2015, p. 71).

We also have partnerships with Sookmyung Women's University (South Korea), Hanyang University (South Korea), the University of Prizren (Kosovo), Nguyen Tat Thanh University (Vietnam), and Vytautas Magnus University (Lithuania). For spring 2017, GGC is planning to host a student researcher from Vytautas Magnus University for four months, and VMU will in turn host a GGC faculty member for one week. Through the combined efforts of two charities—one based in Gwinnett County and another in Kosovo—GGC receives high school students annually for intensive English in the English Language Institute. The students' program has a Friday cultural component, which enables the students to interact with GGC students through class visits and other campus events. The third cohort completed their program in October 2016. The English Language Institute is one of the steps GGC has taken to enhance internationalization of the campus. Jointly established in 2015 by the Office of Internationalization and the School of Transitional Studies, the Institute is a means to further diversify the student body and facilitate the recruitment of international students and scholars as some of the Kosovars have returned and matriculated at GGC after completing high school in Kosovo.

Case Study in Curriculum Internationalization: Georgia College – Vytautas Magnus University

On March 27, Honorable Julius Pranevicius, Lithuania's Consul General based in New York, was scheduled to visit Atlanta and agreed to come to GGC and deliver a guest lecture titled "Challenges and Opportunities in the European Union's Eastern Neighborhood: The Case of Ukraine." Consul General Pranevicius, a seasoned diplomat both in Vilnius and Brussels, has also once held an eight-year tenure in the School of International Relations at Vilnius University. A GGC faculty member agreed to receive Consul General Pranevicius as a guest lecturer in his international relations class. The lecture was quite engaging, with most of the questions coming from students. Afterwards, Mr. Pranevicius met with the staff of the Office of Internationalization to explore opportunities for collaboration between GGC and Lithuanian institutions. Among others, he provided an insightful review of Lithuania's post-secondary education system and the country's academic culture. Based on a briefing on Georgia Gwinnett's profile, he was to recommend a Lithuanian university with characteristics of GGC. Later that summer, he recommended Vytautas Magnus University.

In November 2015, Dr. Dovile Budryte, a GGC Professor of Political Science and Assistant Dean for Faculty Evaluation, visited Vytautas Magnus University (VMU) and met with six members of VMU's political science department who were interested in exploring areas of mutual interest with GGC, including joint teaching. Dr. Budryte is of Lithuanian origin and has a good understanding of the university. The visit resulted in their agreeing to organize 90-minute online seminars which would bring together faculty and students from both institutions. Given the time difference between the U.S. East Coast and Lithuania, the meetings would be scheduled for 9:00 AM U.S. Eastern Time. The format was GGC faculty each making a brief presentation, followed by a question-and-answer session; then VMU would do the same. Dr. Budryte sent the biographies of several GGC faculty, indicating their areas of research and presentation titles, and VMU political scientists would make a choice. Vytautas Magnus University reciprocated. The result was two online mini-conferences, of which the first was on February 10, 2016 and featured two GGC faculty presenters.

Besides the occasional online webinars, there was discussion about cooperation in political science by getting students on both campuses to work on joint projects. Faculty members from Vytautas Magnus University visited GGC in fall 2016. These included a visiting scholar who addressed students and faculty on opportunities for them at VMU; another was the chairperson of the Sociology Department, who discussed with faculty in the School of Liberal Arts possible joint curricular initiatives. Given that

Georgia Gwinnett is an access institution—with 76% of the students receiving need-based scholarships, this type of interactive international programming is an ideal way of bringing the world to students who might never go overseas during their undergraduate years. Ultimately, foreign partners will be hosts to most GGC students pursuing semester or academic-year programs abroad. For students at both ends, such exchanges—by virtue of their duration—provide the greatest opportunity for immersion and intercultural learning.

CAMPUS PROGRAMMING AND INTERCULTURAL COMPETENCE

The Peace Corps Preparatory Program

The Peace Corps Preparatory Program (PCPP) is a formal cooperative endeavor between GGC and the U.S. Peace Corps Program designed for GGC students interested in serving as Peace Corps Volunteers after they graduate. The program has four competencies and career preparation benefits:

1. **Training and Experience in a Work Sector:** This competence requires at least three courses which align with a specific work sector and at least fifty hours of volunteer or work experience in the same sector, preferably in a teaching or outreach capacity. Under this sector is a wide array of courses in six fields: Education, Health, Environment, Agriculture, Youth in Development, and Community Economic Development;
2. **Foreign Language Skills:** Requirements here vary by language and include three options:
   a. **French or Spanish through Course Credit or Language Testing International:** French or Spanish credit at the 2002 level or higher or a score of "intermediate mid" or better on the Oral Proficiency Interview or Writing Proficiency Test through Language Testing International;
   b. **Any other language through Language Testing International:** Credit through the 1002 level in any other language or a score of "novice high" or better on the Oral Proficiency Interview or Writing Proficiency Test through Language Testing International;
   c. **French or Spanish through the College Level Examination Program (CLEP):** The US Peace Corps Program accepts CLEP test results in lieu of high school or college classes. Spanish 1 requires a score between 50 and 62 on the Spanish CLEP in the past six years; Spanish 2 requires a score of 63 on the Spanish CLEP in the past six years; and all French courses require a score of 50 on the French CLEP in the past six years;
3. **Intercultural Competence:** With this learning objective, students will deepen their cultural agility through a mix of three introspective courses in which they learn about others while reflecting upon their own selves in relation to others. The goal is for students to build their capacity to shift perspectives and behavior around relevant cultural differences. They will complete a course from each of these tracks (for a total of three courses): an approved study abroad or service-learning trip abroad, one internationalized course at the 1000 level, or one internationalized course at the 2000 level or higher;
4. **Professional and Leadership Development:** The Peace Corps Preparatory Program requires three specific activities which will strengthen the student's candidacy for the Peace Corps Program (or any other professional endeavor):

a. Have your resume, cover letter, and personal statement critiqued by someone in the Career Development and Advising Center;

b. Attend a workshop or class on career planning, job searching, and interview skills in the Career Development and Advising Center;

c. Participate in a mock interview in the Career Development and Advising Center;

d. Develop at least one significant leadership experience and be prepared to discuss it thoughtfully; for example, organizing a campus event, leading a work or volunteer project, or serving on the executive board of a student organization.

General Campus Programming

The Office of Internationalization engages the campus in intercultural education activities throughout the year through campus-wide and small-group activities, including student club programs and conferences. One such conference is the Georgia International Leadership Conference (GILC), an annual weekend-long conference for international students and study abroad student leaders from Georgia colleges. It seeks to cultivate friendships among the students, promote international understanding and global awareness on Georgia's college campuses, challenge students about the concept of self as leader in global stewardship, and encourage participants to recognize and understand everyone's responsibility in preserving the planet. The conference takes place every spring semester, and activities include interactive workshops led by students and cover, *inter alia*, leadership styles, collaboration, conflict management, and cross-cultural communication. The Office of Internationalization has sponsored international student participation in this conference over the past three years. In January 2016, seventeen students and three faculty/staff members attended it.

Students are integral to the Office of Internationalization's campus programming, and the Office of Internationalization undergirds many student clubs and organizations and funds some of the activities. OI staff advise the International Student Association, the Korean Student Association, and Model United Nations. Plans are underway to establish a campus chapter of the international honor society Phi Beta Delta. The effort will be headed by a faculty member who serves on the Internationalization Committee, which is chaired by the Director of Internationalization. Establishing a Phi Beta Delta chapter was among the goals of the Internationalization Committee for AY 2016-2017. Other student registered organizations whose activities OI supports include Sigma Iota Rho, the Organization of Latin-American Students, the African Student Association, and the Kosovar Student Association. These organizations enhance GGC's co-curricular programs in palpable ways.

International Education Week and Global Awareness Week are among the campus' intense and engaging weeks, and they occur in the fall and spring, respectively. Students are invited and encouraged to stage various intercultural events of general interest. Recurring International Education Week events have included an education abroad returnee symposium—an opportunity for all students who have studied abroad the previous year to share their experiences with the rest of the campus community and help whip up interest among students for education abroad. International Language Tables, coordinated by a member of the Internationalization Committee and GGC's Dean of the School of Transitional Studies, promotes foreign languages by getting faculty and staff who speak foreign languages to man "language" tables where they engage campus community members in brief, structured conversations in each language. Each exchange lasts between five and ten minutes, and then the participant may move to another table and try out another language. Foreign languages represented in the past have included

Albanian, Arabic, French, Kiswahili, Korean, Mandarin, Russian, Spanish, Twi, Urdu, Vietnamese, and Yoruba. Below are some of the "conversation starters" for the exchanges:

- Where did you grow up?
- Do you have any siblings?
- Do you know what your name means?
- What do you like to do in your spare time?
- What is your favorite holiday?
- If you could meet anyone in history, who would it be?

For students taking some of the foreign languages, International Language Tables is an opportunity to hear someone else speak their foreign language or practice it in a different, low-risk, and nonthreatening context. This type of exercise mirrors Leask and Carroll's concept of aligning the formal curriculum and the informal curriculum as they report in a case study at the University of South Australia (2011, pp. 652-54), a study which led them to this acknowledgment: "only by changing the culture and campus environment can students start to feel able and comfortable with moving out of the current silos" (University of South Australia, 2011, pp. 656-57). Language and Cultural Exchange Café, like International Language Tables, provides an environment for students to interact with and learn from each other. As with many other events, there are finger foods, music, and beverages representing various cultures. Like International Language Tables too, the interactions include a quiz—this time about one's country of origin. Here are some of the questions:

- In what continent is my country?
- What does my flag look like?
- What is the capital city?
- Do you know of any foods that we eat a lot?
- What famous people come from my country?
- If you were to visit my country, what would you expect?

Global Competency Quiz has quickly become a staple of the week-long programs. Each day of International Education Week and Global Awareness Week, the campus community has a chance to answer five questions about world cultures, history, and geography and at the end of the week, results are tabulated and shared with the whole campus. The quizzes are modeled after the U.S. Department of State's, only longer. Invariably, students, faculty, and staff have written saying they loved the exercise and wished it were all year long. There have been symbolic prizes for top finishers.

Each week has also typically featured a keynote presenter who engages the campus community on some topical issue. Past presentations have been titled as follows: "A Change to Much of the Same: Cuba" by Georgia State Representative Pedro Marin; "Globalization and the Challenges of Our Future" by Georgia State Representative B.J. Pak; and "Civil Rights in the Global Context: Where Does Africa Fit In?" by Ambassador Robin Sanders. The November 2016 keynote address, titled "Graduate Profile for Today's Youth Workforce: German Businesses in Georgia/U.S. Southeast," was delivered by Meredith Steinmetz, Outreach Director of Goethe-Zentrum Atlanta. The presentations are usually scheduled around the class times of committed faculty members to ensure a good student turnout. These faculty members treat the event as a class, so their students attend, participate actively, and earn class credit.

In November 2016, following Ambassador Robin Sanders' keynote address, about a dozen students, selected from various student organizations and political science and international relations classes, had a luncheon meeting with the ambassador at which the students asked more questions about her career, world affairs, and Foreign Service career opportunities.

The addresses have been intertwined with less serene, informal, but equally engaging presentations, including musical recitals and movie nights (mostly documentaries). The Model United Nations Club staged a mock debate in November 2016 titled "Child Refugees: Receive or Refuse?" to further the raging debate about migration from conflict-ravaged regions of the world into Western Europe, Australia, Canada, and the United States. Global Awareness Week 2017 was themed "Breaking Barriers: Inclusion in the U.S. and Beyond," and most of the week's events addressed the theme and included these: a guest presentation titled—"Love of One's Country: Perspectives from a Muslim marine," Global Dance Showcase (with African and Korean performing groups), a student panel presentation titled "Islam, American Culture and Immigration," and a faculty panel presentation titled "Crisis in Ukraine: A Challenge to the Current International Order."

Beyond the two weeks of intense activities, OI stages various intercultural events intended to engage the entire campus during the year. One of them—Global Café—is a series of occasional informal luncheon presentations by students, faculty, staff, and administrators about global affairs or recent travel abroad. Launched in February 2017, the International Student-Faculty Buddy program pairs international students with faculty for cross-cultural learning. The program, an initiative of the Internationalization Committee, is designed to allow GGC international students to connect with faculty as a way of transitioning to life at GGC and in the United States. It is not academic advising, but rather informal mentoring and a campus resource for the students which provides informal linguistic and cultural support as well as general guidance. Each student is paired with a knowledgeable faculty member for a year, during which each faculty buddy guides the student buddy through any occasional difficult times. It is a campus resource for friendly advice, a conversation, or just a cup of coffee. The College is supporting this endeavor by paying for two campus meals per student buddy per semester.

Conversation Partners pairs English Language Institute students with domestic students for language learning. To guard against unintentionally promoting the so-called "hidden curriculum," every effort is made to ensure the International Student-Faculty Buddy Program and Conversation Partners foster cross-cultural communication and cross-cultural learning from, about, and with each other as Stohl advocates (in Brewer and Cunningham, 2009, p. 212), rather than seek to assimilate one group.

A new campus intercultural event intended to pull campus community members out of cultural silos is the Albanian Cultural Showcase, jointly organized by the Kosovar Student Association and Kosovar high school students who come to GGC every fall to take classes in the English Language Institute. The event celebrates Albanian culture through music, food, fashion, and dance and has drawn large audiences and participants. The event is educational as the students always share with the rest of campus various slices of life in Kosovo through poster presentations.

The Office of Internationalization is also charged with expanding faculty and staff involvement in internationalization initiatives, a responsibility which is also furthered by the Internationalization Committee, in turn charged with all aspects of promoting international education on campus. Consistent with American Council on Education guidelines, committee membership is broad based and includes students and faculty from each of the schools to represent multiple perspectives and different levels of discourse. Here are committee goals for academic year 2016/2017: Promote intercultural programs and activities on campus, increase education abroad participation by students and faculty, promote the study of foreign languages among students, and support the recruitment of international students. The committee members take their work seriously and have always been the core of each year's International Education Week planning committee. All the work of the committee members, GGC faculty and staff and administration, and the student leaders and organizations that is of an intercultural nature is geared towards ensuring students graduate with appropriate competencies for a global society. Leask (2015, p. 55) summarizes graduate capabilities associated with curriculum internationalization at universities around the world as follows:

1. Knowledge of other cultures and times and an appreciation of cultural diversity;
2. Responsiveness to national and international communities;
3. The ability to work effectively in settings of social and cultural diversity;
4. A capacity to work effectively in diverse settings and to relate well to people from diverse backgrounds;
5. Global perspectives—the ability to understand and respect interdependence of life in a globalized world;
6. International perspectives and competence in a global environment;
7. International perspectives as a professional and as a citizen.

In several ways, these capabilities reflect GGC's Integrated Educational Experience outcomes discussed earlier under international partnerships, except that the GGC outcomes are more closely tied to the curriculum. These outcomes also reflect Joe Mestenhauser's (1999) concept of the curriculum as embracing "several knowledges: the conventional disciplinary subject-matter knowledge, and knowledge about countries, self-reflective knowledge about our own culture, and meta-knowledge about how we relate to each other globally" (qtd. in Bond 2006, p. 3).

CONCLUSION

This chapter has reviewed Georgia Gwinnett College's approach to globalizing the campus by strengthening the intercultural competence of its students and employees. The approach is overt—through the curriculum and other aspects of the student's required course of study, and covert—through campus and off-campus programmatic activities. The curricular component is evident in internationalized courses sprouting in each school and with faculty increasingly embracing them as the norm in ensuring diversity in their pedagogy. The co-curricular component is more diffuse and could be limited by availability of resources. Education abroad, while largely viewed as the watershed between a rounded education and a circumscribed education, if not well conceived, could also constitute a further marginalization of students with limited financial means or other challenges. As a result, creative programming that takes advantage of domestic opportunities for intercultural experiences as well as creative use of electronic resources could ensure that GGC graduates will be poised to engage the world as they walk out the door.

As with a lot of endeavors is the issue of assessment. Institutions can hardly ever claim they attained a "goal" of internationalization or intercultural competence for, if well-conceived, curriculum internationalization is an endless cycle. Nonetheless, there always should be an opportunity for an institution to take stock and determine whether it is (still) on track. Internationalized courses, courses taught abroad, intercultural programs and activities, online seminars, overseas partnerships, and other such endeavors could represent mileposts and are easy to identify, document, and measure. Not easily measurable are the less perceptible skills and dispositions, which are often fluid and subject to ceaseless variation based on circumstances, including location, subject matter, and group chemistry. The Office of Plans, Policies, and Analysis and the Office of Co-Curricular Assessment conduct periodic surveys which, long term, could provide a clue as what difference the programs may have made in the lives of students and other members of the campus community.

Georgia Gwinnett College, like many other institutions seeking to globalize their curricula, has identified its key graduate attributes, emphasizes the relevance and role of faculty in the internationalization process, and is battling the age-old issue of varying degrees of engagement between faculty based on their disciplines—with practitioners in the social or applied sciences more readily disposed than their peers in the pure sciences. GGC's School of Science and Technology may be bucking that trend given that, as shown earlier, five of the nine faculty-led programs set for academic year 2016/2017 are in science and mathematics. It is also worth noting that three of the five programs have been led by the same faculty members. Whatever the challenges, globalization is here to stay. International education and intercultural education are no longer options if students are to acquire skills that will enable them to function well in a culturally diverse and ever more complex, interdependent world.

ACKNOWLEDGMENT

I am grateful to Dr. Ellen Cox, former Associate Vice President for Quality Enhancement Programs and Institutional Policy, for reviewing and emending the section on GGC's Quality Enhancement Program; to Dr. Kristina Watkins Mormino, Coordinator of the Global Studies Certification Program and Associate Professor of French, for her assistance with the section on GGC's Peace Corps Preparatory Program and for her review of and comments on the manuscript; to the volume editors for their patience and candid reviews which helped me to refocus the write-up; and Dr. Dovilė Budrytė, Professor of Political Science and Assistant Dean in the School of Liberal Arts, for her assistance with the case study. Without their assistance, the chapter would be quite different. I am ultimately responsible for the material.

REFERENCES

American Council on Education. Center for Internationalization and Global Engagement. (n.d.). Retrieved July 9, 2017 from http://www.acenet.edu/news-room/Pages/CIGE-Model-for-Comprehensive-Internationalization.aspx

Bond, S. (2006). *Transforming the culture of learning: Evoking the international dimension in Canadian university curriculum*. Retrieved October 15, 2016 from http://international.yorku.ca/global/conference/canada/papers/Sheryl-Bond.pdf

Brewer, E., & Cunningham, K. (Eds.). (2009). *Integrating study abroad into the curriculum: Theory and practice across the discipline*. Sterling, VA: Stylus.

De Vita, G., & Case, P. (2003). Rethinking the internationalization agenda in UK higher education. *Journal of Further and Higher Education*, 27(4), 383–398. doi:10.1080/0309877032000128082

Georgia Gwinnett College. (2013a). *Quality Enhancement Program: Internationalization of the curriculum: Engaging the world to develop global citizens.* Author.

Georgia Gwinnett College. (2013b). *Internationalization of the curriculum: Engaging the world to develop global citizens—Quality Enhancement Plan (QEP).* Lawrenceville, GA: Author.

Georgia Gwinnett College. (n.d.a). *History of Georgia Gwinnett College.* Retrieved July 16, 2017 from http://www.ggc.edu/kaufman-tribute/history

Georgia Gwinnett College. (n.d.b). *Internationalized courses.* Retrieved October 23, 2016 from http://www.ggc.edu/academics/qep/internationalized-courses

Leask, B. (2013). Internationalizing the curriculum in the disciplines: Imagining new possibilities. *Journal of Studies in International Education, 17*(2), 103–118. doi:10.1177/1028315312475090

Leask, B. (2015). *Internationalizing the curriculum.* London: Routledge.

Leask, B., & Carroll, J. (2011). Moving beyond "Wishing and Hoping": Internationalisation and student experiences of inclusion and engagement. *Higher Education Research & Development, 30*(5), 647–659. doi:10.1080/07294360.2011.598454

McLoughlin, C. (2001). Inclusivity and alignment: Principles of pedagogy, task and assessment design for effective cross-cultural online learning. *Distance Education, 22*(1), 7–29. doi:10.1080/0158791010220102

Statisticalatlas. (n.d.). *Languages in Gwinnett County, Georgia.* Retrieved October 16, 2017 from https://statisticalatlas.com/county/Georgia/Gwinnett-County/Languages

United States Census Bureau. (n.d.). *Quick Facts, Gwinnett County, Georgia.* Retrieved October 25, 2016 from: http://www.census.gov/quickfacts/table/PST045215/13135

Section 2

Chapter 13
Grounded Globalism:
Regional Identity Hypothesis as a Framework for Internationalizing Higher Education Curriculum

Paulo Zagalo-Melo
Western Michigan University, USA

Charity Atteberry
University of Montana, USA

Roch Turner
University of Montana, USA

ABSTRACT

This chapter explores the internationalization of higher education at four-year institutions in the Rocky Mountain West (Idaho, Montana, Wyoming, Colorado, Utah, Nevada, Arizona, and New Mexico) through the lens of James Peacock's grounded globalism. As global forces increase and impose upon higher education, administrators and faculty must remain mindful of best practices in internationalizing curriculum. This chapter draws on surveys of senior international officers at four-year colleges in the Rocky Mountain West states. It examines existing literature to apply Peacock's concept of grounded globalism. The authors provide shared characteristics of states in the Rocky Mountain West to add context to the challenges and strengths of internationalization in this region. The authors provide recommendations for future research and best practices in internationalizing curriculum.

INTRODUCTION

The internationalization of education demands that educators provide students with globalizing experiences as tools for contextualizing an increasingly interconnected world. Authors, internationalization professionals, and faculty have made efforts to close the global learning circle by redirecting global learning goals and outcomes toward the student's place of belonging. As noted by Peacock (2007, p. 10),

DOI: 10.4018/978-1-5225-2791-6.ch013

"Once we achieve global identities, we must ground them, integrating the global and the local in some way that energizes and sustains both." Grounded globalism, which serves as the theoretical framework for this chapter, assumes that humans contextualize their lives through a sense of place and belonging. For grounded globalism, the progressive globalization of society necessarily and continuously encroaches upon our sense of place and belonging. The same courses of identity promoting a sense of place and belonging constitute barriers to expanding and reintegrating global learning.

This chapter will present cases on internationalization efforts from four-year universities in the Rocky Mountain West. It will highlight challenges and opportunities unique to regional identities and enumerating strategies for internationalizing curriculum in higher education. The authors will discuss the regional identity of the Rocky Mountain West, as well as its impact on comprehensive internationalization efforts. Using Peacock's conceptual framework for grounded globalism, this chapter will describe barriers and good practices in globalism and internationalization efforts seeking to foster a sense of place in Rocky Mountain West universities.

The chapter will begin with an adaptation of Peacock's (2007) seven step model and regional identity hypothesis to define the cultural nuances of the Rocky Mountain West. Building on a detailed understanding of regional identity, the juxtaposition of internationalization efforts and regional opposition to global endeavors will be explored. These findings will be used as a foundation for suggested internationalization efforts in other regions.

The authors will discuss strategies for facilitating grounded globalism in higher education. The chapter will discuss internationalization of higher education and regional impacts of globalism. Integrated approaches to learning abroad, including pre- and post-international experiences, will be presented as best practices and global learning pathway programs connecting disciplines across curricula for faculty, staff, and students at the university level.

The authors acknowledge the help of many individuals, including the senior international officers and reviewers. This chapter came to fruition through these collaborative efforts.[1]

This chapter will identify obstacles faced by educational practitioners in international education. The authors endeavor to provide relevant, illustrative examples of obstacles in the Rocky Mountain West. The expectation is that this chapter will facilitate a dialogue between international education stakeholders. Collective global knowledge will increase while the cultural identity of the Rocky Mountain West is enhanced. Additionally, this work will present a detailed framework for exploring grounded globalism in other regions.

In an effort to clarify the terminology that will be used throughout the chapter, the following terms and definitions are provided:

- **Seven Step Model and Regional Identity Hypothesis - Far Away and Deep Within:** A framework developed by James Peacock that offers parameters by which grounded globalism, a term to "describe and prescribe syntheses of international connections and local traditions that are fueled by energies from both," can be explored (Peacock, 2007, p. ix). Three stages - past, present, and future - are included in Peacock's seven step model, and trends, or hypotheses, explore globalization in a region;
- **Globalism:** The broad economic, technological and scientific trends that directly affect higher education and are largely inevitable in the contemporary world (Altbach, 2006, p. 123);
- **Internationalization:** The process of integrating an international, intercultural, or global dimension into the purpose, functions or delivery of post-secondary education (Knight, 2004, p. 11).

BACKGROUND

The Rocky Mountain West of the United States, like other countries and regions of the world, has specific identities and subidentities. According to Castells (2011, pp. 411-413), "… people identify themselves primarily with their locality." Approximately 13% of the world's population identifies as citizens of the world or cosmopolitans (Castells, 2011). Grounded globalism offers a framework for infusing globalism with specific identities or subidentities (Peacock, 2007).

In this chapter, the authors will align the understanding of globalization with "the tendency for similar policies and practices to spread across political, cultural, and geographical boundaries" (Dimmock & Walker, 2005, p. 13). Through technological advances, geo-political relationships, and an increasingly global economy, citizens from all parts of the world have become neighbors. Interconnectedness and borderless knowledge, skills, capital, and jobs have heightened the importance of learning in a global context. Higher education institutions have meaningfully recognized the need to react to new levels of political, social, economic, scientific, and cultural interconnectedness. With careful consideration, they are integrating it into their academic programs, research, services, and community outreach. In doing so, they are responding to the new needs of students, faculty, staff, administration, and community members, as well as taking advantage of innovative opportunities. In fact, higher education is both a culprit and a victim of globalization. National and global economic, political, and social developments within the last several decades (especially since the end of World War II) were generated by and impacted higher education around the globe (de Wit, 1995).

Higher education impacted globalization through ideas, attitudes, and technologies. While this occurred through research, it was not systematically and appropriately reflected in the curriculum (Katz, 2014). *Comprehensive internationalization* is understood here as "a strategic, coordinated process that seeks to align and integrate policies, programs, and initiatives to position colleges and universities as more globally oriented and internationally connected institutions" (ACE, n.d., para. 1). It is, to some extent, higher education's acknowledgement of the need to complement research-focused transformations previously operated at the graduate level.

Higher education institutions helped to generate interconnectedness, which led to the prevailing understanding of globalization. Today, higher education institutions are being encouraged to develop individual responses to interconnectedness. Higher education's response to globalization is internationalization. To do this, higher education is incorporating global competence into its mindset through coordinated strategic initiatives, including expansion of learning opportunities abroad, integration of international students on campus, and introduction of global concepts and culture across the curriculum.

Globalization also intensified the conflict between the following levels of identity: global; regional; local; and individual. This brought additional complexity to the implementation of internationalization in higher education institutions. Moreover, comprehensive internationalization is becoming a standard reaction of higher education institutions to globalization. For several years, the American Council on Education has promoted comprehensive internationalization in academia as "a strategic, coordinated process that aligns and integrates international policies, programs, and initiatives and that positions colleges and universities to be more globally oriented and internationally connected" (Peterson & Helms, 2013, p. 29). Nevertheless, comprehensive internationalization may not become the sustainable source of change necessary to deliver new programs, curricula, research, and services. It must connect new global levels of identity with the subidentities mentioned as primary sources of identity (Castells, 2011). This is where grounded globalism comes in.

James Peacock, the Kenan professor of anthropology at the University of North Carolina at Chapel Hill, presented a framework for examining globalism's regional impact. Within this study, which focused on regional perspectives of the Southern U.S., Peacock developed a seven-step model and global identity hypothesis titled "Far Away and Deep Within." This framework offered parameters by which grounded globalism, a term to "describe and prescribe syntheses of international connections and local traditions that are fueled by energies from both," could be explored (Peacock, 2007, p. ix). In an effort to acquire a thorough understanding of the depth and breadth of comprehensive internationalization in higher education, Peacock's grounded globalism serves as a tool for understanding regional identity, developing and sustaining international programs that employ best practices, and fusing "a transformative global identity to a sustaining regional identity—a fusion that potentially enhances the strength of both identities and their potential for energizing action" (Peacock, 2007, p. x).

Globalism and grounded globalism will be explored, as well as the adaption of Peacock's seven-step model in examining the Rocky Mountain West's regional identity. In addition, the chapter will discuss barriers and collaborative solutions to the internationalization of higher education rooted in regional identity. Surveys of senior international officers at Rocky Mountain West public institutions of higher education provided insight into regional identity, as well as relevant barriers, unique characteristics, and strategies for fostering comprehensive internationalization. This chapter will suggest ways in which public institutions in higher education in the Rocky Mountain West can build a university of a global century by sustaining regional identity and a transformative global identity.

Peacock's (2007) seven-step model and global identity hypothesis included the following steps to address the past, present, and future:

1. Regional identity
2. Opposition to national identity
3. Rebellion
4. Defeat
5. Resentment and oppression
6. Transmutation by global identity
7. Grounding of identity in sustained regional identity

There are several observations related to grounding globalism once a region's past, present, and future are superimposed on the seven-step model. Steps one through five represent the past. Steps two through five vary as institutions use Peacock's model to explore regional identity and support comprehensive internationalization. The following steps describe the southern U.S. per Peacock's in-depth study and analysis: opposition to national identity; rebellion; defeat; and resentment and oppression. As regions begin to possess individual identities and subidentities, they will also have unique histories and contexts influencing those identities. Step six and seven may be viewed as recursive. These two steps are critical for stakeholders in international higher education.

Reversal of the model's two final steps facilitates a transformative identification. According to Peacock (2007, p. 9), "transformative identification is sustainable only by integrating it into one's life, family, and community that are localized somewhere, including home regions." By avoiding rootless globalism and capitalizing on the integration of a global relationship into regional grounding, the interconnectedness between different regions becomes a powerful catalyst for change. Strong regional identity becomes transformative only when global forces are grounded in that identity.

John Bowlby's (1978) attachment theory provides an explanation for the significance and power of grounding in regional identity. A significant tenet of Bowlby's psychological model is the infant's need for a safe base with a primary caregiver. Assured safety between the infant and caregiver allows the child to explore the world, develop relationships, and effectively regulate emotions. Grounding in regional identity serves as the safe base in which bonds are formed with families and communities. In following Peacock's model, an individual will possess this grounding and be better prepared to embrace global forces.

GROUNDED GLOBALISM AND HIGHER EDUCATION

Inherent challenges exist in comprehensive internationalization efforts in higher education. Barriers are present in the six interconnected target areas for institutional initiatives, policies, and programs. These include: articulated institutional commitment; administrative leadership, structure, and staffing; curriculum, co-curriculum, and learning outcomes; faculty policies and practices; student mobility; and collaboration and partnerships. The value of tradition in higher education in the U.S. can make it difficult to achieve sweeping changes. Comprehensive internationalization requires both short- and long-term investments in time, money, and resources. Regional opposition to global forces can also pose a myriad of barriers. An understanding of regional identity is beneficial when overcoming these barriers. As international programs guide their institutions to embrace global forces and prepare students for living in a global century, grounded globalism identifies barriers and strategizes collaborative and innovative solutions.

Goethe remarked, "The man of action is always ruthless. No one has a conscience but an observer" (as cited in Peacock, 2007, p. 220). This statement is relevant for institutions of higher education seeking to embrace global interconnectedness while honoring regional identity. Peacock's concept of grounded globalism and seven-step model promote the "syntheses of international connections and local traditions that are fueled by energies from both" (Peacock 2007, p. ix). This allows stakeholders the invaluable opportunity to observe before fusing a transformative global identity to a sustaining regional identity.

Following purposeful observation, institutions of higher education must take strategic action informed by best practices research. These must reflect the needs of the region. Through grounded globalism, institutions of higher education can facilitate the institution's ability to embrace global forces both far away and deep within.

To identify characteristics of a quality postsecondary education, the Lumina Foundation created the degree qualification profile (DQP). The DQP provides a standard criterion for credentials earned in higher education. Five learning categories emerged: (1) specialized knowledge; (2) broad and integrative knowledge; (3) intellectual skills; (4) applied and collaborative learning; and (5) civic and global learning. The fifth category addresses the need for internationalization of higher education. According to the DQP (p. 5):

... this category recognizes higher education's responsibilities both to democracy and the global community. Students must demonstrate integration of their knowledge and skills by engaging with and responding to civic, social, and environmental and economic challenges at local, national, and global levels.

This category highlights the need to discuss both local and global challenges. Grounded globalism can be used as a framework for internationalization efforts.

The DQP recognizes the need for varying levels of knowledge. It begins with the student describing their "own civic and cultural background, including its origins and development, assumptions, and predispositions" (Degree Qualification Profile, p. 29). An essential part of grounded globalism, it allows students to better understand their home experiences and the effects of global forces on local culture.

THE ROCKY MOUNTAIN WEST

In this study, the Rocky Mountain West was geographically comprised of the following eight states: (1) Idaho; (2) Montana; (3) Wyoming; (4) Colorado; (5) Utah; (6) Nevada; (7) Arizona; and (8) New Mexico. The U.S. Census Bureau (n.d.) defined this area as region four, west, division eight, and mountain. The Rocky Mountain West expands across 863,970 square miles of diverse terrain and constitutes 23% of U.S. territory (NOAA, n.d.).

While the Rocky Mountain West accounts for nearly one-quarter of U.S. territory, a mere 6.7% of the total U.S. population—approximately 22 million people—resides in this region (U.S. Census Bureau, 2010). Among these eight states, populations range from approximately 600,000 to 6 million residents. Of these residents, population by race in each of the eight Rocky Mountain Western states is predominately white. Five states' populations were calculated as more than 80% white. Three states reported approximately 90% white residents (U.S. Census Bureau, 2010).

To better understand the region's features relevant to comprehensive internationalization efforts at institutions of higher education, surveys were completed by senior international officers at public universities. This correspondence illuminated unique characteristics aiding in the definition of the Rocky Mountain West. Wyckoff and Dilsaver (1995, p. 2) discussed this distinctive region:

Strewn everywhere across the West's vastness are mountains that belie our stereotyped views of a single "western" region. Any physiographic map of the West suggests the pattern. The central problem is this: both the physical and human geographies of these mountain zones have conspired to create a very different West than that encountered in the coastal lowlands, desert valleys, and arid plains below. And even though the Western mountains are a fragmented and discontinuous collection of separate ranges that extend from the Rockies to the Pacific Slope, these seemingly isolated places share a special character and coherence which binds them together as a distinctive American subregion.

The physical and human geographies of the Rocky Mountain West inform the attitudes and perspectives of its residents. Additionally, as Wyckoff and Dilsaver (1995, p. 2) explained, this region is "defined not only by its elevation and slope, but also by its peculiar diversity of environments, by its hoards of concentrated resources, and by a unique convergence of historical events which occurred in these settings during the past 150 years." Such factors sustain characteristic attitudes and perceptions in this region. An examination of these perspectives and attitudes requires lines of inquiry. For example, what is the role of the Rocky Mountain West in American culture? What forces of globalization impact regional perception? Peacock (2007) suggested that two core questions should guide this examination: "How do I relate to the nation?" and "How do I relate to the world?" Answers to these questions result in emerging themes. In the Rocky Mountain West, six dominant themes impact Rocky Mountain Western attitudes and perspectives: (1) independence; (2) healthy lifestyle; (3) work-life balance; (4) pride in Western heritage; (5) frugality; and (6) appreciation of the natural landscape.

Wyckoff and Dilsaver (1995) identified five themes to define the mountainous west, including: (1) barriers; (2) islands of moisture; (3) zones of concentrated resources; (4) an area of government control; and (5) a restorative sanctuary. Of the five themes, three demonstrated relevance to globalism, grounded globalism, and comprehensive internationalization efforts at institutions of higher education in the Rocky Mountain West. These were: (1) barriers; (2) an area of government control; and (3) restorative sanctuary. These themes interweave with the six dominant characteristics identified by senior international officers working in the Rocky Mountain West.

A strong spirit of independence serves as a regional identity characteristic in the Rocky Mountain West. Independence is grounded in the region's unique geography. For example, distance separates rural communities and cities, restricting access to education, culture, travel, and employment opportunities. At one time, independence was imposed on those living in this region and necessitated by geographic barriers. Therefore, it became a part of the Rocky Mountain Western identity. As Wyckoff and Dilsaver (1995) noted, the mountains serve as a historic and enduring barrier. Interestingly, the physical and geographical characteristics attracting residents to the Rocky Mountain West also function as barriers to transportation, commerce, and education. At times, it results in an insular worldview.

With access to mountains, rivers, lakes, and wild and wood lands, residents engage in year-round healthy outdoor recreational activities. According to the Gallup-Healthways Well-Being Index, four states in the Rocky Mountain West (Montana, Colorado, Idaho, and New Mexico) are identified in the top 10 most active states in the U.S. (Willett, 2014). Healthy living also fosters an emphasis on work-life balance for many residents. Time is designated for leisure and physical activity outside of professional obligations. Popular activities include hiking, running, climbing, camping, and fishing. By prioritizing healthy practices and work-life balance, residents experience a high quality of life and report high levels of emotional and physical well-being (Bernardo, 2016).

Pride in Western heritage is also characteristic of the Rocky Mountain West. This pride is rooted in the federal government's historic role in settling the region, as well as the storied interactions between its indigenous peoples and frontiersmen. As noted by Wyckoff and Dilsaver (1995, p. 39), "Ultimately, the region possesses a finite number of prized areas containing crucial transport corridors, surplus waters, other extractive resources, scenes of inspiration, and areas for recreation." Treasured land, such as the region's national parks and forests, is a source of pride and generates controversy. This reflects the emerging theme of a deep appreciation of the natural landscape. One area of controversy, natural resource and environmental restoration, was described by Swanson and Janssen (2012, p. 1) as "… returning resources to a pre-development or pre-damages condition." The "fairly massive extent of past and continuing damage to these lands and their natural environments by a broad array of industrial activities, past and present," offers opportunities for beautification, sustainability, and economic development (Swanson & Janssen, 2012, p. 2). Conversely, such endeavors require funding, as well as state and federal administration. At times, regional hubris results in polarized viewpoints between individuals who were born in the region and those who moved to the region as adults.

In addition to regional hubris, surveys of Rocky Mountain West senior international officers suggested that frugality is characteristic of many residents. Rooted in high economic inequality, such disparity is prevalent in areas considered to be tourist destinations and resort towns. The result is an imbalance among the high cost of living and low income potential.

The six dominant Rocky Mountain Western themes cultivate a distinctive regional identity rooted in space and place. Apprehension of identity unique to this region helps to answer Peacock's (2007) questions: "How do I relate to the nation?" and "How do I relate to the world?" These dominant themes inform the development of a seven-step model and global identity hypothesis adapted for the Rocky Mountain West to address the past, present, and future:

1. **Regional Identity**
   a. Insularity
   b. Indigenous expansion
2. **Westward Expansion**
3. **Resistance and Settler Colonialism**
4. **Displacement and Devastation**
5. **Regional Identity Revisited**
   a. Independence
   b. Healthy lifestyle
   c. Work-life balance
   d. Pride in Western heritage
   e. Frugality
   f. Appreciation of the natural landscape
6. **Transmutation by Global Identity**
7. **Grounding of That Identity in Sustained Regional Identity**

While grounded globalism connects the individual to a primary (local) identity with the world, comprehensive internationalization provides institutions with a systematic facilitation of necessary changes brought by globalization. The next section will discuss how higher education institutions can incorporate both concepts to secure a sustainable approach to internationalization. The approach will respect and endorse primary identities as a key component in implementing changes generated by globalization. The authors will focus on the Rocky Mountain West as a local identity. The internationalization of the curriculum will be a necessary approach to an equitable and sustainable process for providing students with the skills and knowledge for becoming efficient citizens in a globalized society.

COMPREHENSIVE INTERNATIONALIZATION, GROUNDED GLOBALISM, AND THE INTERNATIONALIZATION OF THE CURRICULUM

This research surveyed senior international officers at eight four-year universities in the Rocky Mountain West. Institutions surveyed included the University of Idaho, University of Montana, University of Wyoming, University of Colorado Boulder, University of Utah, University of Nevada, University of Arizona, and University of New Mexico. The following questions and prompts were given:

1. How do you define the Rocky Mountain West regarding the characteristics of those living in this region? (Idaho, Montana, Wyoming, Colorado, Utah, Nevada, Arizona, and New Mexico)
2. What barriers do the characteristics of the Rocky Mountain West pose to comprehensive internationalization?
3. In what ways do the characteristics of the Rocky Mountain West support comprehensive internationalization?

4. Please identify the broad strategies that your institution has taken to support comprehensive internationalization.
5. In what unique ways does the Rocky Mountain West plan for and implement comprehensive internationalization efforts?
6. What recommendations do you have for other Rocky Mountain West institutions embarking on comprehensive internationalization?

Questions were chosen to allow participants an opportunity to expound on their answers. It was expected that senior international officers would differ in perspectives. Therefore, it was expected that they gravitate toward different questions as a means of explaining their unique interpretations of the region. Responses were decontextualized to identify emerging themes. It was expected that participants understood some of the general characteristics of the Rocky Mountain West (for example, the rugged terrain does not allow for ease of travel). It was apparent in the literature that characteristics of the region and the occupants were inextricably linked to the experience of the west. This played a role in the development of questions and prompts.

When developing the questionnaire, the authors allowed participants the opportunity to couch their response in a shared understanding of the region. This was analyzed on an in-depth literature review of Rocky Mountain West characteristics. The survey was an initial step toward understanding internationalization efforts at major universities in the Rocky Mountain West. Supplementary questions added context to the outcomes of this chapter. In addition, they will assist future researchers in understanding the concept of grounded globalism and the unique characteristics of the Rocky Mountain West. These findings may impact how institutions of higher education cope with and respond to global forces.

The questions were designed to understand internationalization efforts in the Rocky Mountain West. Responses included policy and procedural matters regarding internationalization, as well as personal perceptions on the region's characteristics. The study looked at how perceived characteristics influence policies and procedures in internationalization efforts. The results have been useful in better understanding internationalization efforts in the Rocky Mountain West.

As discussed, the Rocky Mountain West is viewed as a distinct source of primary identity and serves as an anchor for grounded globalism. Moreover, its main characteristics define a mindset and lifestyle that impact comprehensive internationalization efforts of higher education institutions. This creates distinctive barriers, as well as opens unique opportunities. In this section, the authors will list important obstacles to implementing a coordinated internationalization effort to result in a globalist mindset.

The Rocky Mountain West's remoteness and insularity, boosted by its rurality and lack of large urban spaces (i.e., Idaho, Utah, and Montana do not have cities with more than 250,000 inhabitants), cause problems and limitations in establishing and developing comprehensive internationalization. The senior international officers pointed out limited international and intercultural experiences, which resulted in a narrow understanding of comprehensive internationalization.

Education abroad, for example, was highly impacted by remoteness and income. Located in small cities, Rocky Mountain West college towns are far from airline hubs. This deters students from going abroad due to costly and lengthy travel costs. With five states (Idaho, Montana, Nebraska, Arizona, and New Mexico) in the bottom half of the income per capita ranking of all U.S. states (Bernardo, 2016), there are limited resources for students to participate in education abroad.

Participation in educational experiences abroad also affected anticipated high-stress factors regarding intercultural experiences (Paige, 1993). Ethnocentrism, cultural distance, and limited intercultural experience due to low diversity levels in the Rocky Mountain West increased anticipated and effective psychological stress of intercultural encounters. This issue was heightened by an insular worldview.

This phenomenon was exacerbated by relatively low intercultural competencies among teachers at all levels. For teachers, intercultural competency is the "ability to effectively respond to students from different cultures and classes while valuing and preserving the dignity of cultural differences and similarities between individuals, families, and communities" (Ladson-Billings, 2001). Many educators believe that diversity is the inclusion of games, cultural festivals, food fairs, and similar social gatherings (Guo, Arthur, & Lund, 2009). This general lack of cultural understanding and awareness leaves students insufficiently prepared to handle forces on local culture.

Another negative impact on student mobility originated from difficulties in recruiting international students to the Rocky Mountain West due to the few number of the region's higher education institutions appearing in the top university rankings consulted by international students and their universities (Boulder). Additionally, the large majority of international students sought out big cities in the U.S. rather than rural or low population areas (Ruiz, 2014). This preference for metropolitan areas may also be related to Paige's theory of anticipated psychological stress of intercultural encounters due to cultural distance as "most foreign students come from large fast-growing cities in emerging markets" (Ruiz, 2014).

Rocky Mountain West senior international officers also mentioned that regionally-oriented faculty had limited intercultural interaction and international travel. This resulted in faculty focusing on local, regional, and national issues rather than international and global perspectives. This narrow international exposure also resulted in few businesses with international ties and multinational focus.

An underlying issue intersecting several of these barriers is the limited exposure of a large majority of the population to higher education. In many states, this results in lower educational attainment levels. In this category, five Rocky Mountain West states ranked in the bottom half for educational level measured by the percentage of the state's population with a bachelor's degree.[2] This may result in a restricted understanding of the increasingly important role of internationalization in higher education. This factor, compounded by the frugality and spirit of independence that at times results in isolation from government and the world, also characterizes the Rocky Mountain West mindset and lifestyle. This may cause limited availability of resources to be invested in comprehensive internationalization of higher education.

These factors can be identified as limitations of higher education. Nevertheless, the same characteristics open the region and its higher education institutions to equally unique opportunities. This connection between seizing opportunities to connect globally and overcoming barriers to internationalization results in the region's approach to the theory of grounded globalism.

GROUNDED GLOBALISM AND OPPORTUNITIES FOR INTERNATIONALIZATION

The potential transformation of the South's identity through Peacock's theory on globalism is translatable to the Rocky Mountain West due to similarities in isolationism and the unique mindset. Comprehensive internationalization is higher education's response to globalization. Therefore, it is one of society's best opportunities to create sustainable change.

The features of the Rocky Mountain West include independence, a sense of isolation, and regional pride in heritage. These have contributed to an identity that comes across in the reactions of the senior international officers. Applying Peacock's thesis for the South and looking at it through the lens of higher education as applied to the Rocky Mountain West results in accepting that comprehensive internationalization has the capacity to transform the region "economically, demographically, and, perhaps, politically, but also culturally and psychologically" (Peacock, 2007). The spirit of independence, isolation, and lack of diversity of the Rocky Mountain West supports Peacock's argument of the possibility of a new and globalist frame of reference for the region "because the rest of the nation is no longer the dominant framework; the world is" (Peacock, 2007).

Despite barriers mentioned in the previous section, the Rocky Mountain West presents opportunities for comprehensive internationalization. For example, senior international officers identified the region's higher education institutions as offering opportunities for high-level networking with state officials and business leaders. Due to limited numbers of large universities in the region, as well as their important roles in small cities and low-population states, higher institutions become essential economic, political, and cultural players. This gives them direct access to key political and economic organizations (i.e., governor's office, state legislature, and state senators). A Rocky Mountain West university can significantly impact its community and state. On the other hand, a metropolitan university's efforts often go unnoticed.

In contrast to faculty members originally from the Rocky Mountain West, faculty who come from cosmopolitan or international locations strongly support internationalization. This countered the perceived underdeveloped level of the university's comprehensive internationalization. These faculty members often led education abroad programs, brought representation of international organizations to campus, invited and hosted international guests, served on internationalization advisory boards and committees, and were supporters of general internationalization initiatives.

Internationalizing the curricula is a fundamental component of comprehensive internationalization. Various pieces of a higher education institution's curricula are essential to develop the globalmindedness required to succeed in this global century. Due to the sense of place and connection to nature, Rocky Mountain West institutions were aware of core issues of global education, including natural resources, the environment, and issues connected to key global challenges. This close connection was a strong starting point and a positive constituency for embarking on global education programs and curricula.

The values given by the Rocky Mountain West to experiential learning contributed to openness to participation in beyond-the-classroom experiences. These included service learning and internships, which are key components of global education and education abroad. Research on experiential learning opportunities sought by students in the region's higher education institutions would be important to support these values.

Initiatives have been established to develop internationalization efforts, including financial incentives to education abroad, international development of faculty, and investment in international student recruitment. In addition, unique challenges and opportunities have prompted strategies and actions by Rocky Mountain West higher education institutions to overcome barriers by taking advantage of the region's specificities. Although some of these strategies do not pertain exclusively to the region, they are perceived as pressing by Rocky Mountain West higher education institutions. Therefore, they receive more attention due to leadership's consciousness of and responsiveness to the region's uniqueness, challenges, and opportunities.

Opportunities for higher education institutions in the Rocky Mountain West can sustain a comprehensive approach to internationalization. Nonetheless, equity in internationalization translates into opportunities for all students. In undergraduate education, it is important to provide students with experiences to enhance their sensitivity to global challenges. The key undergraduate curriculum is a channel for equal opportunity in the acquisition of basic global competence. Internationalization of the curriculum is steadily becoming a strategic discussion within higher education.

INTERNATIONALIZING THE CURRICULUM IN HIGHER EDUCATION

Comprehensive internationalization calls for an institutional and governmental systematic approach to structural change. According to Peterson and Helms (2013), comprehensive internationalization "requires a clear commitment by top-level institutional leaders, affects the curriculum and institutional policies and programs, and involves a broad range of people." Limitations of the two-way traditional dimension of internationalization include student mobility, the limited percentage of students involved (NAFSA, n.d.), and difficulties in integrating domestic and international students (Leask, 2015). Therefore, curriculum and student mobility are an important part of this process. Despite forecasts with a global enrollment in higher education institutions of more than 260 million students by 2025, the respective estimate of 8 million for global international student mobility would set the global internationalization ratio through student mobility at a mere 3% for that same year (Davis & Mackintosh, 2012; Goddard, 2012; Timeshighered). Thus, 97% of global higher education students would be excluded from exposure to a transformative educational experience contributing to global mindedness and global competence.

Global competency is generally understood as the combined proficiency of international issues and a second language with the "ability to learn and work with people from diverse linguistic and cultural backgrounds," as well as with the skills to navigate a highly-interconnected world regardless of how locally or globally one interacts (NEA Education Policy and Practice Department, n.d.). As suggested by Olson and Kroeger (2001), second-language proficiency and international experience are related to ethnorelativism. This could contribute to the "disposition to understand and act on issues of global significance" (Mansilla & Jackson, 2011). Furthermore, there is consensus among key grant making foundations, program development foundations, and other key players in international education that "a framework for a comprehensive global education curriculum must encompass global issues and challenges, global cultures, and world areas," as well as international relations (Barker, 2000).

There are additional reasons for internationalizing curriculum. In fact, one of the arguments in support of internationalizing curriculum is closely connected with the rationale for internationalization (Katz, 2014).

An additional supportive argument is for the educational system or higher education institution to take an ethical stance toward preparing students to be "ethical citizens and professionals, [...] who see themselves not only as being connected with their local communities, but also as members of world communities" (Leask, 2015). Nationally- or regionally-bound conceptualizations of the curriculum may result in limited learning outcomes compared to curricula infused with international perspectives and global issues. This also brings up the issue of inequality. Decisions regarding the content and scope of the curriculum are not value free (Leask, 2015). According to Leask (2015), it is necessary to challenge the paradigms that anchor the curriculum and to bring non-Western models into internationalization (Leask, 2015). The ethical standard is also for "students to examine their implicit and explicit beliefs about whose wellbeing matters, and to develop a more globalized sense of responsibility and citizenship" (Kreber, 2009, p. 49).

Higher education, a birthplace of globalization, faces challenges in incorporating the needs caused by globalization and internationalism into their teaching, research, and service. This includes academia-built research centers, learning of world languages, area studies, and international relations. However, "scholars did not expend time and energy in re-conceptualizing the undergraduate curriculum to reflect internationalism" (Katz, 2014, p. 3).

After starting with research and, to some extent, experiential learning through student mobility, it is now time to turn attention to internationalizing curriculum. The limited reach of student mobility—10% in the U.S. and an estimated 3% for global student mobility by 2025—calls for action to impact massive numbers of students. Inequality is not entirely disconnected from this call for action. Student mobility will continue to be a type of global education until systematic approaches—especially at the undergraduate level—infuse curriculum with global competence elements. The connection between the lack of comprehensive internationalization and inequality, as well as the logical subsequent call for standardization and accreditation in internationalization, deserve more attention from scholars of international education and related areas of study. The curriculum equalizes internationalization opportunities in higher education.

Moreover, some barriers and challenges generated by the Rocky Mountain West's characteristics highlight limitations to student mobility in expanding the reach of global education in higher education. These include: geographical and financial limitations; added psychological pressures; increasing participation in education abroad opportunities; and difficulties in recruiting international students to diversity the campus classroom. Therefore, support is needed to develop curriculum as a central point of education for the global century.

Key strengths of higher education internationalization in the Rocky Mountain West may provide the necessary environment to implement a grounded globalism approach to internationalizing curriculum. For instance, global awareness generated by key academic strengths in the areas of environmental sciences, sustainability, wildlife, and natural resources conservation is an essential component of curriculum aimed at preparing students for "the kind of world we currently live in and the kind of world we would want to create through our graduates" (Leask, 2015). The same reasoning applies to the preponderance of Native American studies scholars and departments in this region, as well as their impact on the development of intercultural competence, which is another fundamental component of internationalizing curriculum. As Leask (2015, p. x) noted, "the intercultural competence required for global contexts is equally important for living and working in today's increasingly diverse and multicultural societies." The faculty, especially those exposed to internationalization, are important players in leading a collaborative approach to internationalizing curriculum. Moreover, the collaborative network between higher education institutions and leadership at the state and city levels provides a nurturing environment for strategic planning and policymaking regarding global education. However, limited awareness of higher education trends and exposure to higher education may limit the potential of such networks. Rocky Mountain West institutions of higher education have essential curricular assets and supportive networks necessary to the internationalization of the curriculum.

Grounded globalism's integrated approach to globalism and local identities is, to some extent, inherent to Rocky Mountain West higher education institutions. Connections between academic strengths generated by place (i.e., environmental and sustainability studies) and culture (i.e., strong presence of Native American cultures) give evidence of the need to root the educational system and curricula in their distinct region. The connection between these grounding elements of higher education and higher education's response to globalization is articulated by comprehensive internationalization and global learning, which can more efficiently and effectively be expressed through internationalization of the curriculum. Nevertheless, that articulation should draw and expand upon the strengths of regional identity.

The Carnegie study pressed for a framework capable of facilitating the inclusion of global issues, cultures, and international affairs to enable "a comprehensive global education curriculum" (Barker, 2000). The authors recommend grounded globalism as a useful and efficient framework for addressing conflicts between global, national, and regional levels of identity. This stems from efforts to implement an effective structural and systemic response to globalization that must rely on the curricular component of higher education.

SOLUTIONS AND RECOMMENDATIONS

Internationalization of higher education successfully prepares students for an increasingly globalized world. Higher education's response will shape posteducational student success. Administrators, faculty, and staff must incorporate civic virtues and global competencies.

Students must understand how these experiences will create improved cultural competencies while deepening their understanding of respective disciplines. To meet this need, higher education institutions can combine service learning and internationalization efforts, as well as provide pre- and postservice education. Collaborative efforts between faculty and staff will result in a program functioning across campus and curricula. When providing pre- and postservice education, faculty must rely on extensive reflection exercises. Through these exercises, students will contextualize experiences and make informed decisions. Bringle and Hatcher (1999, p. 180) said the following about reflection:

Too often, the presentation of a theory by an instructor or in a textbook is viewed by students as an empty, pedantic venture. It is through active learning and the interplay between abstract, remote content, and personal, palatable experience that student learning is deepened and strengthened.

By that logic, faculty must utilize reflection exercises. This will allow students to appropriately relate their experiences at home and abroad throughout their studies. The result will be a greater understanding of all disciplines anchored by valuable experiences and cultural competencies gained while serving abroad.

Serving internationally should be an impactful experience on students. It should spark a dialogue on the similarities and differences of multicultural responses to critical issues. Having experienced the impact of serving abroad and participating in guided self-reflection exercises, students will better understand the nuances of issues faced by their community. This will allow students a greater depth of knowledge when advocating for change at local and state levels. One peculiarity of Rocky Mountain West states is the relative ease of contacting state-level representatives. Due to relatively low populations, elected officials are easily contacted and engaged by constituents. This includes students. This phenomenon extends to individual institutions wishing to implement grounded globalism on their campus.

To take advantage of access to top leadership in government, private sector organizations, and non-profit organizations, some universities (Idaho, Utah) have established nonexecutive consulting or advisory boards and councils. These are made up of the organization's leaders to assist in strategic planning and outreach. Although this is not unique to Rocky Mountain West universities, joining the community and the state's leadership to address international issues is a key factor in the success of advisory structures. This strategic outcome can be enhanced by involving community representatives who have had significant international experience.

Fluency in multiple languages, a factor contributing to education abroad and international faculty collaborations, was strategically addressed in several Rocky Mountain West states through the implementation of K-8 language immersion programs. With the prominence of the Latter-day Saints (LDS) culture, Utah possesses a distinct awareness to world languages and language programs. However, LDS participation in language teaching initiatives is limited by their focus on family and career in early adulthood.

Another approach underlined by Rocky Mountain West universities is finding creative global links to regional affairs and interests. These usually translate into partnerships with universities that have similar regions, related research, and comparable economic interests. These partnerships tend to be sustainable and produce more results related to exchanges of students, sharing of faculty, and stronger research collaborations.

Service learning and education abroad have many similarities. Both result in cultural competencies by forming views based on experience, combining outside experiences with intimate local experiences, requiring extensive self-reflection, and shaping future experiences and perceptions. However, cultural competencies are not innately recognized. Students may need guidance through exercises to understand how their individual experiences will foster cultural competencies.

Faculty across different areas of the curriculum should be included to incorporate quality pre- and postexperience education based on specific disciplines. Without faculty, the process could neglect disciplines. This will decrease potential impacts across the campus.

The suggested strategies rely on the close connection that Rocky Mountain West higher education institutions have with their communities. It also relies on their political, economic, and cultural influence within their cities, states, and region. They are responsible for developing and sustaining local and regional traditions. Concurrently, they are responsible for facilitating change. Therefore, Rocky Mount West higher education institutions are privileged to operate the transformative processes of developing global identity with a regional character.

CONCLUSION

Globalization is the undisputed backdrop in which higher education institutions must operate. Therefore, they must adjust their methodologies and actions to fulfil their mission. Comprehensive internationalization is a key strategy adopted by higher education institutions to infuse institutional culture (or mindset) with values, orientations, strategies, and actions required for those adjustments. Grounded globalism allows for an interpretation of comprehensive internationalization informed by regional and local identity. This enables higher education institutions to become more effective in the implementation of comprehensive internationalization, as well as secures important features of their regional identity.

Grounded globalism is a pathway toward globalism. Made up of global values, international perspectives, and regional characteristics, it represents a culturally homogenous territory. Further studies could reveal if this framework connects other levels of identity, including global and national levels. By applying this concept and framework to institutions of learning, connections between global and regional identifies can simultaneously be implemented and sustained. Through higher education, this is a transformative process in facilitating and promoting enduring change.

REFERENCES

ACE. (n.d.). *CIGE model for comprehensive internationalization*. Retrieved from http://www.acenet. edu/news-room/Pages/CIGE-Model-for-Comprehensive-Internationalization.aspx

Alvaraz & Marsal. (2016). *Healthcare insights report. Post-acute care: Disruption (and opportunities) lurking beneath the surface*. Retrieved November 5, 2016, from https://www.taxanduk.net/sites/default/ files/am_hig_postacutecare_06spreads.pdf

Barker, C. M. (2000). *Education for international understanding and global competence* (Report of a meeting convened by Carnegie Corporation of New York). Retrieved October 5, 2016, from https:// www.carnegie.org/media/filer_public/6d/b0/6db0fdc1-f2b1-4eea-982a-a313cea6822c/ccny_meet- ing_2000_competence.pdf

Bernardo, R. (2016, September 12). 2016's happiest states in America. *WalletHub*. Retrieved November 1, 2016, from https://wallethub.com/edu/happiest-states/6959/

Bowlby, J. (1978). Attachment theory and its therapeutic implications. *Adolescent Psychiatry*, *6*, 5–33. PMID:742687

Bringle, R. G., & Hatcher, J. A. (1999). Reflection in service learning: Making meaning of experience. *Educational Horizons*, *77*(4), 179–185.

Castells, M. (2011). *The power of identity: The information age: Economy, society, and culture* (2nd ed.; Vol. 2). Hoboken, NJ: Wiley-Blackwell.

Davis, D., & Mackintosh, B. (2012). *Making a difference: Australian international education*. Kensing- ton, NSW: University of New South Wales Press.

de Wit, H. (1995). *Strategies for the internationalisation of higher education. A comparative study of Australia, Canada, Europe and the United States of America*. Amsterdam, The Netherlands: European Association for International Education.

Dimmock, C. A., & Walker, A. (2005). *Educational leadership: Culture and diversity*. London, UK: SAGE Publications.

Gibney, E. (2013, January 31). A different world. *Times Higher Education*. Retrieved September 20, 2016, from https://www.timeshighereducation.com/features/a-different-world/2001128.article

Jankowski, N., Hutchings, P., Ewell, P., Kinzie, J., & Kuh, G. (2013). The degree qualifications profile: What it is and why we need it now. *Change*, *45*(6), 6–15. doi:10.1080/00091383.2013.841515

Katz, S. N. (2014, January 17). Borderline ignorance: Why have efforts to internationalize the curriculum stalled? *The Chronicle of Higher Education*, *60*(18). Retrieved from http://www.chronicle.com/article/ Borderline-Ignorance/143865/

Kreber, C. (2009). *Internationalizing the curriculum in higher education*. San Francisco, CA: Jossey-Bass.

Kurosu, M. (Ed.). (2009). *Human centered design, HCII 2009*. Berlin: Springer-Verlag. doi:10.1007/978- 3-642-02806-9

Ladson-Billings, G. (2001). *Crossing over to Canaan: The journey of new teachers in diverse classrooms* (1st ed.). San Francisco, CA: Jossey-Bass.

Leask, B. (2015). *Internationalizing the curriculum*. London, UK: Routledge.

Mansilla, V. B., & Jackson, A. (2011). *Educating for global competence: Preparing our youth to engage the world*. New York, NY: Asia Society. Retrieved from http://asiasociety.org/files/book-globalcompetence.pdf

NAFSA. (n.d.). *Trends in U.S. study abroad*. Retrieved September 12, 2016, from http://www.nafsa.org/ Policy_and_Advocacy/Policy_Resources/Policy_Trends_and_Data/Trends_in_U_S__Study_Abroad/

NEA Education Policy and Practice Department. (n.d.). *An NEA policy brief: Global competence is a 21ˢᵗ century imperative*. Retrieved November 2, 2016, from http://www.nea.org/assets/docs/HE/ PB28A_Global_Competence11.pdf

NOAA. (n.d.). *U.S. census divisions*. Retrieved October 12, 2016, from https://www.ncdc.noaa.gov/ monitoring-references/maps/us-census-divisions.php

Olson, C. L., & Kroeger, K. R. (2001). Global competency and intercultural sensitivity. *Journal of Studies in International Education, 5*(2), 116–137. doi:10.1177/102831530152003

Peacock, J. L. (2007). *Grounded globalism: How the U.S. South embraces the world*. Athens, GA: University of Georgia Press.

Peterson, P. M., & Helms, R. M. (2013). Internationalization revisited. *Change, 45*(2), 28–34. doi:10.1 080/00091383.2013.764261

Ruiz, N. G. (2014, August 29). The geography of foreign students in U.S. higher education: Origins and destinations. *Brookings*. Retrieved from http://www.brookings.edu/research/interactives/2014/geography-of-foreign-students#/M10420

Swanson, L., & Janssen, H. (2012, August). *Natural resource and environmental restoration in Montana: Case studies in restoration and associated workforce needs* [Scholarly project]. Retrieved October 17, 2016, from http://crmw.org/Downloads/Restoration Study Overview.pdf

Top 200 Universities in the World | 2017 World University Web Rankings. (n.d.). Retrieved October 20, 2016, from http://www.4icu.org/top-universities-world/

U.S. Census Bureau. (n.d.). *Census regions and divisions of the United States*. Retrieved October 20, 2016, from https://www2.census.gov/geo/pdfs/maps-data/maps/reference/us_regdiv.pdf

Willett, M. (2014, March 13). *These are the most active states in America*. Retrieved November 1, 2016, from http://www.businessinsider.com/the-states-that-exercise-the-most-2014-3

Wyckoff, W., & Dilsaver, L. M. (1995). *The mountainous west: Explorations in historical geography*. Lincoln, NE: University of Nebraska Press.

KEY TERMS AND DEFINITIONS

Curriculum: Components of a course of study or program at the university level.

Globalism: The impacts of global forces on local cultures, norms, and beliefs.

Grounded Globalism: A concept assuming that humans contextualize their lives through a sense of place and belonging.

International Service Learning: The process by which students contextualize their learning experience with volunteer service abroad.

Internationalization: Actions by individuals, governments, and organizations in reaction to globalism.

Rocky Mountain West: A geographic and cultural region of the United States, including Idaho, Montana, Wyoming, Colorado, Utah, Nevada, Arizona, and New Mexico.

Senior International Officer: A college representative tasked with internationalizing curriculum at a four-year university.

ENDNOTES

[1] The authors are grateful to David Di Maria, Susie Bender, and Sabine Klahr for their valuable contributions to this chapter. They also acknowledge Rita Bacelar, Nancy Bjorklund-Gass, and Ben Hamman for reading and editing several versions of this text.

[2] Nebraska ranks #45 with 23% of the state's population with a bachelor's degree or higher. Idaho ranks #41 with 25%, Arizona #31 with 28%, New Mexico #38 with 26%, and Wyoming ranks at #37 with 27%. (See http://247wallst.com/special-report/2015/09/23/the-most-and-least-educated-states/.)

Chapter 14
Opening the Classroom to the World:
A Grounded-Theory Study of Student Perceptions of Integrating Intercultural Competence Into Curriculum

Xingbei Ye
Eastern Michigan University, USA

Inna Molitoris
Spring Arbor University, USA

David Anderson
Eastern Michigan University, USA

ABSTRACT

Most curriculum internationalization studies have been focusing on international students and study abroad programs, which has excluded the majority of non-mobile students on American campuses. In addition, the existing studies have been conducted from administrator and faculty perspectives. This chapter generates a substantive theory of intercultural curriculum and teaching methods from the experiences of students who have taken intercultural classes in American classrooms. Active interview theory and grounded theory were utilized for data collection and data analysis. Based on the pure voices from both domestic and international students, this chapter has identified three core categories and eight sub-categories representing student-preferred internationalized curriculum. These categories or themes offer new angles to look at curriculum internationalization.

INTRODUCTION

In the contemporary era of globalization, higher education institutions are more important than ever as mediums for continuous global flows of people, information and images, investments, and knowledge at an unprecedented pace and scale (Appadurai, 1996; Friedman, 2005; Rizvi, 2008). American Council of Education published a preliminary report *Internationalization of U.S. Higher Education* claimed that

DOI: 10.4018/978-1-5225-2791-6.ch014

"if we fail to become effective global citizens" with the ability to "move seamlessly between different nations, cultures, and languages," the United States may find itself falling behind the other major players in the world (Hayward, 2000). Therefore, the international dimension of higher education is becoming increasingly important (Knight, 2004). A widely accepted definition describes internationalization of higher education as "the process of integrating an international, intercultural, or global dimension into the purpose, functions or delivery of postsecondary education" (Knight, 2003, p.2). This definition implies that the curriculum plays a key role in university internationalization as it is "the backbone of the internationalization process" (Knight, 1994, p.6). Several researchers have suggested to place curriculum at the center of any attempt to higher education internationalization (Bond, 2003; Knight, 2004; Paige, 2003). The faculty of the Department of Advertising at the University of Texas-Austin pointed toward the need of developing curriculum that are "truly global and less ethnocentric" (University of Texas, 2000, p. 37). The emphasis on the importance of internationalizing curriculum raises some interesting questions: whose knowledge, systems and procedures form the basis for internationalization, and what the power relations are that underpin this (Tribe, 2005)? Who should be the decision maker of the scope, activity, teaching methods of the internationalized curriculum? Who would be the judge to push the "yes" or "no" button pertinent to the curriculum content and how it will be delivered?

Although the goal of internationalized curriculum is mainly to increase global awareness of students, they are usually not the decision makers on what and how the curriculum should be taught. As Bond (2003) stated, it is problematic that the course content and instructional approaches are determined by authority in the university has been accepted norms. She found that most curriculum reform papers were written from an administrative perspective and a few from a faculty perspective. The researchers have identified that it was a weakness of evaluating the course construction and teaching methods from only solid perspectives of administrators. How do students feel about the impact the course has on their intercultural development? What do students have to say about the course content that necessarily benefit to them? Are students receptive to the course delivery approaches? Since students are the receivers of the curriculum, it is necessary to conduct a research of the topic centering on student opinions, beliefs, and experiences.

The purpose of this study was to discover general elements and categories from the selected subject areas, and eventually generate a substantive theory of intercultural curriculum and teaching pedagogy from student perceptions. To achieve this goal, the qualitative method Grounded Theory (GT) first developed by Glaser and Strauss (1967), later refined by Strauss and Corbin (1990), was utilized. According to Klenke (2008), qualitative research values personal voice and informal speech in data collection and is subject to the phenomenon of emergence of categories, patterns, meanings and theories. The participants of this study were students who had finished classes with embedded intercultural components in two undergraduate programs and two graduate programs at two different universities: undergraduate Business Administration (BA), MBA program, undergraduate Leadership Minor (LEAD), and graduate Educational Leadership (EDLD) program. Although there are multiple elements that make up international education, this study solely focused on the areas of *internationalized curriculum* and *internationalized teaching as* they were cited as the most confusing yet most critical concepts in curriculum internationalization (Bond, 2003; Olson & Green, 2003). The following questions were explored:

1. How do students perceive the content of an intercultural course?
   a. How important do students perceive the course content as a factor of their success with becoming interculturally competent?

    b.   How important is the construction of an intercultural course for students?

    c.   What experiences related to the course content have students had that they would like to remain in future courses?

    d.   What elements would students like to add into an intercultural course?

2.   What aspects of teaching method do students perceive as essential to an intercultural course?

    a.   How important is an instructor's delivery methods of the course to the students?

    b.   How important is an instructor's ability to use international-orientated course materials?

    c.   How important is an instructor's ability to use meaningful assessment in an intercultural course?

BACKGROUND

To avoid the theory generating process to be contaminated by preconceived ideas, particularly, from the literature, this section provides only general background information about the two areas of international education: intercultural competence and international pedagogy, but does not contain frameworks, conceptual maps, or hypothesized models that may create leading questions during the interview process.

Intercultural Competence to Internationalized Curriculum

There is an agreement that curriculum internationalization is a main indicator of higher education internationalization, but there is no consensus what specifically constitutes curriculum internationalization. Nilsson (2000) defines an internationalized curriculum as one that "gives international and intercultural knowledge and abilities, aimed at preparing students for performing professionally, socially, emotionally in an international and multicultural context". According to Banks (1999), an optimal learning environment reflects the diverse cultures, perspectives and experiences of students. Haigh (2009) pointed out that the real internationalization of the curriculum should be constructed on multicultural foundations. Likewise, McKenllin (1996) suggested that an internationalized curriculum is to prepare students for professional and social performance in an international context, and designed for both international and domestic students. These viewpoints are similar with the notion made by several other scholars that international curriculum must have the development of intercultural competence as central components (Otten, 1999; Paige, 2003; Knight, 2004). Apparently, to produce students with intercultural competence is becoming an urgent education priority as it enables students to engage in informed, ethical decision-making dealing with problems that involve a diversity of perspectives (Gurin et al., 2002). Therefore, offering intercultural curriculum focusing on intercultural competence can build and maintain human relationship beyond geographical and cultural boundaries.

There has been substantial research on intercultural competence which has been varied, vague, and sometimes conflicting. Scholars have offered various definitions as well as terminologies such as "awareness", "communication", "global competence" and "effectiveness" to describe intercultural development (Ye, 2017). Some researchers have attempted to produce intercultural models based on individuals' traits and attitudes towards foreign culture (Hammer, Gudykunst, & Wiseman, 1978; Abe &Wiseman, 1983), while others argue that behavioral effectiveness is the core criterion of intercultural competence (Ruben, 1977; Hawes & Kealey; 1981). Some scholars offered definitions from their professional fields. Pedersen (1994) views intercultural development as a "continuous learning process based on cultural awareness, knowledge, and skills" from a multicultural counseling perspective. From a science perspective, Dinniman and Holzner (1988) suggest including universal literacy, computer literacy, knowledge of science, mathematics and statistics, underpinning of scientific and technological civilization, and well-structured knowledge of the world (p. 47). Compare with those studies focusing on a single perspective, King and Baxter-Magolda (2005) claim that their "intercultural matrix" framework is more comprehensive with three dimensions of intercultural maturity: understanding (cognitive dimension), sensitivity to others (interpersonal dimension), and a sense of oneself that enables one to listen to and learn from others (intrapersonal dimension). The researcher was intrigued to find out students' options on what elements would be essential to them for internationalized curriculum.

Pedagogical Approaches to International Curriculum

It is unrealistic to achieve effective curriculum internationalization without appropriate pedagogical approaches, because student learning can take place as a result of classroom activities structured by an instructor. Pedagogy refers to the teaching and learning process as well as the context in which the particular curriculum is being taught (Barnett & Coates, 2005). It emphasizes the interactions among instructors, students, the learning environment, and the learning tasks (Murphy, 2008, p.35). There is an absence of literature addressing international pedagogy used in teaching domestic students. Educators have distinguished between internationalization abroad and internationalization at home (Nilsson, 2000). The former describes the more conventional cross border activities of individuals, such as exchange programs, sabbaticals, international research networks. The latter refers to help students develop international understanding and intercultural skills without ever leaving campus (Knight, 2004). However, in the existing literature, the term of internationalization has been mostly referred as "teaching international students to be home students" (Welikala & Watkins, 2008), thus only teaching issues related to international students have been addressed. Even though there is much rhetoric around internationalizing the experience of all students, the reality is that 85% of students who are sitting in their home classrooms have been somewhat excluded (Wächter, 2003). Thus, very few studies were found discussing curriculum and pedagogy from the perspective of internationalization at home.

After examining the course content of international advertising curriculum in eight universities in the United States, Lee, Chen, and Katz (1997) summarized that the courses were generally taught in traditional format through lecture and discussion. This type of course structure covers international issues only "at the surface level" (p. 4). Students failed to construct knowledge or develop skills necessary to "plan and implement" (p. 4). Kelleher and O'Malley (2006) suggested that the technology approach was useful in an international communication project for linking people from the global through internet group work. In addition to teaching activities, Dunn (1965) found that the lack of instructor expertise was another concern in promoting internationalized curriculum. Likewise, Lee et al. (1997) also stated that an inexperienced instructor may limit the program growth. To mitigate this concern, some practitioners in international field recommended to invite guest lectures from the industry who have international experiences (Hachtmann, 2014).

Bond (2003, 2006) mentioned three approaches faculty can use in curriculum internationalization: the add-on approach, the infusion approach, and the transformation approach. The add-on approach refers to simply add something from other cultures onto the curriculum, it has narrow focus, limited participation, and limited impact. The infusion approach integrates international activities and materials into the curriculum, which enables faculty to become more involved in the internationalization process (Cogan,

1998). The transformation approach produces reform, and shift the fundamental way of how faculty and students think about the world (Bond, 2003). Truly internationalized curriculum entails embracing new forms of knowledge and acquiring more than a passing understanding of "multi-varied modes" of thinking and learning (Bond, 2003), therefore, any of these pedagogical approaches would require change from the traditional way of teaching. However, many faculty either reject or are uncomfortable with the concept of internationalizing the curriculum. At the heart of that discomfiture is the implicit threat to the established view of knowledge (Bond, 2006) and the "usual" pedagogical approaches they are comfortable with.

While professors and administrators have shared their opinions on the dimensions of course content as well as international pedagogy, the voices of students who are taking the curriculum have been missing. What do they have to say about the key elements of curriculum? How receptive are they to the assigned curriculum? How much they believe intercultural competence can better prepare them as global leaders? This study intended to explore elements and categories of student-preferred intercultural curriculum and teaching pedagogy through interviews with both international and domestic students.

MODELS OF INQUIRY

This study was designed based on active interview theory developed by Holstein and Gubrium (1995) and followed by Grounded Theory (Corbin & Strauss, 1990, 2008). The purpose of using the grounded theory (GT) was to present a rigorous method of qualitative research that would enable a systematic data collection, coding, and analysis for generating theory that grounded in an inductive data analysis. According to Holstein and Gubrium (1995), active interview was not a "pipeline for transmitting information" (p.3), rather it was a process exploring the true voice of respondents' unique experiences through their narratives, as well as recognizing both interviewer and respondent engaging in meaning making. The interviews were loosely structured as part of the rigor of GT was to avoid the theory generating process to be contaminated by preconceived ideas, which means the researcher should let the shape of an interview itself evolves according to the way the respondent is answering the questions.

Grounded Theory

Grounded Theory (GT) is a qualitative method that can "discover the theory from data systematically obtained and analyzed" (Strauss & Corbin, 1990, p.1) and it allows the researcher to "uncover and understand what lies behind phenomenon" (p. 19). It is an interactive process that consists of three basic elements: concepts, categories, and propositions (Klenke, 2008). "Concepts are the basic units of analysis from which the theory is developed, and categories are at a higher level of abstraction. They are generated through the same analytic process of making comparisons to highlight similarities and differences that are used to produce the lower level concepts. Proposition involves conceptual relationships" (Klenke, 2008, p. 191). The key elements of GT include (a) the systematic obtaining of data, (b) the constant comparative methods of qualitative analysis, and (c) the generation of theory. Therefore, this study did not form a preconceived proposition prior to the interview, but let the data drive the process of generating categories and themes which resulted in a new profile of internationalization curriculum and teaching pedagogy.

Data Collection

Data was collected at one private university and one public university in the Midwest of the United States. The researchers utilized an active interview approach (Holstein & Gurbrim, 1995) with 12 students who had respectively taken leadership courses, international business courses, and MBA courses. All courses had incorporated intercultural competence components into the subject. The interviewees were informed the purpose of the study, confidentiality issues, and their rights to withdraw from the study at any point. The length of the interviews was about 45-60 minutes range as some respondents would elaborate more and some not. All interviews were audio recorded, transcribed, and analyzed. Of those 12 respondents, there were 4 males and 8 females. Table 1 provides a description of participants: the names of participants were changed to pseudonyms.

The active interview is not just simply asking a set of predetermined questions and seeking complete answers which put respondents in a passive position. It is a process that is "both structured and flexible at the same time" (Sunstein & Chiseri-Strater, 2012, p. 220) which allows the respondents to tell stories beyond expected answers and truly speak for themselves. The researchers attempted to collect individual experience through a "close and personal" way (Marshall & Rossman, 1999, p. 62) by listening carefully and asking for further clarification in the spirit of a "friendly talk" (Sunstein & Chiseri-Strater, 2012, p. 219). Open-ended questions like "what do you think about…", "describe how you feel about…" and "would you please talk more about that…" were asked in the interviews.

Table 1. Demographics of the respondents

Table 1
Demographics of the respondents

N	Pseudonym	Gender and Ethnicity	Age	University and Education level
1.	Amy	Female, Caucasian	21	Public university, undergraduate
2.	Stella	Female, Caucasian	20	Public university, undergraduate
3.	Oliver	Male, Caucasian	24	Public university, undergraduate
4.	Sonya	Female, African-American	32	Public university, graduate
5.	Alexis	Female, Asian	28	Public university, graduate
6.	Mike	Male, an international student from Malaysia	24	Public university, graduate
7.	Thomas	Male, Caucasian	46	Public university, graduate
8.	Julia	Female, Caucasian	20	Private university, undergraduate
9.	Maria	Female, African-American	24	Private university, undergraduate
10.	Victor	Male, Caucasian	22	Private university, undergraduate
11.	Jennifer	Female, Caucasian	32	Private university, graduate
12.	Nora	Female, Caucasian	38	Private university, graduate

IDENTIFYING CONCEPTS THROUGH OPEN CODING

As an inductive method, GT analysis generates theory from relevant issues based on data rather than from existing theories (Sousa & Hendricks, 2006). The researchers followed an analysis that consists of open coding, axial coding, and selective coding (Strauss & Corbin, 1990) in order to "identify and describe both implicit and explicit ideas" (Namey et al., 2008, p. 138), and eventually produced a "cohesive theory" (Glaser, 1978). The researchers broken down the data into parts, such as words, phrases, and sentences from the interviews and compared them constantly in order to move to conceptual coding of a set of empirical indicators (Corbin & Struss, 2008). During the open coding process, a constant comparative analysis (Strauss, 1987) was utilized to note similarities and differences from the units of analysis and indicators that would generate the concepts and categories. Through the constant comparative analysis and open coding, 11 concepts were drafted from the identified indicators. Table 2 illustrates the concepts along with the indicators.

EMERGING CATEGORIES THROUGH AXIAL CODING

Axial coding is a process that explicitly examines the relationships between variables or categories (LaRossa, 2005) which leads to identification of the core category (Strauss, 1987). In this study, axial coding was performed as an inductive building up process identifying a set of final categories and relationships among them. Through re-grouping the initial indicators and concepts, six categories represented six essential aspects to construct an intercultural course were emerged. The label of each category

Table 2. Concepts extracted from initial analysis

Table 2
Concepts extracted from initial analysis

Concepts		Indicators
Knowing Self	Knowing my own culture and values; Being self-aware; I am bias, we are bias; Curious about learning cultures; The world is connected; There are people different than me	People may see us differently; Empathetic; Acceptance; Tolerance; Learning foreign language
Knowing others	Walk in other's shoes; Knowing other cultures and values; Female can't be leader; Male dominated society; Knowing why that happens; Knowing the roots; Guest speaker from other countries	No stop signs in China; Lucky and unlucky numbers Saving face; Conformity; Arranged marriage; Yes, or no gifts; Know the taboos
Communication Skills	Business blunder; Did not know how to start a conversation; They seemed not open to us; Start talking about their names; Change my speaking speed; Asking questions; Interact with people from different background	Talking to match the situation; Communication skills; Sharpening the axe; Listen to understand, not to respond; Body language; Inappropriate touching/hand shaking; Embarrassed; Felt offended
Theory	Cultural theories are abstract; They didn't seem useful in the beginning; "Hofstede Dimensions" was pretty cool after the international panel discussion; Low-versus high-context culture	"Iceberg Cultural Model" was hard; Lewis Cross-communication model was helpful when interviewed for job; Cultural Intelligence
Practice	Real-world experience; Theory and practice are twins; Theory doesn't work without practice; Theory and practice interwoven; Study Aboard; Having international student in class	Interact with people from other countries; Wish to have chance to apply cultural theories; Pair with an international student
Assignment	Cultural narrative; Journal; Assignments help know myself better; Paper requires interview an international individual; Analytical paper on international media	Paper on international movies; Assignments need to be thought-provoking; Let students do their own international research; Self-reflection through others
Participative Approach	Less lecture; Involve students; Engage students; Allow individual opinions; Student teaching	Presentation; Open discussion; Let student solve the problem; Survey assessment; In class comprehensive questions
Interactive Approach	Building relationships; Harmony class environment; Pair work; Group work	Student to student interaction; Brain storm; Debate
Activity-based Approach	Creative; Doing things; Self-confidence; Everyone has to participate; Theory into reality; Candy trading activity	International panel; Skit/Role play; Bringing cultural artifacts in class; Story-telling; Cross-cultural exercise
International materials	Use examples not only about the U.S.; Video clips /Movies about other cultures; Materials written by people from other countries; Past and current international issues; Guest speakers from other countries; Culture is more than just race, gender, and sexual orientation	Something new and bigger; Culture is beyond the national boundary; Use international media; See the other side of the world; Be informed with festivals of other countries; Eye opening
Instructor has a story to tell	Instructor has lots of international experience; Instructor challenge students asking to tell stories of their own international experiences; Instructor is from another country; Instructor can teach hands-on cultural skills; Instructor with international-mind; Instructor him/herself has to be passionate about intercultural	Instructor has to be persuasive and advocate for intercultural education; Instructor shares personal cultural experience; Host international students; Learning foreign language; Attending international conference; Attending international events; Working with international people

was obtained through *In-vivo Coding*, which was derived from the original language respondents used during the interviews. According to Charmaz (2006), in-vivo coding is valuable in grounded theory research as it uses symbolic markers of "participants' speech and meanings". See the following for the six identified categories:

1.   Knowing yourself;
2.   Knowing others;
3.   Sharpening the axe;
4.   Feeling and doing approach;
5.   Eye-opening materials and thought-provoking assignments;
6.   International equipped instructor.

These categories are elaborated in the sections below.

Knowing Yourself

This category is the antecedent condition of intercultural competence. When asked their own definition of intercultural competence, almost all participants expressed the concept of being self-aware first and how that pushed them to be aware of "others". Stella, an undergraduate student from the Leadership program, explained, "it is impossible to be culturally competent without knowing 'who you are' first. By knowing yourself, then you realize 'ah, this is me'; there are some people out there who are different, why?' - this is how you start paying attention to others." Similarly, her peer, Amy, stated that she never thought about the real meaning of "self" before taking the class "because everything was the way it was, how would I even think about 'what' and 'why' it was?" She finally started self-reflection, because "the outside stimulation awakened the awareness of self - that is, the others you have to deal with". The experiences of students revealed that self-awareness is the "stimulator" and the "why" factor to motivate them to study and to interact with the others.

Maria, an African-American student in the undergraduate Business Administration program, defined intercultural competence as an ability to effectively communicate with international people and be aware of cultural differences. She shared her observation of her American peers: "a lot of American students I know are not self-aware of their bias. They feel that the American way is the right way, and everybody should learn their way because they [international people] are in America. I have few American friends who seemed open to other cultures, but the majority of those I know do not try."

Thomas, a graduate student in the MBA program, stated, "unfortunately, we as Americans often believe that we are exceptional... part of that, because we are here on a big land with the ocean and no one can get to us, while in Europe all the countries are together. Another part of that is a fear because we do not know how to deal with those people, so we try to stay away from them..." Nora said, "It is ashamed how we here live without any idea how people live and work in other countries... it is embarrassing to me how arrogant we are."

These experiences are consistent with what Papa, English, Davidson, Culver, and Brown (2013) argued that self-awareness helps develop consciousness and ability to step outside oneself and view the world objectively. Jokinen (2005) also believed that being self-aware is one of the primary competencies that fundamentally increase the intercultural effectiveness. Similarly, Bird and Osland (2004) concluded that one of the byproducts of self-awareness, a sense of humility, is an important competency for successful intercultural interaction. High self-awareness also builds a foundation for strategically acquiring new competencies and skills (Mendenhall et al., 2008) because it allows one to strategically involve others in one's work to complement one's personal weaknesses (Goldsmith et al., 2003). For example, Mike from the undergraduate Leadership program, who is an international student from Malaysia, explained:

I have felt so natural and comfortable talking in my own language with people from my own country, even there are Americans around. However, now I am able to jump out of my own comfort zone and adjust myself to suit the situation. I mean, now, I intentionally speak in English, when Americans are around, because I realized it is rude to make other people feel like you might talk something bad about them.

These findings revealed how intercultural competence influences one's learning attitude and learning style which constructs one's personality characteristics. By adding cultural awareness materials into the course content, students will have a better understanding of their own values, strengths and limitations, and what impact their behaviors may have on others.

Knowing Others

This category is about obtaining intercultural knowledge of other cultures. What information and message students should receive from the course? What theories and materials should be included in the course content? Some general elements of intercultural competence cited by the participants included values and social structure, literature and arts, political system, popular social media, history and customs. Other more specific elements included technical skills, conflict management, stress management, verbal and non-verbal communication skills, and situational factors. In summarizing students' comments, intercultural competence theories should consist of general and specific cultural knowledge and skills that can assist students to effectively communicate with individuals or groups from other cultures. Stella shared her positive experience in applying some of the theories; specifically, she explained how cultural theories learned from class helped her to get a job:

My favorite two theories were the Hofstede's cultural dimensions and the communication model... the triangle... I did not like the Hofstede in the beginning but after interacting with some international students from different parts of the world, I was able to categorize them by using Hofstede model, and it made a lot sense to me. When you are able to do that, you know, it is really a cool thing... then... the triangle model helped me when I was interviewing for my current job, a Brazilian company...the manager and the employees in the company were pretty much like the theory described, you know... the whole culture of the company...I tried to embrace their culture by being extremely enthusiastic and passionate...I even talked about the triangle model with the manager, and she was impressed...I got the offer!

It reveals that an effective intercultural class would transfer knowledge of other cultures, as well as development applicable skills, and both will help students successfully interact with persons of diverse backgrounds. Therefore, when choosing a theory for an intercultural course, the course developer(s) should ask themselves this question: Does this theory provide general cultural knowledge that helps increase cultural sensitivity and cultural analysis ability?

Sharpening the Axe

This is another in-vivo code borrowed from the phrase of participants. It refers to intercultural communication skills, the "how" factor of the development of intercultural competence. The participants talked about the importance of mastering "hands-on skills" in intercultural context, such as "knowing how to start conversation" with people from different background, and "understanding the meaning of body language and appropriately use body language". Participants expressed their desires to learn some useful cross-cultural communication skills "actually can be used in practice." Amy said, "I had interest in interacting with people from other cultures, but I did not know how to start talking and they seemed not interested to start the conversation either... so many times I had to let the chance go" ... Thomas emphasized a need for Americans to develop their tolerance to language accents and express appreciation to those non-native English speakers who can "survive" in the United States. Likewise, other participants (Stella, Mike, Alexis, and Victor) pointed out that an intercultural class should cover communication skills that could direct them in "what they should and should not to do" in a cross-cultural context to avoid embarrassment. Mike stated, "Just like before chopping the wood, you have to sharpen your axe." This category is supported by the next category of putting the theory into practice through active teaching approach.

Feeling and Doing Approach

Participants involved in this research seemed to be averse when they discussed about the traditional lecture-based teaching approach, "I am so sick of the lengthy and boring lectures in most classes... honestly, that only makes students sleepy... I learn the best by feeling and doing things..." Oliver, an undergraduate student from the Leadership program, said that it is common that students attempt to miss lecture classes, because "why come to class, if they [students] can learn the same from the book?" Another student, Julia, said that some students in her classes did not go to class, because "lecture dominated classes do not have a Q and A portion". She wished that her professors could make the class more "interactive", however, "it almost never happens, because there always a lot of material to learn and many things to address," she said.

This category is about active learning/teaching, an instructional method that directly engages students in the learning process of doing "meaningful learning activities and think about what they are doing" (Prince, 2004, p. 1). Most participants expressed the desire of having the class taught through active teaching approaches such as role play, games, panels, guest speakers, simulations, media uses, case studies, presentations, and small group activities. Some participants also suggested out-of-classroom experiences such as internships, service learning, and study abroad. It is believed that active learning techniques create an enjoyable learning environment that has a positive impact on comprehension and understanding of the materials (Katula & Threnhauser, 1999). Stella stated, "we played a candy trading game, it was a simulation of how people from different cultures make business... it really helped me understand the theory previously I thought was pretty abstract and confusing..." Another important point was made by Thomas, who said that intercultural activities can be integrated into "any class in the program, even accounting". Likewise, Jennifer and Maria expressed how they liked a statistics class that they learned about differences in the way of writing numbers, and putting comma and period in other countries. Nora also mentioned that cross-cultural tours would help students learn, "In my class tour in Greece, I learned language, geography, history, economy and social life in Greece. It is really cool that I could actually 'touch' the real thing!" Therefore, practitioners in intercultural field should reduce lengthy lecturing and avoid transferring knowledge to passive receivers. Instead, utilizing active teaching approach that can effectively help students develop intercultural competence such as self-awareness, self-reflection, and necessary skills in comparison, analysis, communication and collaboration.

Eye-Opening Materials and Thought-Provoking Assignments

Participants repeatedly talked about how the "eye-opening" and "thought-provoking" class materials and assignments had helped them with self-discovery and self-expansion. What they meant by "eye-opening" was "the materials beyond the American-focused topics" (Victor), "what was written by those who has first-hand experience (Nora), and "video materials that show the real life of people there [abroad]" (Alexis). Stella discovered a new international perspective of the concepts of culture. She said the following:

I liked the [intercultural leadership] class, because some of the materials were something I have never heard before. I had heard about the term 'culture' many times in my life, but never really thought about what it was. Then my instructor really got us started. She asked us to reflect on a poem written by Rudyard Kipling called 'we and they,' that was awesome. That was really my first time started exploring culture. For a long period of time, we talked about culture related to gender, race, and sexuality. I thought that was all culture was about. After this class, I know culture is more than that. It is something bigger, broader, and deeper, as my instructor said, across the physical boundaries... I liked that a lot...

Similarly, Mike, who was an international student, talked about a "global issue" video he thought was "eye-opening and "thought provoking":

For one assignment, I watched a video about child brides in Yemen - I never even knew where Yemen was, not to mention about knowing anything on its education or women's rights, or just anything... however, after that video, I was shocked, shocked, shocked! That video made me so emotional, I wrote a long paper...and then I did more research and found the similar issues also exist in Bangladesh, Tanzania, India...I did lots of self-reflection, and I decided to take initiative as a leader, to do something... I am actually applying for Peace Corps... to go to Tanzania... that really has changed my previously narrow horizon and now I am doing my part to help solve the world issues...

Providing eye-opening materials means that the class materials should extend its range from the Western centric to a global wide view. The researchers combined the initial two categories of "eye-opening materials" and "thought-provoking assignments" into one category as they were almost inseparably linked. Respondents suggested thet all assessments in this type of class should be beyond the traditional methods such as "multiple choices, memorization, or American-focused paper". Stella stated:

One of the most helpful assignments I had in this class was to write an analytical paper on culture dimensions after we had an international student panel in class with panelists from five different countries. Honestly that was the first time I had a real chance to get to know those countries. By knowing the historical and current situations about those countries, I reflected on myself on what do I have, what I have ignored, what are the main differences between my culture and those, what can I do to improve my communication skills in a cultural situation... that was definitely my favorite assignments in college so far. It combined the class activity and assignments together... all assignments should be like that... of course, the class materials should be more international as well, I mean... intercultural assignments should be something 'inter'...

For some students with limited intercultural experience, some materials and/or activities can be overwhelming. Jennifer shared her New York trip which was a required activity for her class:

I have never previously been to New York... never traveled outside of my state... In New York I felt lost, tired, overwhelmed... even New York is America, I was a stranger there... after that trip, when was I reading the [International Business] textbook, I pictured people in places where I have never been and situations I have never experienced... it was overwhelming...but I realized that is why I need to learn more...

When talking about materials and assignments, students emphasized "international," "not western only," "something new and bigger," "help to see the other side of the world," "more global issues," and "international media." Apparently, their main point was that the international materials should be infused into readings, examples, case-studies, and other activities and assignments.

International Equipped Instructor

The International Equipped Instructor category was not among those concepts first considered, but surprisingly it underlays nearly every interview. Respondents expressed how much they enjoyed when the instructors could "tell stories" related to different cultures, or share their own international experiences. An example from Amy demonstrated how much an international equipped instructor was wanted:

My instructor [in the intercultural class] was from Detroit area. She hardly has any overseas experience and did not show her interest or a good understanding of intercultural...Frankly, she did not have any story to tell... Anyways... actually I didn't even think, she really believes in intercultural...sorry to say that...all examples she gave were about things happened here on campus, or within her community... then, one day we had a substitute instructor who was a Chinese. I enjoyed the most when she shared her cultural experiences and how those experiences actually reflected the theories we learned. She even immediately taught me something that I have been using ever since, and it works well every time when I meet a new Chinese person.... I was always wondering what they talk when meet new people...then the substitute instructor told us we could start talking about names with Chinese, because their names usually have specific meaning. Later, I went to a Chinese party and I started talking with a Chinese guy about his name. He really liked to talk about that. His name means "Blue Ocean," because he was born in an ocean city... Since then, I was able to talk more freely with Chinese people and they were actually open to me... I just wished that the Chinese substitute instructor was my instructor for the class...

The interviewees noted that American instructors who have traveled abroad are better prepared to teach intercultural courses. International-minded instructors are not necessarily foreign-born, but those who are open-minded with strong interest and rich experience in intercultural issues. For example, Mike, an international student in the graduate Leadership program, was very satisfied with his instructor:

As an international student myself, I expect the instructor to view things with international perspective. My instructor was an American, but she has lots of international experiences. I found myself enjoyed the most was the time when she shared her international experiences... even some places she never been to, she was knowledgeable about them. For example, she never been to China, she is going to though... she was able to tell stories about education, food, and family structure in China – when we had discussion on Hofstede's cultural theory, she shared her experience having dinner at her Chinese friend's home. She said that she was honest to tell that the food was too salty and she left food in her plate. Her friend's mom never invited her back again... that example helped me understood the "saving face" of Chinese culture, and also helped me know people from a 'directive culture' would really make such mistakes. I mean, it was nice that she was able to tell her own culture blunders... I definitely prefer an instructor who is international, or at least, somewhat equipped with international mind, truly believe in international culture, and willing to learn...

Most interviewees (Victor, Maria, Thomas, Nora) did not think that many instructors from across campus have enough knowledge, experience, and skills to help students turn negative cultural experience into positive learning opportunity. Nora emphasized that, an instructor in any discipline must be "sensitive to cultural differences, must have good communication skills, must be very flexible in switching roles, and must have ability to bring students with different ethnic and cultural origins together to learn and to get along".

CONCLUSION AND DISCUSSION

This study revealed students' perceptions of the essential elements to an intercultural competence course. Most respondents held similar views on what had pleased them while few students reported their unpleasant experience during the intercultural courses. Overall, respondents reported a strong correspondence between course content, teaching approach, the role of the instructor, and the degree of their engagement and intercultural development. They expressed that they engaged and enjoyed the most when the course content was "interesting, eye-opening, thought-provoking, and applicable." At the same time, the teaching approach has significant impact on students' motivation and interest to the course. A preferred instructor for teaching intercultural courses would be a person who "has international-mind, has stories to tell, truly believes in intercultural, and teaches in an unconventional way". Students heavily emphasized the importance of international background/experience of the instructor which was not expected in the beginning of the study.

Integrating Categories and Discovering Relationships

Glaser and Strauss (1967) argued that the purpose of qualitative research is to gain understanding of "theoretical purpose and relevance", not to verify facts (p. 48). Through constantly returning to the beginning, memo writing, and re-analyzing the rich information respondents provided, the researchers were able to reveal relationships among emerged categories which leading to the final establishment of a substantive theory (Figure 1). The final theory consists of three integrated core categories and eight sub-categories representing student-preferred intercultural course. Figure 1 shows each emerged category

Figure 1. Emerged categories and relationships: The integrated theory

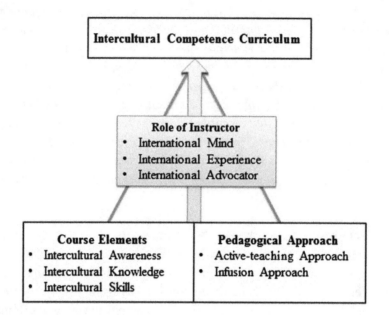

Figure 1. Emerged categories and relationships – the integrated theory

and the relationships among them. In the final theory, all in-vivo terms were replaced with formal terms but still represent the meaning of those in-vivo concepts.

Course Elements

Three sub-categories were emerged into the course content theme: Intercultural Awareness, Intercultural Knowledge, and Intercultural Skills. They represent necessary course elements for a student-preferred intercultural curriculum.

Intercultural Awareness

This sub-category is the intrapersonal aspect of an individual. A part of the course content should focus on awaking and increasing one's intercultural awareness, including understanding one's own values, ethical principles, philosophies, history, behaviors, bias, strengths, weaknesses, learning styles, as well as the ability of analyzing the similarities and differences between one's own culture and other cultures. Intercultural awareness serves as the foundation of further intercultural development, it is part and parcel of growing in consciousness and the ability to step outside ourselves and look objectively at who we are, what we want, and why we want it (Papa et al., 2013). Individuals who have high intercultural awareness understand their own values, strengths and limitations, and how their behaviors impact others. In contrast, individuals with low self-awareness have little concern or interest in knowing themselves or how their behavioral tendencies affect others which promotes self-deception and arrogance (Mendenhall et al., 2008). Besides, Jokinen (2005) believes that self-awareness is one of the primary competencies that fundamentally increase the effectiveness of working with people from other cultures.

Intercultural Knowledge

Moving from "knowing self" to "knowing others", one should be engaged in group activities and explore the world that is bigger than "me" and "my comfort zone." The course content should include the knowledge of people and environment not only at the individual and community level, but also at the national and international level (e.g., the history, literature, arts, political and law systems, language, taboos, costumes, and human rights notion in other cultures). A noticeable finding through the interview was the mutual relationship between these two categories: knowing self and knowing others. It is not a linear but a circular relationship (i.e., *self-others-self*). One has a better understanding of self through the process of reflection on others. This was accurately reflected from one interviewee who shared her experience on how "the other people you have to deal with" pushed her to self-reflect. Thus, the "self" and "others" are "stimulator" and "mirror" for each other.

Intercultural Skills

One cannot effectively communicate with others without mastering interpersonal skills. If the previous two categories were referred to as intangible "paper talk", this category is substantial and can be used in practice. Respondents showed appreciation for the skills they developed during the courses that they could apply to real cultural context. As can be recalled from the data report section, Amy was excited when she successfully started a conversation with a Chinese individual by using the tips the instructor gave her. Some would argue that it is unrealistic to teach intercultural skills in a one-semester classroom as it requires time to develop and it is usually situational. It is true that one cannot be taught to speak a foreign language in an intercultural class, but it is necessary to learn some general starting-point skills. For example, the verbal and non-verbal techniques in a certain culture such as hand shaking, greeting, listening, questioning, clarifying, and apologizing would help students start their cultural journey.

Pedagogical Approach

The quality of an intercultural course mostly relies on the effectiveness of course delivery. The way how instructors construct and teach the course would shape the learning outcomes of the students. Based on students' comments and suggestions, two core categories were emerged for the theme of pedagogical approach: Active-teaching approach and Infusion approach.

Active-Teaching Approach

Active learning uses different activities and interactive teaching styles to involve students more in the learning process (Prentless, 2006). Some studies have suggested using active learning in teaching intercultural competence instead of passive learning methods (Zimmerman, 1995), because students learn best about another culture by experiencing it, analyzing it, and applying their knowledge to other situations (Roose, 2001). Sometimes students are not interested in discovering or learning other cultures because "it seems it is not my business" as there is no direct impact on them. Using active learning can induce students by relating the concept to their "real life" situations and makes information more applicable and engaging (Pare, 2006). For example, Stella mentioned that one class activity required students to bring a cultural artifact to class and tell a story behind it. "I have never realized that a small piece of craft called 'dala horse' was such meaningful to my grandma and her family until she told me the story. I suddenly felt, I was connected to Swedish culture and I wanted to trace back my family history". Other respondents also expressed that class activities such as games and role play helped them to better engage with course materials. According to Koles et al. (2005), students attended classes with active learning approach had a higher attendance rate and reported greater affinity for the course. Overall, active teaching approach reflects what the respondents referred as "participative and interactive classroom." It engages a deeper understanding of concepts as the learner must apply knowledge to an activity (Prentless, 2006).

Infusion Approach

This sub-category was derived from the initial generated two categories of "eye-opening materials and thought-provoking assignments." The reason to merge these two concepts into one category was that the elements described by respondents were fully lined up with the *curricular infusion approach* (Bond, 2006) based on the work of Mesteinhauser (1998) and Banks (1999). According to Bond (2006), there are three approaches to international curriculum: Add-on approach, Infusion approach, and Transformational approach. Among them, Infusion approach best fits the ideal intercultural course the respondents described as "to add international materials and activities to the curriculum". In fact, the infusion approach was suggested as the most appropriate approach for international curriculum in the current stage. Mestenhauser (1998) argued that if enough courses can be enriched with international content of some kind, the cumulative effect will be an impressive international education. Cogan (1998) stated that the main characteristics of the infusion approach include the following requirements: (a) the course goals should be local-global focused, (b) the reading materials should reflect diverse points of view; (c) the assignments should encourage students to think beyond national borders; (d) students should be allowed to discuss about their personal cultural experiences; (e) students should be allowed to do their own international issue related research; (f) students must be encouraged to attend internal conferences; (h) inviting intentional guest speakers must be a norm in an intercultural class; and (i) instructor must taking advantage of international activities at the institution to engage students. These features matched what respondents suggested in the interviews and it was proofed by the students that it was one of the appropriate and realistic pedagogical approaches in teaching intercultural classes.

Role of Instructor

Historically, the relationship between faculty members and international education was vital that professors traveling from city to city, meeting people from different cultures, and teach in different languages (Cleveland-Jones, Emes, & Ellard, 2001). Instructor is the executor responsible for course implementation; his/her own personal quality and characteristics will influence the learning outcomes. Again, this is a newly generated category from information provided by participants. Basically, students prefer an instructor who has an international mind, international experience, and is willing to advocate for intercultural competence.

International Mind

International mind, or global mind is a highly complex cognitive structure characterized by an openness to and articulation of multiple cultural and strategic realities on both global and local levels, and the cognitive ability to mediate and integrate across this multiplicity (Levy et al., 2007, p. 244). By extend this, faculty members who have an international mind are open to differences and able to construct meaning from multiple perspectives. They understand the complexity of global issues without making oversimplified judgments; they prioritize their goal of preparing students as global citizens; and they enjoy integrating their knowledge and skills into the classes they teach. All these will result in a good exchange of ideas and learning from each other's culture.

International Experience

Participants showed deep concerns with instructor who did not have international experience and doubted if they were eligible to teach intercultural classes. Indeed, it is more convincing that an instructor who has extensive international experience can shape the way students view the other side of the world. Faculty who have international experiences would develop ability of reflective thinking, cross-cultural communication, and being non-stereotypical. This finding is in line with Dunn (1965) and Lee et al. (1997) who suggested that instructor expertise and international experience may determine the growth of the internationalized curriculum they teach. Higher education institutions encourage faculty to develop themselves towards the goal of cultural competency through their own "ongoing self-assessment, reflection, and meaningful action" (Seifer & Connors, 2007). However, the challenge is that many faculty remain uncomfortable with this type of development since it is time consuming, naturally introduces issues of ethics and personal development, creates difficulties in grading, and challenges the traditional standards of academic quality (Braskamp, 2008).

International Advocacy

Although there is a general agreement that faculty members take the primary responsibility for internationalizing curriculum, many professors do not necessarily believe that internationalization is an important transformative process can invigorate their courses and teaching (Bond, 2006). Most respondents in this study expressed their enjoyment of having instructors who were internationalization advocators while few complained of having professors who lacked enthusiasm for the course. Students preferred an instructor who "has international stories to tell, who advocates for intercultural competence, who has international mind to learn, and who has to be international first before teaching intercultural courses." Faculty who "truly believe in what they are preaching for" are more likely devoting themselves into the course construction and teach in a genuine way.

MOVING FORWARD

To involve more non-mobile students and faculty members into intercultural competence field, it is necessary to open the American classroom to the world through internationalized curriculum. Although some universities have been making effort on curriculum internationalization, the promise has not been fulfilled due to lack of consideration of students' perspectives. The three identified core categories and eight sub-categories offer new angles to look at curriculum internationalization from students' perspectives.

Participants in this study provided various ideas on what elements they wanted to be included in an intercultural program. While the researchers have extracted three sub-categories "intercultural awareness, intercultural knowledge, and intercultural skills" from the interviews, there were some fragmented information reported, such as funding, institutional attitudes, study abroad opportunities, and government policy. This implies that the internationalized curriculum is more complex than just one dimension. In addition to the elements identified in this study, many other units may also influence the implementation and quality of curriculum internationalization. As Tribe (2005) states, "a curriculum is socially constructed, it is the product of human thought and negotiation" (p. 447).

Participants expressed their preference of active learning and infusion approach in terms of pedagogy. It seems like the infusion approach best fits the intercultural course at the current stage, as it enables students to view the world from multiple perspectives. However, Bond (2003) suggested that the transformation approach would be ideal because it enables faculty and students to move in and out among different cultures comfortably (Bond, 2003). There is still a long way to go to apply this approach as it is the most demanding and difficult approach to achieve. It requires faculty to revise their "usual" pedagogy, and to "embrace a more meaningful definition of internationalizing learning" that involves substantive knowledge about the social-cultural content of other societies; alterations in how one responds to cultural differences; how one behaves in intercultural circumstances, and how one maintains one's own cultural integrity while understanding and working with others" (Bond, 2006). Bond (2003) suggests that faculty members who are bilingual or multilingual, have lived overseas, and have been active in international programs show better understanding of their role in internationalization than those who do not have that international experience. Fortunately, international experience can be gained through training programs and day-to-day practice. Activities such as attending workshops and international conferences, teaching overseas and engaging in international service learning, hosting international students, paying attention to international issues, and networking with international researches would be a good start.

All participants in this study have successfully completed intercultural classes in their degree programs. Therefore, the identified categories from this study are fairly practical to be applied in course design and implementation. For future research, it would be interesting to explore the factors that may have negatively influenced students who have failed or dropped from this type of class. Additionally, comparing perceptions of the course content and teaching methods between students and faculty/administrators would be useful to the field.

REFERENCES

Abe, H., & Wiseman, R. L. (1983). A cross-cultural confirmation of the dimensions of intercultural effectiveness. *International Journal of Intercultural Relations*, 7(1), 53–69. doi:10.1016/0147-1767(83)90005-6

Appadurai, A. (1996). *Modernity at large: Cultural dimensions of globalization*. Minneapolis, MN: University of Minnesota Press.

Banks, J. A. (1999). *An introduction to multicultural education*. Boston: Allyn & Bacon.

Barnett, R., & Coates, K. (2005). *Engaging the curriculum in higher education*. Buckingham, UK: Society for Research into Higher Education and Open University Press.

Bird, A., & Osland, J. (2004). Global competencies: An introduction. In Handbook of global management. Oxford, UK: Blackwell.

Bond, S. (2003). Untapped resources: Internationalization of the curriculum and classroom experience. *Canadian Bureau for International Education Research*, 7, 1–15.

Bond, S. (2006). *Transforming the culture of learning: Evoking the international dimension in Canadian university curriculum*. York University.

Braskamp, L. (2008). Developing Global Citizens. *Journal of College and Character*, X(1), 1–5.

Charmaz, K. (2006). *Constructing grounded theory*. Thousand Oaks, CA: Sage Publications.

Cleveland-Jones, M., Emes, C., & Ellard, J. H. (2001). On being a social change agent in a reluctant collegial environment. *Planning for Higher Education*, 29(4).

Cogan, J. (1998). Internationalization through networking and curricular infusion. In J. Mestenhauser & B. Ellingboe (Eds.), *Reforming higher education curriculum: Internationalizing the campus*. Phoenix, AZ: Oryx Press.

Corbin, J., & Strauss, A. (1990). Grounded theory method: Procedures, canons, and evaluative procedures. *Qualitative Sociology*, 13(1), 3–21. doi:10.1007/BF00988593

Corbin, J., & Strauss, A. (2008). *Basics of qualitative research: Techniques and procedures for developing grounded theory*. Los Angeles, CA: Sage. doi:10.4135/9781452230153

Dunn, S. W. (1965). Cross-cultural research by U.S. corporations. *The Journalism Quarterly*, 42(3), 454–457. doi:10.1177/107769906504200312

Friedman, T. L. (2005). *The world is flat*. London: Penguin Books.

Glaser, B. G. (1978). *Theoretical sensitivity*. Mill Valley, CA: Sociology Press.

Glaser, B. G., & Strauss, A. L. (1967). *The discovery of grounded theory: Strategies or qualitative research*. New Brunswick, NJ: Aldine Transaction.

Goldsmith, M., Greenberg, C., Robertson, A., & Hu-Chan, M. (2003). *Global leadership: The next generation*. Upper Saddle River, NJ: Prentice-Hall.

Green, M. (2002). Joining the world: The challenge of internationalizing undergraduate education. *Change Magazine, 34*.

Gurin, P., Dey, E. L., Hurtado, S., & Gurin, G. (2002). Diversity and higher education: Theory and impact on educational outcomes. *Harvard Educational Review*, 72(3), 330–366. doi:10.17763/haer.72.3.01151786u134n051

Hachtmann, F. (2014). International Advertising Education: Curriculum and Pedagogy. Faculty Publications, College of Journalism & Mass Communications, 82.

Haigh, M. J. (2009). Fostering cross-cultural empathy with non-Western curricular structures. *Journal of International Education.*, 13(2), 271–284.

Hammer, M. R., Gudykunst, W. B., & Wiseman, R. L. (1978). Dimensions of intercultural effectiveness: An exploratory study. *International Journal of Intercultural Relations*, 2(4), 382–393. doi:10.1016/0147-1767(78)90036-6

Hawes, F., & Kealey, D. J. (1981). An empirical study of Canadian technical assistance. *International Journal of Intercultural Relations, 5*(3), 239–258. doi:10.1016/0147-1767(81)90028-6

Hayward, F. M. (2000). *Preliminary status report 2000: Internationalization of U.S. higher education.* Washington, DC: American Council on Education.

Hostein, J. A., & Gubrium, J. F. (1995). *The active interview.* Thousand Oaks, CA: Sage. doi:10.4135/9781412986120

Jokinen, T. (2005). Global leadership competencies: A review and discussion. *Journal of European Industrial Training, 29*(2/3), 199–216. doi:10.1108/03090590510591085

Katula, R. A., & Threnhauser, E. (1999). Experiential education in the undergraduate curriculum. *Communication Education, 48*(3), 238–255. doi:10.1080/03634529909379172

King, P. M., & Baxter-Magolda, M. (2005). A developmental model of intercultural maturity. *Journal of College Student Development, 46*(6), 571–592. doi:10.1353/csd.2005.0060

Klenke, K. (2008). Qualitative research in the study of leadership. Emerald Group Publishing Limited.

Knight, J. (1994) Internationalization elements and checkpoints. Canadian Bureau for International Education.

Knight, J. (2003). Updating the definition of internationalization. *Industry and Higher Education, 33,* 2–3.

Knight, J. (2004). Internationalization remodeled: Definitions, approaches and rationales. *Journal of Studies in International Education, 8*(1), 531. doi:10.1177/1028315303260832

Koles, P., Nelson, S., Stolfi, A., Parmelee, D., & DeStephen, D. (2005). Active learning in a year 2 pathology curriculum. *Medical Education, 39*(10), 1045–1055. doi:10.1111/j.1365-2929.2005.02248.x PMID:16178832

LaRossa, R. (2005). Grounded theory methods and qualitative family research. *Journal of Marriage and the Family, 67*(4), 237–257. doi:10.1111/j.1741-3737.2005.00179.x

Lee, W., Chen, C., & Katz, H. (1997). International advertising education in the United States: A preliminary study and evaluation. *International Journal of Advertising, 16*(1), 1–26. doi:10.1080/02650487.1997.11104670

Levy, O., Beechler, S., Taylor, S., & Boyacigiller, N. A. (2007). What we talk about when we talk about 'Global Mindset': Managerial cognition in multinational corporations. *Journal of International Business Studies, 38*(2), 231–258. doi:10.1057/palgrave.jibs.8400265

Marshall, C., & Rossman, G. B. (1999). *Designing qualitative research* (3rd ed.). Thousand Oaks, CA: Sage.

McKellin, K. (1996). *Anticipating the future.* Vancouver, Canada: British Columbia Centre for International Education.

Mendenhall, M. E., Stevens, M. J., Brid, A., & Oddou, G. (2008). *Specification of the content domain of the Intercultural Effectiveness Scale.* The Kozai Group, Inc.

Mestenhauser, J. (1998). Portraits of an international curriculum. In J. Mestenhauser & B. Ellingboe (Eds.), *Reforming higher education curriculum: Internationalizing the campus*. Phoenix, AZ: Oryx Press.

Murphy, P. (2008). Defining pedagogy. In K. Hall, P. Murphy, & J. Soler (Eds.), *Pedagogy and practice: culture and identities* (pp. 28–39). London: SAGE publications.

Namey, E., Guest, G., Thairu, L., & Johnson, L. (2008). Data reduction techniques for large qualitative data sets. In *Handbook for team-based qualitative research*. Rowman Altamira.

Nilsson, B. (2000). Internationalizing the curriculum. In P. Crowther, M. Joris, M. Otten, B. Nilsson, H. Teekens, & B. Wachter (Eds.), *Internationalization at home: A position paper* (p. 2127). Amsterdam: European Association for International Education.

Olson, C., & Green, M. F. (2003). *Internationalizing the campus. A user's guide*. American Council on Education.

Otten, M. (1999). Preparing for the intercultural implications of the internationalisation of higher education in Germany. In K. Häkkinen (Ed.), *Innovative approaches to intercultural education: International Conference on Multicultural Education* (pp. 238-249). Jyväskylä, Finland: University of Jyväskylä Press.

Paige, R. M. (2003). The American case: The University of Minnesota. *Journal of Studies in International Education*, *7*(1), 52–63. doi:10.1177/1028315302250180

Papa, R., English, F., Davidson, F., Culver, M. K., & Brown, R. (2013). *Contours of great leadership: The science, art, and wisdom of outstanding practice*. Lanham, MD: Rowman & Littlefield Publisher, Inc.

Pare, A., & Maistre, C. L. (2006). Active learning in the workplace transforming individuals and institution. *Journal of Education and Work*, *4*(4), 363–381. doi:10.1080/13639080600867141

Pedersen, P. (1994). *A handbook for developing multicultural awareness* (2nd ed.). Alexandria, VA: American Counseling Association.

Prentless, K. (2006). What is meant by "active learning?". *Education*, *12*, 566–569.

Prince, M. (2004). Does Active Learning Work? A Review of the Research. *Journal of Engineering Education.*, *93*(3), 223–231. doi:10.1002/j.2168-9830.2004.tb00809.x

Rizvi, F. (2008). Epistemic virtues and cosmopolitan learning. *Australian Educational Researcher*, *35*(1), 17–35. doi:10.1007/BF03216873

Roose, D. (2001). White teachers' learning about diversity and "otherness": The effects of undergraduate international education internships on subsequent teaching practices. *Equity & Excellence in Education*, *34*(1), 43–49. doi:10.1080/1066568010340106

Ruben, B. D. (1977). Guidelines for cross-cultural communication effectiveness. *Group & Organization Studies*, *2*(4), 470–479. doi:10.1177/105960117700200408

Seifer, S., & Connors, K. (Eds.). (2007). *Faculty Toolkit for Service learning in Higher Education*. Community-Campus Partnerships for Health for Learn and Serve America's National Service Learning Clearinghouse Health National Service - Learning Clearinghouse. Retrieved from: http://servicelearning.org/filemanager/download/HE_toolkit_with_wo rksheets.pdf

Sousa, C., & Hendricks, P. (2006). The diving bell and the butterfly: The need for grounded theory in developing a knowledge based view of organizations. *Organizational Research Methods*, *9*(3), 315–338. doi:10.1177/1094428106287399

Strauss, A. (1987). *Qualitative analysis for social scientists*. Cambridge, UK: Cambridge University Press. doi:10.1017/CBO9780511557842

Strauss, A., & Corbin, J. (1990). *Basics of qualitative research: Grounded theory procedures and techniques*. Newbury Park, CA: Sage.

Sunstein, B. S., & Chiseri-Strater, E. (2012). *Field working: Reading and writing research*. St. Martin's.

Tribe, J. (2005). Tourism, knowledge, and the curriculum. In D. Airey & J. Tribe (Eds.), *International Handbook of Tourism Education* (pp. 47–60). Amsterdam: Routledge.

University of Texas at Austin, College of Communication, Department of Advertising. (2000). *Thoughts about the future of advertising education* [white paper]. Retrieved from: http://marketingpedia.com/MarketingLibrary/Advertising%20in%20Education/FutureOf AdvertisingEducation2.pdf

Wächter, B. (2003). An introduction: Internationalisation at home in context. *Journal of Studies in International Education*, *7*(1), 5–11. doi:10.1177/1028315302250176

Welikala, T., & Watkins, C. (2008). *Improving intercultural learning experiences in higher education: Responding to cultural scripts for learning*. London: Institute of Education Publishers.

Ye, X. (2017). *Lost and found: Cultural different, intercultural maturity, and self-authorship among international students* (Unpublished doctoral dissertation). Eastern Michigan University.

Zimmerman, S. (1995). Perceptions of intercultural communication competence and international student adaptation to an American campus. *Communication Education*, *44*(4), 321–335. doi:10.1080/03634529509379022

KEY TERMS AND DEFINITIONS

Axial Coding: A data analysis process that explicitly examines the relationships between variables or categories which leads to identification of the core category.

Grounded Theory: A qualitative research method that can discover the theory from data systematically obtained and analyzed. It is an interactive process that consists of three basic elements: concepts, categories, and propositions.

In-Vivo Coding: A data coding practice of assigning a label to a section of data by using the original language of the participants, such as interview transcript, words, and phrases.

Internationalized Curriculum: The academic content of a specific course or program with international orientation aims to prepare students to be interculturally competitive in a global context.

Internationalized Pedagogy: A wide range of activities used to teach internationalized curriculum with an international, intercultural, or comparative focus.

Chapter 15
Fieldwork in Developing Countries:
Preparing Pre-Service Teachers

Michelle Vaughn
Mercer University, USA

Karen Swanson
Mercer University, USA

ABSTRACT

Twenty-first century teachers can become more culturally competent through thoughtfully planned opportunities designed to develop global perspectives. Cultural competence can be cultivated through service-learning experiences such as study abroad, thus maximizing pre-service teachers' global preparation and future success within diverse classrooms. In this chapter, the authors discuss preparing undergraduate and graduate students for fieldwork in Liberia, South Africa, and Belize. The purpose of trips to developing countries is to teach and serve but also requires planning that acknowledges issues experienced by pre-service teachers such as anxiety and low efficacy. Upon completion of the Mercer on Mission trips, several pre-service teachers expressed their views about the usefulness of the preparation activities, which are explored within student narratives. Ultimately, the goal of the service-learning program is to support the completion of fieldwork requirements in exceptional contexts while adequately preparing students to be effective across a variety of diverse settings and activities.

INTRODUCTION

Mercer on Mission

Pre-service teachers can benefit from an international service-learning component while completing their coursework. Mercer University provides an exemplary service-learning model called Mercer on Mission (MoM), which facilitates opportunities for students to participate in acts of service where they participate in academic and cultural experiences. Pre-service teachers who participate in MoM programs

DOI: 10.4018/978-1-5225-2791-6.ch015

expand their global awareness by observing and teaching within an international setting. The design of international fieldwork experiences is directly tied to the Tift College of Education's conceptual framework, which is based on the transformative literature of Noddings (2001), Mezirow (2000), and others. The goal of supporting students towards becoming a transformative educator is exemplified in the teaching and service- learning experiences in Liberia, South Africa, and Belize. The purpose of the MoM program is to provide students with an international experience, which includes cultural immersion, meaningful service, and growth through personal reflection.

The structure and requirements for students is that they completed up to 80 hours of classroom observation and teaching during the MoM programs. The pre-service teachers also conversed with peers, teachers, and university faculty in order to comprehensively prepare prior to and during this international professional practicum experience.

The MoM program teacher candidates visited three destinations, which included Liberia, South Africa, and Belize. South Africa and Belize however were not originally included in program destinations. Instead, program facilitators spent fourteen months preparing for a program to Nepal, planning and meeting with the participating pre-service teachers. Unfortunately, one month prior to departure, a catastrophic earthquake hit Nepal. Plans were quickly changed as less than one month remained to prepare a new program to South Africa. Surprisingly, the trip to Nepal was deterred again the following year due to a trade blockade and, once again, we had to prepare for another destination, Belize.

Description of the Trips

The Mercer on Mission (MoM) program trips helped to facilitate the completion of the pre-service teacher's professional practicum experiences in international settings. Master's level students participated in the Liberia MoM program at Ricks Institute, a K-12 preparatory school. Other master's level and undergraduate students who were part of the Belize and South Africa MoM programs participated in a school outside of Cape Town, South Africa. All of the pre-service teachers within these settings observed, taught, and engaged in numerous service-learning projects.

Goals for Students

The goals for the pre-service teachers encompassed the mission of Mercer on Mission (MoM), "...to teach, to learn, to create, to discover, to inspire, to empower and to serve" (Mercer University, 2017a). The facilitators of each program supported the students' preparation through face-to face meetings during which they discussed topics about schools they would be visiting, the culture of the country, and the expectations of the program. The pre-service teachers were challenged daily to embrace each of the components of the mission set forth by MoM. In addition, the students were expected to observe their new environment. Based on their observations and conversations with the classroom teacher, each pre-service teacher planned lessons that were relevant to the students they were serving. Along the way, they each were able to discover things about their teaching, themselves, and others that would later assist them in their classroom when they returned to the States.

BACKGROUND

Teaching and Service-Learning Abroad

This section is a review of literature that explains the importance and value of providing to students with study-abroad teaching and service-learning experiences that enhance their cultural competencies and global perspectives. Bringle and Hatcher (1995) stated that:

Service-learning [is] a course-based, credit-bearing, educational experience in which students (a) participate in an organized service activity that meets identified community needs and (b) reflect on the service activity in such a way as to gain further understanding of course content, a broader appreciation of the discipline, and an enhanced sense of civic responsibility. (p. 112)

Martines (2005) suggested that the purpose of international teaching experiences is to prepare future teachers for an increasingly diverse population in US classrooms. Darling-Hammond (2010) and Ladson-Billings (1999), both teacher educators, have advocated for changes in teacher education to better prepare a majority white teacher workforce to be better equipped to positively teach a growing minority school population. International study abroad experiences for pre-service teachers provide unique training for exactly the purpose of expanding students' global perspectives and cultural awareness.

Merryfield and Wilson (2005) stated that global awareness is the first step in cultural competence by facilitating communication and interactions with people in cultures different from their own. Furthermore, short-term study abroad experiences for pre-service teachers provides the opportunity for "a new appreciation of both home and host countries, new tools and techniques to bring to the classroom and knowledge of themselves and others as cultural beings and transforms them as educators, learners, and people" (Walter, Green, Wang, & Walters, 2011, pp. 37-38).

Along with the cultural skills gained, short-term abroad teaching experiences have been shown to enhance a student's confidence, maturity, interpersonal skills, adaptability, and problem-solving skills (Armstrong, 2008; Doppen & An, 2014; Quezada, 2004). Further, Prather-Jones (2017) found that international short-term field experiences benefit pre-service teachers in the areas of multicultural education, instructional practices, and confidence in abilities as a teacher.

This chapter focuses on pre-trip processes. The literature reviewed in this section supports the concept that preparing students to teach abroad requires a specialized process. Activities associated with preparing to embark on the international field experience assisted the pre-service teachers with understanding the "course learning goals, the cultural context of the international setting, and an orientation to study abroad required by the university" (Miller & Gonzalez, 2016, p. 256). Many study abroad experiences are designed with a reflective component within the curricular objectives. For teachers, this is referred to as being a reflective practitioner (Brookfield, 2017). Cross and Dunn (2016) encouraged experiences to be designed around collaborative and peer reflection to ease pre-service teacher anxiety of utilizing a new skill in an international context.

Communities of Practice

It is vital for faculty to plan well for a student trip abroad. The course syllabus must reflect instructional space, time, assignments, and pedagogy that support the course outcomes in a non-traditional setting. Requisite pre-departure logistics include in-country considerations of housing, food, transportation, translation, safety, and communication. However, what makes these trips unique or even original is the goal for the members, faculty, and students to be more than a group that performs activities together. The goal is for these individuals to become a community, not bound by coursework, but interconnected by the practice of teaching and learning. The goal of the Mercer aspired to envelope students, teachers, and principals from developing countries into a community of practice. This is one reason that the trips to Liberia and Nepal have become repeat destinations. It is the practice through service-learning that provides for long-term relationships, community impact, and personal transformation.

Wenger (1998) explained that the components necessary in a community of practice include a domain, community, and practice. The domain is comprised of the people in the group who share the same interest whereas the community consists of those people who are a part of the domain with the shared interest and when they come together they interact and learn from each other. Practice is when the participants of the group come together to discuss ways of solving problems. Barab and Duffy (2012) found it beneficial to relate the meaning of community "as a persistent, sustained social network of individuals who share and develop an overlapping knowledge base, set of beliefs, values, and experiences focused on a common practice and/or mutual enterprises" (p. 41). Therefore, Mercer on Mission (MoM) purposefully does not exploit communities in need to meet their service-learning outcome goals. Instead, MoM develops extended relationships that are persistent and engaging for both sides of the experience. As you will read later in the chapter, students from previous years continue to practice with subsequent pre-service student groups. Faculty members remain involved from year to year, and those in-country individuals collaborate annually to grow the collaborative community. The motivation and purpose to belong to the MoM communities have served as important attributes in a community of practice.

Communities of practice are groups of people bound together by a common purpose and in internal motivation. The central feature of a community of practice is "the relationship that develops between the members; it is here that the key to understanding the softer aspects of knowledge is to be found" (Kimble & Hildreth, 2005, p. 103).

Relationships will form while serving in a community of practice, and it is within those relationships where knowledge will be cultivated. Fraga-Cañadas (2011) explained that communities of practice are intended for group members to learn from each other. When group members with the shared domain come together with common goals, interaction and the act of learning takes place among the members (Naude & Bezuidenhout, 2015). Barab and Duffy (2012) offered four features that are central to establishing those relationships in a community of practice:

1. Common purpose or overlapping enterprise;
2. Common cultural and historical heritage;
3. Interdependent system;
4. Reproduction cycle.

The pre-service teachers who volunteered to be a part of the MoM program came together and exemplified a common purpose, created a common culture of pre-service teaching, and were interdependent.

The faculty who planned these programs understood that successful fieldwork experiences required students, faculty, and participants to be more than a group. In the text that follows, we will explain each of these features specifically in the context of preparing for the trip. These features were clearly evident throughout the trip and upon returning.

Common Purpose

Mercer on Mission (MoM) has a twofold purpose, which is "to provide a transformative experience for Mercer students through focused learning and meaningful service and to make an important and lasting difference for people living in the Majority World" (http://religiouslife.mercer.edu/mercer-on-mission/). The pre-service teachers understood the overarching purpose of MoM when applying for the opportunity. However, the educational coursework included additional requirements that were defined at the onset of the program. Three elements of the MoM program were to observe, teach, and serve. The pre-service teachers embraced and employed these elements. During the class meetings prior to embarking on our international journey, we discussed at length what and whom we would observe, whom and how we would teach, and what our service would consist of in the foreign country. Iyer and Reese (2013) explained that, "a community of practice depends on communal meaning-making that assists in identification and belonging for newcomers, while it reaffirms participation and practice for experts" (p. 28). Through ongoing conversations in our community, we were able to discuss our purposes at length. Because the MoM participants shared a common purpose, all members within this unique community of practice contributed to the meaning-making of the program.

Common Culture

The contextual purpose of the Mercer on Mission (MoM) program was to establish a common culture for pre-service teachers while teaching and learning in an international setting. Barab and Duffy's (2012) definition of common culture pertains to participants in the community of practice having "shared goals, meaning, and practice" (p. 41). The pre-service teachers shared the goal of studying and serving abroad. Each pre-service teacher found personal meaning as well as shared a common meaning of what the experience would contribute to themselves and to the group. Participants also understood that each member of the group could possibly contribute different practices, which derived from their personal experiences. When the pre-service teachers came together to discuss the overarching premise of the MoM program, the participants quickly discovered the program was something larger than themselves. As a result of meetings and meaningful discussions about the MoM program, the participants developed deep interconnections within their communities. Although the participants were from different economic and cultural backgrounds, they found common interests in teaching and learning with young children. These interests also helped establish a foundation for communication and relationship building.

The professors of the MoM program maximized opportunities to develop relationships by conducting face-to-face meetings and facilitating digital communication among participants. Cousin and Deepwell (2005) explained how "there has to be time for a group to develop a shared repertoire" (p. 65).

Interdependence System

For communities of practice to develop properly, internal leadership is necessary (Wenger, 1998). The university professors served in this capacity for each program. The role of the faculty members with these pre-service teachers was to support their "navigation of ambiguity and complexity of the experience" (Butin, 2010, p. 5). The roles of the facilitators were significant to the success and preservation of the community of practice. Although the roles of the facilitators within the community of practice were important, the interactions and interdependence among the group members were critical factors that promoted knowledge building. Lathlean and Le May (2002) found that group members tend to look to the facilitator of the group to take the lead of the community of practice. However, it is important that the participants in a group recognize their facilitator as a guide rather than a dictator.

The Mercer on Mission (MoM) group was a complex community that originated around credit hours needed for graduation and related assignments required to complete the courses. A strong community of practice gradually developed as the leadership and faculty created tasks, activities, and conversations as the pre-service teachers prepared to surpass the required responsibilities and engagement beyond the coursework. We came together within our community and focused on a common purpose, which was the MoM program and the upcoming international experience. Our common purpose of coming together as the MoM group was to develop an overall understanding of our upcoming program, which would take us to a developing country where we would observe, teach, and participate in service-learning opportunities. Providing pictures, discussions, ice-breaking sessions, as well as welcoming invited guests to speak to the group allowed the MoM group to unite with the shared goal of understanding the upcoming MoM experience.

Throughout our meetings, each group purposely focused on developing our identity of the MoM group "by building, acknowledging, and sharing collective competencies of members of the communities of practice" (De Waal & Khumisi, 2016, p. 70). Conversations took place regarding multiple topics that would ensure a successful MoM program. Some of those conversations that took place covered topics such as the geography of the country, the culture of the country, what to pack prepare for the experience, which specific grade-levels pre-service teachers would work with while in-country, and the content and focus for the lessons to be taught while in-country. Through conversations, the participants could ask questions to gain clarity, offer insight into specific topics, and share information that could hopefully add to or begin building the necessary knowledge needed for the international experience.

It is worth noting the diversity of the pre-service teachers within each MoM program. Different genders, races, socioeconomic status, and personal ideals and beliefs were among some of the vastly different characteristics of the members. However, what made these groups form a community of practice were their shared interests and learning experiences among all the pre-service teachers (Wenger, 1998). Handley, Sturdy, Fincham, and Clark (2006) argued that the "capacity of individuals to compartmentalize their identities and behaviors according to the community they were currently 'in' might be difficult to achieve, especially given a desire to maintain a coherent sense of self" (p. 650). Although the diversity among the pre-service teachers who were a part of the communities of practice for MoM was evident, the noted diversity added richness to the perspectives represented in each group. Iyer and Reece (2013) found that "communities of practice are possible when there is recognition of difference, respect for difference, and acceptance of diversity" (p. 37). Having the diversity in our community of practice added deep value to the overall experience.

More insight into our experiences is provided in the next section, where we will describe both the Liberia and Nepal MoM trips, including the purpose, coursework, and student quotes that exemplify their experiences and the program's impact on their identity as teachers.

Reproductive Cycle

The reproductive cycle refers to the opportunity for participants of a community of practice to complete the experience more than one time. Each year, pre-service teachers are recruited for the Mercer on Mission (MoM) program, thus not allowing for a reproductive cycle as Barab and Duffy (2012) suggest. Annually, we welcomed "new comers" but did not have the opportunity for "old timers" to share (Barab & Duffy, 2012). Although our community of practice within MoM program did not allow for a reproductive cycle, we cultivated a strong community of practice during each program.

Description of Mercer on Mission (MoM)

The trip was one of the most fulfilling experiences of my life so far, not only personally, but it caused me to change my entire outlook on education. (Marisha, 2016)

The Mercer on Mission academic goals are to address academics and service. The purpose is to serve others and to gain a global perspective. These goals and purposes are present in the MoM experiences. Pre-service teachers develop their views of service with respect as they enter schools that have 30 or more students in them, no air-conditioning, chalk, or books. MoM students gain respect for the school's educators who teach in spite of the lack of resources. The school's teachers and principals serve MoM students while they model and teach together for the good of their students.

The relevance of the education courses for which pre-service teachers are receiving credit and doing additional reflective assignments is perfectly aligned. For example, MoM students experience an authentic cultural diversity course that would be very different if taken on campus among their peers. Culture and respect are illuminated in real and striking ways through exposure to the realities of poverty, language barriers, challenging living conditions, travel challenges, etc. Although the goal is to stretch the MoM students' perceptions of themselves and teaching, that stretching can be ungraceful and painful. However, when scaffolded well, it can be life changing.

We describe the service-learning experiences of pre-service teachers who spent five weeks in Liberia, three and a half weeks in South Africa to fulfill their fieldwork hours for their professional practicum experience, and three and a half weeks in Belize where the students could observe, teach, serve, and learn in the field. We have included lengthy portions of narratives from four pre-service teachers and single quotes from many other pre-service teachers involved in the programs to provide a glimpse into how this unique fieldwork experience added to their understanding of children, teaching, and development of their identity as teachers. It is here, in the heart of this chapter, where the transformation of the students' personal impact and shifting views of themselves as teachers are revealed, as illustrated in the following narrative:

The professors helped us see both a big picture perspective of a foreign education system and also get a pragmatic grounded experience of teaching a group of young people in radically different conditions

Table 1. Mission destinations and settings, university-participant demographics, and university courses

Destination	Liberia, Africa 2011	Mitchell's Plain, South Africa 2015	El Progresso, Belize in Central America 2016
Setting	P-12 Preparatory School, Ricks Institute	P-8 Public School, Caravelle Primary School and Yellowood Primary	P-8 Public School, El Progresso Government School
Participants	9 Graduate Pre-service teachers 2 mentor teachers 2 faculty	5 Graduate Pre-service teachers 11 Undergraduate Pre-service 2 faculty	4 Graduate Pre-service teachers 4 Undergraduate Pre-service teachers 2 faculty
University Courses	Graduate courses: EDUC 618 Issues of Diversity: Language, Cognition and Culture EDUC 625 Culturally and Educationally Responsive Pedagogy EDUC 611: Practicum	Undergraduate courses: EDUC 485 Professional Practicum EDUC 403 Connecting the Home, School, and Community Graduate courses: EDUC 608 Professional Practicum EDUC 618 Issues of Diversity: Language, Cognition and Culture EDUC 625 Culturally and Educationally Responsive Pedagogy	Undergraduate courses: EDUC 390 Special Topics - Culturally Responsive Pedagogy EDUC 403 Connecting the Home, School, and Community Graduate courses: EDUC 618 Issues of Diversity: Language, Cognition, and Culture EDUC 625 Culturally and Educationally Responsive Pedagogy EDUC 699 Special Topics - Development and Culture of Nepal

than our childhoods. Applying both visions to my experience here at home, I can be a transformational teacher and colleague. (Jack, 2016)

The Mercer on Mission (MoM) program at Mercer University are optional summer programs that offer students six credits toward either their bachelor's or master's degree for initial teacher certification. This service -learning program is offered to both bachelor's and master's students. Those students who are a part of the bachelor's degree program take a course in connecting the home, school, and community and a course in which students concentrate on immersion in the classroom before beginning their student teaching experience. Those students who are a part of the master's degree program are required to take a course in culture and diversity as well as a course focusing on immersion in the field before beginning their student teaching experience. The students have class sessions before leaving and while they are in-country. The students also complete specified assignments upon returning from the international program.

The cost of the trip is paid for by Mercer University. Students are only responsible to pay for the credit hours and their own personal spending needs. This is a unique aspect of study abroad and service-learning programs. It does however show the commitment to the program at the university level. The financial support from the university also allows a broader spectrum of students to participate because socio-economics is not a factor. We believe that because of Mercer's urban and multicultural setting, the financial arrangements attract diverse students' participation, as mentioned previously.

Each of the MoM trips is designed and organized by two Tift faculty members. Students who were in the teacher education program may apply for each trip. Students were interviewed to better determine their interest in the program, disposition, and motivation to teach and serve abroad. Student transcript GPAs were reviewed, which needed to be at or above a 3.0 for both undergraduate and graduate. Students were considered for the trip if the courses were required for their program of study. Students who did not need the courses toward graduation were not chosen. Once students were accepted to go on the trip, the training sessions, readings, and preparation activities began. It is important to mention that some students who were originally accepted to participate were asked to leave prior to leaving the country.

Liberia, Africa 2011

The academic courses students registered for the Liberia trip were all at the Master's degree level. This project focused on the elementary students at Ricks Institute, located 16 miles east of Monrovia in the Sub-Saharan Republic of Liberia in Western Africa. Ricks was once the premier private K-12 school in the country but was virtually destroyed during the nation's civil war from 1989 to 2003. The school continues to rebuild and currently has more than 650 students enrolled in kindergarten through high school. Students were assigned to K – 5 classrooms to plan and teach with Ricks' teachers. Graduate students mentored Ricks' faculty and initial certification students. All Mercer students participated in bi-weekly seminars and school facility-related service projects during the weeks of their visit, such as painting the school.

Mitchell's Plain, South Africa 2015

The South Africa trip included both undergraduates and graduates all working towards their initial teaching certification. The project in South Africa was focused on the elementary and middle school students at Caravelle Primary School located in Mitchell's Plain South Africa, which is about 17 miles southeast of Cape Town. Caravelle Primary hosts almost 700 students from Grade R (kindergarten) to eighth grade. The pre-service candidates also were involved in weekly service at Yellowood Primary, also located in Mitchell's Plain. Through a partnership with the Cape Experiential Learning and Development Agency (CELDA), the students worked with the CELDA staff to assist with the mission of transformation efforts.

Pre-service teachers were assigned to Grade R (kindergarten) – 8th grade classrooms to observe, plan, and teach lessons while they worked alongside the classroom teacher. Daily conversations took place between the cooperating teacher and the Mercer students concerning what was observed. The cooperating teacher and the Mercer students were expected to plan together and offer feedback to each other after lessons were taught. While in attendance, Mercer students participated in all events being held during the visit. For example, Mercer students assisted the facilitators of the after-school program each week at Yellowood Primary, also located in Mitchells Plain, South Africa. Programs consisted of art, drama, karate, dance, reading, gardening, and sports such as soccer.

El Progresso, Belize 2016

This project focused on teaching school aged students in the village of El Progresso, also known as Seven Mile Village, which is about 70 miles southwest of Belize City and located in the Cayo District in the Caribbean country of Belize. The Cayo District is an agricultural region located in the interior of the country. Through a partnership with Toucan Education Programs, MoM students were assigned to classrooms to plan and teach with Belizean teachers of the El Progresso Government School, which hosts over 130 students in grades Infant I (kindergarten) through Standard VI (8th grade).

All MoM students participated in school facility-related service projects, depending on the needs at the school in El Progresso. All selected service projects gave MoM students and El Progresso faculty, staff, and students a chance to work together. The eighth-grade students were invited to participate in a half-day seminar conducted by MoM's pre-service teachers where specific topics such as time management and study skills were discussed. Additionally, MoM students embraced multiple opportunities to present to various educators. These experiences included teaching a half-day professional development seminar for teachers of El Progresso Government School, presenting researched based best practices to the teachers, and delivering professional development to faculty of the Belize Elementary School in Belize City. Mercer's pre-service teachers also had the opportunity to provide support to staff and members of the sister Cecelia Home for the Elderly in Belize City.

Preparing to Go Abroad

The success of any trip is in the planning and preparation. Our goal was to build a community, but one with purpose, as defined within the context of communities of practice: "[G]roups of people who share a concern, a set of problems, or a passion about a topic and who deepen their knowledge and expertise in this area by interacting on an ongoing basis" (Wenger, McDermott, & Snyder, 2002, p. 4). Although the word 'or' is used to differentiate what happens when the group of people gathers, the word 'and' could be used to include all the noted components of problems, passions, knowledge, and expertise. Students in the programs shared a common concern regarding the upcoming study abroad teaching and learning experience. All students shared a passion for being a part of the experience and wanting to deepen their knowledge and expertise of teaching.

Preparing for Liberia

For the Liberia trip, students had the advantage that the faculty had taken previous students to Liberia for similar trips. Students met for class prior to leaving with a theology professor involved at Ricks Institute, who had assigned students to read Stephen Ellis' seminal work on the Liberian civil war, The Mask of Anarchy.

A Saturday seminar was designed that brought together pre-service teachers preparing for the 2011 trip with veteran students from the 2009 trip, who facilitated a photo activity. To facilitate the learning experience, faculty printed 1,500 pictures from the 2009 trip. The photos were randomly divided among five groups, each of which included a 2009 student as the narrator and two students who were preparing for the 2011 trip. Together they spent a few hours going through the photos. They categorized them any way they wanted, such as by plane flights, housing, meeting government officials, the school, the teachers, housing, food, cooking, toilets, laundry, and a lot of exhaustion.

The goal of the activity was for the 2011 students to ask questions to relieve their anxiety about safety, living conditions, and most of all teaching the beautiful children. Two narratives from student experiences are provided next. The first is Hannah, a 2009 narrator, practicing teacher, and a mentor teacher for the 2011 trip. The second is Catie, who was a 2011 participant.

Hannah's Narrator and Mentor Teacher Narrative

When I received an email asking me to meet 2011 participants, I instantly said yes. I would do anything to help another student prepare for the trip. It is important to know what to bring, what to do when you get there, and how to tell your family you will make it back in one piece! There were stacks of photos on each table and I quickly could think of nothing but getting my hands and eyes on each picture! It took only a few minutes for me to settle down and begin sharing about photos and just as quickly the questions began.

The women in my group wanted to know who the people were and what their jobs were. They immediately recognized that teachers dressed nicely for work and that prompted questions about their own wardrobe. I told them about my outfits from bras to shoes. I reminded them that washing clothes by hand means they also dry by afternoon air. Clothes that are light keep you cool in the heat and dry faster in the humid weather.

The stories from the photos were real. They all needed to answer the questions they had in order to focus on teaching and learning. I left the seminar knowing that my stories and experiences at the Ricks Institute in Liberia helped a few others prepare for their journey. I hoped their doubts and fears were reduced as they immersed themselves in the good stories about our trip in 2009.

Catie's Pre-Service Teacher Narrative

When I was selected to be a part of the Mercer on Mission experience in Liberia, I was ecstatic; scared beyond belief, but ecstatic. Having heard of the work being done at Ricks Institute for years through my church, I was excited to see first-hand this place, and not only see it, but contribute something to it and put to practice some of the pedagogical lessons I had learned in my MAT program.

I am a highly anxious person by nature. I have a huge passion for travel and novel situations, but I also have a potentially crippling fear of the unknown. So, after the initial shine of being selected began to wane, I really started to worry in earnest about what I had gotten myself into.

After being selected for the trip, one of our first experiences as a group was this on-campus meet-and-greet orientation activity. We were introduced to the faculty, formally, who were to travel with us, as well as a couple of other faculty members with vested interest in the program. Dr. Swanson then took over the meeting, telling us we were going to take part in a more hands-on orientation activity than just being told about the trip. We were introduced to the "oh-niner" at each of our tables, and told that this person would be our guide. We were then told of the 1,500+ photos taken from a prior trip, and told we were going to use these photos and were encouraged throughout to ask questions about Ricks, Liberia, Africa, travel, teaching, and whatever else came to mind.

My group's leader, and apparently all of the '09ers, had not seen these pictures, and they brought back vivid memories. We heard about the meals we were to eat and the tremendous friendliness of Liberians. We saw the "grey house" and learned of bucket bathing and hand laundering. We wondered at drawing pictures on eggshells and grew excited at cultural differences.

We asked questions, and began the bonding process as a group who would eventually share VERY close quarters, stress levels, and experiences. I was not consciously aware of my more basic worries being quelled, but I can now see that this experience began the process of changing my worries from safety and basic need concerns to those of the work we were to do for and with the Ricks Institute—teaching, learning, and creating relationships with those a literal and figurative world away from our own experience.

The goal of the photo narrative experience was to give students an experience rather than primarily providing them with information. All these photos could have been put into a PowerPoint and explained by the faculty. But the first-hand story-telling from the previous participants brought them to life and provided the opportunity for students to ask questions they may not be comfortable asking in a group setting. The anxiety of the unknown was replaced by the excitement of possibility for the 2011 participants.

Preparing for Nepal, No! Wait, We Are Going to South Africa

Plans started for the Mercer on Mission program to Nepal in the early spring of 2014. The program was approved in the summer of 2014 and student recruiting began soon after. At the end of 2014, our group was formed and we started planning as a group for our international experience. For the students to share their thoughts regarding their concerns, stating their problems, or relaying their passions, the students came together through face to face interactions, phone conversations, and email to deepen their understanding of the expectations of the program. The purpose was to relieve some anxiety and create realistic expectations for the experience.

Our group was able to meet face-to-face a few times before our departure. During this time, we provided the group with opportunities to get to know each other by facilitating ice-breakers and allowing the group to share their reason for taking on this learning experience. We also took this face-to-face time to discuss the culture of Nepal and answered questions that related to our upcoming experience.

In late April 2015, Nepal was hit by a catastrophic earthquake. The morning we received word of the devastating incident, emails and calls were made for our group of 18. Thoughts and prayers were being sent to our new family whom the students had never met. Immediately following the earthquake, travel advisories were posted by the United States' State Department, and our University halted our program - for good reason as safety is and should always be of the utmost importance. However, we had a group of 16 students who needed two classes during this summer session to graduate on time.

We quickly started planning for a different international destination, with less than three weeks until our plane left for somewhere. During this time of uncertainty, we rallied together as a group for our final face-to-face meeting before leaving for our unknown destination. Although many questions could not be answered during our final meeting before leaving, we still came together as one group and discussed how we were going to observe, teach, and serve the students we would soon visit. After a week of calling and emailing contacts all over the world, we landed in Cape Town, South Africa.

Frances' and Jack's narratives provide their perception of the preparation process. Frances was a participant in the 2015 program to South Africa. was a participant in the 2016 program to Belize. Both students were graduate level students who were in the initial teacher certification program.

Frances' Narrative

There was no calling my mother to alleviate my anxieties. No dad. No brother or sister. There was no one I could really talk to about how I felt inside about leaving my family - the risk I was taking because of the pull I felt to do something greater than myself. There wasn't anyone for me because in my family, I was that person. With being a senior-aged person being selected to go on this wonderful trip to Nepal, I definitely felt the honor and also the responsibility not only to my own family to return in one piece, but also to the younger members of the mission group to be somewhat of a mentor and to the new students I would soon be assisting in their education. Even though I didn't have a family member to talk to, I soon realized that my family would increase in the way of team leaders Dr. Michelle Vaughn and [other participating faculty member].

Drs. Vaughn and [other participating faculty member] were impeccable in their preparation of us for the trip to Nepal. There were several prep meetings, with tons of information being disseminated, at which they encouraged us all to ask any and all questions – no matter how small they may seem. For those questions they knew answers to, the information was quickly given. What I admired the most was their candor and forthrightness when they didn't have the answers and their willingness to go to whatever lengths to find the information.

That kind of honesty went a long way with me in that it said they held us all in great regard. Besides the meetings, there were LOTS of emails, which I appreciated, because I would rather know than not know. There was never a time when I wondered what was going on. With information being so close at hand, the trip across the world seemed manageable and one that I would not only enjoy but would come back having been of true service.

Prior to departing, days and nights were filled with getting ready for Nepal. Then the unbelievable happened with one of the biggest earthquakes in recent history happening in the same region that we would have been traveling. I remember it being very early in the morning that I heard the news, and my heart went out to the Nepalese people. However, I instantly wondered what would happen to our trip – would we now become rescue missionaries. I sent a quick email to Drs. Vaughn and [other participating faculty member]. Even though it was early, I received a quick reply saying that no news was known yet, but as soon as they could get news they would let the team know.

Both were true to their word and the days that followed were filled with every tidbit they acquired. Soon, meetings were held and we discussed the possibilities and all talked honestly about our anxieties. None of us, though, were willing to let go of going to Nepal. When it became understood that we would not be going to Nepal, we were all worried about the Nepalese but were ready to transition to whatever country we were being sent. The way that Drs. Vaughn and [other participating faculty member] led us through the transition was the only way that we could stay focused. They both stayed steadfast in charge, never wavering that all would work out. Their passionate encouragement was the glue that we needed, and my encouragement to step up in whatever role that was needed of me.

The trip to South Africa went off without a hitch. It felt as if we were always going there. The meetings segued into the same prep meetings as were held for Nepal, the same flurry of knowledge-filled emails and the same impeccably honest and capable leadership from the professors. Between the many meetings, emails, and capable leadership, we were ready to go, and at the end of it – we were the total success we had all hoped to be, because of our very capable professors. Personally, I gained so much from this trip – a sense of new direction, purpose, and fulfillment. Most of all, a new sister, Dr. Vaughn.

A level of anxiety that was evident among the MoM pre-service teachers was apparent when the focus of our preparation was changed due to unforeseen circumstances. Through constant communication among all members of the group, we could grow as a community. Having the same purpose among all members, allowed us to stay focused and not deviate from our initial promise, which was to serve others.

Nepal, No! Wait, We Are Going to Belize

After a successful international experience in South Africa, we started planning for Nepal again. Our recruiting efforts started during the fall semester of 2015. As of early December, our group was formed and we were making plans as a group of how we were going to observe, teach, and serve in Nepal. The excitement was apparent, and communication among our group regarding our learning experience started brewing. While our group was discussing our excitement, Nepal was ratifying their new constitution. This newly ratified constitution was not welcomed by India.

The country of Nepal is landlocked with China to the north and India to the south, with much of Nepal's trade coming from India. India had unofficially blockaded trade coming into Nepal, which made petroleum, medical supplies, produce, etc., scarce. After receiving word of the blockade, a member of our Board of Trustees recommended we halted our planning for Nepal in favor of a different destination. January found us relaying our news to our group and again, attempting to find another international learning experience for our students. After weeks of searching, we decided to embark on the Central American country of Belize. There we would observe, teach, and serve at a remote interior village with no electricity.

Jack's narrative provides a personal recollection of the process we encountered when planning for another successful MoM program.

Jack's Narrative

I began to orient my understanding about Nepal's geography, its language and cultural groups, and its political history (including its current tensions with India). Then we heard in December that we couldn't go to Nepal any longer. Though saddened that I wouldn't get to leave the hemisphere, I understand that placing us in a region where regular 6.0 temblors still shake the un-reinforced structures also meant placing us in harm's way.

I don't exactly remember how I discovered that my math pedagogy classmate Leslie had also applied and been accepted to Mercer on Mission, but sometime in February, she said something in class that sounded like she was thinking internationally. I asked her if she had heard of Mercer on Mission. Her eyes widened as she said that she was going to Belize in the summer. Then my eyes widened. How serendipitous to already know someone in my cohort.

As our first face to face meeting approached, Dr. Vaughn and [other participating faculty member] sent occasional emails about logistics. It was clear they were thinking of us and that they were in regular communication with the CEO of the organization we had teamed with for our experience in Belize. In each email, Dr. Vaughn let us know how excited she was, and that in turned piqued my anticipation and excitement. I usually don't get excited about the trip until I'm on the plane, but I felt myself swell with the thought of serving and being immersed in an international community.

The entire team met a few times at our centrally located campus. My first impression would have been that it was a young group, except that my actual first impression was that as the only male on the team, I was already an outsider, even while being acquainted with two of the teammates from previous classes. During my phone interview, Dr. Vaughn and [other participating faculty member] had mentioned that if accepted, I would be the only male on the team. I said that I was comfortable in that environment, having been raised with two elder sisters and three aunts. I also said that as a feminist, I respect and support women's autonomy and space. But seeing our entire team in person, for the first time, gave me the visceral feeling that I needed to be ready for the isolation that I would face every night as we retired to our quarters. I wondered if Dr. Vaughn and [other participating faculty member] anticipated this; they regularly roped me into group conversation and checked-in with me during the un-programmed time. I think maybe they're just the type of people to be the glue of a community.

The best of several team-building exercises was when in one of the exercises, the [faculty member] emptied a bag of a variety of candy onto a table and we picked the one we liked. We then grouped ourselves with others who picked the same candy and then read out loud, a sheet of paper with a script delineating the attributes of people in our group corresponding to a specific piece of candy chosen. I'm pretty sure this wasn't social-research based, but I liked that it got all us to think about different strengths and sensibilities amongst our teammates. Undoubtedly, in a trip lasting 24 days, there would be personality clashes, stylistic differences, and personal misunderstandings that could unravel a group. Starting with an appreciation of everyone's unique strengths helps minimize those tensions.

The most helpful to me, regarding logistics, were the Skype calls with the CEO of the organization we teamed with while in Belize and with [a professor with expertise in Belize] an assistant professor [at a neighboring university] who had spending extensive time facilitating faculty-led student groups in Belize and conducting research.

The CEO walked us through the proposed schedule day-by-day. Having that a more-resolved schedule gave me an anchor for my imagination and expectations. The CEO described our accommodations throughout the schedule run-down. We would be staying in reputable locations with amenities that, to me, approximated 1st-world accommodations. That was also a relief, yet I remained skeptical. I did feel exceptionally secure knowing that we had professionals working to make our trip as seamless and successful as possible. Just one example: because of the spread of Zika to the Americas, our professors, and the CEO made sure through repetition and through multiple emails that we understood that we must do our utmost to mitigate against mosquito bites. While I knew to be prepared for malaria or dengue, it didn't even occur to me to check for Zika activity.

[The professor's] Skype conversation with us gave us an even better picture of life in Belize. She briefly described the major cultural groups and their origins. She also gave an overview of the development and history of the education system. Her tips on pedagogy aides were invaluable: I borrowed her suggestion of using a sheet-protector (with a piece of paper or card stock within) as a makeshift personal whiteboard. Because of the hour-long interaction with Dr. Casey, we were consistently better-informed than our Belizean guides and presenters recognized.

By the time we arrived in Belize, I was over-packed, confident that our team would gel, and assured that we were in good hands. We were ready to hit the ground running, or rolling, in a group van, traversing across the Belizean country to the edge of the Maya Mountains and the Central American jungle.

Jack's preparation and experience provided the necessary scaffolding for him to feel successful regarding his personal and professional growth.

Common Threads Among Participants

Several threads were prominent in the four student narratives. The first is the development of a common language among the community. The second was the acknowledgement and active pursuit to dispel anxiety. The third was the connection that students made with one another and the faculty for each trip.

The common language for all four narratives is that, as students, they experienced tensions that can and should exist in a vibrant and well-planned community of practice. All students were approaching the unknown of venturing outside of their country in a study abroad experience. The pre-service teachers had not previously traveled to the destinations; therefore, there was a consistent desire among the participants to know more about the country they would be visiting.

One tension was the anxiety of the unknown in play with the desire to accomplish the common purpose. The purpose of looking at photos with a guide was to help students see second-hand and hear first hand the stories and challenges of the trip ahead.

Another tension was the writhe between acting as an individual and working as an interdependent group. These are both evidence of the participation in a community of practice. It is not only the creation by faculty of the community but also the negotiation of how each member will be accepted and participate within the group.

It is also important to mention that because this chapter only focuses on preparing a community to travel abroad to serve and teach, features of the community of practice were not addressed in full. Interdependence of the system was limited, and although it was established, evidence is not presented as to what form it took once students were in-country or had returned. Reproductive cycle is also not discussed because these three trips, while repetitive over the years demonstrate a reproductive cycle, the preparations discussion is limited to each individual trip rather than the one MoM study abroad across multiple years.

ISSUES, CONTROVERSIES, PROBLEMS

One issue within teacher education programs that are designed to develop global perspectives of pre-service teachers is that they often include traveling abroad.

Some teacher education programs provide students with opportunities to complete student-teaching assignments abroad. These programs can place students under financial burdens associated with traveling because many students lack the finances and time for lengthy experiences abroad. However, we contend that even a briefer summer experience abroad that is focused on teaching and learning at the field-work level is effective to challenge students' assumptions about cultures other than their own.

In terms of preparing students to go abroad and teach rather than just travel, faculty must provide specific boundaries, expectations, delineate assumptions, and support for how to belong to a community of practice so they can function as a group.

SOLUTIONS AND RECOMMENDATIONS FOR PREPARING PRE-SERVICE TEACHERS FOR STUDY ABROAD EXPERIENCES

As we prepared our students for the study abroad experience, we learned lessons that could improve upcoming programs. First and foremost, we understood that a community was needed among the pre-service teachers. We facilitated time where the group came together as a community so they could have conversations pertaining to pertinent information regarding the MoM program. During these conversations, the pre-service teachers voiced their concerns, anxieties, excitements, as well as other feelings they were having. Once this environment was established, the students started to build trust with one another, which in turn, assisted in creating the needed community.

Another important piece of preparing pre-service teachers was communication. Each program was very different in location however many of the expectations of the program were the same. It was a necessity to relay the needed communication to the members of the groups. Our way of communicating pertinent information came through face-to-face meetings where we disseminated information regarding the expectations of the program, the culture of the destinations, and travel information. We also corresponded through emails and phone calls. Blanketed emails pertaining to travel itineraries and in-country schedules served to disseminate information needed quickly and effectively to group members. Skype conversations with in-country personnel and experts in the field also served to promulgate information that the pre-service teachers would need while immersed in the international setting.

When changes beyond our control took place, we found it beneficial to keep the student's informed of all changes. As we received our new places of destination, we circulated the information quickly and precisely to diminish some of the anxiety felt by the pre-service teachers.

FUTURE RESEARCH DIRECTIONS

Service-learning experiences in places such as Liberia, South Africa, and Belize allow pre-service teachers to be immersed in cultures different from their own. As the populations of US classrooms become more and more diverse, study abroad experiences can assist pre-service teachers in becoming more culturally aware. In order to prepare the pre-service teachers' responsiveness to the cultural differences, additional research addressing the following questions would benefit facilitators of such study abroad programs:

- What cultural knowledge is known of the place that will be visited?
- What internal biases will need to be dealt with in order to be culturally responsive in the place that will be visited?

CONCLUSION

In terms of skills transferable to teaching, Parker, Webb, and Wilson (2017) explained the benefits of preparing pre-service candidates regarding "curriculum, instructional approaches, and general school norms that may differ from those typical of US schools" (p. 118).

Although this chapter emphasized issues relating mostly to pre-trip aspects of going to a developing country to learn, to teach, and to serve, the reflective narratives suggest that those preparations provided a solid foundation for "doing the work" upon arrival in Liberia, South Africa, and Belize. Noddings (2001) asserted that academic achievement cannot be attained with success unless students learn to care about others and believe that others care about them. Mercer on Mission (MoM) asserts the same depth of impact for those served and those serving.

The four features of a community of practice identified by Barab and Duffy (2012) were initiated in the pre-trip orientation and the purposeful transition from a group of students to a learning community. Students found confidence in their leaders and embraced the opportunity to teach in challenging, unfamiliar circumstances, and they eagerly embraced that challenge.

As faculty, we have learned the necessity to personalize pre-trip orientations and to explicitly create experiences to develop a community of practice. We have learned not only to focus on the destination, preparations, and goals, but also to focus on the student's anxiety and the goal to stretch their visions of teaching, working with others, and themselves in a global context.

REFERENCES

Armstrong, N. F. (2008). Teacher education in a global society: Facilitating global literacy for preservice candidates through international field experiences. *Teacher Education and Practice*, *21*(4), 490–506.

Barab, S. A., & Duffy, T. (2012). From practice fields to communities of practice. In D. Jonassen & S. Land (Eds.), *Theoretical foundation of learning environments* (pp. 29–69). New York, NY: Routledge.

Bringle, R. G., & Hatcher, J. A. (1995). A service-learning curriculum for faculty. *Michigan Journal of Community Service Learning*, *2*(1), 112–122.

Brookfield, S. (2017). *On becoming a critically reflective teacher*. San Francisco, CA: Jossey-Bass.

Butin, D. W. (2010). *Service-learning in theory and practice. The future of community engagement in higher education*. New York: Palgrave McMillan. doi:10.1057/9780230106154

Cousin, G., & Deepwell, F. (2005). Designs for network learning: A communities of practice perspective. *Studies in Higher Education*, *30*(1), 57–66. doi:10.1080/0307507052000307795

Cross, S. B., & Dunn, A. H. (2016). "I didn't know of a better way to prepare to teach": A case study of paired student teaching abroad. *Teacher Education Quarterly*, *43*(1), 71–90.

Darling-Hammond, L. (2010). *The flat world and education: How American's commitment to equity will determine our future*. New York, NY: Teachers College Press.

De Waal, M., & Khumisi, O. (2016). Supporting communities of practice: A reflection of the benefits and challenges facing communities of practice for research and engagement in nursing. *Gateways: International Journal of Community Research & Engagement*, *9*(1), 58–73. doi:10.5130/ijcre.v9i1.4717

Doppen, F. H., & An, J. (2014). Student teaching abroad: Enhancing global awareness. *International Education*, *43*(2), 59–76.

Fraga-Cañadas, C. P. (2011). Building communities of practice for foreign language teachers. *Modern Language Journal, 95*(2), 296–300. doi:10.1111/j.1540-4781.2011.01183.x

Handley, K., Sturdy, A., Fincham, R., & Clark, R. (2006). Within and beyond communities of practice: Making sense of learning through participation, identity and practice. *Journal of Management Studies, 43*(3), 641–653. doi:10.1111/j.1467-6486.2006.00605.x

Iyer, R., & Reese, M. (2013). Ensuring student success: Establishing a community of practice for culturally and linguistically diverse pre-service teachers. *Australian Journal of Teacher Education, 38*(3), 26–40. doi:10.14221/ajte.2013v38n3.4

Kimble, C., & Hildreth, P. (2005). Dualities, distributed communities of practice and knowledge management. *Journal of Knowledge Management, 9*(4), 102–113. doi:10.1108/13673270510610369

Ladson-Billings, G. (1999). Preparing teachers for diverse student populations: A critical race theory perspective. *Review of Research in Education, 24*, 211–247.

Lathlean, J., & Le May, A. (2002). Communities of practice: An opportunity for interagency working. *Journal of Clinical Nursing, 11*(3), 394–398. doi:10.1046/j.1365-2702.2002.00630.x PMID:12010537

Martines, D. (2005). Teacher perceptions of multicultural issues in school settings. *Qualitative Report, 10*(1), 1–20.

Mercer University. (2017a). *Mission Statement*. Retrieved from http://about.mercer.edu/mission/

Mercer University. (2017b). *Mercer on Mission*. Retrieved 17 March from http://mom.mercer.edu/

Merryfield, M. M., & Wilson, A. (2005). *Social studies and the world: Teaching global perspectives*. San Jose, CA: Cowan Creative.

Mezirow, J. (2000). *Learning as transformation: Critical perspectives on a theory in progress*. San Francisco, CA: Jossey-Bass.

Miller, K. K., & Gonzalez, A. M. (2016). Short-term international internship experiences for future teachers and other child development professionals. *Issues in Educational Research, 26*(2), 241–259.

Naude, L., & Bezuidenhout, H. (2015). Moving on the continuum between teaching and learning: Communities of practice in a student support program. *Teaching in Higher Education, 20*(2), 221–230. doi:10.1080/13562517.2014.978752

Noddings, N. (2001). The caring teacher. In V. Richardson (Ed.), *Handbook of research on teaching* (4th ed.; pp. 99–105). Washington, DC: American Educational Research Association.

Parker, A., Webb, K. E., & Wilson, W. V. (2017). Creating a studying abroad experience for elementary teacher candidates: Considerations, challenges, and impact. In H. An (Ed.), *Handbook for research on efficacy and implementation of study abroad programs for P-12 teachers* (pp. 111–132). Hershey, PA: IGI Global. doi:10.4018/978-1-5225-1057-4.ch007

Prather-Jones, B. (2017). The benefits of short-term international field experiences for teacher candidates. In N. P. Gallavan & L. G. Putney (Eds.), *Teacher education yearbook XXV: Building upon inspirations and aspirations with hope, courage, and strength through teacher educators' commitment to today's' teacher candidates and educator preparation* (pp. 119–134). Lanham, MD: Rowman & Littlefield.

Quezada, R. (2004). Beyond educational tourism: Lessons learned while student teaching abroad. *International Education Journal, 5*(4), 458–465.

Walters, L. M., Green, M. R., Wang, L., & Walters, T. (2011). From heads to hearts: Digital stories as reflection artifacts of teachers' international experience. *Issues in Teacher Education, 20*(2), 37–52.

Wenger, E. (1998). Communities of practice: Learning as a social system. *The Systems Thinker, 9*(5).

Wenger, E., McDermott, R., & Snyder, W. (2002). *Cultivating communities of practice.* Boston, MA: Harvard Business School Press.

Chapter 16

From Teaching Software Engineering Locally and Globally to Devising an Internationalized Computer Science Curriculum

Liguo Yu
Indiana University South Bend, USA

ABSTRACT

Software development is the process to produce an information technology solution to a real-world problem. Teaching and integrating non-technical software engineering skills into the curriculum is considered one of the most challenging tasks in an academic environment. This becomes even more challenging when the curriculum is supposed to be internationalized and applied in different countries because of the cultural difference, policy difference, and business model difference. In this chapter, the authors present their experience of teaching a software engineering course both locally and globally, where two universities of USA and China are chosen for this study. Specifically, they describe how they adjust homework assignments and student performance evaluations to reflect different government policies, different business environment, and different real-world customer requirement. The chapter shows that it is possible to create an internationalized computer science curriculum that contains both common core learning standards and adjustable custom learning standards.

INTRODUCTION

Curriculum internalization is a new trend in education. More and more internationalized curricula are being created. The benefits of globalizing education are enormous. However, risks and challenges also exist. This is especially true for engineering education, such as software engineering education, where knowledge and skills should be adapted to local policies and local business environment.

DOI: 10.4018/978-1-5225-2791-6.ch016

Software engineering is a discipline in computer science. Software engineering education is the process we educate computer science students or information technology students with required knowledge and skills to compete in the software industry. The learning objectives of software engineering not only include technical skills, such as modelling, design, and programming, but also non-technical skills, such as communication skills, management skills, documentation skills, and customer interaction skills (Sedelmaier & Landes, 2014; Kuhrmann et al., 2014; Johns-Boast, 2014). Generally speaking, these non-technical skills are hard to deliver in a traditional lecture-based classroom, where it is not effective in providing hands-on experience for students. Instead, problem-based learning (Hmelo-Silver, 2004; Hung, 2011; Kay et al., 2000) has been used in software engineering education to achieve these learning objectives.

Problem-based learning allows students to learn software engineering knowledge and skills through solving a real-world problem. This is in contrast to the traditional lecture-based learning. Under the problem-based learning environment, although instructors no longer need to spend their majority efforts on lectures nor directly participate in the problem-solving process, they are still the key players. Their main tasks include designing the problems, assisting/coaching students, and evaluating students' performance. The new tasks have raised new challenges for instructors, some of which are listed below:

- How to design an assignment so that it is more similar to a real-world problem?
- How to help students solve a problem so that appropriate assistance should be given to students without suppressing their creativity?
- How to evaluate students' performance if the assigned problem is not solved or not completely solved?

Implementing problem-based learning in an internationalized curriculum could be even challenging. First, real-world problems have their own context; they are closely related to business models, government policies, and cultural environment; some problems considered critical in one country might be irrelevant in another country. Second, we are living in a dynamically changing world; problem-based learning in an internationalized curriculum should be revised frequently to reflect the transforming global reality (Kahn & Agnew, 2015).

In this chapter, I present my experience of applying problem-based learning to teach software engineering in two universities of two different countries, Indiana University South Bend, USA and New York Institute of Technology-Nanjing, China. The business environment differences between the US and China provide valuable insights on how to adjust teaching strategies locally in order to design a potential internationalized curriculum.

The remaining sections of the chapter are organized as follows. I first present the ideas to create an internationalized computer science curriculum. Next, I review the background knowledge. Then, I describe the software engineering classes which are taught both locally and globally. Finally, conclusions are presented.

COMPUTER SCIENCE CURRICULUM INTERNATIONALIZATION

Computer science and software engineering education, like other engineering educations, could be standardized and internationalized. This is mainly because the software development process is already standardized with CMM model and ISO 9000 model. Software organizations around the world are following similar practices to produce quality products. In addition, software products needed by different countries and used in different regions could have similar functional requirements and quality requirements. Therefore, it is possible to apply the computer science curriculum created in one country to another country.

On the other side, software products are used to solve real world problems. It is necessary for software developers to follow specific local business procedures and local business policies. Therefore, computer science curriculum must be adjusted before it can be used in a different country.

Based on my teaching experience, I propose an internationalized computer science curriculum model that is composed of two parts: core standards and custom standards. Core standards should include technical aspects of software development, such as modelling, analysis, design, testing, and maintenance; core standards should also be relatively stable and could be localized with little changes. Custom standards include nontechnical aspects of software development, such as requirement engineering, project management, and customer services; these standards should be adapted to the education institution's local policies and regional culture.

Problem-based learning as a common practice in software engineering education should be categorized into custom standards. The local educators should be able to freely design their own problems and grading rubrics. My experience in applying problem-based learning in two counties with different business environment and government policies shows that it is possible to introduce the problem-based learning method into an internationalized computer science curriculum.

The proposed internationalized computer science curriculum model could incorporate ABET (Accreditation Board for Engineering and Technology) recommendations. ABET is a non-profit organization that accredits high education programs in applied science, computing, and engineering fields. The accredited institutions are mainly in the United States. Some international institutions are also accredited. The ABET course requirement for computer science curriculum is summarized in Table 1.

If we carefully examine Table 2, which shows the computer science curricula of Indiana University South Bend (IUSB) and New York Institute of Technology – Nanjing (NYIT-Nanjing), we can see both

Table 1. ABET computer science curriculum course recommendations (Data source: ABET, n.d.a)

Area	Subject
Computer science major	• Algorithms • Data structures • Software design • Concepts of programming languages • Computer organization and architecture • Exposure to a variety of programming languages and systems • Proficiency in at least one higher-level language • Advanced course work that builds on the fundamental course work to provide depth
Mathematics	• Discrete mathematics • Calculus • Linear algebra • Numerical methods • Probability • Statistics • Number theory, geometry, or symbolic logic
Science	• Scientific method • Laboratory work

Table 2. Comparison of computer science curricula of IUSB and NYIT-Nanjing (Data source: Indiana University South Bend, n.d.; NYiT, 2017)

Subject	IUSB Course Number (Credit)	NYIT-Nanjing Course Number (Credit)
General Education		
English Composition I		FCWR 101 (3)
English Composition II	ENG W 131 (3)	FCWR 151 (3)
Speech	SPCH S121 (3)	FCSP 105 (3)
Critical Thinking	Covered in major CS courses	FCIQ 101 (3)
Computer Literacy	Covered in major CS courses	FCWR 304 (3)
Natural World, Scientific Process, Literature, and Philosophy	4 courses (9)	FCSC 101 (3) ICLT 3XX (3) ICPH 3XX (3)
Behavioral Science, Social Values, Global Issues, and Health	3-4 courses (8)	ICSS 309 (3) ICBS 3XX (3)
Art and Visual Literacy	2 courses (6)	
Information Literacy	COAS Q110 (1)	
Foreign Language	2 courses (6)	
Career Discovery		ETCS 105 (2)
Computer Science Major		
Computer and Society	INFO I202 (3)	ETCS 108 (3)
Computer Programming I	CSCI C101 (4)	CSCI 125 (3)
Computer Programming II	CSCI C201 (4)	CSCI 185 (3)
Linux Operating Systems	CSCI C151 (2)	
Computer Organization	CSCI C335 (4)	CSCI 155 (3)
Discrete Structures	CSCI C250 (3)	CSCI 235 (3)
Data Structures	CSCI C243 (4)	CSCI 260 (3)
Theory of Computation	CSCI B401 (3)	CSCI 312 (3)
Programming Language	CSCI C311 (3)	CSCI 318 (3)
Operating Systems	CSCI C435 (3)	CSCI 330 (3)
Analysis of Algorithm	CSCI C455 (3)	CSCI 335 (3)
Software Engineering	CSCI C308 (4)	CSCI 380 (3)
Senior Project	elective	CSCI 455 (3)
Computer Networks	elective	CSCI 345 (3)
Computer Science Electives	(9)	(12)
Mathematics		
Calculus I	MATH M215 (5)	MATH 170 (4)
Calculus II		MATH 180 (4)
Linear Algebra	MATH M301 (3)	MATH 310 (3)
Probability	MATH M260 (3)	CSCI 270 (3)
Statistics	MATH M261 (2)	
Science		
Physical and Life Science	3-5 courses from Physics, Chemistry, Biology (14)	3 courses from Physics, Chemistry, Biology (11)
Electives		
Mathematics and Science Electives		(6)
General Elective	(7)	(3)
Total	**120 credits**	**120 credits**

of them match well to the ABET course requirement. Specifically, computer science major courses, mathematics courses, and physical and life science courses can be grouped as core courses and general education courses can be grouped as custom courses.

In the United States, undergraduate computer science programs largely follow ABET curriculum recommendations, although only a fraction of programs are ABET accredited. It is worth to note that neither IUSB computer science program nor NYIT-Nanjing computer science program is ABET accredited. However, they are all close to ABET requirements. Appendices A and B list the ABET accredited computer science programs in the United States and other countries, respectively. Currently, about 300 computer science programs worldwide are ABET accredited. I believe more programs are following ABET recommendations, although they are not officially accredited yet, like IUSB and NYIT-Nanjing.

Besides ABET, there are some other organizations trying to create an internationalized computer science curriculum. One of them is IB. The International Baccalaureate (IB) is an educational foundation headquartered in Geneva, Switzerland. It offers some educational programs worldwide. International Baccalaureate Diploma Computer Science Program Curriculum model is described in Table 3.

Compared to ABET recommendations, IB model focuses more on career development. However, what we can really learn here is that more and more computer science educators are realizing the importance of creating a standardized international curriculum.

BACKGROUND

Non-technical skills, such as communication skills, team working skills, and documentation skills are considered essential for engineering graduates, especially software engineering graduates. Because any software engineering project is the work of team effort, communication and documentation are surely needed. However, the traditional lecture-based learning is not effective in delivering software engineering

Table 3. The International Baccalaureate (IB) computer science curriculum model (Data source: International Baccalaureate Organization, 2014)

Category	Coursework
Core syllabus content	Topic 1: System fundamentals Topic 2: Computer organization Topic 3: Networks Topic 4: Computational thinking, problem-solving and programming
Extension	Topic 5: Abstract data structures Topic 6: Resource management Topic 7: Control
Case study	Additional subject content introduced by the annually issued case study
Option (Students study one of the following options)	Option A: Databases Option B: Modelling and simulation Option C: Web science Option D: Object-oriented programming (OOP)
Internal assessment solution	Practical application of skills through the development of a product and associated documentation
Project	Group project

knowledge and skills, especially non-technical skills (Yu, 2014). Students often find the lecture-delivered knowledge is hard to apply and few hands-on skills could be obtained in a traditional classroom.

Because problem-based learning is an essential approach in general engineering education (Brodie, 2009), to overcome the aforementioned challenges, software engineering educators have introduced this approach in their classrooms (Huffman, 2002; dos Santos et al., 2009). For example, Weibelzahl & Lahart (2011a, 2011b) described a web-based resource for students to practice problem-based learning; Richardson & Delaney (2010) described how to help students meet industry expectations through problem-based learning.

Despite the benefits, there are also some limitations regarding problem-based learning (Xu & Liu, 2010). Below, I summarize the challenges facing most software engineering educators when applying problem-based learning:

1. It is important to assign interesting real-world problems to students in order to engage them. Therefore, the instructor should be willing to shift their focus from lecturing to problem design;
2. Problems should be redefined or reexamined every time they are assigned to students, if necessary, to reflect the evolution of information technology and the changing of customer interests;
3. Evaluations of students' performance should be based on the industrial environment. This includes the business environment and the social environment.

The author has taught software engineering in both the US and China, specifically Indiana University South Bend and New York Institute of Technology-Nanjing. Problem-based learning is proved to be an effective approach in delivering software engineering knowledge and skills. Table 4 compares the software engineering classes at IUSB (Indiana University South Bend) and NYIT (New York Institute of Technology)-Nanjing.

From Table 4, it can be seen in general that IUSB and NYIT-Nanjing have similar students body. Furthermore, it is worth noting that NYIT-Nanjing follows the curriculum of NYIT-New York City campus; English is the primary language of instruction and most instructors are from the US. From the viewpoint of teaching software engineering, the main difference between IUSB and NYIT-Nanjing is the business environment students are going to enter, including government policies, user requirements, and application domains.

Table 4. Comparison of software engineering courses offered at IUSB and NYIT-Nanjing

	IUSB	NYIT-Nanjing
Campus location	South Bend, IN, USA	Nanjing, Jiangsu, China
Class size	30 to 40	Around 30
Class level	Junior	Junior
Student population	Full time and part time	Full time
Student K-12 education	Northern Indiana	Sate (Jiangsu) wide
Student job market location	Primarily locally	Nationally

Class Description

When teaching software engineering at IUSB and NYIT-Nanjing, I developed two types of assignments: micro-assignments and team projects, which are mapped to different learning objectives. Table 5 summarizes the learning objectives of micro-assignments and team projects.

In the following of this section, I describe how I adjust assignments and their evaluations to adapt to different business environments in the US and China.

Micro-Assignment 1: Advertisement

- **Problem:** Assume that you are the Chief Executive Officer (CEO) of a regional bank that has about 200 employees. Currently, your bank supports ATM banking, telephone banking, and online banking through the regular web access. Due to the recent advancements of 4G and LTE mobile technology, the bank's board of trustees approved a business plan of implementing mobile banking, which will allow customers to access their accounts through smartphones.

Your task is to hire a new Chief Information Officer (CIO) who will report directly to you and be responsible for setting up a new department for this technical upgrade. The current IT department that is under your supervision will not directly participate in this project, but will provide the basic support.

Please write an advertisement (200-300 words) for this position, which will be published in IT magazines. The advertisement should include descriptions of the position, candidate requirement, application procedure, and so on. Please format your advertisement with borders, colours, background, if you think they are needed, and choose the appropriate font so that the document should appear professional just like a real advertisement in a magazine.

Sample Student Submission (With Permission From the NYIT-Nanjing Student; the Original Submission Is Modified to Have Personal Data Removed)

To carry out our business plan of implementing the wireless banking, we are now looking for a new Chief Information Officer (CIO). This position will be one of the top decision-makers in our bank. If hired, you will need to report to the Chief Executive Officer (CEO) and will be responsible for setting up a new department for our technical upgrade. You should have experience working at large hardware / software companies or other engineering fields. You should be able to deal with the complex contract negotiations, supplier management, and the rapidly growing environmental planning. You need to provide

Table 5. Learning objectives of micro-assignments and team projects

Micro-Assignments	Team Projects
Domain knowledge	Team working skills
Requirement elicitation skills	Interpersonal skills
Customer interaction skills	Management skills
Problem identification skills	Leadership skills
Problem analysis skills	Documentation skills
Business design skills	Communication skills
Presentation skills	Technical design skills

system-related technical and business trainings to your subordinates. The current IT department will not directly participate in this project, but will provide basic support. Having the ability of supervising developers and solving various problems in the operation is vitally important for this position.

Requirements

- More than five years of development experience, more than three years of large-scale system design experience, and more than three years of management experience;
- Proficient in TCP / IP protocol, with concurrent network programming experience;
- Strong analytical and communication skills, strong sense of responsibility and teamwork, good quality awareness, and ability to prepare documents.

We offer a competitive salary, along with performance related year-end bonuses and generous benefits. Should you be interested, please kindly send your up-to-date resume to 11111111@qq.com.

- **Experience:** This assignment was given to both IUSB and NYIT-Nanjing students. Although this is a general problem to solve, there are some differences between the students' solutions. For example, in the US, age should not be listed as a requirement for a job. Otherwise, the company might face the lawsuit of age discrimination. However, this is not a problem in China. Some NYIT-Nanjing students specified the age limit for the applicant, which is a common practice in China. So, when these assignments are graded, the government policy should be considered. Moreover, it is important for the instructor to consider the law differences between the US and China when assessing the assignments. Students should understand that no solutions to a real-world problem can be applied in all business environment.

Micro-Assignment 2: IT Solutions to Reducing the Healthcare Cost

- **Problem:** Reducing the healthcare cost is one of the highest priorities of our nation. It is also an important task of every state, every city, and every community. The advance of information technology might be able to provide means helping solve this problem.

We live in an area with several regional hospitals, dozens of clinics, and about 200K people. Your task is to interview someone living in this area and interested in reducing the healthcare cost. This person could be a doctor, a nurse, an insurance agent, someone who manages or lives in a nursing home, someone who needs the long-term care, or someone who worries about the healthcare cost and is looking for a solution to reducing the cost. Through interviewing your client, you should identify one specific problem that causes the increase of healthcare cost. You should then propose an information technology solution to solving or partially solving this problem.

Please write a 1-2 page report that documents your interview, the identified problem, and your proposed solution. The problem you are going to tackle could be a large problem of the healthcare system or a small problem related to a specific issue or a specific group of people.

Your document should include the following information: objective of the interview, who is the interviewee (the real name can be hidden), time and place the interview is taken, problems identified, and your proposed solution. Please also analyse the cost and the benefits of adopting your solution.

Sample Student Submission (With Permission From the NYIT-Nanjing Student; the Original Submission Is Modified to Have Personal Data Removed)

Due to the increasing of healthcare cost, our government is conducting a massive reform of the medical system, especially after the severe acute respiratory syndrome (SARS) epidemic in 2003. As we all know, the SARS epidemic really brought to light the weakness of the rural healthcare system, which is also known as the cooperative healthcare system. The goal of this reform is to create a healthcare system that is able to cover everyone, and focus on bringing rural and urban systems closer. The important feature of this system is low cost. Each participant just pays 20 RMB per month and is eligible to receive partial coverage of any medical expense, up to 65 percent of the total cost or 30,000 RMB. However, the system is not working quite well. People are still complaining about the healthcare cost.

I interviewed a 25 years old young man working in a state-owned enterprise. According to him, the price of medicines is too high and the healthcare cost does not receive enough attention. It is also a big problem that some doctors do not prescribe effective medicines to patients. The current reform seems like a sound solution, because more and more people can participate in this state-wide insurance system. However, after a detailed calculation, we find that the cost of healthcare increases faster compared to the wage increases in the past years. Consequently, citizens cannot really benefit as much as the government anticipated. Therefore, despite so many legislations have passed on medical reforms, there are still numerous challenges in developing a more successful medical insurance system.

My suggestions to reducing the healthcare cost based on the interview are described below:

- First, we can implement an online drug price comparing system to make the most affordable medicines available to patients. We know this approach cannot solve all the problems, but it can make things better;
- Secondly, diseases are more serious in rural regions. Therefore, we should pay more attention to those undeveloped areas. More effort and budget should be allocated to rural regions. Internet can be used as a channel to educate our rural citizens about health and healthcare. The past unbalanced healthcare policy not only lowered the healthcare quality in rural regions, but also led to higher rates of infectious diseases. Therefore, the government should use the Internet wisely to inform the citizens about all kinds of diseases;
- Last but not least, what the current reform fails to consider is the supervision over the health care sector. For example, the doctors often prescribe too many drugs and treatments, some of which are unnecessary for patients. Instead, these prescriptions are intended to boost the hospital's profit. The government should have a tracking system so that if doctors prescribe unnecessary medicines, tests, or treatments, they should be held accountable.

Based on the above discussions, we can conclude that we are still faced with huge challenges in developing an effective national healthcare and insurance system. We should keep reducing the medical cost, pay more attention to rural areas, and reinforce the supervision system. These efforts together can help more and more citizens obtain affordable healthcare in the future.

- **Experience:** The skyrocketing healthcare cost is a common problem in the US and in China. However, the causes could be different. This assignment was used in both IUSB and NYIT-Nanjing. It requires students to identify and solve a real-world problem. It also requires students to meet with a real-world customer. When this problem was assigned, some students did not know how to identify a problem. To help them, at IUSB the instructor gave an example of a pharmacy that provides discharge services helping hospitals reduce readmissions (Walgreens, 2012); the instructor hinted that we might be able to provide an IT solution to this problem, too. At NYIT-Nanjing, the instructor pointed out that one problem in China's healthcare system is the insurance cost and an insurance quote website could provide consumers more choices of affordable health insurance. In both classes, many different problems were identified. For example, in the US, students focused more on unnecessary medical tests and in China, students identified more problems on drug cost. In both classes, students found this question interesting and engaging.

Micro-Assignment 3: IT Solutions to Community/Food Safety

- **Problem 1 (community safety):** Maintaining a safe environment is one of the highest priorities of any community. Gun violence, drug trafficking, and sexual assault, are just examples of many criminal activities threating our citizens. To make our community a better place to live, we should try all different means to prevent crimes. Because we are going to be IT professionals, we are committed to providing information technology solutions to community safety.

Your task is to interview someone living in our area who is interested in improving community safety. This person could be a police officer, a school teacher, a bus (school bus) driver, a community leader, a crime victim, or someone who worries about the safety of their kids or themselves and is looking for a solution. Through interviewing your client, you should identify one specific problem that risks the safety of our community. You should then propose an information technology solution to solving or partially solving this problem.

Please write a 1-2 page report that documents your interview, the identified problem, and your proposed solution. The problem you are going to tackle could be a large problem of the law enforcement system or a small problem related to a specific issue or a specific group of people.

Your document should include the following information: objective of the interview, who is the interviewee (the real name can be hidden), time and place the interview is taken, problems identified, and your proposed solution. Please also analyse the cost and the benefits of adopting your solution.

Sample Student Submission (With Permission From the IUSB Student; the Original Submission Is Modified to have Personal Data Removed)

I am living with my uncle in XXX Ave, YYY City for about 2.5 years. The neighbourhood is ranked as one of most dangerous places in our city. I had an interview with an employee in ZZZ Company on November 2, 2014. Her name is Lady U, who has lived here for about 30 years. I asked her many questions about this neighbourhood.

Because this neighbourhood is too dangerous, some residents have moved to other places. There are many empty houses. Some poor people try to break in the empty houses and live there. There are crimes in this neighbourhood too. The government is trying to break this vicious cycle. They set up a neighbourhood office. We are fortunate to have engaged residents that are involved in a number of endeavours to beautify the neighbourhood, improve the houses, and sponsor the community events.

The most important task for now is that we want everyone to know that our neighbourhood is getting better than before. We would like our neighbours to help each other and form a watch group to prevent crimes in our community. Watch groups are made up with volunteers in our community who will report suspicious activities to the police department. Watch groups could also provide neighbourhood surveillance when police officers are not around, which can effectively reduce the chances of crime.

Based on my interview, I have some suggestions for the neighbourhood. The first suggestion is to set up a website about housing information, so anyone can access this website and get to know our community. Since some of our houses have been improved, we would like to attract new residents to move here.

Second, I suggest our residents setting up a home security system. It is as low as 29 dollars per month and is monitored 24/7 by the fast responders. The security system could also be connected to the police office and the fire department. Alternatively, we could set up a remote video monitoring system for our neighbourhood.

Finally, I suggest using some social media websites, such as Facebook and Twitter, to connect people in our community together. The residents can update the safety information and communicate with each other through social networking.

My suggestions are not difficult nor expensive to implement. The point here is to let everyone know that we all want to change this neighbourhood and we are working on it.

- **Problem 2 (food safety):** Food safety is a growing concern of our community. The government is under increasing public and international pressure to solve food safety problems. Because we are going to be IT professionals, we are committed to providing information technology solutions to food safety.

Your task is to interview anyone in our area who is interested in improving food safety. This person could be a government officer, a school teacher, a community leader, a victim of food poisoning, or someone who worries about the food safety of their children or themselves and is looking for a solution.

Through interviewing your client, you should identify one specific problem that risks the food safety of our community. You should then propose an information technology solution to solving or partially solving this problem.

Please write a report that documents your interview, the identified problem, and your proposed solution. The problem you are going to tackle could be a large problem of the law enforcement system or a small problem related to a specific issue or a specific group of people.

Your document should include the following information: objective of the interview, who is the interviewee (the real name can be hidden), time and place the interview is taken, problems identified, and your proposed solution. Please also analyse the cost and the benefits of adopting your solution.

Sample Student Submission (With Permission From the NYIT-Nanjing Student; the Original Submission Is Modified to Have Personal Data Removed)

Nowadays, food safety has become a big problem in China. We often hear some news about food-safety related incidents on the Internet and on TV.

Like most people, I used to think that food safety problems are far away from my life. Even occasionally I suffer from diarrhea, I seldom think about food safety problems. Several days ago, I had a lunch with one of my friends in a local restaurant. We talked a lot about the meals served to us. I was surprised that the restaurant is so generous to offer beefsteaks for just ten RMB. After my friend told me secretly that the steak in our meal was not real beef but made of soy protein, I was shocked. Fortunately, soy protein is a nontoxic food additive and widely used in daily meals. However, I started to worry about our food safety.

Last Friday, I conducted a survey about food safety in an online newsgroup. The question is "Do you think the food you are eating everyday safe?" The options include:

1.   I do trust the food on market. It is fresh and safe;
2.   I do not totally trust the food on market, but I have no other choices but to eat it;
3.   I completely do not trust the food on market;
4.   I do not care about the question.

I found that most people were very interested about the question and they gave me many responses. Within half a day, I received almost 100 responses. Option B got the most votes, about 60 percent of the total responses. Option D took the second place, about 20 percent. Options A and C each got half of the remaining 20 percent.

To make my survey more accurate and convincing, I interviewed about 20 people in my community and found the answers are similar to the ones obtained from the online questionnaire.

From the results, I can see two problems. First, people have just realized the food safety problem, although some of them never considered the problem before. Second, people hardly have any solutions to solve the food safety problem; they even cannot supervise the cooking process in restaurants and cafeterias.

To solve these problems, I would like to give a short-term solution and a long-term solution. First, it is necessary to inform our citizens about food safety. For example, we could use the Internet to emphasize the importance of food safety. In addition, basic food safety knowledge could be provided online so that our citizens know what kind of food is safe, what kind of food is not safe, and how to identify them.

Second, I would like to suggest a long-term solution: build a food visual identification system. This can be a large project. However, once it is implemented, food safety problem will not be a big concern anymore. Here is my idea. The reason that people have concerns about food safety is that they really do not know what they are eating. A food named chicken might not be made of chicken. If we have a system that could tell us the ingredients of every meal we eat, we will be assured. Actually, Japan has already developed this kind of system. In some areas of Japan, you are able to know the information of the fish you eat through scanning the bar code attached to the fish. I believe building this kind of system is very important and useful.

This system could be regulated and implemented by the government to make sure high standards are followed. Maybe one day in the future, everyone could supervise food safety and we will no longer worry about food safety problems.

- **Experience:** Problem 1 was used at IUSB, because community safety is a major concern in most cities of the US. Problem 2 was used in NYIT-Nanjing, because food safety has always been a major problem in China. Although similar requirement elicitation skills, problem identification skills, and solution design skills are needed to work on these assignments, students are certainly more engaging to solve the problems that they can relate to. Many interesting problems were identified and feasible solutions were proposed. For example, some IUSB students suggested installing a GPS tracking system on school buses to improve student safety. Although there is no correlation to this assignment, this solution was adopted by our local school district a year later. At NYIT-Nanjing, some students suggested creating an official website for disclosing food safety issues and clarifying food safety rumours, because food safety rumours could disturb and harm the society.

Domain Knowledge

One objective of team project is to get students familiar with different application domains. Therefore, at both IUSB and NYIT-Nanjing, I asked students to pick their own team projects. Table 6 and Table 7 list the domains and application types of their team projects, respectively. We can see that varieties of applications and domains of these team projects could provide different knowledge and development experiences to students.

It is interesting to notice that although the projects conducted by IUSB teams and NYIT-Nanjing teams are similar in general, there are some differences: three teams at IUSB worked on projects to help homeless animals and five teams at NYIT-Nanjing worked on projects related to their own university (course management, book management, and test generation). We can see that students' interested projects are related to their living environment, where most IUSB students live off campus and all NYIT-Nanjing students live on campus.

Through allowing students to select their own team projects, I provide opportunities for them to learn the domain knowledge that they are interested in and mostly likely to use when they join the industry. This is one of the approaches I advocate to support software engineering education under real-world business environment.

Using Real-World Case-Studies

Software engineering principles are valued experience assembled by IT professionals through real-word software development, which include software project failures. In teaching project failures, two ill-reputed software projects were examined to help students understand the complexity of real-world projects. They

Table 6. Comparison of application domains of team projects

IUSB (Fall 2013)	NYIT-Nanjing (Spring 2014)
Animal rescue: 3 Nutrition and health: 2 E-Commerce: 2 Media inventory: 1 Game: 3 Education: 1 Scheduling: 2 Business solution: 1 Real estate: 1 Banking: 1	Heath care: 2 Banking: 2 Business management: 1 Game: 3 Inventory management: 3 Course management: 2 Library and book management: 2 Messaging and texting: 1 Exam and test generation: 1 Integration calculation: 1

Table 7. Comparison of application types of team pojects

IUSB (Fall 2013)	NYIT-Nanjing (Spring 2014)
Computer graphics and animation: 3 Web application: 11 Database application: 1 File management: 1 Mobile computing: 1	Computer graphics and animation: 3 Web application: 7 Database application: 2 File management: 2 Mobile computing: 1 Console application: 3

are the *healthcare.gov* project (Heusser, 2013) of the US and the *12306.cn* project (Ong, 2012) of China, which are intensively discussed at IUSB and NYIT-Nanjing, respectively.

HealthCare.gov is the US Department of Health and Human Services' website for health insurance exchange. It was developed to support the *Affordable Care Act* under the Obama's administration. The project was supposed to deliver a functional website on October 1, 2013. However, it did not work as expected. Many technical issues were identified and had to be fixed. Although the website works fine now after a tremendous extra effort and budget was spent, there are many valuable software engineering lessons that can be learned from this project. Similarly, *12306.cn* is China's Ministry of Railway's website for buying train ticket, which was launched in 2011. It is notorious for its failure to support billions of purchase requests around the Chinese New Year Festival, which greatly disappointed hundreds of millions of travellers. The website was later revamped and it now works better.

Although every student of IUSB knew the story of *healthcare.gov* and every student of NYIT-Nanjing knew the story of *12306.cn*, they really did not understand the failure from the viewpoint of software engineering. Through analysing the complexity of these two projects, students learned the importance of project management and quality assurance. Most importantly, they understood that their software engineering knowledge and skills could have real impact on the society after they join the industry; these impacts could be positive or negative depending on how they are going to follow and apply the software engineering principles.

CONCLUSION

In this chapter, I presented my experience of teaching an undergraduate-level software engineering course at Indiana University South Bend and New York Institute of Technology-Nanjing. Problem-based learning is used in teaching this course. I described how assignments are adjusted in two institutions according to the business environment of the US and China. Through solving real-world problems related to their business environment, students could be better prepared for their challenging career as software engineers. The study also shows that it is possible to create an internationalized computer science curriculum that contains both common core learning standards and adjustable custom learning standards, where problem-based learning can be characterized into the custom learning standards.

It is worth to note that the problem-based learning approach only provides one aspect on internationalized computer science program. There are certainly more work needs to do. However, globalization has revolutionized our business and our life, including education. I hope my experience in computer science and software engineering education could be a useful reference for other educators around the world to create internationalized curricula in their fields.

ACKNOWLEDGMENT

The author would like to thank students of Indiana University South Bend and New York Institute of Technology-Nanjing for proving their homework solutions.

REFERENCES

ABET. (n.d.a). *Criteria for Accrediting Computing Programs, 2016-2017.* Retrieved from http://www.abet.org/accreditation/accreditation-criteria/criteria-for-accrediting-computing-programs-2016-2017/#curriculum

ABET. (n.d.b). *Abet Accredited Program Search.* Retrieved from http://main.abet.org/aps/accredited-programsearch.aspx

Brodie, L. M. (2009). eProblem-based learning: Problem-based learning using virtual teams. *European Journal of Engineering Education, 34*(6), 497–509. doi:10.1080/03043790902943868

dos Santos, S. C., da Conceição Moraes Batista, M., Cavalcanti, A. P. C., Albuquerque, J. O., & Meira, S. R. (2009). Applying PBL in software engineering education. In *Proceedings of the 22nd Software Engineering Education and Training Conference* (pp. 182–189). Hyderabad, India: IEEE.

Heusser, M. (2013). Six software development lessons from healthcare.gov's failed launch. *CIO.* Retrieved from http://www.cio.com/article/2380827/developer/6-software-development-lessons-from-healthcare-gov-s-failed-launch.html

Hmelo-Silver, C. E. (2004). Problem-based learning: What and how do students learn? *Educational Psychology Review, 16*(3), 235–266. doi:10.1023/B:EDPR.0000034022.16470.f3

Huffman Hayes, J. (2002). Energizing software engineering education through real-world projects as experimental studies. In *Proceedings of 15th Software Engineering Education and Training Conference* (pp. 192–206). Covington, KY: IEEE. doi:10.1109/CSEE.2002.995211

Hung, W. (2011). Theory to reality: A few issues in implementing problem-based learning. *Educational Technology Research and Development, 59*(4), 529–552. doi:10.1007/s11423-011-9198-1

Indiana University South Bend. (n.d.). *Computer and Information Sciences.* Retrieved from https://www.iusb.edu/computerscience/programs/bs-cs.php

Johns-Boast, L. (2014). Developing personal and professional skills in software engineering students. In L. Yu (Ed.), Overcoming Challenges in Software Engineering Education: Delivering Non-Technical Knowledge and Skills (pp. 198–228). Hershey, PA: IGI Global. doi:10.4018/978-1-4666-5800-4.ch011

Kay, J., Barg, M., Fekete, A., Greening, T., Hollands, O., Kingston, J. H., & Crawford, K. (2000). Problem-based learning for foundation computer science courses. *Computer Science Education, 10*(2), 109–128. doi:10.1076/0899-3408(200008)10:2;1-C;FT109

Kuhrmann, M., Femmer, H., & Eckhardt, J. (2014). Controlled experiments as means to teach soft skills in software engineering. In L. Yu (Ed.), Overcoming Challenges in Software Engineering Education: Delivering Non-Technical Knowledge and Skills (pp. 180–197). Hershey, PA: IGI Global. doi:10.4018/978-1-4666-5800-4.ch010

NYiT. (2017). *Curriculum: Computer Science, B.S.* Retrieved from https://www.nyit.edu/degrees/computer_science_bs/curriculum

Ong, J. (2012). Chinese rail ministry on the defense as $52m ticketing website is widely reviled. *The Next Web*. Retrieved from http://tnw.to/j5V3

Richardson, I., & Delaney, Y. (2010). Software quality: From theory to practice. In *Proceedings of the 7th International Conference on the Quality of Information and Communications Technology* (pp. 150–155). IEEE.

Richardson, I., & Hynes, B. (2008). Entrepreneurship education: Towards an industry sector approach. *Education + Training, 50*(3), 188–198. doi:10.1108/00400910810873973

Sedelmaier, Y., & Landes, D. (2014). Practicing soft skills in software engineering: A project-based didactical approach. In L. Yu (Ed.), Overcoming Challenges in Software Engineering Education: Delivering Non-Technical Knowledge and Skills (pp. 161–179). Hershey, PA: IGI Global. doi:10.4018/978-1-4666-5800-4.ch009

Walgreens. (2012). *Walgreens WellTransitionsSM provides discharge services to help hospitals and health systems reduce readmissions*. Retrieved from http://news.walgreens.com/article_print.cfm?article_id=5648

Weibelzahl, S., & Lahart, O. (2011a). Developing student induction sessions for problem-based learning. *Proceedings of International Conference on Engaging Pedagogy*.

Weibelzahl, S., & Lahart, O. (2011b). PBL induction made easy: A web-based resource and a toolbox. *FACILITATE Conference: Problem-Based Learning (PBL) Today and Tomorrow*.

Xu, Y., & Liu, W. (2010). A project-based learning approach: A case study in China. *Asia Pacific Education Review, 11*(3), 363–370. doi:10.1007/s12564-010-9093-1

Yu, L. (2014). *Overcoming challenges in software engineering education: Delivering non-technical knowledge and skills*. IGI Global. doi:10.4018/978-1-4666-5800-4

ADDITIONAL READING

Altbach, P. G., & Knight, J. (2007). The internationalization of higher education: Motivations and realities. *Journal of Studies in International Education, 11*(3–4), 290–305. doi:10.1177/1028315307303542

Anderson, L., & Krathwohl, D. A. (2001). *Taxonomy for learning, teaching and assessment: A revision on Bloom's taxonomy of educational objectives*. New York: Longman.

Azer, S. A. (2007). *Navigating problem–based learning*. Elsevier Australia.

Ball, S. J. (2012). *Global education inc: New policy networks and the neo–liberal imaginary*. Routledge.

Barrett, T., & Moore, S. (2011). *New approaches to problem–based learning: Revitalising your practice in higher education*. New York: Routledge.

Bennett, R., & Kane, S. (2009). Internationalization of UK university business schools: A survey of current practice. *Journal of Studies in International Education*.

Benson, S. (2003). Metacognition in information systems education. In *Current issues in IT education* (pp. 213–222). Hershey, PA: IRM Press. doi:10.4018/978-1-93177-753-7.ch017

Brindley, J. E., Walti, C., & Blaschke, L. M. (2009). Creating effective collaborative learning Groups in an online environment. *International Review of Research in Open and Distance Learning*, *10*(3), 1–18. doi:10.19173/irrodl.v10i3.675

Bruns, A., & Humphreys, S. (2007). Building collaborative capacities in learners: The M/Cyclopedia project revisited. In *Proceedings of the International Symposium on Wikis* (pp. 1–10). doi:10.1145/1296951.1296952

Cambridge, J., & Thompson, J. (2004). Internationalism and globalization as contexts for international education. *Compare: A Journal of Comparative Education*, *34*(2), 161–175. doi:10.1080/0305792042000213994

Chan, B. T. Y. (2011). Postgraduate transnational education in nonbusiness subjects: Can it fit conceptualizations of curriculum internationalization? *Journal of Studies in International Education*, *15*(3), 279–298. doi:10.1177/1028315310379420

Chan, W. W. (2004). International cooperation in higher education: Theory and practice. *Journal of Studies in International Education*, *8*(1), 32–55. doi:10.1177/1028315303254429

Chang, C. K., Chen, G. D., & Li, L. Y. (2008). Constructing a community of practice to improve coursework activity. *Computers & Education*, *50*(1), 235–247. doi:10.1016/j.compedu.2006.05.003

Childress, L. K. (2009). Planning for internationalization by investing in faculty. *Journal of International and Global Studies*, *1*(1), 30–50.

Clemens, M. A. (2004). The long walk to school: International education goals in historical perspective. *Center for Global Development Working Paper*, (37).

Codd, J. (2005). Teachers as 'managed professionals' in the global education industry: The New Zealand experience. *Educational Review*, *57*(2), 193–206. doi:10.1080/0013191042000308369

Crosling, G., Edwards, R., & Schroder, B. (2008). Internationalizing the curriculum: The implementation experience in a faculty of business and economics. *Journal of Higher Education Policy and Management*, *30*(2), 107–121. doi:10.1080/13600800801938721

Crossley, M. (1999). Reconceptualising comparative and international education. *Compare: A Journal of Comparative Education*, *29*(3), 249–267. doi:10.1080/0305792990290305

Crossley, M. (2000). Bridging cultures and traditions in the reconceptualisation of comparative and international education. *Comparative Education*, *36*(3), 319–332. doi:10.1080/713656615

Daniels, M., Cajander, Å., Pears, A., & Clear, T. (2010). Engineering education research in practice: Evolving use of open ended group projects as a pedagogical strategy for developing skills in global collaboration. *International Journal of Engineering Education*, *26*(4), 795–806.

Downey, G., & Beddoes, K. (2010). *What is Global Engineering Education For? The Making of International Educators*. Morgan & Claypool Publishers.

Evensen, D. H., & Hmelo, C. E. (2000). *Problem–based learning: A research perspective on learning interactions*. Lawrence Erlbaum Associates Publishers.

Felder, R. M., & Brent, R. (2005). Understanding student differences. *Journal of Engineering Education, 94*(1), 57–72. doi:10.1002/j.2168-9830.2005.tb00829.x

Gehlhar, J. N. (2009). Of course they want us at the curriculum internationalization table. *Modern Language Journal, 93*(4), 616–618. doi:10.1111/j.1540-4781.2009.00935.x

Goodman, B., Henderson, D., & Stenzel, E. (2006). *An interdisciplinary approach to implementing competency based education in higher education.* Lewiston, NY: Edwin Mellen Press.

Grayling, I., Commons, K., & Wise, J. (2012). It's the curriculum, stupid! *Teaching in Lifelong Learning: A Journal to Inform and Improve Practice, 4*(1), 21–31.

Green, W., & Whitsed, C. (2013). Reflections on an alternative approach to continuing professional learning for internationalization of the curriculum across disciplines. *Journal of Studies in International Education, 17*(2), 148–164. doi:10.1177/1028315312463825

Green, W., & Whitsed, C. (2015). *Critical perspectives on internationalising the curriculum in disciplines: Reflective narrative accounts from business, education and health* (Vol. 28). Springer. doi:10.1007/978-94-6300-085-7

Gutek, G. L. (2005). American Education in a Global Society, 2/E.

Hansen, R. S. (2006). Benefits and problems with student teams: Suggestions for improving team projects. *Journal of Education for Business, 82*(1), 11–19. doi:10.3200/JOEB.82.1.11-19

Hanson, L. (2008). Global citizenship, global health, and the internationalization of curriculum: A study of transformative potential. *Journal of Studies in International Education.*

Hayden, M. (2006). Introduction to international education: International schools and their communities. *Sage (Atlanta, Ga.).*

Hicks, D. (2003). Thirty years of global education: A reminder of key principles and precedents. *Educational Review, 55*(3), 265–275. doi:10.1080/0013191032000118929

Higgs, M., Plewnia, U., & Ploch, J. (2005). Influence of team composition and task complexity on team performance. *Team Performance Management, 11*(7/8), 227–250. doi:10.1108/13527590510635134

International Baccalaureate Organization. (2014). International Baccalaureate Diploma Programme Subject Brief. Retrieved from http://www.ibo.org/globalassets/publications/recognition/4_computerhl.pdf

Ivanova, M., & Popova, A. (2011). Formal and informal learning flows cohesion in Web 2.0 environment. *International Journal of Information Systems and Social Change, 2*(1), 1–15. doi:10.4018/jissc.2011010101

Jonassen, D. H. (2000). Towards a design theory of problem solving. *Educational Technology Research and Development, 48*(4), 63–85. doi:10.1007/BF02300500

Jones, E. (2013). Internationalization and employability: The role of intercultural experiences in the development of transferable skills. *Public Money & Management, 33*(2), 95–104. doi:10.1080/09540962.2013.763416

Kahn, H. E., & Agnew, M. (2015). Global learning through difference considerations for teaching, learning, and the internationalization of higher education. *Journal of Studies in International Education.*

Kapoor, D., & Jordan, S. (Eds.). (2009). *Education, participatory action research, and social change.* New York, NY: Palgrave Macmillan. doi:10.1057/9780230100640

Kehm, B. M., & Teichler, U. (2007). Research on internationalisation in higher education. *Journal of Studies in International Education, 11*(3–4), 260–273. doi:10.1177/1028315307303534

Kirkwood, T. F. (2001). Our global age requires global education: Clarifying definitional ambiguities. *Social Studies, 92*(1), 10–15. doi:10.1080/00377990109603969

Kniep, W. M. (1989). Social studies within a global education. *Social Education, 53*(6), 399.

Knight, J. (2006). Cross–border education: Conceptual confusion and data deficits. *Perspectives in Education, 24*(4), 15–27.

Knight, J. (2008). The role of cross–border education in the debate on education as a public good and private commodity. *Journal of Asian Public Policy, 1*(2), 174–187. doi:10.1080/17516230802094478

Knight, J., & de Wit, H. (Eds.). (1997). *Internationalisation of higher education in Asia Pacific countries.* European Association for International Education.

Kwok, C. C., & Arpan, J. S. (2002). Internationalizing the business school: A global survey in 2000. *Journal of International Business Studies, 33*(3), 571–581. doi:10.1057/palgrave.jibs.8491032

Lane, J. E., & Kinser, K. (2011). The cross-border education policy context: Educational hubs, trade liberalization, and national sovereignty. *New Directions for Higher Education, 2011*(155), 79–85. doi:10.1002/he.446

Leask, B. (2013). Internationalizing the curriculum in the disciplines—Imagining new possibilities. *Journal of Studies in International Education, 17*(2), 103–118. doi:10.1177/1028315312475090

Manuel, T. A., Shooshtari, N. H., Fleming, M. J., & Wallwork, S. S. (2001). Internationalization of the business curriculum at US colleges and universities. *Journal of Teaching in International Business, 12*(3), 43–70. doi:10.1300/J066v12n03_03

May, B. E. (1997). Curriculum internationalization and distance learning: Convergence of necessity and technology. *Journal of Teaching in International Business, 9*(1), 35–50. doi:10.1300/J066v09n01_03

Mayer, R. E., & Alexander, P. A. (2011). *Handbook of research on learning and instruction.* New York: Routledge.

McTaggart, R., & Curró, G. (2009). *Action research for curriculum internationalization: Education versus commercialization* (pp. 89–105). Palgrave Macmillan, US: Education, Participatory Action Research, and Social Change.

Merriam, S. B. (1988). *Case study research in education: A qualitative approach.* San Francisco, CA: Jossey–Bass.

Merryfield, M. M. (2001). Moving the center of global education: From imperial world views that divide the world to double consciousness, contrapuntal pedagogy, hybridity, and cross–cultural competence. *Critical issues in social studies research for the 21st century*, 179–208.

Merryfield, M. M., & Subedi, B. (2001). Decolonizing the mind for world–centered global education. *The social studies curriculum: Purposes, problems, and possibilities*, 277–290.

Michaelsen, L. K., & Sweet, M. (2008). The essential elements of team-based learning. *New Directions for Teaching and Learning*, *2008*(116), 7–27. doi:10.1002/tl.330

Milton, J., & Lyons, J. (2003). Evaluate to improve learning: Reflecting on the role of teaching and learning models. *Higher Education Research & Development*, *22*(3), 297–312. doi:10.1080/0729436032000145158

Nance, W. D. (2000). Improving information systems students' teamwork and project management capabilities: Experiences from an innovative classroom. *Information Technology Management*, *1*(4), 293–306. doi:10.1023/A:1019137428045

Olds, K. (2007). Global assemblage: Singapore, foreign universities, and the construction of a "global education hub". *World Development*, *35*(6), 959–975. doi:10.1016/j.worlddev.2006.05.014

Osler, A., & Vincent, K. (2002). *Citizenship and the challenge of global education*. Stylus Publishing, LLC.

Patil, A., & Codner, G. (2007). Accreditation of engineering education: Review, observations and proposal for global accreditation. *European Journal of Engineering Education*, *32*(6), 639–651. doi:10.1080/03043790701520594

Patil, A. S. (2005). The global engineering criteria for the development of a global engineering profession. *World Transaction on Engineering Education*, *4*(1), 49–52.

Phillips, D., & Schweisfurth, M. (2014). *Comparative and international education: An introduction to theory, method, and practice*. A&C Black.

Pinar, W. F. (2013). *International handbook of curriculum research*. Routledge.

Poindexter, S., Basu, C., & Kurncz, S. (2001). Technology, teamwork, and teaching meet in the classroom. *EDUCAUSE Quarterly*, *24*(3), 32–41.

Polack–Wahl, J. A. (2001). Enhancing group projects in software engineering. *Journal of Computing Sciences in Colleges*, *16*(4), 111–121.

Prados, J. W., Peterson, G. D., & Lattuca, L. R. (2005). Quality assurance of engineering education through accreditation: The impact of Engineering Criteria 2000 and its global influence. *Journal of Engineering Education*, *94*(1), 165–184. doi:10.1002/j.2168-9830.2005.tb00836.x

Robley, W., Whittle, S., & Murdoch–Eaton, D. (2005). Mapping generic skills curricula: Outcomes and discussion. *Journal of Further and Higher Education*, *29*(4), 321–330. doi:10.1080/03098770500353342

Sheard, A., & Kakabadse, A. (2002). From loose groups to effective teams: The nine key factors of the team landscape. *Journal of Management Development*, *21*(2), 133–151. doi:10.1108/02621710210417439

Sibley, J., & Parmelee, D. X. (2008). Knowledge is no longer enough: Enhancing professional education with team-based learning. *New Directions for Teaching and Learning, 2008*(116), 41–53. doi:10.1002/tl.332

Stella, A. (2006). Quality assurance of cross-border higher education. *Quality in Higher Education, 12*(3), 257–276. doi:10.1080/13538320601072859

Strauss, P., & U, A. (2007). Group assessments: Dilemmas facing lecturers in multicultural tertiary classrooms. *Higher Education Research & Development, 26*(2), 147–161. doi:10.1080/07294360701310789

Tadayon, N. (2004). Software engineering based on the team software process with a real world project. *Journal of Computing Sciences in Colleges, 19*(4), 133–142.

Toole, J. C., & Louis, K. S. (2002). *The role of professional learning communities in international education. In 2ⁿᵈ International Handbook of Educational Leadership and Administration* (pp. 245–279). Springer Netherlands.

Trytten, D. A. (2001). Progressing from small group work to cooperative learning: A case study from computer science. *Journal of Engineering Education, 90*(1), 85–91. doi:10.1002/j.2168-9830.2001.tb00572.x

Tye, K. A. (2003). Global education as a worldwide movement. *Phi Delta Kappan, 85*(2), 165–168. doi:10.1177/003172170308500212

Van der Wende, M. (1997). Internationalising the curriculum in Dutch higher education: An international comparative perspective. *Journal of Studies in International Education, 1*(2), 53–72. doi:10.1177/102831539700100204

Van Gigch, J. P. (2000). Metamodelling and problem solving. *Journal of Applied Systems Studies, 1*(2), 327–336.

Walker, E. L., & Slotterbeck, O. A. (2002). Incorporating realistic teamwork into a small college software engineering curriculum. *Journal of Computing Sciences in Colleges, 17*(6), 115–123.

Weiner, L. (2008). *The global assault on teaching, teachers, and their unions: Stories for resistance* (L. Weiner & M. Compton, Eds.). Palgrave Macmillan. doi:10.1057/9780230611702

Wells, C. E. (2002). Teaching teamwork in information systems. In E. B. Cohen (Ed.), *Challenges of Information Technology Education in the 21ˢᵗ Century* (pp. 1–24). Hershey: Idea Group Publishing. doi:10.4018/978-1-930708-34-1.ch001

Wilkerson, L., & Gijselaers, W. H. (1996). *Bringing problem–based learning to higher education: Theory and practice (No. 68).* San Francisco, CA: Jossey–Bass.

Wilson, B. G. (1998). *Constructivist learning environments: Case studies in instructional design.* Englewood Cliffs, NJ: Educational Technology Publications.

KEY TERMS AND DEFINITIONS

Computer Science Education: A disciplined approach to educate IT professionals, software developers, and computer experts.

Cross-Border Education: The practice to allocate educational resources across regional borders and international borders.

Cross-Cultural Education: The Education that needs to deal with students of different cultural background.

Engineering Education: Teaching engineering knowledge and practices to future engineers.

Global Education: An internationalized approach to teaching students of different countries with different background.

Non-Technical Skills: People skills, such as communication skills, documentation skills, and leadership skills, which are important in a teamwork environment.

Problem-Based Learning: A student-centred teaching approach, in which students achieve learning objectives through solving real world problems.

Software Engineering Education: A disciplined approach to educate software developers.

Standardized Curriculum: A curriculum that can be applied to different education institutions with little changes.

APPENDIX A

Table 8. ABET accredited computer science programs of the United States (Data source: ABET, n.d.b)

State	Universities
Alabama (AL)	Alabama A&M University Auburn University Jacksonville State University The University of Alabama The University of Alabama in Huntsville University of Alabama at Birmingham University of North Alabama University of South Alabama
Alaska (AK)	University of Alaska Anchorage University of Alaska Fairbanks
Arizona (AZ)	Arizona State University Northern Arizona University
Arkansas (AR)	Arkansas Tech University The University of Central Arkansas University of Arkansas University of Arkansas at Little Rock
California (CA)	California Polytechnic State University, San Luis Obispo California State Polytechnic University, Pomona California State University, Chico California State University, Dominguez Hills California State University, Fullerton California State University, Long Beach California State University, Los Angeles California State University, Northridge California State University, Sacramento California State University, San Bernardino San Jose State University Santa Clara University University of California, Berkeley University of California, Davis University of California, Irvine University of California, Los Angeles University of California, Riverside University of California, Santa Barbara University of Southern California University of the Pacific
Colorado (CO)	Metropolitan State College of Denver Regis University United States Air Force Academy University of Colorado at Boulder University of Colorado at Colorado Springs University of Colorado Denver
Connecticut (CT)	Central Connecticut State University Southern Connecticut State University University of Connecticut University of New Haven
Washington DC (DC)	Howard University The Catholic University of America The George Washington University University of the District of Columbia
Florida (FL)	Embry-Riddle Aeronautical University - Daytona Beach Florida A&M University Florida Atlantic University Florida Institute of Technology Florida International University Florida Memorial University Florida State University University of Central Florida University of North Florida University of South Florida

continued on following page

Table 8. Continued

State	Universities
Georgia (GA)	Armstrong Atlantic State University Georgia Institute of Technology Georgia Southern University Kennesaw State University Mercer University Southern Polytechnic State University University of West Georgia
Idaho (ID)	Boise State University Idaho State University University of Idaho
Illinois (IL)	Illinois Institute of Technology Illinois State University Southern Illinois University at Carbondale Southern Illinois University Edwardsville University of Illinois at Chicago University of Illinois at Urbana-Champaign
Indiana (IN)	Indiana University-Purdue University Fort Wayne Rose-Hulman Institute of Technology University of Evansville University of Notre Dame
Iowa (IA)	Iowa State University
Kansas (KS)	Kansas State University The University of Kansas Wichita State University
Kentucky (KY)	Eastern Kentucky University University of Kentucky University of Louisville
Louisiana (LA)	Grambling State University Louisiana State University and A&M College Louisiana State University, Shreveport Louisiana Tech University McNeese State University Nicholls State University Southeastern Louisiana University Southern University and Agricultural & Mechanical College University of Louisiana at Lafayette University of Louisiana at Monroe University of New Orleans
Maine (ME)	University of Maine University of Southern Maine
Maryland (MD)	Bowie State University Loyola University Maryland The Johns Hopkins University Towson University United States Naval Academy University of Maryland Baltimore County
Massachusetts (MA)	Fitchburg State College Massachusetts Institute of Technology Northeastern University Salem State University Tufts University University of Massachusetts Boston University of Massachusetts Dartmouth Wentworth Institute of Technology Westfield State University Worcester Polytechnic Institute

continued on following page

Table 8. Continued

State	Universities
Michigan (MI)	Calvin College Grand Valley State University Kettering University Michigan State University Oakland University University of Michigan University of Michigan-Dearborn Western Michigan University
Minnesota (MN)	St. Cloud State University University of Minnesota Duluth
Mississippi (MS)	Jackson State University Mississippi State University Mississippi Valley State University University of Mississippi University of Southern Mississippi
Missouri (MO)	Missouri State University Missouri University of Science and Technology Southeast Missouri State University Southwest Baptist University University of Missouri - Kansas City University of Missouri-Columbia
Montana (MT)	Montana State University - Bozeman Montana Tech of the University of Montana University of Montana
Nebraska (NE)	University of Nebraska at Omaha University of Nebraska-Lincoln
Nevada (NV)	University of Nevada-Las Vegas University of Nevada-Reno
New Hampshire (NH)	University of New Hampshire
New Jersey (NJ)	Fairleigh Dickinson University (Metropolitan Campus) Kean University Monmouth University Montclair State University New Jersey Institute of Technology Rowan University Stevens Institute of Technology The College of New Jersey William Paterson University of New Jersey
New Mexico (NM)	New Mexico Institute of Mining and Technology University of New Mexico
New York (NY)	City University of New York, City College City University of New York, College of Staten Island Iona College Pace University Rochester Institute of Technology State University of New York at Binghamton State University of New York at Brockport Stony Brook University Syracuse University United States Military Academy University at Buffalo, The State University of New York
North Carolina (NC)	Appalachian State University Fayetteville State University North Carolina Agricultural and Technical State University North Carolina State University at Raleigh University of North Carolina at Greensboro University of North Carolina Wilmington Winston-Salem State University

continued on following page

Table 8. Continued

State	Universities
North Dakota (ND)	University of North Dakota
Ohio (OH)	Case Western Reserve University Cedarville University Miami University Ohio Northern University Ohio University The Ohio State University The University of Toledo University of Cincinnati Wright State University
Oklahoma (OK)	The University of Tulsa University of Central Oklahoma University of Oklahoma
Oregon (OR)	Oregon State University Portland State University University of Portland
Pennsylvania (PA)	Bloomsburg University of Pennsylvania Bucknell University California University of Pennsylvania Drexel University East Stroudsburg University of Pennsylvania Edinboro University of Pennsylvania Gannon University Grove City College Indiana University of Pennsylvania Lafayette College Lehigh University Millersville University of Pennsylvania Saint Joseph's University Shippensburg University Slippery Rock University University of Pennsylvania University of Scranton Villanova University West Chester University of Pennsylvania York College of Pennsylvania
Puerto Rico	University of Puerto Rico at Arecibo University of Puerto Rico at Bayamon University of Puerto Rico, Rio Piedras Campus
South Carolina (SC)	Charleston Southern University Clemson University Coastal Carolina University College of Charleston South Carolina State University The Citadel University of South Carolina University of South Carolina Upstate Winthrop University
South Dakota (SD)	South Dakota School of Mines and Technology South Dakota State University
Tennessee (TN)	East Tennessee State University Middle Tennessee State University Southern Adventist University Tennessee State University Tennessee Technological University The University of Memphis University of Tennessee at Chattanooga University of Tennessee at Knoxville Vanderbilt University

continued on following page

Table 8. Continued

State	Universities
Texas (TX)	Abilene Christian University Baylor University Lamar University Prairie View A&M University Sam Houston State University Southern Methodist University Stephen F. Austin State University Texas A&M University Texas A&M University - Corpus Christi Texas A&M University - Kingsville Texas Christian University Texas State University Texas Tech University The University of Texas - Pan American The University of Texas at Brownsville & Texas Southmost College University of Houston - Clear Lake University of North Texas University of Texas at Arlington University of Texas at Dallas University of Texas at El Paso
Utah (UT)	Brigham Young University Southern Utah University Utah State University Utah Valley University Weber State University
Virginia (VA)	George Mason University Hampton University Norfolk State University Radford University The University of Virginia's College at Wise University of Virginia Virginia Commonwealth University Virginia Military Institute Virginia Polytechnic Institute and State University Virginia State University
Washington (WA)	Eastern Washington University Gonzaga University Pacific Lutheran University Washington State University Washington State University - Tri-Cities Washington State University-Vancouver Western Washington University
West Virginia (WV)	West Virginia University West Virginia University Institute of Technology
Wisconsin (WI)	University of Wisconsin - Eau Claire University of Wisconsin-Milwaukee University of Wisconsin-Oshkosh
Wyoming (WY)	University of Wyoming

APPENDIX B

Table 9. ABET accredited international computer science programs (Data source: ABET, n.d.b)

Country	Universities
Bahrain	AMA International University University of Bahrain
Ecuador	Escuela Superior Politecnica Del Litoral
Egypt	The American University in Cairo
India	VIT University (Chennai) VIT University (Vellore)
Indonesia	Institut Teknologi Bandung
Jordan	Princess Sumaya University for Technology
Kuwait	Gulf University for Science & Technology
Lebanon	Beirut Arab University Lebanese American University
Mexico	ITESM, Monterrey Campus
Morocco	Al Akhawayn University in Ifrane
Philippines	Mapua Institute of Technology Technological Institute of the Philippines Manila Technological Institute of the Philippines Quezon City
Qatar	Qatar University
Saudi Arabia	King Abdulaziz University King Fahd University of Petroleum and Minerals King Faisal University King Saud University Taif University Umm Al-Qura University
Singapore	National University of Singapore
United Arab Emirates	American University of Sharjah
Vietnam	Ho Chi Minh City University of Technology

Compilation of References

Abdi, A., & Shultz, L. (Eds.). (2008). *Educating for Human Rights and Global Citizenship*. Albany, NY: State University of New York Press.

Abe, H., & Wiseman, R. L. (1983). A cross-cultural confirmation of the dimensions of intercultural effectiveness. *International Journal of Intercultural Relations*, *7*(1), 53–69. doi:10.1016/0147-1767(83)90005-6

ABET. (n.d.a). *Criteria for Accrediting Computing Programs, 2016-2017*. Retrieved from http://www.abet.org/accreditation/accreditation-criteria/criteria-for-accrediting-computing-programs-2016-2017/#curriculum

ABET. (n.d.b). *Abet Accredited Program Search*. Retrieved from http://main.abet.org/aps/accreditedprogramsearch.aspx

ACE. (n.d.). *CIGE model for comprehensive internationalization*. Retrieved from http://www.acenet.edu/news-room/Pages/CIGE-Model-for-Comprehensive-Internationalization.aspx

Adams, M. (1992). Cultural inclusion in the American college classroom. In L. L. Border, & E. N. Van Note Chism. *Teaching for diversity New Directions for Teaching and Learning*, *49*(49), 5–17. doi:10.1002/tl.37219924903

Adams, T. M. (1996). Languages across the curriculum: Taking stock. *ADFL Bulletin*, *28*, 9–19. doi:10.1632/adfl.28.1.9

AFCLC. (2017, October 20). *Expeditionary Culture Field Guides*. Retrieved October 26, 2017, from http://culture.af.mil/ecfg/index.html

Agoston, S., & Dima, A. M. (2012). Trends and Strategies within the Process of Academic Internationalization. *Management & Marketing Challenges for the Knowledge Society*, *7*(1), 43-56. Retrieved August 30, 2016, from http://www.managementmarketing.ro/pdf/articole/254.pdf

Altbach, P., & de Wit, H. (2015). Internationalization and Global Tension: Lessons from History. *Journal of Studies in International Education*, *19*(1), 4–10. doi:10.1177/1028315314564734

Altbach, P., & Knight, J. (2007). The Internationalization of Higher Education: Motivations and Realities. *Journal of Studies in International Education*, *11*(3-4), 290–305. doi:10.1177/1028315307303542

Aluisio, F., & Menzel, P. (2005). *Hungry Planet*. New York: Material World Books.

Alvaraz & Marsal. (2016). *Healthcare insights report. Post-acute care: Disruption (and opportunities) lurking beneath the surface*. Retrieved November 5, 2016, from https://www.taxanduk.net/sites/default/files/am_hig_postacutecare_06spreads.pdf

American Council of Education. (2013). *Internationalization in Action*. Retrieved from http://www.acenet.edu/news-room/Pages/Intlz-in-Action-2013-December.aspx

American Council on Education. (2012). *Mapping Internationalization on U.S. Campuses: 2012 Edition.* Retrieved October 21, 2016 from https://www.acenet.edu/newsroom/Documents/Mapping-Internationalizationon-US-Campuses-2012-full.pdf

American Council on Education. Center for Internationalization and Global Engagement. (n.d.). Retrieved July 9, 2017 from http://www.acenet.edu/news-room/Pages/CIGE-Model-for-Comprehensive-Internationalization.aspx

American Council on the Teaching of Foreign Languages. (2014). *Global Competence Position Statement.* Retrieved October 21, 2016, from https://www.actfl.org/news/position-statements/global-competence-position-statement

American Psychological Association. (1997). *Learner-Centered Psychological Principles: Guidelines for School Re-design and Reform.* Author.

American, I.-C. (2015, January 1). *New Americans in Georgia: The Political and Economic Power of Immigrants, Latinos, and Asians the Peach State.* Retrieved September 2, 2016, from American Immigration Council: https://www.americanimmigrationcouncil.org/research/new-americans-georgia

Anderson. (2007). *Being a Mathematics Learner: Four Faces of Identity.* University of Georgia.

Anderson, J. (2008). *Driving change through diversity and globalization: Transformative leadership in the academy.* Sterling, VA: Stylus.

Anderson, L. W. (2009). *A taxonomy for learning, teaching, and assessing: A revision of Bloom's taxonomy of educational objectives.* New York.

Anderson, L. W., Krathwohl, D. R., Airasian, P. W., Mayer, R. W., Pintrich, P. R., Raths, J., & Wittrock, M. C. (Eds.). (2001). *A taxonomy for learning teaching and assessing.* New York: Longman.

Anderson, P. H., & Lawton, L. (2012). Intercultural Development: Study Abroad vs. On-campus Study. *Frontiers: The Interdisciplinary Journal of Study Abroad, 21*, 86–108.

Appadurai, A. (1996). *Modernity at large: Cultural dimensions of globalization.* Minneapolis, MN: University of Minnesota Press.

Apple, M. (1979). *Ideology and Curriculum.* New York: Routledge and Kegan. doi:10.4324/9780203241219

Armstrong, N. F. (2008). Teacher education in a global society: Facilitating global literacy for preservice candidates through international field experiences. *Teacher Education and Practice, 21*(4), 490–506.

Ascher, M. (2010). *Ethno mathematics: A multicultural view of mathematical ideas.* Boca Raton, FL: CRC Press.

Ashcraft, M. H., & Kirk, E. P. (2001). The relationships among working memory, math anxiety, and performance. *Journal of Experimental Psychology. General, 130*(2), 224–237. doi:10.1037/0096-3445.130.2.224 PMID:11409101

Asia Society. (2008). *Going Global: Preparing Our Students for an Interconnected World.* Retrieved October 21, 2016, from http://asiasociety.org/files/Going%20Global%20Educator%20Guide.pdf

Aspaas, H. R. (1998). Integrating World-views and the News Media into a Regional Geography Course. *Journal of Geography in Higher Education, 22*(2), 211–227. doi:10.1080/03098269885912

Atlanta-Regional, C. (2013, March). *Regional Snapshot.* Retrieved September 2, 2016, from ARC: Atlanta Regional Commission: http://documents.atlantaregional.com/arcBoard/march2013/dr_regional_snapshot_3_2013_foreignborn.pdf

Backman, E. (1981). The development of an international commitment: A case study. *Occasional Paper Series in International Education, 1*(1), 3-17.

Baerwald, T. J. (2010). Prospects for Geography as an Interdisciplinary Discipline. *Annals of the Association of American Geographers*, *100*(3), 493–501. doi:10.1080/00045608.2010.485443

Banks, J. (2004). Approaches to multicultural curriculum reform. In J. A. Banks & C. M. Banks (Eds.), *Multicultural education: Issues and perspectives* (5th ed.; pp. 242–264). Hoboken, NJ, USA: John Wiley & Sons, Inc.

Banks, J. A. (1999). *An introduction to multicultural education*. Boston: Allyn & Bacon.

Barab, S. A., & Duffy, T. (2012). From practice fields to communities of practice. In D. Jonassen & S. Land (Eds.), *Theoretical foundation of learning environments* (pp. 29–69). New York, NY: Routledge.

Barber, B. (2007, January). Internationalizing the Undergraduate Curriculum: Opening Commentary. PS. *Online (Bergheim)*, 105.

Barker, C. M. (2000). *Education for international understanding and global competence* (Report of a meeting convened by Carnegie Corporation of New York). Retrieved October 5, 2016, from https://www.carnegie.org/media/filer_public/6d/b0/6db0fdc1-f2b1-4eea-982a-a313cea6822c/ccny_meeting_2000_competence.pdf

Barkley, E. F. (2010). *Student Engagement Techniques: A Handbook for College Faculty*. San Francisco: Jossey-Bass.

Barnett, R., & Coates, K. (2005). *Engaging the curriculum in higher education*. Buckingham, UK: Society for Research into Higher Education and Open University Press.

Barr, R. B., & Tagg, J. (1995). From Teaching to Learning —A New Paradigm for Undergraduate Education. *Change: The Magazine of Higher Learning*, *27*(6), 12–26. doi:10.1080/00091383.1995.10544672

Bates, R. (2005). Can we live together? Towards a global curriculum. *Arts and Humanities in Higher Education*, *4*(1), 95–109. doi:10.1177/1474022205048760

Beare, W. (1964). Tacitus on the Germans. *Greece & Rome, 11*(1), 64-76.

Becher, T. (2001). *Academic tribes and territories: intellectual enquiry and the cultures of the disciplines*. Buckingham, UK: Society for Research into Higher Education and Open University Press.

Bednarz, S., Heffron, S., & Huynh, N. (2013). *A Road Map for 21 Century Geography Education: Geography Education Research*. Washington, DC: Association of American Geographers.

Beilock, S. L., & Carr, T. H. (n.d.). When High-Powered People Fail: Working Memory and Choking Under Pressure in Math. *PsycEXTRA Dataset*. doi:10.1037/e537052012-380

Bell, D., & Kahrhoff, J. (2006). *Active learning handbook*. Retrieved February 26, 2017, from http://www.cgs.pitt.edu/sites/default/files/Doc6-GetStarted_ActiveLearningHandbook.pdf

Bennett, J. M., & Bennett, M. J. (2004). Developing intercultural sensitivity: An integrative approach to global and domestic diversity. In D. Landis, J. M. Bennett, & M. J. Bennett (Eds.), Handbook of intercultural training (pp. 147-165). Thousand Oaks, CA: Sage.

Bennett, M. J. (1993). Towards ethnorelativism: A developmental model of intercultural sensitivity. In R. M. Paige (Ed.), Education for the intercultural experience (pp. 21-71). Yarmouth, ME: Intercultural Press.

Bennett, J. M., & Bennett, M. J. (2004). Developing intercultural sensitivity: An integrative approach to global and domestic diversity. In D. Landis, J. Bennett, & M. Bennett (Eds.), *Handbook of intercultural training* (3rd ed.; pp. 147–165). Thousand Oaks, CA: Sage. doi:10.4135/9781452231129.n6

Bennett, J. M., Bennett, M. J., & Allen, W. (2003). Developing intercultural competence in the language classroom. In D. L. Lange & R. M. Paige (Eds.), *Culture as the core: Perspectives on culture in second language learning*. Greenwich, CT: Information Age Publishing.

Bennett, M. J. (1986). A Developmental Approach to Training for Intercultural Sensitivity. *International Journal of Intercultural Relations*, *10*(2), 179–196. doi:10.1016/0147-1767(86)90005-2

Bennett, M. J. (1993). Towards Ethnorelativism: A Developmental Model of Intercultural Sensitivity. In R. M. Paige (Ed.), *Education for the Intercultural Experience* (pp. 21–71). Yarmouth, ME: Intercultural Press.

Bennett, M. J. (2004). Becoming Interculturally Competent. In J. Wurzel (Ed.), *Toward multiculturalism: A reader in multicultural education* (2nd ed.; pp. 62–77). Newton, MA: Intercultural Resource Corporation.

Benneworth, P., & Osborne, M. (2014). Knowledge, Engagement, and Higher Education in Europe. In *Global University Network for Innovation, Higher Education in the World 5* (pp. 219–232). New York: Palgrave Macmillan.

Berliner, P. (1978). *The soul of mbira: Music and traditions of the Shona people of Zimbabwe*. Berkeley, CA: University of California Press.

Bernardo, R. (2016, September 12). 2016's happiest states in America. *WalletHub*. Retrieved November 1, 2016, from https://wallethub.com/edu/happiest-states/6959/

Bird, A., & Osland, J. (2004). Global competencies: An introduction. In Handbook of global management. Oxford, UK: Blackwell.

Boas, F. (1887). Museums of ethnology and their classification. *Science*, *9*, 589. PMID:17779725

Bohlander, M. (1998), *Bundesministerium der Justiz und für Verbraucherschutz: GERMAN CRIMINAL CODE* [Federal ministry of justice and consumer protection: GERMAN CRIMINAL CODE]. Federal Ministry of Justice, Germany, para. 130 sec. 1. Retrieved June 11, 2017, from http://www.gesetze-im-internet.de/englisch_stgb/englisch_stgb.html#p1241

Bok, D. C. (2006). *Our underachieving colleges: A candid look at how much students learn and why they should be learning more*. Princeton, NJ: Princeton University Press.

Bolhuis, S., & Voeten, M. (2004). Teachers' conceptions of student learning and own learning. *Teachers and Teaching*, *10*(1), 77–98. doi:10.1080/13540600320000170936

Bond, S. (2006). *Transforming the culture of learning: Evoking the international dimension in Canadian university curriculum*. Retrieved June 30, 2016, from http://international.yorku.ca/global/conference/canada/papers/Sheryl-Bond.pdf

Bond, S. (2006). *Transforming the culture of learning: Evoking the international dimension in Canadian university curriculum*. Retrieved October 15, 2016 from http://international.yorku.ca/global/conference/canada/papers/Sheryl-Bond.pdf

Bond, S. (2003). Untapped resources: Internationalization of the curriculum and classroom experience. *Canadian Bureau for International Education Research*, *7*, 1–15.

Bond, S. (2003a). *Engaging educators: Bringing the world into the classroom: Guidelines for practice*. Ottawa, Canada: Canadian Bureau for International Education.

Bond, S. (2003b). *Untapped resources: Internationalization of the curriculum and classroom experience: A selected literature review (CBIE Research Millennium Series No. 7)*. Ottawa, Canada: Canadian Bureau for International Education.

Bond, S. (2006). *Transforming the culture of learning: Evoking the international dimension in Canadian university curriculum*. York University.

Bonds, S. (2003). *Engaging Educators: Bringing the World into the Classroom: Guidelines for Practice*. Ottawa, Canada: Canadian Bureau for International Education.

Bonwell, C. C., & Eison, J. A. (1991). *Active Learning: Creating Excitement in the Classroom*. Washington, DC: School of Education and Human Development, George Washington University.

Boschmann, E. E., & Cubbon, E. (2014). Sketch Maps and Qualitative GIS: Using Cartographies of Individual Spatial Narratives in Geographic Research. *The Professional Geographer, 66*(2), 236–248. doi:10.1080/00330124.2013.781490

Bowlby, J. (1978). Attachment theory and its therapeutic implications. *Adolescent Psychiatry, 6*, 5–33. PMID:742687

Bowles, S., & Gintis, H. (1976). *Schooling in Capitalist America*. New York: Besic Books.

Brake, T., Walker, D., & Walker, T. (1995). *Doing Business Internationally: The Guide to Cross-cultural Success*. Burr Ridge, IL: Irwin Professional Publishing.

Braskamp, L. (2008). Developing Global Citizens. *Journal of College and Character, X*(1), 1–5.

Bremer, L., & van der Wende, M. (1995). Internationalizing the curriculum in higher education: Experiences in the Netherlands. Amsterdam: Academic Press.

Breninger, B., & Kaltenbacher, T. (2012). Intercultural Competence in the 21st Century: Perspectives, Issues, Application. In Creating cultural synergies: Multidisciplinary perspectives on interculturality and interreligiosity (pp. 7-23). Newcastle upon Tyne, UK: Cambridge Scholars Pub.

Brewer, E., & Cunningham, K. (Eds.). (2009). *Integrating study abroad into the curriculum: Theory and practice across the discipline*. Sterling, VA: Stylus.

Brewley, N., Boindala, P., & Sinclair, J. (2014). *Ideation to Execution: Flipping an Undergraduate Pre-Calculus Course to Create Significant Learning Experiences* (pp. 26–41). IGI Global Publications.

Bringle, R. G., & Hatcher, J. A. (1995). A service-learning curriculum for faculty. *Michigan Journal of Community Service Learning, 2*(1), 112–122.

Bringle, R. G., & Hatcher, J. A. (1999). Reflection in service learning: Making meaning of experience. *Educational Horizons, 77*(4), 179–185.

Brock, T. (2010). *Young adults and higher education: Barriers and breakthroughs to success*. Ann Arbor, MI: National Poverty Center.

Brodie, L. M. (2009). eProblem-based learning: Problem-based learning using virtual teams. *European Journal of Engineering Education, 34*(6), 497–509. doi:10.1080/03043790902943868

Bromberger, S. (1992). *On What We Know We Don't Know: Explanation, Theory, Linguistics, and How Questions Shape Them*. Chicago: University of Chicago Press.

Brookfield, S. (1995). *Becoming a Critically Reflective Teacher*. San Francisco: Jossey-Bass.

Brookfield, S. (2017). *On becoming a critically reflective teacher*. San Francisco, CA: Jossey-Bass.

Brosius, M. (2006). *The Persians: An Introduction*. London: Routledge.

Brown v. Board of Education of Topeka, Kansas, 347 U.S. 483 (1954).

Brown, M. F. (2008). Cultural relativism 2.0. *Current Anthropology, 49*(3), 363–383. doi:10.1086/529261

Brown, P. C., Roediger, H. L., & McDaniel, M. A. (2014). *Make it stick: The science of successful learning.* Cambridge, MA: The Belknap Press of Harvard University Press. doi:10.4159/9780674419377

Buerk, R. (2006). *Breaking Ships.* New York: Chamberlain Bros.

Burbules, N., & Berk, R. (1999). *Critical Thinking and Critical Pedagogy: Relations, Differences, and Limits. In Critical Theories in Education.* New York: Routledge.

Burkert, W. (1990). Herodot als Historiker fremder Religionen. In W. Burkert et al. (Eds.), *Hérodote et les peoples non grecs* (pp. 1–32). Geneva: Foundation Hardt.

Burn, B., & Smuckler, R. (1990). *A National Mandate for Education Abroad: Getting on with the Task.* Washington, DC: National Association of Student Affairs.

Butin, D. W. (2010). *Service-learning in theory and practice. The future of community engagement in higher education.* New York: Palgrave McMillan. doi:10.1057/9780230106154

Butt, G., & Lambert, D. (2014). International perspectives on the future of geography education: An analysis of national curricula and standards. *International Research in Geographical and Environmental Education, 23*(1), 1–12. doi:10.1 080/10382046.2013.858402

Caesar, J. *Comentarii de bello gallico.*

Campbell, W. E., & Smith, K. A. (1997). *New Paradigms for College Teaching.* Edina, MN: Interaction Book Co.

Candy, P. C. (1991). *Self-Direction for Lifelong Learning: a Comprehensive Guide to Theory and Practice.* San Francisco: Jossey-Bass.

Carey, J. (2008). Presidential versus parliamentary government. In C. Menard & M. Shirley (Eds.), *Handbook of new institutional economics* (pp. 91–122). Berlin: Springer-Verlag. doi:10.1007/978-3-540-69305-5_6

Carter, M. J., & Fuller, C. (2015). Symbolic interactionism. *Sociopedia.isa.* Retrieved March 13, 2017, from www. sagepub.net/isa/resources/pdf/Symbolic%20interactionism.pdf

Cartlege, P. (2006). *Thermopylae: The Battle that changed the World. Woodstock.* Overlook Press.

Castells, M. (2004). *The Network Society: a Cross-Cultural Perspective.* Cheltenham, UK: Edward Elgar Pub. doi:10.4337/9781845421663

Castells, M. (2011). *The power of identity: The information age: Economy, society, and culture* (2nd ed.; Vol. 2). Hoboken, NJ: Wiley-Blackwell.

Castillo, J., & Cano, J. (2004). Factors explaining job satisfaction among faculty. *Journal of Agricultural Education, 45*(3), 65–74. doi:10.5032/jae.2004.03065

Castles, Miller, & de Haas. (2013). The Age of Migration: International Population Movements in the Modern World. New York: Guilford Press.

Center for Advanced Operational Culture and Learning. (2014). Retrieved from https://www.marinecorpsconceptsand-programs.com/programs/investing-education-and-training-our-marines/center-advanced-operational-culture-and

Chaplinsky v. New Hampshire, 315 U.S. 568 (1942).

Charmaz, K. (2006). *Constructing grounded theory.* Thousand Oaks, CA: Sage Publications.

Charts All Over the World. (n.d.). Retrieved March 9, 2017, from http://www.lanet.lv/misc/charts/

Childress, L. (2010). *The Twenty-First Century University: Developing Faculty Engagement. In Intrinsic motivation and self-determination in human behavior.* New York: Plenum.

Chopp, R., Frost, S., & Weiss, D. H. (2014). *Remaking college: Innovation and the liberal arts.* Baltimore, MD: The Johns Hopkins University Press.

Clarke, I. III, Flaherty, T. B., Wright, N. D., & McMillen, R. M. (2009). Student intercultural proficiency from study abroad programs. *Journal of Marketing Education, 31*(2), 173–181. doi:10.1177/0273475309335583

Clayton, P. H., Bringle, R. G., & Hatcher, J. A. (2012). Research on Intercultural Learning of Students in Service Learning. In Research on Service Learning V2A: Conceptual Frameworks and Assessments (pp. 157-186). Sterling, VA: Stylus Pub.

Cleveland-Jones, M., Emes, C., & Ellard, J. H. (2001). On being a social change agent in a reluctant collegial environment. *Planning for Higher Education, 29*(4).

Cogan, J. (1998). Internationalization through networking and curricular infusion. In J. Mestenhauser & B. Ellingboe (Eds.), *Reforming higher education curriculum: Internationalizing the campus.* Phoenix, AZ: Oryx Press.

College Board. (2015). *AP Human Geography Course Description Effective 2015.* College Board. Retrieved from http://media.collegeboard.com/digitalServices/pdf/ap/ap-human-geography-course-description.pdf

Collins, P. H. (1990). *Black feminist thought: Knowledge, consciousness and the politics of empowerment.* New York: Routledge.

Collins, P. H. (1997). Comment on Hekman's "Truth and method: Feminist standpoint theory revisited": Where's the power? *Signs (Chicago, Ill.), 22*(2), 375–381. doi:10.1086/495162

Cooper, T. C. (1987). Foreign Language Study and SAT Verbal Scores. *Modern Language Journal, 71*(4), 381–387. doi:10.1111/j.1540-4781.1987.tb00376.x

Corbin, J., & Strauss, A. (1990). Grounded theory method: Procedures, canons, and evaluative procedures. *Qualitative Sociology, 13*(1), 3–21. doi:10.1007/BF00988593

Corbin, J., & Strauss, A. (2008). *Basics of qualitative research: Techniques and procedures for developing grounded theory.* Los Angeles, CA: Sage. doi:10.4135/9781452230153

Cornelius-White, J. (2007). Learner-Centered Teacher-Student Relationships Are Effective: A Meta-Analysis. *Review of Educational Research, 77*(1), 113–143. doi:10.3102/003465430298563

Courts, P. L., & McInerney, K. H. (1993). *Assessment in Higher Education: Politics, Pedagogy, and Portfolios.* Westport, CT: Praeger.

Cousin, G., & Deepwell, F. (2005). Designs for network learning: A communities of practice perspective. *Studies in Higher Education, 30*(1), 57–66. doi:10.1080/0307507052000307795

Cox, A. (2016). *Music and Embodied Cognition: Listening, Moving, Feeling, and Thinking.* Bloomington, IN: Indiana University Press.

Crichton, J. A., Paige, M., Papademetre, L., & Scarino, A. (2004). *Integrated resources for intercultural teaching and learning in the context of internationalisation in higher education (University of South Australia, Research Centre for Languages and Cultures Education) The role of language and culture in open learning in international collaborative programs: A case study.* Retrieved June 23, 2017, from: https://www.researchgate.net/publication/224807122_The_role_of_language_and_culture_in_open_learning_in_international_collaborative_programs_A_case_study

Crichton, J. P. M., Papademetre, L., & Scarino, A. (2004). *Integrated resources for intercultural training and learning in the context of internationalization of higher education.* Retrieved from http://www.unisa.edu.au/staff/gratns/archive/2003-integrated-report.doc

Cross, S. B., & Dunn, A. H. (2016). "I didn't know of a better way to prepare to teach": A case study of paired student teaching abroad. *Teacher Education Quarterly, 43*(1), 71–90.

Darhower, M. (2007). A tale of two communities: Group dynamics and community building in a Spanish-English tele-collaboration. *CALICO Journal, 24*, 561–589.

Darling-Hammond, L. (2010). *The flat world and education: How American's commitment to equity will determine our future.* New York, NY: Teachers College Press.

DaSilva, E. B., & Kvasnak, R. N. (2012). Multimedia Technology and Students' Achievement in Geography. *Geography Teacher, 9*(1), 18–25. doi:10.1080/19338341.2012.635080

Davis, D., & Mackintosh, B. (2012). *Making a difference: Australian international education.* Kensington, NSW: University of New South Wales Press.

De Waal, M., & Khumisi, O. (2016). Supporting communities of practice: A reflection of the benefits and challenges facing communities of practice for research and engagement in nursing. *Gateways: International Journal of Community Research & Engagement, 9*(1), 58–73. doi:10.5130/ijcre.v9i1.4717

de Wit, H. (1995). *Strategies for the internationalisation of higher education. A comparative study of Australia, Canada, Europe and the United States of America.* Amsterdam, The Netherlands: European Association for International Education.

de Wit, H. (2002). *Internationalization of Higher Education in the United States of America and Europe.* Westport, CT: Greenwood Press.

Deardorff, D. K. (2006). Identification and assessment of intercultural competence as a student outcome of internationalization. *Journal of Studies in International Education, 10*(3), 241–266. doi:10.1177/1028315306287002

Deardorff, D. K. (2009). Assessing intercultural competence: Issues and tools. In *The Sage handbook of intercultural competence* (pp. 456–476). Thousand Oaks, CA: Sage Publications.

Deardorff, D. K. (2009). Exploring interculturally competent teaching in social sciences classrooms. *Enhancing Learning in the Social Sciences, 2*(1), 1–19. doi:10.11120/elss.2009.02010002

Deardorff, D. K. (2009). *The Sage handbook of intercultural competence.* Thousand Oaks, CA: Sage Publications.

Deardorff, D. K. (2009). *The Sage Handbook of Intercultural Competence.* Thousand Oaks, CA: Sage Publications.

Deardorff, D. K., de Wit, H., & Heyl, J. (2012). *The SAGE Handbook of International Higher Education.* Thousand Oaks, CA: SAGE Publications.

Democracy. (n.d.). In *Oxford dictionary.* Retrieved June 11, 2017, from https://en.oxforddictionaries.com/definition/democracy

Deutsch, D., Gabrielson, A., Sloboda, J., Cross, I., Drake, C., Parncutt, R., . . . Zatorre, R. (n.d.). Psychology of music. In *Oxford Music Online.* Retrieved from http://www.oxfordmusiconline.com.libproxy.ggc.edu/subscriber/article/grove/music/42574

DeVale, S. C. (n.d.). Boas, Franz. In *Oxford Music Online.* Retrieved from http://www.oxfordmusiconline.com.libproxy.ggc.edu/subscriber/article/grove/music/03328

DeVita, G., & Case, P. (2003). Rethinking the internationalization agenda in UK higher education. *Journal of Further and Higher Education*, *27*(4), 383–398. doi:10.1080/0309877032000128082

De-Zan, A.-T., Paipa-G, L.-A., & Parra-M, C. (2011). Las Competencias: Base para la Internationalicion de la Educacion Superior [The Skills as a Basefor Internationalization of Higher Education]. *Revista Educacion en Ingenieria,* (11), 44-54. Retrieved August 1, 2017, from www.acofi.edu.co

Dicken, P. (2011). *Global Shift: Mapping the Changing Contours of the World Economy*. New York: Guilford Press.

Dicken, P. (2014). Global Shift: Mapping the Changing Contours of the World Economy. *Sage (Atlanta, Ga.)*.

Dimmock, C. A., & Walker, A. (2005). *Educational leadership: Culture and diversity*. London, UK: SAGE Publications.

Dolby, N. (2007). Reflections on nation: American undergraduates and education abroad. *Journal of Studies in International Education*, *11*(2), 141–156. doi:10.1177/1028315306291944

Donnelly, J. (1984). Cultural relativism and universal human rights. *Human Rights Quarterly*, *6*(4), 400–419. doi:10.2307/762182

Doppen, F. H., & An, J. (2014). Student teaching abroad: Enhancing global awareness. *International Education*, *43*(2), 59–76.

dos Santos, S. C., da Conceição Moraes Batista, M., Cavalcanti, A. P. C., Albuquerque, J. O., & Meira, S. R. (2009). Applying PBL in software engineering education. In *Proceedings of the 22nd Software Engineering Education and Training Conference* (pp. 182–189). Hyderabad, India: IEEE.

Dostrovsky, S., Cambell, M., Bell, J., & Truesdell, C. (n.d.). Physics of music. In *Oxford Music Online*. Retrieved from http://www.oxfordmusiconline.com.libproxy.ggc.edu/subscriber/article/grove/music/43400

Doubleday, V. (2008). Sounds of Power: An Overview of Musical Instruments and Gender. *Ethnomusicology Forum*, *17*(1), 3-39. Retrieved from http://www.jstor.org.libproxy.ggc.edu/stable/20184604

Doyle, S., Gendall, P., Meyer, L. H., Hoek, J., Tait, C., McKenzie, L., & Loorparg, A. (2010). An Investigation of Factors Associated With StudentParticipation in Study Abroad. *Journal of Studies in International Education*, *14*(5), 471–490. doi:10.1177/1028315309336032

Duke, R., Simmons, A., & Cash, C. (2009). It's Not How Much; It's How: Characteristics of Practice Behavior and Retention of Performance Skills. *Journal of Research in Music Education*, *56*(4), 310–321. doi:10.1177/0022429408328851

Dundes Renteln, A. (1988). Relativism and the search for human rights. *American Anthropologist*, *90*(1), 56–72. doi:10.1525/aa.1988.90.1.02a00040

Dunn, S. W. (1965). Cross-cultural research by U.S. corporations. *The Journalism Quarterly*, *42*(3), 454–457. doi:10.1177/107769906504200312

Dutton, D. (2009). *The art instinct: Beauty, pleasure and human evolution*. New York: Bloomsbury Press.

Egron-Polak, E., & Hudson, R. (2014). *Internationalization Of Higher Education: Growing Expectations, Fundamental Values. In Internationalization Of Higher Education: Growing Expectations, Fundamental Values*. Paris: International Association of Universities. Retrieved from http://www.iau-aiu.net/sites/all/files/iau-4th-global-survey-executive-summary.pdf

Eisner, E. W. (1985). *Learning and teaching the ways of knowing*. Chicago: National Society for the Study of Education.

Elia, A. (2006). Language Learning in Tandem via Skype. *The Reading Matrix*, *6*(3), 269–280.

Engstrom, R. N. (2008). Introductory American government in comparison: An experiment. *Journal of Political Science Education, 4*(4), 394–403. doi:10.1080/15512160802413675

Etherington, N. (2011). Barbarians Ancient and Modern. *American Historical Review, 116*(1), 31-57.

Felder, R. M., & Brent, R. (2009). Active learning: An introduction. *ASQ Higher Education Brief, 2*(4).

Fennema, E., & Sherman, J. A. (1976). Fennema-Sherman Mathematics Attitudes Scales: Instruments Designed to Measure Attitudes toward the Learning of Mathematics by Females and Males. *Journal for Research in Mathematics Education, 7*(5), 324. doi:10.2307/748467

Findlaw. (n.d.). *What are civil rights?* Retrieved June 10, 2017, from http://civilrights.findlaw.com/civil-rights-overview/what-are-civil-rights.html

Fink, L. D. (2003). *Creating Significant Learning Experiences: An Integrated Approach to Designing College Courses.* San Francisco, CA: Jossey-Bass.

Fink, L. D. (2005). *A Self-Directed Guide to Designing Courses for Significant Learning.* Academic Press.

Fink, L. D. (2013). *Creating significant learning experiences, revised and updated: An integrated approach to designing college courses.* San Francisco, CA: Jossey-Bass.

Fink, L. D. (2013). *Creating Significant Learning Experiences: An Integrated Approach to Designing College Courses, Revised and Updated.* San Francisco: Jossey-Bass.

Fink, L. D. (2013). *Creating Significant Learning Experiences: an Integrated Approach to Designing College Courses.* San Francisco, CA: Jossey-Bass.

Fleuhr-Lobban, C. (1995, June 9). Anthropologists, cultural relativism, and universal rights. *The Chronicle of Higher Education*, pp. B1–2.

Fleuhr-Lobban, C. (1998). Cultural relativism and universal human rights. *Anthro Notes, 20*(2). Retrieved from http://anthropology.si.edu/outreach/anthnote/Winter98/anthnote.html

Fluehr-Lobban, C. (2005). Cultural relativism and universal rights in Islamic law. *Anthropology News, 46*(9), 23. doi:10.1525/an.2005.46.9.23

Fordham, M. (2012). Disciplinary History and the Situation of History Teachers. *Education in Science, 2*(4), 242–253. doi:10.3390/educsci2040242

Foucault, M., & Gordon, C. (1980). *Power/Knowledge: Selected Interviews and Other Writings, 1972-1977.* New York: Pantheon Books.

Fournier, E. J. (2002). World Regional Geography And Problem-Based Learning: Using Collaborative Learning Groups in an Introductory-Level World Geography Course. *The Journal of General Education, 51*(4), 293–305. doi:10.1353/jge.2003.0011

Fraga-Cañadas, C. P. (2011). Building communities of practice for foreign language teachers. *Modern Language Journal, 95*(2), 296–300. doi:10.1111/j.1540-4781.2011.01183.x

Frankenstein, M. (1990). Incorporating Race, Gender, and Class Issues into a Critical Mathematica Literacy Curriculum. *The Journal of Negro Education, 59*(3), 336. doi:10.2307/2295568

Frazier, J. W., & Margai, F. M. (2010). *Multicultural Geographies: The Changing Racial/Ethnic Patterns of the United States.* Global Academic Publishing.

Freeman, S., Eddy, S. L., McDonough, M., Smith, M. K., Okorafor, N., Jordt, H., & Wenderoth, M. P. (2014). Active learning increases student performance in science, engineering and mathematics. *Proceedings of the National Academy of Sciences of the United States of America*, *111*(23), 8410–8415. doi:10.1073/pnas.1319030111 PMID:24821756

Freire, P. (1970). *Pedagogy of the Oppressed*. New York: Seabury Press.

Friedman, T. L. (2005). *The world is flat*. London: Penguin Books.

Fuller, T. L. (2007). Study abroad experiences and intercultural sensitivity among graduate theological students: A preliminary and exploratory investigation. *Christian Higher Education*, *6*(4), 321–332. doi:10.1080/15363750701268319

Gallup. (2016a). *Confidence in institutions*. Retrieved February 12, 2017, from http://www.gallup.com/poll/1597/confidence-institutions.aspx

Gallup. (2016b). *Trust in government*. Retrieved February 12, 2017, from http://www.gallup.com/poll/5392/trust-government.aspx

Gallup. (2016c). *Americans trust in political leaders at new lows*. Retrieved February 12, 2017, from http://www.gallup.com/poll/195716/americans-trust-political-leaders-public-new-lows.aspx

Geertz, C. (1973). Thick description: Toward an interpretive theory of culture. In C. Geertz (Ed.), The interpretation of cultures: Selected essays (pp. 3-30). New York: Basic Books.

Gehlhar, J. (2009). Of course they want us at the curriculum internationalization table. *Modern Language Journal*, *93*(4), 616–618.

Gelbman, S. M. (2011). A qualitative assessment of the learning outcomes of teaching introductory American politics in comparative perspective. *Journal of Political Science Education*, *7*(4), 359–374. doi:10.1080/15512169.2011.615187

Gellner, E. (1995). *Anthropology and politics: Revolutions in the sacred grove*. Oxford, UK: Blackwell Publishers.

Georgia Gwinnett College International Student Learning Outcomes. (n.d.). Retrieved from http://www.ggc.edu/academics/qep/internationalized-courses/index.html

Georgia Gwinnett College Quality Enhancement Plan. (n.d.). *Student Learning Outcomes*. Retrieved from http://www.ggc.edu/academics/qep/student-learning-outcomes/index.html

Georgia Gwinnett College. (2013a). *Quality Enhancement Program: Internationalization of the curriculum: Engaging the world to develop global citizens*. Author.

Georgia Gwinnett College. (2013b). *Internationalization of the curriculum: Engaging the world to develop global citizens—Quality Enhancement Plan (QEP)*. Lawrenceville, GA: Author.

Georgia Gwinnett College. (2015). *Internationalized Courses*. Retrieved October 21, 2016, from http://www.ggc.edu/academics/qep/internationalized-courses/

Georgia Gwinnett College. (2015). *Student demographics. About GGC*. Retrieved from http://www.ggc.edu/about-ggc/at-a-glance/ggc-facts/

Georgia Gwinnett College. (2017). *Quality Enhancement Plan Student Learning Outcomes*. Retrieved from http://www.ggc.edu/academics/qep/student-learning-outcomes/index.html

Georgia Gwinnett College. (n.d.a). *History of Georgia Gwinnett College*. Retrieved July 16, 2017 from http://www.ggc.edu/kaufman-tribute/history

Georgia Gwinnett College. (n.d.b). *Internationalized courses*. Retrieved October 23, 2016 from http://www.ggc.edu/academics/qep/internationalized-courses

GGC. (2016a). *Academics: Program Goals*. Retrieved Sept 2, 2016, from Georgia Gwinnett College: http://www.ggc.edu/academics/qep/program-goals/

GGC. (2016b). *Academics: Faculty Professional Development*. Retrieved Sept 4, 2016, from Georgia Gwinnett College: http://www.ggc.edu/academics/qep/faculty-professional-development/

GGC. (2016c). *Academics: Internationalized Courses*. Retrieved September 4, 2016, from Georgia Gwinnett College: http://www.ggc.edu/academics/qep/internationalized-courses/

GGC. (2016d). *Academics: Global Studies Certification*. Retrieved September 4, 2016, from Georgia Gwinnett College: http://www.ggc.edu/academics/qep/global-studies-certification/

GGC. (2016e). *Academics: Student Learning Outcomes*. Retrieved September 5, 2016, from Georgia

Gibney, E. (2013, January 31). A different world. *Times Higher Education*. Retrieved September 20, 2016, from https://www.timeshighereducation.com/features/a-different-world/2001128.article

Giddens, A. (2003). *Runaway World: How Globalization Is Reshaping Our Lives*. London: Routledge.

Gilovich, T. (1991). *How We Know What Isn't so: the Fallibility of Human Reason in Everyday Life*. New York, NY: Free Press.

Glaser, B. G. (1978). *Theoretical sensitivity*. Mill Valley, CA: Sociology Press.

Glaser, B. G., & Strauss, A. L. (1967). *The discovery of grounded theory: Strategies or qualitative research*. New Brunswick, NJ: Aldine Transaction.

Goffart, W. (2006). *Barbarian Tides: The Migration Age and the Later Roman Empire*. Philadelphia: University of Pennsylvania Press. doi:10.9783/9780812200287

Goldsmith, M., Greenberg, C., Robertson, A., & Hu-Chan, M. (2003). *Global leadership: The next generation*. Upper Saddle River, NJ: Prentice-Hall.

Green, M. (2002). Joining the world: The challenge of internationalizing undergraduate education. *Change Magazine, 34*.

Green, M. F., Luu, D., & Burris, B. (2012). *Mapping internationalization on U.S. Campuses* (2012 edition). Washington, DC: American Council on Education.

Green, M. F., & Olson, C. L. (2003). *Internationalizing the campus: A user's guide*. Washington, DC: American Council on Education.

Green, P. (1996). *The Greco-Persian Wars*. Berkeley, CA: University of California Press.

Gurin, P., Dey, E. L., Hurtado, S., & Gurin, G. (2002). Diversity and higher education: Theory and impact on educational outcomes. *Harvard Educational Review, 72*(3), 330–366. doi:10.17763/haer.72.3.01151786u134n051

Gutierrez, R. (2013). The Sociopolitical Turn in Mathematics Education. *Journal for Research in Mathematics Education, 44*(1), 37–68. doi:10.5951/jresematheduc.44.1.0037

Gutstein. (2006). *Reading and Writing: The World with Mathematics, Towards a Pedagogy for Social Justice*. CRC Press.

Gwin, P. (2014). The Ship-Breakers. *National Geographic*. Retrieved from http://ngm.nationalgeographic.com/2014/05/shipbreakers/gwin-text

Hachtmann, F. (2014). International Advertising Education: Curriculum and Pedagogy. Faculty Publications, College of Journalism & Mass Communications, 82.

Haigh, M. (2009). Fostering cross-cultural empathy with non-western curricular structures. *Journal of Studies in International Education*, *13*(2), 271–284. doi:10.1177/1028315308329791

Haigh, M. J. (2009). Fostering cross-cultural empathy with non-Western curricular structures. *Journal of International Education.*, *13*(2), 271–284.

Hainmueller, J., & Hopkins, D. J. (2014). *Public Attitudes Toward Immigration*. SSRN Journal SSRN Electronic Journal.

Hajjar, R. (2006). The TRADOC Culture Center. *The Free Library*. Retrieved from https://www.thefreelibrary.com/TheTRADOC Culture Center.-a0190700220

Hall, E. (1959). *The Silent Language*. Garden City, NY: Doubleday & Company.

Hall, E. T. (1989). *Beyond Culture*. New York: Doubleday.

Hall, J. (1997). *Ethnic identity in Greek antiquity*. Cambridge, UK: Cambridge University Press. doi:10.1017/CBO9780511605642

Hammer, M. R. (1999). A Measure of intercultural sensitivity: The Intercultural Development Inventory. In S. M. Fowler & M. G. Mumford (Eds.), *Intercultural sourcebook: Cross-cultural training* (Vol. 2, pp. 61–72). Yarmouth, ME: Intercultural Press.

Hammer, M. R. (2009). The Intercultural Development Inventory. In M. A. Moodian (Ed.), *Contemporary leadership and Intercultural Competence*. Thousand Oaks, CA: Sage.

Hammer, M. R., Gudykunst, W. B., & Wiseman, R. L. (1978). Dimensions of intercultural effectiveness: An exploratory study. *International Journal of Intercultural Relations*, *2*(4), 382–393. doi:10.1016/0147-1767(78)90036-6

Handbook for Institutions seeking reaffirmation.pdf. (n.d.). Retrieved from http://www.sacscoc.org/pdf/081705/Handbook%20for%20Institutions%20seeking%20reaffirmation.pdf

Handley, K., Sturdy, A., Fincham, R., & Clark, R. (2006). Within and beyond communities of practice: Making sense of learning through participation, identity and practice. *Journal of Management Studies*, *43*(3), 641–653. doi:10.1111/j.1467-6486.2006.00605.x

Hanson, V. D. (1989). *Western Way of War: Infantry Battle in Classical Greece*. New York: Knopf.

Haraway, D. (2004). Situated knowledges: The science question in feminism and the privilege of partial perspective. In S. Harding (Ed.), The feminist standpoint theory reader (pp. 81-102). New York, NY: Routledge.

Harding, S. (1993). Rethinking standpoint epistemology: What is strong objectivity? In L. Alcoff & E. Potter (Eds.), Feminist epistemologies (pp. 49-82). New York, NY: Routledge.

Harding, S. (Ed.). (2004). *The feminist standpoint theory reader*. New York, NY: Routledge.

Harley & Laxton. (2001). *The New Nature of Maps: Essays in the History of Cartography*. Baltimore, MD: Johns Hopkins University Press.

Harley, J. B., & Cosgrove, D. E. (1988). Maps, Knowledge and Power. Cambridge, UK: Cambridge University Press.

Harouni, H. (2015). Toward a Political Economy of Mathematics Education. *Harvard Educational Review*, *85*(1), 50–74. doi:10.17763/haer.85.1.2q580625188983p6

Hart, M., Stevens, J., & Lieberman, F. (1990). *Drumming at the edge of magic: A journey into the spirit of percussion.* San Francisco: Harper San Francisco.

Hartog, F. (1988). *The Mirror of Herodotus: The Representation of the other in the writing of History* (J. Lloyd, Trans.). Berkeley, CA: University of California Press.

Hawes, F., & Kealey, D. J. (1981). An empirical study of Canadian technical assistance. *International Journal of Intercultural Relations, 5*(3), 239–258. doi:10.1016/0147-1767(81)90028-6

Haynes, C. C. (1990). Religion in the Classroom: Meeting the Challenges and Avoiding the Pitfalls. *Social Education, 54*(5), 305–306.

Hayward, F. M. (2000). *Preliminary status report 2000: Internationalization of U.S. higher education.* Washington, DC: American Council on Education.

Heiede, T. (1992). Why Teach History of Mathematics? *The Mathematical Gazette, 76*(475), 151. doi:10.2307/3620388

Helms, R. M. (n.d.). *Internationalization in Action: Internationalizing the Curriculum, Part 1 - Individual Courses.* Retrieved from http://www.acenet.edu/news-room/Pages/Intlz-in-Action-2013-December.aspx

Hendrix, K. S., Finnell, S. M. E., Zimet, G. D., Sturm, L. A., Lane, K. A., & Downs, S. M. (2014). Vaccine Message Framing And Parents' Intent to Immunize Their Infants for MMR. *Pediatrics, 134*(3), e675–e683. doi:10.1542/peds.2013-4077 PMID:25136038

Herdt, G. H. (2006). *The Sambia: Ritual, sexuality, and change in Papua New Guinea.* Belmont, CA: Thomson/Wadsworth.

Herodotus, . (2007). *The Landmark Herodotus: the Histories.* New York: Pantheon Books.

Herzberg, F., Mausner, B., & Snyderman, B. (1959). *The motivation to work.* New York: Johjn Wiley & Sons.

Heusser, M. (2013). Six software development lessons from healthcare.gov's failed launch. *CIO.* Retrieved from http://www.cio.com/article/2380827/developer/6-software-development-lessons-from-healthcare-gov-s-failed-launch.html

Higbee, M. D. (2009). How reacting to the past games 'made me want to come to class and learn': An assessment of reacting pedagogy at EMU, 2007- 208. *The Scholarship of Teaching and Learning at EMU, 2*(4).

Hinde, E. R. (2014). Geography and the Common Core: Teaching Mathematics and Language Arts from a Spatial Perspective. *Social Studies Review, 53*, 47–51.

Hmelo-Silver, C. E. (2004). Problem-based learning: What and how do students learn? *Educational Psychology Review, 16*(3), 235–266. doi:10.1023/B:EDPR.0000034022.16470.f3

Hoffa, W. W., & DePaul, S. C. (2010). *A history of U.S. study abroad: 1965–present.* Carlisle, PA: Forum on Education Abroad.

Hofstede, G. J. (2009). The Moral Circle in Intercultural Competence. In D. Deardorf (Ed.), *Handbook of Intercultural Competence* (pp. 85–99). Thousand Oaks, CA: Sage.

Homan, A. C., Buengeler, C., Eckhoff, R. A., van Ginkel, W. P., & Voelpel, S. C. (2015). The interplay of diversity training and diversity beliefs on team creativity in nationality diverse teams. *The Journal of Applied Psychology, 100*(5), 1456–1467. doi:10.1037/apl0000013 PMID:25688641

Hor, J., & Matawie, K. (2006). An Examination of Institutional Factors for Internationalizing the Business and Accounting Curricula. *International Journal of Learning, 13*(5), 1–7.

Horta, H. (2009). Global And National Prominent Universities: Internationalization, Competitiveness and the Role of the State. *High Educ Higher Education*, *58*(3), 387–405. doi:10.1007/s10734-009-9201-5

Hostein, J. A., & Gubrium, J. F. (1995). *The active interview*. Thousand Oaks, CA: Sage. doi:10.4135/9781412986120

Hudzic, K. (2011). *Comprehensive internationalization: From concept to action – executive summary*. Washington, DC: NAFSA.

Hudzik, J. K. (2011). Comprehensive Internationalization: From Concept to Action. Washington, DC: NAFSA: Association of International Educators.

Hudzik, J. K., & McCarthy, J. S. (2012). *Leading comprehensive internationalization strategy and tactics for action*. NAFSA: Association of International Educators. Retrieved June 23, 2017, from http://www.nafsa.org/pubs

Huffman Hayes, J. (2002). Energizing software engineering education through real-world projects as experimental studies. In *Proceedings of 15th Software Engineering Education and Training Conference* (pp. 192–206). Covington, KY: IEEE. doi:10.1109/CSEE.2002.995211

Hung, W. (2011). Theory to reality: A few issues in implementing problem-based learning. *Educational Technology Research and Development*, *59*(4), 529–552. doi:10.1007/s11423-011-9198-1

In Greer, G. B. (2010). *Culturally responsive mathematics education*. New York: Routledge.

IndexMundi. (2013). *Georgia Hispanic or Latino Origin Population Percentage, 2013 by County*. Retrieved September 2, 2016, from Index Mundi: http://www.indexmundi.com

Indiana University South Bend. (n.d.). *Computer and Information Sciences*. Retrieved from https://www.iusb.edu/computerscience/programs/bs-cs.php

Institute of International Education (IIE). (2015). *Open doors 20/12 "fast facts."* Retrieved from http://www.iie.org/Research-and-Publications/Open-Doors/Data/US-Study-Abroad#.WARf8YVYWt8

International Institute for Democracy and Electoral Assistance (IDEA). (n.d.). *Voter turnout database*. Retrieved June 16, 2017, from http://www.idea.int/data-tools/data/voter-turnout

Internationalization, O. o. (2007). *Office of Internationalization Mission and Vision*. Retrieved July 21, 2017, from Georgia Gwinnett College: http://www.ggc.edu/academics/academic-opportunities-and-support/office-of-internationalization/mission-vision/

Irwin, T. (1990). *Aristotle's first principles*. Oxford, UK: Clarendon Press. doi:10.1093/0198242905.001.0001

Iyer, R., & Reese, M. (2013). Ensuring student success: Establishing a community of practice for culturally and linguistically diverse pre-service teachers. *Australian Journal of Teacher Education*, *38*(3), 26–40. doi:10.14221/ajte.2013v38n3.4

Jacob, W. J. (2015). Interdisciplinary trends in higher education. *Palgrave Communications*, *1*, 1–5.

Jaeger, W. (1939). *Paideia: The Ideals of Greek Culture* (G. Highet, Trans.). Oxford, UK: Oxford University Press.

Jaggar, A. M. (2016). *Just methods*. New York, NY: Routledge.

Jang, W., & Yao, X. (2014). Tracking Ethnically Divided Commuting Patterns Over Time: A Case Study of Atlanta. *The Professional Geographer*, *66*(2), 274–283. doi:10.1080/00330124.2013.784952

Jankowski, N., Hutchings, P., Ewell, P., Kinzie, J., & Kuh, G. (2013). The degree qualifications profile: What it is and why we need it now. *Change*, *45*(6), 6–15. doi:10.1080/00091383.2013.841515

Jarosz, L. (1996). Working in the global food system: A focus for international comparative analysis. *Progress in Human Geography*, *20*(1), 41–55. doi:10.1177/030913259602000103

Johns-Boast, L. (2014). Developing personal and professional skills in software engineering students. In L. Yu (Ed.), Overcoming Challenges in Software Engineering Education: Delivering Non-Technical Knowledge and Skills (pp. 198–228). Hershey, PA: IGI Global. doi:10.4018/978-1-4666-5800-4.ch011

Johnson, J. D., & Tuttle, F. (1989). Problems in Intercultural Research. In Handbook of International and Intercultural Communication (pp. 461-483). Newbury Park, CA: Sage Publications.

Johnson, R. M., Smith, K. H., & Carinci, S. (2010). Preservice Female Teachers' Mathematics Self-Concept and Mathematics Anxiety: A Longitudinal Study. *Global Pedagogies*, 169-181. doi:10.1007/978-90-481-3617-9_11

Jokinen, T. (2005). Global leadership competencies: A review and discussion. *Journal of European Industrial Training*, *29*(2/3), 199–216. doi:10.1108/03090590510591085

Jones, W. R. (1971). The Image of the Barbarian in Medieval Europe. *Comparative Studies in Society and History*, *13*(4), 376–407. doi:10.1017/S0010417500006381

Jorgensen, E. (2002). The Aims of Music Education: A Preliminary Excursion. *Journal of Aesthetic Education, 36*(1), 31-49. Retrieved from http://www.jstor.org/stable/3333624

Joughin, G. (1998). Dimensions of Oral Assessment. *Assessment & Evaluation in Higher Education*, *23*(4), 367–378. doi:10.1080/0260293980230404

Juwah, C., Macfarlane-Dick, D., Matthew, B., Nicol, D., Ross, D., & Smith, B. (2004). *Enhancing Student Learning Through Effective Formative Feedback*. York, UK: Higher Education Academy.

Kaldor, M. (2014). The habits of the heart: Substantive democracy after the European elections. *Open democracy*. Retrieved June 10, 2017, from https://www.opendemocracy.net/can-europe-make-it/mary-kaldor/habits-of-heart-substantive-democracy-after-european-elections

Kartomi, M., & Mendonça, M. (n.d.). Gamelan. In *Oxford Music Online*. Retrieved from http://www.oxfordmusiconline.com.libproxy.ggc.edu/subscriber/article/grove/music/45141

Katan, D. (1999). *Translating Cultures*. Manchester, UK: St. Jerome Publishing.

Katula, R. A., & Threnhauser, E. (1999). Experiential education in the undergraduate curriculum. *Communication Education*, *48*(3), 238–255. doi:10.1080/03634529909379172

Katz, S. N. (2014, January 17). Borderline ignorance: Why have efforts to internationalize the curriculum stalled? *The Chronicle of Higher Education*, *60*(18). Retrieved from http://www.chronicle.com/article/Borderline-Ignorance/143865/

Kay, J., Barg, M., Fekete, A., Greening, T., Hollands, O., Kingston, J. H., & Crawford, K. (2000). Problem-based learning for foundation computer science courses. *Computer Science Education*, *10*(2), 109–128. doi:10.1076/0899-3408(200008)10:2;1-C;FT109

Kazemi, F., Shahmohammadi, A., & Sharei, M. (2013). The survey on relationship between the attitude and academic achievement of in-service mathematics teachers in introductory Probability and Statistics. *World Applied Sciences Journal*, *22*(7), 886–891.

Kimble, C., & Hildreth, P. (2005). Dualities, distributed communities of practice and knowledge management. *Journal of Knowledge Management*, *9*(4), 102–113. doi:10.1108/13673270510610369

Kim, M., Kim, K., & Lee, S.-I. (2013). Pedagogical Potential of a Web-Based GIS Application for Migration Data: A Preliminary Investigation in the Context of South Korea. *The Journal of Geography, 112*(3), 97–107. doi:10.1080/002 21341.2012.709261

Kim, T. (2011). *Globalization And Higher Education in South Korea: Towards Ethnocentric Internationalization or Global Commercialization of Higher Education?* Handbook On Globalization and Higher Education.

King, P. M., & Baxter Magolda, M. B. (2005). A Developmental Model of Intercultural Maturity. *Journal of College Student Development, 46*(6), 571–592. doi:10.1353/csd.2005.0060

Klee, C. (2009). Internationalization and Foreign Languages: The resurgence of interest in languages across the curriculum. *Modern Language Journal, 93*(4), 618–621. doi:10.1111/j.1540-4781.2009.00936.x

Klenke, K. (2008). Qualitative research in the study of leadership. Emerald Group Publishing Limited.

Knight, J. (1993). Internationalization: Management strategies and issues. *International Education Magazine*, 21-22.

Knight, J. (1994) Internationalization elements and checkpoints. Canadian Bureau for International Education.

Knight, J. (1999). *A Time of Turbulence and Transformation for Internationalization.* Ottawa, Canada: Canadian Bureau for International Education.

Knight, J. (2003). Updated Definition of Internationalization. *Industry and Higher Education, 33*(Fall), 2–3.

Knight, J. (2003). Updating the definition of internationalization. *Industry and Higher Education, 33*, 2–3.

Knight, J. (2004). Internationalization remodeled: Definition, approaches, and rationales. *Journal of Studies in International Education, 8*(1), 5–31. doi:10.1177/1028315303260832

Knight, J. (2008). Internationalisation: key concepts and elements. In M. Gaebel (Ed.), *Internationalisation of European Higher Education: an EUA/ACA Handbook* (pp. 1–24). Berlin, Germany: Raabe Academic Publishers.

Knight, J., & De-Wit, H. (1995). Strategies for Internationalization of Higher Education: Historical and conceptual perspectives. In *Strategies for Internationalization of Higher Education: A comparative study of Australia, Canada, Europe and the United States of America* (pp. 5–33). Amsterdam: European Association for International Education.

Koester, J., Wiseman, R. L., & Sanders, J. A. (1993). Multiple perspectives of intercultural communication competence. In R. L. Wiseman & J. A. Koester (Eds.), *Intercultural Communication competence* (pp. 3–15). Newbury Park, CA: Sage.

Koh, H. H. (2003). On American Exceptionalism. *Stanford Law Review, 55*(5), 1479–1527. Retrieved from http://www. jstor.org/stable/10.2307/1229556?ref=no-x-route:c6cf276eeb26e8f80e47cb2d574528e5

Kolb, D. A. (1984). *Experiential learning: Experience as the source of learning and development.* Englewood Cliffs, NJ: Prentice-Hall.

Koles, P., Nelson, S., Stolfi, A., Parmelee, D., & DeStephen, D. (2005). Active learning in a year 2 pathology curriculum. *Medical Education, 39*(10), 1045–1055. doi:10.1111/j.1365-2929.2005.02248.x PMID:16178832

Korostelina, K. (2013). *History Education in the Formation of Social Identity: Toward a Culture of Peace.* New York: Palgrave Macmillan. doi:10.1057/9781137374769

Krakowka, A. R. (2012). Field Trips as Valuable Learning Experiences in Geography Courses. *The Journal of Geography, 111*(6), 236–244. doi:10.1080/00221341.2012.707674

Kreber, C. (2009). *Internationalizing the curriculum in higher education.* San Francisco, CA: Jossey-Bass.

Krebs, C. (2011). *A Most Dangerous Book: Tacitus's Germania from the Roman Empire to the Third Reich.* New York: W. W. Norton & Company.

Kriewaldt, J. (2010). The Geography Standards Project: Professional Standards for Teaching School Geography. *Geographical Education, 23*, 8.

Krutky, J. (2008). Intercultural competency: Preparing students to be global citizens. *Effective Practices for Academic Leaders, 3*(1), 1–15.

Kubik, G., & Cooke, P. (n.d.). Lamellophone. In *Oxford Music Online.* Retrieved from http://www.oxfordmusiconline.com.libproxy.ggc.edu/subscriber/article/grove/music/40069

Kuhrmann, M., Femmer, H., & Eckhardt, J. (2014). Controlled experiments as means to teach soft skills in software engineering. In L. Yu (Ed.), Overcoming Challenges in Software Engineering Education: Delivering Non-Technical Knowledge and Skills (pp. 180–197). Hershey, PA: IGI Global. doi:10.4018/978-1-4666-5800-4.ch010

Kurosu, M. (Ed.). (2009). *Human centered design, HCII 2009.* Berlin: Springer-Verlag. doi:10.1007/978-3-642-02806-9

Ladson-Billings, G. (1999). Preparing teachers for diverse student populations: A critical race theory perspective. *Review of Research in Education, 24*, 211–247.

Ladson-Billings, G. (2001). *Crossing over to Canaan: The journey of new teachers in diverse classrooms* (1st ed.). San Francisco, CA: Jossey-Bass.

Lamb, A., & Johnson, L. (2010). Virtual Expeditions: Google Earth, GIS, and Geovisualization Technologies in Teaching and Learning - ProQuest. *Teacher Librarian, 37*(3), 81–85.

LaRossa, R. (2005). Grounded theory methods and qualitative family research. *Journal of Marriage and the Family, 67*(4), 237–257. doi:10.1111/j.1741-3737.2005.00179.x

Lasky, M. J. (2002). The Banalization of the Concept of Culture. *Society, 39*(September/October), 73–81. doi:10.1007/s12115-002-1008-2

Lathlean, J., & Le May, A. (2002). Communities of practice: An opportunity for interagency working. *Journal of Clinical Nursing, 11*(3), 394–398. doi:10.1046/j.1365-2702.2002.00630.x PMID:12010537

Lazenby, J. F. (1993). *The Defence of Greece 490-479 B. C.* Warminster: Aris & Phillips.

Leask, B. (2014, December 12). Internationalising the curriculum and all learning. *University World News.* Retrieved February 19, 2017, from http://www.universityworldnews.com/article.php?story=20141211101031828

Leask, B. (2014, July 25). Internationalising the curriculum and all learning. *University World News.* Retrieved July 25, 2016, from University World News: http://www.universityworldnews.com/article.php?story=20141211101031828

Leask, B. (2001). Bridging the gap: Internationalizing university curricula. *Journal of Studies in International Education, 5*(2), 100–115. doi:10.1177/102831530152002

Leask, B. (2009). Using formal and informal curricula to improve interactions between home and international students. *Journal of Studies in International Education, 13*(2), 205–221. doi:10.1177/1028315308329786

Leask, B. (2012). *Internalisation of the curriculum (IoC) in action: A guide.* University of South Australia.

Leask, B. (2012). *Internationalization of the curriculum: A guide.* Sydney, Australia: University of South Australia.

Leask, B. (2013). Internationalizing the curriculum in the disciplines: Imagining new possibilities. *Journal of Studies in International Education, 17*(2), 103–118. doi:10.1177/1028315312475090

Leask, B. (2015). *Internationalizing the curriculum*. London: Routledge.

Leask, B. (2015). *Internationalizing The Curriculum*. Taylor and Francis.

Leask, B., & Carroll, J. (2011). Moving beyond "Wishing and Hoping": Internationalisation and student experiences of inclusion and engagement. *Higher Education Research & Development*, *30*(5), 647–659. doi:10.1080/07294360.2011.598454

Leatham, K. R. (2013). *Vital Directions for Mathematics Education Research*. Dordrecht, The Netherlands: Springer. doi:10.1007/978-1-4614-6977-3

Lee, A., Poch, R., Shaw, M., & Williams, R. D. (2012). *Engaging Diversity in Undergraduate Classrooms: A pedagogy for Developing Intercultural Competence*. San Francisco: Jossey-Bass.

Lee, A., Poch, R., Shaw, M., & Williams, R. D. (2012). *Engaging Diversity in Undergraduate Classrooms: A Pedagogy for Developing Intercultural Competence*. San Francisco: Jossey-Bass.

Lee, W., Chen, C., & Katz, H. (1997). International advertising education in the United States: A preliminary study and evaluation. *International Journal of Advertising*, *16*(1), 1–26. doi:10.1080/02650487.1997.11104670

Levi-Strauss, C. (1969). *The elementary structures of kinship*. Boston, MA: Beacon Press.

Levitin, D., & de Grassi, A. (Nov. 3, 2011). Your brain on music: a story of song meets science. In *Inforum: connect your intellect*. San Francisco: The Commonwealth Club. Retrieved from https://www.commonwealthclub.org/events/2011-11-03/your-brain-music

Levy, M. (2007). Culture, culture learning and new technologies: Towards a pedagogical framework. *Language Learning & Technology*, *11*(2), 104–127.

Levy, O., Beechler, S., Taylor, S., & Boyacigiller, N. A. (2007). What we talk about when we talk about 'Global Mindset': Managerial cognition in multinational corporations. *Journal of International Business Studies*, *38*(2), 231–258. doi:10.1057/palgrave.jibs.8400265

Lewkowicz, M. (2017). The law as the language of civil rights: using Supreme Court cases to facilitate an inclusive classroom dialog on difference and equality. In D. Budrytė & S. Boykin (Eds.), *Engaging difference: Teaching humanities and social science in multicultural environments* (pp. 19–30). Lanham, MD: Rowman & Littlefield.

Liaw, M.-L. (2006). E-learning and the development of intercultural competence. *Language Learning & Technology*, *10*(3), 49–64.

Lichter, D. T., & Johnson, K. M. (2009). Immigrant Gateways And Hispanic Migration to New Destinations. *The International Migration Review*, *43*(3), 496–518. doi:10.1111/j.1747-7379.2009.00775.x

Lijphart, A. (2008). *Thinking about democracy*. London: Routledge Press.

Lipset, S. M. (1996). *American Exceptionalism: a Double-Edged Sword*. New York: W.W. Norton.

Lortie, D. C. (2007). Schoolteacher: A sociological study; with a new preface. Chicago: Univ. of Chicago Press.

Mahoney, S. L., & Schamber, J. F. (2004). Exploring The Application of a Developmental Model of Intercultural Sensitivity to a General Education Curriculum on Diversity. *The Journal of General Education*, *53*(3), 311–334. doi:10.1353/jge.2005.0007

Maidstone, P. (1995). International literacy: A paradigm for change. A manual for internationalizing the post-secondary curriculum. Victoria, Canada: Ministry of Skills, Training, and Labour.

Malloy, M. N., & Davis, A. J. (2012). The University of Georgia Avian Biology Study Abroad Program in Costa Rica. *North American Colleges and Teachers of Agriculture (NACTA) Journal, 56*(3), 24–29. PMID:23097857

Malmgren, J., & Galvin, J. (2008). Effects of study abroad participation on student graduation rates: A study of three incoming freshman cohorts at the University of Minnesota, Twin Cities. *NADADA Journal, 28*(1), 29–42.

Mansilla, V. B., & Jackson, A. (2011). *Educating for global competence: Preparing our youth to engage the world.* New York, NY: Asia Society. Retrieved from http://asiasociety.org/files/book-globalcompetence.pdf

Marchesani, L., & Adams, M. (1992). Dynamics of diversity in the teaching-learning process: A faculty development model for analysis and action. In New directions for teaching and learning (Vol. 52, pp. 9-20). San Francisco: Jossey-Bass. doi:10.1002/tl.37219925203

Marginson, S., & Smolentseva, A. (2014). Higher Education in the World: Main Trends and Facts. In *Global University Network for Innovation, Higher Education in the World 5* (pp. 26–31). New York: Palgrave Macmillan.

Marshall, C., & Rossman, G. B. (1999). *Designing qualitative research* (3rd ed.). Thousand Oaks, CA: Sage.

Martines, D. (2005). Teacher perceptions of multicultural issues in school settings. *Qualitative Report, 10*(1), 1–20.

Massey, D. B. (1995). *Spatial Divisions of Labor: Social Structures and the Geography of Production.* Psychology Press. doi:10.1007/978-1-349-24059-3

Ma, X., & Xu, J. (2004). The causal ordering of mathematics anxiety and mathematics achievement: A longitudinal panel analysis. *Journal of Adolescence, 27*(2), 165–179. doi:10.1016/j.adolescence.2003.11.003 PMID:15023516

Mazon, B. (2009). Creating the Cosmopolitan US Undergraduate: Study abroad and an emergent global student profile. *Research in Comparative and International Education, 4*(2), 141–150. doi:10.2304/rcie.2009.4.2.141

McCombs, B. L., & Miller, L. (2007). *Learner-centered classroom practices and assessments: Maximizing student motivation, learning, and achievement.* Thousand Oaks, CA: Corwin Press.

McKellin, K. (1996). *Anticipating the future.* Vancouver, Canada: British Columbia Centre for International Education.

Mckellin, K. (1998). *Maintaining the momentum: The internationalization of British Columbia's post secondary institutions.* Victoria, Canada: The British Columbia Centre for International Education.

McLoughlin, C. (2001). Inclusivity and alignment: Principles of pedagogy, task and assessment design for effective cross-cultural online learning. Distance Education. *Distance Education, 22*(1), 7–29. doi:10.1080/0158791010220102

Mello, D., & Less, C. A. (2013). *Effectiveness of active learning in the arts and sciences.* Retrieved February 24, 2017, from http://scholarsarchive.jwu.edu/cgi/viewcontent.cgi?article=1044&context=humanities_fac

Mellor, R. (1993). *Tacitus.* London: Routledge.

Mendenhall, M. E., Stevens, M. J., Brid, A., & Oddou, G. (2008). *Specification of the content domain of the Intercultural Effectiveness Scale.* The Kozai Group, Inc.

Mendez, et al v. *Westminster [sic] School District of Orange County, et al,* 64F.Supp. 544 (S.D. Cal.1964), aff'd, 161 F.2d 774 (9th Cir. 1947) (en banc).

Mercer University. (2017a). *Mission Statement.* Retrieved from http://about.mercer.edu/mission/

Mercer University. (2017b). *Mercer on Mission.* Retrieved 17 March from http://mom.mercer.edu/

Merryfield, M. M., & Wilson, A. (2005). *Social studies and the world: Teaching global perspectives*. San Jose, CA: Cowan Creative.

Mestenhauser, J. (1998). Portraits of an international curriculum. In J. Mestenhauser & B. Ellingboe (Eds.), *Reforming higher education curriculum: Internationalizing the campus*. Phoenix, AZ: Oryx Press.

Meyer, K. E., Mudambi, R., & Narula, R. (2011). Multinational Enterprises and Local Contexts: The Opportunities and Challenges of Multiple Embeddedness. *Journal of Management Studies*, *48*(2), 235–252. doi:10.1111/j.1467-6486.2010.00968.x

Mezirow, J. (2000). *Learning as transformation: Critical perspectives on a theory in progress*. San Francisco, CA: Jossey-Bass.

Michel, B. (2013). Does offshoring contribute to reducing domestic air emissions? Evidence from Belgian manufacturing. *Ecological Economics*, *95*, 73–82. doi:10.1016/j.ecolecon.2013.08.005

Miller v. California, 413 U.S. 15 (1973)

Miller, K. K., & Gonzalez, A. M. (2016). Short-term international internship experiences for future teachers and other child development professionals. *Issues in Educational Research*, *26*(2), 241–259.

MLA Ad hoc Committee on Foreign Languages. (2007). *Foreign languages and higher education: New structures for a changed world. Profession*. Academic Press.

Momigliano, A. (1966). *Studies in Historiography*. London: Weidenfeld and Nicolson.

Monmonier, M. S. (1991). *How To Lie with Maps*. Chicago: University of Chicago Press.

Montagu, J. (n.d.). Instruments, classification of. In *Oxford Music Online*. Retrieved from http://www.oxfordmusiconline.com.libproxy.ggc.edu/subscriber/article/opr/t114/e3431

Moodian, M. A. (2009). Assessment instruments for the global workforce. In *Contemporary leadership and intercultural competence: Exploring the cross-cultural dynamics within organizations* (pp. 175–190). Los Angeles, CA: SAGE. doi:10.4135/9781452274942

Mubeen, S., Saeed, S., & Hussain Arif, M. (2013). Attitude towards mathematics and academic achievement in mathematics among secondary level boys and girls. *IOSR Journal of Humanities and Social Science*, *6*(4), 38–41. doi:10.9790/0837-0643841

Muir, K. (2016). So what is anthropology anyway? *Anthropology News Teaching and Learning Blog*. Retrieved from http://www.anthropology-news.org/index.php/2016/09/29/so-what-is-anthropology-anyway/

Munson, R. V. (2009). Who are Herodotus' Persians? *Classical World*, *102*(4), 457–470. doi:10.1353/clw.0.0116

Murphy, P. (2008). Defining pedagogy. In K. Hall, P. Murphy, & J. Soler (Eds.), *Pedagogy and practice: culture and identities* (pp. 28–39). London: SAGE publications.

NAFSA. (n.d.). *Trends in U.S. study abroad*. Retrieved September 12, 2016, from http://www.nafsa.org/Policy_and_Advocacy/Policy_Resources/Policy_Trends_and_Data/Trends_in_U_S__Study_Abroad/

Namey, E., Guest, G., Thairu, L., & Johnson, L. (2008). Data reduction techniques for large qualitative data sets. In *Handbook for team-based qualitative research*. Rowman Altamira.

National Education Association (NEA). (2010). *Global Competence Is a 21st Century Imperative*. Retrieved October 21, 2016, from http://www.nea.org/assets/docs/HE/PB28A_Global_Competence11.pdf

National Geographic-Roper. (2002). *Global Geographic Literacy Survey*. Retrieved October 21, 2016, from www.nationalgeographic.com/roper2006/pdf/FINALReport2006GeogLitsurvey.pdf

National Intelligence Council. (2008). *Global trends 2025: A transformed world*. Washington, DC: U.S. Government Printing Office.

National Standards Collaborative Board. (2015). *World-Readiness Standards for Learning Languages* (4th ed.). Alexandria, VA: Author.

Naude, L., & Bezuidenhout, H. (2015). Moving on the continuum between teaching and learning: Communities of practice in a student support program. *Teaching in Higher Education*, *20*(2), 221–230. doi:10.1080/13562517.2014.978752

NEA Education Policy and Practice Department. (n.d.). *An NEA policy brief: Global competence is a 21ˢᵗ century imperative*. Retrieved November 2, 2016, from http://www.nea.org/assets/docs/HE/PB28A_Global_Competence11.pdf

New York Times Co. v. United States, 403 U.S. 713 (1971).

Nickerson, R. S. (1998). Confirmation Bias: A Ubiquitous Phenomenon in Many Guises. *Review of General Psychology*, *2*(2), 175–220. doi:10.1037/1089-2680.2.2.175

Nilsson, B. (2000). Internationalizing the curriculum. In P. Crowther, M. Joris, M. Otten, B. Nilsson, H. Teekens, & B. Wachter (Eds.), *Internationalization at home: A position paper* (p. 2127). Amsterdam: European Association for International Education.

NOAA. (n.d.). *U.S. census divisions*. Retrieved October 12, 2016, from https://www.ncdc.noaa.gov/monitoring-references/maps/us-census-divisions.php

Noddings, N. (2001). The caring teacher. In V. Richardson (Ed.), *Handbook of research on teaching* (4th ed.; pp. 99–105). Washington, DC: American Educational Research Association.

Norris, C. (1996). *Reclaiming truth: Contribution to a critique of cultural relativism*. Durham, NC: Duke University Press.

Nyhan, B., Reifler, J., Richey, S., & Freed, G. L. (2014). Effective Messages In Vaccine Promotion: A Randomized Trial. *Pediatrics*, *133*(4), e835–e842. doi:10.1542/peds.2013-2365 PMID:24590751

NYiT. (2017). *Curriculum: Computer Science, B.S.* Retrieved from https://www.nyit.edu/degrees/computer_science_bs/curriculum

O'Dowd, R. (2006). The use of videoconferencing and e-mail as mediators of intercultural student ethnography. In J. Belz & S. L. Thorne (Eds.), *Internet-mediated intercultural foreign language education* (pp. 86–119). Boston, MA: Thomson Heinle.

Oakley, A. (1985). *Sex, gender and society*. London: Gower.

Odgers, T., & Giroux, I. (2006). *Internationalizing Faculty: A Phased Approach to ransforming Curriculum Design and Instruction*. Paper presented at the York University Annual International Conference on Internationalizing Canada's Universities, Toronto, Canada.

Odgers, T., & Giroux, I. (2006). York University Annual International Conference On Internationalizing Canada's Universities. In *Internationalizing Faculty: A Phased Approach To Transforming Curriculum Design and Instruction*. Retrieved from https://www2.viu.ca/internationalization/docs/odgersgirouxicpaper.pdf

Olsen, S. A., & Brown, L. K. (1992). The Relation Between Foreign Languages and ACT English and Mathematics Performance. *ADFL Bulletin*, *23*(3), 89–93.

Olson, C. L., & Kroeger, K. R. (2001). Global competency and intercultural sensitivity. *Journal of Studies in International Education, 5*(2), 116–137. doi:10.1177/102831530152003

Olson, C., & Green, M. F. (2003). *Internationalizing the campus. A user's guide*. American Council on Education.

Olsson, T. C. (2007). Your Dekalb Farmers Market: Food and Ethnicity in Atlanta. *Southern Cultures, 13*(4), 45–58.

Ong, J. (2012). Chinese rail ministry on the defense as $52m ticketing website is widely reviled. *The Next Web*. Retrieved from http://tnw.to/j5V3

Orton, R., & Davies, H. (n.d.). Theremin. In *Oxford Music Online*. Retrieved from http://www.oxfordmusiconline.com.libproxy.ggc.edu/subscriber/article/grove/music/27813

Otten, M. (1999). Preparing for the intercultural implications of the internationalisation of higher education in Germany. In K. Häkkinen (Ed.), *Innovative approaches to intercultural education: International Conference on Multicultural Education* (pp. 238-249). Jyväskylä, Finland: University of Jyväskylä Press.

Oyserman, D., Coon, H. M., & Kemmelmeier, M. (2002). Rethinking Individualism and Collectivism: Evaluation of Theoretical Assumptions and Meta-Analyses. *Psychological Bulletin, 128*(1), 3–72. doi:10.1037/0033-2909.128.1.3 PMID:11843547

Paige, R. M. (1993). *Education for the intercultural experience*. Yarmouth, Me: Intercultural Press.

Paige, R. M. (2003). The American case: The University of Minnesota. *Journal of Studies in International Education, 7*(1), 52–63. doi:10.1177/1028315302250180

Pandit, K. (2009). Geographers and the Work of Internationalization. *The Journal of Geography, 108*(3), 148–154. doi:10.1080/00221340903099557

Papademetriou, D., Somerville, W., & Sumption, M. (2009). *The Social Mobility Of Immigrants and Their Children*. Migration Policy Institute. Retrieved from http://www.migrationpolicy.org/research/social-mobility-immigrants-and-their-children

Papa, R., English, F., Davidson, F., Culver, M. K., & Brown, R. (2013). *Contours of great leadership: The science, art, and wisdom of outstanding practice*. Lanham, MD: Rowman & Littlefield Publisher, Inc.

Pare, A., & Maistre, C. L. (2006). Active learning in the workplace transforming individuals and institution. *Journal of Education and Work, 4*(4), 363–381. doi:10.1080/13639080600867141

Parker, A. (2003). Motivation and incentives for distance faculty. *Distance Learning Administration, 6*(3). Retrieved August 1, 2017, from http://www.westga.edu/~distance/ojdla/fall63/parker63.htm

Parker, A., Webb, K. E., & Wilson, W. V. (2017). Creating a studying abroad experience for elementary teacher candidates: Considerations, challenges, and impact. In H. An (Ed.), *Handbook for research on efficacy and implementation of study abroad programs for P-12 teachers* (pp. 111–132). Hershey, PA: IGI Global. doi:10.4018/978-1-5225-1057-4.ch007

Parsad, B., & Spiegelman, M. (2012). *Arts education: In public elementary and secondary schools 1999*. Academic Press.

Patterson, T. C. (2007). Google Earth as a (Not Just) Geography Education Tool. *The Journal of Geography, 106*(4), 145–152. doi:10.1080/00221340701678032

Pawson, E., Fournier, E., Haigh, M., Muniz, O., Trafford, J., & Vajoczki, S. (2006). Problem-Based Learning in Geography: Towards a Critical Assessment of Its Purposes, Benefits and Risks. *Journal of Geography in Higher Education, 30*(1), 103–116. doi:10.1080/03098260500499709

Peacock, J. L. (2007). *Grounded globalism: How the U.S. South embraces the world.* Athens, GA: University of Georgia Press.

Pedersen, P. (1994). *A handbook for developing multicultural awareness* (2nd ed.). Alexandria, VA: American Counseling Association.

Pegg, C. (n.d.). Overtone-singing. In *Oxford Music Online.* Retrieved from http://www.oxfordmusiconline.com.libproxy.ggc.edu/subscriber/article/grove/music/49849

Peterson, A. (n.d.). *Civic Republicanism and Civic Education: The Education of Citizens.* London: Palgrave Macmillan.

Peterson, P. M., & Helms, R. M. (2013). Internationalization revisited. *Change, 45*(2), 28–34. doi:10.1080/00091383.2013.764261

Pillsbury, R. (2008). No Foreign Food: The American Diet. In *Time And Place.* Westview Press.

Popkewitz, T. (1991). *A Political Sociology of Educational Reform.* New York: Teachers College Press.

Powell, A. B., & Frankenstein, M. (1997). *Ethno mathematics: Challenging eurocentrism in mathematics education.* Albany, NY: State Univ. of New York Press.

Prather-Jones, B. (2017). The benefits of short-term international field experiences for teacher candidates. In N. P. Gallavan & L. G. Putney (Eds.), *Teacher education yearbook XXV: Building upon inspirations and aspirations with hope, courage, and strength through teacher educators' commitment to today's' teacher candidates and educator preparation* (pp. 119–134). Lanham, MD: Rowman & Littlefield.

Prentless, K. (2006). What is meant by "active learning?". *Education, 12,* 566–569.

Prince, M. (2004). Does Active Learning Work? A Review of the Research. *Journal of Engineering Education., 93*(3), 223–231. doi:10.1002/j.2168-9830.2004.tb00809.x

Pusch, M. D. (2009). The interculturally competent global leader. In D. Deardorff (Ed.), *Sage Handbook of Intercultural Competence* (pp. 66–84). Thousand Oaks, CA: Sage.

Quezada, R. (2004). Beyond educational tourism: Lessons learned while student teaching abroad. *International Education Journal, 5*(4), 458–465.

Rabkin, N., & Hedberg, E. C. (2011). *Arts education in America: What the declines mean for arts participation 2000 and 2009-2010.* Washington, DC: National Endowment for the Arts.

Rachels, J. (2003). *The elements of moral philosophy.* Boston, MA: McGraw Hill.

Rahe, P. (2015). *The Grand Strategy of Classical Sparta: The Persian Challenge.* New Haven, CT: Yale University Press.

Ramsey, G. (n.d.). African American music. In *Oxford Music Online.* Retrieved from http://www.oxfordmusiconline.com.libproxy.ggc.edu/subscriber/article/grove/music/A2226838

Ravenstein, E. G. (1876). The Birthplaces of the People and the Laws of Migration. London: Academic Press.

Rawls, R., & Rawls, J. (2017). Intersectionality and the Spoken Word. In D. Budryte & S. Boykin (Eds.), Engaging Difference: Teaching Humanities and Social Science in Multicultural Environments (pp. 11-17, 134-135). Lanham, MD: Rowman & Littlefield.

Rawls, J., Wilsker, A., & Rawls, R. (2015, Spring). Are You Talking to Me? On the Use of Oral Examinations in Undergraduate Business Courses. *Journal of the Academy of Business Education, 16,* 22–33.

Redmon, J. (2014). *Georgia's foreign-born population up by 5 percent since 2009.* Retrieved September 2, 2016, from AJC.com: http://www.ajc.com/news/news/state-regional-govt-politics/georgias-foreign-born-population-up-by-5-percents/nhQGZ/

Reitano, R., & Elfenbein, C. (1997). American government: A comparative approach. *PS, Political Science & Politics, 30*(3), 540–552. doi:10.1017/S1049096500046801

Relich, J. (1996). Gender, self-concept and teachers of mathematics: Effects on attitudes to teaching and learning. *Educational Studies in Mathematics, 30*(2), 179–195. doi:10.1007/BF00302629

Reynolds, M. (1997). Learning Styles: A Critique. *Management Learning, 28*(2), 115–133. doi:10.1177/1350507697282002

Richardson, I., & Delaney, Y. (2010). Software quality: From theory to practice. In *Proceedings of the 7th International Conference on the Quality of Information and Communications Technology* (pp. 150–155). IEEE.

Richardson, I., & Hynes, B. (2008). Entrepreneurship education: Towards an industry sector approach. *Education + Training, 50*(3), 188–198. doi:10.1108/00400910810873973

Rindfuss, R., & Stern, P. (1998). Linking Remote Sensing and Social Science: The Need and The Challenges. In People and Pixels: Linking Remote Sensing and Social Science (pp. 1–28). National Academies Press.

Rives, J. B. (1999). *Tacitus, Germania.* Oxford, UK: Oxford University Press.

Rizvi, F. (2008). Epistemic virtues and cosmopolitan learning. *Australian Educational Researcher, 35*(1), 17–35. doi:10.1007/BF03216873

Rockwell, S., Schauer, J., Fritz, S., & Marx, D. (1999). Incentives and Obstacles Influencing Higher Education Faculty and Administrators to Teach Via Distance. *Online Journal of Distance Learning Administration, 2*(3). Retrieved from http://www.westga.edu/~distance/rockwell24.html

Roose, D. (2001). White teachers' learning about diversity and "otherness": The effects of undergraduate international education internships on subsequent teaching practices. *Equity & Excellence in Education, 34*(1), 43–49. doi:10.1080/1066568010340106

Ross, A. (2010). Chacona, lamento, walking blues: bass lines of music history. In *Listen to this.* New York: Farrar, Straus and Giroux.

Ruben, B. D. (1977). Guidelines for cross-cultural communication effectiveness. *Group & Organization Studies, 2*(4), 470–479. doi:10.1177/105960117700200408

Rubenstein, J. M. (2010). *Contemporary Human Geography.* New York: Prentice Hall.

Rui, Y. (2014). China's Internationalization Strategy. *Global Opportunities And Challenges for Higher Education Leaders,* 95–98.

Ruiz, N. G. (2014, August 29). The geography of foreign students in U.S. higher education: Origins and destinations. *Brookings.* Retrieved from http://www.brookings.edu/research/interactives/2014/geography-of-foreign-students#/M10420

Rundquist, B. C., & Vandeberg, G. S. (2013). Fully Engaging Students in the Remote Sensing Process through Field Experience. *The Journal of Geography, 112*(6), 262–270. doi:10.1080/00221341.2013.765902

Russell, W. B. (2011). *Contemporary social studies: An essential reader.* Charlotte, NC: Information Age Pub.

Ryan, J. (2013). American Schools vs. the World: Expensive, Unequal, Bad at Math. *The Atlantic Monthly.* https://www.theatlantic.com/education/archive/2013/12/american-schools-vs-the-world-expensive-unequal-bad-at-math/281983/

Salisbury, M. H., Umbach, P. D., Paulsen, M. B., & Pascarella, E. T. (2009). Going global: Understanding the choice process of the intent to study abroad. *Research in Higher Education, 50*(2), 119–143. doi:10.1007/s11162-008-9111-x

Sancisi-Weerdenburg, H. (2002). The Personality of Xerxes, King of Kings. In E. J. Bakker & H. de Wees (Eds.), *Brill's Companion to Herodotus* (pp. 579–590). Leiden: Brill.

Savile-Troike, M. (1984). What Really Matters in Second Language Learning for Academic Achievement? *TESOL Quarterly*, (18): 2, 199–219.

Schenker, T. (2012). Intercultural competence and cultural learning through telecollaboration. *CALICO, 29*(3), 449–470. doi:10.11139/cj.29.3.449-470

Schleicher, A., & Shewbridge, C. (2004). *What Makes School Systems Perform?: Seeing School Systems through the Prism of PISA*. Paris: Organisation for Economic Co-operation and Development.

Schorske, K. (1990). History and the Study of Culture. *New Literary History, 21*(2), 407-420.

Schubring, G., & Karp, A. P. (2014). History of Mathematics Teaching and Learning. Encyclopedia of Mathematics Education, 260-267. doi:10.1007/978-94-007-4978-8_70

Schwandt, T. A. (1998). Constructivist, interpretivist approaches to human inquiry. In N. K. Denzin & Y. S. Lincoln (Eds.), *The landscape of qualitative research: theories and issues* (pp. 221–255). Thousand Oaks, CA: Sage Publications.

Scott, A. (2017, October 17). *Foreign students eye U.S. election with caution. Marketplace*. National Public Radio.

Scutt, C., & Hobson, J. (2013). The stories we need: Anthropology, philosophy, narrative and higher education research. *Higher Education Research & Development, 32*(1), 17–29. doi:10.1080/07294360.2012.751088

Secada, W. G., Fennema, E., & Byrd, A. L. (1995). *New directions for equity in mathematics education*. Cambridge, UK: Cambridge University Press.

Sedelmaier, Y., & Landes, D. (2014). Practicing soft skills in software engineering: A project-based didactical approach. In L. Yu (Ed.), Overcoming Challenges in Software Engineering Education: Delivering Non-Technical Knowledge and Skills (pp. 161–179). Hershey, PA: IGI Global. doi:10.4018/978-1-4666-5800-4.ch009

Seifer, S., & Connors, K. (Eds.). (2007). *Faculty Toolkit for Service learning in Higher Education*. Community-Campus Partnerships for Health for Learn and Serve America's National Service Learning Clearinghouse Health National Service - Learning Clearinghouse. Retrieved from: http://servicelearning.org/filemanager/download/HE_toolkit_with_worksheets.pdf

Serow, R., Brawner, C., & Demery, J. (1999). Instructional reform and research universities: Studying faculty motivation. *Review of Higher Education, 22*(4), 411–423. doi:10.1353/rhe.1999.0018

Shelemay, K. (2015). *Soundscapes: Exploring music in a changing world*. New York: Norton.

Shenefelt, M. (2003). Why Study the Greeks? *The Chronicle of Higher Education, 49*(26), B 11.

Shields, C. (2016). Aristotle. In *The Stanford Encyclopedia of Philosophy*. Retrieved from http://plato.stanford.edu/archives/win2016/entries/aristotle/

Sineema, C., & Aitken, G. (2012). Effective pedagogy in social sciences. Brussels: International Academy of Education, and Geneva: International Bureau of Education.

Singer, A. (2013). Contemporary Immigrant Gateways In Historical Perspective. *Daedalus, 142*(3), 76–91. doi:10.1162/DAED_a_00220

Singing with two voices. (2011). In *Get mouthy*. London, UK: Wellcome Collection. Retrieved at https://www.youtube.com/watch?v=-o31Yg936Ac

Sitar. (n.d.). In *Oxford Music Online*. Retrieved from http://www.oxfordmusiconline.com.libproxy.ggc.edu/subscriber/article/grove/music/25900

Smiley, S. L., & Post, C. W. (2014). Using Popular Music to Teach the Geography of the United States and Canada. *The Journal of Geography*, *113*(6), 238–246. doi:10.1080/00221341.2013.877061

Solijonov, A. (2017). *Voter turnout trends around the world. Institute for Democracy and Electoral Assistance*. Retrieved March 26, 2017, from http://www.oldsite.idea.int/vt/compulsory_voting.cfm

Solomon, Y. (2007). Not belonging? What makes a functional learner identity in undergraduate mathematics? *Studies in Higher Education*, *32*(1), 79–96. doi:10.1080/03075070601099473

Somdahl-Sands, K. (2014). Combating The Orientalist Mental Map of Students, One Geographic Imagination at a Time. *The Journal of Geography*, *114*(1), 26–36. doi:10.1080/00221341.2014.882966

Sorkin, M. (Ed.). (1992). *Variations on a Theme Park | Michael Sorkin* (1st ed.). Macmillan. Retrieved from http://us.macmillan.com/variationsonathemepark/michaelsorkin

Sousa, C., & Hendricks, P. (2006). The diving bell and the butterfly: The need for grounded theory in developing a knowledge based view of organizations. *Organizational Research Methods*, *9*(3), 315–338. doi:10.1177/1094428106287399

Southern Association of Colleges and Schools Commission on Colleges. (2012). *Resource manual for the principles of accreditation: foundations for quality enhancement*. Decatur, GA: Southern Association of Colleges and Schools Commission on Colleges. Retrieved from http://www.sacscoc.org/pdf/Resource%20Manual.pdf

Sowell, T. (1997). *Migrations And Cultures: a World View*. New York: Basic Books.

Speece, D. L., & Keogh, B. K. (1996). *Research on classroom ecologies: Implications for inclusion of children with learning disabilities*. Mahwah, NJ: Lawrence Erlbaum Associates.

Spitzberg, B. H., & Cupach, W. R. (1984). *Interpersonal communication competence*. Beverly Hills, CA: Sage.

Spronken-Smith, R. (2005). Implementing a Problem-Based Learning Approach For Teaching Research Methods in Geography. *Journal of Geography in Higher Education*, *29*(2), 203–221. doi:10.1080/03098260500130403

Stallman, E., Woodruff, G. A., Kasravi, J., & Comp, D. (2010). The diversification of the student profile. In W. W. Hoffa & S. C. DePaul (Eds.), A history of U.S. study abroad: 1965–present. Lancaster, PA: Frontiers: The Interdisciplinary Journal of Study Abroad.

Statisticalatlas. (n.d.). *Languages in Gwinnett County, Georgia*. Retrieved October 16, 2017 from https://statisticalatlas.com/county/Georgia/Gwinnett-County/Languages

Stigler, J. W., & Hiebert, J. (2009). *The teaching gap: Best ideas from the world's teachers for improving education in the classroom*. New York: Free Press.

Stigler, J., & Thompson, B. J. (2009). Thoughts on Creating, Accumulating, and Utilizing Shareable Knowledge to Improve Teaching. *The Elementary School Journal*, *109*(5), 442–457. doi:10.1086/596995

Strauss, A. (1987). *Qualitative analysis for social scientists*. Cambridge, UK: Cambridge University Press. doi:10.1017/CBO9780511557842

Strauss, A., & Corbin, J. (1990). *Basics of qualitative research: Grounded theory procedures and techniques*. Newbury Park, CA: Sage.

Strauss, B. (2004). *The Battle of Salamis: the Naval Encounter that saved Greece – and western Civilization*. New York: Simon & Schuster.

Stroud, A. H. (2010). Who plans (not) to study abroad? An examination of U.S. student intent. *Journal of Studies in International Education, 20*(10), 1–18.

Strunk, W. O., Treitler, L., Mathiesen, T. J., McKinnon, J. W., Tomlinson, G., Murata, M., & Allanbrook, W. J. (1998). Source readings in music history. New York: Norton.

Sunstein, B. S., & Chiseri-Strater, E. (2012). *Field working: Reading and writing research*. St. Martin's.

Swaffar, J., & Urlaub, P. (Eds.). (2014). *Transforming Postsecondary Foreign Language Teaching in the United States*. Springer. doi:10.1007/978-94-017-9159-5

Swanson, L., & Janssen, H. (2012, August). *Natural resource and environmental restoration in Montana: Case studies in restoration and associated workforce needs* [Scholarly project]. Retrieved October 17, 2016, from http://crmw.org/Downloads/Restoration Study Overview.pdf

Sweeney, K. (2013). Frontiers: The Interdisciplinary Journal of Study Abroad. Inclusive Excellence and Underrepresentation of Students of Color in Study Abroad. *Frontiers: The Interdisciplinary Journal of Study Abroad, 23*, 1–21.

Tacitus, . (1991). *Agricola* (H. Benario, Trans. & Ed.). Norman, OK: University of Oklahoma Press.

Tacitus, . (1999). *Germania* (J. B. Rives, Trans. & Ed.). Oxford, UK: Clarendon Press.

Takagi, H. (2015). The internationalisation of curricula: The complexity and diversity of meaning in and beyond Japanese universities. *Innovations in Education and Teaching International, 52*(4), 349–359. doi:10.1080/14703297.2013.820138

Tang, T., & Chamberlain, M. (2003). Effects of rank, tenure, length of service, and institution on faculty attitude toward research and teaching: The case of regional state universities. *Journal of Education for Business, 79*(2), 103–110. doi:10.1080/08832320309599097

Tedrow, B. (2017). Favorite place mapmaking and the decolonization of teaching. In D. Budrytė & S. Boykin (Eds.), *Engaging difference: Teaching humanities and social science in multicultural environments* (pp. 75–82). Lanham, MD: Rowman & Littlefield.

Teichler, U. (2014). Opportunities and problems of comparative higher education research: The daily life of research. *Higher Education, 67*(4), 393–408. doi:10.1007/s10734-013-9682-0

Telles, J. A., & Vassallo, M. L. (2006). Foreign language learning in-tandem:Teletandem as an alternative proposal in CALLT. *The ESPecialist, 27*(2), 189–212.

Thomas, R. (2009). The Germania as a Literary Text. In A. J. Woodman (Ed.), *Cambridge Companion to Tacitus* (pp. 59–72). Cambridge, UK: Cambridge University Press.

Thompson, L., & Clay, T. (2008). Critical literacy and the geography classroom: Including gender and feminist perspectives. *New Zealand Geographer, 64*(3), 228–233. doi:10.1111/j.1745-7939.2008.00148.x

Time Magazine. (1993, November 18). Special Issue: The New Face of America: How Immigrants are shaping the World's First Multi-Cultural Society. *Time, 142*(21).

Top 200 Universities in the World I 2017 World University Web Rankings. (n.d.). Retrieved October 20, 2016, from http://www.4icu.org/top-universities-world/

Trahar, S. (2013). Autoethnographic journeys in learning and teaching in higher education. *European Education Journal*, *12*(3), 367–375.

Treacy, M. J. (2015). *Greenwich Village, 1913: Suffrage, labor, and the new woman (reacting to the past)*. New York City: W. W. Norton & Company.

Tribe, J. (2005). Tourism, knowledge, and the curriculum. In D. Airey & J. Tribe (Eds.), *International Handbook of Tourism Education* (pp. 47–60). Amsterdam: Routledge.

Truscott, S., & Morley, J. (2001). Cross-cultural learning through computer-mediated communication. *Language Learning Journal*, *24*(1), 17–23. doi:10.1080/09571730185200171

U.S. Census Bureau. (2005). *Exports from manufacturing establishments*. Retrieved October 21, 2016, from www.census.gov/mcd/exports/arp05.pdf

U.S. Census Bureau. (n.d.). *Census regions and divisions of the United States*. Retrieved October 20, 2016, from https://www2.census.gov/geo/pdfs/maps-data/maps/reference/us_regdiv.pdf

Ulin, R. C. (2007). Revisiting cultural relativism: Old prospects for a new cultural critique. *Anthropological Quarterly*, *80*(3), 803–820. doi:10.1353/anq.2007.0051

United Nations. (2013). *Migrants by Origin and Destination: The Role of South-South Migration*. Department of Economic and Social Affairs: Population Division.

United State Navy. (n.d.). *Center for Language, Regional Expertise, and Culture*. Retrieved from http://www.netc.navy.mil/centers/ciwt/clrec/

United States Air Force. (n.d.). *Expeditionary Field Guides*. Retrieved from http://culture.af.mil/ecfg/index.html

United States Census Bureau. (2014). *The Foreign-Born Population in the United States: US Census Bureau*. Retrieved from https://www.census.gov/newsroom/pdf/cspan_fb_slides.pdf

United States Census Bureau. (n.d.). *Quick Facts, Gwinnett County, Georgia*. Retrieved October 25, 2016 from: http://www.census.gov/quickfacts/table/PST045215/13135

United States Courts. (n.d.). *Background. Mendez v. Westminster reenactment*. Retrieved March 5, 2017, from http://www.uscourts.gov/educational-resources/educational-activities/background-mendez-v-westminster-re-enactment

University of Texas at Austin, College of Communication, Department of Advertising. (2000). *Thoughts about the future of advertising education* [white paper]. Retrieved from: http://marketingpedia.com/MarketingLibrary/Advertising%20in%20Education/FutureOf AdvertisingEducation2.pdf

Van Maanen, J. (2004). The Role of History of Mathematics in the Teaching and Learning of Mathematics: Presentation of the ICMI Study and the Study Book. *Proceedings of the Ninth International Congress on Mathematical Education*, 374-377. doi:10.1007/1-4020-7910-9_96

Vande Berg, M., Connor-Linton, J., & Paige, R. M. (2009). The Georgetown Consortium Project: Interventions for Students Living Abroad. *Frontiers: The Interdisciplinary Journal of Study Abroad*, *18*, 1–75.

Vasilogambros, M. (2015, April 2). *The Most Diverse County in the Southeast Is Run Almost Entirely by White Politicians*. Retrieved September 2, 2016, from The Atlantic: http://www.theatlantic.com

Wächter, B. (2003). An introduction: Internationalisation at home in context. *Journal of Studies in International Education*, *7*(1), 5–11. doi:10.1177/1028315302250176

Wade, B. C. (2013). *Thinking musically: Experiencing music, expressing culture*. New York: Oxford University press.

Waldron, J. (2012). Conceptual frameworks, theoretical models and the role of YouTube: Investigating informal music learning and teaching in online music community. *Journal of Music. Technology and Education*, *4*(2–3), 189–200. doi:10.1386/jmte.4.2-3.189_1

Walgreens. (2012). *Walgreens WellTransitionsSM provides discharge services to help hospitals and health systems reduce readmissions*. Retrieved from http://news.walgreens.com/article_print.cfm?article_id=5648

Walshaw, M. (2013). Post-Structuralism and Ethical Practical Action: Issues of Identity and Power. *Journal for Research in Mathematics Education*, *44*(1), 100–118. doi:10.5951/jresematheduc.44.1.0100

Walters, L. M., Green, M. R., Wang, L., & Walters, T. (2011). From heads to hearts: Digital stories as reflection artifacts of teachers' international experience. *Issues in Teacher Education*, *20*(2), 37–52.

Wamboye, E., Adekola, A., & Sergi, B. S. (2015). Internationalisation of the campus and curriculum: Evidence from the US institutions of higher learning. *Journal of Higher Education Policy and Management*, *37*(4), 385–399. doi:10.1 080/1360080X.2015.1056603

Ware, P., & Kramsch, C. (2005). Toward an intercultural stance: Teaching German and English through telecollaboration. *Modern Language Journal*, *89*(2), 90–105. doi:10.1111/j.1540-4781.2005.00274.x

Watson, J. R. (2010, March). Language and Culture Training: Separate Paths? *Military Review*, 93–97.

Webber, K. L. (2012). Learner-Centered Assessment in US Colleges and Universities. *Research in Higher Education*, *53*(2), 201–228. doi:10.1007/s11162-011-9245-0

Weibelzahl, S., & Lahart, O. (2011a). Developing student induction sessions for problem-based learning. *Proceedings of International Conference on Engaging Pedagogy*.

Weibelzahl, S., & Lahart, O. (2011b). PBL induction made easy: A web-based resource and a toolbox. *FACILITATE Conference: Problem-Based Learning (PBL) Today and Tomorrow*.

Weimer, M. (2002). *Learner-Centered Teaching: Five Key Changes to Practice. the Jossey-Bass Higher and Adult Education Series*. Jossey-Bass.

Welikala, T., & Watkins, C. (2008). *Improving intercultural learning experiences in higher education: Responding to cultural scripts for learning*. London: Institute of Education Publishers.

Wenger, E. (1998). Communities of practice: Learning as a social system. *The Systems Thinker*, *9*(5).

Wenger, E., McDermott, R., & Snyder, W. (2002). *Cultivating communities of practice*. Boston, MA: Harvard Business School Press.

West, S. (1992). Herodotus and Foreign Cultures [Review of the book *Hérodote et les peoples non grecs: Neuf exposés suivis de discussions* by G Nenci & O. Reverdin]. *The Classical Review New Series, 42(2)*, 277–279.

Whalley, W. B., Saunders, A., Lewis, R. A., Buenemann, M., & Sutton, P. C. (2011). Curriculum Development: Producing Geographers For the 21st Century. *Journal of Geography in Higher Education*, *35*(3), 379–393. doi:10.1080/0309 8265.2011.589827

White, L. Jr. (1965). The Legacy of the Middle Ages in the American Wild West. *Speculum, 40*(2), 191–202. doi:10.2307/2855557

Wiggins, G. P., McTighe, J., Kiernan, L. J., & Frost, F. (2000). *Understanding by design.* Alexandria, VA: Association for Supervision and Curriculum Development.

Wiggins, G., & McTighe, J. (2005). *Understanding by design.* Alexandria, VA: Association for Supervision and Curriculum Development.

Willett, M. (2014, March 13). *These are the most active states in America.* Retrieved November 1, 2016, from http://www.businessinsider.com/the-states-that-exercise-the-most-2014-3

Winberry, J. J. (2015). "Lest We Forget": The Confederate Monument and the Southern Townscape. *Southeastern Geographer, 55*(1), 19–31. doi:10.1353/sgo.2015.0003

Woodin, J. (2001). Tandem learning as an intercultural activity. In M. Byram, A. Nichols, & D. Stevens (Eds.), *Developing Intercultural Competence in Practice* (pp. 189–203). Toronto: Univ. of Toronto Press.

World Bank. (2015). *Foreign direct investment, net inflows.* Retrieved November 1, 2016, from http://data.worldbank.org/indicator/BX.KLT.DINV.CD.WD?year_high_desc=true

Wyckoff, W., & Dilsaver, L. M. (1995). *The mountainous west: Explorations in historical geography.* Lincoln, NE: University of Nebraska Press.

Xu, Y., & Liu, W. (2010). A project-based learning approach: A case study in China. *Asia Pacific Education Review, 11*(3), 363–370. doi:10.1007/s12564-010-9093-1

Yanguas, I. (2010). Oral computer-mediated interaction between L2 learners: It's about time. *Language Learning & Technology, 14*, 72–79.

Ye, X. (2017). *Lost and found: Cultural different, intercultural maturity, and self-authorship among international students* (Unpublished doctoral dissertation). Eastern Michigan University.

Yershova, Y., DeJaeghere, J., & Mestenhauser, J. (2000). Thinking Not as Usual: Adding the Intercultural Perspective. *Journal of Studies in International Education, 4*(1), 39–78. doi:10.1177/102831530000400105

Yu, L. (2014). *Overcoming challenges in software engineering education: Delivering non-technical knowledge and skills.* IGI Global. doi:10.4018/978-1-4666-5800-4

Zenón, M., Perdomo, L., Glawischnig, H., Cole, H., Matos, T., Allende, O., & Gutiérrez, J. (2009). *Esta Plena.* Cambridge, MA: Marsalis Music.

Zimitat, C. (2008). Internationalisation of the undergraduate curriculum. In L. Dunn & M. Wallace (Eds.), *Teaching in Transnational Higher Education.* London: Routledge.

Zimitat, C. (2008). Student perceptions of the internationalisation of the curriculum. In L. Dunn & M. Wallace (Eds.), *Teaching in transnational higher education* (pp. 135–147). London: Routledge.

Zimmerman, S. (1995). Perceptions of intercultural communication competence and international student adaptation to an American campus. *Communication Education, 44*(4), 321–335. doi:10.1080/03634529509379022

About the Contributors

David Anderson has worked in the education field for over 30 years, in a variety of capacities, including as a secondary mathematics and computer science teacher, a researcher for the Bureau of Accreditation and School Improvement Studies, the Executive Associate for Research and Assessment with the National Board For Professional Teaching Standards, the Associate Director for the National Science Foundation Statewide Systemic Initiative in South Dakota, the lead administrator at a professional development school (PDS), and a faculty member in Maryland and Michigan. He is currently the coordinator of the doctoral program in Educational Leadership at Eastern Michigan University. He has published over 40 articles and book chapters, completed over 100 scholarly presentations, and authored over 20 funded grant proposals. He is a past president of the Michigan Association of Professors of Educational Administration, and has been awarded the EMU College of Education Innovative Scholarship Award, the EMU College of Education Special Service Award, the Maryland Association of Higher Education Award for Outstanding Research, and the University of Michigan Award for Outstanding Dissertation in School Administration.

Jenna Andrews-Swann is trained as an environmental anthropologist, and she has well over a decade of higher education teaching experience in Anthropology, Women's Studies, and Environmental Science. Her work outside the classroom focuses primarily on immigration, resettlement, and food studies. Dr. Andrews-Swann is currently an Associate Professor of Anthropology at Georgia Gwinnett College, where she teaches courses in introductory and upper-level anthropology. She is also a co-creator of, and instructor for, the college's new Environmental Science - Social Science degree program.

Charity Atteberry is an Athletic Academic Advisor and Life Skills Coordinator with the Intercollegiate Athletic Department at the University of Montana. Prior to this role, she was a Graduate Teaching Assistant for the Department of Educational Leadership and Academic Success Coach with TRiO Student Support Services at the University of Montana and worked in the Chicago Public Schools as a classroom teacher and reading specialist. Atteberry is a doctoral candidate, pursuing concurrent degrees in Educational Leadership and International Educational Leadership at the University of Montana. She received her Masters of Education degree in Reading from Concordia University – Chicago and a Bachelor of Science degree in Elementary Education from Drury University.

Funwi Ayuninjam is the director of Internationalization and a professor of English for Academic Purposes at Georgia Gwinnett College. He oversees the co-curricular component of campus internationalization, which includes education abroad, international student services, the Peace Corps Preparatory

Program, and general campus intercultural programming. He is a member of NAFSA: Association of International Educators and served as NAFSA Academy Coach from 2014-2015. Funwi is co-founder of the Southern Interdisciplinary Roundtable on African Studies and serves on the editorial committee of the Association of International Education Administrators and on the editorial boards of the Brill Journal of Asian and African Studies and CEREC Publishing. Before coming to Georgia Gwinnett College, he had served as senior international officer at Central State University, Chatham University, Winston-Salem State University, and Kentucky State University. In some of these institutions, he also taught courses in linguistics, research, African studies, and/or interdisciplinary studies. Funwi is the author of A Reference Grammar of Mbili (1998), The Egg Polisher and Other Tales (2010), and Voices from Africa and Beyond: A Collection of Poems (2011). He holds a BA in English and French from the University of Yaounde, Cameroon and an MS and a PhD in linguistics from Georgetown University.

Priya Boindala received her PhD in Mathematics from Tulane University, New Orleans, and her Masters in Mathematics from Osmania University, India. She is an Assistant Professor of Mathematics at Georgia Gwinnett College in the School of Science and Technology. Her research interests include undergraduate course re-design, classroom methodologies for student engagement and learning, faculty learning communities, Biomathematics, and mathematical modeling. Boindala is currently involved in two course imbedded and SoTL research projects. She has been the recipient of the Governor's Teaching Fellowship (2015) and the IPLA fellowship(2014). She is currently pursuing an online M.Ed. program in Learning Design and Technology from the University of Georgia.

Scott Boykin, before joining Georgia Gwinnett College, practiced law in Alabama and Texas and served as a judicial clerk to Judge Patrick E. Higginbotham on the United States Court of Appeals for the Fifth Circuit. Boykin has published research in political theory, constitutional political economy and constitutional law.

Dovile Budryte, Ph.D, is a professor of political science at Georgia Gwinnett College. Her areas of interest include gender studies, trauma and memory in international relations and nationalism. She was a 2004 National Endowment for the Humanities grant recipient, 2000-01 Carnegie Council on Ethics and International Affairs (New York) Fellow, and a 1998-99 Fellow at the College for Advanced Central European Studies at Europa University Viadrina, Frankfurt (Oder), Germany. Her publications include articles on gender issues, minority rights and democratization in the Baltic states and four books, Taming Nationalism? Political Community Building in the Post-Soviet Baltic States (2005), Feminist Conversations: Women, Trauma and Empowerment in Post-Transitional Societies (co-edited with Lisa M. Vaughn and Natalya T. Riegg, 2009), Memory and Trauma in International Relations: Theories, Cases and Debates (co-edited with Erica Resende, 2013) and Engaging Difference: Teaching Humanities and Social Science in Multicultural Environments (co-edited with Scott A. Boykin, 2017). Recently she has published articles in peer-reviewed special issues of The Journal of Baltic Studies, Gender and History, Humanities and co-edited a special issue of Ethnicity Studies on transnational memory. Her current research agenda is reflected in a recent essay published in E-International Relations. In 2016, she recorded a webinar for the University System of Georgia Faculty Development Monthly Series on the use of intersectionality concept in teaching political science. Budryte has delivered invited talks at various colleges and universities internationally, including Florida International University, University of Cincinnati, University of Latvia, Vilnius University (Institute of International Relations and Political Science), Warsaw University, The National Technical University of Ukraine and the University of Tennessee in Knoxville (Center for The Study of War and Society).

David Dorrell is an Assistant Professor of Geography, PhD. from Louisiana State University.

Boyko Gyurov is an Associate Professor of Mathematics, who has taught at Georgia Gwinnett College since August 2012. He obtained his Ph.D in mathematics from the University of Arkansas, Fayetteville in 2008. His research interests are in Semigroup Theory, Algebraic Graph Theory and Networks in his pure mathematics research, and interdisciplinary study abroad, in his education research. In particular, he is developing techniques to effectively embed analytical and statistics methods into science major students' science classes in study abroad setups.

Michael A. Lewkowicz, PhD, is an assistant professor of political science at Georgia Gwinnett College. His academic interests cover a variety of topics in American Politics, including political behavior, election laws, political participation, governmental institutions, constitutional law and public policy, as well as pedagogical topics such as the utilization of Supreme Court cases to teach civil rights in American Government courses.

Todd Lindley is Assistant Professor of Geography at Georgia Gwinnett College. Dr. Lindley's earned his PhD in 2010 at Indiana University, where his research focused on globalization, development, migration, and intercountry adoption, with a focus on the Philiippines.

Rong Liu, Ph.D., is an Associate Professor of English for Academic Purposes at Georgia Gwinnett College, in Lawrenceville, Georgia, USA. His research interests focus on language processing and using technology in second language reading and writing.

Angela (Angi) Lively has a passion for teaching and learning. She has spent the past fifteen years in educational environments, teaching mathematics to students at the high school level, the college level, and helping prepare students to become mathematics educators. She coordinates the Educator Preparation Program in Mathematics at Georgia Gwinnett College, mentoring and teaching students on their journey. Her research is steeped in SoTL: she is currently working on a grant that integrates science labs into the math classroom; allowing students to immediately see the relevance of the curricular topics; as well as a project integrating specifications grading in a corequisite model of College Algebra. She has a BS in Mathematics from Middle Tennessee State University, a Masters in Mathematics Education from Piedmont College in Demorest, Georgia and is currently working on her PhD in Mathematics Education at the University of Georgia.

Ramakrishnan Menon received his PhD in Curriculum & Instruction from the University of British Columbia, Vancouver, British Columbia, Canada in 1993, and also has the following degrees: MA--C & I (Univ of Northern Iowa); BS--Math (University of London, England), BA--Math (University Malaya, Malaysia); and Adv. Dip in TESL (University of W. Australia). He has taught (Math, English Language, Physics, Science, Additional Math--AP Math) in High Schools, and preservice and inservice teachers, in various countries (Australia, Canada, Egypt, Malaysia, Singapore and the USA--Ohio, Iowa, California, and Georgia), for a total of more than 40 years. He has authored more than 50 scholarly articles, presented more than 100 scholalry papers at conferences, and been an external examiner of PhD dissertations, as well as been an external evaluator of large research grants from Australia. He is currently at Georgia Gwinnett College (where he has been for the past 7 years), teaching Math courses for preservice teachers.

Inna Molitoris, Ph.D., is a Lecturer with the Gainey School of Business and is the Lead faculty for the Business Research program at Spring Arbor University, Spring Arbor, Michigan. She serves as the Institutional Review Board Chair and is involved in the International Initiative Committee and Intercultural Office's activities. Dr. Molitoris received her Ph.D. in the field of Educational Leadership from Eastern Michigan University where she been teaching multicultural education leadership courses for as a doctoral fellow and adjunct faculty for 8 years. She was the organizer of international conferences, educational trips to Russia, and hosted on universities' campuses about 100 educators from former Soviet countries, Iraq, China, and Taiwan.

Clemente Quinones has been teaching political science courses for about 19 years, some of these in Mexico, his native country. His doctoral sub-fields are comparative politics and survey research methods. His teaching commitment and interests are in the areas of comparative politics, international affairs and political methodology. In this regard, he specifically teaches Latin American Politics, Inter-American Relations, USA-Latin American Relations, Mexico's Politics, Comparative Electoral Systems and Political Parties, Comparative Foreign Policy, Foundations of International Policy, Comparative Political Institutions, Comparative Democracy and Democratization, Comparative Public Opinion, Research Methods, Survey Research, and Quantitative Analysis in Political Science. Based on the Critical Pedagogy School, he applies the student-centered approach in his teaching. His research focuses on investigating the relationship between political institutions (e.g., electoral systems) and sociopolitical movements on one side and democratization, democracy and public policy on the other, as well as internationalization in higher education. His current work in progress reflects this commitment. His work in progress includes "Impact of Sociopolitical Upheaval and Electoral Reforms on Mexico's Democratization Process, 1946–2015," "Policy Implications of the Current Mexican Electoral System," "Explaining Political Representation in Latin America," "The Role of the Strategic Voting in the 2000, 2006 and 2012 Presidential Elections in Mexico," and "Explaining the Latin American Foreign Policy." Some of his distinctions embrace: Multi-cultural Fellowship at University of Connecticut, Storrs, CT, 1997–2005; Teacher of the Year Award from Cedar Valley College, Dallas, 1992; CONACYT Scholarship from the Mexican government, 1981–1983 to pursue the MA; Best Student of my undergraduate class of 1973–1978; Best Student, Class of 1971–1973, Lázaro Cárdenas High School. Dr. Quinones is affiliated with the following professional organizations: International Studies Association and Southern Political Science Association.

Mark Schlueter is a Professor of Biology, who has taught at Georgia Gwinnett College since August 2007. He obtained his Ph.D in zoology from Miami University in Oxford, Ohio in 1997. His research interest focuses on bees, in particularly native bees and enhancing crop pollination and yield. In addition, he is very active leading and developing study abroad programs in Central/South America and Asia. He has led over 200 students on study abroad experiences over the past 10 years.

Karen Weller Swanson, EdD, is currently an Associate Professor and chair in Tift College of Education at Mercer University in Atlanta, Georgia. Her research encompasses transformative education, faculty professional development and the scholarship of teaching and learning. She has a B.., degree in Biology and an M.Ed. in Secondary Education, and an Ed.D in Curriculum and Instruction all from Northern Arizona University.

Roch Turner is the Director of Program Development at Bitterroot College and a member of the University of Montana Political Science and Educational Leadership adjunct faculties. Turner served six years in the US Navy, after which he earned a bachelor's degree in US History, a Master's of Public Administration focused on early childhood education policy, and a PhD in International Education. Turner's research is currently focused on the impact of international service experiences on subsequent coursework and the institutional impact of facilitated concurrent enrollment opportunities.

Michelle Vaughn, EdD, is an Assistant Professor for the Tift College of Education at Mercer University where she focuses on literacy and teacher preparation. Before becoming a college professor, Dr. Vaughn taught as a kindergarten - fifth grade teacher. She had the opportunity to work with the Florida Department of Education where she served as a liaison between the program offices and budget office. She has traveled internationally presenting at different conferences and providing professional development to teachers around the world. She also has the pleasure of directing international field experiences for pre-service teachers. Research interests include culturally responsive pedagogy, teacher preparation, and teacher professional development. She is currently researching the transformation of pre–service teachers' culturally responsiveness.

Xingbei Ye has been teaching intercultural competence and global leadership classes for years. She has studied and worked in several countries including Malaysia, Switzerland, Australia, and the U.S. Her extensive experiences in international education allows her to pursue her career dream as "an ambassador of international education". Dr. Ye has published over 10 articles and book chapters, completed over 80 scholarly presentations, and received the award of "the most valuable professor" from Eastern Michigan University. Her research interest is focusing on Global leadership, intercultural competence, Chinese Philosophy, International Comparative Education and Study Abroad.

Laura Young, originally from Memphis, Tenn., is a graduate from Purdue University in Lafayette, Ind. She received her Ph.D. from Purdue in August 2013 with an emphasis in international relations. Young specializes in security issues, as well as U.S. foreign and environmental policy. In addition to numerous other research projects, Young is currently working on a book titled, Making States: An Historical Approach to Modern Day State Building, which explores the relationship between resource scarcity and state capacity throughout history.

Liguo Yu Yu received his PhD degree in Computer Science from Vanderbilt University in 2004. He received his MS degree from Institute of Metal Research, Chinese Academy of Science in 1995 and his BS degree in Physics from Jilin University in 1992. Before joining IUSB, he was a visiting assistant professor at Tennessee Tech University. During his sabbatical of Spring 2014, he was a visiting faculty at New York Institute of Technology-Nanjing. His research interests include software coupling, software maintenance and software evolution, empirical software engineering, and open-source development.

Paulo Zagalo-Melo is Associate Provost for Global Education, overseeing the Diether H. Haenicke Institute for Global Education and furthering comprehensive internationalization efforts at Western Michigan University. Previously, Zagalo-Melo served as Associate Provost for Global Century Education, Director of the Global Engagement Office and Associate Professor of Educational Leadership at the University of Montana. Prior to that, he was Director for Science, Technology and Innovation at the Luso-American Foundation (FLAD), in Lisbon, Portugal. Before joining FLAD, Zagalo-Melo served as the U.S.-Portugal Fulbright Commission's Executive Director for 10 years, after 3 years as its Administrative Officer. Additionally, he was a member of the Executive Committee of Fulbright Directors from Europe, and he served as the European Union's Project Coordinator for IMPACT, an E.U.-U.S. ATLANTIS four-year exchange program. Zagalo-Melo is vice chair of the Policy and Advocacy Committee of the Association of International Education Administrators (AIEA) and was a 2015-2016 AIEA Presidential Fellow. He was a TEDx speaker on multilingual education, with a talk titled "Building Global Nations." Zagalo-Melo has a master's degree in public administration from Harvard University and a doctoral degree in political science from the Catholic University of Portugal. He was a visiting scholar at the University of Colorado-Boulder and a visiting professor at the Catholic University of Portugal.

Index

S

Self-directed Learning 106, 108, 111, 113, 115
Senior International Officer 250
Service Learning 218, 221, 243, 246-247, 250, 260, 268
Significant Learning 3, 42, 50, 82-83, 101, 108, 138-140, 143, 145, 147, 150, 155-158, 180
Software Engineering Education 293-295, 305-306, 314
Standardized Curriculum 314
Standpoint Theory 119-124, 127, 129, 133
STEM study abroad 181-182, 186-187
Student Engagement 5, 82, 115, 155, 193
Study Abroad 19-20, 31, 47, 58-59, 135, 157, 160, 181-188, 191-193, 195-201, 203, 217, 220-223, 226, 251, 260, 268, 273, 275, 280, 282, 288-289

T

Tacitus 81, 92-94
Technology 5, 18, 61-64, 109, 134-135, 143, 156, 161, 182-183, 187-188, 191-193, 196, 217, 220, 222-223, 230, 254, 293-295, 298, 300, 302-303
Themistocles 90
TRADOC 91

X

Xerxes 89-90

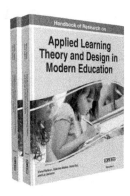

Stay Current on the Latest Emerging Research Developments

Become an IGI Global Reviewer for Authored Book Projects

Premier Reference Source

Emerging GIS Applications for Emergency and Disaster Management

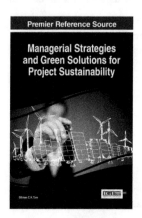

Premier Reference Source

Managerial Strategies and Green Solutions for Project Sustainability

Premier Reference Source

Comparative Approaches to Using R and Python for Statistical Data Analysis

Premier Reference Source

Solutions for High-Touch Communications in a High-Tech World

The overall success of an authored book project is dependent on quality and timely reviews.

In this competitive age of scholarly publishing, constructive and timely feedback significantly decreases the turnaround time of manuscripts from submission to acceptance, allowing the publication and discovery of progressive research at a much more expeditious rate. Several IGI Global authored book projects are currently seeking highly qualified experts in the field to fill vacancies on their respective editorial review boards:

Applications may be sent to:
development@igi-global.com

Applicants must have a doctorate (or an equivalent degree) as well as publishing and reviewing experience. Reviewers are asked to write reviews in a timely, collegial, and constructive manner. All reviewers will begin their role on an ad-hoc basis for a period of one year, and upon successful completion of this term can be considered for full editorial review board status, with the potential for a subsequent promotion to Associate Editor.

If you have a colleague that may be interested in this opportunity, we encourage you to share this information with them.

Information Resources Management Association

Advancing the Concepts & Practices of Information Resources Management in Modern Organizations

Become an IRMA Member

Members of the **Information Resources Management Association (IRMA)** understand the importance of community within their field of study. The Information Resources Management Association is an ideal venue through which professionals, students, and academicians can convene and share the latest industry innovations and scholarly research that is changing the field of information science and technology. Become a member today and enjoy the benefits of membership as well as the opportunity to collaborate and network with fellow experts in the field.

IRMA Membership Benefits:

- **One FREE Journal Subscription**

- **30% Off Additional Journal Subscriptions**

- **20% Off Book Purchases**

- Updates on the latest events and research on Information Resources Management through the IRMA-L listserv.

- Updates on new open access and downloadable content added to Research IRM.

- A copy of the Information Technology Management Newsletter twice a year.

- A certificate of membership.

IRMA Membership $195

Scan code or visit **irma-international.org** and begin by selecting your free journal subscription.

Membership is good for one full year.

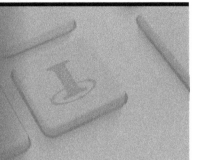

CPSIA information can be obtained
at www.ICGtesting.com
Printed in the USA
BVHW011039061019

560080BV00031B/206/P